The State against Society

The State against Society

POLITICAL CRISES

AND THEIR AFTERMATH

IN EAST CENTRAL EUROPE

GRZEGORZ EKIERT

PRINCETON UNIVERSITY PRESS

PRINCETON, NEW JERSEY

Library of Congress Cataloging-in-Publication Data

Ekiert, Grzegorz, 1956–
The state against society : political crises and their aftermath in
East Central Europe / Grzegorz Ekiert.
p. cm.
Includes bibliographical references and index.
ISBN 0-691-01114-1 (alk. paper) — ISBN 0-691-01113-3 (pbk. : alk. paper)
1. Communism—Europe, Eastern.   2. Europe, Eastern—Politics and
government—1945–1989.   3. Hungary—History—Revolution, 1956.
4. Czechoslovakia—History—Intervention, 1968.   5. Poland—Politics
and government—1980–1989.   6. Communism—Hungary.
7. Communism—Czechoslovakia.   8. Communism—Poland.   I. Title.
HX240.7A6E44 1996   306.2′0943—dc20   96-11807   CIP

This book has been composed in Sabon

Princeton University Press books are printed on acid-free paper and meet the guidelines for
permanence and durability of the Committee on Production Guidelines for Book
Longevity of the Council on Library Resources

Printed in the United States of America
by Princeton Academic Press

1 2 3 4 5 6 7 8 9 10

1 2 3 4 5 6 7 8 9 10
(Pbk.)

IN MEMORY OF MY FATHER

W L A D Y S L A W   E K I E R T

CONTENTS

PREFACE AND ACKNOWLEDGMENTS

EXTRAORDINARY CHANGES are occurring in East Central European countries brought on by the spectacular collapse of state-socialist regimes in 1989, the dissolution of the Soviet Union in 1991, and the rapid transition to liberal democracy and a market economy. The countries' domestic economic and political institutions have been recast, new political forces, parties, and organizations have emerged, private property and markets have been restored, and their social structures have been undergoing radical transformations. These domestic changes have been paralleled by a profound alternation in the international situation. The constraints that governed the global politics during the four decades following the Second World War disappeared with the collapse of the Soviet empire. This rapid unraveling of state-socialist regimes and Soviet-imposed regional institutions left scholars of East European affairs in a state of confusion and uncertainty. Do the knowledge, research, and theoretical approaches developed and accumulated over four decades of the existence of state-socialist regimes have any lasting values? Does the fact that the collapse of state socialism was so sudden and largely unexpected mean that we failed to understand and untangle the political and economic processes taking place in the region? Do the newly open archives reveal new facts that make our analyses and interpretations of events obsolete?

Albert Hirschman once noted that in social sciences "as soon as a social phenomenon has been fully explained by a variety of converging approaches and it is therefore understood in its majestic inevitability and perhaps even permanence, it vanishes."[1] Does this statement reflect the situation of political scientists and sociologists working on contemporary Eastern Europe? State socialism certainly vanished from the European continent. Whether we were able to fully explain it is still an open question. The postmortem assessment of the strengths and weaknesses of the field has been slowly emerging.[2] With a healthy dose of self-criticism, scholars emphasize contributions that added significantly to our understanding of state socialism. Ellen Comisso argues that "although our knowledge and understanding of 'actually existing' socialism is far from complete, it is also quite considerable, and that despite a multiplicity of models, characterizations, and labels, there exists a fairly broad consensus as to the essential features of communist systems, the way in which these features vary over time and place, and the causes of the variations."[3] Moreover, despite well-known difficulties in conducting scholarly research under state-socialist regimes (i.e., almost total lack of access to documents and primary sources, censorship, political constraints on empirical research, etc.), recently opened archives have not yielded any significant revelations. According to one researcher, "one must acknowledge that although these materials answer many questions posed by historians and the interested public over the years . . . none of the documents contains anything that could be called a sensation."[4] Similarly, newly published interviews and autobiographies of former communist leaders have hardly shed any new light on important events of the past, as have official investigations conducted in these countries.[5] To be sure, many interesting footnotes have been added to our knowledge of particular events, but major works in the field were able to withstand the confrontation with new facts, testifying to great analytical skills and meticulous scholarship of many students of state-socialist regimes. In fact, major historical and analytical works on Eastern Europe published prior to 1989 lost little value in the light of recent developments and new evidence. Yet much remains to be done in order to fully explain the experiences of more than four decades of communist rule.

The scholarship on Eastern Europe has been uneven. Despite a great number of excellent and exhaustive single-country studies, there is a consensus among scholars that the comparative studies have been the weakest component in the volume of works on state-socialist regimes. The traditional "comparative communism" approaches developed in the 1960s and 1970s had a number of well-known theoretical shortcomings. They were too often based on simplistic functional and modernization models, focused almost exclusively on elite-level politics, and "provided insights into the origins, but not into the dynamics of political change."[6] These approaches reached an impasse long before 1989. In terms of comparative strategies, many works designed to be comparative in nature were nothing more than chronologically structured narrative accounts (often excellent) of political and economic developments in all or selected countries in the region. The most prominent units of analysis were the country, specific state institutions (military, security police, parliaments, trade unions, etc.), specific social groups (workers, professionals, intelligentsia), or a specific social or political phenomenon (religion, opposition, elections, economic reforms, etc.). Studies of such institutions and phenomena were conducted on a country-by-country basis. Thus, most of the comparative volumes presented collections of country-specific analyses rather than truly cross-national comparisons. Still, as George Schopflin emphasizes, "The post-war history of Eastern Europe actually cries out for a comparative approach."[7] This new comparative approach can only emerge from a serious effort to incorporate comparative studies of state-socialist regimes into mainstream comparative politics. Now more than ever, one should agree with Daniel Nelson that "the unique challenge to those who engaged in comparative studies of communist parties and state . . . is to identify new paths of their own research and analyses."[8]

The closing of the long and difficult postwar chapter in political history of the region offers a unique opportunity to reexamine the events that took place during this period and reevaluate the scholarship developed in the past. Moreover, we can reassess past knowledge and the analytical frameworks developed for the study of state-socialist regimes from the vantage point of the experiences of the last several years, marked by rapid dissolution of these regimes across the region. While state socialism as a coherent political and economic system has disappeared, the study of its history and experiences is not a purely academic exercise. Decades of communist rule reshaped East European societies in many crucial ways. All countries experienced rapid and massive industrialization and urbanization. As a result of communist policies, their traditional political and economic institutions were thoroughly changed, civil societies destroyed and repressed, and social structures transformed. Their people's aspirations, expectations, habits, and behavior were profoundly altered.

The analysis presented in this book rests on the assumption that we cannot adequately grasp the meaning and patterns of the massive changes occurring in the region today without reexamining past developments and their legacies. We have to reconsider specific experiences of particular countries and identify critical historical junctures in order to explain their unique national trajectories both under the communist rule and during the present transition process. The paradox of the persistence of cross-national differences, despite common challenges and pressures and similar formal institutional structures, can only be adequately addressed by employing a macrohistorical comparative approach.

The deceptive clustering of regime breakdowns in the span of a few months in 1989 reinforced the widely accepted but totally mistaken view of the region as a homogeneous entity composed of basically similar countries, with their identical political and economic systems held together by Soviet imperial domination. The rapid changes in all countries of the region also prompted some scholars to deny the usefulness of macrohistorical comparative studies that seek to correlate historical conditions in individual East European countries with the pattern and outcomes of the democratization process.[9] Yet, as William Sewell emphasizes, "History displays both stubborn durabilities and sudden breaks, and even the most radical historical ruptures are interlaced with remarkable continuities."[10] The interpretation of East European political developments proposed in this book is inspired by Sewell's effort to reconsider the Braudelian notion of history as the "longue durée" and to resurrect the notion of events that "constitute unpredictable ruptures of normal causality, moments of fluidity in which small and momentary causes may have gigantic and enduring consequences."[11] I will argue that the most appropriate comparative strategy for the reexamination of political experiences of East European societies should focus not on formal characteristics of state-socialist regimes but on momentous political events that formed "critical junctures" in the development of state socialism. The events I have in mind were major political crises that periodically shook the region. They had profound institutional consequences and decisive impact on political, social, and economic developments in countries where they occurred and in other East European countries. In short, a comparison of such events and their consequences is more effective in our quest to understand varied experiences and forms of communist rule then a comparative analysis that focuses on formal institutions, social groups, or specific political and social processes and phenomena across the region.

In postwar East European history, there were three crucial turning points that produced long-lasting institutional, political, and cultural consequences throughout the region. The Hungarian Revolution of 1956, the reform movement in Czechoslovakia in 1968 known as the "Prague Spring," and the rise of Solidarity trade union in Poland in 1980 sent shock waves across the entire Soviet bloc, shaping domestic politics in other countries and forcing the change of Soviet strategies vis-à-vis dependent countries of the region. Western analysts frequently referred to these political crises as similar efforts of East European societies to reject Soviet domination and one-party rule. In many works, they are grouped together as signs of the persistent party-states' legitimacy deficit or as the most evident examples of the failure of communist policies. However, as I argue in this book, these events shaped the postwar history of Eastern Europe more than anything else, and their nature and impact need to be analyzed in much more detail. They must be understood as consequential political struggles among various political actors embedded in their domestic context, and we must pay attention to their short- and long-term institutional, political, and cultural consequences. As Sewell emphasizes, "events . . . are constituted as well as constitutive."[12] They have the potential of creating new structural conditions as well as cultural and political categories that shape and constrain human action. Moreover, they set in motion path-dependent developments that generate significant cross-national differences. None of the regions can provide a better case for studying the importance of a few momentous historical events on political developments than postwar Eastern Europe. The crisis of Stalinism in 1956 (exemplified by the Hungarian Revolution and a nonviolent political transition in Poland), the collapse of revisionism and communist reformism in 1968 (epitomized by the Prague Spring), the rise of Solidarity in 1980, and above all the collapse of state-socialist regimes in 1989 were critical history-shaping events that reshaped and altered institutions and political practices of states and societies across the region.

As a result of these events, since the mid-1950s, when the uniform institutional patterns and policies imposed on the countries of the region by the Soviet Union were breached, domestic politics played an increasingly important role. This situation produced striking differences in both the political and economic dimensions among the countries of the region, despite similarities in the formal characteristics of their party-states and their common patterns of political and economic dependency on the Soviet Union. Political developments in various countries following the de-Stalinization crisis aptly illustrate the point emphasized by the new institutional approach in comparative politics. According to Kathleen Thelen and Sven Steinmo, "Institutions themselves may be resistant to change, but their impact on political outcomes can change over time in subtle ways in response to shifts in the broader socioeconomic or political context."[13] Moreover, while de-Stalinization did not change the formal characteristics of the party-states, it altered what Peter Hall calls the "relational character" of institutions.[14] In short, as a result of institutional breakdowns in some countries and preventive state responses to such a possibility in others, the nature of political interaction between institutional orders of the party-states and between actors within the state and society has begun to differ increasingly from country to country.

Timothy Garton Ash, one of the most perceptive observers of contemporary Eastern Europe, argued that the dismantling of state socialism should be understood as a process that differed in length and nature from country to country.[15] While it is indeed difficult to correlate directly the outcomes of current democratization and economic transformations in individual countries with their political trajectories under the communist rule, we cannot explain the different modes of extrication of state-socialist regimes in 1989 without references to past experiences.[16] In this book I argue that in order to understand differences in the institutional forms and political practices of communist states, as well as to explain why and how particular East European regimes disintegrated and what political and economic legacies they left, we have to take into account past political struggles and their consequences for actors within the state and society. In order to understand Poland's rebellious history, culminating in the formation of the largest independent trade union movement in the recent European history and peaceful surrender of power by the communist elites in 1989, one has to go back to the peaceful resolution and peculiarities of the de-Stalinization crisis in the 1950s and cycles of political protest and repressions that followed the 1956 transition.[17] The revolutionary pattern of the de-Stalinization crisis, in which all anti-Stalinist forces were crushed by Soviet military intervention and all opposition eradicated by postrevolutionary repression, also accounts for quiescence of the Hungarian society and its reform-minded communist leaders before 1989, and the smooth power transition and relatively stable and moderate policies after 1989. Similarly, one has to go back to Czechoslovakia's experiences in 1968 to understand the persistence of neo-Stalinist rule prior to 1989, the nature of the "velvet revolution," and the recent dissolution of the Czechoslovak state. In short, we have to take seriously domestic political and economic developments in each country, employ the comparative historical approach, and adopt events and their institutional consequences as a central unit of analysis if we are to offer a more compelling explanation of East European developments after the Second World War.[18]

In the chapters that follow, I will focus on three crises in the region: the Hungarian Revolution of 1956, the reform movement in Czechoslovakia in 1968, and the rise of the Solidarity movement in Poland in 1980. These were the three most important cases of institutional breakdown in Soviet-dominated East Central Europe. I will argue that these political crises and their resolution were the most crucial turning points in the history of these particular countries. They formed critical junctures setting in motion unique, long-term, path-dependent developments. I will emphasize the distinctive nature of each crisis, arguing that varied degrees of institutional breakdown, patterns of popular mobilization, intra-elite divisions, and choices of political leaders produced restricted sets of alternatives, especially given the Soviet response and general international situation. I will argue that the specific nature of the particular crisis and constraints it produced limited political opportunities and options for both the actors within society and the party-state. These constraints molded the contours of postcrisis policies, generated different political outcomes, and shaped the institutions of the party-state as well as the relationship between the state and society in each case. It is my contention that by constraining the resources, capacities, and actions of social and political actors, the short- and long-term outcomes of these crises produced cross-national differences among the state-socialist regimes. In turn, these varied domestic conditions influenced not only the patterns of extrication of the East European regimes but also political developments in the postcommunist period.

This book is not a work of history, and it is not intended to offer a detailed historical analysis based on new archival records and primary sources. Although it provides a narrative account of three crises and their aftermaths, it aims to reconstruct political, social, and economic causes and consequences of these events and to propose, if not an entirely new, at least a more systematic interpretation of their impact on the long-term development of state-socialist regimes. Focusing on the interpretation of existing historical accounts and records, I hope to cast new light on specific national experiences in three countries. Central to my reconstruction of the Hungarian, Czechoslovak, and Polish crises is an effort to explain the following paradox: how and why the Hungarian and Czechoslovak communist regimes were able to restore their institutions and party-state domination and stabilize their rule after a major institutional breakdown, and why the post–martial law regime in Poland failed to accomplish any of this. Its failure to recover the party-state's institutional coherence, demobilize oppositional forces, and stabilize the political and economic situation ultimately led to its surrender of power and opened wide the process of radical political change for the entire region.

The book opens with an analytical chapter that offers an overview of traditional analyses within the field of East European studies, discusses some recent contributions in the general field of comparative politics that may be usefully employed in the study of state socialist regimes, outlines the comparative framework constructed for the analyses of specific empirical cases, and summarizes the main hypotheses and arguments. The three case studies follow. They are organized chronologically in order to emphasize their political dynamics and to provide a historically coherent analysis of each case. The more narrative case studies and the chronological organization was designed for readers who are not familiar with details of contemporary East European history and are interested in events themselves as well as in their interpretation. Finally, the conclusions point to specificities of each crisis and its short- and long-term legacies as well as their impact on patterns of democratization in these three countries.

The book has been a long time in the making. I began researching its topic in 1987 for my Ph.D. dissertation in the Department of Sociology at Harvard University. It owes as much to academic fascinations and concerns as to my own personal experience of living through the ecstatic days of the Solidarity movement and disappointments, hopes, and struggles under martial law. When I began writing the first drafts, the extraordinary events of 1989 were unthinkable, although I worked on the assumption that Poland would not experience the fate of Hungary after 1956 and Czechoslovakia after 1968. In fact, from the very beginning the strategies and outcomes of military suppression of the Solidarity movement and the policies introduced by the post–martial law regime were markedly different from those pursued by the Hungarian regime after 1956 and the Czechoslovak regime after 1968. These differences became more apparent with the passing years. During the 1980s, the Polish party-state's elites departed significantly from the orthodox policy patterns common to Soviet-dependent communist regimes. Militant communist rhetoric was absent, the communist party lost its central position, and the traditional structure of relations between the institutional orders of the party-state was recast. As a result, the relationship between the state and actors within society was redefined. Nevertheless, the opening of the negotiated political transition in Poland and the collapse of other state-socialist regimes in 1989 has given me (and all other students of East European societies) a very different perspective on the past events. I deeply believe, however, that this analysis is not an ex post factum exercise, projecting the image of the historical inevitability of 1989 political transitions.

Over the years working on this project, I benefited enormously from the friendly advice, criticism, and wisdom of my teachers and colleagues. I wish to thank Theda Skocpol, who was a caring adviser, a tough critic, and a constant source of inspiration. Daniel Bell, Piotr Sztompka, John Hall, and Ivan Szelenyi were my teachers and advisers, shaping my understanding of social sciences, sharing with me their wisdom and commitment to understanding politics and society, and offering encouragement and support. Martha and Jan Kubik read and commented on countless versions of the manuscript. They were always there when I needed their help, and I am grateful for their friendship. Many colleagues offered their comments on different parts of the manuscript. I am particularly grateful to Peter Hall for his friendly criticism and review of the entire manuscript. Anna Seleny, Kazimierz Poznanski, Andy Markovits, Deborah Yashar, and two anonymous reviewers for Princeton University Press offered many useful comments and suggestions. Krzysztof Owerkowicz and Anna Grzymala-Busse helped prepare the bibliography.

My research and writing was generously supported by grants from the MacArthur Foundation, the Krupp Foundation, the Center for European Studies at Harvard University, and the American Council of Learned Societies. For the last several years, the Center for European Studies offered me an intellectually exciting and supportive environment, and I am indebted to all with whom I share that wonderful space. Finally, I wish to thank my wife, Ela, for her forbearance, love, and unwavering support.

The State against Society

Introduction: Political Crises, Mobilization, and Demobilization in East Central Europe

BETWEEN THE END of the Second World War and the spectacular collapse of communist rule in 1989, several state-socialist regimes of East Central Europe experienced major political crises threatening their domestic political order and the geopolitical relations in the region. The Hungarian Revolution of 1956, the Prague Spring of 1968, and Poland's "self-limiting" revolution of 1980 signaled recurring political instability, fragility of the party-states' institutional order, and the vulnerability of the Soviet-imposed regimes in these countries. Each crisis was followed by massive efforts to demobilize collective actors who emerged to challenge the regime and reequilibrate the institutional system of the party-state. Thus, in spite of conventional political wisdom concerning the stability of state socialist regimes, their remarkable ability to control the population, and coercive capacity to defend their monopoly of power, East Central European countries were an arena of surprising and dramatic political struggles, abrupt leadership changes, daring collective protests, military crackdowns, political repressions, as well as massive institutional reforms, sudden policy changes, reversals, and adjustments instituted by the ruling elites in response to the crisis. The contrast to the Western part of the continent is striking in this respect. As Helene d'Encausse bitterly stated a few years after the imposition of martial law in Poland:

> On the European continent, which has experienced for the first time in its history complete peace for forty years, the only place where weapons are fired and tanks and rifles periodically enter into action is the Soviet empire: Berlin, Budapest, Prague, Gdansk, and Kingir as well as in Soviet territory, so many places where the will of the people has been crushed by military force. The state of war that has been established in Poland for the last several years is an ironic symbol for a Europe at peace.[1]

This historical observation undermines long-held theoretical assumptions about the nature of state-socialist regimes, the relationship between the state and society under communist rule, and the effectiveness of elites' political and ideological control in these countries. The frequent cases of serious political crisis indicated profound tensions and contradictions, which plagued not only the domestic, political, and economic orders of these societies but the whole post–World War II geopolitical arrangement of the region as well. On the one hand, all instances of political instability demonstrated the persistent popular defiance, resistance, and opposition to communist rule as well as the actual ability of actors within society to organize and launch a large-scale collective protest. On the other hand, these crisis situations demonstrated the striking inability of the ruling elites to effectively respond to domestic and international challenges and pressures, institutionalize social and political tensions and conflicts, and prevent the accumulation of grievances and the emergence of collective protests.[2] Thus, in countries of East Central Europe, as in other countries ruled by nondemocratic regimes, "the presence of social mobilizations represent[ed] an authoritarian regime's inability to rule through repression and the existence of pockets of space in civil society for the reconstitution of collective action."[3]

The recurrent crisis situations exposed the institutional and political deficiencies of state socialism and the failure of institutional reforms attempted by their ruling elites. They also showed the resilience of civil society under communist rule. Even a brief overview of political developments in the region after the Second World War effectively challenges the misleading image of a homogeneous and atomized citizenry incapable of exercising any effective political pressure and skillfully manipulated by the rulers, suggested by the concept of totalitarianism and other "one-actor" models developed in the field of Soviet and East European studies.[4] Moreover, actual historical experiences of these countries question the validity of "state-centered" explanatory models according to which only the state elites and/or the hegemonic power in the region were accorded an active role in the shaping of political institutions and processes.[5] In this book I argue that each political crisis that occurred in East Central Europe involved a multiplicity of collective actors, generated contrasting short-term outcomes, produced significant institutional changes and adjustments, and left long-lasting legacies. In fact, the character and policies of these regimes were in a large measure crisis-driven and should be explained by peculiarities of the major crises that they experienced rather than by other kinds of factors that comparative political studies usually adduce to explain the character of such regimes. In short, cross-national differences in the region and distinct characteristics of different state-socialist regimes were a result of successive political crises and complex responses of the party-states, regional power, and actors within society to these crises.

CYCLES OF POLITICAL CRISIS AND POPULAR PROTEST UNDER COMMUNIST RULE

Instances of mass political mobilization, protest movements, and political instability in dependent East Central European regimes[6] form two distinctive historical clusters. These two periods of intensification of conflicts and political struggles mark two turning points in the historical development of state-socialist regimes. They can be conveniently described as the crisis *within* state socialism and as the crisis *of* state socialism, to emphasize the changing nature of the crisis, its causes, and consequences throughout the four decades of the state-socialist regimes.

Contemporary research on collective protest convincingly demonstrates that political mobilization is shaped by the structure of political opportunities offered by the state and has a cyclical nature.[7] David Snyder and Charles Tilly argue that in the modern history of France strikes and other forms of collective protest occurred in waves that coincided with the increased vulnerability of the state.[8] Similarly Theda Skocpol asserts in her research on revolutions that the conditions favorable to mass mobilization emerge when there is "the breakdown of the concerted repressive capacity of a previously unified and centralized state."[9] Such conditions are usually the result of the cumulation of domestic economic and political difficulties reinforced by geopolitical pressures. They precipitate changes in more stable structural characteristics of the state and in informal political alignments that open the political opportunity structure and invite a collective challenge to the existing political status quo. According to Sidney Tarrow, "political opportunities provide the major incentives for transforming mobilizational potential into action . . . ; they signal the vulnerability of the state to collective action and thereby open up opportunity for others—affecting both alliances and conflict systems. The process leads to state responses which, in one way or another, produce a new structure of opportunity."[10] Tarrow identifies five conditions that contribute to the opening of opportunities for collective action: the degree of openness of political institutions, the stability of political coalitions and alignments, elite divisions and/or their tolerance for protest, the presence of support groups and allies, and the policymaking capacity of the state.[11]

The opening of the political opportunity structure is an extended and dynamic process that affects different groups and actors within society to a different degree. As a result, their capacity to challenge power-holders and to influence political outcomes varies across time, space, and social location. Expanding political opportunities created by "changes in institutional features or informal political alignments of a given political system . . . significantly reduce the power disparity between a given challenging group and the state."[12] Altering of the structure of political opportunities often leads to the emergence of the cycle of protest. Tarrow argues that the cycle of protest is characterized by five interconnected processes: (1) the intensification of conflict, (2) geographic and sectoral diffusion of protest, (3) the formation of new organizations, (4) the emergence of new frames of meaning and ideologies, and (5) an expanding repertoire of contention.[13]

The concepts of the political opportunity structure and protest cycles can easily be adapted to the postwar history of East Central Europe. However, one more condition ought to be emphasized. The stability of geopolitical relations, especially in the situation of political and/or economic dependency, can significantly shape the structure of political opportunities. This condition is crucially important for the understanding of major political crises in Soviet-dominated East Central Europe. During two periods—the late 1950s and late 1980s—state-socialist regimes experienced profound instability caused by the overlapping of the domestic economic and political crisis with geopolitical pressures and uncertainty. These situations generated splits and struggles within the ruling elites, led to the fall of powerful leaders, and created openings in the political space. As a result, in both periods the repressive capacity of the party-state was seriously weakened and various collective actors responded to the expanding structure of political opportunities by voicing grievances, demanding changes in the state policies, and calling for reform of political and economic institutions. In short, they display all characteristics of protest cycles that had the regional scope and direct or indirect consequences in all state-socialist countries.

During the first period, commonly described as the period of de-Stalinization, the crisis mainly affected the institutional level of the party-state. Party reformers and revisionist critics focused on the relations between the communist party and other institutional orders within the party-state, condemned the abuses of power, and demanded economic reforms and policy changes. The crisis did not undermine political, economic, and ideological foundations of Soviet-type regimes because the challengers did not question the principal tenets of state socialism, such as the political monopoly of the communist party, state ownership of means of production, central planning in the economy, or the alliance with the Soviet Union. It was diffused by a removal of the Stalinist power elite and a change in the state's economic and political practices without any significant modifications of the institutional architecture of the party-state.[14]

In the second period, the locus of political opposition moved outside the institutional structures of the party-state, and the crisis was compounded by three elements: the exhaustion of the limits of extensive economic development, the identity crisis of the communist parties and the collapse of dominant political discourse, and the erosion of Soviet hegemonic power in the region. This situation not only produced profound economic and political difficulties but, more importantly, indicated the disintegration of the Marxist-Leninist state idea. The principles that gave self-legitimation to the party-state elites and a normative foundation of political and social organization were increasingly blamed for the existing economic and political stagnation. Marxist-Leninist ideals were questioned not only by oppositional intellectuals but increasingly by significant segments of the ruling elite, and new political discourses and frames of meaning emerged.

Cases of political instability and popular mobilization during the de-Stalinization period ranged from a full-blown revolution to localized industrial strikes, student protests, and local rebellions. They may be viewed as a response of collective actors within society and the party-state to the failure of the post–World War II Stalinist domestic and regional policies. During this time, collective protests were prompted by the breakdown of forced industrialization and collectivization policies that led to an acute economic crisis and severe shortages in the consumer market. They also signified the rejection of dominant political practices based on the terroristic political control and personalistic forms of Soviet imperial domination. The opening of the structure of political opportunity was reinforced by the confused policies of ruling communist parties, which tried to respond to the disastrous economic situation, social unrest, and pressure from the Soviet Union by introducing inconsistent amendments to Stalinist political and economic practices. These new policies exemplified the profound uncertainties generated by the struggle for succession in the Soviet Union and the subsequent zigzags of the de-Stalinization process. Stalin's death played an important symbolic role in precipitating the crisis. According to George Schopflin: "Stalin symbolized permanence and changelessness in himself. His death negated and disproved this. At the symbolic and affective levels, the unity of the Soviet system was opened to questioning."[15] De-Stalinization unleashed intense factional struggles at the pinnacle of the power apparatus and produced the half-hearted approaches of ruling elites to the reforms of the Stalinist legacy. All these factors resulted in unpredictable oscillations between more hard-line and orthodox and more flexible and tolerant methods, tactics, and policies employed by East Central European ruling elites during this period.[16] These different responses of ruling elites to the crisis, the level of intra-elite conflicts and divisions, the varied patterns of popular mobilization, the extent of institutional breakdown of the party-state, and the nature of state repressive response to challenges from below produced distinct outcomes and shaped specific national trajectories that characterized particular East European regimes for many years to come.

Mass popular protests occurring during this time frame include the Berlin uprising of June 1953;[17] a small-scale workers revolt in Pilsen, Czechoslovakia, in June 1953;[18] workers' strikes in Hungary, Bulgaria, and Romania; the Poznan uprising of June 1956 in Poland and the subsequent major political crisis in October 1956;[19] and the dramatic revolution in Hungary in October and November of 1956.[20] It seems that ensuing events—such as the political crisis and student revolt in Poland in March 1968,[21] the Czechoslovak reform movement of the same year smashed by the Soviet-led military invasion,[22] and two waves of worker unrest in Poland in 1970 and 1976[23]— should be included in this first historical cluster, as well. These latter events can be perceived as either instances of delayed de-Stalinization (Czechoslovakia) or collective responses to the inconsistent post-Stalinist policies of the Polish communist leadership.

Processes unfolding in East Central Europe during this period should not be seen only as a reaction to the political developments and intra-elite struggles in the Soviet Union. Each occurrence of popular mobilization was the result of a distinct set of domestic causes, unique combinations of domestic, and geopolitical pressures. Each had specific domestic political consequences. The diffusion of unrest and political dissent was apparent on both popular and elite levels. Such events affected and shaped political processes in other state-socialist regimes as well as in the Soviet Union itself. In every case there were significant policy changes in neighboring countries and collective efforts of the Soviet bloc's ruling elites to prevent the spillover of the crisis. These reaction to the crisis show that when similar geopolitical conditions prevail in the region, a crisis in one country tends to foster parallel processes in other countries and generates preemptive responses of their ruling elites. In this respect, mutual impact of the Polish October of 1956 and the Hungarian Revolution or of the Prague Spring and the Hungarian economic reforms of 1968 is easily detectable. Above all, the events of 1989 are striking examples of the interactive nature of political crisis within a unified geopolitical state-system.[24]

It also should be stressed that while the impetus for change came from the groups within the party-state institutions, in all these situations the role of social unrest, as well as its nature, class characteristics, demands, and organizational capacity of the popular opposition, had a crucial effect on political developments. On the one hand, this situation reflects the nature of state-socialist regimes in which the state boundaries and institutional penetration of society were dramatically expanded and spaces for autonomous political action drastically reduced. On the other hand, totalitarian Stalinism, lasting only a few years, was not able to crush social networks, eradicate completely autonomous social spaces, and assert the party's exclusive and undivided rule over all aspects of social and political life. The subsequent contradictions of the post-Stalinist reworking of the system, which David Ost described as an attempt by the ruling elites to find a compromise between the impossibility and the necessity of totalitarianism,[25] are generally responsible for all cases of political instability in East Central Europe up to the 1980s. In short, contrary to state- and empire-centered explanations that prevail in East European and Soviet studies, it was the interaction between the party-state elites and various groups within society expressing themselves by means of dissent, popular pressure, collective protest, and social unrest that played the vital role during the de-Stalinization period and in the period leading to 1989 collapse of state-socialist regimes.

Moreover, political instability was more the result of domestic tensions and struggles between the party-state and society, generated by the uncertainties of the post-Stalinist domestic political environment, than an effect of internal frictions inside and between political elites in the region. These domestic political uncertainties can, in turn, be attributed to the lack of legitimate mechanisms of political succession as well as to society's penetration into the economy and polity that gradually undermined Stalinist institutional practices and the normative basis of state-socialism. Thus, the process of de-Stalinization can be characterized as a turbulent beginning of what Ivan Szelenyi calls "a silent revolution from below,"[26] which led to the profound erosion of state socialism in the late 1970s and its collapse in the end of the 1980s.

In spite of serious institutional breakdown and geopolitical uncertainties, however, the state idea that animated the postwar transformation of East Central Europe remained largely unchallenged in the 1950s, facilitating the swift reconstruction of the party-states institutions and reequilibration of the regime. This confirms Walter Powell's and Paul DiMaggio's argument that "institutionalized arrangements are reproduced because individuals often cannot even conceive of appropriate alternatives (or because they regard as unrealistic the alternatives they can imagine)."[27] Popular demands and grievances voiced during the de-Stalinization period, with the notable exception of the Hungarian Revolution, were mostly formulated in a rudimentary language of social justice and concerned with social welfare and failures in the redistributive role of the state. The almost exclusive economic nature of collective grievances was a striking characteristic of these earlier forms of collective protest. Even though the symbols of the regime, such as pictures of party leaders or the Soviet flag, were destroyed during workers demonstrations, these acts of protest were devoid of any identifiable political symbolism of their own. Similarly, oppositional intellectuals formulated their grievances and demands in the language of revisionism and therefore were not able to develop a real alternative political vision and program. Oppositional intellectuals and members of the party state bureaucratic elites shared the same political language, which perpetuated the distrust and the alienation of important segments of society and inhibited the articulation of political and institutional visions of an alternative sociopolitical order. Therefore, as Jadwiga Staniszkis argues, the instances of collective protest during this period were characterized by "non-transformational political articulation," where the often dramatic rejection of the system in the symbolic dimension was not followed by any alternative political thinking envisioning a new institutional arrangement.[28]

Moreover, collective action during this period was characterized by a significant segmentation along class, social, and regional lines. It was usually confined to traditional workers' strongholds and urban industrial centers. As historical records show, collective protest was more likely to break out in huge industrial complexes located in the peripheral areas of the country. It also affected traditional industries and enterprises that were not disrupted by the war or significantly altered by the postwar industrialization and where there had been a tradition of worker militancy. These early cases of collective protest also displayed the inability of collective actors to develop solid organizational structures and forge any effective alliance among protesting workers, other important social strata such as peasants or professional groups, traditional political forces such as churches, and the new revisionist movements inside or outside of the party-state.

Responding to instances of collective protest and popular mobilization, the party-states decisively and effectively used coercive forces and violence to quell social unrest, and economic measures to defuse political tensions. With the exception of the Hungarian Revolution, state-socialist regimes were able to maintain control of the situation and subsequently to restore order and stability by promising and granting some economic and political concessions and by employing direct repressive strategies. Brutal police and military actions were ordered and performed under the authority of individual states; however, in more serious cases, where the coercive capacity of the party-state was significantly weakened or its willingness to use force against the population was in question, the Soviet military and police forces were promptly employed, as was the case in East Germany in 1953, Hungary in 1956, and Czechoslovakia in 1968. The direct and massive use of the Soviet army in several situations clearly indicated the limited sovereignty of these countries and the imperial nature of Soviet domination in the region.

Although transformed and weakened by the transition to post-Stalinism, state-socialist regimes were able to preserve their institutional coherence, ideological vigor, and political initiative. During the years that followed the turbulent 1950s, ruling elites managed to defuse the most dangerous tensions and to create the appearance of a political consensus and popular support. As a result of de-Stalinization, however, the distribution of power and relations between major institutional orders of the party-states were altered. The power of the security apparatus and its supervision of the party organizations was curtailed. Soviet advisers who personally supervised security police, the military, government institutions, industries, and factories were recalled. In the post-Stalinist period, state-socialist regimes were freer to implement their own policies in both the political and economic spheres. They strived to reproduce the existing type of domination mainly by correcting the redistributive role of the state.[29] Among the factors that facilitated adjustments of social and economic policies during the transition to post-Stalinist environment and helped to ensure the continuing viability of state-socialist regimes, the most important were:

1. the reserves of extensive economic development in the form of natural resources, land, and labor forces, which were relatively easy to mobilize in the context of a low-technology environment, low consumer expectations among the population, and isolation from the global economy;

2. the potential to transform the established pattern of Soviet economic exploitation of the region into a more reciprocal type of economic relations that allowed dependent countries to decrease their indebtedness to the Soviet Union and to utilize plentiful and inexpensive Soviet natural resources and energy in order to maintain their inefficient economic systems;

3. limited political relaxation within the existing political system (post-Stalinist elites could alter terroristic Stalinist practices and grant some political concessions without endangering their political control and the party's monopoly of power);

4. some legitimization capacities based on the policies of economic concessions, revocation of terror, as well as on the regime's attempts to resurrect selected elements of national identity and tradition, which together could produce an appearance of consensus and popular support;

5. the enduring appeal of the Marxist-Leninist project and the state-idea, which sustained the ideological vigor of the ruling elites and supplied their ideological self-justification, and the domination of Marxist political language (the extinction of traditional political discourses hampered the formation of any alternative political discourse that could form new political identities and collective action frames, and posed a real threat to the party-state institutions and its hegemony);

6. The fragmentation of society resulting from the massive reconstruction of social structure caused by the postwar migrations, nationalization, collectivization, and industrialization policies, as well as by the complete reconstitution of political and intellectual elites.[30]

The second historical period that produced the cross-regional cycle of protest had its beginnings in the Polish self-limiting revolution of 1980–1981. The rise of the most powerful and organized opposition movement in the post–World War II period and its destruction by the imposition of martial law had profound political consequences not only in Poland but in the region as a whole. Following the 1980–81 crisis, Poland experienced the precarious political developments reinforced by a growing crisis in other countries of the region. This period was characterized by deepening economic stagnation, the corrosion of the communist party organization and power and the disintegration of its ideology, the rise of independent social and political movements, and the resurgence of traditional ethnic tensions in many countries of the region. The rapid deterioration of the political situation and the growth of political opposition in the 1980s may be seen as a collective response to the encroaching process of decay that consumed the entire socialist state-system. It culminated in the spectacular 1989 collapse of state-socialist regimes throughout Eastern Europe and disintegration of the Soviet Union two years later.

The crisis affecting state-socialist regimes in the 1980s was visible at every level of social, economic, and political organization. It was comprised of six distinct, yet interconnected developments:

1. the profound identity crisis of the communist parties as reflected by the collapse of the official political discourse and the transition from legitimation claims based on Marxist-Leninist ideology to those based on a pseudo-realpolitik with strong nationalistic underpinnings;

2. the gradual disintegration of the party-state's auxiliary institutions such as trade-unions and professional and youth organizations that in the past played the crucial role of "transmission belts," blocking the entire political space and insuring political stability;[31]

3. the failure of centrally planned economies resulting in economic stagnation, the disruption of the consumer market, and a severe financial crisis;

4. the emancipation of a vigorous second economy reflected in the explosive growth of the black market and semilegal and legal private enterprises;

5. the formation of a distinct political society consisting of a wide variety of

independent social and political movements and organizations as well as the revival and "de-privatization" of religion;[32]

6. the relaxation of geopolitical constraints and the expanded party-states' autonomy in dealing with their own internal affairs, granted by a crisis-ridden Soviet Union.

Though similar in makeup, these processes proceeded with varying speeds and intensities within the different countries of Eastern Europe and therefore produced significant diversity among state-socialist regimes at the end of the decade. They were most explicit in Poland as a result of the 1980–81 crisis and the failure of post-crisis policies.

The intensifying crisis was reflected in the increasing anarchy that prevailed within the legal and institutional systems and by the collapse of the state's precarious legitimization based on a goal-oriented rationality appropriate to the teleological nature of the communist ideology.[33] It was also apparent in the rapidly deteriorating economy and in the severe budgetary and financial crisis.[34] This process of decay led to the serious institutional decomposition of state-socialist regimes, the decline of their coercive capacity, and the disintegration of their ideological and theoretical foundations. It resulted in the intensification of emancipatory drives within the society, and the increase of centrifugal tendencies in the region.[35] By the end of the 1980s, the traditional foundations of domestic and foreign policy and the economic organization of state-socialist regimes were no longer viable, and political initiative moved outside the official structures of the party-state. The whole region reached a turning point where the boundaries of what was permissible and possible were unclear. A long, difficult, and uncertain process of fundamental economic and political transformations culminated in 1989 with the collapse of Soviet-type regimes across the region.

The Polish crisis of the 1980s was perhaps the most dramatic illustration of the changes occurring in East Central Europe since de-Stalinization.[36] Political developments in Poland most dramatically reflected the emergence of the new opposition and the dissolution of dominant political discourses and ideological principles common to all state-socialist regimes.[37] In the late 1970s, political initiative gradually shifted outside the official institutional structure of state-socialist regimes, and political language went beyond the revisionist discourse. Accordingly, communist parties no longer were able to set the limits and to design the content of changes. Instead, they were only able to respond to the challenges and processes that developed outside of the political space controlled by the regime.[38] At the same time, oppositional intellectuals in the region developed a new political language and revived old political and cultural traditions that allowed different political actors within society to build new all-inclusive identities and cross-class alliances, to monopolize political initiative, and to mobilize public support.[39] In short, the conditions for the regime transition were in place long before 1989.

This short overview indicates that East Central European state-socialist regimes faced crucial challenges in maintaining political stability during their postwar history.[40] Despite their highly repressive nature, collective protest and popular mobilization often occurred, and there was the ever-present threat of collective action. The danger of popular explosion became an important element of every political and economic decision and calculation made by the ruling elites, and political crises, rebellions, and protests often shattered the deceptive silence and routine of oppressive political regimes in the region. As a result of crisis-generated changes, gradual adjustments of institutions and policies, and changing Soviet objectives toward the region, the overall political context within which political struggles unfolded changed significantly during the four decades of communist rule. The Solidarity movement in Poland confronted a very different set of constraints and challenges than those who pressed for reforms in 1956 Hungary and 1968 Czechoslovakia. This overview also shows the usefulness of the "political process model," synthesizing structural factors with actions and choices of elites and popular actors, in analyzing East European political developments.[41]

The cycles of popular mobilization and the changing character of political crises in various periods of the development of state-socialist regimes attracted considerable scholarly attention in the past. Students of Eastern Europe raised puzzling questions about causes of political conflicts, identity and importance of various collective actors, and the geopolitical ramifications of political crises in the region. All such events received extensive coverage in the Western media. Nevertheless, as soon as a crisis was over, both academic and public interest faded, and the postcrisis periods have remained largely unexplored. This situation is not unique to East Central Europe but characterizes a general tendency in contemporary political science. Although the various forms of political mobilization, their impact on different sociopolitical systems, and the causes for their failure and success have been thoroughly analyzed by scholars of all theoretical persuasions, surprisingly little attention has been paid to processes of political demobilization and reequilibration of the regimes that followed the crises. The present work was specifically designed to focus more explicitly on postcrisis developments and was conceived as an attempt to partially fill this gap in the existing scholarship.

PROCESSES OF POLITICAL DEMOBILIZATION AND REGIME REEQUILIBRATION

Cases and processes of political demobilization have been largely neglected, leaving a surprisingly unexplored field within political sociology and political science. As Karen Remmer observed in her paper on Chile following the military coup of 1973, "Limited research exists on political demobilization

processes even in an historical context in which their relevance seems obvious."[42] Similarly, Piotr Sztompka stressed that "the systematic study of the
consequences of social movements is less developed . . . and virtually non-
existent is the study of the consequences of the movements that were suppressed, crushed, defeated by force."[43] From a more analytical perspective,
Mayer Zald, assessing the tasks facing the theory of social movements,
pointed out that in order to advance our knowledge of mobilization processes "we need to have better understanding of the counterpart processes
of demobilization and deescalation."[44] Unfortunately, despite such assessments, the absence of significant theoretical and comparative work on demobilization processes has remained a persistent feature of sociology and
political science during the last decade.[45] Similarly, the process of reequilibration of nondemocratic regimes that experienced the political crisis and
institutional breakdown has not attracted enough attention to become a
subject of systematic research.[46]

In this book I explore the issues of demobilization and reequilibration of
state-socialist regimes in their theoretical and empirical dimensions. The
chapters that follow present analyses of the conditions and patterns of the
consequential processes of large-scale coercive political demobilization and
institutional reequilibration that occurred several times during the post–
Second World War history of East Central Europe. As I argue, these processes played a crucial role in shaping the political evolution of the region
during the last three decades. Moreover, different trajectories of political
and economic transformations and patterns of collapse of state-socialist regimes in East Central Europe cannot be fully comprehended without understanding how these countries were "stabilized" and their populations demobilized after the previous crises.

For my analyses I have chosen the three most significant instances of
institutional breakdown, coercive political demobilization, and institutional
reequilibration. These case studies include: the Hungarian Revolution of
1956 and the period between 1956 and 1963 following the suppression of
the revolution by the Soviet army, the reform movement in Czechoslovakia
of 1968 and the period between 1968 and 1976 following the collapse of the
reform process initiated from above by the party-state elites and the military invasion by five Warsaw Treaty Organization countries, and the rise of
Solidarity in Poland in 1980 and the period between 1981 and 1989 following the imposition of martial law and the destruction of the Polish self-limiting revolution by coercive forces of the Polish party-state. Among all the
occurrences of mass mobilization, political conflict, and institutional breakdown during the four decades of communist rule in East Central Europe,
these three were comparable in scope and significance. In all three cases, the
entire institutional structure of the party-state both in the polity and in the
economy was affected, and large segments of the population were involved.
Various social groups and political actors both within the society and within

the party-state were able to develop and advance crucial systemic and ideological challenges that threatened the domestic political order and geopolitical relations in the region. And in each case, the party-state was forced to employ large-scale coercive measures in order to restore its domination and stabilize the political system. In this respect, these three crises differ from all other cases of popular mobilization where the party-state either succeeded in pursuing the noncoercive demobilization policies, such as those employed following the 1956 political crisis in Poland, or used small-scale, localized coercive demobilization tactics such as those following the Polish crises of 1968, 1970, and 1976. Moreover, these three political challenges to the party-state's rule occurred within surprisingly consistent time intervals, allowing an opportunity to assess the impact of long-term political and economic transformations of the region and effects of the political learning process among both ruling elites and opposition forces. These contextual changes and the learning process had an easily detectable influence on the tactics and strategies of individual party-states, actions of the hegemonic power in the region, and strategies of oppositional struggle.

Demobilization and reequilibration policies and their outcomes displayed significant variation from case to case and raised interesting questions and puzzles. In the course of the demobilization process following its revolution, Hungary suffered mass terror, enforced collectivization of agriculture, the prosecution of the church, and the decline of economic performance. George Urban pointed out in 1962 that "in a structural sense Hungary is now closer to the Soviet model than she was under Rakosi. The collectivisation of agriculture has completely, and perhaps finally, changed the country's political, social and economic profile."[47] However, this period of highly repressive policies concluded with a general amnesty, an ideological attitude by the party elites that was less rigid, some political concessions to professionals and intelligentsia, a relaxation of censorship, and unjammed transmissions of Western radio broadcasts.

Although the Stalinist institutional framework of the party-state remained unaltered, there was a gradual change in practices of ruling elites and relations between major institutional orders of the state. Over the years, there was some expansion in the role of the Parliament and trade unions, limited competition in elections, as well as a liberalization of contacts with the West and partial reconciliation with Hungarian emigration. Moreover, in the late 1960s, the Hungarian party-state introduced a series of cautious economic reforms that created, according to many commentators, the most successful model for management of economic affairs in the Soviet bloc. In spite of direct Soviet military intervention and involvement of Soviet coercive forces in the restoration of political order, the Hungarian party-state was able to secure more independence in pursuing domestic policies. It also established more favorable economic exchange and cooperation with the USSR than it had had before the revolution.

By contrast, the outcomes of demobilization and reequilibration policies in Czechoslovakia amounted to the establishment of a quasi-Stalinist, highly centralized party-state pursuing a repressive policy and ideologically motivated control over society and the economy. The restoration of the neo-Stalinist regime, however, did not result in the return to a classical form of Stalinism. "Husak's regime lacked both the vigour of true totalitarianism and the elan of real reformism."[48] In contrast to the Stalinist period, strategies of forced political mobilization were abandoned and the secret police's control over the party apparatus was dismantled. The federalization of the Czechoslovak state, drafted during the Prague Spring, changed the institutional structure of the state and partially soothed the national tensions between Czechs and Slovaks. Also, there was less extensive control over the private life of citizens, consumer expectations were encouraged, and the second economy was tolerated. Marxist-Leninist ideology acquired a purely ritualistic character, and the regime achieved an almost total depoliticization of its citizens. After only a few years through the demobilization process, Czechoslovakia was, as Vaclav Havel writes, in a state of "spiritual, moral, and political degradation."[49] Although such a situation differed greatly from the civic activism of 1968, it also did not resemble the artificial mass enthusiasm manufactured during the 1950s.

During the course of the demobilization process, Czechoslovakia became more dependent on the Soviet Union than ever before, not only in the sphere of politics and ideology but in the economic sphere as well.[50] In short, demobilization policies eradicated any organized opposition to the regime and produced a desolate economic, political, and sociopsychological situation in Czechoslovakia. In contrast to the demobilization process in Hungary, these policies blocked all meaningful attempts to reform either the economy or the polity. In spite of such different outcomes of demobilization processes in Hungary and Czechoslovakia, in both cases reequilibration of the regime was effective and successful in the sense that the undivided rule of the party-state and its institutional structure was fully restored; society was forced into quiescence; and the relationship between the state and society characteristic of Soviet-type regimes was re-established.

In this respect, the situation in Poland after the imposition of martial law was significantly different. After a few years into the demobilization and reequilibration process, it became clear that for a variety of reasons the Polish party-state was able to follow neither the Hungarian nor the Czechoslovak scenario. First of all, the institutional framework of the party-state was not fully reestablished, and relations between its core institutions underwent a significant transformation. The role of the communist party and ideology was reduced to a remarkable extent. The shift was toward a statist policy, increasing the role of the army and state institutions at the expense of the communist party. This was emphasized by the transfer of decision-making power to state institutions at all levels and by the takeover of many crucial administrative and political positions by the army elite. Moreover, following martial law, more than two hundred legislative acts were adopted by the Parliament, significantly altering the legal framework of the Polish regime and introducing important institutional changes to the organization of the state.

Despite the militarization of the economy and full state control over resources and labor, a general economic situation and the country's economic performance consistently deteriorated during the 1980s. Jaruzelski's government efforts to introduce changes and to improve economic performance were very inconsistent and largely unsuccessful. This was despite significant structural changes in the economy, such as a relaxing of central control and the introduction of elements of a market economy, as well as a much more lenient attitude toward small-scale private enterprises and farms. Given the poor economic performance, the consumer market was de-stabilized, standards of living fell sharply, inflation and foreign debt substantially increased, while productivity, product quality, and the decapitalization of factories reached alarmingly low levels by the end of the decade.

Moreover, in spite of political repression following martial law, oases of autonomy and liberty survived and even expanded within the political landscape of Poland. Although large segments of the population were effectively demobilized, various forms of collective protest became routine elements of political life. After the initial shock of military crackdown, the political opposition regrouped, diversified, and proliferated. Churches and universities, which were not purged, provided institutional bases and intellectual assistance to Solidarity's organized underground resistance in various factories and regions. As the sole autonomous institution and social force, the Catholic Church became a focal point of oppositional activities and in realization of its growing social power, remarkably increased its independence and intransigence vis-à-vis the state. In response to flourishing underground publications and information networks, censorship was significantly relaxed and almost disappeared by the end of the decade. The policies of the regime regarding travel abroad became for both political and economic reasons more relaxed and emigration became much easier.

The Polish party-state had substantial autonomy in pursuing its internal policies. Yet, because of the deteriorating economic situation, there was a notable increase in dependence on the Soviet Union within the economic sphere. In general, the effectiveness of the Polish demobilization process was remarkably low. Despite persistent efforts, the party-state's domination was not restored nor did society become quiescent or accept forced cooperation with the rulers. The communist party-state was initially able to secure its position due to factors such as a shift in the role of the military and state administration, innovative institutional transformation, and the development of new strategies that forestalled a large-scale confrontation between the state and society. However, after 1988 the collapse of demobilization policies was apparent. Unable to improve the economic situation and confronted with new waves of large-scale workers protests, party and state leaders opened the negotiations with representatives of the banned Solidarity movement. The round-table agreement signed on April 7, 1989, represented the ultimate failure of demobilization policies and opened the way to rapid and fundamental political and economic changes. During the span of several weeks, the Parliament introduced significant constitutional changes and the communist party suffered a crushing defeat in the prearranged elections and was deserted by its satellite parties. These developments resulted in the formation of the first noncommunist government in East Central Europe since the 1940s.

The differences in patterns and outcomes that exist between these three cases of large-scale coercive demobilization and reequilibration policies are due in part to specific characteristics of each crisis, distinct strategies employed by the leaders of each party-state, and the different capacities of actors within the state and society. The aim of this study is to systematically account for these differences by applying a consistent analytical framework to all three cases. A comparative approach to cases of coercive political demobilization may significantly contribute to our understanding of each particular case. By focusing on specific political events and historical trajectories of individual countries, I hope to avoid a problem that too often plagues East European studies. While all comparative works on the region have forcefully emphasized the historically patterned differences and individual peculiarities among these countries, many scholars have surrendered to the temptation to base their research and analyses on uncomplicated macrolevel models, which effectively blurred these differences. Such a practice has reduced the scholars' ability to detect specific national patterns emerging within a seemingly uniform institutional structure imposed on the countries of Eastern Europe following the Second World War.

UNDERSTANDING PROCESSES OF DEMOBILIZATION AND REEQUILIBRATION OF STATE-SOCIALIST REGIMES

Academic interest in East Central Europe has fluctuated considerably over the past four decades. The highly fragmented field of East European studies reflected the changing political fortune of particular countries within the region, vested political interests and intellectual fascinations in the West, as well as theoretical developments of contemporary social sciences. Conforming to a general trend in modern political analysis, scholars and professional commentators have mostly focused on the issue of crisis and change in state-socialist regimes. Spectacular political events in East Central Europe were widely analyzed, but as soon as a crisis ended, both general and academic interests rapidly faded away. Accordingly, we have an amazing number of books and papers dealing with causes and dynamics of crises in East Central Europe but precious few works that look at what happened in particular countries after crises.[51]

State actions and policies following a political crisis have usually been characterized as attempts to reinstate the political and social relationships of domination weakened during the crisis. Czechoslovak government officials euphemistically dubbed this process as a "normalization of the situation," and many scholars make reference to this same term, assuming that it adequately characterizes the nature of post-crisis developments and policies not only in Czechoslovakia but also in Hungary and in Poland. Shortly after the Jaruzelski regime crushed the Solidarity movement in Poland, some scholars explored possibilities of comparing the demobilization policies employed in these three countries. A common analytical framework used in these studies was built around the concept of "normalization." For Jiri Valenta " 'normalization' describes the complex policies developed and fostered by the Soviets, under specific national conditions and over a long period, spanning a decade or more, to partly or fully reverse revolutionary change in a given Eastern European country."[52] Jan de Weydenthal, Bruce Porter, and Kevin Devlin argue that the term refers "to the reestablishment of Leninist norms in all spheres of national life."[53] Similarly, Wlodzimierz Brus contends that "normalization means restoration of the basic elements of the political status quo ante."[54]

In spite of wide acceptance, the basic problem with the concept of normalization is that it assumes the existence of definite political norms; reinforcement of which automatically produces a "normal" social and political order of state-socialist societies, regardless of the nature of the crisis that affected a given society. It also seems to imply the existence of a master plan (designed by the Soviets, as it is argued) that outlines the way in which the political and economic system must be changed and transformed after the crisis. Moreover, it seems that behind the notion of normalization there is an assumption that "normal" refers to the "Stalinist" model of sociopolitical organization.

The notion of what is normal in an empirical and ideological sense is always problematic, and cases traditionally considered to be model examples of normalization raise serious doubts.[55] Moreover, the notion of "normalization" originated as a specific political category that was used in a particularly obscure way to justify repressive policies; its transfer to social sciences discourse retained this ambiguity of meaning. Therefore, the notion of normalization used by scholars to describe the aftermath of political crisis in East Central Europe does not present a satisfactory analytical framework that accounts for the complex nature of large-scale coercive demobilization and regime reequilibration policies.

Demobilization processes should be understood as highly disruptive and costly political processes that reflect a complex relationship between various groups and actors within society and the party-state elites in state-socialist societies. Effective demobilization is a part and necessary condition for the reequilibration of the nondemocratic regime that experienced the institutional breakdown. Following Juan Linz, I define reequilibration as "a political process that, after a crisis that seriously threatened the continuity and stability of the basic [political institutions and mechanisms] results in their continued existence at the same or higher levels of . . . efficacy and effectiveness."[56] Demobilization and reequilibration policies should be viewed as a product of internal struggles within and between institutions and elites of the party-state shaped by ad hoc political decisions in a given country rather than as the implementation of a preconceived political design or the return to a "normal" situation. In all cases, demobilization policies were more or less innovative improvisations that were shaped and forced by the changing domestic and international political and economic conditions and led to a variety of unanticipated political and social consequences. Pierre Kende's assertion that "the policy of Kadarizm has been worked out in the heat of action"[57] applies equally to the situation in Czechoslovakia and Poland. Moreover, the demobilization and reequilibration processes should be accorded their crucial impact in shaping and transforming the entire sociopolitical system in the countries where they occurred.

The short- and long-term outcomes of these policies, reflected in the change of institutional structures and political behavior, can hardly be described as a return to the political status quo ante. Processes of mobilization, demobilization and reequilibration are in fact about making, unmaking, and remaking of the state. They reflect struggles for influence and define boundaries between the state and society.[58] It can be argued that demobilization policies produced, directly and indirectly, the most significant political innovations and institutional and policy changes in the history of state-socialist regimes in East Central Europe. In all cases under study, demobilization policies reshaped the political institutions and relations between them, reshaped the relationship between the party-state elites and actors within society, and changed dominant political practices and political discourse. They also significantly influenced the political, economic, and social conditions in decades that followed.[59]

It is evident that post-crisis developments not only involved a retrogressive and conservative tendency to preserve the essential features of the existing type of social and political organization and protect established institutions, but, more importantly, reflected an urgent need of the new party and state leadership to introduce political and institutional innovations in order to meet new and old challenges and to find a new level of accommodation with important groups within society. In all three cases the rhetoric of the leaders implementing demobilization policies was strikingly similar. They firmly denied the possibility of returning to the situation that existed during the political crisis that they considered as permeated by dangers of chaos and counterrevolution. But they also emphasized that they had no intentions of returning to the same political and institutional environment that caused the crisis. They characterized their policies as middle-of-the-road attempts at "socialist revival." Their actions were meant to eliminate policy distortions or errors committed by the precrisis ruling elites. At the same time they aimed to defend the existing institutional system against alleged counter-revolutionary threats, and to perfect the state-socialist regime's organization and policies in order to create a more effective and stable sociopolitical and economic system. This political rhetoric was often followed by deeds. Eastern European developments provide clear evidence to Anthony Oberschall's point that "a movement can be ruthlessly suppressed and yet many changes it had sought might still be brought about at a later time, for confrontation is a warning signal to the ruling groups that they better change course or else face even more explosive upheavals in the future."[60]

The existing analyses of demobilization processes in East Central Europe advanced by scholars in the field have weaknesses that reflect the more general theoretical difficulties of traditional approaches to state-socialist societies developed over the last four decades. First, the dominant totalitarian perspective radically underestimated the differences between state-socialist regimes and, more importantly, denied nonelite actors any capacity to shape domestic politics. Second, even when varieties of state socialism were admitted to and the significance accorded to domestic forces moderately expanded, changes in the region as a whole were still considered to be determined exclusively by the Soviet Union. Thus, most scholars working in the field overemphasized the role of geopolitical factors, focused on intra-elite struggles and personalities of top leaders, and underestimated the autonomous role of society in shaping social and political processes.[61] Moreover, another problem with the existing scholarship on the subject is a limited use of the comparative approach.[62]

Among explanatory hypotheses advanced by scholars analyzing crisis situations, one can distinguish several recurring themes. One of the most common is the emphasis on the personality of leaders who carry out the policies of demobilization. For some scholars the personality differences between the leaders seems to be the most crucial factor in shaping the outcomes of demobilization processes and in accounting for differences between the cases.[63] This fascination with the personalities of leaders has its source in a previously dominant style of reasoning within American sovietology. Without entering the classical debate concerning the merits or pitfalls of reductionism, one can agree that in a monocentric political order the personality, perceptions, and preferences of a ruler may have added importance.[64] However, it is hazardous to assume that the preferences of a leader can be considered a major explanatory variable in the analysis of complex political and social processes. In Joel Migdal's words, "The state does not merely reflect the will and skill of its leaders."[65] Moreover, leaders' choices may be so constrained as to prevent implementation of any of their personal preferences.

Another common theme in the existing explanations is a focus on Soviet strategies, policies, and actions. As Jiri Valenta argues, "During the years of consolidation, the policies of the Hungarian and Czechoslovak regimes were greatly influenced, if not almost wholly determined by the Soviets."[66] This empire-centered viewpoint reflects a fascination with great-power politics and seems to grossly underestimate the autonomous role of particular national states, their societies, and their elites. During the four decades after the Second World War the Soviet Union built a complex set of institutions and informal practices enhancing their control of East European countries. They included multilateral institutional ties, such as the Warsaw Treaty Organization and the Council for Mutual Economic Assistance, bilateral agreements and informal arrangements. However, these institutions played different roles in various periods, and as Andrzej Korbonski emphasizes, "under the impressive and seemingly impregnable facade of formal and informal arrangements, some major changes have taken place."[67] These intricate mechanisms of control did not prevent defiant and independent actions of East European leaders. The Yugoslav (1948), Polish (1956), Albanian (1961), and Romanian (1960) leaders were able to defy the Soviets and pursue their own policies. These examples aptly illustrate that even in the most obvious cases of political dependence there is room for defiance and autonomous action.

There is no doubt about the extent and significance of state-socialist regimes' political dependence on the Soviet Union and of the Soviet influence on their domestic policies. It would be impossible not to agree that the course of demobilization policies in these countries was significantly shaped and influenced by the Soviet power elites, if only by the fact of direct military involvement. Moreover, it is well documented that the Soviet internal situation had an important impact on both the decision to intervene and policies implemented after the intervention. Scholars like Ferenc Feher[68] and Pierre Kende[69] are right in linking the relative success of Kadarization to Khrushchev's attempts to move away from the Stalinist system in the Soviet Union. Similarly, Valenta has a point when he argues that Czechoslovak's failure to liberalize the system and to soften demobilization policies reflected the conservative policies of the Brezhnev period.[70] Yet even when acknowledging the significance of both geopolitical dependence and the role of external pressure, the argument can be made that geopolitical constraints give only partial insight into complexity of domestic political conflicts and struggles. Thus, reducing complex political phenomena to a simple geopolitical variable cannot be justified by any reasonable methodological standard.

In explaining why Hungarian and Czechoslovak societies did not respond to demobilization policies with lasting and effective resistance and were effectively forced into quiescence and compliance, and why Polish society was able to maintain organized and effective resistance for a period of several years, two sets of factors are most often emphasized. First is the extent and severity of repression. As Kende points out, "Hungary's 'normalization' . . . began with the nation's complete defeat, with the total knock-down of Hungarian society."[71] Hungary stands alone in the severity of repression un-leashed during the demobilization process. The role of repression in Poland and Czechoslovakia, however, is more ambiguous and does not provide a clear-cut explanatory variable.

The scope of postintervention repressions differed greatly in these three cases. At one extreme were the bloody political repressions in Hungary, which Kadar's closest associate characterized in the following way: "In 1949 we missed an opportunity of smashing the forces of reaction—this time we will exterminate them." Recently uncovered data show that four thousand Hungarians were killed and twenty thousand wounded during ac-tual fighting with Soviet troops, whose losses stood at 669 killed, 1,450 wounded, and 51 missing. This was followed by methodical and massive repressions. Between 1956 and 1959, thirty-five thousand people were ar-rested for their activities during the revolution. Of those, twenty-six thou-sand were brought to trial and twenty-two thousand were sentenced. By the summer of 1961, 280 to 300 people were executed and 350 to 400 death sentences were commuted. Moreover, between 1957 and 1960, thirteen thousand people were interned.[72]

By contrast, the death toll in Czechoslovakia was much smaller. One hun-dred persons died, 335 were severely wounded, and some five hundred were injured as a result of the massive military intervention of the WTO forces between August 21 and October 18, 1968.[73] Between August 20 and Sep-tember 3, only 172 persons were arrested, and eight individuals remained in detention on the latter day. The number of people arrested and tried for political reasons after 1968 was surprisingly small. In the most extensive police action, in December 1971 and January 1972, some two hundred per-sons were arrested, among whom forty-seven were sentenced.[74] In Poland the physical terrors of martial law were patchy and mild. There were only thirty-six proven cases of killings by soldiers or the police during the first year of martial law, and a few hundred cases of people wounded during the strike-breaking and street demonstrations. In contrast to Czechoslovakia, however, martial law started with a huge and systematic wave of arrests. Among approximately fifty thousand Solidarity activists, 10,131 were de-tained in internment camps during the first few months after martial law was imposed. Moreover, until the first amnesty of July 1983, an additional 4,173 persons were arrested in connection with political activities, among whom 2,310 were put on trial.[75] Although direct repressions are a significant and indispensable element of any coercive demobilization policy, their use, ex-tent, and severity is determined by other more essential factors. Thus, politi-cal repression should be seen as a dependent variable, which instead of pro-viding an explanation requires one. Moreover, I will argue that the ability to withstand even severe and prolonged political repression is directly linked to the nature of mass mobilization, the level of organization, and the avail-ability of resources at the disposal of oppositional groups and movements.

Second, the argument advanced in many studies states that effective demobilization policies are combined with the party-states capacity to immediately improve the economic situation and offer substantial economic concessions in exchange for political compliance. The notion of a new social contract provides an analytical foundation for this argument.[76] The concept of the new social contract is founded on the assumption that society under Soviet-type regimes collectively, but through atomized decisions, exchanges its political rights, liberties, and aspirations for security and consumer satisfaction. When economic downswings generate a breakdown in the state's ability to maintain a high level of benefits, it is argued that society is likely to withdraw its support and/or compliance, which is purely conditional and rests on the fulfillment of material and other consumer expectations. The trouble with this concept is its perception of politics. Politics is reduced to a simple barter transaction where cars, refrigerators, and sausages are traded for human rights and political liberties. Such a view also implies a vision of society as a perfectly rational actor able to calculate gains and risks and act according to such calculations.

Contrary to such a point of view, it can be argued, as Alain Touraine does, that "Homo socius is not just a variety of Homo oeconomicus"[77] and, therefore, the notion of a new social contract, although elegant in its simplicity, can be considered as one more attempt to reduce politics and complex social phenomena to a simple and rational decision-making process of atomized political actors. To a social scientist, the notion of a new social contract is as artificial a construction as its more famous predecessor in the eighteen century and is as misleading in understanding real historical situations as the original concept of social contract was. There is no doubt, however, that the postcrisis regimes' capacity to improve the economic situation as well as the ability of other bloc countries and the Soviet Union to provide needed economic assistance played an important role. In this respect there is marked differences between the post-1981 situation in Poland and the two other cases analyzed in this book.

This brief discussion leads to a conclusion that scholars in the field were not completely successful in providing satisfactory explanations of large-scale coercive demobilization and reequilibration processes in Soviet-type societies. All explanatory and conceptual efforts analyzed above fail, in my view, to generate a convincing set of hypotheses that account for the variations in the party-states' strategies and the different courses, and outcomes of the demobilization policies. While many scholarly works significantly contributed to our understanding of the crucial aspects of demobilization processes and specific country experiences, there is still an urgent need to systematically reassess the nature and impact of these processes.

In investigating demobilization and reequilibration processes, my ambition is not to discover the causal relations among the multitude of factors shaping the large-scale political processes but rather to establish some correlations between selected variables that, according to Pierre Birnbaum,[78] constitute the only valid task for comparative historical analysis. This, of course, requires some fairly arbitrary choices. In fact, as Sidney Tarrow reminds us:

> Modern states are never more complicated, confusing and contradictory than when they respond to waves of collective action. They are capable of simultaneous facilitating, repressing, co-opting and showing indifference to protestors, and occasionally responding to their claims, depending on the identity of the actors, the demands they make, against whom they are made, forms of action they use and what part of the state is invested with protest.[79]

In the case of state-socialist regimes, patterns of Soviet domination and involvement in domestic affairs of dependent countries make things even more complicated. For many years Soviet involvement and policies in Eastern Europe have been extensively analyzed, often at the expense of analyses focusing on domestic conditions. My choice is to change this perspective. I will focus more on domestic developments and institutions than on Soviet goals and policies. I will try to identify most important domestic factors and conditions that were responsible for the variations in demobilization strategies, policies and outcomes between effective cases of demobilization, and reequilibration in Hungary and Czechoslovakia and Poland, which represents the apparent failure of the party-states' demobilization efforts. In short, I will try to answer the following questions: Why and how was the Hungarian party-state able to conclude its highly repressive period of demobilization with the establishment of a paternalistic regime characterized by a pragmatic approach to economic policies and a relative flexibility in political and ideological matters? Why did the demobilization policies in Czechoslovakia remain highly repressive, produce political and economic stagnation, and freeze any attempts to introduce meaningful political and/or economic reforms for almost twenty years? And, finally, why did the Polish postmartial law regime fail to rebuild the party-state's authority and institutions, to destroy political opposition, to prevent large-scale collective protest, to arrest economic crisis, and to introduce effective political and economic reforms?

Methodologically this analysis illustrates two well-known problems of comparative research—a small number of cases and a large number of variables as well as added influence of additional variables over time.[80] I do not claim to escape from or to find solution to these problems. Instead, I identify with the tradition of historically oriented interpretative work and organize my analysis around cases. According to Charles Ragin: "Case-oriented studies, by their nature, are sensitive to complexity and historical specificity. Thus, they are well suited for addressing empirically defined historical outcomes.[81] As a result of this choice, those who search for a parsimonious, generalizable argument based on a single causal relation tested in these three cases will be disappointed. I agree with David Laitin that "normal models of political conflict, which assume incremental changes within a stable political context and linear relationship between cause and effect, may not be applicable to the political processes involved in the building and breakdown of regimes or the building and breakdown of hegemonic ideas."[82] I consider the cases I analyze as configurations or nests of variables whose importance changes over time. Each crisis developed through three distinctive stages that differed from case to case. They included: (1) sources and patterns of underlying political and economic crisis, (2) patterns and outcomes of the confrontation stage, and (3) patterns and outcomes of the demobilization and reequilibration stage. Combinations of characteristics of early stages constrained the choices and actions of political actors and had the important impact on developments in latter stages. I argue, however, that the stage of demobilization and reequilibration in each crisis left the most enduring consequences.

The additional difficulty for my analysis comes from the fact that these events were highly interlinked and were important elements in a general process of change that characterized state-socialist regimes during the five decades of their existence. This situation presents the problem that Stefano Bartolini describes as the "historical multi-collinearity."[83] Mutual impact of these events weakens the validity and control of cross-temporal causal generalizations. Moreover, these events produced important cognitive changes and provide an excellent illustration of the political learning process across cases with a significant consequences for behavior and actions of both elite and mass political actors.[84] In East Central Europe, the political learning process from case to case may be documented in a most literal sense. For example, Jaruzelski's regime in Poland invited Hungarian experts to seek advice in designing martial law policies. Among other things, Hungarian experts strongly recommended against dissolution of the communist party, arguing that this had been a serious mistake committed by Kadar in 1956.

In the existing scholarship, the process of political demobilization is commonly considered as a simple reversal of the process of political mobilization.[85] While, according to Charles Tilly, the mobilization process involves the accumulation and collective control over coercive, utilitarian, and normative resources; demobilization involves "seizure, devaluation or dispersion of the resources at the disposal of contenders."[86] In the most general sense this view is correct. However, there are different patterns of mobilization that produce varied institutional consequences, opportunities, and constraints for challenging groups. Moreover, the mobilization and demobilization processes are constrained by institutional characteristics of states. According to Pierre Birnbaum, theorists of mobilization too often neglected "the crucial problem of the relations between types of state and the nature of mobilization."[87] Moreover, in every specific historical case, the institutional and political context of mobilization and demobilization processes is drastically different. Between these two phases we are usually confronted with a significant change in the character and capacity of the state[88] either due to internal change and institutional reconfiguration of power, as in the case of a military coup, or due to geopolitical circumstances, such as military invasion and the installation of the new government by the regional hegemon. Such a change sets specific constraints and conditions that not only affect the capacity of the state but also significantly modify the capacity of the political actors resisting the state's actions and policies. Thus, while the type of state and the nature of the crisis shapes political mobilization, the subsequent transformation of the character of the state, which usually involves the enhancement of the state's coercive capacity, is a crucial variable in shaping demobilization processes.

The mobilizational capacities of Soviet-type regimes were often emphasized by students of East European politics.[89] However, the issue of mobilization in itself requires careful examination. The distinction, introduced by Elemer Hankiss,[90] between strategies of quasi-mobilization and demobilization employed by the party-states and strategies of self-demobilization and self-mobilization, which characterized the responses of various groups and collective actors within society to the state's actions under state-socialist regimes, captures the precarious nature of the interaction between the state and society. It can be argued that in Soviet-type regimes, a political crisis arises when self-mobilization efforts of various collective actors within society are no longer controllable nor are they obstructed by routine demobilization and quasi-mobilization strategies employed by the state institutions and agencies responsible for political control.

In the post–World War II period, there were several cases in East Central Europe when self-mobilization, fueled by the accumulation of various, widely held grievances and prompted by the opening of the political opportunity structure, approached a critical level precipitating institutional breakdown of the party-state and threatening the existing type of relationship between the state and society and the prevailing mode of the distribution of power. Patterns of self-mobilizations were shaped by characteristics of both the state and society. On the one hand, due to colonization of political space by state-run institutions, extreme institutional penetration of society, and lack of autonomous organizations of civil society, the mobilizational potential of actors outside the state was seriously limited. On the other hand, as a result of the absence of the organizational infrastructure, the fragmentation of society and "segmented social space," symbolic political articulation played a critical role. In the conditions where the matrix of interests was distorted and unclear, political articulation was only possible through the integrating "symbolic visions" of the sociopolitical system organized around "us" and "them" dichotomy. Thus, the formation of groups' political identity was linked not to social characteristics but to the recognition of being a side in the political conflict.[91] In all cases of mobilization from below, large-scale coercive demobilization policies were employed by the party-state. The coercive response of the state was usually based on the enhanced capacity of the state resulting from organizational changes and mobilization of domestic resources as well as an infusion of external economic and political resources and direct external military aid.

In this book, the process of political demobilization will be generally defined as coercive reappropriation by the state of political spaces that were opened during the crisis through an effort to rebuild and stabilize the party-state institutional order and an attempt to restore a specific type of relationship between the state and society. In the course of this process, previously mobilized social actors within society lose their capacity to act collectively, to be involved in or to shape the political process, and to pursue their collective goals. They are transformed again, as Charles Tilly writes, into "a passive collection of individuals" and lose collective control over coercive, utilitarian, and normative resources they acquired as a result of the crisis.[92] Political demobilization is a complex social and political phenomenon that involves a wide variety of collective actors, political and social institutions, and resources. Methods and means utilized in the state's demobilization strategy may differ from case to case depending on the capacity and strength of the state and the collective actors who are the subject and recipients of demobilization efforts. In some cases, as I shall demonstrate, demobilization efforts and strategies can fail and opposition movements may not only survive but also retain their capacity to shape the political developments in a given country and even to force significant political changes. In every instance, however, political demobilization, whether successful or not, had a profound impact on the shape, functioning, and evolution of the entire sociopolitical system. As Karen Remmer emphasizes, "political demobilization, like political mobilization, is a disruptive process, entailing not only high social and economic costs, but also leading to a variety of unanticipated political consequences that may defeat its intended purpose and accentuate regime weaknesses."[93] Moreover, reequilibration of a nondemocratic regime after the political crisis depends on and requires the effective demobilization of actual and potential political opposition.

I shall argue that the core of effective demobilization strategies is the ability to restore fundamental elements of the regime's institutional order, solidify the state's boundaries, and reestablish a specific type of relationship between the institutional orders of the state and between the state and society that characterizes a given type of sociopolitical system. Thus strategies and tactics employed by the state in the demobilization process, such as political repression and/or economic and political concessions, are the instrumental means to this purpose. The state's ability to restore the desired state-society relationship, however, depends not only on its own institutional and coercive capabilities and resources but also on capacity of actors outside the state to resist demobilization efforts. Peter Hall correctly asserts in another context that "capacities of the state to implement a program tend to depend as much on the configuration of the society as of the state. . . . The state appears as a network of institutions deeply embedded within a constellation of ancillary institutions associated with society and the economic system."[94] This insight, although derived from the study of a democratic regime, has crucial implications for the present analysis pointing to a plausible analytical framework for studying demobilization policies.

Through my case studies, I will demonstrate that the capacity of the political actors to survive demobilization efforts is directly linked to the character of the preceding mobilization process. Contrary to the claims of theoreticians of mass society, who asserted a connection between social atomization and political mobilization,[95] and students of modernization who failed to explain the mechanism of political mobilization,[96] contemporary scholarship convincingly established that political mobilization depends on a previously constituted social organization.[97] According to Charles Tilly, the mobilization potential of a group is largely determined by the degree of preexisting group organization and the existence of strong collective identities.[98] Craig Calhoun argues that in order to mobilize, "people must have strong emotional ties with each other, a faith in their strength, and an identification with the collectivity in which they are to act."[99] These social networks and collective identities are activated by the leaders and solidify by organizational structures in the process of mobilization. If that is the case, then it can be argued that groups with weak collective identities and underdeveloped intrapersonal networks and organizations and that lack their own grass-roots leaders are not only less likely to mobilize but, when political mobilization does occur, they are also more prone to be easily demobilized. Therefore, an enduring oppositional movement able to survive in a repressive environment requires "the cementing together of an organizational network, which is always easier when some group networks already exist."[100]

The capacity to successfully survive political repression is also significantly enhanced when there is a longer time period before the coercive reappropriation of the political space by the state. Given more time, the opposition movement is more likely to develop a movement culture, symbols, language, and ideals that give the movement its distinct collective identity and in turn enhances its organizational capacity.[101] In his analysis, Scott McNall states:

> For a union or any other form of class organization to be successful, people must be educated by the organization in the movement culture, and/or ideology; otherwise, they are not likely to support its long-term goals and purposes. Likewise, if the time between recruitment and attempted mobilization is short, then the likelihood of a group's success is diminished, because its members will not have had time to develop a movement culture or will not understand the organizational policies or tactics that lead to discipline.[102]

This relation between organizational networks, collective identities, and the capacity to mobilize highlights the importance of rapidity and the time span of the mobilization process. If political mobilization is rapid, the organizational structures of opposition movements and organizations are often underdeveloped or nonexistent. Moreover, rapidly arising and expanding movements are likely to loose any organic relation to preexisting social networks.[103] Similarly, if the movement is large in size, the possibility of developing unified organizational networks and collective identities within a short span of time is inhibited. The same applies when the time span of the mobilization process is limited by an immediate and effective counteraction of either the state or dominant power in the region.

Therefore, the very nature of political mobilization is one of the most crucial elements in determining the vulnerability of oppositional movements. From this point of view one can argue that an opposition movement's ability to survive in an extremely repressive environment, which usually characterizes the political situation after the coercive response of the state to mass mobilization, is greater (1) when political mobilization is slow in coming and long in duration and when the movement is well organized and centralized prior to any form of coercive demobilization,[104] (2) when following the crackdown, the movement is able to adopt a segmented and decentralized model of organization,[105] and (3) when the "exit option,"[106] such as a large-scale emigration of oppositional activists and leaders or their withdrawal into nonpoliticized roles and activities, is restricted.

In the same vein, it could be argued that for the state elites to launch an effective demobilization campaign, several factors must be in place. First, the state elites must be able to preserve the state's organizational unity during the crisis and have the ability to mobilize coercive resources either domestically or in conjunction with external help. Second, the state elites must have the ability, resources, and determination to effectively respond to political and economic challenges that give rise to popular mobilization and to resolve major tensions and cleavages destabilizing the sociopolitical system. Finally, the state elites must preserve their organizational identity as well as the viability of the specific state idea that serves to justify a given type of state's institutions, their relationship and organizing principles, and gives motivation and purpose to elites' actions.

Thus, the framework for studying demobilization processes should include several dimensions because varying outcomes of strategic interaction are contingent on resources and capacity of all actors involved. First is the effort and strategies to preserve, enhance, and redirect state resources and policies that may involve a significant level of intra-elite conflict and struggle. Second is the state-society struggle, which involves capacity and resources of collective actors to resist state demobilization efforts and state strategies employed to this end. Finally, in the situation of political and economic dependence, the pressures and strategies of external actors can shape both the capacity of the state and society in their domestic confrontation.

I argue that in order to account for the variation in demobilization processes and success or failure of regime's reequilibration one has to take into account a number of different factors. In each of the cases under study, the strategic interaction of complex and internally divided political actors within three institutional domains shaped the course and effects of demobilization policies. These domains are the party-state, the society, and the regional institutional system based on dominant political power. The contrasting capabilities, goals, strategies and actions of collective actors within these three institutional domains account for the variations, effectiveness, and outcomes among the demobilization policies. In turn, these capabilities, goals, and strategies were significantly shaped by the nature and sequencing of the political crises that preceded demobilization processes. Each crisis had different patterns of cleavages and conflicts and different patterns of popular mobilization. Each produced a varied degree of institutional breakdown. Therefore, in the present analysis I am going to advance a complex argument that attempts to accommodate in a coherent way all these factors in order to provide a new more persuasive interpretation of historical records. Analytically, this interpretation is based on an eclectic synthesis of recent theoretical contributions from a broad range of social sciences literature, including comparative politics, social history, historical and political sociology, as well as East European studies.

While many factors contributed to the character and effectiveness of demobilization processes and success or failure of regime's reequilibration, I focus more specifically on three issues critical to the understanding of post-crisis developments: (1) patterns of cleavages and conflicts within the party-state and between factions of the ruling elite that not only opened the political opportunity structure for protest and reform movements but also set the limits for demobilization strategies, (2) patterns of popular mobilization during the crisis that crucially influenced and limited capacity of actors within society to resist the party-state's demobilization efforts and strategies, and (3) the role of international constraints and pressures as well as the capacity of international actors to shape domestic policies of demobilizing regimes. Thus, I am going to show that in all cases under study the character and effectiveness of demobilization policies were shaped by the nature, extent, and organization of popular mobilization as well as by cleavages, conflicts, and struggles both between the actors within the institutional structures of the party-state and between the state and society during the crisis and after the coercive response to it. This argument challenges existing explanations that strongly emphasize similarities among demobilization policies and place a particular emphasis on relatively stable geopolitical dependency as well as persistent and well defined interests and strategies of the Soviet Union.

In all three cases, the direct role of the Soviet Union in initiating, directing, and conducting the military operations aimed at defending the existing regional status quo and preventing any significant reform of internal political structures as well as its involvement in stabilizing the countries after the crisis is well-known. Even martial law in Poland, although executed by the domestic forces, was prepared in close collaboration with the Soviet military and approved by the Politburo,[107] and has often been described as the "intervention by proxy." Nevertheless, there is a profound contrast between the bloody suppression of the Hungarian Revolution by the Soviet troops, the massive military invasion of Czechoslovakia by the Warsaw Pact armies, and the politics of pressure and cover support for the military and police in the Polish case. While scholars emphasize the continuity of Soviet interests and objectives in Eastern Europe, they also acknowledge that the type and severity of Soviet involvement was dependent upon a variation of domestic factors in both the given country and the Soviet Union, changes within the broader international situation, and a significant evolution in the Soviet policy toward the region. There is no consensus among the students of Soviet foreign policy about the principal motives of Soviet military involvement.[108] The pattern of Soviet involvement, however, displayed a distinct shift. In the 1950s, Soviet troops were immediately mobilized and deployed at any sign of a major crisis. This was the case in East Germany in 1953 and in Poland and Hungary in 1956. Beginning in the 1960s, however, the decision to intervene militarily was preceded by a long period of consensus building and multilateral consultations among the Soviet elites and WTO members.[109]

The shift in Soviet policy of intervention can be traced back to the acceptance of the principle of "many roads to socialism" at the Twentieth Congress of the Soviet party in 1956. This declaration initiated a policy change that is characterized by Ken Jowitt as a transition from "consolidation to inclusion" in which the "individuality" but not "individualism" of dependent countries was allowed by the Soviets.[110] The underlying problem for the Soviet elite was, to use James F. Brown's phrase, "to find the right balance between cohesion and viability."[111] Moreover, within the broader international context, the relations of the Soviet Union with the communist movements in the West and in Third World countries, as well as the Soviet-China split, clearly affected Soviet policies and relations with its satellite party-states of Eastern Europe. After all, it was much easier to justify politically and ideologically the brutal suppression of the Hungarian revolution in the midst of the Cold War confrontation than it would have been in the 1980s following the Helsinki Accords and many years of building political and economic bridges to the West. Also the Soviet bloc's changing relationship to the global economy and the increasing dependence of these countries on the West for credits and technology clearly set limits on more aggressive political behavior.

The objectives of Soviet foreign policy were relatively clear. According to Eric P. Hoffmann, "Soviet leadership has always sought national security, economic growth and political stability at home; dissemination of its ideology and social institutions abroad; territorial expansion and increased influence over non-Communist governments and parties, ruling and non-ruling communist parties, and revolutionary movements."[112] From the Soviet point of view, therefore, Eastern Europe was the most important and sensitive region of the world for all these historical, military, political, economic, and ideological reasons. In spite of a consensus among scholars regarding the Soviet political and strategic goals in the region and the existence of a well defined hierarchical system of political dependency, a review of Soviet policies toward East Central European countries in the post–World War II period reveals a striking lack of consistency. In contrast to prevailing views about stability of Soviet goals and strategies in Eastern Europe, Brown asserts that during periods from Stalin's death until 1956, from Khrushchev's dismissal until the Prague Spring, and from 1975 to the end of the 1980s, Soviet policy toward the region exhibited remarkable indecision, contradictions, and uncertainties.[113]

Moreover, the political history of the region also exposes inherent weaknesses and paradoxes of Soviet imperial domination. In this context it is interesting to explore the applicability of the dependency theory to the East European hierarchical regional organization. William Zimmerman argues that "dependency theory shares with much of the traditional literature on Soviet foreign policy the assumption that the nature of the domestic system of the hegemonic state explains that state's relations with other, lesser states. Where the two differ is that one sees in the American socioeconomic system—capitalism—the explanation for the observed dependency relationships, whereas the other focuses on the Soviet political system—socialism—for an explanation."[114] The efforts to systematically compare Eastern Europe with other regions dominated by hegemonic powers did not yield, however, convincing evidence to support dependency theory. Jan Triska admits this difficulty when he points out that "as a consequence of the many differences between the two regions [Latin America and Eastern Europe] as well as between the two kinds of domination, the list of regional similarities is not very long. There are no inherent regional similarities except for the common resentment against domination."[115] In contrast to the classic characteristic of hegemonic power where political domination is exercised for the purpose of economic exploitation, and the dominant state enjoys socioeconomic advantages and cultural primacy, Soviet–East European relations exhibit striking qualities. First, the standards of living, economic performance, and technological advancement were higher in Eastern Europe than in the Soviet Union, with the exception of the military sector. Cal Clark and Donna Bahry argue that in comparison to most of Eastern Europe, the Soviet Union was less developed. It was the natural-resource and primary-goods exporter and manufactured-goods importer.[116] Second, the economic relations between state-socialist regimes and the Soviet Union did not present a clear picture of economic exploitation, especially after the mid 1950s and evolved into mutually disadvantageous economic bonds.[117] Finally, in the cultural and ideological dimension, the situation was equally paradoxical. The Soviet Union was not a hegemon in the Gramscian sense. It failed to establish itself as an ideological and cultural center of the empire.[118] But in spite of these weaknesses, the Soviet Union followed a path of all imperial powers, cumulating more international obligations than it was able to fulfill.[119] This is especially important when one takes into account that foundations of the Soviet empire were based on military might not on economic, technological, or cultural superiority.

The nature, complexity, and change in relations between the Soviet Union and other state-socialist countries provides a fascinating subject in itself. Above I have raised points to make clear that despite a seemingly uniform and hierarchical system of regional dependency, East European states had considerable room for maneuver. The policies and choices of their ruling elites were much less constrained by the Soviet power than is often assumed and they were willing to admit. Moreover, the nature of these relations and constraints evolved in a notable way during the four decades of communist rule. In this book I will focus primarily on internal forces and domestic conditions. I will emphasize the fact that in all three countries under study, postcrisis policies were carried out by domestic political forces, although with varying degree of the involvement by the Soviet coercive and political apparatus. Subordination of these East Central European countries to Soviet hegemony was, in fact, ensured by these internal forces and the essential institutional features of the political system imposed on those countries after the Second World War.

Given the focus of this book on domestic policies, I will analyze several processes and dimensions important to understanding the crises, their aftermaths, and their outcomes. First, I describe the causes and nature of each crisis, emphasizing the degree of institutional breakdown of the party-state, struggles within the ruling elites, and the modes of organization and the nature of popular mobilization. Second, I will look at the party-state's and Soviet coercive response to the crisis, cleavages that emerged as the result of military action as well as resources and capacity of actors within the state and society in the postcrisis environment. I will also analyze policies of postcrisis regimes and their short- and long-term outcomes. Finally, in each case, I will explore changing regional and broader international pressures and constraints. I will show how external actors shaped domestic policies and increased capacity of domestic actors in each case.

In the case studies that follow, I will suggest that the revolution in Hungary, crushed by bloody Soviet intervention, established a clear division between the Soviet-imposed party-state and society, which perceived Kadar's government as a tool of antinational policy. Paradoxically, this highly polarized political situation produced a strong party-state, which by selectively accommodating both reformist and conservative factions within the communist party had relatively more space to implement flexible policies. Moreover, given the conditions of the Cold War confrontation at that time, the Hungarian party-state was shielded from any effective pressure by Western governments and international institutions. As a result, the Soviet-restored Hungarian party-state was able to preserve the impetus for change, to flexibly choose and pursue both the Stalinist-type terrorist policies and practices, as well as the more pragmatic policies of concessions, reforms, and humanization of the regime.

On the other hand, in Czechoslovakia and Poland the crisis and its military solution produced weak party-states, though for quite different reasons in each case. Although in Czechoslovakia challenging groups within society did not emerge as united and organized political force, the party-state was locked in paralyzing internal divisions and conflicts. The prolonged period of intrastate political stalemate that followed the WTO military intervention was resolved by the shift toward highly repressive policies and neo-Stalinist practices. This shift resulted in the eradication of all reformist forces within the party-state and the effective pacification of society. The triumph of the party's conservative faction and its inability to accommodate more pragmatic forces, blocked any possibility for policy adjustment and inhibited the impetus for reforms. As a result the postcrisis Czechoslovak regime failed to pursue more pragmatic policies that characterized the postrevolutionary Hungarian regime and established itself as one of the most orthodox regimes in the region.

In Poland the party-state confronted a society organized in complex territorial and professional networks that survived the imposition of martial law and retained their oppositional capacity. Moreover, Poland was highly vulnerable to international pressures given her commitment to the Helsinki Accords, opening up to the West, the extent of economic crisis, and economic dependency on Western goods, credits, and expertise. As a result neither the party-state nor the opposition was able to break the political stalemate produced by the imposition of martial law. This situation generated a deepening decay and anarchization of the political and economic institutions. The Polish party-state was caught in a contradictory attempt to liberalize and reform the economy without any liberalization of the polity while facing a restive population and acute external pressures and constraints. Thus both domestic and international factors account for the failure of the Polish party-state to reequilibrate the regime after the crisis.

PART I

The Political Crisis and Its Aftermath in Hungary, 1956–1963

The Hungarian Revolution of 1956 represented the unprecedented challenge to communist rule in the postwar history of East Central Europe and was the most tragic event in the cycle of political changes following Stalin's death and unraveling of Stalinist regimes in the region. It lasted only thirteen days and had three distinct phases marked by changes in country's leadership. From October 23, when mass demonstrations erupted in Budapest, to October 28, the leadership of the party and the state remained in the hands of old Stalinist leaders, who asked for the Soviet military intervention against the popular insurgency. On October 28 Stalinists were ousted and Imre Nagy's government announced its support for the revolution, a ceasefire was declared, and the Soviet troops withdrew from Budapest. Janos Kadar proclaimed the formation of the new communist party, to be named the Hungarian Socialist Workers' Party, and the consolidation of new revolutionary institutions started. On November 1 the Soviet leaders decided to launch the second military intervention. Responding to the Soviet military buildup in the country, the desperate Hungarian leadership declared Hungary's neutrality and the country's withdrawal from the Warsaw Pact. They also appealed to the United Nations and Western powers for help and protection. On November 4 Soviet tanks overrun the country and Nagy's government was overthrown. During these few days, Hungary underwent profound political changes. As a result of mass popular mobilization, the Hungarian communist regime experienced almost complete institutional breakdown and was de facto overthrown by the revolutionary popular movement from below. Only a massive and brutal Soviet military intervention abruptly ended revolutionary political changes taking place in the country, allowed the installation of the Soviet sponsored government headed by

Janos Kadar, and commenced the harsh process of restoration of the Soviet-type regime in Hungary.

The new, Soviet-imposed leader of Hungary, Janos Kadar, faced the a more difficult situation than any communist leader in East Central Europe ever as he announced the formation of the new Worker Peasant Revolutionary Government on November 4, 1956. Somewhere nearby, Soviet troops were fighting the desperate Hungarian resistance. The communist party that had dissolved and reorganized during the revolution hardly existed, and among its seven founding leaders, five had received asylum in the Yugoslav embassy and one was already under arrest. Some members of Kadar's government learned of their nominations from the Soviet-run radio. Thus, in order to rebuild the party and the government, "Kadar had to start from scratch. There was no continuity with the past. The Stalinist followers of Rakosi, the dogmatists, were as unsuited as the followers of Nagy, the revisionists, to join the new leadership."[1]

Similarly, the whole state apparatus with its central and provincial institutions was in a state of disarray, and the coercive forces of the regime were in chaos. The secret police, the pillar of Soviet-type regimes, was disbanded during the revolution. At the same time, the regular police force had been reorganized during the revolution, and the majority of its functionaries joined the ranks of the freedom fighters resisting the Soviet invasion. The army was paralyzed and divided, unable to take a decisive action against the Soviet troops and unwilling to fight against the popular resistance. The auxiliary institutions of the regime, the Stalinist "transmission belts" that controlled the political space, secured stability of the regime, and enforced the compliance of the population either ceased to exist (such as the youth league DISZ) or were drastically changed during the revolution (such as the trade unions).

The population, represented by a myriad of independent institutions, political parties and organizations, resisted the Soviet invasion not only by a general strike but by taking up arms to defend their revolution. The most desperate armed resistance was mounted in the industrial areas of Csepel, Ujpest, Pecs, Miskolc, and above all, Dunapentele—the new industrial complex formerly known as "Stalin-town." The mountains near Miskolc and Pecs were the main strongholds of partisan resistance. Intense fighting in the capital and the provinces between poorly armed insurgents and a vastly superior Soviet army lasted until November 9. Skirmishes continued in isolated areas until the beginning of December. In the country's industrial centers, a general strike lasted by and large until mid-January of 1957. Thus, the new government and its founder were not only hated as traitors but also actively opposed by a majority of the nation. More importantly, the new regime had no domestic institutional means of asserting its control. New rulers had to rely fully on the Soviet forces and were forced to resort to bloody terroristic policies so as to reestablish the political order and regain control.

It took several years to fully restore and consolidate the party-state institutions, to stabilize the political and economic system, and to ensure the
population's compliance and cooperation. But during the Seventh Congress
of the Hungarian Socialist Party held at the end of 1959, Kadar proudly
announced:

> The domestic political situation in the Hungarian People's Republic is today char-
> acterized by tranquility, stability, and rapid progress. People's power is stronger
> than it was before the counter-revolutionary uprising, the foundations of social-
> ism have been considerably extended and socialist construction is going ahead in
> an orderly and vigorous manner.[2]

By the middle of the 1960s, despite its postrevolutionary political terror and
repression, Hungary gradually and unexpectedly turned into one of the most
liberal regimes in the Soviet bloc. "Kadar has been less 'dogmatic' than the
pessimists would dare to imagine," wrote the editors of *Survey* in 1962,
analyzing the policies of the postrevolutionary regime.[3]

Much has been said about Kadar's political skills, personality and good
intentions, which prompted him to stop political terror, introduce gradual
liberalization, and implement some innovative economic reforms, which,
although they did not bring about any significant structural changes to the
polity or the economy, nevertheless turned Hungary into "the happiest bar-
rack in the Soviet camp" and a socialist consumer's paradise.[4] In the two
decades following the revolution, he became an internationally recognized
statesman, a sponsor of state-socialism with a human face, and an un-
equaled model for desperate Polish communist leaders in their struggle for
the restoration of the party-state undermined by the self-limiting revolution
of 1980. After 1956 Hungary replaced Yugoslavia as the country both the
elites and people of East Central Europe sought to emulate.[5] In this context,
"both Kadar and the 'Kadarization' of Hungary—the person, the process,
and the product—are indeed remarkable phenomena."[6]

In the following chapters I intend to explore the puzzle of "Kadarization." I would like to emphasize that it is not my purpose to present a detailed historical account of the analyzed period or to contribute new archival
findings to the existing analyses. This work was designed as a reinterpreta-
tion of existing evidence with an overriding comparative agenda in mind.
While a truly comprehensive analysis of the Hungarian Revolution and
its aftermath is still to be written, the existing sources are quite adequate
for the purpose of such analysis.[7] I shall analyze the demobilization processes in Hungary after the revolution with two question in mind. First, how
was it possible that the brutally crushed revolution produced a state-socialist
regime with liberal and reformist leanings; second, what were the conditions
that allowed for the relatively fast and effective restoration of the Hungarian party-state and reequilibration of the regime. Addressing these general
questions, I shall refrain from analyzing Kadar's personality and investigating nuances of internal frictions and conflicts among political elites. I will

focus instead on the more general domestic and geopolitical structural conditions and constraints that shaped political actors' choices and the process of the restoration and reequilibration of the state-socialist political order in Hungary.

In the existing scholarship, the success of demobilization policies in post-revolutionary Hungary and the gradual shift from political terror and repression to more pragmatic and liberal policies has been explained by two general sets of factors. In more geopolitically oriented explanations, Soviet-Hungarian relations, direct Soviet interference, and indirect reflections of the power struggles at the Kremlin were said to account for all significant changes and shifts in the Hungarian domestic politics. Another group of explanations emphasized the internal divisions and struggles within elites of the Hungarian party-state, where different factions gaining an upper hand were able to shift the state's policies in one direction or another. While these traditional explanations often overemphasize the role of one or the other of the above sets of factors, they nevertheless must be seriously taken into account. What I would like to suggest in this analysis is that a more comprehensive explanation of demobilization processes is needed and must take into account the set of factors that may be described as the nature of relations between the party-state and society. Only when these three sets of factors are taken together can a more persuasive explanation of the successes and failures of Hungary's demobilization policies emerge.

As many scholars emphasize, the Hungarian demobilization process is the product of a crushed revolution. Patterns of popular mobilization, a degree of institutional breakdown of the party-state, intra-elite struggles and cleavages, and the broader political situation in the Soviet bloc during this period created a unique set of conditions and constraints. Thus, the Hungarian crisis differed in many crucial respects from the 1968 crisis in Czechoslovakia and the 1980 crisis in Poland. I will argue that these specific conditions limited a number of viable political choices of post-1956 elites and crucially shaped the capacity of different actors and groups within both the Hungarian state and society. The general contours of the Hungarian demobilization processes were shaped by (1) the rapid mobilization and reinstitutionalization of the diverse and fragmented political society during the revolution and its subsequent annihilation following the Soviet intervention; (2) the collapse of the communist party and the state institutions that paradoxically created more room for maneuver for the Kadar's group. This allowed the rebuilding of institutional structures without the inclusion of extreme Stalinist and reformist factions and limited the power of entrenched political forces; and finally (3) the capacities and the character of the Soviet leadership during the period of demobilization and the specific nature of the broader international context. The political choices made during this period and consequences of demobilization policies left the distinct imprint on political and economic developments in Hungary in the next three decades. In

1989, Janos Kis noted that "Hungarian society has yet to come to terms with the total defeat it suffered at that time, and those in power have yet to overcome the burdens of their victory. The economic and political crisis which in the '80s overwhelms Hungary is the crisis of the restoration regime which came into existence thirty years ago."[8]

The Party-State and Society during the Hungarian Revolution

THE CONSEQUENCES of the Second World War made all East Central European countries highly susceptible to radical political change and transformations of all prewar political and economic structures and social relations. Foreign occupations devastated their economies, crushed national independence, destroyed existing political and social structures, and compromised prewar political and social organizations. Hungary, having been unable to disassociate herself from Germany, suffered not only severe devastation at the end of the war and found herself under the Soviet occupation but also had her past entirely condemned and all her political leadership discredited. In contrast to other East Central European states, Hungary was a defeated and occupied country. The initial Soviet policy toward Hungary, however, displayed significant hesitancy and ambivalence in comparison to its policy toward other countries in the region.[1]

For the first two years following the war, the Soviet Military Command allowed nonfascist parties to organize, and a progressive, democratic coalition, the National Independence Front, was established. It included five political parties: Smallholders, Social Democrats, National Peasants, Radicals, and Communists. According to Joseph Rothschild: "On balance, the Communist political program in 1944 and 1945 was remarkably self-effacing and self-abnegating. It called for the rule of law, free culture, free intellectual inquiry, free political dialogue, a free press, free enterprise, and free election."[2] This political hesitancy on the side of the Soviet leadership and the caution of the Hungarian communists was aptly illustrated by official political practices during this period. In the relatively free electoral contest of 1945 and 1947, the Communist party remained in the minority in spite of the significant real power it could have exercised under the umbrella of the Soviet occupational administration.[3]

Although there has been a debate among historians concerning the interpretations of Soviet policy during the first years after the war, the Stalinization of the country was the Communist party's goal from the very beginning.[4] During these first postwar years (1945–47), in spite of the generally temperate political behavior of the Communist party, the systematic prosecution and purge of real and alleged pro-Nazi elements and war criminals was launched.[5] Purges were quickly extended to include leaders and members of noncommunist political parties, churches, and social organizations and those employed in state institutions. At that time, economic objectives dominated Soviet policy toward Hungary, and "the roots of the Rakosiite police state, its political excesses, were deeply conditioned if not determined by Soviet demands and exploitation in the immediate postwar period."[6] The ruthless economic exploitation of the country by the Soviets additionally crippled the economy dislocated by the war.[7] The period of relative restraint in monopolizing power by the Communists ended in 1947, once the peace treaty with the Allies came into effect and the representatives of the Western nations left the country. The gradual Stalinization of the country involved a concerted assault on traditional political forces and institutions and included the destruction of existing political parties, the purge of the bureaucratic apparatus of the state, the confrontation with and subjugation of the churches,[8] the nationalization and centralization of the education system[9] and the economy,[10] and the destruction of the independent press and public opinion. In 1949, after the organized political opposition was entirely destroyed, a single list of candidates drafted by the Communists received 95.6 percent of the votes in so-called new-type parliamentary elections; a Soviet-emulated constitution was adopted, and Hungary officially became a "people's democracy." As a result of these developments, the Communists achieved full political control, broke down the social fabric of Hungarian society, and secured themselves against any challenge. At the same time, all resistance and opposition were eliminated. The new institutional framework was created and Communist-controlled mass organizations firmly penetrated all dimensions and segments of society. Yet, despite organizational success, "there was no sign of reintegration of society through new, approved associations and organizations commanding loyalty and solidarity."[11]

By 1949 all institutional instruments of power characteristic of the Soviet-type regime were firmly established. The Communist party, which started with two thousand members in 1945, claimed 1.5 million members in 1949. The political police, about 140,000 strong, and the army, expanded to 210,000 soldiers by 1952, were organized and controlled by the Soviet advisers. All independent political and social institutions and organizations were either destroyed or were under full state control. Churches, with their schools nationalized and youth organizations dissolved, were penetrated and supervised by the party-state. Political space was fully colonized by new public institutions and mass organizations united under the umbrella of the People's Patriotic Front (Hazafias Nepfront). Formerly independent sources of social power were taken over by the party-state.

At the end of 1949, all enterprises with ten or more employees and all income-bearing properties were nationalized. The collectivization of agriculture that began in 1948 gradually extended the party-state's control over the land and the system of compulsory delivery of crops and excessive taxation suffocated agricultural production.[12] Massive industrialization policies were launched on January 1, 1950, under the auspices of the First Five-year Plan. Oriented entirely toward heavy industry, they were set in motion and maintained through the constant raising of work norms and reduction in consumption.[13] State control was imposed on labor mobility and discipline. Arts and intellectual life in all its variety was harnessed to the purpose of the party-state and its Marxist ideology. The party-state began a full-scale assault on society, attempting to politicize the entire network of social relations. The efficient system of secret police, supported by an extensive network of informants, implemented a reign of terror aimed not only at the middle classes but at all segments of society, including the high echelons of the party itself.[14]

As I argued in the preceding chapter, the severity of the Stalinist period in various Soviet-dominated countries can be explained not only by the shift in Soviet policies in the region after 1948, but also by the internal composition of the Communist party and by the strength or merely the presence of traditional political and social forces. Hungary represents an illustrative example in this respect. The democratic interlude that followed the war allowed noncommunist political forces to organize. Moreover, Hungarian political society was not wiped out by the war as it was in Poland. Although during the consolidation of power by the communists hundreds of leading members of social organizations and political parties were arrested, disappeared, or were forced into exile, the majority of professionals and civil servants remained in the country.[15] This physical presence of middle and professional classes in Hungary greatly contributed to the severity of political repression by giving an easy pretext for the extension of "class struggle" against "reactionary elements" and "foreign agents."

At the same time, the Communist party was split into two broad factions. On the one hand were leaders who had spent the war period in hotels and party schools in the Soviet Union (so-called Muscovites). On the other were those who were involved in the communist underground organization within Hungary. When the monopolization of power was de facto accomplished by the end of the 1940s, the rift between Stalin and Tito overplayed this division and resulted in a series of political purges within the highest ranks of communist parties in the region. The conflicts and purges in Hungary were especially drastic, involving many leaders and hundreds of low-ranking party members. The arrest and execution in 1949 of the minister of interior—Laszlo Rajk, who was one of the major architects of communist victory—was a triumph of the Muscovite faction in the HCP. His subsequent rehabilitation and reburial on October 6, 1956, drew more than 150,000 people and was one of the most significant events leading to the revolutionary explosion. Through this process of permanent purge, the personal dictatorship of Matyas Rakosi was built to imitate that of his master, Stalin. Rakosi and his three closest associates—Erno Gero, Jozsef Revai, and Mihaly Farkas—constituted Hungary's powerful "quadrumvirate" during the Stalinist period, and in no other country did the personality cult reach such proportion. Thus in comparison to other countries of the region, the

Stalinist period in Hungary was significantly more repressive and therefore more prone to alienate not only almost the entire population but also significant segments of the party-state elites. As Rothschild bluntly states, Stalinism in Hungary presented the "orgy of political sycophancy and economic irrationality"[16] and therefore gradually created conditions for a violent confrontation, which came about in 1956.

HUNGARIAN STALINISM IN CRISIS, 1953–1956

As those who study the breakdown of nondemocratic regimes have contended, domestic difficulties are most likely to precipitate a serious political crisis when coupled with geopolitical pressures. The developments leading to the revolution in Hungary comply well with this assertion. The crisis of Stalinist order in Hungary became apparent shortly after Stalin's death. It was caused and reinforced by several interconnected factors: (1) the collapse of forced industrialization policies and the economic breakdown as well as the related widespread social unrest among workers and peasants, (2) the intensifying internal struggle and the stalemate between Stalinist and anti-Stalinist forces within the Hungarian Communist party, (3) uncertainties within the Soviet bloc precipitated by Stalin's death, the subsequent succession struggle within the Soviet leadership, and the campaign of de-Stalinization in the Soviet Union.

The most evident sign of the crisis in Hungary was the collapse of forced industrialization policies designed to imitate the Soviet pattern with total disregard for the natural resources, limitations, and peculiarities of the Hungarian situation. While heavy industry developed rapidly, the volume of industrial production and power generation lagged behind demand. Such a situation forced additional imports, which distorted the country's trade balance. Light industry and agriculture were severely weakened by the low level of investment and strained by the heavy system of taxation and compulsory deliveries. Such polices caused acute shortages of food and consumer goods. The shift of labor force away from the rural to urban areas further disrupted agricultural production and generated critical housing shortages in the cities. The drastic diversion of funds from consumption to investment significantly reduced already low standards of living. From 1951 to 1953, real wages and standards of living fell well below their 1949 level.[17] The effects of irrational economic policies were coupled with and compounded by the extent of political terror, the bureaucratization of political and economic institutions,[18] the suppression of individual initiative, the silencing of any criticism by censorship, and the dictatorial party elites control over the country. The dismal social and economic consequences of Stalinist policies produced a very tense and serious political situation. Social unrest was mounting and workers' wildcat strikes and peasants demonstrations spread across the country.[19] The party's leadership was quick to realize the serious-ness of the situation. Rakosi himself admitted that "if we don't make a change at once, we will be threatened with the most serious of crises."[20]

The situation in Hungary seriously concerned the Kremlin as well, and the new Soviet leadership was prompted to react decisively. In the middle of June 1953, Hungarian leaders were summoned to Moscow and severely crit-icized for bringing the country to the verge of political explosion. Soviet leaders demanded the introduction of new political and economic initiatives and forced Hungarians to institute "collective leadership" and to change economic priorities. The notion of "collective leadership" implied the sepa-ration of party and state posts, and Matyas Rakosi was pushed to transfer the prime ministership to Imre Nagy. Although this change did not mean the end of his power—Rakosi still retained the leadership of the party—it sig-naled the end of one-person rule and the upcoming changes in policies and the shift in the political opportunity structure. Thus direct Soviet interven-tion began the slow process of the unraveling of the Stalinist regime in Hun-gary. Paradoxically, as George Schopflin notes, "de-Stalinization was very like Stalinism in one central respect—it was imposed by the Kremlin on East-ern Europe without regard for the appropriateness of the de-Stalinization strategies."[21] Therefore the most immediate result of the Soviet pressure was a split within the ruling elite, which only aggravated the economic and polit-ical conditions and created de facto a dual power situation lasting until March 1955.

The new-course policies have been associated with Imre Nagy, whose speech in Parliament on July 4, 1953, presented an open critique of Stalinist policies and outlined a program of reform.[22] However, Bill Lomax in his penetrating essay convincingly argues that "the New Course had been nei-ther composed by nor initiated by Imre Nagy. . . . Nor did the reforms an-nounced by Imre Nagy represent as radical or as heretical a break with the past as is often supposed."[23] New Course policies were collectively designed by the top party leaders, including Rakosi, Gero, and Hegedus, and ap-proved during the session of the full Central Committee on June 27–28, 1953. Nevertheless, it was Nagy who for better or worse became the symbol of change, and his "speech was received throughout the country as a life-restoring breath of fresh air. The response it called forth from writers and intellectuals was the most immediate and the most apparent, as the entire literary world seemed to take on a new life, but many an ordinary worker and peasant too felt it promised them new hope."[24]

This relatively sudden political relaxation and the official critique of Sta-linist policies were interpreted by many as a sign of weakness on the part of the party-state. From this time on, anti-Stalinist groups within the party-state and among the student and intelligentsia slowly gathered force and rallied around Nagy. The release and rehabilitation of political prisoners in 1954 additionally strengthened the anti-Stalinist forces as hundreds of Com-

munist leaders and intellectuals who were incarcerated because of their opposition to Rakosi's policies were set free. Yet in spite of the urgency of the
situation, the New Course policies in Hungary did not bring about the expected radical changes.[25] This was due to the power and influence the Stalinist forces were still able to exert. Nagy failed to build a political base within
the party and state apparatus, where Stalinists still dominated. Thus, modifications to economic and political practices launched in 1953 were sabotaged. They only served to initiate the period of protracted political crisis,
internal struggle, and paralysis, which was followed by Nagy's ouster in
April 1955[26] and finally culminated in the popular revolution.

The fall of Nagy in 1955 did not signal a return to Stalinist status quo
ante. Although concessions to peasants and artisans made under the New
Course were abolished, the emphasis on heavy industry and collectivization
was renewed, and Nagy's supporters were purged from high party and state
offices; the Stalinist restoration was doomed to failure both for domestic
and geopolitical reasons. The Soviet Union's Twentieth Party Congress and
Khrushchev's "secret speech" in February 1956 inflicted a final blow to the
survival of the Stalinist regime in Hungary. By March 1956 everybody in
Eastern Europe knew that the Soviet Union was setting out on a new course
and reassessing the Stalinist legacy, and in Hungary changes were imminent
as well. After the Twentieth Congress, the political situation in the country
and intra-elite divisions were aggravated further when intellectuals, students, and former prisoners openly criticized the party's policies and demanded radical changes. Nagy became a rallying point for all opponents of
the regime. Yet, the emerging political opposition was confined to a narrow
circle of humanistic intelligentsia and former party activists who still clearly
adhered to the principles of the communist ideology.[27]

In March of 1956 the institutional basis for the revisionist opposition
emerged. The Petofi Circle, a discussion forum of university students organized by the official youth organization (DISZ), provided a platform for
communist intellectuals and innocent victims of Stalinist terror to criticize
the ruling elite. In a few months it became the center of the growing opposition movement. The demands voiced during the circle's meetings, however,
did not go beyond calls for moderate reforms. "Our demands—as Paul
Jonas concedes—were essentially the demands of 'revisionist' Czechoslovakia in 1968."[28] They included "economic reform and decentralization, the
end of police terror and censorship, guarantees of 'elementary' freedoms."
Similarly, Paul Kecskemeti argues that "up to the actual outbreak of the
revolution the stirrings of opposition and agitation for reform had very
much the character of an internal family affair within the Party itself."[29] The
revisionist opposition not only failed to question the basic tenets of the socialist organization of the state and the economy but also failed to construct
any consistent political program of reforms. "The intellectual movement
had neither time nor, perhaps, enough energy to work out a program, an

alternative, to the party's quickly collapsing political and moral power. The price for the lack of a well-prepared, coherent and positive program was paid on October 23, 1956 when institutional power collapsed, leaving the country in political void."[30]

During this period of growing dissent, Rakosi's faction within the party was strong enough to strike back, and on June 30 at the Central Committee meeting, the Petofi Circle was condemned and its activities suspended. However, full-scale repressive action against the opposition was prevented by the Soviets.[31] In July, Rakosi was finally ousted and replaced by Erno Gero as the first secretary of the Central Committee, signaling the definite end of the Stalinist period. But as Lomax emphasizes, "In the popular mind Gero was too closely associated with the Stalinist years for his leadership to be able to put an end to the growing popular alienation from the regime. . . . Gero's appointment thus whetted the appetite for change without satisfying it, and made even more probable the eventual outbreak of revolt."[32]

From this point on, the Communist party was in full retreat. The party policies were even criticized in articles published in its own newspapers. The Writers' Union openly defied the authorities, the Petofi Circle resumed its activities, and similar debating societies emerged at university campuses across the country. "The concealed anti-regime campaign reached and permeated many institutions and Party organizations. Youth organizations were especially affected by it. . . . Party cells, Party branch organizations and local groups of People's Patriotic Front also provided cloaks for disguised resistance."[33] On October 6 the reburial of Laszlo Rajk, a rehabilitated victim of the political show trial, brought thousands of people in a symbolic manifestation against the Stalinist rule. George Schopflin notes that "this proved to be the dress rehearsal, the moment when thousands of atomized individuals recognized that they were not alone and lost their fear of the system, the moment when the possibility of changing the regime from below returned to the agenda."[34] While political dissent was spreading throughout the country, university students formed their independent organization—the Hungarian University Youth Association (MEFESZ). The movement lasted only four days, yet was instrumental in mobilizing the students for a pro-Polish manifestation on October 23, which started the revolution.

Thus far, this short review clearly illustrates the intricate interplay of domestic and geopolitical pressures that shaped the crisis of the Stalinist regime in Hungary. The Hungarian regime was not able to resolve basic political challenges in a time when economic crisis prevented it from continuing its existence through sheer inertia. It also proves that political splits in the ruling elites over economic and political changes are essential in opening the political opportunity structure and in activating society's oppositional potential. From the spring of 1953 to the fall of 1956, the cleavages and factional struggles in Hungary resulted in a protracted political stalemate within the ruling elite. Such a situation opened the political opportunity structure and produced conditions favorable for the occurrence of violent

outbreaks of social tensions and rapid political mobilization. Zinner emphasizes this point, arguing that "without profound internal decay in the Hungarian party, no revolution would have taken place regardless of the amount
of popular hatred against the regime."[35]

Neither the party-state elites nor the emerging opposition was prepared
for the rapid social explosion that came in October 23, 1956. The revolution
in Hungary was one of those rare examples of large-scale collective action
that erupted with lightning speed and smashed the existing state institutions
in a matter of hours. At the same time, the sheer speed of events prevented
the effective organization of the opposition and the efficient acquisition and
consolidation of power. Miklos Molnar writes: "The Hungarian uprising
had no technicians, no organizers. Once more, for a historical moment, perhaps for the last time, poets, dreamers, and thinkers prepared the social and
national uprising of a people."[36]

THE REVOLUTION AND THE PARTY-STATE

According to Molnar, the Hungarian Revolution, which erupted on October
23, 1956, "was perhaps the last of the revolutions of the nineteenth century.
Europe will very probably never see again this familiar and romantic picture
of the rebel, gun in hand, cries of freedom on his lips, fighting for something."[37] Although different political actors in the Hungarian party-state
and society as well as their Soviet supervisors were aware of the grave political crisis plaguing the country, neither those who pressed for reforms nor
those who resisted being swept from power expected a revolutionary explosion.[38] Moreover, neither organized nor unorganized political forces were
ready to respond in an effective way to the rapid political mobilization of the
Hungarian population. The revolution itself, as Lomax argues, was "far
from being a revolutionary coup in which organized bands of insurgents
seize the focal points of power and communications—government ministries, party offices, police stations and post offices—this was a spontaneous
revolutionary mass movement in which the people threw themselves at the
symbols of the old regime."[39]

The Hungarian Revolution has an extensive bibliography, but its truly
comprehensive history is still to be written. In this chapter I will use selected
primary and secondary sources to illustrate several processes that formed
the main contours of the revolution and shaped the pattern of the subsequent suppression and demobilization policies that followed. I will focus on
two crucial aspects of the revolution, describing first the extent of the institutional breakdown of the Hungarian regime and the collapse of the Communist party and state institutions and, second, the nature of mass mobilization
and the emergence of revolutionary institutions.

In the existing historiography of the revolution, these two issues have
been highly contested. There has been disagreement concerning the extent of

the party-state's collapse, the scope of the popular support for revolutionary forces, and, finally, the nature of the insurgents' goals, including their political and ideological makeup. Official communist interpretations always underestimated the extent of the state collapse and support for the revolution. They described insurgents as counterrevolutionaries seeking to reestablish capitalism and to return to a fascist-type political regime. The official recognition of the revolution in Hungary as a popular and fully legitimate uprising in the end of the 1980s, however, underscored the validity of interpretations advanced in Western social sciences, which always stressed the democratic and popular character of the revolution. After 1989 the Institute for the History of the 1956 Hungarian Revolution was founded in Budapest in order to review archival sources and facilitate new research and interpretations of the event.[40]

The Collapse of the Party-State

The Hungarian Communist party was literally crushed as an organization during the revolution. Its collapse, however, was more a result of internal paralysis and divisions than the effect of direct action by revolutionary forces.[41] On the night of October 23–24, the party's striking impotence was highlighted at the meeting of the Central Committee convened to deal with the street demonstrations. According to Molnar: "The crisis of the party at the crucial moment of October 1956 was part of an infinitely greater crisis. If the party found itself completely paralyzed at the decisive moment, if its powerful organization disintegrated all at once, if its combat forces were condemned to remain in their quarters, it is because . . . of a series of crises, conflicts, and ailments, which had already manifested themselves with more or less acuteness throughout the preceding decade."[42]

On the eve of the revolution, the Hungarian Workers party had 811,135 members and 42,406 candidates for membership.[43] When Matyas Rakosi was replaced by Erno Gero in July 1956 in order to quell growing political discontent, nobody still realized how fragile this carefully built and run institutional machinery really was. It came as a surprise to everybody, from the party leaders to the people on the streets and from party ideologists to social scientists, that such a system of totalitarian rule, which was supposed to have been impregnable from any internal threat, disintegrated within a few days and was swept away by the popular revolution.

In response to popular demands voiced in the streets of Budapest and in a desperate attempt to quell the demonstrations, previously expelled members of the revisionist faction, including Imre Nagy, were co-opted to the Central Committee during the first night of the revolution. On the same night the Politburo was reconstructed. Several compromised Stalinists were removed and replaced by reformists, but Gero was still able to retain his post as the first secretary of the party. That same night the Soviet troops stationed in Hungary were asked for help in putting down the demonstrations. The next day, in the face of a full-scale revolutionary uprising and fierce fighting between the Soviet troops and the armed insurgents, Gero was relieved of his duties, and Janos Kadar, himself imprisoned during the Rakosi reign, was appointed to replace him. At that time, however, the whole party organizational machine was in a state of disintegration, with its leaders either barricaded in party's buildings, going into hiding, or seeking refuge in the Soviet Union. On October 28, in view of the "extraordinary conditions" the Central Committee placed the party's leadership in the hands of a six-member Presidium headed by Kadar. But on November 1, Kadar announced the dissolution of the Hungarian Workers party and appealed for the formation of a new, reformed communist party. He proposed the convening of a party congress to formalize these decisions and to begin a new chapter in the history of the Hungarian communist movement. For this purpose, a new preparatory committee was formed under Kadar's leadership. The same day, however, Kadar disappeared from Budapest to return on November 7 in the footsteps of the Soviet army as the head of the new Workers Peasants Revolutionary Government.

When the Soviet troops launched the mass military invasion on November 4, the Communist party virtually did not exist. During the eleven days of the revolution both the central and local parties' structures collapsed. Its members and functionaries either joined the revolutionary movements and institutions or quietly disappeared. In factories around the country, the party's basic organizations either vanished or were expelled by the workers. Thus Kadar's decision to dissolve the party was only an official acknowledgment of its actual disappearance from the Hungarian political scene. Following frequent criticism for his decision to dissolve the party on November 1, Kadar still argued in 1982: "There was no other possibility. The Party collapsed, lost all credibility, and there was a need to organize it from scratch."[44]

Our knowledge of what happened in provincial towns and in the countryside during the revolution is still very fragmented and limited. Most of the historiography of the Hungarian Revolution has concentrated on the events in Budapest and political struggles and decisions on the national level. Lomax's history of the revolution published in 1976 is one of the preciously few works that gives a more systematic account of the situation outside Budapest. From his account it is apparent that in provincial cities officials of the old Stalinist regime put up little or no resistance to the revolution. In some places like Gyor, the old authorities quietly disintegrated almost overnight, and old officials slipped away. In others, the old regime continued to exist without change through the first few days of the revolution. In Pecs, Lomax observes, "The Stalinist functionaries in both the town and party administration and in the factories sought to maintain control for several days with the support of a force of over a thousand armed security police (AVH) men." Finally, in some places party-state functionaries joined the revolution. In Miskolc, for example, "from the start of the revolution the local party leadership declared its solidarity with the people's demands, and local party leaders and activists took a leading role in organizing the revolutionary forces."[45]

The only force that desperately resisted the revolution through the country were units of the security police AVH. The regular police and army units either remained uncommitted or joined the emerging revolutionary institutions. Although the history of the revolution outside Budapest is still incomplete, the scattered information we have clearly leads to the conclusion that the whole institutional structure of the party-state on the local level collapsed either instantly or in a matter of days, and the political vacuum that emerged was rapidly filled up by new revolutionary institutions. The vivid indication of the rapid dissolution of the party-state's institutions was the almost total lack of effective resistance on the side of the old regime. The number of functionaries killed opposing the revolutionary forces was surprisingly small. The postintervention government eager to justify the Soviet intervention and political repression, was able to produce only 220 cases of victims of "counter-revolutionary" terror throughout the whole country, of whom 164 were members of the state armed forces, mostly the AVH.[46] But the attitude of the coercive forces of the regime is even more surprising than the collapse of the civilian party and state institutions.

The Revolution and Coercive Forces of the Communist Regime

Before the revolution, the coercive forces of the party-state comprised the People's Army, the State Police, the armed formations of the AVH, and the Frontier Guard under the control of the AVH. The Army had around two hundred thousand men, and the AVH and the Frontier Guard between forty thousand and ninety thousand men.[47] Given the organization and strength of the coercive forces, the total collapse of the repressive capacity of the Hungarian party-state is one of the most intriguing aspects of the revolution. During the night session following the first day of the revolution, the Central Committee instructed the Council of Ministers to issue a decree of martial law throughout the Hungarian territory. The communique stated that the Council of Ministers "has ordered summary jurisdiction throughout the country to be applied against acts designed to overthrow the People's Republic: revolt, incitement, appeal and conspiracy to revolt, murder, manslaughter, arson, keeping of explosives and crimes committed by the use of explosives, force applied against the authorities, force against private persons, illicit possession of arms. Crimes falling into the categories of summary jurisdiction must be punished by death."[48]

But the martial law decree was not implemented. Despite the announcement of repressive measures and the presence of the sixty-seven hundred soldiers and fifty tanks of the regular Hungarian army as well as at least thirty-five hundred strong and well-armed AVH forces in the city,[49] within hours Budapest was in hands of insurgents, and the official authorities were confined to a public building that had been guarded by the AVH units. Moreover, the request for Soviet military help issued during the same meeting, which brought Soviet troops to the city the next morning, did not result in the recovery of military and political control and led to the further escalation of conflict. It is clear, therefore, that the coercive capacity of the regime collapsed within hours and even the direct Soviet military engagement was not sufficient to prop up the power of the party's leadership, stop the disintegration of the state, and prevent continued rapid popular mobilization.

Many commentators explain the reluctance of Hungarian coercive forces to act decisively against the popular demonstrations as the result of the deep state of confusion and lack of authorized orders from the communist authorities during the first days of the revolution. Tibor Meray's account of his visit to the headquarters of the Budapest police during the first day of the revolution gives credence to such views. "I had seen confusion before—he observed—in war and in peace, but the agitation that I observed there was nothing like anything I had ever seen . . . a kind of bewilderment disguised by the semblance of doing the job."[50] And, in fact, from the outbreak of the revolution on the evening of October 23, the uniformed police did not intervene or attempt to restore order. Later it became known that Sandor Kopacsi, the head of the Budapest police, instructed his units to stay in their stations and not move against the people. Following his orders, the state police not only did not actively move against the insurgents but also became their first major source of arms. Weapons spirited away from the police stations headed to the revolutionaries.[51]

While the police clearly sided with the revolution, the situation within the regular Hungarian army was more complex. The peace treaty signed in Paris in 1947 limited the size of the Hungarian army to seventy thousand men, and prior to 1948 the army played a marginal role in Hungarian political life.[52] Beginning in the summer of 1948, however, the armies of newly consolidated people's republics in East Central Europe began playing an active and important role in Soviet military strategy and planning. Thus on the eve of the revolution, the highly expanded, reorganized, and politicized Hungarian army consisted of ten divisions, and its total strength was two hundred thousand men. The army was supervised by Soviet military advisers assigned to almost every unit to the level of battalion; Soviet regulations were introduced to all areas of military life. Moreover, most high-ranking officers were trained in the Soviet Union.

Comparative studies of revolutions show that the attitude of armed forces always plays a significant role in revolutionary upheavals.[53] In Hungary, in spite of its strength and subordination to the Communist party, the army did not prevent the revolutionary outbreak. Moreover, the army did not play any decisive part in the revolution. The most desperate resistance the Soviet army encountered in Hungary both during the first and the second intervention was not that of the regular units of the Hungarian army but of the fierce, improvised, and unorganized resistance of civilian groups of workers and students.

Janos Berecz in his book defending the communist regime claims that "no unit of the armed forces of the People's Republic of Hungary went over completely to the side of the revolutionaries."[54] In fact, at first the army tried to maintain a policy of neutrality in the armed combat between the insurgents and the Soviet units. However, many individual soldiers joined the battle on the side of revolution from the very beginning. Moreover, in many instances army units sent into action either did not follow orders and remained passive or joined the side of the insurgents in battles against the Soviet troops and the Hungarian security police guarding public buildings. But even Berecz admits that the political situation in the country "was aggravated by the treason of some police and army officers already in the first hours. An uncertain and procrastinating approach by the officers of the general staff, by the commanders of the armed services, by the officers of military academies as well as conscious sabotage or open treason on the part of certain officers caused serious damage especially in Budapest."[55]

Two factors significantly weakened the morale and the capabilities of the Hungarian army before the revolution. First, the paralyzing crisis within the party acutely affected the armed forces. According to Meray, among the young officers there was a movement similar to that of the communist intellectuals opposed to the Stalinist leadership. He argues that "the Soviet party's Twentieth Congress had shaken everything in these men: their confidence, their faith, their unity."[56] The second factor was the reduction and reorganization of the armed forces. Kiraly argues that after the Soviet contingency plan of aggression on Yugoslavia, in which the Hungarian army was to play an important role, was abandoned after 1951, the army experienced profound crisis and decline. "In the fall of 1956 . . . the People's Army of Hungary was already only a shadow of what it had been in 1950–51. Without a war plan against Tito, the army was as useless as it had been prior to 1948."[57] On August 1, 1956, the Council of Ministers reduced the size of the army by fifteen thousand men and the Hungarian army underwent a process of reorganization that included the dismissal of over ten thousand commissioned and noncommissioned officers. This large-scale reorganization clearly weakened the army's strength and its organizational capabilities.

The Collapse of Auxiliary Institutions of the Party-State

In the political organization of the party-state, the auxiliary institutions and organizations as well as coercive forces played a crucial role in enhancing political control. Under the state-socialist regimes, institutions such as youth organizations, trade unions, and other functional social organizations constituted what Philip Selznick called "organizational weapons of communism."[58] Their organizational function was to take up the political space and to insure extensive penetration by the state agencies of all groups in society. As Leszek Nowak argues, they were designed to place a bureaucratic inter-mediary in natural social relations between the social actors.[59] These auxiliary institutions were "transmission belts" between the decision-making organs and the population and were meant to manufacture social support for the regime's policies by extensive mobilization campaigns common during the heyday of Stalinism.[60] In Hungary such organizations included: The National Council of Trade Unions (SZOT), The Hungarian Federation of Democratic Women (MNDSZ), The Association of Working Youth (DISZ), The National Association of Freedom Fighters (OSZSZ), The National Association of Cooperatives (SZOVOSZ), and many other smaller movements and professional organizations. All these organizations were collective members of the National Front—an umbrella organization in charge of coordinating their activities, organizing elections, and creating the symbolism of national unity. These organizations were in charge of dispensing the state's social benefits and privileges to specific professional and social groups. This gave them the control of powerful material incentives and the ability to establish stabilizing networks of clientelistic relations.[61] But with the eruption of the revolution, these complex instruments of political and social control disintegrated in a similar fashion as the institutions of the party and the state.

There were two youth organizations in Hungary before the revolution: the Association of Working Youth (DISZ), which organized all young people between the ages of fourteen and twenty-six, and the Pioneer Movement, formally under the control of the DISZ, which organized children between the ages of six and fourteen. In August of 1956, there were fourteen thousand DISZ organizations with eight hundred thousand members and approximately one million children organized under the Pioneer Movement.[62] In the mid 1950s, the DISZ, like all other organizations, was in a state of political crisis and ferment. In October 1956, university students formally quit the DISZ and set up their own independent organization, the Association of Hungarian University and College Students (MEFESZ), which played an important role during and after the revolution.

During the revolution both communist-controlled organizations ceased to exist, and a wide range of new youth organizations was formed, which declared their independence from all political parties and the state.[63] Alongside these new organizations, revolutionary students' committees and councils were formed at colleges and universities across the country, and students worked to form a National Student Parliament. After the suppression of the revolution, only the MEFESZ survived as a viable movement, while the remaining organizations that were centered along political lines and lacking a distinct social basis, quietly disappeared. The communist youth organizations were the weakest link in the chain of auxiliary institutions; the trade unions were stronger and more powerful instruments of communist rule.

From the beginning of the revolution the National Council of Trade Unions (SZOT), commanding approximately two million members organized in functional branches, repeatedly appealed for support for the government and for an end to strikes and a resumptions of production. At the same time, workers' delegations from around the country demanded that the trade unions become independent, free of Communist-party influence, and representative of the authentic interests of the workers. On October 31, during an extraordinary session, the Presidium of SZOT resigned, and leadership was transferred to the temporary executive committee of the National Association of Free Hungarian Trade Unions (MSZSZOSZ). The temporary committee stated that "this revolution also made it possible for the trade union movement to become free and independent of every kind of Party and government influence." The committee also declared that the trade union organization "is now the true, consistent and fighting representative of the workers' interests."[64] The newly refurbished leadership of trade-union organizations declared support for Nagy's government and called for new trade-union elections and continuation of the strike. In a move parallel to the changes in the central unions' bureaucracy, presidiums of various branches of trade unions were renewed and old leaders replaced. Some unions were taken over by the workers' councils, which from the beginning of the revolution posed a major challenge to the unions in factories and enterprises. Also, several new trade union organizations emerged.

Although the SZOT endorsed the immediate organization of workers' councils, trade unions rapidly lost their influence, and the balance of power within enterprises and factories shifted to the newly created workers' councils, which took over most of the traditional functions of the trade unions. By October 31 trade unions were completely on the defensive, surrendering their prerogatives to the councils and struggling for the right to represent and safeguard narrowly defined worker economic interests. For most of the trade-union leaders, the Soviet invasion was a gift that saved the organization as a whole and secured their positions of power within the bureaucratic structures.

The New Government and the Reconstitution of the Party System

The nomination of Imre Nagy as prime minister by the Central Committee and the formation of the new government during the first night of the revolution was hoped to fulfill one of major political demands drafted by the students and to stop the further aggravation of the political situation in the country. But Nagy's abrupt return to politics was too late and too little to arrest the revolutionary process. For the next twelve days, until the final Soviet assault, the changing Hungarian government tried in vain to catch up with the radicalization of demands coming from the emerging revolutionary movements and organizations. Already by October 25, as Lomax points out, "Imre Nagy gradually consolidated his power and moved slowly but surely into step with the revolutionary demands of the Hungarian people."[65]

The first spontaneous and unorganized phase of the revolution came to an end on October 28, with the following announcement from Prime Minister Imre Nagy: "The Government of the Hungarian People's Republic, in order to prevent further bloodshed and ensure a peaceful settlement, hereby orders a general and immediate cease-fire." At that time the revolution was victorious and the country was firmly in hands of insurgents organized in worker and territorial councils and the units of national guard that were already formed in Budapest. The day before the new government was formed—which, for the first time, included not only twenty-one members of the Communist party but also three members of the Smallholders party and one member of the National Peasant Party, which had been destroyed during the Stalinist period.[66]

The cease-fire began the process of stabilization of the revolutionary authority and the integration of the surviving institutions of the party-state with newly emerged revolutionary institutions. Nagy announced the formation of a new armed forces consisting of "the units of the army and police as well as the armed units of workers and youth"[67] and the dissolution of the security police. The People's Patriotic Front called on the population to form county, town, district, and villages national committees. SZOT appealed to its members to join the National Guard. At the same time, new coordinating institutions emerged with the aim to coordinate locally elected revolutionary councils. These included the Hungarian National Committee and the National Council of Free Revolutionary Hungarian Youth. The Communist party's newspaper, which regained its independence, called the revolution "a great national democratic movement."

During the next several days there was a lightning eruption of new political and social organizations as well as a fundamental recomposition of existing state institutions. The Revolutionary Council of National Defense was established with the task of creating of new armed forces of revolutionary Hungary.[68] Ministries of the Defense and Interior issued statements backing the new government, and the Hungarian Frontier Guard announced its support for the struggle for freedom and independence. The presidium of the Hungarian Trade Union Council resigned, and a provisional board of the National Federation of Free Hungarians Trade Unions was formed.

On October 30 Nagy announced that the one-party system would be abolished and the post-1945 coalition parties restored. An inner cabinet designed to represent the new balance of forces was formed and included Nagy, Kadar, and Losonczy (Communists); Tildy and Kovacs (Smallholders); Erdei (National Peasant party), and one person to be nominated from the Social Democratic party. Two days later Nagy announced the government decision to withdraw unilaterally from the Warsaw Pact and to declare Hungary's neutrality. The next day the formation of a new enlarged cabinet was announced. Twenty-three members of the former government were relieved of their posts, and the leaders of the revived political parties as well as representatives of the new revolutionary institutions were co-opted. The new government declared its firm adherence to the maintenance of socialism in Hungary. This declaration was echoed by all major political forces and organizations emerging in the country. Reporting on the events in Hungary for the official Polish press, journalist Wiktor Woroszylski noted: "It seems that we will be able to observe here a curious synthesis: a basic realization of a popular democracy (land in the hands of the peasants, nationalization of factories and banks) and of a pluralism of parties, freedom of press, and all the other liberties inherent in a liberal democracy."[69]

The political phenomenon that was not repeated in any other crisis in East Central Europe until 1989 was the revival of political parties suppressed under the Stalinist regime. According to the official evaluation of events by the Information Bureau of the Council of Ministers, approximately seventy different political parties emerged during the revolution.[70] First to reappear were the parties of the coalition existing between 1945 and 1948. Already on October 30, the national center of the independent Smallholders party and the Provisional Committee of the National Peasant party began their activities. The next day the center of the Social Democratic party was formed. On November 1 these three parties began publication of their official newspapers. Besides the coalition parties, a multitude of smaller political parties emerged representing the whole political spectrum from the far right to the far left. When the Soviet army crushed the revolution on November 4, there were at least sixteen new and revived political parties in Budapest.[71]

The Institutionalization of Revolutionary Power

Bela Kiraly, one of the leaders of the revolution said: "One of the most remarkable features of the revolution—and what made it a revolution in the real sense of the word—was the rapid establishment of new institutions from the lowest level to the central state administration."[72] Within a few days, the power vacuum left by the paralysis and collapse of party-state institutions was filled by hundreds of revolutionary committees and councils formed both on territorial and functional bases. Thus, when on October 26 the People's Patriotic Front called for the creation of territorial national committees, and the Communist party and SZOT called for the formation of workers' councils "in factories, enterprises, mines and other places of work"; "they were merely giving"—as Lomax points out—"official recognition to an already accomplished fact."[73] Recent research confirmed that there were twenty-one hundred worker councils with twenty-eight thousand members and tens of thousands of local revolutionary committees.[74] Most of the newly formed revolutionary institutions issued resolutions proclaiming their political demands and many sent delegations to Budapest to present these demands to the government.

In the last days of October, workers' councils and national committees formed coordinating bodies and larger political structures. Several district workers' councils were created, and on October 31 a Parliament of Workers' Councils was formed for the whole of Budapest, which included delegates from most of the city factories. Similarly new territorial institutions joined forces. Several area councils were formed, and among the biggest was the Trans-Danubian National Council, headquartered in Gyor. In a similar fashion, councils representing specific social and professional organizations formed coordinating bodies. They were especially active among students, intellectuals, and soldiers. The growing cohesion among the revolutionary forces was one of the most striking features of the revolution. Despite the chaos and disorganization of the first days of the revolution, the revolutionary committees, workers' councils, and student parliaments that sprang up everywhere within a matter of days gradually took over the functions of the local administration and even some prerogatives of central power.

The first clear expression of the popular attitudes that animated the revolution were the Sixteen Demands of the students enrolled at the Technical University in Budapest, which were distributed in leaflets on October 23. Shortly before the revolution, similar lists of demands addressed to the Hungarian Communist party's Central Committee were prepared by the students, writers, and members of the Petofi Circle. And from October 23 on, as Edmund Stillman writes in his analysis of the ideology of the Hungarian revolution, "the Hungarian nation issued demands in astonishing volume, and in the form of resolutions, manifestos, handbills, and brief tracts. Later, as radio stations were seized by the revolutionaries, political demands were broadcast daily, and almost by the hour. It was as if a nation, long silenced, were indulging itself in the sheer functional pleasure of speech."[75]

After the revolution official Hungarian propaganda portrayed the insurgents as reactionary forces attempting to destroy the country's socialist system. In Kadar's words, the revolutionaries "sought to destroy the prestige and undermine the foundations of our people's democratic society [and] to restore the capitalist system." But an analysis of revolutionary demands and manifestos clearly shows that the revolution's political discourse barely went beyond revisionist language firmly grounded in the socialist tradition. Recent research has identified four major political trends that emerged and were articulated to different degrees during the revolution: (1) the reform communism trend represented by Imre Nagy, (2) the national democratic trend represented by the noncommunist politicians, (3) the Christian-Conservative trend represented by Cardinal Mindszenty, and (4) an extreme right-wing political trend represented by some groups of fighters.[76] Nonetheless, the reform communism was a dominant ideological idiom. As Lomax points out, "Throughout the final days of the revolution Nagy and his ministers . . . consistently stressed their adherence to the maintenance of socialism in Hungary." Similarly, he emphasizes that the "leaders of the other parties in [Nagy's] government also declared their firm stand against any return to the old capitalist regime."[77] Even Jozsef Dudas, epitomized by the postrevolutionary propaganda as the prime example of reactionary and fascist currents in the revolution, told Polish journalist Wiktor Woroszylski that "no right wing and fascist organizations should be allowed; socialism must be preserved" in Hungary.[78] Thus, while the communist political system and practices were resolutely rejected, a clear institutional alternative to the existing social and economic system did not emerge—in Bibo's words the revolution was "the beginning of one of the most exciting socialist experiments of this century."[79]

The failure to develop a consistent alternative political discourse and a competing institutional vision of social and political organization despite the revolutionary situation and the ensuing Soviet military intervention were the results of the nature of political dissent that existed before the revolution. Dissenting intellectuals, as Tamas Aczel argues, "had still retained their faith in the viability of certain Marxist ideals: the conviction that society's moral force would eventually triumph over the party's physical power and that the only a truly socialist-humanist transformation of society could answer the questions left unanswered by totalitarian regimes."[80] Similarly, Paul Zinner claims that "the great majority of those who were at odds with the system made no break with its fundamental Leninist premises. They developed neither an independent political platform nor distinct ideology. They were content to associate themselves with the June Program of Imre Nagy."[81] In place of the existing system, "they envisioned a more or less ideal model of Communism, adapted to human needs generally and to Hungarian national requirements specifically. They did not want to abolish one-party government, but to reform it." The opposition to the Stalinist regime remained confined to the Marxist political vision, fatalistically accepting a historiosophical principle expressed by Nagy who believed that "all nations will arrive at socialism—this is inescapable—but they will not arrive there in a completely identical fashion. . . . The concrete ways and means of achieving this change are necessarily very diverse and they must remain so."[82] Zinner summarizes the attitude of the socialist opposition in Hungary on the eve of the revolution by arguing: "The inconsistencies of thought and emotion of a majority of the intellectuals that opposed Rakosi caused further differentiation among them, especially in the heat of revolution, which revealed that many of the views they held were incompatible with one another. Some, who were already susceptible to democratic ideas, capitulated to them completely. Others were driven back to the acceptance of a line of reasoning more consistent with orthodox Leninism. The former joined the revolution. The latter stayed neutral in it and later found it possible to serve Kadar."[83]

The characteristic example of these contradictions typifying the Hungarian political dissident's imagination may be found in the ten-point program whose proclamation ended the last discussion of the Petofi Circle and was published by all Budapest papers on the morning of October 23. These demands were as follow:

1. In view of the present situation in Hungary, we propose that the Central Committee of the Workers' party be convened with the minimum possible delay. Comrade Imre Nagy should take part in the preparatory work of this session.

2. We consider it necessary that the party and the government reveal the country's economic situation in all sincerity, revise the second Five Year Plan directives, and work out a specific constructive program in accordance with our special Hungarian conditions.

3. The Central Committee and the government should adopt every method possible to ensure the development of Socialist democracy by specifying the real functions of the Party, asserting the legitimate aspirations of the working class and introducing factory self-administration and workers' democracy.

4. To ensure the prestige of the party and of the state administration, we propose that Comrade Imre Nagy and other comrades who have fought for Socialist democracy and Leninist principles occupy a worthy place in the direction of the party and the government.

5. We propose the expulsion of Matyas Rakosi from the party Central Committee and his recall from the National Assembly and the Presidential Council. The Central Committee, which wishes to establish calm in the country, must offset present attempts at a Stalinist and Rakosiite restoration.

6. We propose that the case of Mihaly Farkas be tried in public in accordance with Socialist legality.

7. The Central Committee should revise resolutions passed in the period which just elapsed—resolutions which have proved wrong and sectarian—above all the resolutions of March 1955, the December 1955 resolution on literature, and the June 30, 1956, resolution on the Petofi Circle. We propose that the Central Committee annul these resolutions and draw the proper conclusions as to the persons concerned.

8. Even the most delicate questions must be made public, including the balance sheets of our foreign trade agreements and the plans for Hungarian uranium.

9. To consolidate Hungarian-Soviet friendship, let us establish even closer relations with the Soviet party, state, and people on the basis of the Leninist principle of complete equality.

10. We demand that at its meeting on October 23 the DISZ Central Committee should declare its stand on the points of this resolution and adopt a resolution for the democratization of the Hungarian Youth Movement.[84]

These demands were moderate in tone and called for policy changes that did not go beyond the existing political framework. Revisionist critics demanded changes in political practices of the regime fully accepting its institutions and leaving the basic premises of the Marxist-Leninist state idea intact.

During the course of the revolution, the issue of national independence became predominant. According to Edmund Stillman, among all demands voiced during the revolution 35 percent were concerned with national independence, 31 percent with political reform, 28 percent with economic reform, 3 percent with the end of censorship, and 3 percent with religious freedom.[85] Interestingly enough, among hundreds of demands articulated during the revolution, there were no demands for a return to the prewar form of government, for the reversal of Marxist-type economic and social transformations, or for the restoration of capitalism. The demands for economic reform did not include calls for the reprivatization of industry or the restoration of a market system. Thus, the majority of demands had, as Stillman points out, "a distinct left-wing flavor, and were in every sense normal demands of a militant Central European working class."[86] They included worker participation in management, the right to strike, the existence of free trade unions, and the abolition of the norm system in factories. Within the political dimension, the demands concerned a restoration of "true Socialist democracy" with a pluralism of parties, freedom of the press, and other political liberties. Thus, the political language of the revolution reinforced the semantic hybrids used by communist propaganda to mix socialist and communist ideals and blur the meaning of institutional guarantees and political liberties that characterized democratic political systems.[87]

The Hungarian Revolution and the Soviet Empire

The pressure for Rakosi's dismissal and the political transition within the Hungarian Communist party elite was orchestrated by the Soviet post-Stalinist leadership, which was concerned about Hungary's economic crisis and growing political instability.[88] Despite Soviet pressure, however, Rakosi had enough domestic control and support within the party-state elites to resist surrendering of his power until July 1956. This internal stalemate within the party's top elite brought the country to a state of political paralysis. At the same time, the anti-Stalinist opposition gained strength and became bolder. The country was moving quickly to the verge of social explosion. During the summer of 1956, Soviet concerns deepened and special delegations of Soviet leaders visited Hungary in order to assess the political situation. In July 1956, the Soviet envoy Anastas Mikoyan reported to the Soviet Central Committee: "As a result of the Hungarian situation there is an atmosphere of uneasiness prevailing in our Central Committee and in the ranks of the Socialist camp, which is due to the fact, that it cannot be permitted for something unexpected, unpleasant to happen in Hungary. If the Hungarian comrades need it, our Central Committee is ready to give them a helping hand by giving advice or else, in order to put things right."[89] But as Rainer concluded, "although the Soviet leaders received serious signals about the further exacerbation of tensions in Hungary, they were distracted by crises in other locations (Poland, Suez). Evidently, in assessing the Hungarian situation, they did not think in terms of social movement, but only in the context of more or less narrow political factions."[90] Thus, the revolutionary uprising came to them as a surprise. After the first confused days of the revolution, the Soviet leaders decided to support Nagy and Kadar and to allow the replacement of Gero and the other hard-liners. On October 28, Hungarian Stalinist leaders were evacuated on board a Soviet plane to Moscow. At that time, Soviet military forces had been fighting with insurgent units on the streets of Budapest for four days without much success.

The Soviet army stationed sixty-five thousand troops in Hungary before the revolution. These included three armored divisions, two air divisions of jet fighters, and several bomber units.[91] When the threatened Hungarian leaders requested Soviet help to put down the demonstrations on October 23, the ninety-second armored division was immediately sent to the capital. The first Soviet tank units entered Budapest in the early hours of October 24. Both the Hungarian and Soviet leadership assumed that the mere presence of these troops in the city would calm down the demonstrations. But after four days of unexpected armed resistance waged by ad hoc organized and poorly armed groups of freedom fighters, the Soviet troops, lacking experience and equipment suitable to fighting in the city, were not only demoralized[92] but in fact, militarily defeated. Yet while the fighting in Budapest was gaining momentum, the Soviet troops stationed in the provinces remained inactive, avoiding any contacts with the population. After the announcement of the cease-fire on October 28, Nagy's government moved to fulfill the major demand of the Hungarian population and asked for the immediate withdrawal of the Soviet troops from the city. However, the supreme commander of Soviet forces in Hungary, General Mikhail Malinin, informed the Hungarian government that he was not prepared to order the evacuation of the capital unless the insurgents surrendered. The next day, nevertheless, an agreement was reached, and on October 30 Soviet troops left Budapest and took up positions outside the city.

While the Soviet troops were evacuating the capital, Anastas Mikoyan and Mikhail Suslov were dispatched from Moscow to oversee the situation and to find a compromise with the new Hungarian government. It is hard not to conclude that this was a political deception to cover the real Soviet plans. At the time when the Soviet ambassador to Hungary, Yuri Andropov, Soviet and Hungarian military commanders, and the Politburo envoys negotiated the withdrawal of the troops, sixteen new divisions crossed the Hungarian border from Carpathian Ukraine and Romania and surrounded airports, train stations, and other strategic points during the first days of November. This was a clear indication that a military solution to the Hungarian crisis was the Soviet Union's most likely choice. We now know that during the Politburo meeting on the morning of November 1, Soviet leaders decided to crush the revolution and to restore order through the country under firm communist control.

The decision to use troops to resolve the crisis was clearly preceded by a complex process of consensus building within the Soviet Politburo, as well as between the Soviet leaders and its communist allies. Consultations with allies included meetings with the Poles in Brest, with the Chinese in Moscow and with Tito in Brioni.[93] The possible responses of the United States and other Western powers were also considered. The final decision was made only after the Americans gave a clear signal that they were not prepared to intervene in the conflict. According to Ferenc Vali: "Not only the stability of the Communist camp but also the Soviet view of power politics in the world must have weighed heavily in persuading the [Soviet] Presidium to resort to massive military action. The relinquishment of Hungary as a Soviet dependency would have upset the basic considerations of Soviet policy as it had been conducted since the end of World War II."[94] Similarly, Charles Gati argues that "the Soviet leaders responded primarily to their sense of threat, to their fear of vulnerability, to their concern about the reputation and hence the power of the Soviet Union."[95] Also the rapid collapse of the communist control in Hungary must have push the Soviets to act quickly and decisively. The Soviet leaders clearly realized that in Budapest, and even more so in the provinces, rapidly emerging revolutionary organizations had displaced the party-state administration. The development of events clearly indicated that within days the remnants of the former Communist administration would be swept away, and the country's new regime would be consolidated on an anticommunist and anti-Soviet basis.

The final decision to invade Hungary and destroy the revolutionary movement was reached on November 1, but the contingency plans were in place days before that date. Thus, the argument that the Hungarian declaration of independence and her withdrawal from the Warsaw Treaty were the real reasons for the Soviet intervention is not supported by the facts. It is absolutely clear that these decisions of the Nagy government were made when the Soviets had already made up their minds. As Vali points out: "The Soviet die had already been cast when Hungary declared her neutrality. The movements of the army to occupy all strategically important points of the country outside Budapest, to seal off the Western border of Hungary and to prepare for the deadly blow, were already under way when the withdrawal from the Warsaw Treaty was conveyed to the Soviet government."[96] During the next three days, the Soviet decision was communicated to other communist leaders, and Soviet troops moved to all strategic positions within Hungary. At dawn on November 4, the Soviet army launched a general attack throughout the country.

The Soviet Invasion and the Defeat of the Revolution

THE SOVIET MILITARY INVASION

In words of a distinguished student of Hungarian politics, "Hungary's normalization . . . began with the nation's complete defeat, with the total knock-down of Hungarian society."[1] In contrast to the invasion of Czechoslovakia, where troops of other Warsaw Treaty Organization countries participated in the military operation, and to martial law in Poland, where domestic forces were used, this defeat came exclusive at the hand of the Soviet army, which invaded Hungary early on the morning of November 4, 1956. The Soviet troops were militarily involved in Hungary since the beginning of the revolution, but the first Soviet intervention in Budapest on October 24 was ill-planned, badly executed, and relied on unprepared and insufficient forces. Fighting with the insurgents ended on October 30 following the cease-fire agreement. The second military operation was well-planed and executed systematically in order to smash all armed resistance and to crush the population's will to resist. Although Soviet leaders received the request for military assistance from the Hungarian government at the outset of the revolution, during the entire period the invading Soviet troops acted without any significant cooperation from Hungary's political institutions, its armed forces, or its other political organizations.[2]

The invasion plan called for a simultaneous attack on all urban centers so as to wipe out the territorial bases of the revolution. In preparation for military action, units of the Soviet army stationed in Hungary were replaced and reinforced by a massive number of additional units from the USSR and Romania, and Soviet forces took control of all strategic points within the country. Several days before the invasion, nineteen Soviet divisions reinforced by two thousand tanks had already occupied airports, train stations and communication centers, road junctions, and bridges, supposedly to cover a Soviet withdrawal from Hungary. When the Soviet army attacked at dawn on November 4, Hungarian leaders understood the hopelessness of armed resistance. Budapest had no organized defense, and Hungarian armed forces were not only unprepared but also had never received an explicit order to resist the Soviet invasion. Facing the overwhelming Soviet strategic advantage, Nagy's refusal to issue clear-cut orders to the Hungarian army, either to fight or to lay down their arms, must be seen as a responsible way of avoiding vain bloodshed.[3] In such a situation, improvised military resistance carried on by groups of students, workers, and some military personnel collapsed before it even began. During the first twenty-four hours of the invasion, Russian tanks and cannon fire crushed the principal resistance centers. The desperate armed resistance was quickly reduced to isolated pockets in industrial strongholds and a few spots in the countryside. But despite the overwhelming superiority of the Soviet forces, the battle for Budapest lasted until November 7, the ill-armed workers of Csepel Island continued their armed resistance until November 14, and a few centers of resistance held out until November 18.

While military resistance gradually died, new political institutions that emerged during the revolution disintegrated within hours. In the early morning of November 4, the government melted away and political leaders of the revolution disappeared. Imre Nagy, with five of the seven members of the organizational committee of the renewed Communist party escaped to the Yugoslav embassy. Together with the central institutions of the state, the political society reborn in Hungary collapsed as rapidly as it had emerged during the revolution. The myriads of old and new political parties and organizations rapidly disappeared or fell prey to the Soviet forces and to returning hard-line communist functionaries, who were eager to reclaim their lost positions. Leaders of revolutionary organizations went into hiding, and the flood of refugees escaped from the country, crossing Yugoslav and Austrian borders. As a result, when the fighting stopped, neither any central nor local administration existed to take over the tasks of running the country.

The provisional Soviet military administration promptly filled the vacuum left by the destruction of revolutionary institutions. During the first weeks of the intervention, the Soviet army and military police not only carried out arrests and purely repressive actions but also maintained order and political control throughout the country.[4] Local Soviet military commanders in all cities within the country issued orders suspending civil and political rights and imposing a curfew. Acting as a civil administration, they arranged for food supplies, the continued service of public utilities, and provided for urgent administrative needs. The country, however, remained in a state of chaos. According to Paul Zinner: "For a period of several weeks, Hungary lived under a veritable *interregnum* with the Soviet military wielding effective power, the Hungarian government in the throes of painful reconstruction, the object of derision and ridicule, and the workers' councils, spontaneous bodies of the people's will, exercising *de facto* political power to the point of being consulted by the Soviet military as well as Hungarian government organs."[5] Very soon, however, the first foundations for the reconstruction of the Hungarian state were laid down. The complete Soviet takeover of the country offered favorable opportunities and created facilitating conditions for the domestic communist forces to regroup, claim back their positions and resources and launch a political struggle to regain full control over the country and its institutions. Following the successful extension of the

Soviet grip over the country, gradually more authority was transferred to the new consolidating Hungarian regime and after January 1957, and direct Soviet military administration slowly disappeared. But the Soviet control over newly recreated coercive institutions of the state remained extensive.

The process of reconstruction of the party-state in Hungary after its institutional breakdown was similar to the strategy the communists used to capture power after World War II. Control of the means of coercion was the first priority, followed by the strengthening of the party and the extension of full control over the state administration and the administration of the economy, and, finally, by the reconstitution and consolidation of secondary social and political mass organizations under communist control.

COERCIVE FORCES OF THE NEW HUNGARIAN REGIME

On November 8, 1956, Kadar's government hurriedly began to create a unit of special forces to serve as a coercive arm of the new regime. In the process of reconstructing the party-state and its institutions, the newly installed regime realized that the reconstruction of and its exclusive control over the state coercive forces was the utmost priority. The first special force units were organized in the capital and gradually spread to all counties and districts in the country. The new forces were recruited from the core supporters of the prerevolutionary regime—"former partisans and employees of the Ministry of Interior."[6] After the annihilation of the security police during the revolution, many of its members went into hiding or were arrested. Following the Soviet intervention, those who had been in hiding or liberated from prisons were the first to offer their service to the Soviets and the new government. By mid-December these ad hoc organized units gradually assumed control over the maintenance of law and order from the Soviet troops. They served as a basis for the reorganization of regular police forces and the army. By early 1957 the total strength of these improvised special forces was close to eighteen thousand.[7] The units were known as Security Force Regiments, R-Groups, Mixed Action Groups, or Factory Guards. From their inception, the new security forces began to apprehend those who were either still resisting or conspiring against the regime. They also arrested, on the basis of private denunciation, the persons who had committed individual violent actions during the revolution. In April and May, these semiregular forces were gradually demobilized, incorporated, and replaced by reorganized units of the police in capital and provincial centers. The formal dissolution of all special security formations took place on December 20, 1957, when all regular formations of the regime's coercive forces were firmly in place.[8]

But before the special forces disappeared from the political scene, the Workers Militia was created on February 18, 1957, to ensure "order and protection of factories and work places." Kadar, in his toast at the central staff and unit commander training school of the workers militia, explained its role in the following way: "The Workers' Militia is an armed body. The member of the Workers' Militia carries out his duty with arms in hand. That weapon is an instrument of the state [and] the purpose and function of the Workers' Militia is the protection and consolidation of workers' power."[9] The Workers Militia was a part-time, paramilitary organization composed mainly of party members; their activities were limited to maintaining general control over factories and enterprises in the event of internal disturbances. Units of the militia were stationed in all larger factories, plants and mines.

The police in Budapest and in provincial towns had proved to be the weakest link in the chain of coercive institutions protecting the communist regime. The police practically joined the insurrection, although they did refrain from direct participation in the fight against the Soviets. Immediately after the invasion, the orders were issued to the police to resume their regular duties. Surprisingly, as Ferenc Vali points out, "no large-scale purges of its officers and men were reported."[10] The main task in the reorganization of the police, involved incorporation of the Security Police (AVH) into the regular police forces.

Although Kadar himself announced on November 11, 1956, that the hated AVH had been abolished, the organization was in fact restored in a different institutional form. To regain political control, which included the enormous task of repression and investigation of insurgents and other opponents of the regime, the existence, stability, and reliability of the political police run by trained and seasoned security police personnel was essential. Following the government's decree on December 30, 1956, the duties of the security police were transferred to the regular police. For this purpose the new Department of Political Affairs in the Ministry of Interior was created, with a very extensive nonuniformed apparatus that dealt with political activities against the state. This department was staffed by former AVH men, and in spite of its new form it effectively carried on all the functions of a security police. According to Vali:

> The 'new' Security Police showed itself as ruthless as during the Stalinist era. During Kadar's first year, it was often accused of brutality in its treatment of prisoners, and there is no doubt that the repression after the Revolution was carried out with the usual totalitarian methods of torture and 'brain-washing' that must have led to a number of extorted confessions, the victimization of innocent, and illegalities on a large scale. After this initial year of terrorism the activities of the Security Police became more discreet and less provocative. Indiscriminate and arbitrary arrests were stopped, and those who kept themselves aloof from politics seemed no longer to have reasons to fear arrest.[11]

But regardless of its renewed importance, the AVH's freedom of action was curtailed, and some of its privileges were reduced. These restrictions can be attributed to both Kadar's own experience with imprisonment and torture under Rakosi's regime and more cautious behavior of the security police themselves due to their vivid memory of the hatred and vengeance their former victims exhibited during the revolution.

Before the revolution the Hungarian Border Guards were well trained military formations under the supervision of the AVH, but in the stormy events of the revolution its units swiftly sided with the revolutionaries. Bela Kiraly writes: "When the Soviet Union started its second attack, a mass exodus from the country of more than two hundred thousand people began. . . . The Border Guards would have had no difficulty in stopping the refugees and keeping them inside the Iron Curtain, but it did not do so. Instead its members helped them cross the Austrian and Yugoslav borders."[12]

After the invasion, therefore, the Soviet troops had to be assigned to guard the western frontiers of the country. Mine fields and barbed wire installations that had been removed in 1956 were reinstalled in February and March of 1957. But the Soviet troops, not familiar with the terrain and operating in large units for security reasons were highly ineffective as border guards. As a result the country's borders remained porous for weeks following the invasion. In the meantime, the Hungarian Border Guards were screened and purged of all "undesirable" elements. They were reorganized as a branch of the armed services under the supervision and jurisdiction of the Ministry of Interior. Officers were selected from among the most reliable noncommissioned officers of the army and former members of the Security Police. In the summer of 1957, Hungarian units were again able to take over the task of policing the country's borders. During the several months following the invasion, the Border Guards were gradually restored to their pre-revolutionary strength of around fifteen thousand men. The vast majority, about eleven thousand, were conscripts.[13]

The army, largely inactive during the revolution, also did not resist the Soviet invasion as a unified force, and most of the fighting was carried out by groups of armed workers. As Janos Berecz claims, "Thanks to the activities of the officers loyal to socialism, the Hungarian Army did not turn against people's power, but they did not have enough strength to prevent the disintegration of the Army." After the Soviet invasion, many left the army. Berecz admits that "as from November 5, thousands of servicemen deserted their barracks and returned to their homes. The highways were packed with Hungarian soldiers on their way home."[14] Thus, initially the armed forces were in a state of disintegration and were highly unreliable; they had to be rebuild almost from scratch, as did all the other institutions of the party-state.

Immediately after November 4, the Soviet forces started to disband those Hungarian units whose members had assisted the revolutionaries. Most of the officers of the Hungarian army were placed under Soviet guard in a barracks camp near the Soviet headquarters at Tokol. An official document describing the party's policies toward the armed forces states that the first task of Kadar's regime was to "purge the entire army and specifically the officer corps of traitors, those who had taken part in the counterrevolutionary events, who are politically unstable, and who were cowards."[15] Accordingly, every officer was subjected to the repeated screening by special Soviet-Hungarian control commissions, regardless of whether he was in active service or on reserve. The purge of the army began on November 16, when Ferenc Munnich, the minister of Internal Affairs, demanded all officers sign a declaration of loyalty to the new regime. The screening process lasted until March 1957, and, as Ivan Volgyes states, "all officers joining the army had to sign an officers' declaration condemning the revolution, announcing their desire to fight against it, accepting the necessity of Soviet military intervention, and unconditionally accepting the Kadar government."[16] Those who refused to sign this declaration were immediately expelled from the armed forces. As a result of the purge, several thousands officers, including nine generals, were dismissed. Those who were dismissed were replaced with newly appointed officers selected from the ranks of the Workers Militia, who were quickly prepared for military duties through accelerated training courses.[17]

With the purge of officers completed, the reorganization of the army slowly began after March 1957. While all former methods of control and supervision were reestablished, new guidelines were introduced that further reinforced the power of the communist military commanders and secured the full supervision of higher party authorities over the army. At the same time, Soviet control of the Hungarian army was reimposed, and Soviet advisers were allocated down to the level of regiment; the army command structure was revamped and fully integrated into the Warsaw Pact command structure. The reorganized army was more rigidly ruled by Soviet military organs than it had ever been before the revolution. After 1958, following the reorganization of the Hungarian army, the number of Soviet troops in Hungary was reduced to four divisions and several air force units, with a total strength around eighty thousand men, which remained the same until their withdrawal after 1989.[18]

Despite these radical actions, it took a full year to reorganize the army. Volgyes points out: "Not until November 1957, could one speak of a relatively complete party control over the army. Since that date, however, it is clear that the army has been a solid partner in the control of the party over society."[19] The strength of the reorganized Hungarian army was reduced to about one hundred thousand, which was roughly half its size before the revolution. The smaller size and more carefully selected and trained officer corps were chosen as a the best means of insuring the army's loyalty to the state. The smaller army also allowed the state to cut military spending by more than 50 percent from 1956, making it four times smaller than in 1953.[20] Moreover, because of the reorganization, the Hungarian army bypassed one round of upgrading military equipment, which also saved additional resources. In 1964 the system of defense education was introduced in all secondary schools, and in a parallel move the political education of the draftees was renewed and expanded in an effort to strengthen the party's control and integrate the army into society.[21]

By the summer of 1957, coercive forces of the party-state were purged, reorganized, and firmly placed within the institutional design of the state. The reorganized police, Border Guards, and the newly formed Workers' Militia were reestablished under the authority of the Ministry of Interior, and the army was transformed into a fully reliable political force. Having its coercive arm in place, Kadar's regime shifted its efforts to other institutional domains of the party-state. The process of restoring the coercive power of the state was paralleled by the efforts of both the Soviets and the new regime to break any effective resistance in the country.

THE COLLAPSE OF THE RESISTANCE MOVEMENT

The only revolutionary institutions to survive the Soviet invasion and continue their existence and activities were those based on organic social relations, cohesiveness and solidarity: the workers' councils, especially around industrial centers and in large factories, and the institutions of intellectuals in Budapest. They became the sole institutional bases of the resistance movement. Bill Lomax writes:

> While the Soviet military intervention had crushed overnight the purely political achievements of the revolution, it led at the same time to the strengthening of the real social base of the revolution. In the weeks which followed 4 November, the Hungarian workers seized the opportunity to establish a revolutionary structure of workers' councils which would ensure that power remained in the hands of the working people themselves. . . . Through the strike and the workers' councils they were to carry on the struggle of the revolution and to withstand for several weeks the counterrevolutionary assault of both the Kadar regime and the Soviet authorities.[22]

Thus, the first months of the restoration of a Soviet-type regime remains to a great extent a history of its struggle against workers' councils.[23]

While the armed resistance gradually subsided, workers' councils and organizations of intellectuals resumed their activities, this time directed against the Soviet troops and the newly imposed government. Janos Kis points out, "While the government had virtually no organised apparatus behind it, the resistance movement had the organisations inherited from the revolution and those brought into being after the dying away of armed fighting."[24] Three organizations played a crucial role in organizing the resistance: the Central Workers Council of Greater Budapest, the Revolutionary Council of Hungarian Intellectuals, and the Revolutionary Council of Young Workers. Unable to resist with arms, workers brought the country to a virtual halt by widespread industrial action. The general strike that followed the invasion was one of the most full-scale and united worker actions in the modern history of the European working-class movement. The strike was purely political in character,[25] lasted over a month, and represented the most serious challenge to the Soviet invaders and the new rulers of Hungary. According to Lomax: "In its beginnings the strike had been an instinctive reaction of the working class, completely spontaneous and neither centrally directed nor organised. Having realised their power, however, the workers proceeded to consolidate and organise it in a revolutionary structure of workers' councils set up at the level of the factory, the district, the city, and eventually the country itself."[26]

With the country in the grip of a general strike, the intellectuals attempted to support the workers and defend the achievements of the revolution by demanding concessions from the new regime. The Writers Association convened its first meeting after the invasion on November 12, during which the invasion was strongly condemned and the basic demands of the revolution—national independence, democratic socialism, and the withdrawal of Soviet troops—were upheld. During this meeting, prominent Hungarian writers and intellectuals voted against the continuation of armed resistance and left a question of general strike for workers' councils to decide. The intellectuals, realizing their weakness and lacking of any effective power, limited themselves to issuing appeals and manifestos and making informal suggestions both to the striking workers and the new government. The effectiveness of such actions was, however, severely limited. In one of its first moves, the new government took over control of the press and radio as well as other means of mass communication. On December 20 the State Information Office was established, mainly to control the press. The creation of the office effectively reimposed censorship on the media.

By the end of November, in an effort to broaden its base, the Writers Association revived the Revolutionary Council of Hungarian Intellectuals, in whose name it issued appeals to the government.[27] But the spiral of repression was already set in motion, and the Revolutionary Council of Intellectuals was banned by the government on December 11. Attempts to organize underground resistance were also unsuccessful. The Hungarian Democratic Independence Movement—which intended to unite all democratic political forces and started the underground journal *October 23*—collapsed in December 1956, when its leader Miklos Gimes was arrested and Pierre Kende and Miklos Molnar fled the country. Among all organizations of intellectuals, the one that survived longest under the repression was the Writers Association, itself not a creation of the revolution. On December 8, after the suppression of workers' councils and the forced return of the majority of workers, the Writers Association held its last full meeting. Its 250 members, with only five dissenting votes, passed a highly critical resolution against the Kadar regime and once more condemned the Soviet invasion as a "historical mistake." This session, as Vali points out, "was rightly called the last 'free meeting' in Hungary."[28] Angered by the continued opposition of the intellectuals, the government struck back—and after the communist leaders condemned the writers, their organization as well as the Journalists Association and other associations of creative intellectuals were temporally suspended on January 17, 1957, with some well-known writers and journalists being taken into custody. On April 21, the Writers Association was permanently disbanded by the government. The Association was legalized and reorganized again only in October 1959, which gives the testimony to continuing resistance of the leading Hungarian intellectuals and their rejection of the Kadar regime. But before the protest of the intellectuals was crushed, the new government focused its all efforts on breaking the back of the workers' resistance.

The Destruction of Workers' Councils

While territorial revolutionary councils were crushed and immediately banned by the Soviet military commanders, initially workers' councils were not banned by either the Soviet authorities or the new government, and they continued to control all factories in the country and called a general strike to protest Soviet intervention. For the first weeks after the invasion, both the Soviet command and Kadar's government, in attempting to break up the general strike, were forced to negotiate with representatives of the councils. With the other institutions of the revolution annihilated, the workers rallied even more strongly to their freely elected councils, and as Zinner points out, "The oft-heralded but seldom demonstrated power of the working class that stems from its concentration, cohesiveness, and superior self-consciousness was apparent beyond the shadow of a doubt in the Hungarian situation of November, 1956."[29]

Although the trade union leadership almost immediately sided with the new government, Kadar's attempts to turn the workers' councils into instruments of the party-state failed, and worker organizations grew increasingly defiant in the weeks following the invasion. Workers' councils rapidly consolidated their power over the factories and even widened their scope of activity by creating broader territorial federations. The emergence of centralized structures was a dangerous challenge for the new government. On November 14, representatives of the workers' councils of all the major factories of the metropolitan area of Budapest founded the Central Workers Council of Greater Budapest (CWC) and empowered it to present the workers' demands to the government.[30] Kis writes, "It rapidly became evident that the CWC was not just capable of harmonising the resistance of the factories, but that through its existence the illegal resistance groups, the legal organizations of intelligentsia and, indeed, even the restive peasantry could establish connections with the striking workers."[31]

Thus with the formation of the CWC a center was formed which was potentially capable of coordinating the non-violent resistance of the entire nation. The CWC sought to expand the power of the councils, but on November 21, the attempt to set up a national council designed as a parliament of all workers' councils[32] led to the first clash between the government and the CWC. The establishment of the council was prevented by the Soviet troops and the Hungarian militia, which surrounded the intended meeting place. Although the representatives of councils from around the country met in a different location, they did not officially constitute the national council.[33] The delegates decided to postpone the establishment of the council and sought instead to transform the CWC into a national center of opposition. By the end of November, the worker-council movement was at the peak of its power. Even official Hungarian historiography admitted as much. Molnar argued that the immense power of workers' councils stemmed from the facts that the Communist party was in disarray, the kidnapping of Imre Nagy by the Soviets outraged public opinion,[34] and support for the councils was increasing since the radicals were prevailing over those who wished to collaborate with the regime.[35]

Kis says, "The Kadar group—old Communists raised on Lenin—immediately recognized the danger of dual power"[36] and, therefore, the confrontation between the CWC and the government escalated in the last week of November in spite of almost daily meetings between Kadar and CWC leaders.[37] The Kadar government's policy toward workers' councils became gradually more decisive. At first the government, lacking the power to break the strike by force, used the tactics of delay and evasion. It called for collaboration between councils and committees and regular institutions of the state administration and urged councils to purge all "counter-revolutionary elements" from their membership. It also supported trade unions in their confrontation with the councils over control of the factories. But the Kadar group needed council cooperation to end the strike in order to show to the Soviets and the population the first anxiously awaited sign of political stabilization and the recognition of the new regime. When this strategy failed, the government did two things. First, it resorted to successive legal regulations that reduced council functions and activities and deprived councils of any real power.[38] Second, it employed purely repressive actions designed to intimidate the councils.

Thus, as Zinner points out, "the workers' councils operated under grievous difficulties. They were harassed in the most brutal fashion by the Soviet military and by Hungarian authorities, who resorted to police and military interference, to infiltration agents, to deliberate misinformation, and to directives issued by the Trade Union Center . . . and who further wear down the councils' resistance by means of meetings, procrastination, and false promises."[39] On November 22, the government issued a decree that restricted the activities of the workers' councils to those that were purely economic and gave the state the exclusive right to control all managerial appointments in factories and enterprises. The decree also prohibited the establishment of councils in several strategic sectors of the economy (railway, postal service, transport). The government also tried to persuade the workers to operate within the framework of the official trade unions, which had in meantime been reestablished under communist control. Although the negotiations between Kadar and representatives of workers' councils were in a deadlock and repressive actions intensified, this situation did not break the councils' determination to defend the political achievements of the revolution.[40] While easing its stance on the original political demands, the CWC launched a series of symbolic confrontations with Kadar's regime. On November 23 the streets were deserted for one hour, on December 1 official newspapers were boycotted, and on December 4 a silent procession of black-robed women placed flowers on the Tomb of the Unknown Soldier. The purpose of these symbolic demonstration was to show the influence of the CWC, to revive the morale of the nation, and to demonstrate support for the ideals of the revolution.

The political stalemate between the government and councils was broken by a series of provocations. In December the government moved with force against workers' councils following Kadar's radio declaration of November 26: "You don't fight counter-revolution by making concessions to its demands but by smashing it." This shift in government policy can be, at least, partially attributed to direct Soviet pressure.[41] On December 2, Kadar rejected all the councils' demands, and the arrests of the councils' leaders began in the provinces.[42] During the first days of December, two hundred members of various workers' councils were arrested. Moreover, the militia and Soviet troops used firearms against demonstrators. Among five similar incidents in the span of one week, the most violent provocation took place in Salgotarjan, where Soviet and Hungarian units opened fire at a crowd protesting the arrest of two members of the workers' council. The volley killed thirty-nine and wounded at least one hundred. These actions prompted the CWC to proclaim a forty-eight-hour general strike on December 11 and 12. To prevent the strike, the government on December 8 decreed a law that banned all territorial and functional revolutionary committees and councils as "harming and impeding the activities of regular authorities." The next day the CWC and all workers' councils above the factory level were outlawed. The majority of the CWC members were arrested and its headquarters occupied. The decree issued on December 9 stated that the "counter-revolution was trying to use workers organs, the workers councils in particular, for its own purpose. In spite of government warnings, district councils had been set up. At the national conference held illegally during the past few days the majority of Budapest workers councils incited to bloodshed, armed provocation and strike."[43]

The strike on December 11 and 12 showed the overwhelming support for the CWC. It was, at the same time, the last major manifestation of concerted opposition by the workers. According to Kis, "the question why the CWC and other like-minded territorial workers' councils could be eliminated from the political arena with such speed" presents itself as a challenge to historians and political scientists. He suggests that the failure of the CWC to prepare for the underground activity, the short period of time the opposition had before a frontal attack by the government, the fear of the economic collapse spread by the government, and the exhaustion of the masses may point to an answer.[44] The banning of the Central Workers Council and the imprisonment of its leaders gave an added urgency and impetus to the strike of December 11 and 12. During the two-day protest action, a number of demonstrations, disturbances and even armed clashes with the authorities occurred in several provincial towns. In response to widespread protest, the government declared the state of emergency, banned all meetings and demonstrations, introduced detention without trial, internal deportation, and summary jurisdiction, putting the whole country under de facto martial law. On December 13, the concentration camp system was reestablished, and by the middle of December the first executions under the state emergency law had been carried out.

These tough repressive measures effectively closed the possibility for legitimate protest actions and caused the rapid deflation of the resistance in the second half of December. By the end of the month the government was the unchallenged master of the situation. When on January 5, 1957, the government extended the death penalty to cover all forms of resistance, including striking and inciting a strike, and further reduced the legal competence of the workers' councils, the organized resistance collapsed, and open defiance against the new regime came to an end. With the resignation of the workers' council of Csepel on January 8, on the ground that it was unable to fulfill its tasks because of continuous harassment by the authorities, the organizational base of effective resistance ceased to exist. The worker demonstration in Csepel organized in support of the council was brutally dispersed by the Soviet troops. It was the last major collective action inspired by the workers' council movement against Kadar's regime. In its last act of resistance, the CWC, still functioning underground, issued on January 15 its final appeal to the workers to continue their passive resistance. This marked the end of the second phase of the restoration, during which, as Kis argues, the parallel process of building the institutional structures of the state and the resistance movement occurred, and the liquidation of the opposition began. From the middle of January, there were still isolated cases of sabotage and passive resistance, and even the occasional strike and demonstration. They continue throughout 1957, but the organized power of the Hungarian workers' councils had been broken.[45]

Even with the suppression of open resistance, the campaign against the workers' councils was not over. In the months that followed, the press and representatives of the party and trade unions launched a series of attacks describing the councils as tools of the counterrevolutionaries organized as a weapon in the fight against working-class power. Finally, after months of hesitation and in an effort to eradicate any independent worker organizations, while still maintaining the semblance of worker participation in the factory management, the workers' councils were dissolved by the decree on November 16, 1957, and replaced by the factory councils.[46] Gyorgy Varga, secretary of the Trade Union Council, justified this decision in the following way: "The workers' councils misled the working masses by their social demagogy. They introduced a series of measures that seemed to serve the interests of the workers. [In fact] The workers' councils were not formed with the purpose of becoming organs of the broadening of factory democracy. [Thus] The workers' councils have lost the confidence of the masses."[47] The newly established factory councils, fully controlled by party and trade union officials as well as the plant management, were said to be created in order to "make it possible for the broad masses of the workers to participate in the management, and control production in their factories, plants, enterprises."[48] The chief function of these new bodies was to "strengthen the dictatorship of the proletariat and to protect public property." The following months witnessed intensifying political terror and ideological campaign against the legacy of the revolution.

Legalized Repression against the Opposition

The demobilization policies in Hungary were the most repressive and bloody of the cases analyzed in this work. Nonetheless, the repression was legally grounded in a framework of extraordinary legal measures introduced by the government in response to the changing political situation within the country. Starting from the Decree Law No. 22 of November 12, 1956, which extended the rights of the public prosecutor, a whole series of ever tougher summary jurisdiction decrees was passed, extending both the range of acts and crimes falling under the provisions of summary jurisdiction and increasing the severity of punishments. The most far-reaching was Decree Law No. 4 of January 15, 1957, which extended the mandatory death sentence to cover not only all political oppositional activities, but even "all acts of non-cooperation over practically the whole field of nation's economy."[49] This decree also applied retroactively to all offenses committed at any point before its official enactment, with the concession that the death penalty was not applicable to past offenses. Under summary jurisdiction, crimes were tried before special councils attached to County Courts and appointed by the Presidential Council of the Republic, Military Courts, and the Supreme Court. To cope with the number of cases when repression was intensified during the spring of 1957, a special People's Court Bench in the Supreme Court of Hungary was created by the decree issued on April 6, 1957, specifically designed to conduct summary trials.

This extraordinary legal framework,[50] designed to prosecute and punish all acts of political opposition and noncooperation with the regime, included a whole range of preventive measures that gave the security authorities virtually a free hand in using any repressive strategy. From the point of view of the communist legal tradition and practices, the extraordinary legal regulations and judicial repression that followed the revolution were only a somehow harsh interpretation of the socialist law that was always understood in a purely instrumental way as a tool of class struggle. Among other provisions the detention of any person without trial for a period not exceeding six months was enacted. A presidential decree of December 13, 1956, revived internment camps for "whoever endangers public order or public security by his activities or behavior." Beginning on March 19, 1957, internment could be ordered by the police, subject to later approval by a state attorney; its duration became indefinite, and interned persons could be put to work. Moreover, police surveillance and internal deportation[51] could be imposed on any person considered "dangerous to the state, to public security or to Socialist order . . . or disquieting important state interests . . . or detrimental for economic reasons."[52] This legal machine was put to use first to only prosecute and prevent any acts of open resistance, but later on it was widely employed to punish those who had participated in the revolution. The restraint in punishing those participants, which had initially characterized the Kadar regime, had been entirely abandoned by the summer of 1957.

According to the recently uncovered evidence, the repressive actions following the revolution were massive.[53] By 1959, thirty-five thousand people were arrested for their activities during the revolution. Among those twenty-six thousand stood trial and twenty-two thousand were sentenced. After the summary jurisdiction had been imposed, thirteen thousand people were interned. Between 1956 and 1961, 280 to 300 people were executed and 350 to 400 death sentences were commuted. The death sentence was still used to punish participants in the revolution, as well as persons accused of conspiring against the state, well into 1960. The postinvasion repression targeted especially three groups: the armed insurgents, the representatives of revolutionary and workers' councils, and the representatives of the pre-1956 party opposition and intellectuals. Without any doubt, the political repression that followed the revolution was comparable in scope and terror to Hungary's worst years of Stalinist rule.

After 1958, however, the extraordinary legal measures were slowly toned down. Already by November 3, 1957, the government announced the introduction of the Decree Law No. 62, which abolished summary jurisdiction. The decree stated, "The success attained in last year in the reestablishment of law and order make it possible to abolish the summary jurisdiction which was introduced for a transitory period."[54] But as George Urban argues, the summary procedure was retained, although in somewhat different form. He claims that "the Presidium's decree abolishing summary jurisdiction does not affect the validity of the rules of summary procedure. . . . the only noticeable difference is that some of the more extraordinary measures have been repealed. . . . The summary procedure currently in practice is thus technically not identical with the summary procedure abolished on 3 November 1957, but the practical effect of abolishing summary jurisdiction has been very limited."[55] Other repressive measures such as internment for security reasons were abolished only in 1960 under the decree on partial amnesty introduced on March 31. The special People's Courts, which conducted summary trials, were abolished on April 14, 1961.

The gradual abolition of extraordinary legal measures was followed by the introduction of a new criminal code enacted at the end of 1961. This new legislation, "with its more liberal tone [was] an unmistakable sign of retreat and relaxation."[56] Introducing the legislation in the Parliament, Minister of Justice Ferenc Nazval said that socialist legality has been completely restored since 1957, and "no innocent person can be punished within the People's Republic. Counterrevolutionary cases are mostly completed, and recent political crimes are rare, which indicates the result of the enormous evolution of social, economic, and cultural life of the State. Nobody can be punished for political conviction. But by maintaining socialist legality, our law enforcement organs must effectively defend the political, social, and economic order of the State."[57] To this purpose, all politically motivated crimes such as crimes against the people's republic, against public security and public order, or against the state property were included in a special section of the criminal code and carried the most severe sentences. This partial relaxation of the repressive legal framework aimed at all antistate activities reflected the progress of the regime's demobilization policies. Urban writes: "The slow petering out of repression has coincided with a spectacular growth in the number and importance of those public bodies and organizations which control, cajole, bait, bribe or admonish the citizen at all levels of his private and public life. Rakosi's brutal policies, and the reprisals of 1956–58 have gradually given way to gentler but equally effective ways of keeping a check on the population and conditioning its responses."[58]

To fully understand why resistance against the regime collapsed so rapidly and did not survive state's repressive policies, additional points need to be made. The first concerns the often-emphasized issue of the general losses suffered by Hungarian society. Together with the number of persons arrested and executed after the Soviet invasion, we must add the number of people killed and wounded during the revolution and the Soviet invasion, as well as the number of refugees, in order to fully appreciate the demographic impact of these losses on the ability of Hungarian society to resist. Official figures on the dead and wounded released by the government listed twenty-five hundred to three thousand dead and about thirteen thousand wounded as of January 15, 1957. Recently disclosed Soviet figures estimate that four thousand Hungarians died, while Soviet loses were 669 killed, 1,450 wounded, and 51 missing.[59] Moreover, until Hungary's border were sealed again, 193,216 refugees escaped to Austria and Yugoslavia by the end of April 1957. A significant number of these people were the real or potential leaders of the resistance movement. The revolution, therefore, cost Hungary a total demographic loss of at least 250,000 mostly young and capable citizens, which had significant political consequences for the small nation of less than ten million people. The Hungarian resistance movement lost its leaders and activists, making the demobilization policies much more effective.

The resistance movement was equally impaired by the collapse or dismantling of its potential allies and independent institutional bases following the invasion. With the reconstruction of the party-state institutions and structures, no political or social organization was allowed to survive without full subordination to the government's directives and control.[60] The Catholic church, which provided autonomous institutional spaces for the opposition movement in Poland in the 1980s, and other churches were brought quickly into line in postrevolutionary Hungary.

During the revolution, both the Hungarian Catholic church and Protestant churches regained their independence and quickly removed their leaders, who cooperated with the communist regime.[61] The state's security arm within the Catholic church, the infamous movement of "peace priests," was abolished; they were removed from their positions within the church by Jozsef Cardinal Mindszenty upon his release from internment. After the Soviet invasion, Cardinal Mindszenty, who sought refuge in the American legation, was not allowed to exercise his prerogatives as the head of the Hungarian Catholic church.[62] At the same time the State Office for Church Affairs, under the direct supervision of the Council of Ministers, resumed its functions of control over the church and church appointments. Additionally, several legal acts were passed designed to recover the state's full control over ecclesiastical organizations.

On February 24, 1957, the government declared that the peace priests "relieved of their offices because of their progressive views are taken under the protection of the Office of Church Affairs." A month later, a government decree subjected all senior church appointments, transfers and dismissals to the governmental approval.[63] The state's rights vis-à-vis the church were extended even further by a new law enacted on April 6, 1957. This law required an oath of allegiance to the state from all clergy and gave the state the right to appoint its own nominees to all vacant positions within churches' hierarchy. These legal regulations were reinforced by the church's dependence on annual subsidies from the state, which were granted after 1948 in exchange for the confiscation of church property.[64] The churches financial dependence gave the state additional leverage in its dealings with organized religion.

The Protestant churches were subjected to measures similar to those taken against the Catholic church. And because of their smaller size and lack of centralized authority, they were much more likely to succumb to state pressure. Already in January 1957, the Ecumenical Council agreed that the prerevolutionary status quo should be reestablished.[65] Accordingly, church leaders who were actively opposed to the regime or supported the revolution were removed and all new bishops and lay persons elected to church positions were the nominees of the Office of Church Affairs, which actively supported the regime policies both in the domestic and international dimension. It did not take long for all Protestant churches to become again fully subservient to the state.

It should be pointed out that while the government arrested Cardinal Mindszenty's secretary and some other priests and pastors and staged a few show trials of the clergy as late as the early 1960s, it did not conduct mass arrests of the clergy or close churches. But the state policies vis-à-vis organized religious denominations were harsh and decisive enough to leave no possibility for churches to support oppositional political activities or even to retain any independence in dealing with their own internal affairs.

THE RESTORATION OF THE PARTY-STATE

The new Revolutionary Worker Peasant Government under Kadar's leadership, formed under still-obscure circumstances, announced its existence on November 4.[66] The newly appointed officials had to wait for three days before they could be brought safely to Budapest by a Soviet armored car and sworn in by Istvan Dobi, the chairman of the Presidential Council. Once installed the newly created government took full responsibility for requesting that the Soviet military "help our people to destroy the sinister forces of reaction and to restore calm and order in our country." Originally the government included Janos Kadar as prime minister, and only seven other members. For weeks, Kadar had considerable difficulty in persuading influential communists to join his cabinet. The people selected by the Soviets to staff this puppet government included only those former communist leaders who represented Kadar's centrist faction within the party and former Stalinists who were less compromised in the past. They were brought to power by the foreign troops and given the country, which experienced total institutional breakdown. Consequently, new rulers of Hungary, even after weeks of residence in Budapest, were vulnerable and totally dependent on the Soviet armed forces. They were also closely supervised by the Soviet command.

The problems faced by newly installed leaders were immense by any standard. First, they had to put down the armed resistance, break the general strike, prevent further escalation of protests and demonstrations, and destroy the institutional remnants of the revolution, which could have provided the base for antiregime opposition. As Kadar himself emphasized, "the first unavoidable step in the interest of consolidation of the dictatorship of the proletariat is to crush the armed groups of the counter-revolution. Therefore all other tasks are subordinated to this primary duty."[67] Second, they had to rebuilt the Communist party institutions and membership almost from scratch. Third, they had to purge and reconstruct the coercive forces of the state. Fourth, they faced the task of recreating the entire local and central state administration. And finally, the new regime had to win international recognition.[68] This was the only case in the history of state-socialist regimes in East Central Europe that such a mammoth task had to be undertaken. In all cases analyzed in this work, only Kadar faced the challenge of reconquering power before he could proceed with the further "construction of socialism." As Lomax points out, "in retrospect the surprising thing is that Kadar managed to stay in power at all and was not ousted once he played out his conciliatory role, in a way similar to the removal of Alexander Dubcek in Czechoslovakia twelve years later."[69]

Initially, Kadar's government presented a rather confusing set of goals and ideas about the restored state-socialist system in Hungary once the destruction of the "counter-revolution" was completed. The different aspects of the governmental program presented by Kadar were largely borrowed from the programs of successive cabinets that existed during the revolution, and from the popular demands put forward by revolutionary organizations.[70] Although Kadar repeatedly suggested during the first weeks after the Soviet intervention that significant changes and concessions would be forthcoming—including free elections, democratization, national independence, and even withdrawal of Soviet troops—his government immediately began a full-scale reconstruction of prerevolutionary party-state institutional structures. As Janos Berecz stated, "the new government began its activities in defence of and in the spirit of the constitution of the People's Republic of Hungary."[71]

In fact, apart from Kadar's conciliatory rhetoric, the Soviet-imposed regime neither changed the Stalinist legal structures of the country nor introduced any institutional and political innovations that could set Hungary apart from the other state-socialist regimes. In this context, as Vali emphasized,

> in both institutional and intellectual matters relating to the Revolution, Kadar displayed a gradualism which was reminiscent, to some extent, of what Rakosi had once called 'salami tactics' (slice by slice). Until the beginning of January, Kadar inspired hopes that a multi-party system might be re-established. . . . He also kept alive the hope that other revolutionary achievements would be maintained: participants in the revolutionary events would not be prosecuted, compulsory instruction of the Russian language would not again be introduced, and so on. Later, however, he disavowed all these and other promises.[72]

There has been a lively debate among the students of Hungarian politics regarding the initial intentions and goals of Kadar's government policies. Some commentators assumed that he lied at the beginning in an attempt to deceive the population and hide real goals of the new rulers. It seems— argues Vali—"that Kadar was even encouraged at this time by the Soviet authorities to make empty promises for the sake of placating the regime's foes and for promoting the much required consolidation of the country."[73] Other scholars take his promises at face value but point to his helplessness and total dependence on the Soviets, who controlled and shaped the restoration objectives and policies.[74] It is clear, however, that whatever Kadar's original intentions might have been, he willingly responded to Soviet pressures and objectively never departed from a very orthodox vision of how a socialist state should be organized and managed, especially during the first years of his rule. Kadar's initial promises and concessions should be seen as a sign of confusion during the first weeks of restoration, not as a significant change in the political program of communist leaders. Kadar himself made this point very clear. He told the May 11, 1957, session of the Parliament:

"In all honesty I have to tell you that this part of the leadership was in a state of serious confusion during those grave days. Speaking on my own behalf, I can tell you that it was not easy to understand what was happening in the drift of the events. And it was even more difficult to foresee the next step, what should be done. So it was difficult to realize what was happening and it was difficult to see what to do."[75]

Following the meeting of five communist party leaders from the Soviet Union, Romania, Czechoslovakia, Bulgaria, and Hungary held in Budapest between January 1 and 4, any initial confusion and doubts concerning the policies and direction of Kadar's government were put to rest. On January 5, Kadar announced a declaration describing the "major tasks" facing his regime. This time without any confusing rhetoric he stated that the major aim of the government was to promote the "dictatorship of the proletariat." He emphasized that policy directions would emanate only from the Communist party and political activity was to remain an exclusive privilege of the party members and those who strictly follow its lead and policies. He asserted that the People's Patriotic Front, guided by the party, would unite all democratic forces and that the government would retain an exclusive right to appoint directors of enterprises, who would be solely responsible to the government.[76] This official statement made clear the policies and objectives of the regime that began to be implemented a few days after the Soviet troops crushed the Hungarian Revolution.

In accordance with these policy objectives, the principal effort of Kadar's newly installed government went into the reconstruction of the party-state institutions that collapsed during the revolution. The restoration of the party-state, designed to reimpose a specific type of relationship between the state and society, was the core of the Kadar regime's demobilization strategy. In this effort, despite an impression to the contrary, the new Soviet-imposed government could count on the active and passive collaboration and support of many Hungarians. The heroic vision of the Hungarian Revolution and mass resistance against the Soviet intervention painted by refugees, journalists, and scholars obscures important political developments on the domestic level, which eventually guaranteed the success of demobilization and restoration policies. Lomax makes similar point by arguing that

> the failure of so many commentators even to be aware of the actual developments in the first year of Kadar's rule may have been due partly to the revulsion felt at the Soviet intervention and the almost unquestioning rejection of anyone associated with it, but partly also to the assumption that so few Hungarians were prepared to collaborate with the regime imposed on their country by Soviet tanks, that those who were must have been only the most unrepentant, dogmatic Stalinist. . . . This picture . . . is one that stands more than a little distant from the truth.[77]

First, thousands of party and state functionaries displaced during the revolution by revolutionary committees and workers councils returned to reclaim their lost positions of authority. This vast entity of state's functionaries and bureaucrats was the product of the postwar economic and political transformation and state-building strategies of newly imposed regimes. This group owed its social and economic advancement solely to the Communist party; their job security and career advancement were completely dependent upon the preservation of the institutional structure of the Stalinist party-state. Therefore, for party and state officials, the revolution meant the loss of political and social status, all related advantages and privileges, as well as their very livelihood. These groups of party and state employees were the social forces behind the successful restoration and reequilibration of the state-socialist regime in Hungary after the revolution. The resistance movement was never able to establish a foothold inside this group to make consolidation of the party-state more difficult. The new regime made it clear from the very beginning that it would protect and defend the party and state nominees.[78] Thus, the communist party became, de facto, a "trade union" of the party-state employees.

This group of people represented a significant segment of the population. In the middle of the 1950s, the state administration alone was three times larger than in the 1930s, with almost three hundred thousand employees. Similarly, the bureaucratic apparatus in the nationalized economy expanded on an even more massive scale. In the machine-making industry alone, it increased by 357 percent from 1938, employing nearly 250,000 people. Thus, the often-emphasized point that state-building strategies in East Central Europe were designed to give the party-state full control of the population and to expand the state's repressive capacity must be broadened. Through a politically shaped process of promotion, state-building strategies tied the large segment of the population to the survival of newly established political and economic institutions. The massive expansion of the state, through which masses of undereducated manual laborers, peasants, and hitherto excluded members of intelligentsia were promoted to the positions of authority was a major strategic tool in achieving political stability and undercutting any real or potential opposition to the regime. In this process, political repression and indoctrination played a secondary role. The rapid reconstruction of the party and state institutions following the destruction of the revolution, illustrates the recuperative power of once established and consolidated institutional structures even after their breakdown under the revolutionary tide.

The Restoration of the Communist Party

The new Hungarian Socialist Workers party, announced by Kadar on November 2, 1956, as a successor to the Hungarian Communist party, which fell apart and vanished in the course of the revolution, started to organize only after the Soviet intervention. The four-member group (Janos Kadar, Antal Apro, Istvan Kossa, and Ferenc Munnich), co-opted a new Provisional Central Committee, which already on November 6 issued an appeal concerning the reorganization of the party. It held its first meeting on November 11 and its first official session, including all twenty-three members of Central Committee, from December 2 to 5. In February the number of Central Committee members increased to thirty-seven. Berecz, in his hard-line official account of the revolution, argues with a curious Marxist insight that Kadar's group clearly recognized that

> it is the internal forces that play decisive role in the socio-political events in any country. Reconstruction of the political super-structure cannot be directed by foreign military personnel. . . . Chaos and ideological confusion in a society cannot be overcome by arms: it can only be surmounted in an ideological and political struggle, through debates, and through persevering educational and ideological work. [Thus] in addition to crushing the armed counter-revolutionary gangs, the regrouping of Communists and the reorganization of the party were the other major tasks.[79]

The difficulties in restoring the Communist party, its organizational structures, and membership were more formidable than the reconstruction of the state administration or the coercive forces of the state. In November and December, the party cadres were on defense, fighting for their survival. The party's membership increased very slowly. On December 1, 1956, the party had 37,818 members and 1,980 active branches, an average of less than twenty members in each branches. By the end of December, membership increased to 101,806; in April it reached 227,420; and by June 1957 the party had 345,000 members, as compared to its prerevolutionary membership of around 800,000. The party's membership rose to 416,646 in January 1959 and increased to around 500,000 by January 1962.[80] In spite of its numerical growth, the party had problems recruiting workers[81] and intellectuals into its ranks. Nonetheless, it quickly persuaded the employees of the state and industrial bureaucratic machineries to join in order to secure state dependent employment.[82] Also, as Molnar points out, when the Communist party was reorganized after the events of 1956, "the ratio of the 'old-timers' CP members since 1945 or before increased to 35 percent of the members,"[83] even though those party members, especially among the party's top echelons, discredited during the Stalinist period were prohibited from joining the new party. Thus, Kadar rebuilt the party apparatus from a large pool of functionaries who had never sided with Nagy and who had been less disgraced for their activities during Rakosi's regime. As a result of this turnover of cadres, 50 percent of basic party organizations had a change in their leadership, and 80 percent of secretaries of these organizations were replaced.[84]

The party held its First National Conference on June 27–29, 1957. During this conference, Kadar's assessment of the causes of the uprising as well as the principle of a "struggle on two fronts" (i.e., against hard-line Stalinists and reformers) were approved. The conference elected a fifty-three member Central Committee, an eleven-member Politburo, and a five-member Secretariat. All members of the Provisional Central Committee were elected as official representatives of the party, and Kadar was confirmed as the party's first secretary. In an effort to establish the organizational foundations of the new party, the conference adopted a new statute that was "by and large a replica of the 'old' Party's statute of 1954."[85] The conference also invalidated all the resolutions of the Hungarian Socialist Workers party adopted before November 4, 1956. This conference decided the organizational shape and the leadership of the party for years to come. The party congresses in December 1959 and November 1962 did not introduce any significant changes to the party rules and leading personnel. As Molnar argues, analyzing the postrevolution period: "The principal political fact must be noted: stability at the top. Until the Tenth Congress of 1970, the Politburo majority were men 'of the first hour,' members of the Executive Committee of November 1956, members of the Central Committee reelected by the Conference of 1957 and the Seventh Congress of 1959."[86] The most notable personal change during the first decade after the revolution involved Kadar's resignation in January 1958 from the position of prime minister, which went to Ferenc Munnich, apparently in the effort to enhance the principle of collective leadership. The only other notable changes in the party's and the government were announced in September 1961, which clearly strengthened Kadar's position by elevating his supporters to key posts.

This remarkable stability and the lack of significant personnel changes at the pinnacle of the party's hierarchy were reflected by the fact that there was no major purge in the ranks of the postrevolutionary communist party. As Kende argues, "Kadar's party has become the only East European CP which after 1956 and 1968 not only abstained from liquidating the reformist wing but integrated it."[87] This more pragmatic internal party policy did not indicate, however, the absence of serious disagreements among its leaders. According to Lomax, the view that the postrevolutionary party was "one of monolithic unity, with little internal disagreement, dissension or debate" is definitely inaccurate.[88] The internal stability of the party may be more accurately attributed to the fact that Kadar had the chance to rebuild the party from scratch, excluding both the most hard-line Stalinist and the most radical reformist wings within the former party. Moreover, because the major line of conflict divided the party-state and society, and the resistance movement did not have any significant basis within the party-state, the intraparty struggles were less confrontational and their outcomes less repressive than in Czechoslovakia after 1968. In comparison to the situation in Czechoslovakia after 1968, this task was much easier because both wings of the party found themselves outside the political process. The former Stalinist leadership sought refuge in the Soviet Union during the revolution, and its most influential members were barred from returning to Hungary for quite some time. The reformists who led the revolution were either interned to be executed later on or escaped to the West in order to avoid prosecution.

From its beginning the new party was based on a centrist platform that was consistently advocated as the principle of a "struggle on two fronts," that is, against the former Stalinist leadership and the leaders who emerged during the revolution.[89] The November 6 proclamation stated that in order "to restore our Party's strength and to enable it to lead the masses, we must definitely break with the harmful policies and criminal methods adopted by the Rakosi clique." But at the same time it advocated that "a definite break has to be made also with the Imre Nagy-Losonczy group which, surrendering the positions of the working class and people's power, and adopting a nationalist-chauvinistic stand, opened the way to the counter-revolutionary forces and in so doing actually betrayed the cause of socialism."[90]

The new Hungarian Communist party had one important advantage that was so sorely lacking in Poland after the imposition of martial law. As in the 1940s, the Communist party elites knew what they wanted, had a program and codified ideology, a model of internal organization, and a clear set of policies not only for themselves but for the whole political and economic system of the country. Kadar said in his address to the Tenth Plenary Session of the Central Council of Hungarian Trade Unions on January 26, 1957: "When on November 3, 1956 we were thinking of forming the present government . . . I was well aware what we would have to face but I was convinced that truth was on our side and that the people would understand our action, would approve and appreciate that we were coming out in opposition to the counter-revolutionary flood, and that we were saving the Hungarian dictatorship of the proletariat."[91] From the very beginning, the party leadership gave first priority to rebuilding all the institutions that were indispensable components to the organization of political and economic life under the "dictatorship of proletariat." They never had any doubts that it was the Communist party that should have an exclusive and absolute monopoly of power within the country. In short, the state-idea that animated the postwar transformation of East Central Europe was still a powerful vision behind the politics of mass demobilization that followed the revolution.

The Restoration of the State and Local Administration

Immediately after its relocation to Budapest on November 7, 1956, the new government set about to recover the full control of the organs of state administration. In the resolution passed on November 8, the government ordered that: "all officials of ministries and higher organs of administration . . . should report without delay in order to resume work. . . . All civil servants, including employees of local organs . . . must report for duty by November 10, 1956 [and] Revolutionary Committees should remove from their ranks without delay counterrevolutionary elements opposed to the People's Republic."[92] Executive power was placed in the hands of appointed local council chairmen, and the revolutionary committees operating in state offices were stripped of their authority. Moreover, all public officials were reconfirmed to the posts they had held on October 1, 1956, whether or not they had been removed by a workers' council or any other organ of self-government. Next, the government appointed county commissioners in order to consolidate state administration in the provinces. The appointment of commissioners began the reconstruction of the local councils. The county commissioners were to guarantee that council leaders carried out government instructions despite pressures from revolutionary councils.[93] In a similar move, the ordinance of the Council of Ministers no. 4/1956 enacted on November 24, 1956, established the position of the government's commissars in all factories with more than two thousand workers and in all other enterprises important to the national economy, regardless of the number of employees. Commissars were granted wide prerogatives, including the nomination of managers and mediation between management and the workers' councils. Their major function was to maintain order and to supervise industrial production.

But a sweeping purge aimed at regaining full control over the state administration was delayed until the general strike ended and the struggle against workers' councils came to a close in December. On the twenty-ninth, the government ordered (Decree No. 15/1956) the so-called rationalization of the inflated state apparatus, which simply meant a purge of all undesirable people from the positions within the administration. As a part of this operation, the number of government ministers was reduced from twenty-two to seventeen, and some administrative national bodies that had come directly under the Council of Ministers were dissolved. In the purge of the state administration, 28.9 percent of all civil servants (a total of 21,876 employees) were dismissed. They included three ministers and ten deputy ministers. Almost six thousand had worked on the local level.[94] At the same time the party and state cadres sacked during the revolution regained their old status. As Kis states, "essentially by June 1957, the pre-October situation had been restored for that part of the Rakosi-era officials who had made no serious concessions to public opinion either during the revolution or in the first stages of the restoration; the waverers who survived the purges increasingly gravitated towards them."[95]

On May 31, 1957, the government reinstated the personnel departments in all factories and enterprises and the state administration, bringing back the hated cadre control system abolished during the revolution. The reestablishment of personnel departments was followed by general screening of all workers and employees. On December 28, 1957, the government reaffirmed the system of nomenclature by issuing a decree (No. 66/1957) that laid down the confidential political preconditions for appointments, promotions, and the transfer of people to important positions within the entire institutional structure of the party-state.

After the reorganization of the state administration, the government revived the state's representative organs, which before the revolution consisted of the National Assembly (298 representatives and 155 alternate representatives) and 3,253 local councils. In January selected committees of the National Assembly started to work, but the first meeting of the full Assembly was reconvened by the government only on May 9, 1957. During the three-day meeting, the number of cabinet posts was increased from twelve to twenty-one. It was also announced that twenty-eight members of the Assembly had resigned or been dismissed because of their actions during the revolution. Among them were the Stalinist leaders of Hungary including Rakosi, Hegedus, and Gero. It is puzzling, indeed, how small was the number of Assembly members who joined the revolution and were dismissed and punished for this reason. The Assembly also postponed the general elections and extended for an additional two years its own mandate, which would have formally expired on May 17, 1957.

While political and social organizations were purged one by one, reorganized, and then established under the party's full control, the People's Patriotic Front remained dormant for the first several months after the invasion. Its revival was implied in the resolution of the National Party Conference in June 1957: "The one-party system which is characteristic of our country does not exclude, but rather in the given circumstances increasingly demands that under the guidance of the Party we should unite in the Patriotic People's Front all those persons who do not belong to the party or who earlier were active in other parties and are loyal to people's power, all progressive forces in the nation who are ready to participate in the socialist construction of the country through their public, scientific, cultural and professional activities."[96] The National Council of the People's Patriotic Front met for the first time in October 1957. The council decided that the front would be open to people "who adhere to Communist ideology and even to individuals who may entertain religious beliefs." On January 27, 1958, Kadar's close associate, Gyula Kallai, became president of the People's Patriotic Front and in the speech before the National Assembly stated that the front was now led by the Hungarian Socialist Workers Party. The fully controlled front was given the task of preparing for the first elections since the Soviet invasion.

The general and local elections were held on November 16, 1958. At that time, full political control was already effectively restored and all organizations were sufficiently subservient to the Communist party. The single list of candidates was officially presented by the People's Patriotic Front, and a complete election turnout was insured. According to Vali: "Before the elections the regime did everything in its power to defend the 'democratic character' of the single ticket, and to play down the conspicuous Communist character of the ballot. The People's Patriotic Front, the official sponsoring agency, was referred to as representing the nation as a whole, 'embracing all Hungarian citizens who wish to work for the future of their country for the building of socialism.'"[97]

In these carefully engineered and grossly falsified elections, communists surpassed the "achievements" of the Stalinist era. According to official statistics, 98.4 percent of those eligible cast their votes, and among those 99.6 percent voted for the single list of the People's Patriotic Front. In the local council elections, out of 89,192 candidates, only ninety-one were defeated. The new National Assembly had 338 representatives, among which 139 were paid functionaries of the party, including fifty-three members of the party's Central Committee. After the elections, however, according to Vali: "the Party, not wishing to see its creature get out of hand, reduced the tempo of the front activities. All in all the People's Patriotic Front remained what it had been in the pre-revolutionary era: a tool of the Party and government for attracting non-Communists and inducing them to follow a course of limited cooperation with the regime."[98]

To secure the position of the party-state and create an efficient machinery to punish the political opposition, the judiciary system had to be once again brought under the state's strict control. Similar to all state institutions, courts, in Vali's words, "had become genuinely independent during the Revolution, and as long as the newly reorganized Communist Party was unable to extend its grip over the Courts again many judges shrank back from implementation of the repressive measures against the counter-revolutionaries, whom they, no doubt, regarded as national heroes rather than criminals."[99] At the beginning of 1957, many government officials bitterly complained that the courts were not properly fulfilling their punitive tasks, that too many persons were acquitted and sentences were too lenient. The acting minister of justice, Ferenc Nezval, speaking at the National Conference of Law Presidents in February 1957, said: "Our jurisdiction must be tough, quick and merciless. . . . the most important task of the courts is to defend and strengthen the people's democratic order, to pass sentences in the spirit of the class struggle—both in summary and accelerated proceedings as well as in ordinary criminal jurisdiction—against subversive counterrevolutionary elements."[100]

While the screening of judges and the creation of substitute court institutions for trying crimes falling under the summary jurisdiction was quickly accomplished, it took almost two years to bring the lawyers under the party-state's full control. Laszlo Bajor, the deputy president of the Budapest Military Tribunal, said, "after the liberation (of 1945) the political and moral screening of lawyers was not achieved in full. . . . A spirit of counter-revolution was gaining ground amongst lawyers and after the counter-revolution lawyers were often admitted to the Chamber without due consideration being given to matters of principle. All this had made it necessary that the ranks of the lawyers should be reordered."[101]

The purge of lawyers had already begun on December 29, 1956, when the minister of justice suspended the autonomy of the Budapest Chamber of Lawyers. New elections to the chamber had been ordered and a number of attorneys, including the president of the Budapest Bar, had been arrested or convicted. On January 22, 1957, the Chamber of Lawyers in Miskolc shared the fate of the Budapest Chamber. Yet it was not until the issuing of Decree

No. 12 on March 30, 1958, that the work of private lawyers in Hungary was virtually stopped. The decree replaced the National Committee of Chambers of Lawyers with a new government-controlled body and appointed the committee to screen all applicants to lawyer collectives. At the same time, the decree stipulated that only those lawyers admitted into the lawyer collectives were permitted to practice at the bar. After the screening procedure in Budapest, only 830 lawyers, grouped in fifty-four collectives, had been licensed to practice out of sixteen hundred who applied for membership.[102] With this decree, Urban writes, "the government made sure that prosecution, judgment and defense were ultimately in the hands of the same authority. Socialist legality was repeatedly upheld as a class concept—judges, prosecutors and councils were expected, and were gradually made, to act as so many voices, ultimately pleading the same case."[103]

The Restoration of Auxiliary Institutions of the Party-State

As mentioned before, effective control of the political space was assured under state-socialist regimes by the formation of a network of auxiliary institutions, which blocked and penetrated the whole public sphere. It was precisely these auxiliary institutions, which Selznick called "the organizational weapon" of communism, that guaranteed political stability and extended party-state control over the entire population. The revolution, however, largely destroyed this carefully built system of organizations, and Kadar's government faced the task of regaining control over some organizations (for example, the trade unions), destroying those that were firmly on the side of the revolution (such as associations of writers and journalists), and creating new organizations to replace those that disintegrated during the revolution (such as the Association of Working Youth). The battle for control of the trade unions was the first action of the new regime in restoring the auxiliary institutions of the party-state.

From the very beginning, the Soviet-imposed government attempted to play the trade unions off against the workers' councils.[104] The trade-union leadership sided with Kadar's regime and on November 6 issued a statement calling for a return to work and stating that "the population received with satisfaction the assistance of the Soviet Army which knocked the weapons out of the hands of the reactionary and counterrevolutionary elements posing as revolutionaries."[105] During this time, many former Stalinist union leaders reappeared. On November 12, the National Council of Trade Unions proposed that workers' councils elections be regulated, suggesting that the elections should be arranged by the trade unions in the factories and that representatives of the trade unions should be included in the councils. The government's decree of November 21, which regulated the activities of the workers' councils, incorporated all suggestions made by the trade unions leaders. But in spite of government support, the unions faced a growing challenge from the worker-council movement, which increased in power during the first weeks after the invasion. Relations between two organizations were hostile from the beginning. Although each acknowledged the other's specific role, at the same time each tried to bring the other under its control. In this struggle, the trade unions were backed by the government and the workers' councils by the workers. The trade unions demanded that workers social interests be protected and Kadar's regime quickly responded to these economic demands in order to enhance the position of the trade unions in the eyes of workers. As long as no political demands were attached to social ones, the later were generously promised and fulfilled. For example, in November, the government raised wages and pensions by 8 to 15 percent, effective January 1, 1957; introduced unemployment relief; abolished the norm system; and extended social benefits. Despite these concessions to the unions, popularity of the workers' councils was rising.

By the end of November, due to increased pressure from the workers' councils and the workers themselves, the trade-union organizations were pushed to the brink of collapse.[106] To save their organization, trade unions began to distance themselves from the government and sought to cooperate with the councils. This change of trade-union policy modified also the attitude of workers' councils toward the trade unions, and both organizations held joint meetings and recognized each other's right to exist.[107] But after the government began arresting members of the councils in December, the National Council of Trade Unions again changed its political stance and firmly sided with the government. On December 11, the Council of Trade Unions issued the statement condemning the general strike called for by the workers' councils and praised "the definite measures taken by the government against the counter-revolutionary forces and individuals."

With pressure from the workers' councils for the democratization of trade unions gone, the Presidium of National Council held a meeting on January 5, 1957, where planned elections to trade unions' branches were annulled and the decision was made to hold the elections "after normal life has been started." Moreover, the Presidium re-examined the results of previously held local elections and suspended most of the newly elected trade union officials. At this meeting the Council also rejected the demand for independent trade unions and recognized the "leading political role" of the Communist party as a condition for the stabilization of "people's power and further social progress." With this meeting, the government's effort to turn trade unions again into obedient instruments of the party-state was successfully accomplished. This relationship was sanctioned by the Nineteenth Trade Union Congress in March 1958, at which the principle and practice of the trade-union movement under the guidance of the party was formally reasserted. Elections to the basic trade-union organizations were held in April and May of 1959; more than one hundred thousand trade union officials were elected by two million members.[108] By 1959 the prerevolutionary character of the trade-union movement was fully restored. The unions resumed their old function of stimulating the increase of productivity by forcing workers to go beyond the imposed work-norm. To this purpose the unions began the socialist work-brigade movement in 1958.

Hungarian youth were the most active segment of the population during the revolution, and young people were among the principle victims of the Soviet intervention and political repression that followed. Students and young workers formed the majority of freedom fighters, and 85 percent of those killed during the revolution were sixteen to thirty-five years old. Approximately 70 percent of the revolution's two hundred thousand refugees were below thirty years of age.[109] However, after the Soviet invasion, the youth organizations did not have the same organizational strength and resources that allowed the workers' council movement to wage an effective struggle against the Soviet-imposed regime. Nonetheless, young people were strongly opposed to the new regime, and it took some time for the party to reestablish control in schools and universities. In fact, while primary schools began to reopen already by the end of November, the universities and colleges did not begin to reopen until January 14, 1957, and the Budapest universities did not reopen until February 1. Yet even after the schools reopened, Urban writes, "three months after the revolution there were demonstrations in practically every school. They ranged from wearing mourning ribbons with the Hungarian tricolor to burning Russian books in public. In places even processions were organized."[110] Such acts of defiance provoked harsh responses from the government, including the expulsion of teachers, police supervision of the schools, and the detention of children.

Among all the youth movements and organizations that emerged by the end of October, only the Association of Hungarian University and College Students (MEFESZ) continued to operate. It remained the center of the resistance against the new government. In its attempt to rebuild the institutional structure of the party-state, the government set up various new youth organizations from November to January so as to gain an institutional foothold among the youth. These organizations included the Young Hungarian Revolutionary Workers Association (MAFISZ), the National Association of Unified Peasant Youth (EPOSZ), and the National Association of Hungarian Students (MDNSZ). These new organizations were not able to attract any significant membership but, as Sandor Balogh and Sandor Jakab claim, "these youth organizations undoubtedly helped the Party and government in restoring order."[111] The initial failure to organize pro-government youth organizations resulted in more radical actions against the resistance of youth groups. On January 12, 1957, the MEFESZ leaders were arrested, and the last surviving center of student resistance was broken. Other organizations were forced to adopt a progovernment position. In mid-February, the Hungarian Pioneer movement for children was reestablished.

On March 17, 1957, the Provisional Party Central Committee passed the resolution calling for the establishment of a unified youth organization under the name KISZ (Communist Youth Association). The resolution assessed the present state of the youth movement as unsatisfactory and stated that "it is necessary to bring socialist unity of Hungarian youth, in order to further the Communist education of youth and to guarantee a new generation of cadres for the Party."[112] To fulfill these objectives, the resolution emphasized that "KISZ is the Party's youth organization. Party resolutions are obligatory for KISZ organizations. The chief KISZ tasks are: to serve in the building of socialist society, to propagate Party objectives among the youth, and to educate youth in the communist spirit." As a symbolic statement, the opening ceremony of the association took place on March 21, 1957, the thirty-eighth anniversary of the declaration of the Hungarian Soviet Republic in 1919.

The newly created KISZ took over the property of the prerevolutionary DISZ, including its hostels, offices, sports facilities, and equipment. Among the nine members of the KISZ national founding committee, there were seven former DISZ leaders.[113] KISZ's relationship to the state was clearly emphasized from the very beginning. As the head of the preparatory commission of KISZ, Zoltan Komocsin emphasized: "We are not independent of the party. Each member of the League accepts the resolutions of the party voluntarily as binding. The Communist Youth League rallies youth ready for any sacrifice for the cause of the party."[114]

Since there now existed a new unified association, other organizations were forced to merge with it, and by the end of 1957 they either joined the KISZ or withered away. However, by the end of June 1957, the association could only claim 120,000 members and four thousand basic organizations within schools, universities, and factories, as compared to the eight hundred thousand members in DISZ before the revolution. Moreover, according to Urban, "KISZ's record in 1957 is one of a series of dismal failures: its political initiatives died of indifference, its drive for organizing youth brigades . . . were sabotaged . . . lecture courses were laid on . . . but lecture halls were empty. At the secondary schools, where school discipline made recruiting a technically simple operation, KISZ recruits were ostracized."[115] But the constant effort and generous party support combined with repressive actions in schools and universities, helped KISZ to establish thirteen thousand basic organizations and to increase its membership to 470,000 by the end of September 1960. This number, in fact, was not a dazzling achievement when one realizes that approximately 1.7 million people in Hungary were eligible for membership. Nevertheless, four years after the revolution, KISZ became a smaller but exact replica of the Stalinist Association of Working Youth.

Together with the restoration of the unified youth organization, the whole education system was slowly forced to return to prerevolutionary conditions. Universities and schools were purged; in the universities alone, two thousand teachers lost their jobs.[116] All teachers were subjected to special party instruction and courses on Marxism-Leninism. Instruction in Marxism-Leninism was again made compulsory in all high schools and universities and the mandatory instruction in the Russian language was restored. Soon the religious education in the schools, introduced after the invasion as a conciliatory gesture, was abolished. In 1958 an educational reform in Hungary, closely resembling reforms in the Soviet Union, was inaugurated. This "reform" placed strong emphasize on a polytechnic education and real experience on the production line at the expense of a liberal education. Thus, in a short time all educational demands, changes, and gains achieved during the revolution were officially wiped out.

With the restoration and consolidation of the party, the state administration, representative organs, coercive forces of the state, and finally the whole plethora of party-state's auxiliary institutions, the process of rebuilding the regime shattered by the revolution was completed. This process was accomplished more or less within the two years following the Soviet invasion. In his speech to the Seventh Party Congress on November 30, 1959, Kadar claimed that "We can say that the counter-revolution now belongs to the past."[117] But this assertion did not indicate any significant changes in regime's policies. At the same congress the minister of the interior stated, "Though the internal enemy has been rendered harmless it does not follow that we can now set out to weaken still less to liquidate, the security functions of the state. . . . Let our enemies not think that we will be liberal toward them. . . . We will further strengthen those organizations to which the defeat of our enemies is entrusted."[118]

Hungarian society, decimated by severe repression and the escape of almost two hundred thousand people and the destruction of all independent institutional bases not only for political but for any independent social activities, was at that time fully demobilized. The political space was again colonized by state-controlled institutions, and the party-state was firmly in control of all aspects of social and political life. The regime was also able to induce the cooperation, even if unwilling, from large segments of the population. While the restoration of the party-state was fundamentally accomplished by mid-1957, its full consolidation took two more years. The last organizations revived in the process of consolidation were the journalist and artist associations, re-established in June 1958, and the Writers Association, which was allowed to reorganize in September 1959. But the full reequilibration of the state-socialist regime culminated with the "socialist reconstruction of agriculture." This was began in December 1958 and was accomplished by 1961, institutionally converting Hungary into a model Stalinist state.

The Collectivization of Agriculture

Individual peasants were the first to receive substantial concessions from the new regime. The government issued its first directives regarding agricultural policies on November 12, 1956, in which it declared the system of compulsory deliveries abolished and collectivization stopped. The government condemned the forced formation of collective farms and pledged to support any farming organization which would increase agricultural production. At that

time most of the "socialist sector," built during the two previous collectivization drives had collapsed. The majority of peasants had already left the
collectives either at the beginning of Nagy's "new course" in 1953 or during
the revolution. At the end of October and during November 1956, 28 percent of the remaining collective farms were dissolved or collapsed, leaving
only around seven hundred state and collective farms in the country controlling 8.5 percent of arable land.[119]

Yet while private farming was allowed by the new regime, during the
party conference in June 1957, the principle of agricultural collectivization
was strongly reaffirmed. In July 1957, the Central Committee published a
list of propositions concerning agrarian policy. It stated, "The gradual
transformation of our agriculture into one of modern, large-scale socialist
farming is to be one of the most important tasks."[120] Although the real collectivization drive started at the end of 1958, the economic pressures used to
force peasants into collectives were already employed during 1957, when
the taxes of private farmers were raised by 11 percent. In 1958 the tax rose
34 percent above the 1955 level, a clear effort to make independent production unprofitable and to force peasants to join collective farms. This milder
strategy can be largely attributed to the difficult situation facing Kadar's
regime. William Robinson argues:

> Between December 1956 and December 1958 Kadar respected the realities of
> power politics on the Hungarian scene. Realizing that the country could not afford
> the economic dislocation and sabotage that forced collectivization would bring in
> its wake, and needing the quiescence if not the support of the peasantry if the
> regime were to eliminate popular resistance and regain its strength, he opposed the
> creation of a cooperative system during this period and sought to win over the
> rural population by a policy of economic aid and political concession. Even after
> the decision to renew the collectivization drive had been made, however, he recog-
> nized that the peasants would not enter the cooperatives of their own volition, and
> the heavy political persuasion and economic incentives were thus necessary to
> prevent physical opposition and maintain production.[121]

The first phase of collectivization began at the end of 1958 and was temporarily halted by the government in March 1959. By that time approximately
40 percent of the country's arable land was cultivated by cooperatives and
state farms.[122] After the second phase of collectivization in the winter of
1959–1960, 76.1 percent of arable land was owned by state farms and cooperatives. The third phase started in the fall of 1960, and by February 1961
the Central Committee reported that, "the massive numerical developments
had ended, and socialist production relations had become dominant in agriculture too."[123] By that time 93 percent of Hungary's agricultural land was
controlled by cooperatives and state farms. Although, according to Urban,
"activists were supposed to convert the peasants by word of mouth only and
farmers were, in theory, expected to join the producers' cooperatives out of

their free will, the first two phases of the campaign (an especially the first) were marked by intimidation and brutality."[124]

The collectivization of Hungarian agriculture poses two puzzles. The first is the question of where the impetus for collectivization came from? The second is the question of whether collectivization was the logical culmination of political repression as is often assumed? It was widely held that the initiative for reintroducing this unpopular policy came from Moscow. Given, however, the statements on agricultural policy issued by the HSWP after the revolution, it is clear that collectivization was its primary agricultural objective. The differences within the Hungarian leadership were over the means of achieving the principle of "socialist production in agriculture." The end itself was never questioned. From this point of view, the argument that collectivization was the final stage of postrevolutionary repressions is not convincing. During this time it was an undisputable dogma among communist leaders that extension of the socialist sector into agricultural production was a required step in building the foundations of the socialist system. Thus the impetus for collectivization can easily be traced to domestic sources. It was the result of the ruling elites' vision of how a socialist society should be organized rather than a conscious repressive strategy.[125]

Regardless of the motivation behind it, collectivization retarded the overall growth of agricultural output and resulted in a decline of the national grain harvest and per-hectare yields after 1959. It also caused a significant drop in the agricultural labor force. The government attempted to solve these difficulties by encouraging members of the collectives to farm private plots allocated to every member of the state farms and cooperatives. According to Urban, already in 1960, "private plots, although not exceeding in acreage more than five per cent of arable land, covered (together with the farms still privately held) 40 per cent of the population's beef consumption, 60 per cent of milk and pork consumption and 98 per cent of all eggs and poultry consumed."[126] Also, for the first-time investments in agriculture were significantly increased, creating a situation in which the workers were forced to make sacrifices for the benefit of the peasants. Such ideologically unorthodox methods of dealing with economic difficulties became a characteristic mark of Kadar's regime in years to come. What may be identified as the essence of Kadarism was the effort to find ways of increasing production and the supply of goods to the market without altering the fundamental principles of state socialism. The creative attempts to reform the economy without reforming the political institutions was Kadar's way of seeking a philosophical stone that would make state socialism work.

Collectivization of agriculture concluded the process of recovery and institutional reconstruction of the communist regime in Hungary. The heroic revolutionary struggles and the chaos of the regime's institutional breakdown became a suppressed collective memory. Political and ideological struggles among the party-state elites were over. Even potential opposition

was eradicated, and the structure of political opportunities drastically con-
tracted making a renewed challenge to party-state authority highly unlikely.
By 1963 the Hungarian regime was fully reequilibrated. Kadar granted a
general amnesty in March 1963 for those who were prosecuted for the participation in the revolution and for postrevolutionary opposition. Political
activities returned to routine practices of a centralized and ideologically motivated party-state. But the legacy of the failed revolution shaped the development of Hungarian state-socialism in a powerful way. The events of 1956
served as a remainder to the absolute rulers that their power has its limits
and that in order to stay in power they have to remember that the forbearance of society should not be tested too often.

CHAPTER 4

The Political Crisis, Demobilization, and Regime Reequilibration in Hungary

THE HUNGARIAN revolution was the most tragic and dramatic culmination of the political decompression in East Central Europe following Stalin's death and the de-Stalinization campaign launched by Khrushchev at the Twentieth Party Congress. The political crisis bore characteristic marks of this period, which Hungary shared with other East European regimes undergoing the transition from Stalinist rule. Legacies of Stalinist rule, with its political terror, ideological belligerence, desecration of national traditions, the Soviet-style industrialization drive, and disastrous economic policies, created preconditions for a political cataclysm. The impetus for change came from within the regime and caused profound intra-elite splits and struggles. Only then did the political opportunity structure open to allow other groups and actors to organize, articulate demands, and press for policy changes and reforms. During this period, revisionism or reform communism dominated the discourse and imagination of collective actors challenging the Stalinist ruling elites. Critics of Stalinist policies framed their demands in terms of "true" and "just" state socialism and condemned Stalinist elites for distorting a real potential of economic and political transformations instituted in these countries. Thus, in Leszek Kolakowski's words, "1956 was the year of ideological delusion."[1] The crisis, however, also reflected specific features of the Hungarian situation and developments before 1956, such as the brutality of the regime, the depth of the economic crisis, and an unwavering and prolonged attempt of the Stalinist elite to stay in power. The result was a popular revolt and rapid institutional breakdown of the regime. The period of successful demobilization policies following the revolution and the restoration of the party-state in Hungary was decisively conditioned by the radical character of the political crisis and the equally radical Soviet military response to this crisis aimed at preserving communist rule in the country at all cost. The revolution itself and the bloody Soviet intervention established a set of conditions that, paradoxically, made the restoration of state socialism in Hungary easier than the intensity and consequences of the conflict would indicate. The relatively rapid decline of popular resistance in the face of postrevolutionary repression and the unexpected long-term effects of demobilization policies that turned Hungary into the quite tolerant and reform-minded country of the Soviet bloc are puzzles that have confronted the students of contemporary East European politics since 1956.

The analysis presented in the previous two chapters suggests that we can identify several parallel sets of circumstances and processes both on the side of society and the state that made demobilization policies pursued by the Kadar regime more effective. Never before or after did a party-state in Soviet-dominated Eastern Europe collapse so thoroughly. Never did a society mobilize so radically and rapidly, and never were emerging social movements and revolutionary institutions so brutally suppressed. I shall argue that these conditions account not only for the extent of postrevolutionary political repression but also for subsequent political relaxation and quasi-liberal economic policies of the Hungarian regime. These factors were the product of the revolution and were specific to Hungary. The contrasting nature of political crises may explain the different scenarios and outcomes of the other two cases of large-scale political demobilization in Czechoslovakia after 1968 and Poland after 1981. Postrevolutionary Hungary was a model of successful demobilization strategies and reequilibration of the regime, especially for the Polish regime after the imposition of martial law. However, the conditions in Hungary and challenges faced by its post-1956 regime were never to be repeated and, therefore, the policies Hungary's communist elite chose to restore the party-state were not possible to imitate or repeat, despite an officially declared desire to do so.

I already suggested that political repressions alone cannot account for the nature and outcomes of the demobilization process following the revolution. This process was shaped by the available resources, specific goals, and capacities of popular resistance, the party-state elites, and the leaders of the Soviet Union. Moreover, I have emphasized that domestic developments and struggles played a more important role in this process and that elite choices were less shaped by the pressures coming from the Soviet Union than it is often assumed.[2] In this concluding chapter, I will briefly summarize these three sets of factors and show how the combination of developments in these three dimensions shaped the postrevolutionary regime in Hungary and set it on a unique historical trajectory. As I argue throughout this work, the way in which a serious political crisis was resolved produced significant differences among these three East European countries and generated path-dependent developments that shaped their history for decades. From 1956 on, Hungarian society and politics displayed unique characteristics in comparison to other state socialist regimes, and their distinctive features are present even today in peculiarities of the process of democratic transition after 1989.

THE CAPACITY OF RESISTANCE AND OPPOSITION MOVEMENTS

The demobilization process in Hungary and its outcomes are the products of the crushed revolution.[3] After the Soviet invasion, the political achievements of the revolution and newly emerged institutions and organizations were destroyed and the wide-open political opportunity structure rapidly closed. The new, Soviet-installed government consequently reestablished and consolidated institutional structures of the party-state. In this pursuit new rulers of Hungary were not hampered by any significant divisions or internal conflicts. Their policies, after a short period of confusion, were consistent and decisive. The success of demobilization policies was initially assured by highly repressive methods and political terror designed to erase all institutional traces of the revolution and to make everybody in society painfully aware that none of the achievements of the revolution would be spared or preserved. This strategy entailed not only a concerted effort to crush revolutionary institutions and forces but also an effort to erect a legal and institutional framework securing the regime from any challenge from below. These actions were supplemented by an intense propaganda campaign designed to destroy the ideological underpinnings of the revolution by imposing the official interpretation of revolutionary events as reactionary assault on socialism's achievements. Political terror and brutality of the demobilization policies left their distinctive marks on subsequent developments in Hungary. Their impact was still emphasized by Istvan Lovas and Ken Anderson thirty years after the revolution: "In spite of a lack of overt repression and the continuation of some economic reform, the basis of the state in Hungary was and is terrorism. This is so because terrorism is not merely the unbridled exercise of violence with certain special features—it is also the *memory* and the *threat*, even the implied threat, that under certain circumstances it could return."[4]

Despite mass popular mobilization from below, the revolutionary character of the political crisis hampered the survival of any effective resistance and opposition in the long run. After years of systematic assault on all groups and institutions of society, which Elemer Hankiss described as "carpet bombing" of civil society,[5] Hungary experienced the rapid political mobilization that resulted in the emergence of fragmented political forces lacking well-defined social bases, established organizational structures, and developed collective identities and collective action frames. I have argued that such rapidly mobilizing movements and organizations are more vulnerable and are more easy to destroy and demobilize through concerted repressive counteraction of an authoritarian regime than are slowly built networks of political opposition and resistance. In Hungary the active phase of mass mobilization lasted only thirteen days and proceeded in conditions of rapid political and organizational decompression and deinstitutionalization as well as in the situation of armed insurgency. The organizational weakness of the revolutionary movement reinforced by the mass emigration of its most active participants after the Soviet invasion may be seen as primarily responsible for the vulnerability of the mass resistance after the revolution. The new organizations, movements, and parties of Hungarian political society, reborn with the speed of light, did not have time to establish firm networks of relations, produce effective leadership, mobilize resources, develop collective action frames, or build any solid organizational bases. Therefore, facing military invasion and political repression, they collapsed with almost the same speed, and organized resistance against the Kadar regime was ineffective and short lived. The case of the workers' council movement, which survived the longest as an organizational base of the resistance, supports this argument. Workers' councils were the only revolutionary organizations built on the solid social foundations and were able to secure the support of well-defined social constituencies bound together by the established networks of close intra-personal relations. It is for these reasons, not for any abstract strength of the working class in general, that they were most difficult to penetrate and destroy.

The survival of organized and effective resistance was inhibited by two additional factors. Research on collective protest shows that the presence or absence of influential allies can greatly influence the survival or success of the protest movement.[6] According to Sidney Tarrow, "the existence of influential allies takes on particular importance in stimulating protest in non-democratic systems."[7] The Hungarian resistance movement was in a disadvantageous position in this respect in comparison to other similar countries and cases. Stalinist rule destroyed all independent social and political organizations, and they barely reestablished themselves during the revolution. Moreover, these potential domestic allies were crushed and made powerless by the Soviet invasion. As a result the emerging resistance movement could not count, for example, on churches to provide autonomous institutional space and support the way Polish Catholic church did in the 1970s and 1980s. The resistance movement also did not have any potential allies within the institutional structures of the party-state as revisionist opposition and reform communists were first to be purged and decimated after the invasion. Finally, the international linkages and channels of support were absent in the heights of the Cold War. The Hungarian resistance movement did not have any support from West European communist parties and left-wing movements the Czech reformers in 1968 had. But more importantly, the international network of human rights organizations did not exist and democratic governments did not have any effective economic or political leverage to support the internal opposition to the communist regime. The case of the Solidarity movement presents here a striking contrast.

The second additional factor contributing to the failure of Hungarian resistance was the inability to develop alternative political discourse and identities that form cognitive frameworks that justify and guide collective action. While the revolution produced an eruption of various political programs and produced a revival of traditional political discourses, fundamental Marxist-Leninist ideas were hardly challenged. Miklos Molnar observes: "The revolution showed that the communist system was clearly rejected on the political level; this does not necessarily imply the rejection of the new economic and social structure. This event well demonstrated the hostility of the population, if not toward socialism and some of its economic and social accomplishments but in any case toward the communist political system."[8] Moreover, revisionist ideas of reforming and improving the existing state socialism provided the backbone of the "collective action frame,"[9] which shaped the discourse of the revolution and action of revolutionaries. During the de-Stalinization crisis, revisionism was clearly the most important master frame in East Central Europe, in some cases blending with nationalistic values and symbols. Other political discourses, including pure forms of nationalism, failed to be articulated and did not capture the attention of important collective actors. Although the revisionist program rejected Stalinist political practices and economic policies, it did not provide an alternative institutional vision to the Soviet-type state socialism. The revisionist strategy was centered on lobbying state and party authorities for change to be implemented from above not on organizing and mobilizing groups and movements within the society to press for reforms from below. Thus it was easily subverted by the post-Stalinist elites that rejected and criticized the Stalinist past as nothing more than sectarian distortions and errors and easily promised some economic and political reforms. As a result revisionists were either co-opted to new ruling elites and quickly abandoned their dreams to reform state socialism or were pushed aside into political void. The ambiguity surrounding the notion of socialism and the unchallenged domination of the single political discourse constructed on the basis of distorted and blurred terms, concepts, and semantic hybrids[10] greatly facilitated the demobilization process in Hungary.

The brutal suppression of the revolution, the collapse of organized resistance, and the elimination of any autonomous institutional spaces left Hungarian society totally powerless. This situation, however, produced specific patterns of social adaptation and defiance. According to Mihaly Vajda, "brevity and tragic outcome of the events of 1956, followed by the relatively rapid consolidation of the new regime, served to create an atmosphere in which nobody wanted or was able to call into question the basic structures of the regime."[11] While clearly alienated from the Soviet-imposed regime, deprived of any channels of political articulation and resources for collective protest and resistance, Hungarian society was able to maintain a type of silent pressure and stood as a reminder of what may happen if the Stalinist methods and practices were to be repeated. Kadar and his colleagues responded to this pressure by an effort to improve living standards and consumption level as well as to make their policies relatively more liberal in comparison to other state-socialist regimes. This is the source of the Kadar regime's obsessive focus on improving economic performance, even if necessary measures ran contrary to the Marxist-Leninist orthodoxy. Hungarian society responded to this repressive paternalism with different strategies. Hankiss argues that withdrawal into indifference and apathy was only one way of coping with the post-1956 regime. Others included massive involvement in the second economy, "socialization from below of mass organizations and state agencies," preservation of intellectual traditions and

independent lifestyles.[12] Many years later Ivan Szelenyi described this interaction between the state and society as "the silent revolution from below,"
in which atomized social groups forced concession from their bureaucratic rulers[13] and prompted others to argue about "the advantage of being
atomized."[14]

The reversal of repression and concessions granted to the Hungarian population can be in part explained by the nature of major fault lines and fis-
sures opened by the political conflict. The Hungarian case provides us with
the example of a crisis in which the main line of conflict completely sepa-
rated the externally imposed political regime from society. As my analysis
shows, the intensity of state-society conflict is a crucial factor in accounting
for the intensity of political repression and in explaining the shift in state
policies towards a more tolerant and accommodating direction. The post-
crisis periods in Hungary and Poland show that it was the absence of serious
intra-elite challenges and struggles that produced both the short-term political repression and long-term concessions. In this context the post-crisis period in Czechoslovakia shows the opposite regularity.

The weakness of society coupled with the severe collapse of the party-
state institutions brought about by the revolution opened wide the political
space for the postrevolutionary regime. Institutional breakdown of the state
provided the new ruling elite with ample room for a variety of strategies and
political choices. Shielded from a direct political challenge from below and
from devastating intra-elite conflicts, Kadar's regime had more freedom in
selecting and screening the cadres for the new regime and in changing its
strategies and policies. Thus, without drastic purges of the top party leadership, new rulers removed any foothold the resistance movement might have
had within the newly restored party-state as well as left most orthodox Stalinist forces outside power structures. This made the restoration and consolidation of the state easier to accomplish. In fact, for Kadar's regime, the real
core of the demobilization strategy was the successful restoration of the
exact institutional architecture of the party-state and its distinctive relationship with society while claiming a sharp break with the Stalinist past in
terms of policies and personnel. In the institutional dimension, the Kadar
regime even "perfected" the organization of its party-state, bringing it into
closer conformity to the orthodox Stalinist model, with the successful collectivization of agriculture. Thus, by the beginning of the 1960s, postrevolutionary Hungary became a more fully "developed socialist society" than its
Stalinist predecessor. In this context Ferenc Feher and Agnes Heller are absolutely right when they point out that "for the first time in Hungarian history, a revolution was so radical that none of its main objectives [were]
discarded by the subsequent . . . developments."[15] However, it should also
be emphasized that the radical mass challenge from below, despite its defeat,
left profound legacies, which shaped policies of the Hungarian regime. Paradoxically, the tragedy of total defeat paid off by producing a state socialist
regime with a more "human face" than most of other Soviet bloc regimes.

THE CAPACITY AND STRATEGIES OF THE PARTY-STATE

As this analysis suggests, the process of demobilization and reequilibration of the state socialist regime in Hungary did not follow a preconceived plan designed by the Soviets or the new Hungarian rulers. This was an open-ended process, which could easily have taken different directions and produced significantly different outcomes. Janos Kis emphasizes this point by arguing that "the process of restoration was not decided by a predetermined plan, but by the amalgam of reciprocal moves and countermoves. . . . The logic of the Kadar government's situation dragged it toward ever more extreme neo-Stalinist positions. It was neither strong nor independent nor determined enough to satisfy the resistance movement it was increasingly subordinated to the Rakosists gathering at its back."[16] But while it is true that Stalinist forces that survived the revolution were the first to benefit from the invasion and laid an exclusive claim for the shaping of demobilization policies, Kadar and his colleagues had critical personal interest in resisting the return of Stalinists. There was hardly a single person in a leading position in the party or government who did not have reason to be afraid of the Stalinists gaining the upper hand. They all said or did things during the revolution that could have been easily used against them. The centrist forces gathered around Kadar also had an important asset at their disposal, namely, they had a relatively clear vision of what they wanted to accomplish. The major objectives inherent to this vision were followed during the demobilization process. As Paul Zinner points out: "Kadar's formulations were strikingly reminiscent of the terms set by the Communists for coalition cooperation in the initial stages of power seizure immediately after the war. The promise of moderation was there, dependent on Communist good will, as was the premise of multilateral accommodation based on prior acceptance of the defense of socialist achievements such as the Communists defined them."[17] Finally, and what was the most important, they had firm Soviet backing cemented by the close personal relationship between Khrushchev and Kadar.

One of the most important advantages of the Kadar regime in designing and implementing demobilization strategies was its belief and sincere adherence to the specific institutional vision of the socialist state. This state-idea, which provided cognitive framework for the new regime, was strikingly orthodox. All political and institutional experiments were rejected and the advocated vision of the institutional order was very familiar to those who created it before 1956. Kadar recalled the convictions of the members of his government two decades latter: "Apart from the fact that all of us were followers of the idea of communism there was complete agreement on one issue: we must save people's power, preserve socialist character of the country and assure its socialist future."[18] The more specific details of what was necessary to defend socialism were aptly summarized by Kadar himself in his report to the National Assembly on the activities of the Revolutionary Workers' and Peasants' Government in May 1957. He said:

> For us one of the most important lessons of October is that the party, the working class, the working people are able to solve all problems which emerge in the course of building socialism as long as they hold to the purity of Marxism-Leninism in the face of all distortions and disfigurations and as long as the working class allied with the working peasantry holds power firmly in their hands. In firm possession of power the working class and the working people are able to attain all set goals, but without it they can only live as prisoners of the bourgeoisie; *therefore power is the most important matter in the life and well-being of the people.* The first and indispensable precondition for the strength of the people's democratic state and the firm power of the working class is the *existence and leadership of a revolutionary workers' party; a party which is capable of working out the teachings of Marxism-Leninism correctly and using Marxism-Leninism as a guiding principle in applying these teachings to the given situation of the day*; a party which enjoys the confidence of the working people; a party which relies on the masses and demands their active support and is able to develop it. . . . A precondition for the sound development of our People's Republic is that the political unity and leading role of the working class are guaranteed in our public life.[19]

Thus the "construction of a socialist society" understood along the lines of the prevailing communist orthodoxy was the first objective of the postrevolutionary regime. Although there were doubts and disagreements as to how to proceed, these were the questions of tactics; the goal itself was never in doubt.

Accordingly, the restoration process strove for the exact recreation of the institutional form of "people's democracy" down to the last detail. Consolidated Hungary was, in fact, a perfect institutional model of a "socialist society" as outlined in Soviet political theory and practice. It was a single party-state with an absolute Communist party monopoly on political and economic decisions and personnel appointments. Although the Communist party itself never fully recovered its prerevolutionary size (nine hundred thousand or 9.1 percent of the population), but with the membership consisting of 6.5 percent of the population in 1971 and 7.2 in 1976, it did not significantly contrast with other East European regimes. Representative institutions of the state did not play any significant role,[20] and elections followed the communist routine without any surprises. The economy remained highly centralized and monopolized, especially before 1968, and the private sector in services and agriculture was kept small and restricted. After the revolution, unified and centralized mass social organizations were restored and full monopoly of the party-state over the mass media, information, and education was secured. Thus the party-state recovered exclusive control of the political space, bringing the relationship between the state and society to its classical Stalinist form with unrestricted power of the state, political rights of citizens suspended, and extensive institutional penetration of society.[21]

The characteristic reflection of this restoration of institutional status quo ante was Hungary's legal system. After the extraordinary legal regulations were dropped in the course of increasing political stabilization and the decline of resistance, the legal system returned to its Stalinist form. The Stalinist constitution of 1949 remained in force without any change. The only constitutional amendments introduced by the Kadar regime were to include the Kossuth emblem in the coat of arms and to delete the communist emblem from the national flag. While some specific legal acts were amended, for example the Criminal Code, they remained exactly in the spirit of Stalinist legal thinking[22] and were characterized by ambiguous and imprecise formulations that gave the monopolistic power the flexibility to interpret and to use the law for its advantage.

But in spite its obvious continuation of the Stalinist institutional legacy, the Kadar regime was neither in its practices nor in its personnel a simple extension of the hated Rakosi regime. The significant change in the party-state's political practices became a symbol of post-revolutionary Hungary. After the ruthless suppression of the revolution, viewed as a necessary element in the reconstruction of the party-state, the Kadar regime embarked on a gradual process of "humanization"[23] of political practices. It was marked by more discreet uses of repressive strategies and epitomized by a series of amnesties for the victims of political prosecutions. The first partial amnesty was granted in April 1959 as a sign of growing confidence of the government and an attempt to show its benevolence. It was limited in its scope and left most of those imprisoned for their participation in the revolution virtually unaffected. The second partial amnesty was granted on March 31, 1960, and as a result several hundred prisoners were released, including writers Tibor Dery and Gyula Hay, whose continuing imprisonment provoked Western protests and appeals. Together with genuine political prisoners, some Stalinist functionaries imprisoned for "serious violation of the law" were also released. This was followed by the general amnesty in March 1963, when all political prisoners were released. Such acts of clemency had the function of easing internal tensions and the international isolation of Hungary, contributing in this way to further consolidation of the regime and its effort to establish legitimacy and international respectability. The decline of repression was followed by less intervention in people's private lives and the recognition of their consumer aspirations. Also travel restrictions were eased.

At the Eighth Party Congress in November 1962, Kadar announced the completion of the process of building the foundations of a socialist society. Accordingly he declared a change in appointment policies to party-state positions. "With the exception of high-level Party offices, he said, from now on any leading post may be filled by non-Party members. We only require from non-Party members that they are loyal to the cause of socialism and to the Hungarian People's Republic."[24] This opened the possibility of the inclusion of nonparty experts in the economic and social decision-making process.[25] Some concessions were made to intellectuals and professional and cultural elites. "Those who had been expelled from their professions were allowed to steal their way back into their fields; the writers whose works had been purged could publish again; the ideological crusades came to a halt; and everyday life was made more bearable."[26] In general, however, the terms of these concessions to different social and professional groups robbed them of any meaning whatsoever. They were granted not as rights but rather as privileges that could be instantly withdrawn as an act of punishment for any kind of undesirable or unapproved behavior. The accommodation the Kadar regime engineered between the party-state and society, therefore, never amounted to a genuine political compromise between the state and the people. According to Feher and Heller, "Kadar's regime, born out of a murdered revolution, [was] not a compromise but goal-rational oppression."[27] Similarly, Kis argued in 1986 that it is important to remember that while the policies of Hungarian regime changed significantly over the past three decades, "the monocentric party-state system restored [in 1956–57] is not the only thing to survive to our days. The practices of power adopted while breaking the back of the resistance still retain their validity."[28]

The change in political practices of the post-revolutionary regime from the political terror of the 1950s to the limited concessions of the 1960s still presents an interesting puzzle for many students of Hungarian politics. A majority of scholars agree that such a change was the legacy of the revolution. While post-revolutionary terror stood as ever present memory and threat for Hungarian society, the revolution itself remained the most important political lesson for the Hungarian ruling elite. As Andrey Amalrik stated it in his letter to Kiraly: "Hungary now enjoys the greatest freedom of any country in East Central Europe precisely because the Hungarians demonstrated their ability to resist with weapons in hand. Although the revolution was suppressed, the Communist powers cannot but remember this lesson."[29] Moreover, for Kadar and his colleagues experiences of the revolution provided a few fundamental policy guidelines that were in force until the late 1980s. Kis summarizes these rules in the following way:

> Firstly, there was the rule that separated [Kadar] from Rakosi's practice: there must be a stop to the limitless exploitation of the population and the people must be offered tranquil, satisfactory conditions of living; [Second] if the leadership does not harass or provoke the population, then it can hold onto politics for itself. It can shape the system as it likes on the condition that it not cause chaos in the everyday lives of the people; [Third] concessions must never be made to groups making political demands [but] great care must be taken to preempt excessive dissatisfaction; Finally . . . nothing is more dangerous than the party's inability to appear as a unified block towards the outside world. Discord of this kind has the

result that, instead of taking a determined stand against its opponents, the party capitulates and tries to regain control over the crisis situation by making political concessions.[30]

There seems to be an established consensus that both domestic and international pressures prevented Kadar's regime from pursuing a more humane course in dealing with the revolution after 1956, and only in the 1960s was he able to return to promises he had made in the tragic days of November 1956.[31] Kadar himself, however, provided a more plausible explanation for this change of regime's policies. Commenting on the repressions following the revolution, he simply stated that during this period "the dictatorship side of the dictatorship of the proletariat received greater emphasis."[32] This statement captures both the philosophy of the postrevolutionary regime and the flexibility of political practices within a given state-system. For the Kadar regime, as long as the major principles of state socialism were in danger, terrorist policies were seen as legitimate means used to accomplish the greater end—that is, the preservation of the party-state.[33] With the consolidation of his regime and the domination of the political space enjoyed by Kadar's group, more flexible policies could be pursued and, in fact, the Hungarian regime did not miss the opportunity to relax its political practices and to establish a more humane and sophisticated form of domination.

There are several additional factors that worked in Kadar's favor and were not present in Czechoslovakia and Poland. The postrevolutionary regime could define itself in clear opposition to both its hated Stalinist predecessors, whom it could blame for precipitating the revolutionary outbreak, and the leadership of the revolution, which it could accuse of betraying the cause of socialism and thus provoking the Soviet intervention. Kadar was in a position to establish a consistent centrist platform with his proclamation of "the struggle on two fronts." Such a position was relatively safe and easy to maintain because both factions of the former communist party were significantly weaker. The Stalinists were swept away by the revolution and their leaders sought refuge in the Soviet Union. As a result they lost their influential position within the recreated Communist party and state apparatus. The reformers were crushed by the Soviet invasion and either were executed or arrested or escaped to the West to avoid imminent prosecution. Thus, the internal situation within the party-state elite after the revolution was characterized by absence of crystallized factions which did not mean the absence of disagreements and conflicts among the leaders.[34] The elimination of both extreme wings of the party left the relatively unified new regime, firmly backed by its Soviet protectors, in full command of the political situation in a country where a brutally defeated society was its main and powerless adversary.

Another factor working in favor of the new regime was, paradoxically, the very disintegration of the party-state. The collapse of the party and state institutions left the political field clear and allowed the Kadar regime to adopt a strategy of selective co-optation of key political personnel. Both stalwart Stalinist and revisionists were excluded from the new Communist party. Such a situation reduced internal tensions and divisions within the party-state and eliminated a need for destructive internal struggles and purges. Thus, Kadar, blessed by firm Soviet backing, was relatively free to select his personnel, and facing an inherently weak resistance movement, was almost from the very beginning an unchallenged master of the party-state institutions and of the country.

In all cases analyzed in this work, I emphasize the importance of institutional and political factors, however, the important element in the success of demobilization policies in Hungary was the regime's ability and will to stabilize quickly the severely dislocated economic system. In fact, as Feher and Heller accurately point out, "in order for the nation to be crushed it also had to be bribed."[35] The relative economic success of the Kadar regime permitted it to achieve the separation of politics and the economy and to test one of its most cardinal beliefs. "The significant part of the working masses," Kadar argued, "are not interested in the general problems of politics, but in the correct solution of the economic and cultural questions affecting their everyday lives. They do not form their opinions of the party or the system . . . on the basis of political issues."[36] The stabilization and reform of the Hungarian economy was not, however, a simple matter.

Economic reforms that became the hallmark of the Kadar regime's pragmatic policies took twelve years to be implemented. In the meantime, the economic policies followed the orthodox pattern with some temporary changes in investment policies and minor structural adjustments that allowed the improvement in the living standards of the population. These included the introduction of the profit-sharing system in 1957, abolition of uniform wage tariff, which allowed wages to be decided by enterprises within centrally determined limits, industrial price reform, and the departure from the drive for economic autarky and the "investment for the sake of investment" approach. Such rationalizing measures were, however, contradicted by forced collectivization of agriculture and the policy of concentration of industrial units in order to simplify the planning system. When at the beginning of the 1960s the GNP growth stagnated and economic difficulties reappeared, the regime maintained the living standards and rose consumption by increasing its foreign debt.[37]

More than Poland or Czechoslovakia, Hungary suffered extensive damage to its economy as a result of the revolution and Soviet military invasion. The fighting alone destroyed twenty-five thousand housing units in Budapest. Moreover, the general strike that followed the invasion brought the whole economy to a virtual stand still for more than two months. As a result, Hungary lost one fifth of its national income in 1956. It experienced a heavy drop in industrial and agricultural output; a scarcity of raw materials, fuel, and electricity; and significant deterioration in its balance of payments. At the same time, the tax and wage concessions granted to different segments of the population by the government created strong inflationary pressure. Immediately after the Soviet invasion, the Kadar regime raised all wages by 8–15 percent, and in 1957 the real wages rose by additional 26 percent. Some strategically important groups benefited the most from the policy of economic concessions. For example, the wages of miners rose by 33 percent in 1957, and during this year more apartment buildings were built for the miners than during the previous ten years.[38] In spite of these problems, Hungary's economy had recovered by the end of 1957, and the following years showed a steady rise in national income and real wages. The economic recovery occurred over three stages. In 1957 the government introduced a one-year reconstruction plan that was designed to put the economy back on its feet. This was followed by a three-year plan (1958–1960) conceived as a period of transition during which economic stabilization and a return to the five-year plan would be achieved. The first five-year plan after the revolution covered the years 1961–1965.

The reconstruction plan for 1957 was aimed at reviving production and combating inflationary pressure. To stabilize the economy and reduce the budget deficit, investments were significantly reduced, state administrative expenses and defense expenditures were cut, and the production of the heavy industry sector was restricted. At the same time, stress was placed on the production of consumer goods to keep up with increases in wages and consumption. To speed up the economic recovery, Hungary received significant help from other state-socialist countries. The principle and the interest on Hungary's earlier debts, especially on those to the Soviet Union, were forgiven. On March 28, 1957, a new economic agreement between Hungary and the Soviet Union was signed, promising large economic assistance involving 750 million rubles in credit and 110 million rubles in finished goods and raw materials. The Soviet aid comprised approximately 75 percent of foreign assistance received by Hungary. The next biggest contributors were China, Czechoslovakia, and East Germany. Moreover, Hungary exported only one-third of its goods stipulated in international agreements. According to George Urban,

> all these factors plus an exceptionally good harvest, made it possible for the Hungarian economy largely to recover its balance by the second half of 1957. Unemployment had been conquered, the consumer goods industries were fully stretched, heavy industry worked at 70–75 percent of its capacity partly fulfilling Czechoslovak and Soviet orders. Raw materials and consumer goods purchased with foreign loans began to flow again, wage demands were checked, and a slow start was made in communal investment programs (housing, school building, etc.).[39]

After 1957, international support for the Hungarian economy was gradually reduced, and the three-year plan spanning 1958 to 1960 was introduced to maintain the country's economic balance by relying on domestic resources. This plan continued to limit heavy industry and to increase social programs. However, by 1958 the reconstruction phase of Hungary's economic plan with its higher standard of living had achieved its purpose and in August 1958 economic policies changed. The earlier trends were reversed and heavy industrial investments were increased by 20 percent and the housing program correspondingly reduced. Introduction of austerity measures illustrated the weaknesses of a centrally planned economy in overcoming the failure of the traditional method used to increase productivity (i.e., worker competition and a "socialist brigade" system). At the same time, it pointed to the success of the demobilization policies. All the highly unpopular austerity measures that were re-introduced—the general rise of production norms that again suppressed real wages, wide use of unpaid "social work," and the price reform that increased producer prices by 70 percent and the cost of transportation by 50 percent—did not generate any significant resistance or protest. The three-year plan was corrected several times and supplemented by such fundamental adjustments as the decision to begin collectivization of agriculture. At the same time, the small private businesses, which recovered after the revolution due to more relaxed policies, were again squeezed. In 1958, 117,000 people were employed in private shops and artisans' workshops. By the summer of 1960, this number dropped to 82,000, and the number of independent artisans fell from 92,000 in 1958 to 64,000 in 1960. Trade licenses for small private businesses were withdrawn, the supply of materials limited, and excessive taxes imposed. Artisans were pressed to join cooperatives. This policy had significant impact on services, particularly in the provinces.[40]

According to the report evaluating the achievements of the three-year plan, national income had risen by 20 percent and consumption by 10 percent. The main contours of economic policy, with its emphasis on heavy industry and import-substituting development remained unchanged. The greatest portion of investment (more than 75 percent) during this period was still allocated to heavy industry with metallurgy, energy, and chemical industry receiving the most funds. While the efforts to further develop iron and steel industry persisted on the 1960s, the major new focus of import-substitution policy was the development of chemical industry. But, there was also a substantial increase in investments in agriculture stimulated by the effort to build the infrastructure for a newly formed "socialist sector." These policies were, according to Ivan Berend, "the surviving effect of earlier development endeavors, the scarcity, and the limited scope of international cooperation."[41]

Thus, in spite of the disastrous economic consequences of this type of industrial policies during the first five-year plan (1950–1954), during the period of the three-year plan and the second five-year plan, the development of heavy industry and the expansion of energy basis remained in the focus of policy decisions and continued without interruption. This direction of economic policy was shaped not only by the effects of past development and the ideologically grounded policy objectives in the economy but also was forced by intraregional policies of the revamped and activated Council of Mutual Economic Assistance after 1956. At that time, the Soviet Union pressured other bloc countries toward specialization of production, harmonization of development, and even joint preparation of long-term economic plans.[42] In sum, Kadar's government did not go beyond the principles of Stalinist industrialization policies common to all state-socialist countries in the region during this period.[43] Ivan Berend summarizes the economic policies in Hungary after the revolution:

> Industrialization policy in the decade after 1956 underwent a very significant change. In spite of the considerable structural changes among and within branches, however, the nature of industrialization persisted. Industrial development was, invariably, characterized by extensive, quantitative growth and bore the typical stamps of a policy which we may call the second phase of import-substituting industrialization. . . . This phase was characterized by the objective of fullest possible self-sufficiency in domestically produced raw materials (intermediary products). A concomitant to this was establishment of the production of widest possible range of investment goods and also embarking on the production of consumer durables produced by the heavy industry. . . . The main development projects, absorbing the most significant resources, remained of an import-substituting nature and the replacement of import, as we have witnessed in the case of ferrous metallurgy, the chemical and even the machine-building industries, has kept its economic-political value. . . . On the whole—with the exception of a few products—the launching of the production of a few, but mass-produced, up-to-date, competitive products, saleable on external markets, and integration into the international division of labor did not materialize.[44]

The issue of economic reforms had been on the political agenda before, during the revolution, and through the first years of Kadar's rule. He and his colleagues were aware that in order to allow for a consistent rise in living standards and consumption levels and to keep his countrymen pacified, the performance of the economy must be significantly improved. The economic policies of prerevolutionary Hungary could not guarantee this. Therefore, postrevolutionary Hungary witnessed the first comprehensive discussion of a new economic mechanism designed to introduce elements simulating market conditions and boost productivity of the centrally planned economy. Early in the 1957, the government created a committee comprised of two hundred experts headed by Istvan Varga. The task of the committee was to survey national economy and to suggest necessary remedies for avoiding past problems.

The report of the Varga committee was ready by the end of 1957. It contained three parts: an analysis of the economic situation, the survey of prerequisites for economic development, and suggestions for the reforms of the system of economic management and coordination.[45] The committee accepted the principle of state ownership of the means of production and its recommendation were more modest than the reform of economic mechanism introduced in 1968. The committee suggested, however, that the system of strict centralized control and management should be replaced by indirect coordination through economic regulators such as price and credit policy and that the economic independence of enterprises should be guaranteed. According to the committee's view, the significant change of the existing system of direct centralized management and planning was needed in order to create a more efficient and rational planned economy. But the unexpectedly fast economic recovery after the revolution made the issue of economic reforms less pressing for the cadres of Kadar's regime. Moreover, for the majority of the party leadership, the critique of directive planning was still equal to a critique of socialism in general and to a hidden threat to restore capitalism. The recommendations of the committee were flatly rejected, and in the official government response the primacy of political objectives over economic ones was reaffirmed with an especially strong attack on the notion of decentralization and indirect economic control and coordination.[46]

But while the proposal as a whole was rejected, some elements of the program were implemented, such as the reform of producer prices and reduction of the number of plan targets. Overall, such changes contributed to the emergence of a less rigid, planned economy. According to Laszlo Antal, "it made the given system tolerant, a little wider possibilities were given to enterprise initiative . . . and these slow changes helped in putting the reform proposals on the agenda again."[47] A renewed effort to introduce changes to the economic system came in the mid 1960s, when it became clear that partial measures (i.e., producer price reform, the introduction of quality norms, and the profit-sharing system) were not working. According to William Robinson: "This can be ascribed to the fact that in a strongly interdependent system the effectiveness of partial changes is greatly limited by the absence of change in the system as a whole. That is to say, the maintenance of the essential features and framework of the old structure acted as a barrier to and a brake on the influence and operation of the new components that had been installed."[48]

The growing economic stagnation that became evident during the second five-year plan and the resulting new austerity measures that fueled popular resentment forced the regime to put debates about economic reforms back on the agenda. Once again the party established a committee of experts to work out a reform proposal. This time, however, as Antal points out, "everybody agreed that the reform was needed [and] the reform proposal enjoyed unambiguous political support."[49] The reforms eventually introduced in 1968 are known as the New Economic Mechanism.[50] Under the new system, the decentralization and indirect regulation of economic activities were introduced and the compulsory character of planning eased in order to raise productivity and to stimulate the worker initiative and involvement. However, while the economic reforms did not significantly improve Hungary's economic performance vis-à-vis other bloc countries,[51] they introduced stability into the economic system and assured Hungarians higher living standards than those in neighboring countries.

The economic experiments of the Kadar regime are tied to the demobilization process in many ways. First, it can be argued that Kadar's promises made immediately after the intervention and his realization of the need of changes in economic performance and organization survived the repressive policies at the end of the 1950s and reappeared again in the middle of the 1960s, when the domestic and international political situation allowed the relaxation in the party's economic policies. Lomax tends to support such a proposition by arguing that the period immediately following the suppression of the revolution foresaw a subsequent reformist stand of the Hungarian regime.[52] Alternatively, it can be argued that it was the complete success of political demobilization that allowed the Hungarian regime to experiment with economic mechanisms in the situation where their political supremacy and control over society was fully secured and no challenge to their authority was expected. Moreover, Kadar's regime learned during the demobilization process the value of political flexibility where certain political principles may be sacrificed to achieve more tangible political gains. This pragmatization of political practices was clearly detectable in the postrevolutionary history of Hungary. Finally, the political crisis that led to the revolution imprinted on the Hungarian Communist party leadership a conviction that people require humane treatment and the policy securing a consistent raising of living standards and consumption is the best protection from the recurrence of political tensions and conflicts. At the same time, it should also be kept in mind that in the course of Stalinist industrialization policies, the living standards were so drastically depressed that it was relatively easy for the postrevolutionary regime to significantly raise them simply by using foreign aid and making some adjustments in investment strategies.

THE INTERNATIONAL CONTEXT OF THE DEMOBILIZATION PERIOD

International context has been kept in the background throughout this analysis for two reasons. First, there has been a prevailing tendency to analyze the domestic policies of East Central European regimes as a direct reflection of Soviet internal struggles and policies designed to protect Soviet strategic and political interests and influence. As I argued before, even a superficial overview of the Soviet goals, strategies, and policies toward Eastern Europe suggest that inconsistency and indecision were their prominent features, especially in times of leadership succession and major regional crises. This situation, however, as Gati suggests, did not result in an "accommodating Soviet foreign policy."[53] Despite the de-Stalinization campaign, he detects a significant continuation in Stalinist foreign policy as exemplified by Soviet aggressive behavior in East Central Europe and elsewhere. Second, it is the intention of this analysis to suggest the relative independence of domestic politics of East Central European regimes vis-à-vis the Soviet Union. I would argue that while direct Soviet pressures and influence should never be underestimated, the space left for East European leaders was much wider than has often been assumed. The tendency to attribute all choices, decisions, and problems to the Soviet influence and pressure long served as a good excuse to party leaders in dependent countries and provided a convenient tool for forcing their personal views and decisions against the opposition within the power elite. In fact, the takeover of Polish Communist party leadership by Wladyslaw Gomulka in 1956 was opposed by the Soviet leaders, and both the introduction of economic reforms in Hungary in 1968 and Edward Gierek's reforms in Poland after 1970 took place precisely when the most conservative winds were blowing from Moscow.

The Hungarian crisis was clearly a reality check revealing both the capacity of Western powers to influence events in Eastern Europe and Soviet determination to preserve its sphere of influence. It also showed the gap between political rhetoric and realpolitik on both sides. As a result of the 1956 events, the American foreign policy myth of "rolling back of the Iron Curtain" collapsed, the bipolar order that emerged from the Second World War was reinforced, and Soviet hegemony over its East European dependencies was reconfirmed long before it was codified in what became known as the Brezhnev Doctrine.

The sudden eruption of the popular revolt in Budapest caught both the Soviet leaders and Western governments by surprise. Initially, while the military action against "counterrevolutionary elements" in Hungary had significant support both within the Soviet leadership and among its East European allies, the uncertainty about a possible Western response to such an action was higher than at any other time of the postwar history.[54] Western governments, however, while expressing moral outrage and condemnation for the Soviet action, very soon declared the hands-off position. Despite its official phraseology of "rolling back communism" and liberating "captive nations" of Eastern Europe, the United States signaled from the very beginning of the crisis that it would not intervene militarily in Eastern Europe. Thus, according to Hans Morgenthau, the Hungarian events proved that "the United States was actually pursuing a policy of containment conceived in terms not of liberation, but of an implicit and thus-far unacknowledged agreement to recognize the existence of spheres of influence."[55] American leaders feared that the loss of control over the dependent East European country might provoke the Soviet Union to start a world war and decided to remain passive spectators of the events unfolding in Hungary. But more importantly, the United States did not have any prepared diplomatic or military contingency plans in the case of a political crisis in Eastern Europe. Moreover, Western responses to the Hungarian crisis were seriously impaired by the Suez events. Although often-alleged causal links between the Anglo-French-Israeli intervention in Egypt and Soviet intervention in Hungary were never confirmed, it is clear that the Suez crisis "overloaded the decision-making networks of the Western powers and was given top priority."[56] Also, the UN action on Hungary was delayed and muted by the

Suez problem until it was too late to do anything. The Security Council discussed the Hungarian situation briefly on November 2 and 3, and the United States agreed to postpone further deliberation until November 5.[57] This situation proved that despite its belligerent rhetoric of liberation, the Western countries had no effective leverage over the Soviet Union's action in its sphere of influence at that time. According to Gati: "The main reason for the US acquiescence in the status quo is self-evident. Lacking appropriate power, military, political or economic, to challenge Soviet power, the United States had no option but to accept prevailing reality."[58] Thus, the Soviet invasion was not effectively challenged and in a few years was forgotten and eclipsed by the need to build stable and predictable relations between military blocs.

After the suppression of the revolution, the international position of the Kadar regime was a reflection of its domestic position. The Soviet military intervention and the repressive actions of the new regime isolated Hungary from Western countries, and the United Nations kept the question of Hungary on its agenda for several years. During that time, the countries of the Soviet-bloc provided the only source of international support for the Hungarian regime. Similarly, foreign aid and Hungary's trade was confined to these countries. Leaders of state-socialist regimes tried hard to compensate Kadar for the boycott and hostile attitude of the Western countries. Immediately after the invasion, Kadar and other communist leaders visited each other's countries on an almost constant basis and with big official ceremonies.[59] Kadar's first trip to the West was not until September 1960, when he addressed the Fifteenth Session of United Nations. It took, however, two more years of behind-the-scene negotiations before the United States submitted the resolution for removing the "Hungarian question" from the agenda of the United Nations. This was followed by the visit to Budapest by Secretary General U Thant in July 1963. Shortly after its Eighteenth Session, the General Assembly accepted Kadar's Hungary as a legitimate member of the international community.[60] Thus, the Soviet bloc countries provided effective sources of economic and political support for Kadar's regime, significantly reducing the effectiveness of Western protests, pressures, and boycott. Moreover, Western political and economic sanctions did not have any significant effect due to the relative isolation of Soviet bloc economies from the world markets. This intra-bloc capacity was significantly missing in post-martial law Poland, when the bloc countries, themselves trying to cope with acute domestic economic difficulties, were unable to grant any significant economic aid to the Polish regime to offset the international political and economic pressures and sanctions.

Paradoxically, Hungary, which remained one of the most independent regimes in pursuing domestic policies was, at the same time, the country where the extensive direct involvement of the Soviets in the country's internal affairs was unprecedented. In no other instance of a large-scale demobilization process were the Soviets so heavily engaged in organizing and running the day-to-day activities of the state. It is clear that Kadar did not exercise any genuine power for the first several weeks following the invasion. The Soviet commanders and advisers were in full control of the country and only gradually transferred their prerogatives to the consolidating Hungarian administration and coercive forces. Moreover, even when the key institutions of the Hungarian party-state were restored Soviet advisers continued to operate in such important organs as the Ministries of the Interior, Defense, Justice, and Foreign Affairs, as well as within the police and the army. Thus, for some time, the Soviet Union exercised significant control over internal political developments in Hungary.

With the progress of consolidation, the focus of Soviet control shifted from open, everyday involvement to more indirect and strategic influence exercised through the political channels of interparty and interstate cooperation. To place the Soviet-Hungarian relations within the official framework of relations between two sovereign states, a series of formal agreements were concluded between the two countries. The first such agreement, of May 27, 1957, legitimized the presence of the Soviet troops on the Hungarian territory "as long as necessary" and formalized their legal status. This agreement was followed by several other less important treaties signed during the summer of 1957.[61] With these political agreements in place came a series of economic agreements designed to supply Hungary with significant economic aid and to help restore her economic balance.

But the extensive cooperation between Hungary and other bloc countries was also built on the basis of more informal meetings and visits. Khrushchev's frequent visits to Hungary and Kadar's trips to the Soviet Union resulted in an intimate relationship between the two leaders that was without precedent in the history of state-socialist regimes. According to Vali: "Kadar and his group aligned themselves so closely to Khrushchev's policies and leadership that the Kadar regime depended, for its stability, more heavily on the personal successes and prestige of Nikita Sergeyevich than any other Soviet satellite regime in East-Central Europe."[62] From the very beginning, Kadar and his centrist policy had Khrushchev's unconditional backing. Also, as Andrew Felkey points out: "Kadar never forgot his indebtedness to Khrushchev and found his de-Stalinization policies admirable. To prove his loyalty, Kadar never made any major decisions without Khrushchev's approval. Thus, the sixty-three-year-old Khrushchev and forty-five-year-old Kadar gradually grew fond of each other. As a consequence of this personal and working relations, Hungary received favorable economic considerations from the Soviet Union, while Kadar was granted more freedom to manage the country's domestic affairs."[63]

It is clear, as it was often argued, that Hungary's domestic policies reflected important developments within the Soviet-bloc during this period. The renewed de-Stalinization campaign launched at the Twenty-second Party Congress in 1961, coincided with the partial liberalization and so-called alliance policy, as well as with the attack on the remnants of Stalinism in Hungary, pursued by the Kadar regime after 1961. Kadar also resolutely supported the Soviet leadership in the growing Sino-Soviet split and the Soviet Union's break with Albania. Yet while the events within the Soviet bloc had a visible imprint on Kadar's policies, Felkay is right when he writes that "in most instances, Hungary was not directly affected by [these] events."[64] Further confirmation of the relative autonomy of the Hungarian regime can be found in the fall of Khrushchev in 1964, which in spite of the close relations between the two man, did not result in any personal or political changes in Hungary. Nor did the new orthodoxy at the Kremlin prevent the Kadar regime from working on and introducing comprehensive reforms of the economic mechanism in 1968 although they were never fully supported by the Soviet leaders.[65]

Yet there was still a more elusive way in which the Soviet Union shaped the postrevolutionary policies and practices of Kadar's regime. As Feher and Heller persuasively argue, the success of demobilization policies and "the main reason for the *pax Dei* reigning supreme in Hungary is the sociological constellation that Kadar's Hungary [was] the only Khrushchevite country in a post-Khrushchevite environment. This, in a word, is a summary of Kadar's statesmanship." They emphasize that Kadar's "Khrushchevism [meant] the preservation of Khrushchev's experimental spirit, or at least the claim (not necessarily the practice) of some rationality, a limited but undeniable respect for the consumer in man, a cynical belief in the de-ideologised everyday life of the 'man in the streets.'"[66]

In conclusion, the success of large-scale demobilization policies in Hungary as well as their long-term consequences, which made Hungary a tolerant and reform-oriented regime, were the effect of several conditions specific to the country and its international environment at this time. The Hungarian road of restoring the state-socialist regime following severe political crisis and institutional breakdown was an unattainable model for any subsequent demobilization policies in the region. The historical conjunction that produced Kadarism was never to be repeated. Successful reequilibration of the state socialist regime was the result of the nature of political mobilization and the internal configuration of the postrevolutionary party-state, the nature of relations between the state and society, as well as the peculiarities of the international political and economic environment. The 1956 crisis and its aftermath made their mark on the three decades that followed the revolution and led to the distinct pattern of the final collapse of Hungarian statesocialist regime in 1989. In fact, one of the critical events of the Hungarian transition was the official reassessment and redefinition of the 1956 events by Imre Pozsgay, one of the top Communist party leaders. The official acknowledgement that the 1956 events were not a counterrevolution but a popular uprising undercut the legitimacy of the communist regime. It offered a powerful symbolic resource to emerging political opposition.[67] In Janos Rainer's words: "The 1956 revolution prefigured the recent democratic changes in Hungary. The memory of thirty year old events and the chance that demands of that time might be satisfied, have acted as a considerable integrating force."[68] Thus, the process of extrication of the Communist regime in 1989 and 1990 as well as political experiences of the first years of democratization reflect the legacies of the revolution but even more importantly the legacies of demobilization policies that followed 1956 events. The failed revolution and the collective memory of struggle and defeat became a powerful political factor in Hungarian political discourse and alignments. Moreover, as George Schopflin argues, the sources of many specific feature of the Hungarian post-communist politics "are partly to be found in the remote past, in the origins of the Kadar regime and in the ways in which that system was put together after the revolution of 1956."[69]

PART II

The Political Crisis and Its Aftermath in Czechoslovakia, 1968–1976

In the mid 1960s, at the time when Hungarian communists were successfully concluding the process of reequilibration of their regime and were relaxing their demobilization policies and political practices, another major political crisis was slowly unfolding in neighboring Czechoslovakia. The consequences of the Stalinist reconstruction of the economic, social, and political order in Czechoslovakia after the communist coup in 1948 produced a political and economic crisis similar in nature to the one swept the other countries of the region in the 1950s. According to Harold Skilling, the political tensions and struggles emerging in the 1960s were the end result of the "profound crisis of the whole society under Novotny . . . the product of the imposition of an alien system, Stalinism, on a country with vastly different circumstances and traditions, and of the impulse for substantial change in that system given by Khrushchev's denunciation of Stalinism and his call for the elimination of its worst evils."[1] Throughout the 1960s, Czechoslovakia experienced growing economic difficulties and political pressures, and reformist groups within the party slowly gathered strength. The country's leadership, which had remained unchanged since Stalin's death, found itself in a situation that required decisive measures to avoid economic stagnation and avert a potential political crisis. The intellectual ferment that culminated in the reform movement emerged gradually within the party-state institutions as a response to the persistence of Stalinism and Czechoslovakia's political and economic ills. Thus, the country's political crisis was a case of delayed de-Stalinization. In Antonin Liehm's words, "The Czechoslovak attempt to reform 'real socialism' was an attempt at a constructive answer to the collapse of the Stalinist system in its entirety."[2]

In contrast to dramatic transitions from Stalinist rule in Hungary and Poland in the mid 1950s, the de-Stalinization process in Czechoslovakia was long lasting and gradual. It did not coincide with a sharp economic decline, open splits among the ruling elites, or significant activation of society and popular unrest. In fact, the state-socialist regime in Czechoslovakia was more stable and more firmly embedded in the 1960s than were the communist regimes in either Poland or Hungary a decade earlier. The degree of state institutional penetration and etatization of Czechoslovak society measured by the percentage of the population belonging to official organizations and associations was much higher here than in other state-socialist regimes. By 1967 more than half of the Czechoslovak population belonged to some formal organizations. The ratio of party members to entire population was the highest among the Soviet bloc countries and stood around 12 percent in the 1960s. Moreover, from the beginning of the postwar period, the Czechoslovak Communist party was stronger and more secure than its Polish and Hungarian counterparts. It could, therefore, respond more effectively to emerging economic and political problems and challenges and maintain more effective political control of the country.[3]

The reform movement of the 1960s, similar to other de-Stalinization efforts in the region, originated within the core institutions of the party-state. The impetus for reform and change came from the younger segment of the party elite and, as Zdenek Suda points out, was socially embedded in "a triple alliance of intellectuals, economists, and young party apparatchiks, with the unaffiliated public waiting and showing various degree of interests."[4] These groups benefited from the gradual opening of the political opportunity structure and had resources necessary to challenge the party and the state establishment. In Galia Golan's words, "They have both the protection and the legitimacy to exploit the situation."[5] In contrast to Hungary, however, the struggle for change led by the party intelligentsia remained almost entirely contained within the party-state institutions and did not spread to the disaffected groups within the society. The political mobilization of important segments of the population, including workers and peasants, was surprisingly low and controlled during the entire period before the Soviet military invasion. Moreover, despite constant appeals for the alliance between the intelligentsia and workers or the party and workers, genuine political alliances between party reformers and important strata of the population did not emerge. As a result of the low level of political mobilization, the reformers were able to keep political initiative within the official institutions of the party-state, to hold popular mobilization in check, and to maintain political control of the reform process.

The reform movement was conceived and realized as a classical reform from above. It did not pose a serious challenge to either the political and economic principles of state socialism or to the dominant Soviet position in the region. The party reformers intended to keep their proposed solutions and strategies firmly within a general framework of political order established in 1948, without questioning any fundamental tenets of the existing Marxist-Leninist state-idea. As has often been emphasized, the Action Program—a Magna Carta of the reform movement—was hardly a revolutionary document and in effect advocated an approach that would preserve all political and economic institutions of state socialism and strengthen the party's position and effectiveness. It could, therefore, be argued that even at its peak in the spring and summer of 1968, the Czechoslovak reform movement did not pose a fundamental challenge either to the domestic political order or to the postwar geopolitical system in the region in the way the Hungarian revolution or the emergence of the Solidarity movement did.[6] Soviet domination and the stability of the Soviet bloc's economic, political, and military relations and institutions never came close to becoming an open political issue. On the other hand, however, reformists of the Prague Spring aimed at the realization of a highly contradictory program that would establish elements of pluralist politics within the framework of a one-party state. As has often been noted, such an endeavor resembled the attempt to "square the circle."

During the whole Prague Spring, the reform process did not undermine or weaken any of the core institutions of the Czechoslovak party-state. While all official institutions and organizations underwent a process of internal democratization, they did not collapse or lose their vitality. Communists retained their positions of authority and were able to exercise a significant degree of control over the situation in the country. Controlled liberalization from above allowed the Czechoslovak party-state to maintain its influence over all segments of the population, retaining their support and cooperation. The development of the reform movement did not produce a sharp split between the state and society similar to Hungarian and Polish crises. Paradoxically, instead of facilitating popular mobilization directed against the state, which often follows the elite attempts to reform nondemocratic regimes, Czechoslovakia's de-Stalinization from above strengthened the authority of the Communist party and further legitimized its rule. As Otto Ulc argues, "The attempt at humanizing socialism in 1968 considerably narrowed the gap between the Party and society."[7]

The reform movement, however, split the party-state internally—generating conflict between reformist and conservative factions, which affected its power structure from the central down to the local agencies and institutions. It also brought into open the underlying ethnic tensions between the Czechs and Slovaks, splitting many institutions and organizations along ethnic lines. Different groups and factions within the party-state struggling for political influence attempted to form alliances with both the internal and external forces and to induce controlled pressure from social groups remaining on the peripheries of the party-state and outside of its formal structures. Mobilized groups and individuals from outside of the power structure, however, were co-opted to informal pressure groups within the party-state rather than being allowed to form independent centers of influence and authority in the less restrictive political space that emerged as a result of reforms. Thus, while the political opportunity structure in Czechoslovakia significantly opened during the Prague Spring, no independent political society emerged. In contrast to Hungary and Poland, Czechoslovakia did not experience any instant groundswell of civic activity represented in organizational structures independent from the party-state. Nor was the prevailing Marxist-Leninist state-idea and official political discourse significantly challenged; none of the emerging collective actors developed any consistent oppositional political discourse. The political struggle focused primarily on the political practices of a one-party regime, leaving the major tenets of the state-socialist economic and political order unquestioned.[8] Ivan Svitak argues: "The democratization movement provided the common cover for various contradictory tendencies, frequently hazy, but not antisocialist, anticommunist, or anti-Soviet. Communists were the mainspring of this process, and the toleration of opposing views was rather an expression of their force than of their weakness."[9]

In the chapters that follow, I will argue that these peculiar characteristics of the Czechoslovak political crisis determined specific demobilization strategies and policy choices employed by the Czechoslovak post-invasion leadership. The peculiar nature of the political crisis with its cleavages and specific institutional locations of conflicts restricted the regime's scope of policy choices. Yet the character of popular mobilization and the relationship between the party-state and society before and during the political crisis, strongly constrained the effectiveness of any popular resistance once the reform process was aborted by the military invasion. Among cases analyzed in this book, the Czechoslovak demobilization process was the most conservative and regressive in the long run. The policies of post-invasion regime, although not violent, remained highly repressive, led to eradication of reformers from the Communist party, and blocked any political and economic reform in the country for more than two decades following the Soviet invasion. I believe that the reasons for this repressive and antireformist reequilibration of the regime can be found in the ways in which the de-Stalinization process unfolded. The original strategies and objectives of the reform movement and the relationship between the party-state and various actors within the society that emerged during and after the country's political crisis are important parts of the explanation.

The scholarly literature on the Prague Spring is enormous. The attempt of factions within the party-state elite to liberalize the state-socialist regimes, the drama of pressures and intimidation exerted on the Czechoslovak leadership by the Warsaw Pact countries, massive military invasion, and the crisis following the Soviet military intervention attracted significant attention. In terms of information and research quality, most of these works are truly outstanding.[10] In fact, scholars and journalists were able to gather much more information about the Czechoslovak case than it was possible to gather in the 1950s in Hungary or Poland. Moreover, for the first time in the history of East European state-socialist regimes, there were public opinion surveys conducted by social scientists, which gave an interesting insight into opinions of Czechoslovak society. The following chapters are not intended to chronicle the events of the Prague Spring and its aftermath. I will draw selectively on diverse sources in order to emphasize specific developments that contributed to peculiarities of this crisis and constituted its unique legacies.

The Party-State and Society during the Prague Spring

ESTABLISHED as an independent state by the Paris Peace Conference in 1918, Czechoslovakia before the Second World War was the most industrialized and prosperous country of East Central Europe. It was also the most democratic, with a relatively well functioning and stable parliamentary system. Additionally, Czechoslovakia was the only country in the region that between the wars had a legal and established communist party, which controlled most of country's trade unions. In spite of the Communist party's opposition to the First Republic and its full subordination to Moscow, it operated with little restriction and was able to achieve considerable electoral support in the industrial centers of Bohemia.[1] The agreement in Munich in September 1938, in which the Western powers bowed to Hitler's territorial claims vis-à-vis Czechoslovakia, destroyed country's independence and freedom and led to its full-scale annexation by the Third Reich six months later. Bohemia and Moravia together were established as a German protectorate, and Slovakia, where the Germans easily exploited anti-Czech nationalist sentiments, was converted into a fascist puppet state. While Czechoslovakia was not spared the horrors and devastations of the war, it suffered less in human and material terms than its neighbors.

Liberated by the Red Army at the end of the war, Czechoslovakia was destined to fall prey to Soviet geopolitical ambitions and to become another victim of the shift in the international balance of power on the continent. But as Joseph Rothschild observes, "For more than two years after the end of World War II the Czechoslovak Communists refrained from any extravagant flexing of their political muscles."[2] At the end of the war, the Czech government-in-exile headed by Eduard Benes was able to return to the country, although on Soviet insistence a sizable representation of communists was co-opted. While the government included representatives of major political parties (Communists, Social Democrats, National Socialists, Czechoslovak Populists, and all members of the Slovak National Council), the Communists slowly moved into key positions within the state structure in preparation to assume exclusive control over the country. The government implemented wide-ranging economic reforms including nationalization of industry and banking and land reform. In October 1945 President Benes signed a decree that nationalized all enterprises employing more than five hundred workers, and in some sectors of the economy, like mining, steel, and the power industry, all enterprises were nationalized. Thus, immediately after the war 70 percent of industrial production was in the hands of the state. The state also confiscated the property and assets of all Germans and Hungarians in Czechoslovakia as well as those who collaborated with the Germans during the war. In the first postwar year, no other state in Eastern Europe apart from the Soviet Union had carried out nationalization and expropriation policies to such a degree as Czechoslovakia. These policies had crucial political and social consequences and changed the very foundations of Czechoslovak society.[3]

At the same time, the Communist party emerged as the largest and best-organized political force in the country. In the first and last free and competitive elections, held in 1946, the Communist party of Czechoslovakia, as the only communist party in the region, was the clear winner. It pooled 38 percent of the votes, almost twice as many as the next political force—Benes's National Socialist Party.[4] While considerable popular support for Communists and other leftist political forces set Czechoslovakia apart from other East Central European countries, the party owed its post-1945 success to a number of factors other than the left-wing political sympathies that existed among the population of Czechoslovakia. Because of their war experience and the political and economic difficulties of the 1930s, Czechs and Slovaks, similar to other East Central European peoples, were disillusioned with the traditional political and economic order. They were ready to embrace the sweeping changes advocated by the Communists. Furthermore, in contrast to all other countries, Czechoslovakia had a historically friendly relationship with Russia and in contrast to Hungary was considered by the Allied powers as an ally and spared, therefore, from the presence of foreign troops and the burden of reparations. The American and Soviet forces withdrew from Czechoslovakia by the end of 1945, but the country, in Hans Renner's words, "remained surrounded by Soviet troops. They were encamped in Hungary, the eastern parts of Austria, in the Soviet occupied zone of Germany and in Poland. Admittedly, the moving to and from of the Soviet occupying forces over Czechoslovak territory could hardly be regarded as interfering in internal affairs. Yet it was a means of political blackmail, especially when the Soviet government demanded transportation of troops at politically sensitive times, such as just before the elections."[5]

In contrast to Poland and Hungary, whose communist parties were intrinsically weak and in effect were nothing more than externally induced creations, the Czechoslovak Communist party (CPCz) enjoyed significant indigenous support and authority. Given the failure of the democratic republic in preventing German takeover of the country, the Communists emerged from the war far stronger than they had been during the interwar period. After the war two groups in Czechoslovak society embraced the policies of the CPCz with considerable enthusiasm. The first was the younger generation of Czechs and Slovaks, who had grown up during the war, and second was a significant body of Czech workers. Moreover, the party not only enjoyed unreserved Soviet backing and significant domestic support but also had important resources at its disposal. The mass expulsion of three million of Czechoslovakia's Sudeten Germans gave the Communists control over sizable assets. These assets included German property and land as well as assets confiscated from those who collaborated with the Germans. German property was promptly distributed in exchange for political support. As a result, the electoral success of the CPCz was greatest in Sudeten counties.[6] Finally, noncommunist parties were weakened by political squabbling and divisions and were unable to form an effective noncommunist coalition. Their leaders, Renner states, "were all too easily persuaded by the communists to take measures that caused irreparable damage to the pre-war political structure of the republic."[7] For example, six coalition parties agreed on the National Front system, which banned two strongest prewar parties and de facto ruled out any political opposition. They also accepted massive social and economic reforms amounting to a creation of a new kind of regime as well as endorsed integration into the Soviet sphere of influence in Europe. Thus, it was clear that the democratic parties themselves effectively contributed to their own downfall.

After three years of political maneuvers and the building of organizational strength and membership by the Communist party, the period of relative political freedom and hopes for the restoration of the parliamentary system came to an end. In February 1948, the communists executed a bloodless coup, which Pavel Tigrid described as an "elegant takeover,"[8] and assumed exclusive political power over the country. During the years leading to the coup, the political space was gradually colonized by communist-controlled organizations, among which the strong procommunist trade union federation ROH played the most important role. The intensifying campaign of harassment and intimidation isolated and atomized democratic forces and potential opponents of the communist rule. Moreover, like all East Central European societies, Czechoslovakia had lost a considerable portion of its intellectual elite during the German occupation, which significantly weakened liberal and democratic currents and impeded the potential for political opposition and resistance of the population.

After several years of fervent recruitment and the forced incorporation of the social democrats in June 1948, the Communist party became the biggest mass party in the region, with almost 2.7 million members in a country of 14 million people. A new constitution adopted in May 1948 finalized the establishment of a "people's democracy" in Czechoslovakia along the orthodox Stalinist lines. Immediately after taking power, the Communists closed all independent newspapers and purged all political and social organizations, universities, and civil and military services, transforming them into institutional agencies of the party-state.[9] Nationalization of industry, which had begun in 1945, was rapidly completed; forced collectivization was intensified;[10] the central planning system was established; and the first five-year plan was introduced for 1949–53. The Stalinist reconstruction of the polity and the economy was concluded by 1960, when the new constitution approved by the National Assembly proclaimed the victory of socialism in Czechoslovakia and the beginning of the transition to communism.

The consolidation of the Stalinist regime was soon followed by repressive policies and extensive intraparty purges. Following Stalin's thesis on the intensification of class struggle in the process of building socialism, political repression was escalated and the system of forced labor camps under the authority of the Ministry of the Interior was established. People were committed to these camps without trial, and sons of "bourgeoisie families" were sent there in place of military service. Between 1949 and 1955, eighty-three thousand people were tried for political offenses and more than 150,000 people, including a significant number of Communists, were arrested or interned in labor camps. The churches and especially the Catholic church were systematically prosecuted. Monastic life was prohibited, and some five hundred monasteries and convents were confiscated. The Catholic church's schools were nationalized, its youth and social organizations disbanded, and publication activities prohibited. All bishops and some eight thousand monks and nuns were imprisoned or interned in labor camps. The same fate was shared by the members of the Catholic laity and all prominent Catholic intellectuals.[11] During the same period, more than one million party members were purged.[12] Political repression culminated in a series of spectacular political trials involving the top leaders of the party and resulting in more than two hundred death sentences, which were instantly carried out. According to Joseph Rothschild, the purge in the party was overtly anti-Semitic and did not involve any real disagreements over important policy issues. It was rather "a raw power struggle among ambitious and insecure persons, exacerbated to a hysterical pitch by Stalinist framing."[13] Thus, in the short time following 1948, "the Czechoslovak Communists, who seemed to be the 'softest' in East Central Europe—with their initial postwar stance toward democratic institutions, competing parties, and the West—were to emerge during the 1950s as the area's arguably most Stalinist party—with their combination of repressiveness, rigidity, xenophobia, and ferocity of internal 'anti-Titoist' purges."[14]

The nationalization of industry, the collectivization of agriculture, and the introduction of central planning did not have, however, such devastating effects in Czechoslovakia as they had in Hungary. According to official statistics, in 1955 industrial production increased by 243 percent over 1937, while agricultural production was 93 percent of the 1937 level. At the same time, real wages increased by 30 percent over the prewar level.[15] While Czechoslovakia experienced far less acute economic problems than her neighbors, the Czechoslovak economy suffered, nevertheless, from all the characteristic problems of other centrally planned economies, such as shortages of raw materials and energy, disproportions in levels of investments and growth between different sectors of the economy, and food and consumer goods shortages. The Communists, strictly following the Soviet pattern, promoted the development of heavy industry and neglected or destroyed the traditionally well-developed branches of light industry. More-over, the expansion of heavy industry in the country with poor natural re-sources made Czechoslovakia entirely dependent on the Soviet Union for its supply of raw materials. The damaging consequences of such policies were already evident by the end of the first five-year plan.

In 1954 and 1955 the growth of heavy industry was slowed down and more resources were transferred to agriculture and light industry in an effort to remedy an unbalanced and deteriorating state of the economy. This lim-ited adjustment, however, neither changed the strategies of economic devel-opment nor resolved the growing economic difficulties. The much higher level of industrialization and the initial strength of the Czechoslovak econ-omy made the economic crisis less disrupting and devastating in comparison to those suffered by Poland and Hungary in the first half of 1950s. The destructive effects of Stalinist economic policies were delayed in Czechoslo-vakia for almost one decade. As Martin Myant argues, the overall per-formance of the Czechoslovak economy from 1948 "must be judged dis-appointing but not disastrous."[16] Yet by the beginning of the 1960s, it was evident that the targets of the second five-year plan would not be realized. In 1962 and 1963 there was an actual decline of industrial and agricultural production, and the third five-year plan was abandoned in August 1962. This growing economic crisis was compounded by rising popular dissatis-faction, the dissent of intellectuals, and by increasing ethnic tensions be-tween the Czechs and Slovaks. When external pressure came into play in the form of a renewed de-Stalinization campaign originating at the Twenty-second Congress of the Soviet party, this conjunction of domestic and geo-political factors triggered the delayed process of de-Stalinization in Czecho-slovakia.

THE DELAYED CRISIS OF STALINISM, 1962–1968

The first wave of de-Stalinization swept the region in the mid 1950s culmi-nating in a revolutionary upheaval in Hungary and a serious political crisis in Poland. It did not, however, affect the situation in Czechoslovakia. Nei-ther the localized worker unrest in Pilsen[17] nor the deaths in 1953 of Stalin and the Stalinist ruler of Czechoslovakia, Klement Gottwald, had any no-ticeable effect on the country's domestic situation and policies of the ruling elites. The Soviet "New Course," the Twentieth Congress of the Soviet party, and the events in Poland and Hungary in 1956 also failed to bring about any significant change in the Czechoslovak party's leadership and its policies. These events caused only mild ferment among the students and in-tellectuals. They did not provoke any pronounced conflicts within the ruling elites and failed to alter the political opportunity structure of the regime. Thus, Czechoslovakia remained as the most conservative state-socialist regime through the stormy 1950s, and the statue of Stalin towered over Prague until October 1962. Stalinism in Czechoslovakia, however, was gradually loosing its teeth, and over a period of two decades, it underwent some important transformations. Otto Ulc distinguishes three phases during two decades of the Stalinist regime in Czechoslovakia: pure Stalinism (1948–1953), Stalinism mellowed (1957–1963), and Stalinism paralyzed (1963–1968).[18] The protracted continuation of the Stalinist regime in Czechoslovakia, although more relaxed as opposed to the "heroic" early fifties, was the effect of several political and economic factors.

The political crisis of the 1950s, which had such significant repercussions in Poland and Hungary, was contained by the cohesiveness and shrewd tactics of the top political elite of Czechoslovakia. During the 1950s, Czechoslovakia lacked alternative communist leaders who could rally support within the party-state and split the ruling elites, such as Imre Nagy or Wladyslaw Gomulka, partly as a result of bloody internal purges. All members of CPCz Presidium (with the exception of Gottwald's son-in-law) survived the first wave of de-Stalinization and retained their party positions. In fact, the continuity of power in the highest party offices was unparalleled. In 1960 seven out of nine Politburo members of 1954 were still in power. Gottwald's successor Antonin Novotny and all other members of the ruling elite were too personally involved in the repressions, purges, and political trials to be able to begin a self-incriminating ritual of controlled de-Stalinization. Moreover, as Renner acknowledges: "Gottwald's death came at a very good moment for the Czechoslovak party leadership. With him the most powerful man, and the first one to be blamed for the Stalinist trials and prosecutions, disappeared from the political scene. The succession of Gottwald passed off without any internal wrangling; after the Soviet example a sort of 'collective leadership' was installed, by distributing Gottwald's functions, and with this the Kremlin seemed to be satisfied."[19]

Another element absent in Czechoslovakia's political scene in the 1950s was widespread popular dissatisfaction among workers and intellectuals. In contrast to Poland and Hungary, in Czechoslovakia Stalinism did not produce any significant collective grievances and tensions among the workers, peasants, or students and intellectuals; nor did it make possible any alliance between dissatisfied workers and disenchanted intelligentsia—for several reasons. First of all, despite economic disbalances and difficulties resulting from the Stalinist reconstruction of the economy, Czechoslovakia suffered no devastating economic crisis that could provoke workers unrest and transform economic grievances into political demands.[20] Moreover, the Czechoslovak regime skillfully prevented the formation of alliances between important social groups. According to Renner: "The Party applied a 'divide and rule' policy towards the population, which had a strong effect. By means of a systematic smear campaign, the Party managed to stir up an anti-intellectual mood, and even feelings of hate towards the Czechoslovak intelligentsia among the workers. . . . [T]his is a specifically Czechoslovak phenomenon. No other communist east-bloc country in the 1950s suffered from such a powerful 'anti-intellectual complex as the CPCz."[21] Finally, after 1948 the Czechoslovak intelligentsia were systematically pacified in a manner hardly repeated in any other East Central European state-socialist regime. Those voicing independent opinions had no 'liberal' faction within the party or any institution outside the party-state such as the church, which could offer protection from the state's wrath.

The Czechoslovak Stalinist regime's survival of the first de-Stalinization wave was by all means a Pyrrhic victory, which resulted in growing economic stagnation[22] and a paralysis of the oppressive machinery created by Czechoslovak communists after 1948. By the beginning of the 1960s, another conjunction of domestic and external tensions and pressures began the delayed unraveling of the Stalinist economic and political order. This time around, poor economic performance was coupled with a growing popular discontent and intellectual dissent, as well as with emerging divisions within the top political elite and the reemergence of the Slovak national question. These internal tensions were reinforced by the renewed de-Stalinization campaign announced by Khrushchev during the Twenty-second Congress of the Soviet party in October 1961.

The instability of the Czechoslovak economy had root causes similar to other crisis cycles of centrally planned economies in the region. It was related to the weakness in agricultural production, the growing disproportion between industrial production and the necessary raw material base needed to sustain it, an excessive level of investment limited to certain sectors, and an increasing lack of competitiveness on the world markets due to the low quality of manufactured goods. The economic problems became more glaringly apparent in 1961, when Czechoslovakia had twenty-two thousand unfinished investment projects and the government was forced to respond to developing difficulties by making an extraordinary cut in the level of investment. In 1962 and 1963, the economy was in crisis. This was reflected in the decline of national income, output, productivity, and even employment, as well as in the difficulties the country was having with its internal and external balance of payments.[23] The growth figures for national income showed a decrease from 6.77 percent in 1961 to 1.40 percent in 1962, to −2.17 percent in 1963 and 0.89 percent in 1964. By 1963, the third five-year plan collapsed and there was an urgent need to identify the sources of the crisis and to devise policy responses that would stabilize the economic system, restore its balance, and stimulate economic growth.

In 1963 a governmental commission of economists headed by Ota Sik was created. It was given the task of reviewing existing economic policies and designing a new system of economic management that was a euphemistic name for the reform of the central planning mechanism. The commission became a rallying point for reformist economists and pragmatic technocrats who were critical of the highly centralized system of running the economy imposed after 1948. And, as Myant writes, "Members of the commission could use their new-found status to ensure publication of their views. Within the prevailing political system[,] that was tantamount to giving them an appearance of official acceptance."[24] In 1965 the proposal for modest reforms suggested by the commission was presented to and approved by the Central Committee; but its implementation encountered growing difficulties and resistance. As a result, the partial measures designed to restrict and rationalize central planning failed to solve the country's economic problems and were effectively paralyzed by resistance from dogmatic leaders and obstructed by managerial and bureaucratic apparatuses within the state and industrial bureaucracy. The stalemate on economic reforms coupled with the economy's dwindling performance continued by and large until 1968 and became a powerful factor in the strengthening of opposition to the Novotny leadership. While reform economists initially believed that the proposed reforms might be introduced under Novotny's regime, the experience of dogmatic resistance against the economic reforms clearly showed that without political changes, any efforts to improve the economy were bound to failure. The difficulties in implementing economic proposals clearly contributed to the radicalization of young party economists and technocrats. They saw party leader Novotny and his dogmatic followers as a main obstacle to their efforts to save the economy from the widening crisis. It was Ota Sik who delivered the most devastating critique of Novotny's policies during the Central Committee meeting in December 1967. His criticism opened the way to the transition of power within the party elite and launched the Czechoslovak reform movement.

While the problem of economic reforms divided the top party leadership, serious political divisions slowly emerged within the party and penetrated its lower ranks. Encouraged by the obvious signs of de-Stalinization (i.e., the release of remaining communist prisoners from the 1950s, the removal and cremation of Gottwald's embalmed body previously displayed in a Mausoleum, and the demolition of the enormous Stalin monument in Prague), young party intellectuals and students began advocating the need for economic and political reforms and the party organizations in universities and research institutes became strongholds of the reformist camp. These people belonged to the generation that after the war enthusiastically embraced communism and provided the intellectual shock troops for the new communist regime. In the 1960s, however, according to Renner, "they lost their illusions about the nature of Soviet communism, but they had not lost their belief in a reform of the communist state in Czechoslovakia, which had long been in a state of severe crisis."[25] The young party reformists found allies among the prominent communists who were the victims of political trials and who demanded political rehabilitation upon their release from prison in the 1960s. To accommodate the demands for rehabilitation, a new party committee was formed to review the trials; some members of Gottwald's old guard who were directly implicated in political trials lost their positions in the Politburo, the party's secretariat, and the government.

From the mid 1960s on, intra-party opposition against Novotny grew stronger. This opposition was by no means cohesive nor did it have common political opinions or visions of reforms. What kept it together was discontent with Novotny's policies. Very soon, however, other hidden political issues surfaced. The new emerging political force that joined the reformers was the Slovak bloc within the Communist party, whose interest in upgrading its nationality status turned it against Novotny. The multi-ethnic character of the Czechoslovak state was, therefore, an additional powerful element that contributed to the unraveling of the Stalinist rule. The communist drive for centralization after 1948 liquidated all areas of Slovak autonomy. The attempted solution of the Slovak national question after the war that gave Slovakia some residual institutional autonomy through the National Council and the Board of Commissioners was reversed by the communists. The power of these institutions was gradually curtailed during the 1950s, and the Board of Commissioners was abolished altogether under the 1960 constitution. In similar fashion Slovakia's separate trade unions were merged with Czech unions and the Slovak Communist party was stripped of its autonomy, becoming only a territorial branch of the organizationally unified all-national bureaucratic structure. Additionally, Novotny's lack of diplomacy offended not only the Slovak population but also the Slovak functionaries within the party-state. Moreover, the economic and cultural gap between the Czechs and Slovaks was never bridged and the Slovak region still remained well behind Bohemia and Moravia in all major economic and social aspects. By the late 1960s, the situation was aggravated to such a degree that the Slovak branch of the Communist party became one of the most significant bases of opposition against Novotny. The serious intraparty divisions along national and political lines that emerged in the second half of the 1960s paralyzed the resoluteness of both the Stalinist power base within the party-state and Stalinist leaders. As a result, writes Renner, "the criticism of Novotny became stronger and louder, more and more members from the highest Party echelons joined the ranks of the opposition. They were spurred on by opportunist considerations or personal rivalry with the Party chief rather than by fundamental disagreements with his policies."[26] Thus, in the late 1960s, the political opportunity structure was significantly altered, allowing the younger generation of party activists to challenge the Stalinist status quo.

For a long time, the reformist opposition was confined to the upper echelons of the party. The population as well as the lower party ranks were unaware or confused concerning the disagreements within the top ruling elite. There were two reasons for this confinement of political debates and conflicts within the narrow elite. First, according to Myant: "Novotny was firm in attacking those who pushed for change from outside the apparatus of power. At the Thirteenth Congress in 1966 he openly attacked 'some cultural journalists' for propagating anti-party's ideas and his battles with the writer's union are well known."[27] The leaders of the student section within the official youth organization were prosecuted after calling for the right to be more critical of the party leadership. Thus the political space that would allow for any public airing of criticism was highly controlled and restricted during the whole period before the Prague Spring. Second, the reformist opposition, including the high-ranking officials of the central party-state's apparatus, the Slovak party organs, and certain provincial party leaders consciously kept their struggle against Novotny within the boundaries of the highest institutions of the party and the state. They feared potential political destabilization caused by the involvement of the public in intraparty political struggles.

Only by the end of the 1960s did the intraparty discontent and disputes spread outside the core institutions of the party-state. At the Fourth Congress of the Union of Writers in June 1967, the party leadership was openly attacked for the first time for its cultural, social, and economic policies. Vladimir Kusin wrote: "What had begun, and continued until 1968, as a search for literary assertion outside the constraints of socialist realism, became one of the major political conflicts in the country. Once again, as in the nineteenth century, the Czech writers were deputising for politicians."[28] However, repressive measures advocated by Novotny against the writers were not approved by all members of the Central Committee, indicating the growing strains within the top ruling elite. The "writers incident" made the rift between the dogmatic leaders on the one hand and the more moderate ones on the other hand increasingly visible. From the time of the Writer's Congress, the perception that something was seriously wrong in country's political life continued to grow inside and outside of the party-state institutions. The situation was the most explosive in Czechoslovakia's universities. On October 31, 1967, some two thousand students staged a candlelight march in Prague to protest living conditions in their dormitories. The demonstration was brutally dispersed by the police. The repressive action against the students caused an flood of protests from the academic community and further heightened political tensions within the country.

During the fall of 1967, Novotny's opponents in the highest ranks of the communist hierarchy, representing reformers as well as moderate and hard-line functionaries opposed to Novotny for different personal and political reasons, formed a loose coalition that was strong enough to challenge the party leader. At this moment the stage was set for the coup within the party's leadership. The Central Committee meeting at the end of October developed into a rebellion against Novotny; he was no longer able to prevent the emergence of open opposition and conflicts within the highest party structures. Yet as the conflict and struggle among party leaders tore apart the core institutions of the Czechoslovak party-state, "the Party rank-and-file members and the Czechoslovak public were—as usual—completely unaware of these developments."[29]

On December 8, 1967, Brezhnev paid an unexpected emergency visit to Prague to discuss the internal difficulties of the Czechoslovak party with its leadership. As Valenta claims: "Brezhnev surprised the Czechoslovakia leaders with his flexible attitude. After he became aware of Novotny's weak position, he reportedly told the Czech leaders, Eto vashe delo [That is your own affair] and left."[30] The refusal of the Soviet leader to back Novotny spelled the end of Stalinism in Czechoslovakia and opened the gate for a pivotal leadership turnover within the Czechoslovak Communist party. At the beginning of January 1968, the party Presidium replaced Novotny with the little-known leader of the Slovak party organization, Alexander Dubcek. This change at the pinnacle of the Czechoslovak party-state initiated the reform process that produced significant political liberalization and laid the foundations for significant changes in the political and economic system several months later. This reformist drive from above ended when Czechoslovakia was invaded by the massive military forces of the Warsaw Pact. All the achievements of Czechoslovakia's brief experiment—"socialism with a human face"—were destroyed.

The Stalinist order in Czechoslovakia spanned more than two decades. Its gradual erosion produced a unique domestic political situation that shaped the subsequent reform process. Unlike Hungary's political and economic crisis, which ended in a popular revolutionary explosion, Czechoslovakia's lingering crisis was more conducive for the formation of a strong, moderate reformist alliance with a relative consensus regarding the direction the country should take—and careful not to provoke the Kremlin by overstepping the boundaries of what was permissible. As Kusin emphasizes: "In 1967 Czechoslovakia was not on the verge of collapse, economically or otherwise. The reformers were not prompted into action by imminent doom, although in some fields relationships had been near breaking point. . . . Reform theories . . . were formulated as an alternative national aim of a long-term nature rather than as a plan for an immediate rescue operation."[31] Moreover, this was a new generation of party leaders who were slowly replacing the old-guard Stalinists throughout the 1960s; before the culmination of the intra-party conflict, they even shared the belief that reforms could take place under Novotny's leadership.

Additionally the domestic situation in Czechoslovakia during the 1960s was not affected by any significant political pressures from below, nor did the country experience any outbursts of collective workers or peasants protests. This notable absence of social unrest was in part the result of higher living standards and a much less dramatic economic situation than the one experienced during the last years of the Rakosi regime in Hungary. Therefore, the nature of political developments in 1968 differed significantly from any other political crisis in East Central Europe after the Second World

War. This was the only instance of major reform from above attempted by a strong reformist movement within the party-state and initiated by the party's highest leadership, which was gradually embraced and supported by the population. Until the reform movement was aborted by the Soviet-led military invasion, the authority, integrity, and survival of the party-state was not in any imminent danger of collapse.[32]

The peculiar nature of the political situation in Czechoslovakia during the crisis of 1968 certainly influenced the demobilization process that followed the Soviet-led intervention. In the next section, therefore, I will look at the period of the Prague Spring and try to identify these political developments, which later on had significant impact of the demobilization policies and process.

THE RULE OF THE REFORM MOVEMENT

The roots of reformist ideas in Czechoslovakia can be traced back to the 1950s and the early 1960s.[33] Nevertheless, the reform movement as a distinctive political force emerged from three Central Committee meetings held at the end of 1967 and the beginning of 1968. The internal coup d'etat began at the Central Committee meeting held at the end of October 1967. This meeting developed into a full-scale rebellion against the party's reigning first secretary, and it was the first occasion that Ota Sik explicitly asked Novotny to resign. But Novotny was not effectively removed until two months later, at the beginning of January 1968. During the entire period, Soviet leaders proclaimed their noninterference in the personal struggle occurring within the Czechoslovak leadership. On the night of January 4, the Czechoslovak party's Politburo directed the Slovak party boss Alexander Dubcek to replace Antonin Novotny as the first secretary of the Communist party. What seemed to be, however, a routine palace revolution to replace compromised leadership acquired a dynamism of its own, and in the coming months this shift in party's leadership radically changed the political practices, if not political structures, of the Czechoslovak party-state.

Dubcek became the leader of the Czechoslovak party as a result of a compromise between various factions within the Central Committee. As Renner states, "the outsider Dubcek had been 'pushed' into that position, not because of his aura of a reformist, not because he was someone with a clear perception of how to help Czechoslovakia, but because at that moment in time he was the most obvious compromise figure."[34] He was acceptable not only to all competing factions within the Czechoslovak leadership, but more importantly, he was seen by the Soviet leadership as a credible replacement of Novotny.[35] Dubcek was little known, especially in the Czech lands, and his elevation to the highest party post surprised everyone. Nobody at that time believed that this rotation of leaders could bring any significant change to Czechoslovak politics, especially in light of the fact that Novotny retained his post as president of Czechoslovakia and the members of his faction stayed in the party's Presidium.[36] Society remained apathetic during the events of January 1968, and the transition of power within the top ruling elite was not disturbed by any collective actions or pressures from outside of the party-state structures and institutions. During his first four months in office, Dubcek's support wavered between conservatives and the reformists, yet in May and June he unequivocally sided with the reformists in the Central Committee. In so doing, he significantly strengthened the reformist wing of the party. But despite the change in party leadership, the political stalemate and indecisiveness that had previously plagued and divided the top party echelons persisted. Giuseppe Di Palma convincingly argues that a political stalemate and paralysis among the top leaders is often conducive in triggering a process of political transition.[37] In fact, the political opportunity structure during the first months of Dubcek's reign expanded rapidly, but the activation of non-elite actors did not occur, despite the political ferment that spread among intellectuals and party activists. The important segments of the population watched the power struggle at the top with suspicion and reservation.[38] Ivan Svitak characterized the political situation in Czechoslovakia at that time in the following way:

> At the beginning of spring the intellectuals and the workers went their different ways, in fact, as regards the aims of their programs they had never come together. The leading Communist intellectuals were so dominated by their feeling of solidarity with the new leadership that they tried only to expand the freedom of the press and to popularize the program of political rehabilitations. . . . The intellectuals' program therefore cut itself off from the people, because the leading Communist insisted on the leading role of the party made no attempts to formulate any goals and contended themselves with supporting the progressive faction. So political life went on in the form of mere back room quarrels with no mass involvement and no support among the population.[39]

Political apathy and inaction among the workers persisted for several months, but the Czechoslovak intelligentsia were quick to make use of the unexpected opening in the political space to voice grievances and demand changes in political practices and extension of political and intellectual freedoms. Renner writes: "up to the middle of February 1968 we can still speak of a 'revolt at the top'; after this date we cannot. In the second half of February and early March the floodgates of criticism opened at annual meetings and conferences of the local organizations of the CPCz. The tide of criticism had now reached the bedrock of the Party and could no longer be stemmed. Soon it had reached every layer of society."[40] The event which contributed the most to the political radicalization of the intelligentsia was major general Jan Sejna's escape to the West at the end of February. Sejna was the chief of the secretariat of the Ministry of Defense and Novotny's close friend. This event triggered a wave of criticism directed against Novotny and culminated in his resignation as president on March 22, 1968.

The radical change in the Czechoslovak political climate was felt first in the mass media. Already at the beginning of March, censorship was suspended and two months later abolished altogether. As a result, Czechoslovakia experienced an explosion of information and the press played a major role as a voice of social criticism, stimulating political debates. Various party controlled newspapers and journals became platforms for propagating various points of views, a substitute for the nonexisting public opinion, and assumed the role as the guardians of the reform process. According to Renner, "without the free press, radio and television, the Czechoslovak reform process would have been completely different. . . . they mobilized millions of citizens in favour of reform policies and made them politically aware."[41] Thus, one can convincingly argue that the freedom of opinion was the most tangible result of the Prague Spring, and journalists became its most dynamic political force.

In the meantime, Novotny's followers and old-guard Stalinists were gradually loosing their positions in the party and state apparatus while the reform advocates were slowly increasing their strength within the core institutions of the party-state. Ludvik Svoboda's election as the country's new president by the National Assembly on March 30 (using the secret ballot for the first time in postwar history) started the process of selectively replacing party-state functionaries in important party and government positions. On April 18 the new government was formed under Oldrich Cernik with many reformists being promoted to ministerial and deputy-premier positions. The popular reformer Josef Smrkovsky became chairman of the National Assembly, and another reform leader, Frantisek Kriegel, became chairman of the National Front. There were also changes in the makeup of the party Presidium and in the secretariat of the CPCz. The promotion of many reformists into high offices gave reformist forces the upper hand. But, as Renner argues, this personnel exchange did not resolve political stalemate in the country. "On the one hand, Dubcek's position in the Party leadership was substantially strengthened, but on the other, the divisions in the Presidium and the secretariat remained. Instead of having to deal with the Novotny group, the Party leader now had to face a fierce and in some respects even more dangerous Bilak-Indra-Kolder group."[42]

The first official expression of intentions by the new reformist leadership was preparation of the Action Program of the CPCz, drafted already in February but approved by the Central Committee only on April 5 and officially published a few days later.[43] This document reflected the goals of party reformers and became a symbol of the reform movement. The Program criticized the previous dogmatic approach to social and economic problems and condemned the distortions of the political system (i.e., arbitrariness, excessive concentration, and misuse of power). It also exposed the deficiencies of central planning and the economic policies. The Program advocated the necessity of political reforms and democratic procedures within the Communist party and other organizations. Additionally, it spoke of the need for other social and political organizations belonging to the National Front to be granted autonomy and to play a larger role in the country's affairs. It also pointed to the need for a new electoral law, the revision of the relationships between the Czechs and Slovaks as well as guarantees of basic political freedoms for all citizens. Moreover, the Program supported economic reform and the democratization of economic institutions. It envisioned a new role for the trade unions and suggested the possibility of small-scale private enterprises in the trade and service sectors. Overall, however, this was not a radical document calling for a decisive transformation of the state-socialist system. It advocated what soon became known as "socialism with a human face," which essentially meant a substantive change of political practices without any radical transformation to the institutional framework of the Czechoslovak party-state. Moreover, in the words of Milan Hauner, "it was already clear then at the time of its delayed appearance . . . that the speed with which political events were moving ahead must have outpaced the document itself: young people were disappointed, workers remained indifferent, and many intellectuals reacted critically."[44]

There has been long discussion about the meaning of changes championed by the leaders of the Czechoslovak reform movement.[45] The abrupt end of the reform process does not allow us to see what institutional elements and social and political forces emerging in Czechoslovakia could have taken a leading role in the reformed polity and economy. I would argue, however, that the reformist institutional vision of the political and economic system did not depart radically from the major tenets of the Marxist-Leninist state-idea. The reformers wanted to preserve the Communist party's leading role, extensive state involvement in the economy, and the dominance of collectivist property rights. As an acute observer and analyst of the Prague Spring, Kusin points out:

> The strongest body of views, which seemed to emerge from the highly volatile exchanges of the Prague Spring, whatever its merits and demerits, favoured a cautious combination of adapted parliamentary democracy with elements of direct democracy (self-management) under the umbrella of enlightened Communist supervision. Such a three-cornered system had many good arguments speaking in its favour. Separation of legislative, executive and judicial powers, pluralistic elections, accountability of all State agencies to elected bodies, etc., were to ensure that political decisions would be taken by genuinely elected representatives of the population at large. In the spheres of production and local government the self-management principle was to apply. Workers' councils were to generate participation of producers in autonomous enterprise action. A multicameral parliament was to provide room for a flow of expertise into political decisions. Local government was to discontinue acting as the executant of central will at town and village level, and reverse its orientation towards representation of local interests and immediate responsibility to the local public for indigenous policy. Finally, the 'reality' of twenty years of development and of looming Soviet presence on the nation's

horizon was to be taken into account by curtailing all newly won autonomies through the continued, even if 'modified', leading role of the Communist Party. . . . 'Democracy', or whatever of it would have been made available to the Czechoslovak people, would remained largely dependent on the good will of the new Communist leadership.[46]

Yet the Action Program, represented a radical break with the political practices of the post-Stalinist regimes in the region and as such, was completely unacceptable to Brezhnev and the other communist leaders. The constant assurance of allegiance to the alliance with the Soviet Union could not change that, nor could the promise of a more active Czechoslovak involvement in activities of the Warsaw Pact and the Council for Mutual Economic Assistance (CMEA). Domestically, the Action Program was too radical for the conservative groups in the party because they were afraid it would extinguish their power and privileges. At the same time, it was too tainted with compromise to appeal to the more radical political forces emerging in Czechoslovak politics. The Program, however, enjoyed strong support among the population. As public opinion polls conducted during this time showed, the Program was approved by 76 percent of Czechs and 77 percent of Slovaks.[47]

After publication of the Action Program, the suspension of censorship, and the liberalization of political life, party organizations and other official institutions of the party-state began the process of internal democratization. In most organizations, old Stalinist leaders lost their positions of authority to newly elected leaders. At that time, despite Dubcek's objections, reformists began pressing for a new party congress that would complete the personnel change at all levels of the party's hierarchy. By the end of May, the Central Committee bowed to the pressures from reformists and decided to convene an Extraordinary Fourteenth Party Congress in September. The reformers won a major victory in the elections of delegates held in June and July; 80 percent of delegates elected represented or backed the reform movement, and the conservative backers came away with only 10 percent of the delegates. The Congress was expected to finalize the process of the party's internal democratization and remove remaining conservatives who held important party posts. This prospect, however, reactivated the antireformist coalition and caused a polarization within the Czechoslovak leadership. Ulc writes: "The lack of orderly cadre exchange did not jeopardize the totalitarian system of self-perpetuation before 1968, but proved to be a great handicap in the following period. Reform could not be carried out by conservative functionaries, and their reluctance to abdicate was completed by the reluctance of Dubcek's regime to force them out."[48]

Another event that heightened political tensions within the country was the publication on June 27 of the Two Thousand Word Manifesto, drafted by the Czech writer Ludvik Vaculik.[49] The manifesto, intended to boost the reform process, pledged support for the progressive forces within the party and for the Action Program. But it also urged an acceleration of the reform process and demanded the "resignation" of party officials opposed to reforms. As Valenta points out: "The manifesto truly reflected the polarization within the Czechoslovak ruling elite, particularly that within the anti-Novotny coalition, which had begun after publication of the Action Program. The manifesto also reflected the internal political atmosphere in the summer of 1968. The authors who seem to be trying to influence the outcomes of the regional Party conferences, were primarily concerned with the slow momentum of Czechoslovak reform and with the activization of anti-reformist forces."[50] Publication of the manifesto became a crucial factor in the transformation of the Czechoslovak ruling elite, which up till then was united in its opposition against Novotny, into two fairly crystallized coalition. The antireformist forces used the manifesto as a convenient pretext to attack and expose the allegedly counterrevolutionary character of the reform movement as a whole.

The publication of the manifesto was also used as a convenient pretext by alarmed East European and Soviet leaders concerned over the possible impact that the Czechoslovak reform movement might have on their own political situation. The first warning and critique of Czechoslovakia's internal developments was delivered at the meeting of Communist Parties leaders held in Dresden on March 23. During a Moscow gathering on May 4–5, Soviet leaders expressed further dissatisfaction with continuing the liberalization of domestic politics in Czechoslovakia. In July the Soviet Union and other countries (especially East Germany, Bulgaria, and Poland) intensified their psychological warfare against the Czechoslovak leaders and escalated their political pressure to stop the reform process. The pressures on Czechoslovakia during the spring and summer of 1968 involved not only a hostile propaganda campaign in neighboring countries and official political interference in Czechoslovakia's domestic affairs. The Warsaw Treaty members employed the whole range of explicit military threats, including the concentration of troops on Czechoslovakia's border. Czechoslovakia was forced to allow foreign troops on its soil under a pretext of joint military maneuvers of the pact members.[51] At the beginning of July, Czechoslovak leaders were summoned to attend the summit meeting of Warsaw Pact members in Warsaw. Yet having already attended two such meetings in Dresden and in Moscow, the Czechoslovak leadership, over the objections from antireformist leaders, rejected the "invitation" and decided that they would accept only bilateral negotiations and only on Czechoslovak soil. Nevertheless, the conference took place. The participants agreed that the political situation in Czechoslovakia was very serious, but they failed again to agree on what to do. The Warsaw summit did send a joint letter that constituted a kind of ultimatum to the Czechoslovak leadership. The letter implied that Dubcek's team had lost control over political developments in the country and harshly criticized many aspects of the country's internal political situation. It contended that revisionist forces had taken over Czechoslovakia's press, radio, and television and that the Two Thousand Word Manifesto created an organizational platform for the forces of reaction and counterrevolution. It also warned that the socialist community was firmly committed to defend the unity of the socialist camp and the revolutionary gains already achieved in Czechoslovakia. The Warsaw Treaty countries promised to provide assistance to uphold the socialist system in Czechoslovakia and help defeat the anti-socialist elements. They also maintained that the reinstatement of censorship, the banning political clubs, and the defeat of "rightist forces" within the party should constitute the foremost objectives of the Czechoslovak leadership.

The charges contained in the letter were officially rejected by the July 19 session of the Czechoslovak Central Committee and Dubcek's supporters received almost unanimous backing for their reform policies. "As had happened several times before during the crisis, the increase in Soviet pressure backfired. The Warsaw Letter did not strengthen the hand of the antireformist coalition as intended by participants in Warsaw; on the contrary, it created a feeling of national unity, and it was used by the reformist coalition led by Dubcek to strengthen their position. The members of the antireformist coalition were afraid to take political action. Soviet pressure played a decisive role in moving Dubcek and some of his supporters, after several months of indecisiveness, to act like leaders of an independent state and to defy the Soviet leadership."[52]

By July's end, the Soviets were demanding the dismissal of several Czechoslovak officials and in particular general Vaclav Prchlik, who was an ardent and most important supporter of reforms and the head of the Department of Defense and Security of the Party's Central Committee. At the same time, the Soviet leadership acquiesced to bilateral negotiations with Czechoslovak leaders to be held in Czechoslovakia's border city of Cierna.[53] Before the negotiations started, however, the Soviet Union announced the largest military maneuvers yet that involved thousands of Soviet reservists and the armies of the other Warsaw Treaty countries. Facing an apparent threat of military invasion, internally divided, and inexperienced in international affairs, the Czechoslovak leadership was confronted in Cierna with charges and accusations already elaborated in the Warsaw summit letter. Sensing what they hoped was Soviet willingness to compromise, Czechoslovak leaders provided new assurances of their loyalty to the Warsaw Pact and CMEA and promised to curb all "anti-socialist tendencies" by suspending political clubs and preventing the revival of the Social Democratic party. They declared that these measures would be completed by the end of August. In what seemed to be a working compromise reached after four days of negotiations, both delegations promised restraint in mutual polemics, and the Soviets assured the withdrawal of the troops that remained in Czechoslovakia after the early summer maneuvers. Both delegations also agreed to hold another multilateral summit of the six Warsaw Pact countries in Bratislava shortly following the meeting in Cierna.

The Bratislava summit confirmed the results of the Cierna negotiations and produced a joint declaration, which concluded that the socialist countries "will never allow anyone to drive a wedge between the socialist states or undermine the foundations of the socialist system." It also stressed that communist parties should "advance firmly along the path of socialism by strictly and consistently following the general laws governing the construction of a socialist society." As Valenta emphasizes, "the declaration did not specifically give approval either to Czechoslovak reformism or to the September Party Congress. Regarding Czechoslovak domestic affairs, the ambiguous and contradictory text of the Bratislava Declaration, like the verbal agreement made at Cierna, obligated the Czechoslovak leadership only to vague tenants of maintaining political stability."[54] Despite its ambiguity and vagueness, the declaration seemed to achieve a compromise between Czechoslovakia and other Warsaw Treaty countries; "the outcome of the Cierna and Bratislava negotiations suggests that the Soviet leadership had not accepted the doctrine of 'unity in diversity.' The leadership decided not to drop the pressure on Czechoslovakia, but, for the time being, to withhold military force as an instrument in resolving the crisis."[55] At that time the domestic situation in Czechoslovakia was relatively stable, but on August 11 new military maneuvers along Czechoslovakia's border were announced. Only seventeen days had passed since seemingly successful negotiations when the Soviet Union authorized a full-scale military invasion.

The domestic political developments in Czechoslovakia created a principal bone of contention among Czechoslovak and other Soviet bloc leaders. In the remaining part of this chapter, I will look more closely at the nature of popular mobilization and the development of an independent political society during the crisis. I will argue that for a variety of reasons the popular mobilization was highly restricted and that, despite significant opening in the political opportunity structure and emergence of relatively unconstrained public space, we cannot speak about the revival of political society in Czechoslovakia. The institutional structure of the Czechoslovak regime remained almost intact and the reform movement was channeled through existing institutional structures. It failed to build independent institutions that could provide the base for challenging the party-state when reformists were ousted from power.

The State and the Local Administration

In striking contrast to the Hungarian Revolution, the political crisis in Czechoslovakia neither significantly threatened the institutional coherence of the party-state and patterns of political domination nor produced an explosion of independent initiatives, movements, and organizations competing with the party-state institutions and challenging the Communist party's authority. The reform movement had most significant influence at national-level party institutions, had its strongholds in a few selected organizations representing country's academic and intellectual elites, and was largely restricted to the country's capital city—Prague. Political struggles and changes only gradually filtered down to other organizations, lower institutional levels of party-state, and other regions of the country. Even during the most dramatic months of spring 1968, bureaucratic and political inertia permeated almost the entire institutional structure of the party-state, which in 1965 employed 11.7 percent of the country's labor force. This huge bureaucratic apparatus survived the reformist efforts of 1968 without great damage, just as it had managed to survive many earlier attempts at change.

The central and local party institutions did not experience any significant structural or organizational changes. Pressures for internal democratization resulted in some personnel changes within the party's hierarchy but did not alter the party's social and political composition. Moreover, the rank-and-file party membership remained relatively stable during the entire reform period. In contrast to Hungary, there were no major defections from the party's ranks. Even though the Action Program advocated restriction of the Communist party role in society and limitation of its power vis-à-vis the state administration, the relationship between institutional orders of the regime experienced inconsequential change. The shadow departments within the central party's apparatus duplicating the functions and structures of administrative units within the state and parallel party structures in all organizations and institutions were never abolished.[56]

Although the policies of Novotny regime were often sharply criticized, Stalinist party apparatchiks, especially on the local level, were never purged. Some prominent supporters of Novotny were dismissed during the spring of 1968, and the remaining old-guard leaders were removed from the party's Presidium at the April 4 meeting of the Central Committee.[57] However, as the rule, in places where the reformers had the upper hand, the opponents of the reform movement were only transferred to less influential positions or to diplomatic posts and removed from the decision-making process. This practice was dubbed by some scholars as "horizontal demotion."[58] While the members of the reformist faction were able to achieve prominence and acquire a majority in important central institutions, this success also crystallized and united all forces of the old regime threatened by their imminent loss of power and privileges. The strength of the Stalinist faction representing mainly the party's local and middle-level functionaries and bureaucrats was estimated to be at between two hundred thousand and four hundred thousand people. They were eager to rally around conservatives within the party leadership in order to obstruct all reformist efforts. In sum, despite far-reaching internal democratization of the party and general liberalization, the Communist party was characterized by the institutional and personnel stability. At the same time, however, it was torn apart by escalating internal conflicts, especially at the national level.

The central state bureaucracy, which employed more than twenty thousand people in ministries and other central offices, also survived the reform period without significant transformations. A number of government ministers were replaced, reorganization of the government's economic organs was undertaken to curtail the extent of central planning and to increase enterprise autonomy, but many other ministries and state institutions were not touched. Overall, although the Action Program promised change in the relationship between the state and the party, along with decentralization and more autonomous economic units; the command system within the economy was not notably altered, and bureaucratization of political life was not curtailed.

The representative institutions of the state were also spared from significant transformations and personnel exchange. For years, the National Assembly served as a rubber stamp for the party's Central Committee. In 1968 its three hundred deputies who were elected in 1964 constituted a extraordinary collection of old party apparatchiks and remnants of the deposed Stalinist order. As a result of growing prominence of the reform movement, the Assembly began to experience some revival of independent opinions, open debates, and increasing polarization, reflecting the political developments and conflicts within the party and society at large. But as Barbara Wolfe Jancar states: "Despite such conspicuous development, there is no indication that the national Assembly ever acted as a bona fide legislative power during the Prague Spring. Its work remained under Party control and all legislative activities were initiated by the Party."[59] Moreover, its deputies were shielded by the parliamentary immunity and many prominent Stalinists, with the exception of Novotny, who lost their positions in the party apparatus still held their parliamentary seats. In the only significant development of this period, Josef Smrkovsky, a prominent party reformer, became chairman of the Assembly. While representatives of various political factions within the party often fought heated battles over policy changes, the Assembly was not able to enact any significant legislative acts changing the country's legal and political framework with the exception of repealing the censorship law of 1967. Thus, although the representative bodies of the state experienced some revival and attempts at regaining at least a semblance of autonomy during the pre-invasion period, they did not emerge as an active political actor and in fact often remained strongholds of Stalinist forces.

Similarly to the parliament, the local state administration, a three-layer structure including 10,565 local people's committees (MNV), 118 district people's committees (ONV), and eleven regional people's committees (KNV), did not undergo any decisive changes or transformation. The people's committees reorganized in 1967 were supposed to represent their specific constituencies and at the same time represent the state interest and supervise the implementation of state policies. In either role they were unable to function properly, being plagued by a lack of resources and staff, insufficient authority and prerogatives, and structurally built dependency on the local party apparatus. In 1968 reform and major political conflicts were taking place mainly on the national level and they produced scarcely significant outcomes on the local level.

The reform movement also did not alter the situation of the peripheral political parties that were permitted to exist in Czechoslovakia after 1948. The existing noncommunist parties were politically insignificant organizations within the framework of the Czechoslovak state. The two Slovak parties (the Freedom party with 248 members and the Slovak Rebirth party with 364 members) and the two Czech parties (the People's party with some 21,000 members and the Socialist party with almost 11,000 members), although represented in the Parliament and in the government were totally compromised and fully controlled by the Communist party authorities. They did not play any role in political developments leading up to and during the Prague Spring. While these parties, like many other organizations in Czechoslovakia, underwent internal democratization, dismissed their Stalinist leaders, and made their newspapers more independent, they nevertheless avoided any confrontation or open conflict with the Communists during the entire period. Given their humiliating record of servility to Communists in the past, they were not in a position to become credible political forces. The only lasting result the liberalization had on them was an increase in their membership that was previously restricted and tightly controlled by the Communists.[60]

The discussion of electoral procedures stirred some controversy concerning the institution of the National Front, the party-controlled umbrella organization uniting all official mass organizations and responsible mainly for preparing and running national and local elections. Despite arguments that the preservation of the National Front posed a serious limitation to democracy, the majority of reformists sought instead to strengthen the institution with a certain plurality granted to its components. The Action Program explicitly rejected the idea of allowing the existence of political opposition and ruled out the formation of new political parties or revival of old parties. In sum, as Galia Golan argues, "There were signs that even party liberals were opposed to genuine competition for power. . . . Some, such as Goldstuecker, took classical Marxist approach to political parties, rejecting them as class phenomena; others such as Husak opposed a large opposition party 'in the present situation.' "[61] The majority position expressed during the May-June Plenum of the Central Committee accepted that the Front should respect its founding principles—to represent the common socialist program guaranteed by the leading role of the Communist party.

Coercive Forces of the Regime

Czechoslovakia had one of the largest and most extensive police forces in the Soviet bloc, and police supervised every aspect of life in the country. Shortly after 1948 the Ministry of the Interior became an enormous power apparatus that was designed to control everything and everyone. Its units consisted of the regular police forces, the State Secret Security Forces (STB), the Committee of Defense Security (OBZ), and the People's Militia under the direct control of the Communist party. At the height of its power during the 1950s, the budget of the Ministry of the Interior was about $1 billion higher than entire military spending of the country, which constituted more than 11 percent of the state budget.[62] In the 1960s, with growing political paralysis and calls for reforms, much public attention focused on the police. The security apparatus, which in 1967 had more than 20,000 full-time employees and 147,000 part-time agents, became increasingly viewed as an instrument of foreign domination, alien to traditional Czechoslovak values and the new vision of the "socialism with a human face" advocated by the party leaders. In 1968 Stalinist political terror and coercion were denounced by the new party leadership as being unacceptable and past abuses of power were condemned. The criticism and political attacks on the STB solidified its ranks. In Ulc's words: "Unlike the early 1950s, when one group of STB thugs was prepared to liquidate another, the late 1960s found the organization turned into a kind of mutual protection society. A belief that its very existence as an institution was in danger led the STB to arrange for quiet dismissals of its more compromised members, providing them with sinecures either as pensioned invalids, as nominal employees of research institutes, or better still, as instant diplomats who could be dispatched abroad."[63]

On the wave of the reform movement, the party leadership contemplated a substantial reduction in power of the Ministry of the Interior and the imposition of tight governmental control over the ministry activities. Also, the investigation of past abuses of power was intensified, and members of officially constituted investigative commissions were given access to party and police archives. Any actual attempt to reform police apparatus proved to be, however, very difficult. As in many other state institutions, where it was not possible to completely purge the old-guard Stalinists, they were only pushed aside and their power was restricted by the reform advocates. But as Condoleezza Rice states: "This policy of ignoring residual pro-Soviet and other old line elements backfired in the long run. [Stalinist functionaries] took it upon themselves to lobby full-time with the Soviets, filing alarmists reports about the state of affairs in Czechoslovakia."[64] During the reform period and military invasion they became an important internal network protecting Soviet control over the security apparatus. As it has often been emphasized, the STB forces were involved in the Warsaw Treaty military operation, cooperated with the invading forces, and supported the objectives of the Soviet invasion. It can be argued, therefore, that in contrast to Hungary the police and security forces remained relatively insulated and barely affected by the reform movement during the Prague Spring. They served as an important element of political stabilization and institutional continuity between the old Stalinist regime and the postinvasion regime.

Between 1948 and 1956, the Czechoslovak armed forces were reorganized and purged of their pro-Western and noncommunist officers, and the Communist party's control and indoctrination was firmly established. The army was integrated into the Soviet structure of command by an extensive network of Soviet military advisers. The Sovietization of the armed forces was assured by adoption of Soviet symbols, practices and organization. The officer corps was already 64.9 percent Communist by 1952, and 67.7 percent of officers came from worker or peasant backgrounds.[65] In the 1960s, more than 90 percent of the officers were members of the Communist party. During 1949, the rapid buildup of Czechoslovakia's armed forces was fueled by the Soviet expectation of the armed conflict with the West, and in 1951 the army numbered 250,000 men and consumed more than 11 percent of the state's budget. It is estimated that in the 1950s, Czechoslovakia had 1.5 million people in arms including police detachments, secret police forces, and paramilitary organizations.[66] This amounted to more than 10 percent of the population. After 1956 the modernization and professionalization of the army increased the level of education of the officer corps. At the same time there were signs of discontent and problems within the military establishment, but it was not until 1968 that the army established itself as a political actor.

Czechoslovakia shared with other East European regimes the characteristic features of civil-military relations common to all state-socialist regimes. They included the virtual isolation of the military personnel from the political processes, the careful separation of civilian and military functions and positions, as well as strong Soviet interference in the military affairs of the region. In fact, the semisovereign status of the armed forces provided the Soviet Union with an additional layer of control over dependent bloc countries. To a significant degree, these structural characteristics account for the surprisingly passive role of the army in both the Hungarian and Czechoslovak crises and swift reconsolidation of the armed forces after the invasion. In Czechoslovakia, Rice argues: "The constraints upon party-military interaction emanating from client military status were obvious in the period of liberalization. The military's participation in the liberalization was demanded by its domestic constituency, but the military stood isolated from the national revival by the character and nature of its ties to the Soviet Union. In an era of rapid and fundamental change, the military elite addressed the issues of reform with one eye firmly riveted upon Soviet reaction."[67] Thus, while the 1968 political crisis in Czechoslovakia did produce some internal ferment and conflicts within the armed forces, their cohesion was not threatened, the Soviet control was preserved, and their political role remained relatively marginal.

The defection of General Jan Sejna to the West and rumored preparations for a military coup to defend Novotny against the reformist forces had political implications for the military establishment. Sejna's revelations caused

great embarrassment and discredited many high-ranking conservative officers. As a result several senior commanders lost their positions. These demo-
tions, however, did not lead to any significant personnel turnover within the
military hierarchy, and antireformist, pro-Soviet officers remained in majority and control of the armed forces. These changes, nevertheless, led to a
surge of reformist ideas within the army advocated mostly by younger officers, and the military press underwent a small degree of liberalization. The
new ideas concerning internal reforms of the military and modification of
the role of the armed forces vis-à-vis the party and the state were quickly
sidetracked. As in many other institutions, the professional military elite
wished to frame the issues of military reform in terms of correcting the existing patterns of party control and involvement in the military affairs, but a
significant role for the Communist party in armed forces was not questioned. Despite the weakness of reform forces within the military, the debates and reform proposals circulating within the Czechoslovak armed
forces during the Prague Spring worried the Soviet leadership and the leaders of the Warsaw Pact. Beginning in July there was mounting pressure to
keep the Czechoslovak military in line and further isolate it from the reform
forces within the party. Soviet military commanders frequently visited the
Czechoslovak military leaders and units under the pretext of ongoing Warsaw Pact military exercises. Each time they conveyed a simple message. As
Marshall Koniev stated in his speech to military commanders, "the preservation of militant revolutionary traditions of the proletariat and the defense of
Soviet-Czechoslovak ties must be assured."[68] To undermine the influence of
reformists in the army, Soviet leaders attacked general Vaclav Prchlik, then
head of the Central Committee department in charge of national security
and a declared reformist. He became a direct object of Soviet wrath after
making several official statements criticizing the organization of the Warsaw
Pact and approaching Dubcek with a proposal to prepare military resistance
in the event of the Soviet invasion. In response to Soviet pressure, at the end
of July the Department he headed was abolished and Prchlik returned to his
duties in the army. After the invasion he was expelled and spent two years in
jail. At the same time, several high-ranking conservative officers were promoted to important positions, effectively blocking the influence of reformers
within the army.

   Overall during the Prague spring, the leadership of the Czechoslovak
armed forces was caught between two contradictory pressures: on the one
hand, the process of domestic liberalization caused internal ferment and
pushed for reforms; on the other hand, all reformists measures were constrained by the Soviet Union's hostility toward the reform movement and its
efforts to keep full control over its military partner. By the end of July, the
Soviet leadership demanded the dismissal of all reformist leaders in the
Czechoslovak army and the party leadership struggling to avert a direct Soviet intervention and anxious to negotiate the compromise, bowed to these
pressures. As a result, the period of quasi-liberalization within the Czecho-

slovak army ended several weeks before the invasion. It could be argued that the reassertion of Soviet control over the army's leadership was an important precondition for the bloodless character of the Soviet military intervention and success of demobilization policies that followed the invasion.

Auxiliary Institutions of the Party-State

During the spring of 1968, core institutions of the party-state experienced internal conflicts, factional struggles, and leadership changes. But they were in no danger of imminent collapse, and the regime did not experience institutional breakdown that could hamper the governing capacity of the party and the state. Change did come relatively fast, however, to the auxiliary institutions of the party-state, especially to professional associations and organizations that operated on the periphery of the party-state's institutional structure. Some of them, such as unions of writers and artists, were the first to claim autonomy and independence from the party and the state. In fact, long before the political space was opened during the spring of 1968, the writers and artists unions defied communist authorities and provided strongholds of opposition against the Stalinist establishment. In 1968 they became the spearhead of the reform movement. But although their members had high social visibility, their power and resources were not significant enough to threaten the stability of the Czechoslovak regime.[69]

In the early stages of the Prague Spring, professional and artistic unions devoted most of their time and energy to their own internal problems and conditions. By the end of April, however, the unions were able to establish horizontal ties by forming coordinating committees of creative unions in several cities. Despite the open political space and emerging organizational ties between the unions as well as their role as a promoter and defender of the reform process, they rarely formulated their own direct political demands during the pre-invasion period. While the organizations of the intelligentsia firmly sided with the reformist camp from the beginning, the internal changes were much slower in coming to such critical mass organizations as trade unions or the youth organization.

Czechoslovakia's Revolutionary Trade Union Movement (ROH) had over five million members assembled in twelve unions, organized along industry lines, and run by fifty-five hundred basic organizations.[70] The unions were not exclusively working-class organizations, and all employees, including the managers, within a given branch of industry belonged to the union. The trade union organization was highly centralized and bureaucratized and stuffed with officials in lifelong positions. In the second half of the 1960s, the hierarchical structure of the trade-union movement faced mounting pressure from below. Fears among the workers that the New Economic Model might cause unemployment and lower wages propelled the unions to push harder for worker interests, and already before 1968 union functionaries were supporting worker demands concerning the wage policy. While the centralized structure of the trade-union movement was criticized by the reformers in the early stages of political crisis, actual changes in the structure and practices of the unions came later. It took three months and a considerable push from the party's reformers before the presidium of the ROH responded to the new situation.

As Kusin points out: "The reformers were aware that for the sake of reforms the workers must be induced to rise against the two main sources of passivity, the politico-organizational and the professional. In political terms the two avenues that opened before them during the Prague Spring lay in reactivating trade unions and in introducing self-management."[71] Thus, the movement toward greater independence of individual unions vis-à-vis the Central Trade Union Council was encouraged, and unions were united in asking for more independence in both organizational and financial matters. Although the principle of organization along industry lines was never questioned, some big unions broke up. As a result, by the summer of 1968 Czechoslovakia had thirty-two unions instead of the original twelve. This situation, however, could hardly be regarded as a disintegration of trade-union organizational unity. Unified and centralized unions were still considered the only viable way of organizing employees, and there was no pressure coming from either rank-and-file or from unions' leadership to change the union structure. Moreover, the party leadership resisted calls for further fragmentation of the unions and insisted on the principle of one factory, one union—thereby prohibiting competition between the unions.

Although the basic organizational structure of the trade-union movement was not significantly altered, the federation of the unions into Czech and Slovak components were permitted, allowing more autonomy for individual union organizations and more emphasis on interest representation. These changes from above coupled with the pressure from below. In some enterprises there were attempts to oust old unions functionaries and elect new members to trade-union committees, often excluding party members from holding positions in the committees. Yet, the ousting of Communists and the replacement of existing trade-union committees were not significant features of the reform process. Thus, in spite of the debates over the role of the trade-union movement as well as proreform pronouncements at the national conference of the Czechoslovak Trade Unions in June 1968, the scope and character of changes that occurred within the trade union organization did not alter its fundamental role and place in the institutional design of the party-state. Unions remained almost fully controlled by the party authorities and followed party's policies vis-à-vis the workers.

The introduction of enterprise councils designed to involve employees in the decision-making process in Czechoslovak industry met with a similar fate. In contrast to 1956 Hungary, where workers' councils emerged as spontaneous organs of workers control, the Czechoslovak councils were not designed as worker councils in a strict sense of the word. The reformers envisioned enterprise councils as similar to the Western board of directors,

with freely elected employee representation but also with outside participants such as bank representatives, members of scientific institutions, and
representatives of the management. Given the extent, popular appeal, and
radical nature of the workers' council movement in the Hungarian Revolution, the failure of the council movement to became a major political actor
in Czechoslovakia is a further indication of the low level of popular mobilization and the highly controlled and imposed from above nature of the reforms. The government, after the debate concerning their organization, role,
and functions, announced the establishment of enterprise councils, to be
implemented in three stages starting on June 29. There was an immediate
response to this decision, and preparatory committees for the establishment
of enterprise councils were formed under the auspices of the enterprise
branches of the Communist party and the trade unions in a number of enterprises.[72] But in the end, the councils failed to open the floodgates for spontaneous workers' participation, and they played no major political role during
the crisis. The only organizations with openly political goals that were set up
in some factories were the press freedom committees. But again, as Kusin
emphasizes: "the committees cannot be regarded as more than a worthy initiative which, although promising spontaneous working class action and an
alliance between workers and the intelligentsia, did not in fact go very far.
No meaningful action by such committees is on record."[73]

Farmers, lacking their own interest representation under the Stalinist regime, used the opportunity created by the reform movement to press for the
formation of their own organization. In April preparatory committees for
the Farmers Union emerged spontaneously in the Czech lands with the aim
to create a unified organization for collective and private farmers. By the end
of May, committees were organized in 50 percent of districts and had registered some 150,000 members. Central collective farm management efforts
to control the movement and Slovak pressure for a separate organization led
to the formation of two unions: a Czech Union of Collective Farmers and a
Slovak Union of Private and Collective Farmers. In the process the collective
farm hierarchy succeeded in preventing the formation of an independent
organization. According to Wolfe Jancar: "The success of the farm leadership in organizing these unions was indicative of the lack of political restive-
ness among the farmers in 1968. . . . The two new unions filled the gap,
although they could not be considered autonomous interest groups."[74]
Overall, farmers representing 11.5 percent of the population were the least
active group during the Prague Spring.

In contrast to the relative calm in the factories and among farmers, young
people, especially students, formed a dynamic political force with vocal
presence on the political scene before and during the political crisis. In fact,
the only major party-state mass organization that collapsed during the
Prague Spring was the Czechoslovak Youth Union (CSM). For some time
before the Prague Spring, the union, designed to duplicate the organizational pattern of the Soviet Komsomol, was a large bureaucratic structure

employing an army of career organizers. However, it faced longstanding difficulty in attracting young people to its ranks.[75] Membership as a percentage of eligible young people decreased from 54 percent in 1961 to 32 percent in 1967. On the eve of its fifth and last congress in 1967, the membership of CSM totaled 983,000. Although there were more than a million trade unionists under age twenty-six, only two hundred thousand workers belonged to the youth organization.[76] In Kusin's words: "Corroded from within and increasingly pushed to the periphery of action and thought by the progress of reformist thinking, the Youth Union had become a sick man by 1967. If there was an organization with clay feet in Czechoslovakia, the CSM must have been considered a front runner for the title."[77]

Given the union's shaky internal situation, by the middle of February, when other state-sponsored organizations were still conducting business as usual, its Central Committee was torn apart by conflict. The impetus for change came from students who represented the core of dissatisfied groups within the organization. By the end of March, after ousting its former chairman and several other members of the Central Committee, the new leaders proposed the union be reorganized along representative and federative lines. But the union was so severely compromised that it had no support for its reorganization proposals—"no one in power in 1968 was willing to save the CSM in any form—centralized, federalized, confederalized, or otherwise," Ulc notes.[78] In spite of the party leadership's appeals for the continuation of the CSM's role as the monopolistic and unifying organization for the youth, the union dissolved and ten youth organizations emerged. At first, students set up independent student councils, which developed into separate student organizations. Then, the Pioneer organization proclaimed its independence from the union, and the Boy Scouts and Sokol movements, banished and prosecuted for twenty years, started to reorganize. The new youth organizations and especially the student movement had their finest hours during the invasion as the most committed group of defenders of the reform policies. It was students who organized the only significant protest actions in the post-invasion period and attempted to build coalitions with workers and intellectuals. The student organizations were also the first to be crushed after the fall of Dubcek in April 1969. The remaining youth movements that emerged as a result of the Prague Spring were merged again in 1970 into a unified youth organization, the Socialist Union of Youth.

Independent Organization of Society

While many official institutions of the party-state were arenas of intense political struggle and the reformist groups within the party were developing and strengthening their position during the Prague Spring, scarce few attempts were being made to develop independent organizations outside the official institutional channels. Moreover, it should be emphasized that the democratization efforts of 1968 were confined primarily to the Czech lands and that in Slovakia neither the Communist party nor the old noncommunist parties or new organizations showed any notable signs of revival. Despite the marginal character of efforts to form political organizations outside the party-state, the formation of independent groups was one of the main issues that the Soviet Union and its allies held against the Czechoslovak leadership.

In the Czech lands three attempts were made to organize independent political forces. All were met with strong party resistance and hardly got off the ground. In 1968 the former officials and members of the Social Democratic Party, which was forced to merge with the Communists in 1948, demanded restoration of their party. This demand met with strong opposition. Both the Communist party Central Committee and the National Front refused to consider the revival of the Social Democratic party on the grounds that it would endanger the unity of the workers' movement.[79] Accordingly, on May 24 the Ministry of the Interior announced that all organized activities for the establishment of a political party were illegal. Faced with such obstacles, the preparatory committee of the Social Democratic party never filed a request for official approval of its statutes. There were two new proto-parties that had emerged during the Prague Spring. A group of some 150 intellectuals, mainly from the Czechoslovak Academy of Sciences, established the Club of Committed Non-Communists (KAN), designed as a platform for citizens without party affiliation to engage in the political process.[80] To this purpose KAN announced its intention to present its own candidates for elective offices. KAN, however, was little more than an idea. It carefully restricted its membership, and when its Preparatory Committee applied for registration with the appropriate authority, it received no response within the thirty-day limit prescribed by law. Thus, KAN never acquired the legal status necessary for serious organizational and political activities. In July, under mounting pressure, KAN announced that it did not want to evolve into an independent political party and declared that it supported the progressive policies of the Communist party.

Another independent organization was the Klub 231, which formed as an interest group to unite all individuals who were former political prisoners during the Stalinist period.[81] The stated goal of the group was to press for rehabilitation and justice for the victims of political prosecution. Its potential membership was given as eighty thousand and included many influential politicians and intellectuals. But the Klub 231 shared the fate of the KAN in failing to gain legal status and official recognition. Along with KAN, it was accused during the Prague Spring of being a cover behind which the class enemy was organizing a political party hostile to the communists. In summary, as Ulc notes: "All three emerging political participants—the Social Democrats, KAN, and K-231—were occupied with the problem of whether or not to join the National Front. They had to assess, in other words, the realistic range of dissenting and even alternative political action. This dilemma was premature, however, because all three aspiring forces were ultimately prevented from entering the political arena."[82]

While in 1968 eighteen churches and religious societies legally operated in Czechoslovakia, in contrast to Poland during the 1970s and 1980s, neither religion nor the churches were of major significance to the reform movement.[83] Among all East European regimes (with the exception of Albania, where religion was formally banned), religious organizations in Czechoslovakia were the most repressed and tightly controlled. By the Prague Spring, the churches had barely recovered from two decades of Stalinist prosecution. They, and especially the Catholic church, which was the biggest denomination in the country, received some concessions from the new government. The Stalinist director of religious affairs in the Ministry of Culture was replaced, several bishops were permitted to take up unoccupied posts in dioceses, a number of priests was released from prison and rehabilitated, the reopening of monastic orders was promised, the circulation of religious press was significantly increased, and freedom was granted to religious gatherings and recruitment of new priests. Also the regime-controlled Peace Movement was abolished and in its place a new organization (Work of Council Renewal) was founded. Overall, however, as Kusin writes: "The reformers certainly did not have a religious outburst on their hands. Bishop Tomasek, Chief Rabbi Feder and other religious leaders were more than willing to co-operate without much ado. Tomasek [the head of the Catholic Church] endorsed socialism, which he did not see as necessarily atheistic."[84] As a result none of the churches, including the Catholic church, constituted a political force outside the official structures of the party-state. None acquired a position that would have forced the reformist leadership to actively include it in their plans. Churches were not able to provide alternative institutional bases or support networks for potential opponents of the regime. After the invasion even meager concessions granted by the party-state were swiftly withdrawn.

THE PRAGUE SPRING AND THE SOVIET EMPIRE

One cannot understand the internal political developments in Czechoslovakia without taking into account geopolitical factors and pressures. The crucial element shaping the political behavior of collective actors during the hot months of the Prague Spring was the pressure coming from the Kremlin and other East European leaders, concerned over the country's internal political developments. Mounting political pressure and military threats, eventually culminating in a military invasion, shaped the direction, demands, and action of collective actors in Czechoslovakia. It also opened the debate of what could have been done to avoid the Soviet military action and how any direct interference in Czechoslovakia's internal affair should have been handled.

The emergence of the reform movement in Czechoslovakia was viewed as a serious threat to the internal stability of other state-socialist regimes that, like Poland, were experiencing economic difficulties and growing internal dissent among intellectuals and students. The Polish and East European leaders, Wladyslaw Gomulka and Walter Ulbricht, were the most fervent critics of the reform movement and the earliest proponents of military intervention.[85] But, according to Valenta, from the beginning of 1968, "all senior Soviet decision makers were disturbed by the Czechoslovak reformism. They all agreed that the political situation in Czechoslovakia had to be stabilized, and they recognized that military force might be required. Thus, covert preparations for military action and possible intervention probably began as early as February—March 1968, in the early stages of the crisis. . . . In fact, the buildup had been accomplished by June–July, but the political decision to invade Czechoslovakia was taken only in August after much pulling and hauling among senior decisionmakers."[86] Similarly, Zdenek Suda argues that "the peaceful counterrevolution in the very core of the Czechoslovak system must have caused more panic in Moscow than the armed insurgency of Hungarian workers and soldiers in October 1956."[87] The seriousness of Soviet concerns was reflected by the fact that from January to August there were six meetings between Dubcek and Brezhnev and an almost constant series of consultations on different levels between the Kremlin and other East European party-states.

The first open warning that the Warsaw Pact regimes were displeased with the reform process was delivered to the Czechoslovak delegation at the summit meeting in Dresden on March 23, just one day after the ultimate fall of Novotny. From this time on, the media in neighboring countries mounted a smear campaign against Czechoslovakia and her new leaders, which intensified as the reform process went on. Major accusations focused on liberalization of the media, the alleged growth of antisocialist forces, and the alleged threat to the leading role of the party. The strong criticism of internal political developments was followed by direct military threats.[88] There are detailed analyses concerning the geopolitical context of the Prague Spring and reasons behind the military intervention.[89] Scholars emphasized the military and strategic considerations, the potential impact of the reform movement on internal security of the Soviet Union and other Warsaw pact regimes, and concerns about the effectiveness of control exercised by the Soviet party over the communist parties in the region. Some of these issues require further exploration, given new access to previously unavailable documents, yet because the primary focus of my analysis concerns the internal political developments, the geopolitical factors will be treated only in a cursory way in the remaining part of this chapter.

The decision to intervene militarily in Czechoslovakia was not taken without much reluctance and deliberation. Valenta argues: "Soviet attempts to negotiate with Dubcek regime during the various stages of the crisis were not a ruse designed to create a false sense of security while plans for the intervention were being perfected. . . . the Soviet leadership decided to intervene only after the long period of hesitation and vacillation."[90] In this context the question of what principles were violated that provoked the direct Soviet action is difficult to answer. While it has been argued that withdrawal from the Warsaw Pact inevitably invites military action (Hungary), Valenta clearly demonstrates that the final decision to use force was shaped by many factors and was a result of a complex process of consensus building between different segments of the bureaucratic elites and different forces both within the Soviet Union and within the Soviet bloc in general. It is certain, however, that the Extraordinary Party Congress scheduled to take place at the beginning of September established a deadline for the decision on using force. If the Czechoslovak reform movement was validated at the party congress and the members of the conservative faction were ousted from the new party's leadership, it would have been much more difficult for the Soviet leaders to control developments in the country.

The Soviet Union's reaction to the Prague Spring was the obvious indication of the dependent status of East European regimes validated ex post factum by the infamous Brezhnev doctrine. The military intervention in Czechoslovakia clearly showed that the broader military and strategic concerns as well as the preservation of Soviet control over ruling apparatuses in dependent countries and perpetuation of specific relations between the party-state and society were the foremost concerns of the Soviet leadership. Ken Jowitt concluded that "the Soviet invasions of Hungary in 1956 and Czechoslovakia in 1968 prove that the Soviet Union does not ideologically tolerate regime individualism and will destroy it when possible."[91] The Czechoslovak crisis also showed that the Soviet factor was an important element that placed crucial constraints on the country's political liberalization even in absence of direct Soviet military presence.[92]

Summing up the above analysis, it should be emphasized that the roots of the political crisis in Czechoslovakia in 1968 were similar to those that led to crisis in Hungary and Poland in 1956. The crisis of the Stalinist system altered the political opportunity structure and allowed the younger and more pragmatic segments of the ruling elites to challenge the Stalinist old guard. The outcomes of the crisis, however, presents the striking contrast to events in Hungary in 1956. While the Prague Spring lasted for several months, as compared to the fourteen-day explosion in Hungary, the institutional structures of the party-state experienced no significant decay or anarchization. Nor did any serious independent organizational bases emerge within society to challenge authority of the party-state. In short, political stability of the regime was never seriously threatened during the whole period of the Czechoslovak reform movement.

Despite the opening of the political space, popular mobilization never reached a significant level before the invasion. The often-emphasized participation explosion was restricted to Czech lands, to big cities, and mainly to party activists and intelligentsia. Moreover, political activism was confined to and channeled through the existing party-state's institutions and organizations. The underlying social and political grievances did not find independent expression and did not trigger the emergence of independent popular movements and organizations. Even existing ethnic grievances did not fuel mobilization from below or find organizational expression.[93] Kusin emphasizes: "It might seem, if one goes by the various general descriptions of the Prague Spring, that hundreds of new organizations queued up for legalization or simply set up shops without asking anybody. In fact only seventy applications for registration had been received by the Ministry by mid-June 1968, of which thirty-one submitted draft statues while the others merely wished to conduct tentative talks about procedural matters. At that time the Ministry [of Interior] had sanctioned only one organization, the Society for Human Rights."[94]

This underdevelopment of independent political society can be explained by several factors. First is the issues of time that should be seen as a major factor hampering the development of interest groups and new organizations. Although the political crisis in Czechoslovakia matured for several years, the time period during which the political space was open, allowing room for less constrained political activity, lasted barely four months. It stretched from the suspension of censorship in March to the Soviet invasion in August. During this politically tense period old and new organizations were grappling with complex theoretical and organizational issues and trying to respond to a multitude of internal and external pressures. According to Kusin, the one condition lacking in Czechoslovakia

> was sufficient time for open crystallisation of ideas. All the ingredients of a new system were there: an economic arrangement combining framework planning with the market, a theory of unconventional political pluralism . . . a nationality solution of the federative type, a participatory economic-cum-political system of workers' councils . . . a cultural policy protecting the public from the two *diktats* of power and commercialisation. Unfortunately, more time was needed to translate the generally prevailing opinions into workable majority solutions of a more detailed nature.[95]

Second, despite the explosion of theoretical and political debates touching almost every element of the economic and political system, the reform movement was plagued by the lack of a crystallized vision of political reforms, the absence of working consensus among the top leadership, and the inability to provide detailed policy options. Working toward the removal of Novotny was a task that unified the reformist groups within the party leadership together. Once this was accomplished, however, the policy choices became the subject of fierce debates and struggles. Moreover, "there is every reason to conclude that the reform regime in Czechoslovakia believed it could realize its program within the context of Communism and alliance with Moscow."[96] The reformers had no alternative political vision that would overcome the ambiguities of Marxist-Leninist political discourse and provide a consistent political platform for their program of political reform. In fact, the socialist identity of the reform movement was indisputable during the whole period of political crisis. As Golan writes: "A key element in the movement . . . was its party nature. While non-communists joined in, and in many instances non-communist and pre-communist measures were recommended and even introduced, none of this was within the specific context of anti-communism. It was not an attempt to undermine or overthrow the Communist Party but rather to find for it a proper, defensible, more genuinely and positively effective role in society."[97] Thus, the state-socialist state-idea was not fundamentally challenged and remained a powerful motivating force behind the reform movement. Rice is not far from the truth when she calls the political crisis in Czechoslovakia the "second Communist revolution."[98]

Third, popular mobilization was constrained, on the one hand, by the conscious strategy adopted by the reformist elites to keep the reform process under control and to confine it to official organizational channels and, on the other hand, by a conditioned habit of inaction engraved into the population by the Stalinist legacy. Ulc states: "The centrifugal trend toward differentiation and autonomy was marked by ideological uneasiness among the reformers, amateurishness among spokesmen for emerging special group interests, and by considerable disparity in their activism. In context of the energetic action of some of the professions, that of other groups, notably the peasantry, was timid and hesitant."[99] The Czechoslovak reform movement was brought to life and led by the party affiliated intelligentsia; workers' actions (what little of it there was) produced no push for change as happened several times in Poland. The absence of independent action from below hampered the formation of an alternative leadership and independent social networks. Even during the Prague Spring, as Kusin points out: "It may seem that working class action remained half-hearted, and the impression is probably correct in so far as organised and determined behavior, typical of workers' movements in comparable historical situations, is concerned. This can most likely by explained by the preceding twenty years of enforced inaction. By the same token, the organisational structure had as yet been little revivified and new leaders at factory level had as yet not emerged in adequate numbers."[100] Although both conservatives and reformists were trying very hard to sway workers to their side during the whole period of reform, be it for ideological or purely practical reasons,[101] it is wrong to assume that the objectives of the progressive wing of the Communist Party, more precisely, the party intelligentsia, have a wide backing among the masses. Moreover, political activism was unproportionally concentrated in only a few urban centers. Again, as Svitak emphasizes: the "basic political illusion is the assumption that the atmosphere of Prague, which is in fact exceptional, extends to the provincial towns and villages as well; . . . The political structure of power in the towns and villages has remained almost untouched by the recent changes."[102]

Finally, the hostile reaction of the Soviet Union and other communist leaders expressed by constant criticism, political threats, and military black-mail had a chilling effect on the Czechoslovak society and leadership and imposed a consciously self-limiting character on the political behavior of all collective actors in Czechoslovak society. In Hungary, external pressure had from the beginning the tangible shape of Soviet tanks on the streets of Budapest. In Czechoslovakia, however, this pressure was applied verbally, through a barrage of meetings and negotiations[103] reinforced by hostile mass media campaigns in the neighboring countries. The continuous dialectics of threats and negotiations created profound uncertainty among the collective actors in Czechoslovakia as to what actions would provoke more hostility and direct intervention. The result was that Czechoslovak leaders became overcautious in selecting their political actions and strategies. It should be stressed that some leaders, while realizing the real possibility of military action, were convinced that the internal situation in the country was far from being one that would provoke a military response.

As I will show in the next chapter, these peculiar characteristics of the political crisis in Czechoslovakia had a decisive role in shaping demobiliza-tion policies after the Soviet intervention as well as in restricting the capacity of the Czechoslovak society to resist them.

The End of Socialism with a Human Face

DURING THE NIGHT of August 20–21, 1968, the joint forces of the Warsaw Pact invaded Czechoslovakia. This action was the biggest military operation in Europe since the Second World War and, according to the official statement of the Soviet press agency TASS, was launched by request of "the Party and government leaders of the Czechoslovak Socialist Republic." However, the names of those who supposedly issued the invitation were never disclosed.[1] The invasion was preceded by several months of preparations, which had included joint maneuvers, extensive troop movements along Czechoslovakia's borders, and the establishment of communication and co-ordination centers. It was massive, swift, and well executed. The invading forces from the Soviet Union, East Germany, Poland, Bulgaria, and Hungary crossed Czechoslovakia's four borders at eighteen different points. Initially, the invading forces numbered around two hundred thousand men and more than sixty-three hundred tanks. Ultimately the occupying forces reached between four hundred thousand and five hundred thousand men.[2] The troops primary targeted airports, communication centers and important cities. They quickly secured important party and government buildings, public places of gathering, and all the country's strategic facilities.

In striking contrast to the invasion of Hungary in 1956, the invading troops did not attempt to assume full control of the country, take over the institutions of the party-state, and carry out the functions of maintaining public order. The troops did not occupy factories, did not prevent legitimate political organs from convening meetings, and more importantly, did not carry out mass arrests or impose martial law regulations. Only few top leaders of the Czechoslovak party were arrested during the outset of invasion. Given the scale of the military operation, it was remarkably bloodless, with few casualties on both sides. Some one hundred civilians and less than twenty soldiers of invading armies died during the invasion and subsequent occupation of the country. While the invading troops used tanks and guns to subdue the crowds, there were no armed clashes either with the Czechoslovak army or with any civilian groups.

In facing the invasion, Czechoslovakia's Communist leaders did not call upon the Czechoslovak People's Army to defend the country's sovereignty, and the army units stayed in their barracks, while foreign tanks rolled over the country. They also issued orders to the security organs and the militia to make sure that arms were secured and not available to "unauthorized" persons. Even though the Czechoslovak army (175,000 men) did not have the

necessary capacity to defend the country against the invasion from its Warsaw Pact neighbors, the party leadership unanimously opposed resistance to
the invasion based on political and ideological considerations rather than on
a rational assessment of military capabilities. But while no attempt at armed
resistance took place, shortly after the invasion the party Presidium, which
was in session at that time, adopted the proclamation criticizing the intervention. Yet at the same time, it urged all citizens not to resist the foreign
troops.[3] The proclamation was broadcast over the Czechoslovak radio the
next morning and soon became the founding document of the spontaneously emerging resistance movement.

While the military objectives of the invasion were successfully and swiftly
accomplished, its immediate political objectives were very unclear. In contrast to Hungary in 1956, the Soviet leadership installed no new revolutionary government to replace the arrested leaders of the CPCz at the outset of
the intervention. The students of the Soviet policy toward Czechoslovakia
have argued that, because of the unity of the Czechoslovak population in the
face of the intervention, its support for the leaders of the reform movement,
the weakness of the conservative faction inside the Czechoslovak party,
and the opposition of the country's president, Ludvik Svoboda, the Soviet
Union was not able to organize and impose a new pro-Soviet government
and was forced to start negotiations with the arrested leaders of the Czechoslovak party. It has been argued that the Kremlin did not make any serious
preparation to form a new government and, as Fred Eidlin states, "it seems
more appropriate to view the entry of Warsaw Pact forces as an escalation
of political pressure to the maximum, rather than as an attempt to change
Czechoslovakia's leaders."[4] Recently discovered evidence suggests, however, that the Soviet leaders relied on the assurances of the Bilak's faction
within the party's Presidium that they would oust Dubcek and other reformers and set up a provisional government after the intervention. They
claimed to have support of a majority in the party's Presidium, Central
Committee, and National Assembly. "The anti-reformists were unable to
make good on any of their promises, and the Soviet Union ended up having
to reinstate Dubcek's government for several months."[5]

The leaders of the Czechoslovak party—including Dubcek, Smrkovsky,
Cernik, Kriegel and Spacek—were arrested by the Soviet army with the help
of members of the Czechoslovak secret police in the building of the party's
Central Committee. They were taken out of Czechoslovakia in the early
morning on August 21. Eidlin explains the arrest, arguing that "considerable evidence suggests that the arrests of Dubcek and his reformist allies
were not part of the original intervention plan, but were organized and carried out in an *ad hoc* manner after these individuals failed to behave as
expected."[6] In spite of these arrests, the remaining leaders of the central
institutions of the party-state, including President Svoboda, were neither
dismissed nor detained. After the initial confusion and some rumored and

apparently failed attempts to form a new government dominated by pro-Soviet opponents of the reforms,[7] on August 23 the official Czechoslovak delegation headed by Svoboda, and including members of both conservative and centrist factions, arrived in Moscow for negotiations with the Soviets. On Svoboda's insistence, the arrested party leaders were brought to Moscow two days later and joined negotiations with the Soviet leaders. Michel Tatu believes that "the negotiation, which took place in Moscow on August 23–26 between the leaders of the two countries, was one of the most peculiar in modern times." And, he argues, "the apparent strategic predominance of the Kremlin could not conceal one major weakness: it had to deal with the very leaders it had labeled 'revisionists' and needed their help to get out of the political mess the intervention had produced."[8] It seems, however, that after all, the cooperation of Czechoslovak leaders was one of the basic foundations of the intervention plan and the negotiations in Moscow simply established this cooperation as a political reality after the unexpected (from the Soviet point of view) hesitation of the Czechoslovak leaders to endorse the "fraternal help" immediately upon the arrival of the foreign troops.

The negotiations, conducted in an atmosphere of intimidation and overpowering Soviet pressure, produced a fifteen-point protocol signed by members of the Czechoslovak delegation on August 26.[9] The Moscow Protocol constituted in fact total surrender to the Soviet demands. The protocol stipulated that the Fourteenth Party Congress, which had convened clandestinely in Prague the day after the invasion, was to be invalidated and that

> the CPCz representatives declared the necessity for the speedy implementation of a number of measures fostering the consolidation of socialism and a workers' government, with top priority to measures for controlling the communication media so that they serve the cause of socialism fully by preventing antisocialist statements on radio and television, putting an end to the activities of various organizations with antisocialist positions, and banning the activities of the anti-Marxist social democratic party.[10]

The protocol also assured party workers and officials who "struggled for the consolidation of socialist positions against antisocialist forces and for friendly relations with the USSR" that they would not be "dismissed from their posts or suffered reprisals." On August 27, after exhausting and humiliating talks, the Czechoslovak delegation returned to Prague and all its members assumed the party and state positions they had held before the invasion.

After their arrival in Prague, members of the delegation went on the radio to explain to the population the results of negotiations. They appealed to all citizens to accept the presence of the foreign troops and some temporary measures restricting freedom of speech and other liberties achieved during the Prague Spring. But the reformers also declared that they were not prepared to capitulate and still intended to follow the course outlined in the Action Program. The final passages of Dubcek's speech represented in a nutshell the new strategy of "reforms without extremes" and an attempt to save as much as possible of the reform policies. He said:

> A people, of which everybody is led by both reason and consciousness, will not go under. I beg all of you, my dear fellow citizens, Czechs and Slovaks, communists and members of other political parties, the National Front, I beg all workers, farmers, I beg intelligentsia, all our people—let us stay united, calm and, especially, cool-headed. Let us understand, that only in that, in our allegiance to socialism, in our honesty, in our endeavour and character the way forward can be found.[11]

Despite claims that the return of reform leaders to their positions in the party and the state was a sign of the weakness of the Soviet political strategy, it seem that in terms of stabilizing the situation and forestalling popular resistance it was the best solution the Soviet Union could hope for. It was not some despised Soviet stooges brought to power by foreign tanks but the trusted founders and animators of the reform movement who were asking for moderation and, in fact, for acceptance of the invasion. The population responded to Dubcek's pleas with self-restraint, and the resistance movement that spontaneously exploded during the first week of the invasion rapidly lost its momentum.[12] As Adam Roberts argues: "Perhaps the greater price the Czechoslovaks had to pay was the calling off the more overt, massive and striking manifestations of Czechoslovak opposition to the invasion. Certain quieter forms of opposition could and did continue . . . but almost everything was curtailed. The Czechoslovak people accepted this new situation with very great reluctance, but with a unanimity and discipline which was characteristic of them in crisis."[13]

In the next few days, in spite of some reluctance, the government, the Central Committee, and the National Assembly succumbed to the Soviet dictate and formally accepted the Moscow Protocol. Moreover, the party-state organs and their leaders proceeded to implement Soviet demands. Already on September 13 the National Assembly enacted several legislations that restricted the right to assembly, reintroduced censorship, and made new political parties and organizations illegal. Thus, while the reform proponents were able to secure their positions within the official institutions, which as it later turned out was only a temporary success, they had to pay for this Pyrrhic victory with their full and conscious cooperation in introducing the first round of demobilization policies. The concessions made in Moscow compelled the Czechoslovak leaders to invalidate the Extraordinary Party Congress, to shut down political clubs, to reimpose a degree of censorship on the mass media, to request that the Czechoslovak issue be dropped from the UN agenda, and to force the resignation of the few liberals who were absolutely unacceptable to the Kremlin. Frantisek Kriegel, the only leader who had not signed the Moscow Protocol, did not return to the party's Presidium. Cestmir Cisar left the party's Secretariat and Minister of

Interior Josef Pavel, Minister of Foreign Affairs Jiri Hajek, and Deputy Prime Minister Ota Sik resigned from their posts. Also the director of Czechoslovak television, Jiri Pelikan, and the director of radio broadcasting, Zdenek Hejzlar, were dismissed.[14] Yet despite these actions, Dubcek and many of his colleagues in the party leadership assumed that it would be possible to overcome the crisis and keep the substance of the reform process intact. They also hoped that "it would be possible for the progressive cadres to 'hibernate' in their functions, in order to be able to continue democratization when a suitable occasion arose in the future."[15] Very soon, however, it became clear that the Soviet Union had its own plans regarding the shape and composition of Czechoslovak political structures and elites.[16] Accordingly, the postinvasion period was to be one of successive crises culminating in the final removal of the reform leaders and the systematic destruction and reversal of their program and policies.

RESISTANCE TO MILITARY INVASION

While the Czechoslovak leaders negotiated in Moscow, popular resistance against the invasion was gaining momentum in Czechoslovakia. The protest against the invasion issued by the party's Presidium was followed by similar statements by the government, the Parliament, and the National Front. The National Assembly, the government, and the Prague city party committee met in continuous sessions during the first week of the invasion. The immediate occupation of editorial offices, radio and TV stations, and printing facilities did not silence the Czechoslovak mass media. Some newspapers and journals emerged underground, and clandestine radio stations coordinated the resistance movement. In a spontaneous expression of protest, thousands of people gathered on the street of the capital and other cities, blocking the movement of occupying troops. While the youth, students and workers played a leading role in protest actions during this week, they had done so spontaneously and as individuals not as members of organizations. This situation persisted for some months following the invasion, and even the disturbances and street protests on October 28 and November 7 in several cities were not formally organized or sponsored by any organization but by small groups of mainly secondary schools students. The most extraordinary event, however, which took place during the first days of invasion, was the convening of the Extraordinary Party Congress, which had been originally scheduled to open on September 9.

On August 22 the Prague city committee of the CPCz called the previously elected delegates to convene the Party Congress in a factory located in the Prague workers' district of Vysocany.[17] More than twelve hundred delegates disguised as workers managed to reach the secret meeting place undetected by the Soviet forces occupying Czechoslovakia's capital. The one-day Congress condemned the intervention and demanded an immediate withdrawal of the foreign troops and the release of arrested party leaders. The delegates elected a new Central Committee and party Presidium, which included all the known reformers, ousted all the members of the conservative faction, and unanimously chose Dubcek as the party's first secretary. The delegates appealed to all communist parties for support and called on the Czechoslovak workers to hold a one-hour long general strike, which was promptly carried out the next day. This unexpected show of party unity created a difficult political problem and made the issue of invalidating all resolutions adopted by the Congress the foremost Soviet demand during the negotiations in Moscow. As a result, the Moscow protocol rendered the Congress illegal and in violation of the party's status. Its resolutions were declared null and void.

The Czech party's defiant action was not repeated during the Slovak Party Congress scheduled on August 26. The Slovak Party Central Committee, which met on August 25, made few personnel changes and issued a statement condemning the invasion. Then, the Presidium decided to convene the congress on schedule. The delegates initially moved forward supporting the results of Vysocany Congress, and the Slovak Central Committee circulated an appeal condemning the invasion. But immediately upon his return from Moscow, Gustav Husak met with the delegates and convinced the Slovak party to reverse its decision to support the clandestine Prague meeting.[18] This was the first important sign and the first precedent of the strategy of splitting party-state organizations along national lines, which was consistently used during the entire demobilization process. In the postinvasion period, the Slovak party and other institutions became the stronghold of dogmatic forces and a tool for shifting the balance of power within party-state's institutions in favor of the dogmatic, pro-Soviet forces.

Although on August 21 Prague Radio and Radio of Czechoslovakia were trying to discourage people from holding demonstrations against the invasion, the first days were marked by widespread nonviolent resistance coordinated by a network of underground radio stations.[19] Protest strategies included total noncooperation with invading forces, attempts to confuse the troops by taking down road and street signs, peaceful demonstrations during which Czech citizens tried to engage the soldiers in political discussions, graffiti and poster campaigns protesting the invasion, and synchronized symbolic protest actions announced at specific times by the radio. At the same time, all official organizations, institutions and factories issued an avalanche of resolutions, letters, appeals, and protests denouncing the invasion, which were printed as leaflets or reproduced in mimeographed issues of newspapers.[20] Galia Golan writes, "there probably was not a journal, paper, organization or group that did not issue words of encouragement to the public, support for the legitimate leaders of the country, and condemnation of invasion."[21] The resolution campaign begun by official institutions and organizations, rapidly developed into a major tactic of the resistant movement; "this flood of messages and constant repetition of the themes they contained created an impression of absolute unity and solidarity of the population, its leaders, and institutions. It is not surprising that news of the invasion immediately triggered such responses throughout the country. This pattern of response to crisis had been well-rehearsed and had become almost habitual during the months preceding the invasion."[22]

Despite its intensity and extent, the collective protest and resistance during the first week after the invasion was the result of the highly spontaneous and rapid popular mobilization. It did not originate from any organized oppositional networks, did not lead to the formation of independent opposition organization and movements, and did not produce well-known leaders and spokesmen. Adam Roberts writes: "Even the most technically accomplished operations of the week following the invasion . . . were all organized on the largely *ad hoc* basis. There is no evidence of a 'secret plan', and a great deal of evidence of confusion, chaos, and hasty improvisation."[23] Moreover, there was a striking absence of prolonged and decisive protest actions such as occupation strikes in factories or nationwide protests. After the successful one-hour general strike called by the clandestine party congress, the strike weapon was abandoned and no longer figured as an element of the resistance strategy. The highly spontaneous street demonstrations that dominated repertoire of collective protest indicated the absence of organizational foundations and resources for sustained protest actions. But, nevertheless, the period up to the fall of Dubcek in April 1969 was characterized by acute political conflict and protest as well as marked by several serious crises.

The short and spontaneous collective protests, coupled with attempts to use official channels to articulate demands and express disagreements concerning the country's political situation decreased in frequency during months following the invasion. The major street demonstrations dispersed by the police took place on October 28 (Czechoslovakia's national holiday) in Prague, October 30 in Bratislava, and November 7 (the anniversary of the October Revolution) and November 11 in Prague. The impatiently awaited resolution of the Party's plenum published on November 19, was seen as a sign of retreat from the reforms. Although the plenum results were considered by the reform leaders to be a compromise, in fact they meant their serious defeat.[24] This aggravated the political situation and spurred another series of protests, open letters, and resolutions, as well as student strikes.[25] The exclusion of Smrkovsky from the delegation of Czechoslovak leaders attending meeting in Kiev in December, sparked another round of protests aimed at defending Smrkovsky, and by extension other reformist leaders. This time the opposition's demands were reinforced by threats of strikes issued by the Czech Metal Workers Union and the Czech Student Union. But the Smrkovsky affair was skillfully defused by the party leadership, and despite the fact that on Husak's insistence Smrkovsky was replaced as the chairman of the Federal Assembly by a Slovak, Peter Colotka, the strikes never materialized.

Political tensions were heightened even further by the popular reaction to self-immolation of twenty-one-year-old history student Jan Palach on January 16, 1969. He became the national martyr and symbol of resistance, and his death triggered student demonstrations in Prague, Brno, Bratislava, and Olomouc forcing the federal government to take special security measures on January 24 in order to preserve peace and public order. On January 25 thousands of people took part in the funeral procession and ceremonies in Prague, while memorial services were held in other parts of the country as well.

The fate of remaining leaders of the Prague Spring was sealed when street demonstrations and disturbances broke out on March 28 after the Czechoslovak ice-hockey team's victory over the Soviet Union and ended with people ransacking Soviet offices and installations in Prague and several other locations. According to official reports, sixty-five policemen were wounded and thirty-nine demonstrators arrested in Prague alone. The demonstrations provided the Soviets with the argument that Dubcek's leadership had failed to enforce the provisions of the Moscow Protocol. This set the stage for the final victory of the pro-Soviet, dogmatic forces. The anti-Soviet demonstrations in March 1969 were the last major collective protests of the postinvasion period and led directly to the reconstitution of the Czechoslovak leadership and the removal of reformist leaders from the party-state's highest positions. It also indicated the progressing erosion of the resistance movement and the success of initial demobilization strategies. According to Golan, this last crisis

> had something artificial about it. The demonstrations after the ice-hockey games had almost none of the potential dangers characteristic of several crises in the post-invasion period. The populace was not organized into active groups around specific demands with threats of greater action if satisfaction were not forthcoming. Neither the unions nor intellectuals nor students nor individual factories or organizations brought pressures to bear on, they had at the time of the Smrkovsky affair or even in reaction to Jan Palach's death. Indeed all of these usual channels of pressure acquiesced to the regime's demand for condemnation of vandalism. . . . At the very least one can say that these still relatively powerful groups were caught unprepared for the spontaneous demonstration.[26]

The last spontaneous protest of the postinvasion period was held during the week of the first anniversary of the invasion. Despite preparations by the regime to prevent any unauthorized action and warnings against possible provocations of the security forces, the demonstrations took place in thirty-one cities, with the most intensive clashes with police occurring in Prague and Brno.[27] The police decisively crushed the demonstrations and the federal Ministry of Interior reported that 3,690 persons were detained. On August 22, emergency repressive legislation was passed to "protect and strengthen public order." The following day the mass media broadcast official thanks to the police, army, and militia for their success in resolving a "complicated situation." Subsequently, some of these emergency regulations were enacted as elements of a new criminal code and the labor code, strengthening the repressive capabilities of the legal system.[28] A year later, the second anniversary of the Soviet occupation passed without incident.

Why did spontaneous resistance in Czechoslovakia not evolve into any organized underground movement but quickly subside after an initial peak? It has often been arued that the reasons lie in the traditional political culture of the country, which gave moral sanction only to "individual and concealed non-compliance" in the face of foreign occupation, as well in the historical experiences of 1938 and 1948, when Czechoslovakia was abandoned by the Western countries.[29] I will argue, however, that the absence of a significant organized resistance movement and the relatively rapid decline of protest actions can be explained, first of all, by the low level of popular mobilization before the invasion, the failure to establish organizational foundations of independent political society, and the absence of independent allies who could support fledgling opposition movements.

As Eidlin argues: "The occupation came as a surprise and was a *fait accompli* by the time people awakened. Resistance had not been prepared for and those individuals who possessed the personal authority to lead the population into organized resistance had been almost completely isolated by morning on 21 August."[30] The absence of resources or organizational networks available to the resistance movement was additionally reinforced by the demobilizing effect of the reinstatement of reform leaders following the signing of the Moscow Protocol. While the rudimentary alliances between the workers, students, and intellectuals began to gradually emerge, the continued presence of "heroes" of the reform movement at the top of party's and state's apparatus created a precarious relationship between the state and society. On the one hand, it effectively restricted open defiance and organized resistance against the domestic authorities who, in spite of the presence of occupying troops, were in charge of maintaining internal law and order. Additionally, in hundreds of resolutions, workers and students pledged support for the party leaders and acceptance of all their decisions[31] and, as public opinion surveys showed, the invasion paradoxically produced the very high approval ratings for the party's leaders among the population.[32] In short, reformist members of the party's leadership became symbols of national solidarity against the foreign intervention.

On the other hand, this wide support for the reform leaders as well as for the ideas contained in the Action Program prevented the post-invasion popular mobilization from developing into a powerful opposition movement and blocked the emergence of any alternative political discourse. All resolutions expressed only general support for the post–January 1968 policies, and as Ivan Svitak emphasizes, "ideological illusions, carefully fostered by the ruling ideology, were a real force which prevented the two basic social groups [workers and intellectuals] from coming to an understanding"[33] necessary for the preservation of an effective opposition movement. Therefore, as Skilling argues:

> For eight months after the occupation a paradoxical situation, full of strange contradictions, prevailed. Although the context of politics had been fundamentally changed by the occupation, the two sets of opposing forces which had been present from January to August continued to operate. . . . The Dubcek leadership again found itself between two mutually opposed pressures, internal, and external. On the one hand, Moscow, in spite of the enormous shift of balance of power in its favor, was unable to impose its will fully on occupied Prague. On the other hand, the Prague regime was unable to win complete support for its policy of compromise from the Czech and Slovak people.[34]

The fact that the Czechoslovak resistance had a sanctioned and official character and was carried out through official channels and organizations initially strengthened the noncooperation movement. In the long run, however, the lack of independent organizational bases or alternative oppositional discourse and a political platform independent of the state significantly hampered the capacity of the resistance movement to survive. This situation remains in striking contrast to both the Hungarian revolution and its aftermath and to the political crisis in Poland in the 1980s.

The correlation between political mobilization and the intensity and extent of collective protest following the invasion is further confirmed by the significant difference in the political situation between Czech and Slovak lands. As I mentioned before, the center of the proreform activities and the most active political groups in the reform movement were confined mainly to the Czech lands and major urban centers. In Slovakia, despite popular approval for the reforms, the reform movement itself both within the party and within official organizations never seriously got off the ground. Slovak officials in general were less interested in reform and more in federalization than the Czechs. As George Klein argues: "Many Slovak communists . . . participated in the reform movement for narrow nationalists reasons, with the specific aim of establishing parity between Slovaks and Czechs within the state. [They] did not share the liberal leanings of their Czech counterparts. Once their demands for autonomy had been fulfilled, they broke the solid front of the reform movement by advocating a return to greater orthodoxy."[35] This different attitude to the reforms was reflected in the developments that occurred after the invasion. Slovakia remained generally quiet during the whole period of demobilization; collective protests and popular resistance as well as repression and purges affected the Czech lands to a much greater extent. The organizations of workers, students, and intellectuals in Slovakia quickly accepted the reality of the invasion, and Slovakia's party organs became the stronghold of conservative and "realist" forces within the party. Clearly the nationality question played into hands of antireformist forces. The lack of popular mobilization during the Prague Spring was reinforced in Slovakia by the fact that, as Golan points out, "many of the post-invasion issues were easily side-tracked by the conservatives (and the realists) along national lines."[36]

The Collapse of the Reform Movement

The return of top Czechoslovak leadership from Moscow on August 27 has often been considered a turning point in postinvasion political developments. It should be noted, however, that at the end of the first week of the military intervention, the situation in Czechoslovakia was already highly stabilized, spontaneous popular mobilization was tempered, and official party-state institutions exercised fairly extensive control across the country. By the second day of the occupation, in response to appeals and resolutions of Czechoslovak authorities broadcast by the radio, workers resumed their work in factories, and the production was not far from a normal level. Simultaneously transportation was restored and most of the stores and services were open. On August 26, the Ministry of Education announced that the school year would begin as scheduled on September 2. Moreover, after the return of Czechoslovak leaders from Moscow, the occupying troops gradually withdrew from communication and media facilities, evacuated public buildings, and moved away from urban centers. Soon after, the radio, television and press started to function in an almost normal way. Thus, in a very short time the life in the country seemed quite normal despite the presence of half a million foreign troops. Eidlin is right when he argues that

> "normalization" began, not after the return from Moscow of the top Czechoslovak leadership, but already on the first day of the occupation. On the one hand, the occupation forces settled in and their presence became an established fact. On the other hand, Czechoslovakia's institutions quickly reconstituted themselves and proceeded to work toward the normalization of life in the country, despite various impediments created by the occupation. By the time of the return of the top leadership from Moscow, much of the country was already normalized.[37]

This situation seemed to be highly paradoxical given the overwhelming popular condemnation of the invasion expressed even by many party and state officials known as opponents of post-January reform policies. As I have already stressed, one factor that may account for such a turn of events was a low level of popular mobilization before the intervention and the absence of independent centers of power as well as organizational foundations for autonomous political action. Moreover, the intervention did not paralyze Czechoslovakia's official institutions and did not precipitate either their collapse or any significant weakening of their position. Quite the opposite, lacking independent centers of authority people rallied around official institutions, expressed their confidence and pledged unreserved support for their leaders. Using their strong position, the party-state leaders and institutions immediately called for order and restraint in protest actions. They appealed to citizens not to use strikes as a means of protests because they could damage the country's economy. They warned that street protests could be used as an excuse for coercive responses by the occupying forces and might give some credence to Soviet claims about counterrevolutionary activities in Czechoslovakia. Thus, the commitment to the maintenance of calm and order was one of the major objectives of both the official Czechoslovak authorities and the spontaneous resistance movement. As Eidlin concludes:

> A major strand of resistance consisted of concerted, cooperative efforts of the population, its institutions, and leaders to maintain and/or restore normal conditions of life . . . Such efforts at normalization began immediately, on the first day of the occupation, as institutions began to mobilize and settle into more or less routine patterns. As shock and confusion evoked by the invasion subsided, life throughout the country progressively returned to normal, despite the tension, anxiety, and excitement in the air while negotiations dragged on in Moscow. By the time the country's highest leaders returned to Prague, normalization had already been realized to a significant extent.[38]

While the resistance movement was highly constrained, the response of the Czechoslovak leadership to the intervention was even more subdued. It amounted to capitulation, accompanied by mild protests, and reflected considerable indecision about what to do. Very soon, however, almost all reform leaders within the party became, willingly or unwillingly, effective agents of demobilization policies, and they actively assisted in dismantling their own reform programs as well as political and organizational bases of support for reform policies. According to Renner, "time after time, making concessions to the Kremlin dominated the political behavior in Prague, in spite of all the sentiments and desires of the overwhelming majority of the population."[39]

Shortly after the return of the top leadership from Moscow, the government introduced a series of measures restricting freedom of speech and imposing control over the media. On August 30, the government decree established the Committee for Press and Information, with offices in Prague and Bratislava designed as an organizational foundation for the reintroduction of censorship. The next day, the Central Committee plenum carried out and announced a series of measures aimed to fulfill various obligations contained in the Moscow Protocol. Among others some personal changes were announced, and Dubcek declared that the Fourteenth Extraordinary Party Congress could not be valid due to inadequate Slovak representation. Announced restrictive measures were then quickly enacted by the National Assembly on September 13, when it passed the National Front bill and a bill on public order, which effectively obstructed the right of assembly and reintroduced censorship through a bill presented as a temporary measure pending the promised new Press Law. After enacting a new restrictive legal framework for domestic politics, which, in fact, abolished all achievements of the

Prague Spring and blocked all unofficial expressions of protest and opposition, the question of the presence of foreign troops was resolved by giving them a legitimate status. After negotiations in Moscow at the beginning of October, both governments signed the treaty in Prague on October 16 stipulating the temporary stationing of Soviet troops on Czechoslovakia's territory. The National Assembly ratified the treaty a few days later with only 4 votes against.

At the same time, however, reformers tried to safeguard their dominant position in the party leadership. The party Presidium was enlarged to twenty-one from eleven members in the process strengthening significantly the reformist bloc. But as Golan argues: "Despite the majority achieved by the reformers, a serious split was beginning to take shape within the reformers' ranks. As distinct from the 'conservatives' such as Piller, Barbirek, and Bilak, and from liberal reformers such as Dubcek, Smrkovsky, Simon, and Spacek, a third centrist group around Husak emerged, known as the 'realists' because of their pragmatic more compromising attitude to the 'harsh realities' of the country's position."[40] The centrist group with its bases of political support mainly in Slovakia dominated the party and state leadership in months following the invasion, slowly departing from post-January reform projects and pushing aside more uncompromising and liberal members of the Czechoslovak leadership. As a result, as Kusin observes: "the post-invasion power centre became much more of a battleground than it was previously. At the same time Moscow had propelled itself back into the position of a recognised supreme arbiter and day-to-day supervisor of Czechoslovak politics, a place from which it was being pushed out in the reformist period."[41] Already the plenary session of the Central Committee in November effectively restricted the influence of Dubcek's group with the creation of the Executive Committee of the party Presidium consisting of eight members with only Dubcek and Smrkovsky representing a liberal position. Thus, from November onward the power of the reformers rapidly declined. Smrkovsky and Dubcek were outnumbered and increasingly isolated by the "realists" in the Executive Committee. Dubcek had to rely on the cooperation of Husak and Lubomir Strougal, who were not friends of the reform movement. In this situation a continuation of the "reforms without extremes," which Dubcek desperately advocated, was a completely unrealistic goal.

With each successive Central Committee meeting, reformers were more effectively isolated and Czechoslovakia's leaders departed further from post-January policies and presented more critical assessment of the political situation during the spring of 1968. This clearly reflected the constant Soviet pressure to terminate all surviving policies and political practices that emerged during the Prague Spring. The Soviet supervision of the beginning of the demobilization process was directed by Soviet Deputy Foreign Minister Victor Kuznetsov, who was dispatched to Prague in the first week of

September. Also, as Kusin points out, "a permanent line of liaison between Czechoslovak authorities and the foreign troops structure of command was established at all levels, giving the Soviet military easy access to the Czechoslovak officials and virtually the right to discuss all matters with them, especially those concerning law and order."[42] Similarly, all Central Committee meetings and important decisions were preceded by consultations with the Soviet leadership and party, and government officials were frequently summoned to Moscow to receive instructions and to submit progress reports.[43] Thus, all important decisions involved extensivey consultation with the Soviet leaders, who undoubtedly exerted heavy pressure to curtail all remaining signs of defiance both on the side of Czechoslovakia's leadership and on the side of the population. Tigrid describes this "occupation diplomacy" in the following way: the official Soviet overseers of the demobilization policies

> paid visits to top Party and government leaders, stressing Soviet arguments in favour of speedy "normalization", and later voicing discontent at the fact that the process was restricted and slow. At the same time, these emissaries and Soviet generals paid visits described as friendly and camaradely to the hardcore conservatives, even if the latter's actual functions in the Party were minor. These visits were meant as public encouragement to these men who were despised by the people and distrusted in the Party, a sign of Moscow's confidence in them. Soviet generals, in their turn, negotiated directly with pro-Soviet officers who held no major posts. At times of crisis, as in January or in April 1969, Soviet emissaries delivered ultimatum-like demands to Dubcek, Cernik and Svoboda, bringing to their notice (and that of the public at large) in the crudest and rudest terms who was the true master of the country.[44]

Moreover, the changes in the composition of Czechoslovak delegations to successive meetings clearly indicated that reformers were being pushed aside and that Dubcek's position and role were gradually being undermined by Gustav Husak, representing the realist faction.

The gradual surrender to Soviet demands and the demobilizing role of Czechoslovak leaders was perfectly illustrated by the Smrkovsky affair. Smrkovsky, the symbol of the reform movement, was excluded from the Czechoslovak delegation meeting the Soviet leaders in Kiev at the beginning of December–clearly suggesting that his continued role in the country's top leadership was in question. The rumors about imminent demotion of Smrkovsky from all his functions caused widespread popular protest. There was a general demand for Smrkovsky to be made chairman of the new Federal Assembly. Smrkovsky's plight mobilized various forces and organizations in defense of liberal leaders gradually loosing their influence in the party leadership. A flood of protests and resolutions denouncing any attempts to remove reform leaders came from universities, public institutions, organizations, and factories. They were reinforced by strike threats issued by the powerful Metal Workers Union and the Union of Students. This was by far the most coordinated and widespread political action after the intervention. But in a characteristic manner, the reform leaders did not use this popular support and mobilization to their advantage. Instead, they vigorously attempted to defuse the tensions and prevent any collective action on their behave. On January 5, Smrkovsky went on television appealling for calm and assuring the public that "'no obligations were taken anywhere' regarding his continuation in office, and literally begging the public to reconsider the threats to strike in view of the consequences such action might bear 'for state, its internal stability, and its international relations'."[45] Shortly after, Dubcek, Cernik, and Smrkovsky met with the students, trying to dissuade them from any action. They also sent a letter to the Metal Workers Union asking them to call off their strike threat. This desperate action of appeals and persuasion was successful in paralyzing a potentially powerful protest movement and a similar strategy was repeated once more in the eve of Jan Palach's funeral in Prague when Dubcek made a radio appeal for calm and order.

As a result of this demobilization strategy carried on by the popular reform leaders, their temporary presence in leadership positions was assured (Smrkovsky was made a deputy chairman as well as chairman of the new People's Chamber of the Assembly) but in the long run such a strategy of undercutting their bases of political support was self-destructive. With every action aimed at diffusion of political tensions and prevention of collective protests, the position of reform leaders further eroded. Moreover, the failure of reform leaders to abandon the traditional Marxist political discourse with its class struggle rhetoric contributed to a gradual redefinition of the situation in the country and vilification of their own reform efforts. As Tigrid emphasizes:

> By resorting to dogmatic language Alexander Dubcek inadvertently played his opponents' game. And once again, there was a tragic logic in the process; what the men of the Prague Spring (as Marxists) had admitted, soon after the invasion to have been 'misunderstandings', 'an under-estimation of the situation', 'underrating the strength of non-socialist forces', 'negligence of the consequences of internal reforms in international relations'—all these notions were gradually but inevitably transformed into 'anti-socialism', 'rightist opportunist deviation', and finally into 'counter-revolution' and treason.[46]

After January 1969 both the power of reformers within Czechoslovakia's leadership and the oppositional potentials of the Czechoslovak society were broken. The party leadership now dominated by the realists started to realize a consistent effort to weaken various groups and organizations that preserved their autonomy and emerged as powerful advocates for the continuation of the reform process after the invasion. The regime began to crack down and exploit the factional splits in various organizations especially those between Czechs and Slovaks. But the opportunity for decisive action came in the aftermath of street disturbances after the Czechoslovak ice-hockey victory over the Soviet Union. For the conservative elements in the party, the situation created by the disturbances was favorable because "the population was not organized for crisis, ready to strike in defence of its reform heroes as it had been upon occasions in the preceding months. For the Russians, too, the situation was convenient, for finally they had an open and even violent defiance of the Soviet Union."[47] The crisis was followed by the flurry of Soviet official visits, confidential talks and negotiations, and new Warsaw Pact military maneuvers were announced. This time it was clear that the major personnel change was pending.

In his speech in the Slovak city of Nitra on April 11, 1969, Gustav Husak, the representative of realist forces, assessed the political situation in the country: "the anti-socialist and various opportunist forces strove to crush and destroy the political power of the working people in this state, and loosen the leading role of the Communist Party, the state power and the state apparatus, to wreck . . . to divide." On April 17, Husak was elected by the Central Committee with the recommendation of the party's Presidium to replace Dubcek as a first secretary of the Czechoslovak Communist party. The number of members in the party Presidium was again reduced to eleven, and this time the reformers, including Smrkovsky, Simon, and Spacek, lost their seats in the most powerful organ of the party-state. To secure the take-over of power by the dogmatic faction, on the eve of the Central Committee plenum there was a demonstration of the police strength and devotion to the defense of socialism throughout the country. In Czech lands 894 people were detained, and in Slovakia 2,300 persons were searched and 135 of them detained. This action was the most extensive police operation during the entire period of demobilization in Czechoslovakia. With the successful demobilization of the Czechoslovak society already accomplished and with the defeat (to a large degree self-inflicted) of the reformist wing within the party leadership, the process of erasing the legacy of the reform movement began in full swing. The role of reformers, who contributed intentionally or unintentionally so greatly to forestalling the development of political oppo-sition to the occupation, was fulfilled. As Tigrid put it: "The curtain was falling on the Prague Spring, and its unwilling hero, Alexander Dubcek, still smiling his slightly embarrassed but now saddened smile, the sentimental Marxist who had wanted to give socialism distinctly humane features, could be seen three days after his fall clapping in the good old Stalinist style, at a celebration of the Ninety-ninth Anniversary of Lenin. 'Long live the Soviet Union', 'Long live the Communist Party of the Soviet Union', shouted several hundred fanatics brought in by buses and trucks to the congress hall in Prague. It seemed that, once or twice, Alexander Dubcek attempted to join the chorus. It was a terrifying sight. A few days later he was 'elected' chairman of the Federal Assembly with a sad man by the name of Josef Smrkovsky as his deputy."[48]

STRATEGIES OF NEO-STALINIST CONSOLIDATION

The final defeat of the reformist faction within the top leadership of the Czechoslovak Communist party in April 1969 initiated a new, highly repressive stage of the demobilization process. By that time, Czechoslovak society was effectively demobilized, organized opposition was non-existent, and conditions for concerted collective protest were absent. The supporters of reforms in official institutions and organizations were increasingly isolated and outmaneuvered by the supporters of the invasion and by realists who were quick to seize the opportunity. The potential for a direct challenge to the party-state's position and authority either from outside or inside official institutions was defused. The next task for the new Soviet-backed leadership, however, was to reassert its undivided control over these institutions, which had acquired a degree of autonomy during the spring or after the invasion and to rebuild those elements of political and social organization weakened during the crisis. To this purpose, a wholesale campaign of dismissals of all suspected reform sympathizers began in what became the most extensive internal purge in the history of East European state-socialist regimes. As Milan Simecka emphasizes:

> It was not the tanks and infantry of the fraternal armies that crushed the orderly expression of the Czechoslovak people's aspiration to a democratic way of life, but the bureaucrats in charge of personal files at every level, who wielded the power to issue dismissal notices, reorganize or redeploy the work-force, provide damning character references and use other ingenious methods, thereby avoiding bloodshed, fuss, trials and mass protests.[49]

Already by the spring of 1970 almost nothing was left of the reform program, although Husak continued to pay lip service to the post-January policy. Economic reforms were almost dead and the necessity of central planning and state control was reasserted. The enterprise councils were dissolved. Discipline was restored in the Communist party and dissenters were expelled. The purge of reform sympathizers taking place in all institutions and on all levels of the party-state organization was supplemented by a reversal of policies and laws introduced during the Prague Spring. Debates on already advanced projects of political and economic reforms, for example federalization of the Communist party, were discontinued. The new laws that aimed to strengthen the party-state's repressive capacity and control over crucial aspects of social and political life were introduced. Freedom of expression was completely curbed, and no independent organs of opinion were left. The press, radio, and television were fully controlled and used to disseminate the regime's propaganda and conduct vicious attacks against reformist ideas and individual persons. In the process of dismantling real and potential basis for opposition and dissent, some organizations that had become dominated by the reformers were dismantled or suspended, their leadership was exchanged, and their subordination to new party authorities was insured. Organizations of intellectuals, especially the Academy of Sciences, the universities, and cultural institutions, were subjected to ever closer party and state control. However, "the Party leadership realized the magnitude of . . . passive resistance and in 1970 offered a compromise modus vivendi by granting political legitimacy to nonparticipation. Echoing an earlier maxim of the Hungarian leader Janos Kadar, 'the who is not against us, is with us,' Husak was somewhat less generous declaring that 'the who is not against us is our potential ally."[50] The new leaders also echoed Kadar's policy of fighting on two fronts: against liberal, reformist forces and against neo-Stalinists sectarians. Yet, despite all attempts to create an image of centrist position in opposition to either "Novotny bureaucracy" or to "Dubcek's anarchy," Husak's regime remained highly orthodox and followed policies of repression directed exclusively against the former reformers.

The destruction of the reform movement forces and their program was implemented gradually and accomplished through routine institutional mechanisms. Demotion from the position of authority, followed by the expulsion from the party and loss of employment rather than arrests and political trials formed the core of the repressive strategy. As in Hungary after 1956, the stabilization of the Communist party become the most urgent task.

The Purge and Consolidation of the Communist Party

The eight months of Dubcek's postinvasion tenure saw not only the termination of the party's reform program but also the destruction of the reformist bloc, which had achieved a majority after the invasion through the enlargement of the party Presidium and Central Committee. The end of the reforms within the party and the defeat of reformers meant in fact the end of the Czechoslovak experiment with reforming state socialism. As Kusin points out:

> It is impossible to overemphasize the significance of the virtual ending of reforms in the party. They had been conceived, rightly or wrongly, as the alpha and omega of the reform process. A democratised party, albeit still the leading force and possibly still the only real political party, was meant to preside benignly over social changes and eventually over the new model of socialism that would emerge as their result. Party reforms were absolutely essential for the success of reforms in all other departments. No benign party, no reforms and no new model of socialism.[51]

While the reformers were gradually isolated and/or joined in the dismantling of their own projects, a powerful dogmatic bloc took shape at the same time, and Husak clearly emerged as an alternative leader of the party. After the street demonstration of March 28, the Soviets increased political and military pressure to annihilate the reform movement, and this time they had a consolidated and powerful domestic counterpart within the highest authorities of the Czechoslovak party-state. Finally on April 17, a crucial reshuffling of the top political elite took place. The new party leadership represented an alliance of people like Husak and Strougal who were considered centrists or realists with a conservative pro-Soviet faction led by Bilak. This new team was destined to lead Czechoslovakia for the two decades that followed the aborted attempt to democratize the Czechoslovak political system.

The eradication of reformist party leaders began at the Central Committee session on April 17, where Dubcek was demoted to the chairmanship of the Federal Assembly. Immediately after the April meeting, other personnel changes followed. By the end of May, Kriegel was expelled from the party and Sik with several other prominent reformers lost their seats in the Central Committee. At the beginning of June, Husak appointed six new party secretaries and started the first-round of purges in the Municipal Party Committee in Prague, which was a stronghold of the reformist forces. At the end of September, Smrkovsky, Cisar, Mlynar, Spacek, Hajek, and several others were removed from the Central Committee, and Dubcek lost his seat in the party Presidium as well as the chairmanship of the Assembly. In January 1970, Cernik was demoted from the premiership and removed from the party Presidium. In March and April, most of those who had previously lost their party and state positions, including Dubcek and Smrkovsky, were expelled from the party. Thus, by the middle of 1970, the leaders of the Prague Spring were effectively eradicated from the institutions of the party-state. A reflection of these changes was the fluctuation of cadres in the party's Central Committee. During this period seventy members out of 170 were dismissed, and at the Fourteenth Party Congress in May 1971, a new Central Committee was elected in which there were sixty-one incumbents and fifty-four newcomers. In all cases the removal from party positions was immediately followed by the loss of other responsible positions in the government or other important public institutions.[52]

The purge of the central party institutions was followed by the removal of all reformers in regional, district, and local party branches. During this period nine regional and fifty-nine district first secretaries were dismissed, and more than one-third of party functionaries elected to various central, regional, and district committees were forced to resign or were expelled from the party ranks. Several party organs were disbanded altogether, including the party committees at universities, at Radio Prague, and at Czechoslovak Airlines. This process of cleansing the party apparatus soon filtered down to the rank-and-file of the party. At its January 1970 plenum, the Central Committee decided to introduce new party membership cards and used the occasion to screen the party members' political commitment and loyalty. For this purpose, 70,217 screening commissions were formed, staffed by party activists representing "the sound core of the CPCz." During the next seven months, the commissions interviewed 1.5 million party members, reviewing their activities during the Prague Spring and up to Dubcek's dismissal. Despite Husak's assurances that the purge was aimed only at the unreformable "enemies of the party"[53], according to official figures 326,817 people were refused new party cards and at the same time some 150,000 people resigned from the party on their own accord. Altogether, the CPCz lost a total of 473,731 members—28 percent of its membership—as of January 1968.[54] It should be stressed that dismissal from the party was often followed by the loss of other positions and jobs held by the purged persons, as well as by various forms of political harassment, including interrogations, surveillance, and a bar on higher education for their children. For the purpose of creating a semblance of legality in job dismissals, the discriminatory provision in the labor code, invalidated in 1965, was reenacted. This provision allowed the termination of employment on the basis that the person could not be trusted to perform his duties.

The purges disproportionally affected certain regions and professional groups. Most of the expulsions were concentrated in Prague and in the Czech lands, leaving Slovakia relatively unaffected (17 percent of Slovak party members were expelled from the organization by the end of 1971 compared to almost 42 percent of Czech party members).[55] The hardest hit were the intelligentsia, especially those working in the mass media, universities, schools, and scientific institutions. A number of papers and journals, including twenty-five literary and cultural journals, were closed, and those that remained were supplied with a new editorial staff. For example, in the party organ *Rude Pravo*, forty-five of eighty editors were dismissed, and in the entire country two thousand journalists—half of the membership of the Union of Czechoslovak Journalists—lost their jobs. In the Czech section of the Writers Union, almost half of the members, including the best and most famous authors in the country, lost their publishing rights, and in the twelve publishing houses more than 80 percent of the editors and executives lost their jobs. Similarly nine hundred of thirty-five hundred of Czechoslovakia's professors were dismissed, and in the Czechoslovak Academy of Sciences, five departments were closed and twelve hundred researchers, a majority of whom were economists, sociologists, and philosophers, were expelled. Additionally, departments of Marxism-Leninism at universities and the Military Political Academy in Prague were disbanded. Most of the people who lost their professional or teaching positions were forced to become menial laborers (janitors, oven-stokers, etc.) with the result that for years to come Czechoslovakia was described as an intellectual and cultural desert.

After the purges, the Communist party adopted a document at the plenum of the Central Committee in December 1970 that fully accepted the Soviet interpretation of the Prague Spring as a counterrevolution. It lauded the Soviet intervention as "international assistance to the Czechoslovak people in defense of socialism." The ideological repudiation of the Prague Spring and the justification of Soviet intervention was followed by the Fourteenth Party Congress in May 1971, which Brezhnev appropriately called "the

Congress of victory over the enemies of socialism." Delegates to this congress concluded that "a serious crisis in the party and in society has been overcome on the basis of a policy pursued by the party central committee headed by comrade Gustav Husak."[56] The Congress condemned Dubcek and other reform leaders for neglecting Marxism-Leninism, allowing revisionist forces to take over and creating a serious threat of counterrevolution. The Congress also thanked the Soviet Union and other "socialist friends" for responding to the appeals of genuine Czechoslovak Communists and helping to avert the counterrevolutionary plot backed by reactionary international forces. It also highly commended Husak's policies since April 1969 aimed at restoring the leading role of the party. For the future, the Congress recommended the further strengthening of the party's leading role and an uncompromising struggle against revisionist tendencies. It also postulated further improvement in planning and management of the economy and a rise in the living standards of the population. Internationally, it urged a further strengthening of friendly relations with the Soviet Union and other members of the community of socialist nations.

The Congress also reflected the thorough purge and exchange of party cadres accomplished after the invasion. None of the 1,219 delegates who participated in the clandestine Vysocany congress was among delegates elected in 1971, and the newly elected members of highest party organs not only represented the new "healthy core" of the party, but also were destined to preside over the most orthodox policies in East Central Europe over the next two decades. After the Fourteenth Congress, there were very few personnel changes in the party Presidium, Secretariat, and government. Two changes (federal minister of interior and a new alternate member of the Presidium) followed the deaths of incumbents. In May 1975 Husak took over of the presidency; in this way he combined the two most powerful positions in the country. The impact of the purges on postinvasion policies and developments can hardly be underestimated. As Kusin argues: "If the purge of the party and other institutions of the state and the infrastructure was conducted leniently, more change-oriented people would have remained in positions of influence to enable the crystallisation of a moderate conservative regime which would preserve some reforms even under the overall umbrella of ideological orthodoxy. Kadarisation would have been possible. The economic reform could have continued."[57] The next party congress, held in April 1976, brought few personnel changes and declared the party's satisfaction with the achievements of the previous five years. It praised the fact that during those five years, the party's leading role consolidated, and 334,000 Czechs and Slovaks joined its ranks. Given the improvement of the country's political situation, the congress offered to consider any person for the readmission to the party who had not been actively involved in the revisionist deviations of 1968 and who was now ready to support wholeheartedly the party's policies. The explanation of this rush to join the party is not very complicated. In Czechoslovakia, as in all other state-socialist regimes, more than half a million higher offices and positions in all sectors of the economy were under direct party control, meaning that the party recommendation was a necessary condition for a job or promotion. Thus, at the beginning of the 1980s, one in seven adult citizens of Czechoslovakia was a party member, and 40 percent of all members had joined since after 1971.[58]

The State and Local Administration

It did not require too much effort to bring the legislative and executive branches of the government back into line. In spite of its defiance in the week following the invasion, by September 1968 the National Assembly approved the Moscow Protocol and voted in the package of laws curtailing freedom of speech and association. In October the Assembly ratified the treaty on stationing Soviet troops in Czechoslovakia with only four dissenting votes. Thus, "the sheer weight of party pressure which had been the parliament's way of life before the Prague Spring prevailed fairly easily."[59] The parliament elected in June 1964, which had already legislated itself into prolonged tenure of office in June 1968, was clearly not a stronghold of reformist forces and never displayed any significant political courage. Its signs of revival during the spring of 1968 were mostly opportunistic gestures of officials afraid to lose their positions and privileges.

The invasion immediately ended all debates and work on various reform projects that were presented to the legislature. Shortly after the invasion, however, one of the most fundamental reforms conceived during the Prague Spring was completed and implemented. On October 28, the fiftieth anniversary of the republic, the establishment of a federal system was legislated and on January 1, 1969, Czechoslovakia became a federal state with two formally equal republics. The federalization of the country was the only major reform dating back to the Prague Spring that survived the invasion. It had an important impact on the country's political stabilization and on the restoration of order by the postinvasion regime. According to Carol Skalnik Leff, "The federal solution for multinational states . . . had impeccable Soviet credentials [and] permission to proceed with federalization was a politically safe way to gratify a significant minority of the population by salvaging a long term Slovak objective."[60] It could be argued that after the invasion, just as before the Prague Spring, when the national question was one of the most significant issues disrupting Czechoslovakia's politics and precipitating the crisis, the tensions between Czechs and Slovaks once again played a crucial role. As Skilling points out, "The immediate aftermath of the intervention revealed continuing political differences between Czechs and Slovaks, particularly regarding the relative priority of democratization and federalization."[61]

After the invasion, it slowly became obvious that Slovak leaders were ready to sacrifice democratization and economic reforms if only their national ambitions were fulfilled and their grievances were acknowledged through federalization of the republic. Slovak popular feelings about Czech domination and support for greater autonomy were swiftly adopted and articulated as a cardinal political issue by the country's leaders. In the absence of any significant political activation among people of Slovakia and support for the program of democratization advocated by the Prague reformers, Stalinist elites were able to survive behind patriotic rhetoric. These differences in levels of political mobilization and major issues structuring political objectives between two parts of the country made federalization a convenient counterbalance to democratization. In fact, the resolution of the national question in the aftermath of invasion was a crucial condition of political stability and significantly contributed to the swift consolidation and restoration of political control and order. By giving immediate concessions to the Slovaks, who remained less mobilized during the Prague Spring and less defiant after the intervention, federalization helped to neutralize the Slovak nationalist movement and their opposition against the central authorities, thereby weakening the opposition movement in the Czech lands as well.[62]

After hectic and stormy debate, the constitutional federalization law was quickly enacted.[63] Under the new law, both republics were to exercise a broad range of exclusive powers, including justice, education, culture, trade, health, and construction through their own independent organs of government. The federal agencies were to possess exclusive powers in matters dealing with foreign and defense policies, federal legislation and administration, and state material reserves as well as some other common affairs including agriculture and food policies and industry. The National Assembly was to consist of two chambers equal in status and competence and directly elected. The problem of elections was solved by the constitutional amendment stipulating that the existing National Assembly was to continue to function as the new Chamber of the People, and the Chamber of Nations was to be formed by delegations from the two national councils expanded by co-optation. Thus, the selection of membership to the new federal institutions and agencies was strictly controlled and decided by the party organs. The recasting of the structure of the legislative branch was followed by the restructuring of executive power. On the federal level, seven ministers and seven federal committees were established, and the structure of governments on the republican level was transformed. The federalization of the state set the stage for imposing federal structures on all countrywide professional and mass organizations. However, it was not followed by the federalization of the Communist party, which was opposed by the Soviets[64] and rejected because of concerns about the strength of reformers in many party organizations in the Czech lands. As a result, the formation of a new Czech party organization, parallel to the existing Slovak organization (KSS), was halted and the central party organs doubled as Czech organs.

The constitutional reform solved a number of problems that had produced recurring ethnic tensions, although it fell short of the Slovak proposals.[65] It also had crucial institutional consequences that changed the political situation in favor of antireformist forces. In practical terms, federalization meant the construction of two regional bureaucratic hierarchies in the Czech Lands and Slovakia and expansion of federal institutions. Instantly, Slovakia, which acquired parity on the federal level, had thousands of new posts to fill. By contrast the number of Czechs in federal agencies had to be reduced. This new expansion of regional and federal power apparatus became a great opportunity for Slovak communists and contributed to further demobilization of Slovakia. At the same time, it increased the isolation of Czech reformers striving to preserve the remnants of the democratization policies. It served as a convenient political tool for breaking the dominance of reform sympathizers in state and governmental agencies and in many other organizations in the country by splitting them along national lines and using the more conservative Slovak counterparts to paralyze the more defiant Czech branches. In a symbolic example of this policy, Husak claimed for a Slovak the chairmanship of the Federal Assembly, which many thought should go Smrkovsky. Following federalization, all nongovernmental organizations prepared to reshape their internal structures by adopting the pattern of two national hierarchies and one federal hierarchy. By forming more conservative Slovak branches open to political pressures, party leaders acquired the internal leverage they needed to push these organizations into submission through personal and political manipulations on the federal level.

Federalization was used, for example, in consolidating coercive forces of the regime behind the conservative policies of the post-invasion leadership. In the effort to eradicate reformist influences in the Ministry of Interior, which attempted to introduce some internal reforms during the Prague Spring, requirements imposed by federalization became a very useful instrument. Although Josef Pavel, reformist minister of interior, lost his position immediately after the Moscow Protocol was signed, the full consolidation of the ministry under conservative control came only after federalization. The ministry was one of those that existed at both the federal and the two national levels, and the new structure provided the occasion for the appointment of new ministers at all three levels. The new appointees swiftly won the battle over "internal bases of the enemy and against ideological subversion" within the Ministry by carrying on a thorough review and screening of cadres and dismissing all those suspected of reformist sympathies.

Generally, it did not require any extensive effort to restore the dogmatic leadership and policies and full party control over the security forces, the police, and the army. The coercive forces of the regime survived the reform period relatively intact and did not undergo any significant changes with the exception of some appointments made at the highest level. The police, security forces, workers' militia, and army remained the strongholds of conservatives and pro-Soviet forces during the entire reform period. Nevertheless, there were some examples of cooperation between military and police functionaries and the resistance movement during the first week of the occupation, testifying to both the influence of reform ideas in the apparatus of coercion and its uneasy reaction to the Soviet-led military intervention. Therefore, while bringing coercive forces quickly back into line was not a major problem, eradication of politically suspect individuals became an important priority. Both the security forces and the People's Militia underwent personnel review and screening, after which some "wavering people, fellow travellers and dissenters" were purged. The exact number of these dismissals was never disclosed. In the years following the invasion, the Husak regime strengthened its coercive and controlling capabilities by almost doubling the strength of the police from fifty thousand to ninety-five thousand, establishing a Police Academy with three faculties and introducing modern computerized technologies to keep the records and to monitor the flow of mail and information. For this purpose, the Institute for the Utilization of Computer Techniques in the Ministry of Interior was established.[66]

The armed forces proved to be more prone to revisionist influences than the security forces and the police. But there was no immediate action to eradicate the reformist influence in the army.[67] At first there were no significant personnel changes in the command structures. But at the same time, the conservative pro-Soviet officers quickly attacked the army reformers for departing from the fundamental principles of the socialist armed forces. Proposals aimed at reducing the party's ideological supervision in order to achieve a more professional character of the army were sharply criticized. This criticism was followed by the accelerated process of strengthening of party control, dismantling some minor changes that were already introduced, and abandoning additional reforms contemplated during the Prague Spring. During this process, the Central Committee's Eighth Department, securing party's supervision of the armed forces, was reestablished. But more radical steps, including the screening of army personnel began only after April 1969. The purges started in full swing with the expulsion of General Prchlik (who was later sentenced to three years in prison) from the party in September 1969.[68] Thus, the coercive forces of the Czechoslovak regime, despite their general antireformist stand and cooperative (or at least a neutral position) during the invasion, were screened and purged by the party-state as all other institutions. In this respect, however, the situation in Czechoslovakia was in marked contrast to the demobilization process in Hungary, where the security forces and police had to be rebuilt from scratch and the size of the army cut by half.

The drastic change of demobilization policies after April 1969 also affected the local government and national committees, which in Czechoslovakia constituted a centralized instrument of state power in all communities. According to Kusin: "Just under 10 percent of members at all levels were being replaced by more trusted persons. In Czech lands 2,798 had been recalled and 9,923 had resigned out of 147,409 by April 1970."[69] This low degree of purges on the local level suggests that both pre-invasion political mobilization and postinvasion resistance did not significantly spread beyond the big cities and some specific organizations and groups. The absence of any major repressions in hundreds of national committees around the country corroborates Svitak's point that "the political structure of power in towns and villages remained almost untouched" during the Prague Spring and was unaffected by the resistance movement after the occupation.[70] After everyone suspected of reformist sympathies was purged in 1969 and 1970, the organs of the state administration were stuffed by the co-optation process, insuring that the "healthy core" of Czechoslovak society could exercise exclusive control over the institutions of the party-state.

The representative organs of the new federal state, with their membership either dating back to 1964 or hand picked by the conservative leaders, were "legitimately" validated and reestablished in November 1971, when the general and local elections took place after two extensions of the constitutional deadline. Before the elections were held, the electoral law adopted in 1967, which introduced a small element of choice into the electoral process, was replaced by a traditional Stalinist electoral system in which the public had only to endorse the candidates chosen by the party authorities. Following a carefully conducted "electoral campaign," during which each household in the country was visited twice by special teams of agitators, 99.45 percent of eligible voters cast their ballots endorsing the single list prepared by the National Front, whose candidates received between 99.77 and 99.94 percent of votes.[71] The elections concluded an important period in the process of reequilibration of the regime. They gave the ruling elite the opportunity to reward those who contributed to the swift defeat of the reform movement. Thus, representative organs of the state underwent a notable exchange of personnel, especially at the national level. For example, among the seven hundred deputies of the Federal Assembly, 614 were newcomers.

Generally, the process of reimposition of strict party supervision over the institutions and organs of the state was easily accomplished. The federalization of the Czechoslovak state proved to be a very convenient tool for the exchange of state personnel whose activities during the Prague Spring and the invasion cast some doubts about their political allegiance and convictions. The fact that state institutions and organs survived the reform movement relatively untouched, greatly contributed to their swift submission to the rules of political game brought about by the Soviet invasion. This also made much easier the process of regaining domination by the conservative, pro-Soviet bloc within the top leadership of the Czechoslovak party-state. The consolidation of the party's grip over the auxiliary institutions of the party-state, which had acquired some autonomy during the reform process, presented a more difficult problem. It should be stressed, however, that reimposition of control over non-governmental organizations was not as serious a problem in Czechoslovakia as the rebuilding of the these institutions after the Hungarian revolution.

Auxiliary Institutions of the Party-State

In Hungary, the Kadar regime used trade union organizations to break the workers' council movement and to reimpose state control over the enterprises and factories. In Czechoslovakia, the trade union movement regained some autonomy during the Prague Spring but never fully reasserted its rights vis-à-vis the party-state as a defender of working class interests willing to use legitimate methods of worker protest such as strikes. The Czechoslovak trade unions were much slower to revive than other organizations, partly because of the solidly conservative character of the unions leadership, partly because of workers' fear that the New Economic Policy may bring unemployment and lower wages. Only in March 1968 were hard-line leaders of the Central Council of Trade Unions forced to resign, opening the way for slow change in unions' personnel, structures, and organizations. The reform proposals that advocated more independence in relations with the state and Communist party and internal democratization were prepared during the summer. At its plenum in the end of September 1968, the Central Council of the ROH reaffirmed its intention to carry on internal reforms and to approve the new statutes for its member unions. The selection of delegates for the Seventh ROH Congress, held on March 4–5, 1969, reflected these more democratic procedures. For the first time, three quarters of the delegates were elected by secret ballot in individual unions. The congress, however, was dominated by trade union bureaucrats and failed to declare unions' independence or fully support the reform movement. The Czechoslovak trade unions, in the words of their chairman, Karel Polacek, during the Congress, could not "restrict their views . . . but it will never be our wish to stand in opposition to the Communist Party of Czechoslovakia."[72]

Before the Congress and especially throughout the period of heightened political tensions during the winter, the unions, especially in the Czech lands, were trying to resist ever-increasing pressure to limit their autonomy and involvement in protecting workers' interests and their desire to exert political influence.[73] Between November 1968 and January 1969, some union organizations (particularly the Czech Metal Workers Union) issued strike threats backing demands that the reform party leaders not be relieved of their official positions in the party's hierarchy. In many of these actions, the union leaders were responding to radical demands and pressures coming from "below" from local union groups in individual enterprises. The threats of strikes and protests, however, were never carried out, and the trade unions never became a focus of resistance and opposition during the demobilization period. This situation was especially evident in Slovakia, where the national issues were skillfully played in the demobilization strategy by the party leaders. Facing double pressure from the more radical rank-and-file as well as from the party-state, the Congress elected a moderate leadership. Although there were both hard-liners and reformers present among the elected leaders, the whole organization moved decisively in a conservative direction in the several months that followed the Congress. While the involvement of unions in politics was always renounced as going beyond a proper trade-union role, it was only after the fall of Dubcek that "the regime insisted that the unions abandon [their] claims to protect workers' wages and return to the concept of their primary task as that of protecting the country's all-over economic interests."[74]

It is not difficult to explain why the trade unions both earlier in Hungary and later in Czechoslovakia easily returned to its function of transmitting and implementing party directives. As Kusin argues, under a state-socialist regime the trade union movement

> was not really a workers' movement, but an essentially bureaucratic organization into which the successive regimes breathed only as much life as they wanted. . . . The link between the shop floor and the office holders and policy formulators was, to say the least, tenuous—in many instances non-existent. . . . Indigenous worker functionaries were few and far between. . . . Even the best intentioned reformers belonged to the social group of trade union bureaucracy, connected through many visible and invisible threads to the power structure of an authoritarian mono-party society. When it came to the crunch and they were to choose between a firmly given party orders and a rank-and-file action, they opted for the former no matter how they felt about it.[75]

Thus, well before the conservative faction ousted reformers from the party leadership in April 1969, the trade unions were pacified and consolidated behind the new ruling elite.

As with many other institutions and organizations, trade unions were more radical and militant in the Czech lands than in Slovakia. According to Golan: "The Slovak Unions were not as active as the Czechs . . . in part because of the more rapid deterioration of the reform movement in Slovakia, the backbone of the realists. Moreover, many of the post-invasion issues were easily side-tracked by the conservatives (and the realists) along national lines [and] the Slovak Council of Trade Unions even condemned the 'ill-considered' Czech workers' decisions."[76] Therefore, the federalization of union structure was an indispensable part of the strategy used to demobilize the Czech branches of union organizations. Already in January 1969, two separate congresses of the Czech and Slovak trade-union councils were held, which clearly indicated the different assessment and approaches to the post-invasion situation existing in the two parts of the country. During the fall and winter, constituent congresses were also held for fifty-nine new unions: thirty Czech, twenty-seven Slovak and two country-wide unions. At the same time, ninety applications for the formation of new unions were rejected. While, during the first year after the intervention, trade unions attempted to influence the situation within the country and to negotiate some concessions from the party-state leaders, by 1972 the trade union movement was entirely consolidated under the conservative leadership. The Eighth Trade Union Congress of June 1972 nullified all measures and declarations adopted during the 1968–69 period and restored the function of the organizations as a classical "transmission belt" between the party-state authorities and the workers.

The Czechoslovak Youth Union (CSM) was the only major mass organization of the party-state that for all practical purposes disintegrated during the Prague Spring. The Pioneer organization announced its independence in March 1968, Boy Scouts and Sokol movements were revived, and independent student councils replaced the CSM at universities. Thus, it was replaced by several smaller groups, most of which were not able to achieve any significant level of organization, and membership before the intervention.[77] However, in spite of the actual fragmentation of the youth organizations and their criticism of the former centralized and bureaucratized federation, the commitment to continue some form of federation was strong among the leaders of the new organizations. It was also clearly encouraged by the party leadership. After the invasion, the youth were the most radical segment of the population, and it was mostly young people who were involved in the resistance movement and protest actions. Therefore, it took some time and effort before youth organizations could be fully controlled and recentralized in keeping with the traditional institutional design in most state-socialist regimes.

The most active youth organization in the resistance movement was the Czechoslovak Student Union (SVS). It held its first parliament in Pilsen from October 31 to November 11 and was instrumental in organizing student strikes in November as well as sponsoring the protest campaign on behalf of Smrkovsky. The SVS, however, was plagued, as were most organizations, by the differences between Prague radicals and moderates who identified with Brno. This division shaped the experience of the organization in the post-invasion period.[78] After failing to reimpose control over the union and oust its radical leaders through internal manipulations, and after the SVS's congress rejected the 'moderates' proposal to join the National Front, its newspaper *Studentske listy* was banned on May 6, 1969. This action was followed by the rejection of the SVS's statute by the Ministry of Interior on June 20 and the union was finally outlawed on August 29. The Slovak Student Union was much less radical than its Czech counterpart. At its constituent congress in May 1968, it voted to join the National Front, and throughout the entire period of the reform movement and after the invasion, it pursued moderate policies with an emphasis on Slovak rights. On February 2, 1970, a new regime-lead student organization was founded, which was soon absorbed by the new centralized youth organization.

The recentralization of the youth movement was accomplished with relative ease. Already by September 1968, the Central Committee of the still existing CSM decided to create a preparatory committee for a new youth federation that would provide a loose structure for various youth movements and organizations. But with the reluctance of existing movements and groups to join the discredited organization, the plan was put on hold, and the CSM itself was formally dissolved on March 5, 1969. At the same time, several youth groups were formed by former CSM functionaries and joined mostly by children of party functionaries and officials. The new Leninist Youth Union, which was able to attract only twelve thousand members, dissolved itself in the fall of 1970. But the formation of a centralized youth organization was a central priority of the Husak regime. As one of the regime commentators said: "The act of discrediting and destroying the unified youth organization after January 1968 was a crime against young people, and also an attempt to divert the youth from socialist perspectives. [Therefore] after a pause of almost two years, a unified organization has once again been created—the Socialist Union of Youth. It has inherited the lesson of past mistakes but, above all, it has the opportunity to restore the correct ideological, political, and organizational principles of the Czechoslovak Union of Youth."[79] By the fall of 1970, a new Socialist Youth Union (SSM) had its Czech and Slovak constituent congresses and forcibly absorbed all youth organizations that had emerged during and after the Prague Spring. Organizations not willing to merge with the SSM—for example, the Boy Scout movement—were outlawed. At that time, the SSM had three hundred thousand members, which was one-third the membership of the previous centralized youth union at the peak of its strength. But at its first congress in September 1972, the SSM chairman announced that the union had regained its former standing as a mass organization; with nine hundred thousand children organized in the Pioneer movement and eight hundred thousand young people belonging to the SSM. The new organization, however, never acquired the militant character of Stalinist youth organizations and accepted the passive character of its membership. Young people joined the organization as the result of school pressures and an attempt to avoid any possible problems in gaining admission to universities and access to jobs.[80]

The only organizations that persistently resisted demobilization efforts of the postinvasion regime were the professional organizations of intellectuals and intelligentsia, who had formed the spearhead of the reform movement before the military intervention. During the Prague Spring, the unions of writers, journalists, musicians, architects, and artists established a Coordination Committee to facilitate cooperation among the unions and to give more force to their pressure and support for various social and political issues. The committee was used in the post-invasion period to preserve a common front in face of the regime's attempts to force the unions into submission. The demobilization strategy of Husak's regime vis-à-vis professional organizations was similar to the one used to pacify mass organizations, and once again the Slovak branches of the professional unions were often used to exert political pressure on the Czech branches. Miloslav Bruzek, the Czech minister of culture, formulated this strategy in the following way: "The goal in the Czech provinces is to gradually widen the circle of those who are prepared to commit themselves to [cooperation with the regime]. While in Slovakia the goal is to get rid of those in the artists' associations who, by their opinions and attitudes, hinder the accomplishment of ideological political tasks."[81]

The Journalists Union was the first to be cleansed, given the special role of mass media and the fact some newspapers and journals in the first months of the occupation and even after the fall of Dubcek were still defiant, despite reintroduction of censorship immediately after the invasion.[82] Several popular publications were already banned by April and May of 1969, and major changes took place in many central and local party newspapers. At the beginning of September 1969, the Ostrava and Prague sections of the union were disbanded, and its central committee was taken over by trusted collaborators of the Husak regime. In December, the union was purged and almost half of its four thousand members were expelled. During this time, some newspapers and periodicals were banned. With the reimposition of control over the Journalists Union, the time had come to deal with other professional organizations.

Although most professional organizations formed centers of defiance in the postinvasion period, they did not transform themselves into organized oppositional institutions. Some of them gave in to the regime's pressures easier than others. For example, the Union of Czechoslovak lawyers called a special conference in February 1970 at which time its reform program and demands issued during the entire period of the Prague Spring up until Dubcek's fall were completely retracted and the leading role of the party was proclaimed as a fundamental principle. But the Union of Czech Physicians did not acquiesce in a similar way and was outlawed by the Ministry of the Interior in February 1970. The unions of creative intelligentsia, however, remained the most stubborn and defiant in the face of demobilization efforts. Having successfully resisted pressures to change their leadership and renounce their past resolutions and statements, they were officially outlawed and liquidated in the course of 1970. The Czech unions of composers, painters, architects, theatrical artists, film artists, and writers ceased to exist in the first half of 1970. This action was reinforced by a ban on publication, staging, exhibition, or performance of works by those artists who refused to submit to the regime's dictate and repudiate their loyalty to the policies of reform. In Slovakia, according to Kusin: "The cultural offensive of the 'normalisers' had a less vehement pace. . . . Only the Slovak Union of Film and Television Artists was liquidated *in toto* while transition to a new leadership and policy in the other unions was accomplished comparatively smoothly. For example, the Slovak Writers' Committee met on 15 December 1969, re-appraised some of its former decisions and 'expressed its sincere and honourable interest in maintaining its existing relations with the leadership of the party'. Even the journalists' union in Slovakia survived without too much damage to the membership base."[83]

In December 1970 the preparatory committees of new unions, formed by state functionaries, committed communists, and third-rate members of former unions, were set up and acquired the assets confiscated from the outlawed organizations. The Interior Ministry quickly endorsed their new statutes, but these organizations were in for a rough start. The new unions were boycotted by almost all influential and well-known intellectuals. By 1972, when the inaugural congresses of the revived unions were held, their membership was at approximately one-quarter of its pre-invasion number. Nevertheless, according to the Minister of Culture, the process of pacifying professional organizations was successfully accomplished. "We have isolated," Bruzek said, "the representatives of the Right in the sphere of art and culture sufficiently to preclude their influence in cultural life."[84] With the liquidation of some and the pacification of other organizations of intellectuals and professionals, which by virtue of their position on the fringes of the party-state and their revival before and during the Prague Spring were the most reluctant to adopt to new conservative policies and to resubmit to the party's exclusive control, the remaining institutional basis for potential opposition were destroyed.

The Czechoslovak churches, especially the Catholic church, failed to gain any political influence during the reform period. Churches that had been struggling for survival since 1948 did not recover any of their former status or independence during the Prague Spring and remained dependent on the state for subsidies and supervised in all matters concerning their organizational life. After some degree of relaxation allowed by the reformist leaders before the invasion, Churches were again submitted to detailed state scrutiny and faced a revival of antireligious propaganda. The old head of the Office for Church Affairs (K. Hruze) returned to his position, and the organization of priests that emerged during the Prague Spring was outlawed. The new proregime clerical association, Pacem in Terris, had a federalized structure and was established in August 1971. The churches, especially the Catholic church, were threatened with administrative sanctions should they not comply with state's directives. In 1973, following this threat, five hundred of some thirty-five hundred Roman Catholic priests were barred from exercising their ministries.[85]

After purging those suspected of reformist sympathies within the party and state apparatus, and after either consolidating existing organizations and institutions under a dogmatic leadership or disbanding those too infested with reformers and replacing them with new-state imposed and controlled organizations, the regime moved to eradicate all remnants of the political opposition outside the institutional structures of the party-state. The prime targets were groups of people who tried to organize a socialist opposition around those who were expelled from the party but, nevertheless, remained loyal to the ideal of socialism and reform movement. But these were isolated groups of individuals with no significant support from either "the party of the expelled" or the population at large. The program they proposed was contradictory and divorced from popular expectations and sentiments. For example, the "Ten Point Manifesto" was addressed to the state and Party leadership, and in this way legitimized the existing regime. It also implied that the authors had no intention of forming a party or a movement but wanted to act within the framework of existing laws and institutions. The Revolutionary Socialist party founded by Petr Uhl, while criticizing the post-invasion regime, declared its unequivocal support for socialism. In the same vein, several documents issued in 1970 defined the position of opponents of the Husak regime as a restrictively socialist one. As Jiri Pelikan stressed, "The Manifesto of 28 October 1970, as well as the other documents issued by the socialist opposition, do not just underline the socialist character of the movement, but furthermore reject every form of anti-Sovietism even though this is a stance which has spread among the population since the invasion."[86] And, according to Kusin these documents "represented a last-ditch effort by reform communists to oppose their former fellow party members, now in power, by traditional communist means."[87] These programs—which did not question the basic tenets of the Marxist-Leninist state idea but simply posed the question, who was a true communist: those who ruled or those who were expelled from the party?—would have little chance of mobilizing popular support in a country that had just experienced a Soviet military invasion. The population, pacified in the name of socialism and friendship to the Soviet Union, was deeply disillusioned and felt too betrayed by both the expelled reform politicians and the new dogmatic rulers to respond to a new vision of genuine socialism.

But despite their isolation and marginal influence, these groups quickly became the prime target of political repression because the regime could not allow expelled reformers to form a quasi-party and carry out their activities in opposition. The first arrests began in 1969, when three signatories of the Ten Point Manifesto were detained and jailed for over a year. The first political trials began in the spring of 1971, including the trials of the writer Vladimir Skutina, General Vaclav Prchlik, and nineteen members of the Revolutionary Socialist party. But despite some impressions to the contrary, the judicial repressions were neither extensive not severe. Kusin writes that "only lesser known figures would be tried and detained, people from the most exposed fields of political science, culture, the media and the younger generation. In addition, a certain number of equally selective trials would be held in those regions where the authorities feel that the level of intimidation requires a boost. It was hoped that this procedure would have the requisite punitive and intimidatory effect."[88] Arrests and trials for political offenses continued to decline through 1972, and through the 1970s no major trials were staged. At the same time, the opposition refrained from overtly challenging the regime. Thus the political climate had stabilized.

During the next five years, the Czechoslovak regime consistently pursued hard-line policies. The Hungarian-type shift toward more accommodating and reform-minded policies, expected by many, never materialized. According to Kusin: "Too much of the party's activity remained backward oriented, in constant search for deviation and heresy, and too little energy was directed towards the future. In the process the innovative spirit had died. The leadership has based its behaviour on ideological aggressiveness, police powers and a social contract between party and people whereby consumerism is exchanged for political compliance."[89] In the 1970s, Czechoslovakia emerged as one of the most dogmatic and conservative regimes in Soviet-dominated Eastern Europe. Although the formation of the Charter 77 civil rights movement signaled a new chapter in postinvasion development,[90] Czechoslovak society remained apathetic and unable to challenge the postinvasion regime for almost two decades. Even at the end of the 1980s, despite growing signs of serious economic and political difficulties, neither a new mass opposition movement nor the network of independent political structures emerged. As Jan Tesar emphasized, "Political crisis in Czechoslovakia is the result of neither the activities of the opposition nor the passive resistance of society."[91]

As the above overview indicates, the demobilization policies in Czechoslovakia produced the results intended by the pro-Soviet dogmatic political forces within the party-state and expected by the Soviet Union relatively quickly and easily. During the first eight months after the intervention, the reformers themselves had already restored political stability and defused any attempts to mobilize the population and organize any form of collective protest or movement from below in defense of their reform program. In his critical assessment of the postinvasion policies, Pelikan rightly argues:

> Instead of encouraging the activity of the working class, everything was being done to maintain calm and discipline by a constant series of appeals. Instead of standing up to Soviet pressure more concessions were made, and the demands of the ultras were being met. . . . Such a position could save nothing; on the contrary, both reforms and people were being sacrificed—in short, the entire policy of the Prague Spring was coming to nought.[92]

This first stage of demobilization was accomplished so easily, as I have suggested, because of weak popular mobilization during the Prague Spring, the failure to build institutional bases outside the party-state (which could have sustained an effective resistance movement in the changed political environment), and the absence of independent allies and sources of support for a potential opposition movement. Moreover, the peculiar absence of a well-pronounced split between the party-state and society was not conducive for building active or passive resistance against the state, which could sustain effective pressure from below. It also prevented attempts to isolate the postinvasion regime. This situation has to be attributed to the nature of the reform movement in Czechoslovakia. Initiating the reform from above, the communist party and its leaders became the symbols of the reform movement. Pelikan writes that Dubcek and his reformist colleagues, "had such authority in the Party and among the population at the time that there was no chance for anyone to enforce a different point of view without being accused of treason."[93] Moreover, the ethnic cleavage that was activated during the crisis blurred the state-society division and impeded the formation of an opposition movement against the post-invasion regime.

After the fall of Dubcek in April 1969, the basis of potential political opposition within the party-state was effectively destroyed. In one of the most extensive purges in the history of the communist movement, the party and all institutions and organizations of the party-state, which had served as an institutional platform for the reform, were thoroughly screened. All people suspected of harboring reformist tendencies were expelled from the party and often lost their jobs and positions. But while almost half a million people were the victims of such purges, there was no violent prosecution of the opponents of the new regime. The number of political prisoners remained insignificant in comparison to Hungary after the revolution, and no single person was executed for political offenses. Also, none of the deposed reform party leaders was put on trial or otherwise prosecuted. Hardly a year after the invasion, the new conservative leadership had firm control of the situation in Czechoslovakia; the population was effectively demobilized, and neither the spontaneous acts of protest nor the organized resistance had survived. By 1972, the whole institutional structure of the party-state, beginning with the party central committee and ending with professional organizations and associations, was thoroughly purged and firmly consolidated under the new leadership. According to Skalnik Leff: "The hard core would no longer have to compete with active reformers for domination in the party and over their dormant partners. With the might of the state behind them, they scaled the commanding heights and made them unassailable to others."[94]

The reform program developed before and during the Prague Spring was eradicated together with the people who represented it and pressed for its implementation. None of the specific reforms advocated during the Prague Spring, with the exception of federalization, survived. The debates on the Enterprise Bill, which formed a centerpiece of the economic reforms, were already thwarted by April 1969. In May the self-management reforms were rejected and the formal disbandment of enterprise councils quickly followed. In many areas, such as culture, education, and electoral policies, the Husak regime even rejected changes introduced under Novotny's rule by instituting new regulations and laws that moved the clock back to the Stalinist times. Even the federalization of the Czechoslovak state, which was swiftly implemented after the invasion, served a function that was hardly anticipated by the reformers and was quickly revised to increase control of federal authorities.[95] It was used by the pro-Soviet forces as a main vehicle to break down reform strongholds within the institutional structure of the party-state and to force more defiant Czech institutions and organizations to submit to new conservative policies. In effect, according to Kusin: "Czecho-slovak economic and political life was once again directed from Prague, with greater Slovak participation and with residual powers over Slovakia vested in a Slovak party-governmental set-up. The Slovak may not have gained as much as they wanted, but the Czechs lost more than they thought."[96]

The Political Crisis, Demobilization, and Regime Reequilibration in Czechoslovakia

A FEW YEARS after the Soviet intervention, many students of Czechoslovak politics compared the situation in Czechoslovakia to that of Hungary after the defeat of the revolution. They wondered why the Husak regime never attempted even a partial reconciliation with Czechoslovak society or used its undivided and unchallenged power to introduce at least partial economic or political reforms that resembled policies of the Kadar regime. Scholars explained the persistent repressiveness, dogmatic character and policies of the Husak regime by pointing to three factors. First, they emphasized the role of geopolitical constraints, arguing that the Soviet Union under Brezhnev's highly conservative leadership was unwilling to tolerate any experiments with the practices or theory of state socialism. The continued Soviet pressure forced Czechoslovakia's leaders to implement ever tougher measures to completely eradicate the bacillus of revisionism that threatened not only Czechoslovakia's neighbors but also the Soviet Union itself. Second, they pointed to the character of the postinvasion political elite in Czechoslovakia. The purge of the reform-oriented faction left the party and the state in the hands of dogmatic or even archconservative forces, which step by step pushed more pragmatically oriented realists like Husak or Strougal toward ideologically driven and orthodox policies.[1] Moreover, the core of the demobilization policies was directed against the very notion of reform and every policy proposal designed to modify and liberalize any aspect of economic and political life had a sacrilegious character that contradicted the basic foundations of the postinvasion regime and threatened legitimation claims of Czechoslovakia's ruling elite. Finally, they argued that lingering popular pressure and the potential danger of a reformist revival within the party and society at large did not allow the leaders, who were afraid of the population and uncertain of their basis of support, to break with the ideologically driven routine and repressive strategies and practices of domination.

In comparison to Czechoslovakia, the Kadar regime, as it has been argued, had a much less difficult external and internal political situation. It dealt with Khrushchev, who was more reform oriented and prone to political and economic experimentation. It did not have to confront any dogmatic majority within the party, and was founded not on the principle of reversing reforms but on the basis of promises and claims that were in many respects similar to those that animated the Czechoslovak reform movement.

Moreover, Hungarian society was more violently pacified, thus giving the Kadar regime more elbow room for experimentation, concessions, and liberalizing gestures without the fear of renewed challenge either from the inside of the party or from forces outside the institutional structures of the party-state. Generally, it has been assumed that the nature of political crises and their major contours in both countries were very similar, with comparable demands and analogous political actors struggling for the reformation of the Stalinist system. In both cases, the Soviets reacted in a similar way, sending in troops and crushing the reform movements. Thus, it was commonly held that what really accounted for the failure to change policies from repression to reform in Czechoslovakia were the three factors mentioned above, which operated in and shaped postinvasion developments in both countries.[2]

A systematic comparison of Hungarian and Czechoslovak crises challenges these traditional interpretations, which emphasize general similarities between cases and focus on the elite-level politics. The general contours of the de-Stalinization crises were similar, and the political crises in both countries were precipitated by and can be seen as a response to a similar set of conditions created by the Stalinist reconstruction of the economy and society. However, the actual crises and their courses, immediate results, and consequences were significantly dissimilar. The domestic and external situation of the Czechoslovak and Hungarian regimes after the military resolution of the crises differed in many respects. Two were most important.

First was the extent of cleavage between the elites of the party-state and various groups and movements within society that emerged during the crisis and underlined the subsequent demobilization process. In this respect, the crisis in Czechoslovakia was much more reminiscent of the crisis in Poland in 1956 than similar to the Hungarian revolution. One could agree with Mark Wright that 1968 "represents nothing more than temporary breakdown in the equilibrium of the upper party, in which faction fighting got out of control and threatened the integrity of the whole machine."[3] Thus, the crisis in Czechoslovakia was more an intra-elite conflict than the struggle between the actors within the state and society that characterized the situation in 1956 Hungary and 1980 Poland.

Second was the extent of the institutional breakdown of the party-state. In this respect, in contrast to the almost total disintegration of the Hungarian state, the Czechoslovak state survived the crisis almost intact. During the demobilization process, its institutions had to be stabilized by elimination of reform supporters not rebuild practically from the scratch. Both political terror and concessions offered by the Kadar's regime as well as anti-reformist stand of the Husak's regime cannot be explained without taking into account these patterns of cleavages and conflicts and institutional legacies of the crisis.

The external conditions of both events were also remarkably different. While the Soviet response to the Czechoslovak crisis was similar to the 1956 response, the military invasion was surprisingly bloodless and the behavior of occupying armies temperate. Fred Eidlin rightly emphasizes that in Czechoslovakia "the concept of 'occupation' does not comfortably fit the behavior of the foreign troops. Neither does the concept of 'resistance' comfortably fit the Czechoslovak response to the intervention."[4] Both the occupation and the resistance had the most classical and true meaning when the Soviet troops crushed the Hungarian Revolution. Legacies of the intervention, therefore, have to be taken into account. Moreover, although the capacity of Western powers to influence Soviet behavior and the domestic situation in both countries was minimal, I will argue that paradoxically Western responses to the Czechoslovak crisis were less effective then in the case of the Hungarian Revolution. Sustained international isolation of the Kadar regime was a significant element in transformation of its domestic policies. In turn, Western responses to the invasion of Czechoslovakia were much more restrained and timid, and such a situation did not encourage the Husak's regime to alter its domestic policies.

While emphasizing differences between two countries, it is obvious that they share one general similarity. In contrast to the Polish case in the 1980s, the demobilization policies of Hungarian and Czechoslovak regime were effective and resulted in institutional reequilibration of the regime. Postinvasion elites accomplished the restoration and stabilization of the party-state institutional structures, eliminated any opposition or even a potential challenge to the Communist party role and authority, and successfully closed the political opportunity structure for many years to come.

In the following sections, I will briefly summarize the weaknesses of resistance against demobilization policies, the advantages of the Czechoslovak party-state in implementing its demobilization strategies, and finally the impact of international conditions on the demobilization process.

The Capacity of Resistance and Opposition Movements

In contrast to the explosive popular mobilization in Hungary, the entire period of the Prague Spring did not produce a comparable level of activation of non-elite actors. The de-Stalinization process, which started in the early 1960s only gradually altered the political opportunity structure, allowing the elite actors to fully control the character and extent of political and economic changes. The accelerated reform process started with the assumption of power by the reformist wing of the Czechoslovak communist party in January 1968, and only slowly gathered momentum. Moreover, during the whole duration of the Czechoslovak crisis, the reform process was monopolized by the narrow political and intellectual elite and was confined to the official institutions of the party-state. In fact, it never slipped out of party control or went beyond the spaces controlled by the party-state. As Antonin Liehm emphasizes, "despite the great openness that accompanied this period, and despite the absolute disappearance of the official censorship—

indeed amidst a real practical self-management of the news media—the entire process of the social reform unfolded in a calm and orderly manner, with increasing participation of the citizenry."[5] In a sense this was a classical case of reform from above in which popular mobilization remained restrained and the proponents of the reform, instead of relying on the broad popular participation and mobilized pressure from below, decided to work through official channels and institutions to achieve their political, economic, and social aims. Ivan Svitak criticized the strategies of party reformers, arguing that "the so-called progressive Communists persistently tried to keep the drive for reform under the control of Party apparatus and did not wish to do more than make certain concessions to the broad movement for democratic rights and civil liberties."[6] Thus, the fate of the popular movement was tied to the fate of the reformist party leadership.

While popular political participation increased with the progress of the reform movement, the emerging political and social activities were directed toward reforming existing institutions and organizations. As a result of growing public involvement, many of these organizations underwent a gradual process of internal democratization. Channeling popular pressure through existing organizations kept the lid on political mobilization but at the same time constrained the nature and extent of political demands and impeded the formation or restoration of independent political society that could effectively challenge the party-state and provide an autonomous institutional basis for the formation of genuine political opposition. This channeled and restrained popular mobilization was characterized not only by the absence of alternative institutional centers of social authority and independent organized political forces but also by the lack of real alliances between various collective actors. As Svitak argues, reformist leaders, despite their rhetoric, tried to impede the formation of genuine political alliances because their "fear of the people, of the workers and intellectuals, made [them] incapable of creating an alliance between those who work with their heads and those who work with their hands. Such alliance was diametrically opposed to the elite's group interests, because it challenged its privileges and called in question not only its policy but its very existence."[7] Moreover, there were significant disparities in the levels of political activation between the regions of the country, especially between Czech lands and Slovakia, and between urban centers and the countryside. The country's capital Prague was almost an exclusive center of most initiatives and activities during the entire period.

The low level of popular mobilization, its regional and social segmentation, and the lack of independent organization of society proved to be fatal when the invasion of foreign troops terminated the reform from above. The military invasion and the arrest of the top party leaders provoked the short-lived outburst of non-violent collective protests and produced a deep sense of solidarity among the population. But this spontaneous popular mobilization was hampered by the swift capitulation of the reform movement's leaders and the necessity to build the potential resistance movement in a highly constrained political environment. The reformist leaders' return to power after accepting the Soviet dictate—which initially seemed to be a victory of the reform movement—quickly proved to have profound demobilizing consequences. The reformers attempted to salvage some parts of the reform program by calling for the termination of protests and an immediate resumption of normal functioning of all institutions and organizations. They were afraid of provoking foreign troops and hoped that political restraint and calm would convince the Soviets that the military intervention was a political mistake and that Czechoslovak society was united behind its party's leadership and ready to resume its usual duties and responsibilities. The commitment to the maintenance of calm and order also became one of the major objectives of the spontaneous resistance movement, which in turn implied implicit acceptance of the political realities of the Soviet-led occupation.

The reformist leadership's strategy was a contradictory effort to preserve and consolidate the achievements of the reform movement and strengthen intra-party opposition to domestic hard-line forces. They claimed and defended their positions of authority within party and state institutions at the cost of undercutting popular mobilization and preventing formation of any organizations outside the official structures of the party-state. By opting for this strategy, the party reformers, in Jan Kavan's words, "had cut all the branches on which they were sitting and become dispensable."[8] This lack of political imagination on the side of the reform movement leaders may in part be explained by deep-seated distrust and fear of society and a conditioned conviction of all communist leaders in East Central Europe that Soviet acceptance and support of their faction within the ruling elite are more important than domestic legitimacy and popular support.

After the fall of Dubcek in April 1969 and expulsion of all reform leaders, the possibilities of maintaining and consolidating reformist forces within the party and converting them into strong intraparty opposition ended once and for all. Ousted reformers could not count on the public running to their defense. The society was already effectively demobilized as a result of Dubcek and his fellow reformers' strategy of keeping law and order. The result was that reformers found themselves isolated both inside and outside of the Communist party and unable to restore support of citizens who became more and more disillusioned and cynical about political developments in the country. In the long run, in Kusin's words, "a reasonably well-fed and well-clad citizen, devoid of political aspiration and unperturbed by official ideology, emerged as the product of reinstated 'normalcy.' "[9]

To account for the weakness of the popular opposition and resistance, four more factors should be mentioned. First, similar to the situation in Hungary, in months following the Soviet invasion, there was a significant number of people who emigrated from the country. More than one hundred thousand citizens left the country before October 9, 1969, when Czechoslovakia's borders with the West were closed to all private travel.[10] Most of those who left were young, well-educated, skilled individuals, with Czechs heavily outnumbering Slovaks. Additionally, those who emigrated were the most likely political opponents of the regime. The pattern of emigration differed significantly from the Hungarian experience, however, where most of the refugees left shortly after the Soviet invasion. In Czechoslovakia, according to Kusin, "most people did not apparently opt for permanent emigration immediately after the invasion, although a number did. There was a great deal of wavering, marking time and waiting to see what would happen next [and] most emigres had not made their choice so much because of the Warsaw Pact invasion as because of the turn that 'normalization' took under the Husak leadership."[11]

The second weakness was the absence of a consistent oppositional political discourse and symbolic resources that would allow for a sustained popular mobilization, appeal to various social groups, and facilitate alliance-building between groups and forces opposing the Soviet occupation and postinvasion policies. The representatives of socialist opposition pushed outside the official party-state institutions were not able for ideological reasons to use and mobilize offended patriotic pride and national resentments against the Soviet Union, or to utilize the deep undercurrents of anticommunist sentiments among the population. Instead, oppositional groups were careful to ascertain their allegiance to the Marxist-Leninist vision of the social and economic order, the idea of a national front policy based on the leading role of the communist party, and continued loyalty to the Soviet Union. Thus, the socialist opposition was not able to present a credible political alternative to those who experienced twenty years of political oppression and the shock of foreign military intervention in the name of saving socialist achievements. Moreover, they appealed to those who were expelled from the party as their natural social basis. As Kusin emphasized: "This large constituency of ex-communists could not, however, be expected to act in unison. Many of its members had left the party in disgust and disenchantment and no longer felt any kinship with communism, however democratic it might pretend or aspire to be."[12]

Third, the national conflict that became an open political issue during the Prague Spring contributed decisively to the abatement of resistance and opposition against the invasion. Slovak national grievances were skillfully manipulated and Slovak leaders were too willing to trade democratic reforms for more independence and a bigger share of federal positions. Czech reformers were often removed from federal institutions in the name of greater Slovak representation, and Slovak branches of many organizations were used to pacify more defiant Czech branches. Thus, the national divisions prevented the utilization of nationalist rhetoric, and symbols and helped to destroy the solidarity of Czechoslovak society. The new ruling elite took full advantage of this opportunity.

Finally, in contrast to Hungary, the economic situation and standards of living in Czechoslovakia were good enough to prevent the rise of undercurrents of social discontent that could fuel political unrest and opposition as well as force the regime to look for political remedies to compensate for the economic deprivation. As a result of pressure from the trade unions, wages were raised in the several sectors of the economy in July of 1968, and on November 11 an agreement was signed between the government and trade unions that covered a wide range of issues affecting living standards.[13] The agreement secured gradual changes in housing policy and work safety; raised the lowest pensions, family allowances, and wages;[14] increased maternity leave to two years; and promised a continuation of price control on basic consumer goods. Moreover, the military intervention did not cause any significant damage to the economy. Consumer market shortages, which resulted from panic buying, were quickly eased by boosting production and imports.

The combination of the political factors discussed above effectively accounts for the rapid deflation of the collective protest and the inability of the resistance to organize and to exert effective political pressure from below to force changes in demobilization strategies and policies of the party-state. In this context, the argument blaming the Czech national character for the country's lack of firm resistance does not hold weight. As Milan Simecka rightly emphasizes:

> There is no need to conceal the fact that the behavior of people in the era of renewed order has given rise to a number of reflections about the national character of the Czechs and Slovaks. Such reflections provide ample scope for erudition and clever distortions of historical facts and moral reality. But although I do not deny that such reflections appeal to me, I doubt whether speedy resignation and subsequent apathy have anything to do with national characteristics.[15]

The above analysis clearly supports this point, suggesting that structural and political factors are more important in understanding the demobilization process in Czechoslovakia than arguments emphasizing the national character and historical legacies of twentieth-century experiences of Czechoslovakia. The political capacity of both the resistance movement and the postinvasion regime can only be adequately understood if we focus on the institutional dimension that shaped the opportunities and actions of collective actors during and after the crisis.

The Capacity and Strategies of the Party-State

As we have seen in the first part of this work, the Hungarian revolution smashed the entire party-state's institutional structure. The collapse of the Communist party, mass organizations, and most of the state institutions created a very complex situation for the Kadar regime, which was literally brought to power by the Soviet tanks and inherited the institutional ruins of the state-socialist regime. As I emphasized, however, it also created paradoxical advantages for the newly imposed regime. The disintegration of the old and the formation of the new party allowed Kadar's regime to eliminate or significantly weaken two radical wings of the party: one formed by the opponents of Kadar, party reformers, and revisionists and another that included a highly dogmatic group of former Stalinists. This was the primary reason why in years following the revolution the Communist party as a whole was able to became the instrument of centrist, pragmatic policy and its leaders achieved a high level of political security, which in turn created added opportunity for further experimentation.[16] In this respect, the situation in Czechoslovakia was diametrically opposed to that of Hungary. The postinvasion Czechoslovak regime did not enjoy the advantages that allowed Kadar's regime to rebuild the party's apparatus on the centrist platform, and afforded a relatively open set of policy choices. This aspect of the postinvasion situation in both countries has been often overlooked in existing comparative analyses. As Karel Kovanda points out, "The differences between purging an existing party and founding a new one are important but have not been sufficiently examined."[17]

The reform-from-above nature of the Prague Spring did not fundamentally disrupt the organization of the party-state or the specific state-society relationship characteristic of Soviet-type regimes. Moreover, while antireformist leaders were "horizontally demoted," there was no large-scale exchange of personnel within party and state institutions. With the exception of the removal of a few of the most conservative top leaders, the members of the Central Committee, deputies of the National Assembly, and leadership of the major institutions of the Communist party, state, and mass organizations remained largely the same. They provided a base of support for the advocates of political moderation during the reform period and for the opponents of reforms after the invasion.[18] Therefore, groups and individuals—who came to be known as a "healthy core of the party" during the postinvasion period—were well entrenched in all Czechoslovak institutions and organizations. When after the Soviet military intervention the balance of political power shifted in favor of the dogmatic forces, these people formed the new vanguard and were entrusted with the implementation of the demobilization policies.[19]

As this case study showed, the Czechoslovak Communist party, although debilitated by internal struggle and polarization, remained nevertheless in effective control of the country's political situation. Following the invasion the party and state institutions did not break apart or even stop performing their normal duties, despite the arrest of a few top party leaders and the presence of foreign troops. Moreover, after the first confused week of the invasion, the entire party and state apparatus resumed its routine activities, responding to the appeals of Czechoslovakia's leaders returning from Moscow. Thus, the organization and functioning of core institutions of the Czechoslovak party-state was not significantly endangered or paralyzed during the Prague Spring and after the invasion. In particular, the coercive forces of the regime remained cohesive and tightly controlled. Throughout the duration of the crisis they remained responsive both to Soviet influence and concerns of the conservative faction within the domestic leadership. Similarly, the central and local state administration as well as representative institutions did not undergo any significant changes and sheltered the most conservative element of the party-state apparatus. Only two major legal acts were adopted before the invasion. One was an amendment to the existing press law, abolishing censorship. Another, providing for rehabilitation of victims of unjust political prosecution, was enacted but never been implemented. Moreover, none of the major mass organizations presented an effective political challenge to the party's rule and its self-claimed right to remain the leading and dominant political force within the country. The monolithic unity of the institutional design of the party-state was questioned by some organizations, and all began to seek more autonomy, internal decentralization, and democratization. However, the process, with a few exceptions, did not go far enough to alter their internal situation. After the invasion, all official institutions and organizations became squeezed between Soviet pressure and demands and the unrelenting push of domestic dogmatic forces to regain full control. Almost immediately after the invasion, these organizations were forced into submission and step by step were consolidated under the control of the hard-liners. This process began with the consolidation of the core institutions of the party and state, including the coercive forces of the regime and the mass media, and was concluded by reestablishing control over professional associations of artists and intellectuals.

With the elevation of Husak to the party's top position in April 1969, the process of breaking the reformist wing in all party-state institutions and organizations was drastically accelerated. What followed was the most extensive purge in the history of the Czechoslovak Communist party. All those suspected of reformist sympathies were expelled; those identifying with the reform movement lost their jobs and positions; and a few organizations that were still defiant were disbanded. By 1971, when the Fourteenth Party Congress and the elections took place, all traces of the reform movement were destroyed. From that point in time, the pro-Soviet hard-liners controlled every aspect of Czechoslovak political, economic, and social life and exclusively shaped the developments of the country for almost two decades.

The strategy used to regain political control closely resembled the reformists' strategy employed during the Prague Spring. The leadership changes in core institutions and top offices filtered down through the hierarchic bureaucratic structures of the party and the state, gradually extending the power and control of the antireformist forces. The gradual takeover of the party-state institutions by the dogmatic forces was followed by the repressive, ideology-driven policies, which reversed not only the gains achieved during the Prague Spring but also many changes in political practices and the legal framework introduced during the last years of Novotny's rule. This highly regressive pattern of the Czechoslovak demobilization process puzzled many students of East European politics, who compared the Czechoslovak situation to postrevolutionary developments in Hungary. As Zdenek Mlynar points out:

> Normalization in Hungary went through a brief phase of mass terror and was accompanied for about five years by the brutal suppression of all that had led to the 1956 uprising; after this phase it was characterized by a constant pragmatic search for compromise. In Czechoslovakia, on the other hand, normalization began with a brief phase of unsuccessful search for compromise; after that it was marked by the constant, systematic suppression of everything that had facilitated developments long before 1969.[20]

As I have argued, a consistent comparative approach to analyzing the situation of the Czechoslovak party-state after the Soviet-led invasion may indeed shed some light on why political relaxation and the search for compromise and accommodation between ruling elites and society was blocked. I would like to argue, despite suggestions to the contrary in the existing literature, that the regressive pattern of demobilization policies was not a result of the persistent passive resistance and uncertain position of the new leadership. My analysis suggests quite different reasons for the continuation of the ideologically driven, repressive policies. Such policies continued uninterrupted after their commencement in April 1969 because of the weakness of the resistance, the absence of significant popular mobilization, the lack of independent centers of social and/or political authority, the strength of the party-state institutions and organizations, and the prominence of the national question. In short, it should be attributed to the absence of a clear state-society cleavage that characterized both the Hungarian and Polish crises.

The postinvasion period was marked by the two distinctive phases: the first spanned the period between the invasion and the ouster of Dubcek in April 1969 and the second between the April reconstitution of the party leadership and 1976 when the Czechoslovak regime was fully reequilibrated. During the first phase, groups, movements, and organizations within Czechoslovak society were effectively demobilized and unable to exert any pressure from below due to Dubcek's team efforts to pursue "reform without extremes." Their actions, designed to save reforms, instead proved to be an effective demobilization strategy. Their choice sealed the fate of the reforms and of Dubcek himself. As a result, Dubcek and his supporters found themselves in the position of the most dangerous "revisionists and right-wing opportunists." In the second period, after the fall of Dubcek, the process of demobilization was additionally reinforced by the ideologically motivated and highly repressive policies of Husak's regime. As a result the "leading role of the party" was completely restored and all signs of dissent or even disagreement with official views were crushed. Thus, in contrast to Hungary, the postinvasion Czechoslovak regime was not compelled to adjust its demobilization policies in order to fend off internal and external pressures and to rebuild its shattered image and institutions.

There are several additional political factors that are important in accounting for the persistence of the highly dogmatic and regressive nature of demobilization policies in Czechoslovakia. They may also help in explaining why, despite their repressiveness, the policies of the postinvasion regime were nonviolent in character and use of judicial repression was limited.

First of all, after the invasion the Czechoslovak Communist party was incomparably stronger (even after the purges) and the level of penetration of society was much more extensive than in Hungary. The percentage of the population belonging to the Communist party in Czechoslovakia was 11.7 in July 1968, 11.4 in April 1969, and 8.3 in 1970. In Hungary the comparable percentage was 1.1 in December 1956, 3.5 in June 1957, and 5.8 in December 1966.[21] Thus, the Hungarian regime was not only forced to employ terroristic strategies to restore its grip over society, but later on, it needed to offer concessions and introduce more inclusive policies in order to redeem its use of terror, to rebuild the mass character of the Communist party, to regain a minimum of popular acceptance, and to create at least the impression of cooperation between the state and society. In this context, it could be argued that the absence of the shift toward a more pragmatic policy pattern in Czechoslovakia was caused not by the strength of the resistance and the Husak regime's persistent lack of legitimacy, as is often implied. Quite to the contrary, popular resistance was weak, sporadic, and disorganized, while the party-state was well organized, strong, and able to penetrate and control society through nonviolent means. In short, communist party leaders were not forced or encouraged to change their political strategies and demobilization policies in order to search for a compromise with society.

Second, in Czechoslovakia there was no opportunity for the party leadership to reclaim the centrist, moderate position and to identify itself with any commitment to reform and change, as was the case with the Kadar regime. The return to power of the orthodox antireformist forces and the spiral of political purges pushed those who wanted to survive in the party to accept highly dogmatic attitudes and policies. Kadar excluded revisionists from his new party but also managed to keep out the most dogmatic groups. Husak did not have this option. After the purge, the most dogmatic forces became the ideological guardians of the party and the prime contenders to power. Husak willingly bowed to their pressure and became the captive of the neo-Stalinists. As a result, instead of choosing the path of moderation and accommodation, the party leadership opted for a war with all suspected revisionists. The aggressive, ideologically driven policies dominated the regime's political practices and its political discourse. In such a political climate, every departure from the orthodox routine was viewed with suspicion, as a sign of retreat, and as a political compromise with the condemned ideas of the reform movement. Therefore, every proposition of reform or liberalization was by definition sacrilegious and as such, principally rejected.

Third, as I have argued before, the cyclical crisis of centrally planned economies was an important factor in precipitating political crisis, forcing policy adjustments, and fueling significant undercurrents of popular dissatisfaction and unrest. While the invasion of Hungary only aggravated an already disastrous economic situation and forced the Kadar regime to constantly search for new solutions that would raise the living standards and remove economic grievances from the highly tense political situation, the postinvasion Czechoslovak leadership did not face any urgent need to introduce significant economic adjustments in order to boost the economic performance or improve the market situation. At the end of the 1960s, the Czechoslovak economy had already recovered from the difficulties that occurred earlier in the decade and experienced a period of sustained economic growth. Kusin concludes that the

> Czechoslovak economy under the short impact of an economic reform did not work worse than before 1968, and that in the post-reformist period it did not start working worse than during the Prague Spring. In other words, Czechoslovakia has experienced a steady economic growth from 1966 (or 1967) to 1978, perhaps not buoyant and confident, but more than satisfactory in East European conditions. This development was assisted by agricultural success. The years 1968–69 mark no substantial deviation from the trend. If anything, they showed an improvement in the standard of living of the population.[22]

Furthermore, some of the economic difficulties of 1969 were blamed on the departure from strict central planning during the Prague Spring and gave yet another occasion to condemn the economic reforms introduced and contemplated during the Prague Spring. These difficulties were used to reverse the changes in the management of the economy and to justify the re-imposition of the strict central planning mechanism. Given this relatively satisfactory economic performance, the Soviet bloc countries were not forced to extend any significant economic aid program to Czechoslovakia in order to compensate for possible losses caused by the military intervention or to defuse potential tensions that may have been caused by the aggravation of the economic conditions, as was the case in Hungary. In general, the major stabilizing factor in Czechoslovak demobilization policies was the ability to satisfy the consumer demands of the population without any need to restructure the economy.

Fourth, the federalization of the country became a valuable asset in the hands of the ruling elite. The only reform proposal that survived the Soviet invasion, federalization, facilitated the demobilization process by directing Slovak longing for more political influence and independence against efforts at political and economic liberalization led by Czech reformers. This situation reflects the peculiarities of Czechoslovak federation. In the Czechoslovak federation, the state comprised only two republics facing each other and competing for resources and power. As Carol Skalnik Leff observes, "This 'us versus them' framework of controversy means that the confrontations of politics are sharply delineated; policy victories and defeats all occur with respect to a single and obvious rival. Slovak gains come clearly and unavoidably at Czech expense, and vice versa." Moreover, Slovakia was always a "permanent minority" on any economic or political issue that seriously polarized the country along regional lines.[23] Thus, while federalization had important short-term political advantages, given these characteristics of the Czechoslovak federation, it did not solve the country's national problems in the long run. The Slovak drive for independence that followed the collapse of the communist regime in 1989 and the split of Czechoslovakia into two states has been a predictable outcome of the postcommunist political transition. The post-1968 policies, cynically exploiting ethnic tensions and grievances, greatly contributed to the failure to preserve the Czechoslovak federation after 1989.

Finally, the international dimension and consequences of the invasion were paradoxically less conducive in influencing domestic policy changes of the post-invasion Czechoslovak regime than they were during the peak of the cold war in the 1950s or after the Helsinki Accords in the late 1970s and early 1980s.

The International Context of the Demobilization Period

The political crisis generated by the Prague Spring had profound intrabloc consequences. It involved the issue of Soviet control over the domestic policies of its client regimes as well as the more general issues of the Soviet perception of its military security and requirements to maintain the geopolitical balance in Europe. The reform movement also challenged the perceived uniformity and unity of the Soviet bloc and stimulated domestic dissent in other countries. As Svitak writes, "The reformists were unable to grasp the consequences of their own policy in the international context, and they failed to see that they unintentionally generated destabilizing pressures within the Soviet bloc, pressures that were unacceptable to Brezhnev"[24] and even more so to other East European leaders like Gomulka and Ulbricht, who strongly lobbied the Soviet leadership to respond decisively to Czechoslovakia's revisionist policies and their contagious effects.

However, the decision to intervene militarily did not come easily.[25] It was preceded by a protracted process of consensus building among political and military leaders in which the other Soviet bloc leaders played a significant role. Throughout the duration of the Prague Spring, the Soviet leaders sent or received thirty-three high-level delegations who discussed events in Czechoslovakia. In the process, the Soviet Union also clarified the legal basis for possible intervention in another Soviet bloc country, later dubbed the Brezhnev doctrine.[26] This principle asserted that the Soviet Union has a right and an obligation to intervene in every situation where socialism is threatened either by domestic or external forces. While the Brezhnev doctrine was widely condemned by such diverse political bodies as NATO (meeting in Brussels in November 1968) and many Western communist parties, the reality of the postwar division of Europe, which gave the Soviet Union virtual freedom of action within its own sphere of influence, was at that time universally condoned as perhaps unpleasant but, nevertheless, a real and unassailable outcome of the Second World War and the postwar world's balance of power.

Like the invasion of Hungary, the Soviet-led invasion of Czechoslovakia produced a remarkable outburst of international protests and a storm of outcry in the West, but the governmental responses were highly restrained and did not present any effective challenge to the Soviet action. The United States and West European states condemned the invasion but, at the same time, implicitly recognized Czechoslovakia's place within the Soviet sphere of influence. Moreover, the international protest and pressures that exploded after the invasion were stifled for reasons similar to those that hampered the development of the resistance movement within Czechoslovakia. A full condemnation and possible diplomatic and economic sanctions became highly problematic when the kidnapped Czechoslovak leaders were returned to Prague and resumed their governmental duties. Similarly the United Nations' response was muted and ineffective. The UN Security Council met on the evening of August 21 to discuss the situation in Czechoslovakia, but the Soviet Union vetoed a resolution condemning the invasion, and three other members abstained. As a result, the Czechoslovak question was not referred to the General Assembly. Immediately after the invasion, Jiri Hajek, the foreign minister of Czechoslovakia, who was at that time in Yugoslavia, flew to New York to present the Czechoslovak case against the occupation to the Security Council. However, in his efforts on behalf of the Czechoslovak government, he displayed the same ambiguous attitude that characterized the policies and rhetoric of the Czechoslovak reformist leadership all along. As Milan Hauner argues: "Hajek's pathetic appearance before the U.N. Security Council on 24 August had all the features of absurd clownery. He was more concerned about declaring his fidelity to socialism and the Soviet people, more about condemning American imperialism in Vietnam, than about the Warsaw Pact aggression of his own country."[27] Czechoslovakia's complaint, presented by Hajek, was withdrawn immediately after the signing of the Moscow Protocol, which specified this withdrawal as one of the major conditions. Thus, in contrast to Nagy's government in Hungary, the Czechoslovak leaders did not attempt to internationalize the Czechoslovak crisis. They did not appeal for support to communist movements and countries that opposed the Soviet-led intervention, nor did they ask the Security Council of the United Nations to intervene. As a result, unlike the Hungarian question, which remained on the UN agenda for several years and provided a means for the embarrassing political isolation and exclusion of the Kadar regime from the international arena, the international pressure following the Soviet-led intervention in Czechoslovakia was much more restrained and less damaging to the post-invasion regime.

In contrast to the situation in the 1950s, when the hostile relations of the cold war allowed and encouraged uncompromising political responses to the Soviet action in Eastern Europe, in the 1960s the international situation was more complex with the growing American involvement in Vietnam, the right-wing military coup in Greece, and the Israeli occupation of Arab territories as a result of June 1967 war. Moreover, the relaxation of tensions between the West and the East became one of the most important foreign policy objectives. Confronted with a potential return to cold war hostilities, the United States and especially other Western countries easily yielded to the temptations of relieving cold war tensions through the policy of detente and upcoming arms negotiations with the Soviet Union.[28] The stabilization of West-East relations was clearly too significant a goal to be sacrificed for the sake of some questionable Soviet behavior within its own sphere of influence, which was unlikely to be reversed short of provoking a military conflict with the Soviet Union. This policy was clearly articulated by Richard Nixon, who stated: "We are aware that the Soviet Union sees its own security as directly affected by developments in this region. . . . It is not the intention of the United States to undermine the legitimate security interests of the Soviet Union. . . . Our pursuit of negotiations and detente is meant to reduce existing tensions, not to stir up new ones."[29] Thus, the Western concern for improved relations with Moscow gave the Soviets a free hand in dealings with their dependencies in Eastern Europe.

Generally, Western countries did not have any political or economic leverage that could have been used to influence Soviet or Czechoslovak policies. As Zbigniew Brzezinski admitted, analyzing the impact of the Czechoslovak crisis on East-West relations, "Clearly, Western policy is not itself the decisive factor of change in the East."[30] In the economic dimension, the trade relations of Czechoslovakia with the West were rather insignificant and economic sanctions would have only been symbolic. By the end of the 1960s, Czechoslovakia had the lowest share of western foreign trade of all Soviet bloc countries, with the exception of Bulgaria. Almost 80 percent of her trade was conducted within the Soviet bloc, and a significant part of the remaining trade was with Third World countries.[31] Czechoslovakia also did not have any financial links with the West. The proposal to seek Western loans was condemned after the intervention as one of the prime examples of revisionist and counter-revolutionary policies attempted by Czechoslovak reformers in the field of the economy.

While Western responses to the intervention were devoid of any effective means of exerting pressure either on the Soviet Union or on Czechoslovakia, and considerations of the global realpolitik quickly moved the problem of the invasion to the back stage, the consequences of the invasion for the world communist movement were far more important. The relations of the Soviet Union with other communist parties suffered a severe blow. The majority of the communist parties, including the Chinese, Italian, Yugoslav, and Swedish parties, condemned the invasion and disassociated them-

selves from the Soviet Union. In this dimension, the invasion of Czechoslovakia clearly gave added impetus to Eurocommunism. However, as Mlynar
argues:

> Among the Eurocommunists . . . tactical interests prevailed in the end: what they
> wanted, above all, was Soviet recognition of certain principles of the relative inde-
> pendence of the West European Communist parties. As far as Czechoslovakia was
> concerned, the Eurocommunists simply maintained their verbal condemnation of
> the 1968 intervention but were willing to accept the Soviet principle of 'non-inter-
> ference in the internal affairs of other parties'.[32]

In the end, the Berlin meeting of European communist parties in June 1976
broadly endorsed Soviet foreign policy and put the Czechoslovak question
to rest.

Therefore, during the 1960s the international context was paradoxically
even more favorable to the Soviet aggressive intrabloc action than it was in
the 1950s, despite decreasing isolationist policies of the Soviet bloc countries
and receding East-West hostilities. Western countries not only lacked political or economic leverage but were also constrained by potential costs of
abandoning the emerging detente policy. Lacking other means of effective
pressure, diplomatic isolation was the only means available to the Western
states for expressing their dissatisfaction with the internal policies of Soviet
bloc countries. However, the broader international isolation used against
any state-socialist regime was, as had been the case earlier with Hungary,
effectively compensated for by its socialist friends. Accordingly, between
1969 and 1977, the Czechoslovak leader Gustav Husak made twenty-six
trips to the Soviet Union and twenty-one visits to other countries of the
Soviet bloc.

The international pressure or sanctions that clearly influenced the policies
of the Kadar regime and played such an important role in the Polish crisis in
the 1980s were, for the reasons outlined above, less effective in pressuring
the postinvasion Czechoslovak regime to reconsider its demobilization strategies. As Karen Dawisha concludes in her analysis of the 1968 intervention:

> In assessments of the lessons which Western countries derived from the invasion
> it has often been noted that, although the invasion widened the splits in the inter-
> national communist movement, its impact on East-West relations was practically
> negligible. . . . In the first half of the 1970s American recognition of the symbolic
> relationship between detente and Soviet hegemony in Eastern Europe was en-
> shrined in the so-called "Sonnenfeldt doctrine".[33]

I would like to argue, therefore, that the international context further reinforced the specific domestic conditions and political factors in Czechoslovakia, which contributed to the rapid demobilization of society, the swift
reestablishment and consolidation of the highly orthodox neo-Stalinist regime, and blocked, or at least did not encourage, any departure from highly
repressive and ideologically driven demobilization strategies.

The Political Crisis and Its Aftermath in Poland, 1980–1989

As I have argued that the political crises in Hungary in 1956 and Czechoslovakia in 1968 were the result of, and a reaction to, the Stalinist policies of forced industrialization and political terror that produced profound reconstitution of economic, social, and political structures in these countries. From such a point of view, both the Hungarian Revolution and the Prague Spring were forms of de-Stalinization expressed through a political crisis. In both cases, shortages and disbalances of centrally planned economies, abuses of power and political repressions, as well as pressures from the international environment, led to deep divisions within the ruling elites and produced protracted political conflicts and struggle among the party leaders. In Hungary, the conflict acquired a more dramatic character and rapidly spilled outside the party-state institutions. It coupled with growing popular dissatisfaction and released lightning revolutionary mobilization, which quickly swept away the entire institutional structure of the Hungarian party-state. In Czechoslovakia, the decay of the Stalinist system and the development of intra-elite conflicts was more subdued and prolonged, but it eventually led to a reform movement from above initiated and carried out by the new elites of the party-state. In contrast to Hungary, however, the reform movement did not trigger popular mobilization that could threaten the integrity and survival of the Czechoslovak party-state.

In both cases, the impetus for change came from political actors inside the party-state. The advocates of reforms within the Communist party operated through the existing institutions and never seriously questioned the major tenets of the Marxist-Leninist state-idea and outcomes of postwar economic and political transformations. Originally, both groups of party reformers, represented by Imre Nagy and Alexander Dubcek, sought to establish a variant of the socialist state that was more democratic and responsive to national conditions. They did so by altering the political practices instituted during the Stalinist period. This moderate reformist program changed dramatically during the revolutionary upheaval in Hungary but was consistently pursued in Czechoslovakia. It could be argued that in both cases the crisis was precipitated by an effort on the part of the ruling elite to reform some elements of existing state socialism in favor of a more humane and more efficient economic and political system. In both cases, the defeat of the revolution and of the reform movement led to rebuilding and consolidation of the party-state institutions and produced at least a short term return to neo-Stalinist political practices.

This was not the case of Poland in the 1980s. First, the Stalinist period in Poland ended for all practical purposes in 1956. The controlled de-Stalinization crisis reconstituted Poland's political elite and led to limited concessions to various social groups and organizations. Repressive political practices were abandoned or altered, despite the preservation of social and economic legacies of the Stalinist transformation and the institutional structures of the party-state. Although the post-1956 regime gradually retreated from its promises of political liberalization and economic reforms, Poland never came close to a reestablishment of Stalinist-type political control. Moreover, even at the height of the Stalinist period, political developments in Poland were markedly different from those in neighboring countries. As Joseph Rothschild emphasizes:

> An erroneous impression has gained currency that Communist and Soviet behavior was more brutal in Poland than elsewhere in East Central Europe. But this is not quite true. . . . Stefan Cardinal Wyszynski was treated more gently than were clergymen in several other people's democracies; traditional Polish military uniforms and other national symbols were uniquely retained even under Konstantin K. Rokossovsky's tenure as defense minister; the peasantry was approached more gingerly than elsewhere; and . . . the so-called Polish Titoists were dealt with more civilly and less violently than were the victims in any neighboring purge.[1]

The Polish de-Stalinization culminated in the bloodily suppressed worker revolt in Poznan in June 1956 and the dramatic change in party leadership in October of the same year. It resulted in institutional adjustments and important concessions to the Catholic church, the peasantry and artisans, the youth, and the country's intellectual and academic elites. The 1956 crisis practically ended the effort to collectivize the Polish agriculture, and Poland became the only Soviet bloc country where the bulk of arable land (83.7 percent in 1970 and 75.8 percent in 1979) remained in private hands. Also, the private sector in retail trade and services remained sizable. It generated a notable part of national income (5.5 percent in 1970 and 6.0 percent in 1980) and employed nearly one million people by 1980. The Polish Catholic church secured its independence and became the most powerful organization outside the party-state. Its place and role in Poland's social and political life was unparalleled in comparison with other state-socialist regimes. New party leaders, enjoying genuine popular support, renegotiated discriminatory trade relations with the Soviet Union and ended personal supervision of the Polish army and police by the Soviet officers. Although these newly regained concessions and freedoms were significantly curtailed during the 1960s, the overall political situation in Poland never came close to the systematic oppression of the churches and intellectuals and the rigid, ideology driven policies found in other state-socialist regimes. After 1956 dogmatic Marxism was mortally wounded and the party's policies became more pragmatic and guided by "a narrowly conceived political realism based upon geo-political considerations."[2] This tendency was further reinforced by the political crisis in 1968, in which liberal and revisionist groups within the party were virtually eliminated. The defeat of Polish revisionists and the dramatic collapse of the Czechoslovak reformist experiment underscored the impossibility of reform from within the party-state and further eroded the ideological foundations of the communist system.[3] Despite the important de-ideologization of the Polish regime, however, the country's political institutions and its system of bureaucratic command economy remained almost completely unaltered through the 1960s and 1970s. In sum, the 1956 transition produced institutional, political, and cultural legacies that set Poland apart from other state-socialist regimes. The structure of political opportunity was permanently altered, and Poland became the most unstable country in the Soviet bloc, plagued by endemic political and economic failures and waves of collective protests. For these reasons it became a virtual laboratory of state socialism's systemic crisis.[4]

Second, the Polish crisis in 1980–81 was the culmination of a series of political crisis that occurred periodically after 1956 and led to unexpected popular protests and abrupt leadership changes (since 1956 virtually all Polish top leaders had been deposed as a result of popular unrest) as well as to the further erosion of Stalinist features of the Polish party-state. During these crises, different social groups and organizations challenged the party's policies and were able, despite their ultimate failures, to extract some concessions from the regime and to maintain a threat of collective protest as a constant element of leadership's political calculation.[5] Successive political crises were the result of the inconsistent and interrupted de-Stalinization coupled with recurrent economic difficulties and growing economic stagnation. These political crises not only led to a further weakening of the party-state's political position, but also generated a militancy among the industrial working class and lingering dissent among Polish intelligentsia. Unlike any others in the Soviet bloc, Poland's restive workers were able to defend their standard of living through collective protests, strikes, and demonstrations. Students and intellectuals were also quite ready to voice their opposition against the party-state's policies. In March 1968, Polish students and intellectuals led a wide-spread protest against cultural policies of the Gomulka's regime and its efforts to curtail concessions given in 1956. In December

1970, workers of the Baltic Coast launched fierce protest actions against state's attempt to raise the prices of consumer goods in an effort to stabilize the economy. The bloody suppression of this protest, in which forty-five workers were killed and twelve hundred wounded, led to the fall of the Gomulka regime. The new party leadership led by Edward Gierek promised economic reforms and adopted more inclusive policies to improve relations between the party-state and society. Yet in the second half of the 1970s, Poland experienced a multidimensional crisis. The unraveling of Gierek's effort to create a socialist consumer society by using Western credits plunged the country into a disastrous economic crisis, dashing the high expectations produced by the regime's more pragmatic policies and a four-year economic boom that had occurred at the beginning of the 1970s. The growing crisis provoked another workers rebellion against price increases in 1976. Repressions against those participating in this wave of strikes and demonstrations resulted in a conscious effort by independent intellectuals to aid prosecuted workers, form independent organizations, and develop effective cooperation among groups and forces opposed to the party-state. The emerging political opposition organized around the Committee for Workers Defense (KOR) and aided by the Catholic church with its institutional resources and moral authority, which was boosted when Polish-born Karol Cardinal Wojtyla became Pope John Paul II in 1978. His first papal visit to Poland in 1979 became a mass political manifestation and a critical symbolic challenge to Communist party rule. At the same time, the anarchization of the party-state institutions, the collapse of Marxist-Leninist political discourse, and the moral bankruptcy of the ruling elite opened the political opportunity structure for the organized challenge from below.

While the early collective protests were hampered by social segmentation, the absence of independent organizations, inability to articulate distinct political claims (which would go beyond redistributive issues), and the lack of alternative institutional visions of economic and political order, they nonetheless had important political and institutional consequences. The growing political insecurity forced the party elites to further relax their ideological principles, to accept differentiation of interests among important social strata, to adopt more inclusive policies,[6] and to employ a specific strategy of "protest absorption,"[7] which put an increasing strain on the party-state's resources. Mass protests also underscored the urgency of reform to step up economic performance in order to raise living standards and improve relations between the party-state and society. The segmented nature of collective protest was gradually overcome in the wake of the 1976 workers rebellion, and efforts to develop an alternative political vision and cross-class alliances became an important element of political opposition's agenda and were more successful.

Third, throughout the 1970s there was a significant generational change within the Polish ruling elite. It was marked by the departure or removal of veterans of the communist struggle, who had formed the new ruling elite of the Soviet imposed regime, as well as those who acquired their positions within the state and party apparatus immediately after the war as a reward for their political loyalty and commitment to the communist cause. The fall of Wladyslaw Gomulka and his replacement by Edward Gierek, the leader of the powerful regional party organization in Silesia, was followed by rejuvenation of the party and state bureaucracies. Gierek supporters were quickly promoted to important positions within the party and social organizations, and the Sixth Congress of the Polish United Workers Party in December 1971 replaced two-thirds of full members of the party's Central Committee with younger party functionaries. Moreover, in the election to the country's Parliament in March 1972, more than half the elected deputies were new. Among the Politburo members elected by the Seventh PUWP Congress in 1975, only three out of seventeen had been the full members of the Politburo before 1970. This turnover of party and state leadership was partly a result of the political crises in 1968 and 1970 and partly due to the natural departure of aging cadres. It resulted in a notable de-ideologization of state policies, which acquired a more ritualistic and pragmatic character.[8] Moreover, it opened channels of organizational mobility within the ruling elite to a new, well-educated, and technocratic generation of leaders and managers. Professional expertise and qualifications were now used as criteria for advancement within the nomenclature system over adherence to political principles of Marxism-Leninism. Such policies of inclusion significantly affected the role and functions of the state, economic bureaucracy, and auxiliary institutions of the party-state. They were ideologically weakened and no longer able to maintain the same level of political control over society. They became more pragmatic channels of personal advancement as well as outlets for the creation of clientelistic networks with important economic functions for their participants.

The generational change in the party-state apparatus was paralleled by changes within the country's working class and work force in general.[9] In the 1950s, the new working class migrating from the countryside at a rate of 10 percent a year, could find employment with no upgrading in skills or education. Forty-seven percent of these workers had only an elementary education, 41.9 percent had not accomplished even this. By 1978, 54.2 percent of workers graduated from elementary schools (while only 4.9 percent had not); 35.1 percent emerged as a new category of skilled workers with basic vocational training; and 5.3 percent had secondary vocational training. As George Kolankiewicz and Paul Lewis emphasize: "Differences in education have been shown to influence lifestyle, sociopolitical involvement and the perception of deprivation. . . . It is the relatively highly educated workers, those with secondary education, that have given most evidence of a qualitative change in the nature of working-class evolution. It was these workers who came to the fore in 1980."[10] Moreover, the workers who formed the mainstay of the protest movement were young—in their twenties and thirties.

The significant change in the composition of Poland's work force prompted some scholars to interpret the emergence of the Solidarity movement as a reflection of changing social structures and the emergence of a new middle class.[11] However, the new generations entering different sectors of the economy and different professions had significantly divergent perceptions of government policies. The workers and peasants benefited much less from the Gierek's economic policies in the first half of the 1970s than did the bureaucracy and intelligentsia, and suffered more from the pervasive shortages in the housing and consumer markets. This situation created new sources of discontent among the working class. According to Alex Pravda, "What exacerbated the workers' dissatisfaction, particularly among the young ones, with housing, as well as with consumer goods in general, was not so much that living standards had fallen but that availability of goods failed to meet the workers' rising expectations."[12]

Lastly, during the 1970s, Poland opened up to the West. This change in Poland's international situation and policies was the result of several factors. The new ruling elites believed they could revive economic development and raise living standards (and thus insure political stability) by using Western credit to purchase new technologies and consumer goods and by conducting business in the Western markets. Moreover, with the policy of detente and the Helsinki process, important political and economic links were established between the West and East that ended three decades of political isolation and autarkic economic policies.

The political opening to the West forced the Soviet bloc countries to commit themselves, at least in principle, to the adherence to international laws. Additionally, their dependence on Western economic aid and credits and their acceptance of international legal obligations[13] gave Western countries important leverage, and the ability to influence domestic policies of East Central European countries. But Eastern Europe's attempts to join the global economy were ill-timed. They came at a time when the global economy was undergoing a revolution in commodity prices, which had longterm implications for both capitalist and communist countries. The inflexible, centrally planned economies were suddenly exposed to the strains and crises that rocked the world economy in the 1970s.[14]

There were important social ramifications to Poland's new relationship with the West. In the 1970s, Poles made 4 million business and personal trips to Western countries.[15] The relaxation in travel restrictions were designed to placate the public, by offering foreign travel privileges to all those not engaged in unauthorized social and political activities. What resulted, however, was that people were better able to assess the misery and inefficiency of life under state socialism; also, there was a dramatic rise in consumer needs and expectations.

In conclusion, at the end of the 1970s, the Polish party-state was facing a political and economic crisis that differed significantly from the classical de-Stalinization crisis. The post-Stalinist crisis in Poland was a much more complex political and ideological phenomenon occurring in a more complex social, political and international environment than the de-Stalinization crises in Hungary and Czechoslovakia. For the first time, the impetus for change shifted from the dissatisfied factions within the party-state to the new political forces within the society. The Communist party lost its militant character and its sense of mission, and international political and economic isolation of the Soviet bloc countries ended.

The Party-State and Society during the Solidarity Period

THE CRISIS OF THE POST-STALINIST REGIME, 1970–1980

The crisis that engulfed Poland during the second half of the 1970s was a reflection of the multi-dimensional process of decay of state socialism. In December 1970 Edward Gierek came to power as a direct result of the worker rebellion against Gomulka's economic policies. Gierek skillfully calmed the worker protests by freezing food prices and scraping the unpopular economic reform. He stabilized the political situation by advocating direct relations between the party and society and a "frank direct dialogue" with all social groups concerning the country's economic and social problems. Moreover, Gierek hoped to rejuvenate the image of the Communist party as the party of economic prosperity, rejecting Marxist orthodoxy and remaining open to economic and political innovations. The political style of the new leaders was a notable departure from the narrow-mindedness of Gomulka's regime. According to George Sanford: "Gierek's programme of economic prosperity and consumerism and reforms designed to improve the political, economic, educational and local-government structures within the existing framework of PUWP hegemony produced a mood of cautious and realistic optimism. This was strengthened by a four-year economic boom and by Gierek's personal popularity, justly gained in this period, as a result of his direct, man-to-man approach and efficiency as a political leader."[1]

Initially these policies were very successful. During the first half of the 1970s, the average income in Poland rose by 40 percent, there were greater varieties of foods and consumer durables on the market, housing availability and transportation were greatly improved. At the same time, the regime made some concessions to the farmers by eliminating hated compulsory deliveries of agricultural products for low, state-set prices and by extending the state health system to the countryside in 1972. The intelligentsia gained some breathing space when the anti-intellectual campaign that followed the events of 1968 subsided under the new party leadership and a new policy of accommodation with the church was introduced. Yet during the second half of the 1970s, Poland's economy began to decline, dashing the high expectations of the first half of the decade. Frustrated expectations have often been seen as one of classical preconditions for revolutionary upheaval. Following this argument, Jacek Kurczewski wrote that the 1980 crisis was not "a rebellion of people in despair but a revolution of those whose hopes remained unfulfilled."[2] However, factors that led to the political social and economic crisis in Poland at the end the 1970s and shaped the character of the Solidarity movement were more complex and reflected a set of various domestic and international developments. In the following section, I will briefly focus on three dimensions of the Polish situation that decisively influenced the course and outcomes of the 1980–81 crisis and its aftermath: Poland's economic decline, the decay of the party-state institutions, and the formation of a new independent political society.

The Polish Economy in the 1970s

Gierek's economic policies constituted a fundamental departure from the "small stabilization" policies characterizing Gomulka's regime.[3] The new policy makers, encouraged by the normalization of relations with West Germany, the general climate of detente, and the availability of Western credits and low interest rates, opted for an aggressive import-led growth strategy. As Kazimierz Poznanski argues,

> the expansionary policy Edward Gierek selected in 1971—different more in degree than in kind from the expansionary policies of many other leaders in Eastern Europe—would have caused Poland serious economic difficulties had there no been intervening factors. However, it was Poland's inability to institute an adjustment policy which worsened the crisis far beyond what one would have predicted on the basis of Gierek's policy alone, and this is exactly what made Poland's the worst crisis in Eastern Europe.[4]

Gierek's economic program involved the acceleration of investment and the rapid expansion of the country's industrial capacities, as well as a restructuring of industry by placing more emphasis on the technologically advanced sectors. By 1975, the volume of investment exceeded the 1970 level by 133 percent, and the share of investment in the gross national product reached 29 percent.[5] No other East European countries pursued such an aggressive investment policy in the 1970s. Gierek based his investment strategy entirely on Western credits that were to be repaid by the export of new technologically advanced products to Western and Third World markets. However, the additional resources pumped into the Polish economy did not facilitate any major structural changes in the country's economic mechanism. The easy access to external resources was regarded by the ruling elite as a golden opportunity to improve consumer market conditions and economic performance without changing the country's economic institutions and their economic strategy was seriously flawed. First, it did not entail necessary institutional reform that would change the behavior of economic actors. Second, the rapid growth of import did not lead to an expected but not correctly stimulated expansion of export. With no significant institutional changes, the industrial sector was not prepared or capable to compete effectively in the international markets for manufactured goods. Third, the relaxation of centralized control over the economy produced what Bartlomiej Kaminski calls a "centrally planned anarchy" characterized by shortages and bottlenecks across the entire economy. Finally, the strategy focused on the rapid expansion of energy-intensive industries and preserved the bias against the private sector both in agriculture and production.[6] As a result, while Polish foreign debt soared from $1.2 billion in 1971 to $23.5 billion in 1980 and the cost of servicing the debt owned to Western financial institutions nearly equaled the annual hard currency earnings in 1980,[7] Polish industry was unable not only to produce high-quality products and to compete on the foreign markets but also failed to respond to growing domestic demands.

Moreover, Gierek's promise to maintain stable food and consumer goods prices, which was an indispensable part of his political strategy to end the 1970–71 workers' strikes and restore political stability, became a significant problem. The negative effects of the policy to hold prices artificially stable was compounded by a wage expansion policy that caused a sharp rise in the real income of the population. Gierek hoped that the real wage expansion policy would allow for an increase in consumption, stimulate domestic production, and at the same time have positive political effects, buying him the support of strategic social groups.[8] In the long run, however, the economic consequences were disastrous. People had more to spend, but the country still did not produce enough for them to buy, and the results were shortages on the consumer market and rising inflation during the second half of the 1970s.

An important component of Gierek's economic strategy was his program of economic reform labeled "improvement of the system of planning and management," prepared in 1972, selectively introduced in 1973 and 1974, and practically abandoned by 1975.[9] The program was abandoned despite the fact that the proposed reforms were very limited and the project did nothing to alter the main features of the centralized economy, such as direct obligatory targets and physical allocation of resources. "In fact, the actual modifications amounted to only one important organizational change, namely amalgamating enterprises into associations and converting them into 'account units' with greater authority over wages, investment, and production decisions."[10] As a result of reforms, Polish industry became even more centralized and monopolistic. Additionally, firms grew less responsive to changes in consumer demands, monopolistic pricing practices were encouraged, and the state's control over wages diminished. The reforms were suspended in 1977, but by this time almost 75 percent of Polish industrial output was concentrated in large economic organizations created during the 1970s.[11] This excessive concentration of industrial activities resulting from Gierek's reform program meant that "in theory"—as Poznanski argues— "the economy looked more like a market economy, but in practice the scheme merely produced more chaos into the operation of the economy and weakened incentives for efficiency."[12] Thus, it can be argued that one of the major causes of the Polish economic crisis was the failure in bureaucratic coordination of economic activities and the erosion of the central planning system. Chaotic planning procedures were reinforced by frequent changes in planned production targets and investment priorities, which became the subject of informal negotiations between industry pressure groups, central bureaucracy, and local authorities. There were important political consequences of reforms as well. Large industrial organizations got into the distributional game through direct access to the central state institutions and by bypassing local and regional party and state authorities. This erosion of mediating and controlling functions of party-state structures on the local level started in the middle of the 1970s and was an unanticipated result of Gierek's regime policies. It lead to the escalation of demands of both the managers and the workers and to the overstretching of the distributional capacity of the party-state.

By the middle of decade there were signs that Gierek's ambitious industrialization program to build a "second Poland" was in trouble. In 1975 industrial investment, which had risen to more than 20 percent of the Gross Domestic Product during the previous three years, dropped to 10.9 percent and in next year was slashed to 1 percent. Deep investment cuts halted hundreds of projects in different stages of construction and resulted in "a staggering figure of 821 billion zlotys frozen in unfinished projects (worth about 50 percent of the 1980 national income)."[13] Concurrently, growth in industrial output declined and agricultural output plummeted to –2.1 percent in 1975 and –1.1 percent in 1976, while the trade deficit and foreign debt rose dramatically. But it was agriculture that proved to be the Achilles' heel of the Polish economy, not because much of the land was privately owned but because of the state's shortsighted, discriminatory policies.[14] The share of agriculture in total investment expenditures declined from 16.5 percent between 1961 and 1970 to 15.7 percent from 1971 to 1980. As a result, about 34 percent of all credits granted to Poland by 1980 were used to purchase agriculture and other consumption products in the West.[15]

With food prices frozen since 1971, declining agricultural output, and general economic difficulties, the need to raise consumer prices in order to stabilize the market and to cut state food subsidies became urgent. In June 1976, Premier Piotr Jaroszewicz announced price increases between 30 to 100 percent on basic commodities. As in 1970, the sudden announcement produced spontaneous and nationwide protests, the biggest being the workers' riots and strikes in Radom and Ursus. Facing serious political instability, the regime revoked the price increases the next day and moved decisively to quell the protest. The 1976 riots constituted a crucial turning point in Polish politics. Despite swift repression of strikes, the political damage suffered by the regime was perhaps greater than that of 1970. The events incited growing oppositional activities that the regime was not able to quell and provided foundations for the alliance between the workers and intelligentsia based oppositional groups.[16]

The failed attempt to adjust consumer prices coupled with a worsening domestic economic situation and ballooning national debt led to the virtual economic disaster during the second half of the 1970s, with far-reaching domestic as well as intrabloc consequences. During the period between 1978 and 1981, the largest contraction in aggregate economic activity in postwar Poland was registered. The country's GNP growth declined from 9.0 percent in 1975 to −2.3 percent in 1979 and −6.0 percent in 1980; growth of industrial output fell from 10.9 percent in 1975 to 2.7 in 1979 and −0.2 in 1980; growth of agricultural output declined to −1.5 percent in 1979 and −9.6 in 1980; growth of investment dropped to −7.9 percent in 1979 and −10.5 in 1980; and the foreign debt rose to $20.7 billion in 1979 and $23.5 billion in 1980. Moreover, the consumer market was increasingly disorganized and plagued by pervasive shortages of basic commodities. In a response to growing shortages, a system of rationing of basic consumer goods was gradually introduced throughout country. I do not believe it is possible to place enough emphasis on the importance of economic factors in facilitating the political crisis of 1980. There were, however, other important dimensions to the Polish crisis.

The Party and the State in the 1970s

After 1956 the Polish party-state appeared to have a more pluralist institutional structure than any of its neighbors. The country's political system, dominated by the Communist party, had a relatively active Parliament, which included other organized although highly controlled political parties: the United Peasant party with a membership of 428,000 in 1977 and the Democratic party with a membership of 96,000, as well as three minor Catholic groups. From 1957, the Polish electoral law allowed more candidates to run than the number of seats available in the Parliament. The quotas of seats were allocated in advance to different organizations represented in the Front of National Unity. In 1976 and 1980 elections, out of 460 seats 261 were allocated to the Communist party, 113 to the Peasant party, 37 to the Democratic party, 36 to activists not associated with any party, and 13 to Catholic activists. Also, following the demise of the Union of Polish Youth in 1956, the youth movement was never again fully centralized and included relatively autonomous unions of Polish Scouts, Polish Students, Socialist Youth, and Peasant Youth.[17] Finally, there was the Polish Catholic church, which, despite the vicissitudes of Church-state relations, was a clear beneficiary of successive crises. It retained and even extended its strength and independence during the entire postwar period.[18] As a self-appointed guardian of the Polish national tradition it played an important role in shaping the country's public opinion through its independent, although heavily censored, publications and Clubs of Catholic Intelligentsia, which survived from the 1956 political thaw. Moreover, following the election of a Polish pope in 1978, the prestige of the church and its political influence were reinforced, and public participation in church activities increased dramatically. According to Christopher Cviic: "Religious processions and pilgrimages attracted even larger crowds than before. Catholic believers became even bolder than in the past. A public petition to allow the Church access to radio and television attracted nearly a million signatures. All this [happened] while morale in the ruling party slumped and the credibility of Gierek's regime was further eroded by serious economic problems."[19]

At first glance, the institutional structure of the Polish party-state and the leading role of the Communist party did not seem visibly shaken during the 1970s. The party congresses, official public appearances, trips abroad, elections, and activities of mass organizations were more carefully orchestrated than ever before. There were no obvious signs of change or a growing political crisis. The Gierek regime presented itself to the population as a pragmatic force interested in economic and social progress and as a champion of reforms. Between 1972 and 1978, alongside its highly publicized but scarcely effective economic changes, the Polish regime carried out a reform of the local administration in which 4,315 lower-level territorial units were replaced by 2,365 larger units. The former middle tier of the administrative structure (county units) was abolished, and the country's twenty-two provinces were reorganized into forty-nine new ones.[20] The structure of the Communist party organization was accordingly changed and forty-nine provincial party committees were established. Apart from the implicit aim of the reform, which was designed to strengthen the central authorities by limiting the power and influence of provincial party secretaries, the reform opened up thousand new, higher-level party and state administration positions in order to allow the new generation of party cadres to move upward. The territorial administration reform, however, had profound consequences for the party's authority and the strength and performance of provincial party organizations. The reform, as Lewis convincingly shows, significantly weakened this crucial tier of party structure and diminished its status and its capacity to control the political and economic developments. Thus, the reform contributed to a gradual decay of party's institutional capacity and authority.[21]

At the same time, the political rituals required by the constitution were efficiently prepared and managed. The results of the elections of March 23, 1980, were identical with those of March 1976, and the Electoral Committee reported that 98.8 percent of those eligible voted, with the National Unity Front receiving 99.5 percent of the valid votes. These elections were accompanied to a lesser degree by a classical show of enforced popular mobilization, but the extent of irregularities and crude rigging of elections results were much more extensive than ever before.[22] The party's rituals were similarly well organized. The seventh and eighth party congresses in 1976 and 1980 did not depart from the usual festive acclamation of the party leadership's policies and did not produce any important personnel changes in the highest party organs. Moreover, membership in the party and party controlled mass organizations was rising throughout the 1970s and the party elites were seemingly united around the program of building a "second Poland." Between 1970 and 1980, membership of the PUWP increased from 2,296,000 to 3,158,000, despite the expulsion of almost four hundred thousand party members during the same period, mostly for failing to pay dues and for gross negligence of party activities.

Yet, despite all "correct" appearances, the institutional structure of the Polish party-state underwent a serious process of internal decay. The pragmatic attitude of the party's leadership and unintended consequences of institutional changes not only weakened the organizational capacity of the party-state but also caused a deep ritualization of ideology and widespread moral malaise. As Andrzej Szczypiorski writes: "Gierek's era brought a destructive erosion of all the structures of power. It also led to the moral decay of the whole party apparatus and of the state administration, and compromised the whole principle of Communist rule. The Polish crisis that began many years ago, and was articulated in 1980 [was] not only an economic crisis. It [was] a spiritual crisis which encompasses everything and everybody."[23]

Scholars studying the emergence of Solidarity emphasized the institutional and ideological dimension of the crisis. According to Wlodzimierz Pankow, the crisis that shook Poland in 1980 was primarily "a crisis of a definite conception of the organization of society, a conception which founded its manifestation in the system of power established in Poland over 30 years ago. It [was] thus a crisis of a certain conception of State, which not long ago was . . . accepted as the only correct model or pattern of the socialist State."[24] In a similar vein, Staniszkis argues, "The evolution of the Polish political system in the 1970s from a totalitarian to an authoritarian-bureaucratic regime was more responsible for the events of August 1980 than was the worsening economic situation."[25] Similarly, Lewis claims that the 1980 crisis was more a result of the crisis of political authority than an effect of the economic crisis.[26] Thus, despite a popular perception that the failure of the economy was the most important factor in precipitating the rise of the Solidarity movement, the crisis of state socialism in Poland was more the outcome of political developments. Unintended consequences of Gierek's reform efforts undermined the relatively coherent system of institutions established after World War II. The progressing decay of the Polish party-state in the 1970s affected their internal organizational structures, their ideological foundations, the relationship between institutional orders of the party-state, and their relations to different segments of society.

Policies of Gierek's regime, described by Staniszkis as a "process of detotalization from above," produced neo-corporatist modes of interest articulation and mediation as well as new modes of protest absorption. This gradual process was characterized by the institutionalization of "lame plu-ralism,"[27] horizontal and vertical segmentation of state activities, and the development of the informal corporate structure of interest representation.[28] Staniszkis argues that "the blockade of interest articulation that was built into the political system led to a situation in which informal competition and negotiation in the economy became the only form of interest articulation left."[29] The formation of semi-institutionalized corporatist networks be-tween the party-state and some professional groups within the society sig-nificantly weakened the official structures of domination, diluted the role of the communist party, and reinforced its de-politicization. According to Daniel Chirot, there was an inherent contradiction between the gradual cor-poratization of social institutions under state-socialist regimes and the mo-nopolistic role of the Communist party, which contributed to the political destabilization. The party, endangered by the development of corporate in-stitutions, periodically attempted to reassert its absolute control and to "dis-organize emergent corporate challengers."[30] Moreover, as Staniszkis argues, corporatist arrangements involve hidden social and political costs. She claims that it was precisely "the social cost of corporatism, i.e., social differ-entiation, the corrosion of law, demoralization, and frustrations of the exec-utive power apparatus [that] led to the explosion of August 1980."[31]

The de-ideologization of the Polish party-state and the development of corporatist practices was followed by a dramatic departure from the party's endorsement of the egalitarian ethos and the ascetic life style of the party functionaries promoted by Gomulka and his regime in the 1960s. Brus de-scribes this situation:

> Dwarfed ideologically and incapable of embarking upon the road of genuine re-newal, Gierek stacked his political fortunes on the prospect of material success, especially for the bureaucracy. The party, state, and economic apparatus were already on the whole removed from any traces of old-fashioned egalitarianism, and hardened enough by experience to eagerly accept "*enrichez-vous*" as a crite-rion of success. [Moreover], the ideological and moral degradation of uncon-trolled power was combined with increased opportunities from corrupt practices due both to gross imbalances in domestic markets and to the complex temptations of business dealings with the West; the state's desperate scramble for every piece of foreign currency and the resulting semilegal parallel circulation of Western money multiplied the opportunities for elicit gains.[32]

The tolerated corruption within the party-state institutions was further re-inforced by the opening of the second economy at the end of the decade in an attempt to deal with the country's escalating economic crisis. During the years 1978–1980, there was considerable growth in small private industry and trade in Poland, which contributed to the differentiation in wages and standards of living among the population. Moreover, a process developed in Poland similar to the one observed in Hungary. The new entrepreneur-ial class and a significant portion of the party-state elite who learned how to exploit market opportunities rapidly accumulated privileges and re-sources.[33] Yet at the same time, large segments of the population were worse off than ever before because they did not have access either to the old redis-tributive system or to market-generated income. Thus, the party-state func-tionaries took full advantage of their political power, which in the 1970s was accompanied by spectacular material benefits and ostentatious con-sumption. This notable change in the motives and behavior of ruling elites was an explosive contributing factor to the emergence of the Solidarity movement. In Aleksander Smolar's words, "Of all unsavory and unpopular features of the Communist system in Poland, perhaps none aroused more hostility and outrage, or contributed more to the outburst of discontent in the summer of 1980, than the existence of widespread social inequalities; blatant disparities of income, social privileges, and material well-being be-tween the bulk of the population on the one hand and the small ruling elite on the other."[34]

In conclusion, it was the institutional and ideological decay of the Polish party-state in the 1970s, the dramatic economic decline, and growing popu-lar outrage resulting from the elaborate system of privileges and corruption and increasing social inequalities that produced all the preconditions for a major political crisis. There was, however, one additional factor that had the crucial impact not only for the impending political crisis, but its aftermath as well. This was the party-state policy of repressive tolerance introduced by Gierek. In describing this policy, Staniszkis writes: "Analogous politically to the creation of the system of lame pluralism was the introduction of a pattern of repressive toleration, in which informal political opposition was tolerated. . . . Gierek's team hoped that the social and political costs of per-mitting the existence of such opposition would be outweighed by the advan-tages. Among the latter was the image of 'the most liberal ruling elite in Eastern Europe', which increased Poland's access to foreign credits."[35] The introduction of repressive toleration was a further indication of the de-ideol-ogization in the political practices of the Polish party-state. However, it had unexpectedly crucial consequences that shaped political crisis in 1980. The political space was opened for creation of independent political and social organizations whose activists supplied cadres for the Solidarity movement.

The Formation of Independent Political Society

Relations between the Polish ruling elite and the country's intellectuals, characterized since 1956 by the ever-widening gap between the two groups, entered a radically new stage in the 1970s.[36] For the first time, the Catholic intellectual movement, which survived the shifting phases of the state-church relations largely intact and benefited from Gierek's attempt to im-prove these relations and the revisionist intellectuals from the mid-1950s, who were either expelled or left the party, realized that only their united front against party policies would result in an extension of intellectual freedoms. The manifesto of this difficult alliance, which had to overcome decades of mutual hostilities and suspicions as well as political and ideological differences, came from than a young left-wing intellectual, Adam Michnik, in his 1977 book published in Paris. Michnik analyzed without any prejudice misunderstandings and ill-intentioned relations between the main currents of the Polish intellectual life after the war and paid long overdue respect for an uncompromising stance of many representatives of the Catholic intelligentsia. He emphasized: "It has been many years since the Catholic Church in Poland has tried to protect the wealthy of this world. The Church now stands stubbornly on the side of the prosecuted and the oppressed. The enemy of the Left is not the Church but totalitarianism. The central conflict in Poland is the conflict between the totalitarian authorities and a society systematically deprived of its rights. In the struggle against totalitarianism, the role of the Church cannot be overemphasized."[37] This alliance was possible both due to the strength of independent Catholic intellectuals sheltered by the church from party-state repression, and the virtual collapse of anti-clerical and party oriented revisionist movements within left-wing Polish intellectual circles. The political crisis of March 1968, the anti-intellectual campaign that followed, and the Soviet invasion of Czechoslovakia produced the ultimate separation between the Polish intellectuals and the Communist party and its ideology. This also meant the collapse of revisionism as a distinct political program. Leszek Kolakowski points out that March 1968, "despite all prosecution and repressions, finally liberated Polish culture from the ties with the Communist system and its ideology. There was nothing left to 'revise' anymore, and nobody was ready to expect any improvement from one or another party faction."[38]

The first outward sign that Polish intellectuals had recovered from the repressions of 1968 and again assumed an active role in Polish political life was an open letter issued in December 1975. Sent to the speaker of the Parliament, it protested the proposed amendments to the Polish constitution, designed to legalize and reinforce the "leading role of the communist party" and the country's allegiance to the Soviet Union and the socialist community. The letter was signed by fifty-nine prominent representatives of Polish cultural and academic life and included a critique of civil rights violations committed by the party-state. The signatories stated that the guarantees of basic freedoms "cannot be reconciled with the official recognition of the leading role of one party in the state system of power. . . . This kind of a constitutional statement would confer on a political party the role of an organ of state authority, which would be neither responsible nor controlled by society."[39] Despite this and other protests, the intended amendments to the constitution were adopted, but the question of the party's leading role became a critical issue in the years to come. Jack Bielasiak writes that "even before August 1980, and certainly afterward, all disputes touched in some way and to some extent on the concept of the party's 'leading role', from the November 1980 registration of Solidarity as an independent trade union to discussion on factory self-management and Solidarity's right to appoint factory directors."[40] The protests against changes in the constitution galvanized intellectual circles and students in the country's most prestigious universities, yet the real stimulus for the development of independent political activities came with the worker rebellion in 1976.

In June 1976, the unexpected announcement of substantial food price increases triggered immediate worker response. Strikes and street demonstrations erupted in several industrial cities,[41] and the militarized police were dispatched to suppress workers' protests. The riot police brutally suppressed the demonstrations, and those who participated in either the demonstrations or the strikes were arrested, fired from their jobs, and black-listed. There were several political trials where the penalties ranged from fines to lengthy prison sentences. Although the price increases were canceled the next day, the savage treatment of detained workers at police stations caused an outrage across the country. According to Michael Bernhard: "The June 1976 strikes had significance beyond being an example of collective action that achieved its goal, namely cancellation of the proposed price rises. . . . The case of June 1976 was a landmark event for two politically active social groups—the working class and the critical intelligentsia."[42]

In September 1976, a group of thirteen intellectuals founded an organization whose goal was to defend and provide legal and material support for prosecuted workers, known as the Committee for the Defense of Workers (KOR).[43] The founders of KOR adopted a strategy of selective openness, and their addresses and telephone numbers were distributed with every document they issued. At the same time, certain parts of the organization, such as its publishing outlets and printing facilities, remained underground. KOR published the clandestine *Information Bulletin*, challenging the state's monopoly of information. It also published the literary periodical *Zapis*, which printed the works of Polish writers and academics banned by the censors. The emergence of, and strategies employed by KOR established the model for oppositional activities, expressed in Jacek Kuron's famous dictum "Don't burn down committees, found your own." This irreversibly changed the Polish domestic political situation by starting the gradual process of independent organization of Polish society.[44] For three years after 1976, a multitude of independent oppositional groups emerged in various cities across Poland, among different professional groups and segments of the population. They adopted similar patterns of activities and focused most explicitly on defending human and political rights and on documenting abuses of power, incompetence, and corruption of the party-state functionaries. Independent publishing and distribution networks based on clandestine publishing houses, the so-called second circulation, soon became a rapidly expanding industry and a powerful tool in shaping the country's public opinion.[45] The formation of new opposition groups was stimulated by the existence of others, and they were often linked by personal contacts and elaborate networks for the distribution of underground publications. The oppositional movements in Poland have attracted much scholarly attention.[46]

Examples of oppositional activities during this period include the formation of the Movement for the Defense of Human and Civil Rights (ROPCiO) in March 1977. Its goals were similar to those of KOR. In May 1977, the first Student Solidarity Committee was created in Cracow and soon the initiative was extended to all important academic centers of the country. The students set out to establish clandestine printing houses and to promote self-educational activities, such as seminars and lectures covering political and historical issues prohibited in official classrooms. In September, KOR redefined its agenda, accepted broader objectives, and changed its name to the Committee for Social Self-Defense-KOR. During the fall of 1977, there was a proliferation of independent cultural and political periodicals targeted at specific groups such as workers, peasants, intellectuals or students. In 1978 a group of academics and artists announced the foundation of the Society for Scientific Courses (TKN), which sponsored lectures and seminars organized by the clandestine Flying University in all major academic centers.[47]

Alongside officially existing Clubs of Catholic Intelligentsia, several other lay Catholic organizations emerged, such as the Young Poland Movement, and some priests even became the leaders of oppositional activities. The priest from the village Zbroza Wielka organized one of the Farmers' Self-Defense committees, which were established in several local communities in 1978. In Gdansk and Katowice, the first committees of Free Trade Unions were organized during the same year. Oppositional activities expanded even more in 1979. The already existing groups were supplemented by a strictly clandestine group Polish League for Independence (PPN), which published an elaborate political program that placed the regaining of the country's independence as its foremost objective. The Confederation for Independent Poland (KPN) was formed as the first explicitly political party representing a radical nationalistic program. At the same time, a group of intellectuals with ties to both the regime and the opposition founded a debating society, Experience and the Future(DiP), which despite problems with authorities, soon issued a series of reports revealing the extent of the Polish economic, social, and political crisis. Also, the official professional associations such as the Polish Sociological Association, became important centers of debate and oppositional activities. By the end of the decade, the democratic opposition (a collective term including all the groups) became a significant political force capable of mustering intellectual and material resources for various clandestine activities and open campaigns, recruiting an increasing number of new members and sympathizers, and penetrating all segments and important groups in society—even the apparatus of the party-state, through its personal contacts and independent publications.

In comparison to any other movement that opposed the existing state-socialist regimes, the size, organizational strength, and capabilities of the Polish democratic opposition were unparalleled. However, its impact on the course of the 1980 crisis has been often overemphasized. As Kolakowski rightly points out: "The strikes occurring in the summer of 1980 were by no means caused by KOR's activity. They were rooted in the economic and social disaster that the power system had produced, and they were organized on the spot by embryonic independent workers' unions. Yet KOR's influence on the way the workers voiced their grievances and articulated their demands was certainly essential."[48] Thus, one of the most important achievements of the democratic opposition in the 1970s was the creation of a new political discourse, which laid a powerful claim to the Polish national and historical legacy. The Communist party used national rhetoric to bolster its political image, suffering from the erosion of communist ideology since 1956. Now the party faced a challenge that finally destroyed this effective legitimizing device. Beginning with the mid-1970s, Polish intellectuals developed a new political language and revived old political and cultural traditions and identities that allowed seemingly unreconcilable political actors within society, such as the Catholic church and the democratic left, to build new all-inclusive identities, monopolize political initiative, and win public support. This new political discourse decoupled social analysis from traditional Marxist language and was built around the concepts of human and political rights, legality, individual responsibility, personal rights, and neo-evolutionism.[49] These ideas, according to Roger Scruton "constitute[d] a decisive reaction against the previously accepted alternative of 'socialism with a human face.'"[50] The redefinition of political language facilitated an intellectual reconciliation between various opposition movements and the church, and revindicated progressive national traditions. It also facilitated what Jan Kubik calls "the public counterhegemony," which "prepares public consciousness for a revolution in such a way that once a precipitating factor does occur, large numbers of people mobilize in a short time and form an organization with relative ease."[51]

There was, however, one more important event with immense impact on Polish society and political developments. In October 1978, a Pole, Karol Cardinal Wojtyla was elected pope, and in June 1979 he made his first return visit to Poland. The election and the visit created an overwhelming sense of joy and unity among Poles, and the church as never before became a symbol of the independence of Polish society and resistance to communist rule. The pope's visit witnessed the biggest peaceful manifestations in the nation's recent memory. It was an extraordinary show of unity and provided final evidence of the political and moral poverty of the Polish party-state. Although the role of the Catholic church in the emergence and politics of the Solidarity movement has been treated with a certain ambiguity by many Western scholars, one can hardly find a more important element in the Polish political conundrum. A perceptive observer of Polish developments, Timothy Garton Ash emphasizes the role of Polish pope not only in precipitating August 1980, but also in the whole political evolution of the region in the 1980s:

> If I was to name a single date for the 'beginning of the end' in this inner history of Eastern Europe, it would be June 1979. The judgement may be thought excessively Polonocentric, but I do believe that the Pope's first great pilgrimage to Poland was that turning-point. Here for the first time, we saw that massive, sustained, yet supremely peaceful and self-disciplined manifestation of social unity, the gentle crowd against the Party-state, which was both the hallmark and the essential domestic catalyst of change in 1989. . . . The Pope's visit was followed, just over a year later, by the birth of Solidarity, and without the Pope's visit it is doubtful if there would have been a Solidarity.[52]

The Pope's election and visit came in a period when a great number of activists associated with the Clubs of Catholic Intelligentsia and contributors to official but independent Catholic periodicals participated in unauthorized, and to some extent oppositional activities. Also, despite objection from the church hierarchy, many priests joined or even organized oppositional groups. Thus, the church's premises were often places of unauthorized meetings, lectures, and debates. Moreover the unauthorized Catholic youth movement (Oazy) had attracted more than two hundred thousand students. Kubik points to four features of Catholicism that reinforced the influence and political role of the church:

> First, the Church's discourse was reinvigorated and its influence among the predominantly Roman Catholic populace increased. This must be attributed to the impact of the Second Vatican Council. . . . Second, the Catholic discourse frequently invoked such popular ethical principles as the dignity of the human person and the dignity of human work. . . . Third, the Church's pronouncements, such as Sunday sermons or pastoral letters, were the only widely accessible cultural media through which such political principles as (liberal) democracy, pluralism, or full national sovereignty were consistently propounded. Fourth, the discourse of Polish Catholicism has developed symbolic means to anchor the political in the ethical and in the religious.[53]

The Catholic church's moral authority was paralleled by its organizational strength. In the late 1970s, the Polish church had considerable human and material resources. It was organized in twenty-seven dioceses divided into 7,118 parishes. It had seventy-seven bishops and 15,444 priests. Its male monasteries had 7,716 members, including 3,977 monastic priests. There were also 26,586 nuns and, in 1980, 6,285 man were training for priesthood. The church had 12,213 churches and chapels and 2,449 convents. It ran forty-six seminaries, four papal faculties, the nonstate Catholic University, and the Academy of Catholic Theology. The Catholic presses published fifteen religious publications, of which the most successful reached some two hundred thousand readers.[54] In short, the church became a powerful force in Poland's social and political life that nobody could ignore.

Poland entered the 1980s in the state of multidimensional crisis. The unraveling of the Gierek regime's effort to create a socialist consumer society plunged the country into a disastrous economic crisis. The workers' rebellion of 1976, the defiance of intellectuals and students, the anarchization of the party-state institutions, the collapse of official political discourse and moral bankruptcy of the ruling elite opened the political opportunity structure for the organized challenge from below. Emerging opposition movement and organizations were protected by the Catholic church with its institutional resources and moral authority. The repressive capacity of the party-state declined significantly as a result of its internal weakness and pressures for respecting human rights coming from the West and backed by considerable economic leverage. In July 1980 the Polish regime attempted once more to increase food prices. In response the wave of worker strikes rapidly spread across the country. Gradually the strikes acquired a determined and organized character. The striking workers had organizational, intellectual, and material resources they lacked in the past. Networks of independent communication linking all segments of the population, potential independent leaders and organizers, political and social agendas, and a powerful and independent center of authority provided by the Catholic church already existed in Polish society. For the first time, the triple alliance of the church, the workers, and the intelligentsia laid a firm foundation for the successful revolt against the party-state apparatus. From the first days of the strike in the Lenin Shipyard through the first months of building the official structures of the independent trade-union movement, the resources provided by the democratic opposition, combined with growing popular mobilization and sheltered by the authority of the church, created a powerful revolutionary movement from below. For the first time in the postwar history of the region, the Communist party was forced to negotiate with independent organizations and was forced to surrender its control over vast areas of social and political life. These characteristics of the Polish crisis in the late 1970s set it decisively apart from the two previously analyzed cases. The independent self-organization of Polish society and the presence of a powerful ally fundamentally changed the rules of the political game and made it impossible for the subsequent demobilization policies to succeed in a way they did either in Hungary after 1956 or in Czechoslovakia after 1968.

THE SELF-LIMITING REVOLUTION

The open political crisis in Poland started with the worker strikes in the summer of 1980, which brought almost the entire country to a standstill. The government desperately tried to stabilize the situation and dealt first with short-term protest actions in July by granting immediate pay raises, often unsolicited, to workers in individual factories. The demands for economic concessions were soon combined with a wide range of political demands.[55] The extent of the strike action, which affected more than four thousand enterprises by the end of August, and the determination of strike committees culminated in the Gdansk Agreements, in which the Polish party-state was forced to accept the right of workers to form organizations independent of party and state control.[56] This unprecedented agreement led to the emergence of the first independent trade-union movement in the Soviet bloc and resulted in a protracted political crisis that lasted sixteen months. This period had three distinct phases. From September 1980 to March 1981, the new trade union movement was institutionalized, overcoming the resistance of the party-state apparatus on provincial and local levels. From the "Bydgoszcz crisis" to July 1981, Solidarity attempted to go beyond the constraints of the trade union formula and redesign its goals and strategies. Its congress in September 1981 adopted a more politically assertive agenda, and the confrontation with the state became imminent. The crisis caused internal turmoil in Poland and destabilized political relations within the Soviet bloc. The political stalemate between the party-state and the newly formed independent organizations that emerged was broken on December 13, 1981, when the Solidarity movement was suppressed by an internal military operation and the imposition of martial law. The sixteen months of Solidarity's legal existence have been one of the most extensively analyzed periods in East European politics after the Second World War. Dramatic political events and struggles that shook Poland captured the imagination of scholars and public opinion around the world and produced a wealth of journalistic and scholarly accounts and analysis.[57] Therefore, in this section I will focus only to those factors that became decisive for demobilization policies and efforts to reequilibrate the regime that followed the imposition of martial law. I will briefly look at the organization and actions of independent political actors, the situation of the party-state, and its responses to the changing domestic and international circumstances.

The successful conclusion of the strikes and somewhat unexpected concessions forced upon the Polish party-state by the striking workers made the political conflict in Poland qualitatively different from the two previously analyzed cases. The summer of 1980 not only witnessed rapid popular political mobilization, which involved all social strata and regions of the country, but perhaps more important, the new organization established as the result of agreements sign between the government and strike committees won significant political concessions and the time necessary to secure and consolidate the achievements of the successful country-wide collective action. By the end of the summer, Polish society had the new organizational structures that emerged during the strikes and the network of old embryonic oppositional organizations that were formed in the end of the 1970s. For the first time, the state-socialist regime faced an independent opposition movement with the capacity to mobilize millions, independent resources, and experienced grass-root leaders. As David Ost emphasizes:

> In August 1980 strikes in Gdansk and Szczecin resulted in the facto legalization of the independent trade-union Solidarity. Literally overnight, the party-state juridical monopoly on public life and on the representation of social interests was destroyed. An independent, legal civil society had suddenly been created. The opposition's main goal had been accomplished. The period for which the program of societal democratization was appropriate came to an end. A new historical period had begun. No one was ready for it.[58]

However, Solidarity, as it came to be known, did not emerge overnight as a powerful, nationwide, and unified organization. The intellectual and organizational groundwork for its creation was built during the several weeks following the Gdansk Agreements. Staniszkis writes that "the most striking characteristic of the initial period of the movement's history was the painful process of cramming that radical wave of protest and class war into a 'trade union' formula. Nearly all other features of the movement stemmed from this self-limitation of the Polish revolution."[59]

Although the right of workers to form independent trade unions was approved by the party-state, the Gdansk agreements were not altogether clear over who had the right to form new unions nor did they prescribe the shape these new worker organizations were to follow. The Polish ruling elite hoped for fragmented factory-based unions coordinated through reformed industrial-branch structures of the existing unions. However, one of the most effective organizational innovations developed during the strikes was the network of regional interfactory strike committees that represented all factories and state-run institutions. These strike-generated territorial organizations were a powerful driving force in establishing the unions' structure. When the activists of some thirty-five new union organizations met in Gdansk on September 17 to discuss the problems of union structure, the decision was made to form one national union based on the Gdansk statutes and to borrow its name, Solidarity.[60] The participants estimated that at that time more than three million people from approximately thirty-five hundred enterprises declared their willingness to join the new unions. However, the process of organization was well advanced only in those enterprises that went on strike during August. The decisions adopted at the September 17 meeting started the parallel process of organizing the factory and regional branches of the unified movement across the country and struggling for its legal recognition. On September 22, the National Coordinating Committee (KKP) representing all thirty-five regional organizations was formed to approve the final draft of the union's statutes. The battle for registration, which forced Solidarity to declare a highly successful one-hour nationwide warning strike and to issue a threat of a general strike, ended on November 10, when Solidarity's charter was accepted by the Polish Supreme Court.[61]

From the very beginning, the authorities tried to restrain union organizing and delay the implementation of the agreements. There was widespread police harassment of unions organizers, especially in provinces and small cities, as well as repressive actions by enterprise management and party organizations. At the same time, efforts were made to boost the prestige and resources of the existing state-controlled unions. However, according to Ost:

> Discredited and isolated, none of the official unions won over many workers during the Solidarity period. Despite (and, no doubt, because of) all the official support and media coverage that they received, they could not shake their image as defenders of the old way at a time everyone was pressing for something new. In November 1980, when Solidarity was at last officially registered as a national union, the government dropped its campaign to present the old unions as a viable alternative.[62]

Additionally, the government tried to delay and evade acting on various elements of the agreements dealing with economic concessions and social benefits. Finally, having full control over the media, the government launched a smear campaign warning against the increasing penetration of the new workers organizations by "anti-socialist elements." This campaign was meant to discredit KOR and KPN activists who often advised various regional and factory union committees and undermine the cooperation between the workers and independent intellectuals. Party members were encouraged to join the union in an effort to secure some influence on the organization's activities from within.[63]

Yet despite all obstacles, by the end of November Solidarity had established its organizational structure and become a powerful and dynamic social and political force. The union was designed as a federation of largely autonomous regional chapters coordinated by the National Coordinating Committee (KKP). After the Solidarity congress in September 1981, it became the National Committee (KK), with a Presidium of twelve members headed by Lech Walesa and headquartered in Gdansk. It served as a consulting and mediating body and represented the entire union in its dealings with the state and foreign organizations. The KK also controlled the organization's finances. The union's basic structure included thirty-eight regional committees and two smaller districts as well as enterprise committees in factories and institutions. Nearly forty thousand full-time employees worked for the Solidarity organization. The union's membership reached approximately 9.5 million by September 1981, and chapters of the union were organized not only in industrial enterprises but also in nonindustrial sectors of the workforce, including education, health service, other public services, and even in many state institutions. Alongside the basic regional structure, there were also two other types of structures. First were coordination committees organized along industry and sectoral branches that cut across the regional structure. The second was "Siec," which emerged in March 1981 as a network of enterprise committees representing the biggest and most important industrial plants in the Polish economy. The Siec focused on economic reform and emerged as a prime advocate of industrial self-management proposals. Thus, in the span of several months, Solidarity evolved into a huge, well-designed organizational structure possessing massive human and material resources as well as a massive and disciplined following, supported by all segments of society.[64] The institutionalization of Solidarity also provided the impetus for the independent organization of other social groups that were unable to join the union because they were not employed by state enterprises or public institutions.

University students were the first such group to start their own independent organization. Already in September 1980, founding committees emerged in several major universities, whose representatives formed the Independent Student Union (NZS).[65] By the end of October, the National Organizing Committee was established, but it took several months of bitter struggle with state authorities before the organization was legally registered in February 1981. It held its first congress that April, established its offices at ninety-two universities and colleges, and had eighty thousand members (more than 30 percent of the student population in Poland). That same spring, the student self-government was established at universities, providing another independent structure for student activities. For the rest of the Solidarity period, the structure of Polish universities was highly pluralistic, with the old, state-approved student organization (SZSP), the new independent one (NZS), the student self-government, the party organization, the Solidarity organization, the old reformed trade union (ZNP), and democratically elected traditional academic self-governing bodies all represented.

Organizing an independent union of farmers was the most difficult undertaking.[66] At that time, 42 percent of the population lived in the countryside, and Poland had three million private farms. Polish farmers, however, did not represent a cohesive political force, due to four decades of exploitation, cultural and political mistreatment and abuse. Beginning in September, efforts to organize peasants began in several regions. The three organizations (Rural Solidarity, Peasant Solidarity, and the Union of Agricultural Producers) that emerged in the fall adopted common statutes in December and applied for registration. But the application was rejected by the court in February 1981.[67] Peasant activists responded by organizing a protest campaign with activities ranging from hunger strikes to occupation of public buildings. In March, the three independent farmer organizations united, calling themselves the Independent Self-governing Trade Union of Individual Farmers "Solidarity." The battle for registration intensified, becoming one of the most divisive political issues in the nation. After the Bydgoszcz crisis,[68] the Solidarity union made the legalization of the peasants' Solidarity one of its foremost demands. Finally, the farmer organization was registered in May 1981. At the same time, the state-sponsored farmer organization—the Union of Agricultural Circles and Organizations—was registered, creating a party-state controlled balance to independent organizations in the countryside. As Jerzy Holzer points out: "The unity of the farmers movement in the countryside was very fragile. . . . In the united Farmers Solidarity the unity was often only a formal position. In reality groups of activists intensely competed with one another."[69] Despite political divisions among peasant organizations, the farmers' Solidarity and several smaller farmer unions represented a considerable social force with 3.5 million members.

Artisans, craftsmen and small businessmen also organized their own independent union. In March of 1981, there was the first meeting of representatives of organizing committees from several regions. At the end of April, the registration application of the Independent Self-governing Trade Union of Individual Artisans "Solidarity" was presented to the court, and the organization was officially recognized in June 1981. However, similar to the peasants' union, the organization was plagued by internal rivalries and conflict between different groups of activists.

The explosion of popular participation following August 1980 transformed the existing state-controlled professional organizations, which underwent a rapid process of internal democratization. The Polish Writers Union, the Polish Journalists Union, and other organizations of creative intelligentsia, which had always kept a measure of autonomy and harbored people representing oppositional undercurrents, emphatically declared their independence from the party-state. At their congresses, persons known for their independence and oppositional activities in the past were elected as new officers. By September 1980, the Coordinating Committee of Creative and Scientific Unions was formed to strengthen the political position of small professional associations and unions. This committee with close links to Solidarity tried to become a moderating voice of Polish intellectuals and often used its prestige to act as mediator in the emerging conflicts. There was also a change in executives at the Polish Academy of Sciences and at the universities. New officials worked to establish independent horizontal links with each other in order to increase their political influence. To this purpose, the newly elected rectors established the Convention of Polish Rectors in the fall of 1981. However, they became entangled in mediating the student strikes in November and December, and this prevented them from playing a more significant role in the country's politics.

Among the independent organizations that existed prior to the summer of 1980, those affiliated with the Catholic church grew rapidly. Clubs of Catholic Intelligentsia expanded in number from four to approximately sixty by December 1981. While the Catholic intelligentsia and many individual priests were deeply involved in the Solidarity movement, the church's hierarchy attempted to position itself as a mediator of conflicts between society and the state. The notion of a Grand Coalition, uniting the Communist party, Solidarity, and the Catholic church, was discussed in the fall of 1981 and most clearly presented by Ryszard Reiff, the chairman of the PAX (a historically pro-regime Catholic organization), who advocated the establishment of a corporatist arrangement between major political actors as the only way to stabilize Poland's political situation and resolve the deepening economic crisis.[70]

From the onset of the strikes, former organizations of the democratic opposition were involved in the creation of independent trade unions. The majority of members of KOR, ROPCiO, and Ruch Mlodej Polski joined Solidarity either as organizers or advisers. They were later elected to many important positions within the movement. Some organizations, however, such as the Society for Scientific Courses, clandestine publishers, and underground papers, continued their activities alongside Solidarity without becoming incorporated within the movement itself. Besides publishing its reports, the organization of reform-minded elites—the DiP—played a major role in trying to bridge a growing gap between the party-state elites and Solidarity. The KPN, the only self-declared political party, despite the imprisonment of its core leaders, continued its activities within the framework of a cadre political party, expanded its networks, and won many supporters among the workers. Only KOR, the most famous and influential oppositional organization, officially disbanded and entrusted its original mission and goals to Solidarity.

The civic fever, sparked by Solidarity, spread to all social groups, cities, and villages in the country, and to all organizations and institutions of the Polish party-state. Even the police and the military were not immune and their members attempted to organize independent trade unions. Thus the emergence and conscious self-organization of independent democratic civil society became the most striking characteristic of the Solidarity period.[71] Unlike Hungary, rapid mass mobilization from below was followed by a relatively long and unconstrained period of the self-organization of society. Polish society and the emerging organizations had sufficient time to establish their own organizational structures, mobilize resources, and develop their own distinct identities, symbols, political language, and programs. And, according to Richard Spielman, the tactics of the Solidarity movement were vaguely familiar to those of the ruling elite. "For sixteen months, Solidarity's revolution . . . proceeded in the manner of Stalinist salami tactics in reverse, as the union slowly sliced one professional organization or public institution after another from Leninist organizational control. . . . this was Leninist history repeating itself not as tragedy but as farce."[72] For the first time after World War II, the party-state in Eastern Europe faced a very powerful and well-organized opponent capable of destabilizing the entire country and even of seizing political control. The developments that followed the imposition of martial law were a telling testimony not only to the weakness of the Polish party-state but also to the strength of independent political society that emerged during the crisis.

Despite its political strength, the limitations Solidarity placed upon itself and its "anti-political" program inherited from the democratic opposition in the 1970s saved the party-state from imminent collapse and dispelled the danger of Soviet military intervention. It produced, however, increasing tensions and the identity crisis within the movement, which resulted in more radical efforts to redefine its agenda after August 1981. This situation created a peculiar paradox. While Solidarity had enough political power to block the state's policies, it was excluded, mostly by its own choice, from participating in important political and economic decisions. The movement's political limitations caused increasing frustration among the leaders as well as the rank-and-file members. This frustration was reflected in "symbolic politics" based on "falsely articulated or surrogate conflicts, which expressed superficially the real cleavages dividing society from the ruling elite."[73] Moreover, preparing martial law, the Polish party-state stopped pursuing any active policies of reform, so as to aggravate the existing political situation.[74] A political vacuum was created by the inaction of the state, which Solidarity was not prepared to fill.

As the self-organization of society from below was an exceptional characteristic of the Polish crisis, so were the situation and internal developments within the Polish party-state. The party-state was not smashed as it was in Hungary in 1956 nor was it split by paralyzing internal conflict as in Czechoslovakia. As Alain Touraine emphasizes:

> The military interests of the Soviet Union in Poland were never directly threatened during the Solidarity period; there was no civil disturbance, not even mass demonstrations outside official buildings; the daily press, radio and television remained throughout under the control of the Party, as did Parliament, the economic administration, and, of course, the army, the militia and the secret police. If the power of the Party weakened and even disintegrated, then it was through its own impotence and decay rather than any direct pressure from the masses, who never went beyond short national warning strikes.[75]

During the crisis, however, a very peculiar political development occurred. The regime's center of gravity gradually shifted from the party to the state, and within the state it shifted from the civilian institutions and personnel to the military. The following section will briefly explore the situation that existed in the Polish party-state during the Solidarity period.

THE PARTY-STATE DURING THE SOLIDARITY PERIOD

The political crisis and emergence of the Solidarity movement did not lead to the institutional collapse of the Polish party-state. It accelerated, however, the party-state's transformation toward an authoritarian state that was taking place since the beginning of the 1970s. This meant the de-ideologization of the state and abandonment of its Marxist ideology as well as the diminution of the Communist party's role in country's politics. In the words of Staniszkis, with the formation of Solidarity, "the five roles characteristic of the communist party in a totalitarian regime (politicization of the masses, use of trade unions as fully controlled transmission belts, recruitment and training of a new political elite, guidance and leadership through the permanent presence of party members in the authorities of many organizations, and direct control over the economy) have now become seriously limited."[76] Facing so powerful a challenge from below, the party-state's institutions had to greatly modify their political practices. As Jan de Weydenthal points out: "The authorities faced very different problems: that of institutional adjustment to the new situation, and of rebuilding their lost credibility as well as their morale and self-confidence. In fact, the growth of social activism that followed the August–September agreement affected the system's routine so much that many of its institutions, procedures, and programs appeared to the public and to many officials themselves as simply irrelevant."[77] But the ruling elite was not prepared for and/or able to begin radical changes and reform to respond to accelerating popular demands and pressures, and so from the very beginning the regime was on the defense. As the new party secretary, Stanislaw Kania, declared in October 1980: "The much needed renewal of public life can only be a socialist renewal, and the leading force in the process will be the Polish United Workers' Party."[78]

Several strategies were employed by the Polish state in order to protect its dominant position in society and stem the magnitude of political changes. First, the regime procrastinated in any dealings they had with the newly formed union and delayed implementing the concessions they granted Solidarity. Local officials harassed union organizers, and every effort was made to co-opt the emerging leaders and organizations. At the same time, the existing party-state institutions and organizations were repackaged. Changes in their leadership and programs were designed to enhance their credibility. The regime's hope was that the popular political mobilization would gradually subside and that the system would return to its routine political practices as it happened in past political crises. The second strategy involved an attempt to insulate some core institutions of the party-state, especially its coercive forces, from the wave of popular civic activation and reformist actions. The special effort was made to reduce any conflicts and tensions within the Communist party in the attempt to preserve its organizational coherence. The third strategy, used frequently since the Spring of 1981, was the attempt to shelter the party from direct responsibility of running the day-to-day affairs of the state and the economy. This was accomplished by enhancing the role and visibility of the government and the state apparatus, which acted as a protective belt between the party and society so as to avoid any direct confrontation between the Communist party and Solidarity. Finally, the party also modified its political rhetoric. The notion of the "vanguard" of the working class and the ardent ideological commitment were replaced by the notion of the "social contract" and traditional patriotism expressed in terms of the national interests of all the Polish people. This signaled that the ruling elite was building a new, quasi-legal legitimacy based on nationalistic foundations and pragmatic appeals. It should be noted, however, that these strategies were developed in the heat of confrontation and, as Staniszkis emphasizes, "the evolution of the Polish political system following the wave of strikes in Summer 1980 was more the result of a web of spontaneous processes and uncontrolled political forces than the effect of purposeful, reform-oriented action."[79]

While for several months the ruling elites were retreating under Solidarity's pressure, after the Solidarity congress, held in September and October of 1981, relations between the union and the authorities deteriorated noticeably. It was becoming clear that the significant policy change was implemented, and the party-state's actions became purposefully confrontational. During talks focusing on economic reform in October 1981, Solidarity pressed for the creation of a Social Council for the Economy, which would supervise the work on resolving Poland's economic crisis. In response, the government formally charged the union with attempting to "undermine the state structures and to overthrow the existing constitutional order and the principles of people's power." Attacks on the union escalated after the Central Committee meeting on October 18, during which General Wojciech Jaruzelski replaced Stanislaw Kania as first secretary of the party, monopolizing the three most important party-state positions—prime minister, minister of defense, and the head of the party. During this meeting the Central Committee issued a strong resolution blaming the union for the economic crisis and appealed to all party members who belonged to Solidarity to define their political position.[80] The party's increased hostility was followed by renewed press restrictions, reflected by the removal of several daily and weekly newspaper editors. On October 28, Solidarity staged a one-hour general strike to protest both the government refusal to relax its control over economic policies and the hostile propaganda campaign that had been launched against it. Shortly after, a resolution was passed in the Polish parliament that demanded an immediate end to all strikes. The same session debated granting special emergency powers to the government. Also in October, the first military "operational groups" were sent to the countryside to "supervise food distribution" and "assist" in the work of local administration and the economy.[81] At this time, preparations for military action, which had began in the early Spring of 1981, were already in full swing; the stage was set for final confrontation.

The Polish Communist party survived the initial Solidarity challenge largely intact by deposing its leader, Edward Gierek, and a few of his cronies in the Politburo. Because the impetus for change came from outside its structures, the party was able to avoid a major internal split within its ruling elite, similar to one that destroyed the Hungarian party in 1956 and paralyzed the Czechoslovak party in 1968. Although there was a pressure to democratize the party from within and factional struggles over policies and strategies for dealing with Solidarity during the whole period, Kania (who replaced Gierek as first secretary in September 1980) was able to muster a necessary unity and discipline to keep the party together. He was also able to successfully manipulate the Extraordinary Ninth Party Congress that met in July 1981 to prevent any major challenge to the party's leadership. During the entire period the party leadership was able to maintain the appearance of party unity and its institutional coherence, but the party experienced significant amount of turmoil at all its levels.

During the crisis, the party experienced a wholesale exchange of cadres in key positions at all organizational levels. The first major reshuffle in the top positions followed Gierek's removal in September 1980. It was followed by more top personnel replacement in April 1981 but the most dramatic change in the composition of the party leadership came as a result of the elections held during the Ninth Extraordinary Party Congress. At this congress, 1,964 relatively democratically selected representatives of the party (among them almost four hundred who were at the same time Solidarity members and many who represented a reformist orientation) elected the party's new Central Committee, from which many prominent incumbents were absent.[82] The delegates to the Extraordinary Congress, however, did not accomplish any revolutionary transformations that could alter the character and fundamental policies of the party. Kania was reelected as first secretary and many established party authorities and practices survived. Yet, as potentially dangerous as the significant turnover of leadership positions was, facing the party was the steady decline in membership throughout the entire Solidarity period. By June 1981, the party lost about three hundred thousand members and lost twice that number in the second half of the year, with a landslide exit of members coming after the imposition of martial law.[83] In 1982 the membership stood at 2,327,000 down from 3,092,000 in 1979. The voluntary departure of almost one-third of the party members reflected a deep state-society cleavage. Staniszkis argues: "The polymorphic status of the party led to a situation in which the polarization of society between those who rule and those who were ruled also polarized the party between its leaders and the powerless masses. The lower level of the party fully identified with the powerless rest of the society. An indication of this was the nearly full participation of rank-and-file party members in the March 1981 warning strike that followed the Bydgoszcz crisis."[84]

This exit of dissatisfied members had a crucial stabilizing impact on the situation within the party and significantly contributed to its survival. The existence of Solidarity created a platform that attracted all those party members who were politically active and yet opposed current party policies. It is estimated that almost one million members of PUWP, especially workers and intellectuals, joined Solidarity, and many of them left the party. A second factor accounting for the party's survival was the defensive consolidation of the party apparatus in a face of an increasingly hostile political environment. The professional party apparatus was pressured from two directions. First, the so-called horizontal structures within the PUWP emerged in the fall of 1980. These networks of activists challenged the Leninist principle of "democratic centralism" and tried to revitalize and democratize the party organizations and to defy its domination by the party bureaucratic apparatus. Despite organizational repression, these networks played a role in selecting candidates for the extraordinary party congress. The congress, however, witnessed the final defeat of these attempts to change the party from within.[85] As Andrew Arato writes: "The real victor of the party congress was the apparatus. From then on, the leadership adopted their 'policy' of no retreat."[86] The collapse of the "horizontal structures" movement was caused to a large degree by an almost complete lack of public interest in any intraparty struggles, after experiences dating back to 1956 any plans to democratize the party were received with distrust and often were considered to be a deliberate deception. Solidarity also completely ignored intraparty squabbles.

The real challenge to the party apparatus was coming from the outside. The party and state functionaries were increasingly attacked by regional and local Solidarity organizations demanding not only the removal of certain functionaries in the regions but also a limitation of the party's role in the local government. There were even increasing calls for the expulsion of party committees from industrial enterprises supported by militant Solidarity activists. The Party's authorities resolutely rejected such demands even at the cost of provoking protracted protest actions in many regions. This policy was summarized by the party secretary of the Silesian region, who emphasized, "we must before all defend our cadres."[87] In turn, fears of the party functionaries were deliberately used as a devise in enforcing the party integration through overblowing an external threat, especially during final preparations to martial law. For example, during the fall of 1981, rumors were spread among the party apparatus and industry managers concerning the existence of alleged black lists of party members and functionaries prepared by Solidarity. It was implied that they became a target of repression once Solidarity was in power.

As a result of the political crisis and internal developments, the party's strength and position in society were significantly weakened, and its role within the political system gradually changed. After the party congress, the stalemate both within the party and between the party and the new organizations of society persisted, while more and more responsibilities and power slowly shifted to other organs of the party-state. This process was accelerated after Jaruzelski assumed the party leadership in October 1981. As Staniszkis argues: "Jaruzelski began a series of delicate maneuvers aimed at redefining the political system. Signs appeared that the Communist party was being removed as an active part of that system and that an effort was being made to rebuild the regime around the state instead the party."[88] Such a shift of power and influence between the fundamental institutional pillars of the state-socialist political system was the culmination of a long-term evolution of the Polish political system from a totalitarian to authoritarian regime. This trend was reinforced during the Solidarity period by the opposition's strategy to ignore and isolate the party. The union refused to conduct any negotiations with party authorities and instead regarded the government and legislative institutions as the only legitimate partners. The fundamental shift in the center of political gravity was further accelerated by the increasing role of the military and institutional changes introduced after the imposition of martial law. In Andrzej Walicki's words, Poland's political system assumed "a nontotalitarian form of 'really existing state socialism.'"[89]

The emergence of Solidarity also affected the institutional capacity of the Polish state. Its major institutional components, however, experienced different amounts of pressure from below and were weakened to a varying degree by the political developments occurring after August 1980. The structures and institutions of the state administration suffered a disruption of their routine activities as well as internal political and organizational turmoil. The problems of the state administration were compounded by the fact that the Polish economic situation deteriorated steadily in 1980 and 1981. The consumer market was almost in a state of collapse and the extensive rationing system, covering wide range of goods from basic food stuff to luxurious products, was introduced. Additionally, frequent protest actions and strikes intensified inherent difficulties of the mismanaged and shortage-plagued centrally planned economy. The representative institutions of the state were less affected by the crisis. Fortunately for the regime, the country's parliament and local councils were elected in the spring of 1980 and were not threatened by the looming problem of elections for the next four years. The parliamentary representation of the Communist party and its allies remained stable. Two other political parties represented in the Parliament (United Peasant party and Democratic party) experienced internal pressures for democratization and changes in the leadership during their party congresses. But despite some stormy events, they survived the crisis with little change of their internal policies and role in the power structure of the country. The coercive forces of the regime remained effectively sheltered from political pressures and were the least affected and disrupted segment of the Polish state. They provided the basis for state's countermobilization and the coercive solution of the crisis.

Reflecting the leadership changes within the party and its futile attempts to arrest the economic crisis, the government itself became an arena of numerous exchanges of the top personnel. During this period, Poland had three prime ministers: Edward Babiuch was replaced by Jozef Pinkowski in August 1980, who in turn was replaced by Wojciech Jaruzelski in February 1981. These changes at the top of the government produced an almost constant replacement of deputy prime ministers, ministers, departments' heads, and other senior officials.[90] With the nomination of Jaruzelski, some thirty ministries changed hands and gradual militarization of the civilian administration through appointment of senior military officers to important positions within the country's administration became particularly visible during the second half of the year. By the end of 1981, at least five ministries were headed by military officers, and many other posts, both at the central and the local levels were taken over by army personnel.[91] However, these personnel changes, in the words of de Weydenthal, "had little discernible impact on the government's operations. . . . The government merely stayed in place and drifted, as if kept afloat by the hope of riding out its problems and difficulties, without any attempt to resolve them. Its strategy seemed to be procrastination; its tactics were delay and dissemblance; its goal was survival."[92]

Poland's coercive forces were perhaps the only core institutions of the state not seriously affected by political turmoil and disorganization. This was remarkable given the size of these forces. At that time, Poland, as other state-socialist societies, was highly militarized country with an extensive military and security apparatus. In the 1970s, under Defense Minister Jaruzelski's command, the Polish People's Army became the third largest army in Europe, smaller only than the Soviet and West German armies. It had almost 350,000 men in arms and a highly trained officer corps. In addition to the regular armed forces under the auspices of the Ministry of National Defense, the Ministry of Internal Affairs controlled a force of 250,000 men, which included the regular police, the security police, the frontier guard units, and the twenty-five thousand specially trained and equipped riot police units. This huge internal coercive apparatus was backed by an army of part-time informers, including members of the official Voluntary Reserve of Citizens' Militia, numbering more than three hundred thousand men.[93] Any widespread confusion or turmoil in these forces would have been catastrophic for the party and the state. Therefore, there was an intensive effort made to insulate the army and police from any political crisis and turmoil pervading Polish society.

The main strategy of the army's leadership was to reduce contact between the soldiers and the population to an absolute minimum. The last major army draft took place before the summer of 1980, and for the entire period of the political crisis, the military restricted its intake of new conscripts who were members of Solidarity and/or participated in any protest actions and political conflicts. Draftees who had been involved with Solidarity were isolated from the other soldiers. Moreover, in the fall of 1981, the army deferred the release of all those who had completed the compulsory twenty-four months of military service. The army also fought frantically against any initiatives by the civilian employees of military institutions to form a trade union; and they were formally prohibited from joining Solidarity.

While the military worked to secure its institutions and forces from outside influences, most of its time was spent on ideological indoctrination and propaganda. This type of brainwashing was accomplished according to the following script:

> Show the extent of the threat from counterrevolutionary forces and the roots, aims and methods of anti-Socialist forces; create ideological and organizational resistance to enemy propaganda, and develop close cooperation with the Army Security Service and the militia; highlight in all party work the Polish reason of state, especially the importance of the political, economic, and defense integration of the Warsaw Pact countries as well as the brotherhood-of-arms with the Soviet and other Socialist armies.[94]

However, even the best laid plans have holes, and there were members of the army who were sympathetic to Solidarity's program. The result was that a significant number of reform proposals came from inside the armed forces, along with a fair number of critical assessments regarding various aspects of military life. Yet, this internal criticism did not set in motion any significant political, structural, or organizational changes. If anything, it produced an intensification of the military's ideological and political supervision exercised by its political departments.[95] As a result of all these measures, the Polish Army was one of a very few institutions that, on the whole, not only remained committed to the defense of the party-state but also retained its ideological and organizational integrity. Moreover, the Polish army had the necessary resources and well-trained personnel to fill posts in the civilian sector that were essential for consolidating its political position in the country. Thus, while the locus of political power was slowly shifting from the party to the state, within the state itself it shifted in favor of the armed forces and military personnel.

The Ministry of Interior's coercive forces passed the Solidarity period relatively unscathed as well. These were the forces that were used most extensively in the implementation of martial law. The tactics used to insulate the police and security forces from the population were similar to those used by the army. They were reinforced by the strong resentment the population bore toward the internal security forces. Images of the execution of members of the Hungarian security police by an infuriated mob during the Hungarian Revolution were quickly invoked to serve as a constant remainder of the chasm between the state and society. There was, however, an attempt by some police officers to establish their own labor union, and preparatory meetings took place in May and June of 1981. It seems that the Ministry of Internal Affairs used this opportunity to identify the "unreliable" members in its ranks. The ministry reacted decisively, and some five hundred officers involved in the attempted organization of the union were dismissed from the force.

The institutional domain of the Polish party-state that was most affected by the crisis was the protective belt of mass organizations and auxiliary institutions blocking the political space and serving as transmission belts between the state and society. In dealing with these auxiliary institutions, the party-state would obstruct or delay any attempt to democratize them or relinquish the party's supervision over their governing structures. In a situation where these state-controlled organizations were challenged by the new independent organizations, the party-state would prop up the resources of the existing institutions in a desperate effort to maintain some kind of organized institutional presence in all the important spheres of the social and political life. In fact, none of the party-state–supported mass organizations that existed before the summer of 1980 entirely collapsed, although their significance and membership decreased radically. Some even became defiantly independent and opposed the continuing interference of the party-state in their internal affairs. The first organizations that moved from under the wings of the party-state and insisted on pursuing their own independent internal policies were the professional associations. Many of these organizations allied with Solidarity or at least attempted to play the role of an independent mediator in the conflict between the state and the union. These organizations lobbied for essential economic and political concessions for their members and advocated broader social and political reforms. The primary battle, however, involved the mass organizations.

In Eastern Europe, the trade union movement had a tradition of being especially groomed and controlled by the party and the state. In Poland, trade unions were the most dramatically altered with the emergence of Solidarity, which assumed political and organization form of a trade-union movement. The existing state-controlled federation of trade unions tried to adopt to the new situation by allowing its member organizations, based upon sectors of the economy and embracing all employees, to convert into "independent, self-governing trade unions" and withdraw from the Central Council. Overhauled organizations started to advocate the new relationship between the trade unions and the state. In November 1980, the unions established the Coordinating Committee of Branch Trade Unions. Soon after, their former bureaucratic power center, the Central Trade Union Council (CRZZ), was abolished. Through this radical change of tactics, which caught many Solidarity organizers by surprise, the official unions secured their survival. At the beginning of 1981, the twenty-four branch unions claimed between 3 and 6 million members vis-à-vis Solidarity's 9.5 million. While the branch unions were transformed from previously existing organizations, during the Solidarity period thirty new unions that were organized along industry branches emerged. These so-called autonomous unions claimed around six hundred thousand members. The organizational and political changes within the trade union movement, even in those organizations aligned with the government, were so significant that after the imposition of martial law all union organizations were suspended and ultimately dissolved.

The youth movement underwent similar changes. Although the Socialist Union of Polish Students, Union of Polish Scouts, and Socialist Union of Polish Youth continued their activities, these organizations lost a large number of members and were thrown into a state of internal turmoil. Additionally, even these traditional cradles of the party cadres became more and more independent and militant and many of their leaders were sympathetic to the "horizontal structures" in the party. At the same time, new organizations emerged. Two of those were the Rural Youth Union and the Union of Democratic Youth, who were allied with two minor parties in the Polish political system, but their political agendas remained somehow unclear. That was not the case of the newly organized Independent Student Union (NZS), which was the most vocal and radical organization allied with Solidarity. Approximately one-third of Polish university students were represented in this union. The union was active in organizing protest actions demanding changes in curricula and in the legal framework governing universities. The NZS activists also participated in protest actions organized by Solidarity. The party dogmatists attempted to establish the Union of Communist Polish Youth, which, while officially registered, never attracted any noticeable following.

In summary, the Solidarity period produced a precarious political situation unprecedented in the postwar history of the region. The powerful independent movement that emerged established its institutional presence within the political system and secured significant resources for itself. On the other hand, the party-state institutions, although weakened and sometimes disorganized, were able to regroup and survive both the internal and external challenges. The political stalemate between these two forces shaped the course of the crisis. The party-state, while loosing control over vast areas of social life, was nonetheless able to protect its core institutions, particularly its coercive forces. Paradoxically, the state was able to secretly plan and prepare a complex military operation in the most open political system Poland had known since the Communists took power. The political stalemate that characterized the Polish crisis, however, cannot be fully understood without taking into account its geopolitical constraints.

The Self-limiting Revolution between the West and East

As Andrzej Walicki argues: "If Poland were not a part and parcel of the Soviet empire, one would only ask why a powerful, all-national movement demanded so little, and how it would be possible to combine a fully-fledged participatory democracy on the local level with a communist-dominated government and, more important, with full communist control over the coercive powers of the state. In the existing situation, however, these demands were not moderate at all—they meant in practice that communist power in Poland should be reduced to safeguarding the interest of the Warsaw Pact. How could it be expected that the Soviet Union accepted such a curious arrangement?"[96] In fact, in 1980 and 1981 there was a growing conviction in Eastern Europe and in the West that the Soviet Union would inevitably invade Poland. By mid-December 1980, however, any serious preparations for a Warsaw Pact military intervention were abandoned and the Soviets endorsed the Polish regime plans for an internal military solution. Since January 1981, the full-scale preparations for the introduction of martial law begun. The Interior Ministry's forces were repeatedly put in the state of combat readiness, different elements of the operation were tested, coordination plans between the army and security forces prepared, and the entire communication and command infrastructure organized.[97]

The Soviet and other bloc countries' reaction to political developments in Poland bears many similarities to the reactions that surrounded the 1968 crisis in Czechoslovakia; the official propaganda emphasized the imperialistic threat, accused the United States of interference in the domestic affairs of Poland, warned about the Federal Republic of Germany's revanchist intentions, and drew a direct parallel between the events in Czechoslovakia in 1968 and developments in Poland pointing to counterrevolutionary danger. While the Soviet Union repeatedly expressed its grave concerns over Polish domestic developments, it also gave the Polish party leadership considerable latitude in managing the crisis. But the longer the crisis dragged on, the more impatient the Soviet leaders became. The Kremlin tried to influence Poland's domestic situation and made it very clear that it wanted decisive action to be taken against Solidarity by criticizing the union in the media and issuing repeated warnings against antisocialist forces, economic chaos, and Solidarity extremists getting ready to destroy the PUWP. This propaganda campaign was promptly picked up by Poland's neighbors. According to Andrzej Korbonski, "It was Czechoslovakia and East Germany that took the lead in criticizing Polish developments, partly as Moscow's proxies and partly in order to forestall potential spillover of labor unrest into their respective countries."[98]

The repertoire of external pressures followed a familiar pattern. It included a constant flow of criticism and accusations in the media, which at some points reached a tone of near hysteria; an extensive buildup of Warsaw Pact forces along the Polish borders and joint military maneuvers crossing into Polish territory; summit meetings of Warsaw Pact leaders and unexpected visits of Soviet leaders to Poland; and letters expressing concerns about the domestic situation sent to the Polish party.[99] Moreover, writes Arthur Rachwald, for the first time in addition to traditional political and military means, "Moscow used its economic weapons to exert pressure on Poland . . . and in September 1981 Moscow implied that it would insist on balanced trade with Poland in 1982. Instead of a planned 4.4 billion rubles' worth of imports from the Soviet Union, Poland's imports would be reduced to 2.7 billion rubles—the amount of Polish export to the Soviet Union."[100] During the crisis the Polish leadership attempted to reconcile various pressures and secure important economic and political objectives. In Jaruzelski's words: "Polish foreign policy faced three fundamental tasks. First, to assure access of the economy to financial and material assistance from both the

CMEA and Western partners. Second, to secure the understanding of Poland's internal policies by the East and West. Third, to prevent the use of Poland as an element of increasing confrontation between two political and military blocs."[101] These objectives were increasingly difficult to reconciliate with the deepening of the Poland's crisis.

The events in Poland presented the Soviet Union with some very difficult choices. Its earlier military invasion in Afghanistan had already caused a serious deterioration in relations with the United States. Another Soviet military action, this time in Europe, could result in its total international isolation. As de Weydenthal emphasizes:

> The broader European consequences of a Soviet invasion of Poland . . . were likely to be multiple and far-reaching. First, there would probably be a considerable drying up of Western financial credits and technology transfers. Second, some of the formal structures of East-West detente, such as the Helsinki Final Act of 1976, could be jeopardized; a follow-up session of the Conference on Security and Cooperation in Europe (CSCE) was due to open in Madrid in mid-November, and Poland was certain to be on the agenda. An invasion might well precipitate the collapse of the CSCE process, rendering a great blow to Soviet prestige, since the original convening of the conference in Helsinki had been the fruit of years of patient diplomacy on Moscow's part. Third, there would likely follow a significant cut-back in East-West exchanges and human contacts of all kind.[102]

Therefore, the geopolitical context of the Polish crisis differed radically from the two previous crises, when the Soviet Union had virtually a free hand in dealing with intrabloc problems and the economic and political leverage of the West was negligible.

At the same time, the official existence of the Solidarity union and its independent international contacts and relations further complicated the relations between Poland and her allies. During the entire period of the crisis, Solidarity was involved in various activities abroad. Solidarity's leader, Lech Walesa, traveled four times to Western Europe and to Japan; Solidarity delegations frequently met with foreign officials, politicians, and the leaders of various organizations; crowds of foreign journalists became a common element of any important Solidarity event; and the Solidarity congress was attended by numerous Western labor delegations. The union also received extensive foreign aid from other labor organizations, including significant material support in money and equipment, which allowed the union to dramatically expand its communication and publishing capacities.

Yet despite international constraints, the Soviet Union was determined by the fall of 1980 to crush the Solidarity movement either through a military invasion of Warsaw Pact forces or through an internal action of the Polish military. The second option clearly emerged as the preferred choice and was carefully planned and prepared through 1981.[103] According to a high-ranking Polish military official who defected to the West, Ryszard Kuklinski:

The decision to impose martial law in Poland, made under pressure from the Soviet Union, was in early November 1981 virtually irrevocable. Were General Jaruzelski to reject it at the last moment, the radio and TV address to the nation would be made by General of Arms Eugeniusz Molczyk, or by another general resolved to take this step. [Moreover] martial-law operations were to be conducted exclusively by Polish police and army forces. If, however, for some reason, they were to prove incapable of crushing the resistance of the society then fully combat-ready Soviet, Czech, and German divisions waiting at Poland's frontiers would march in.[104]

The extent and efficiency of the preparations for martial law became evident only after military action had already begun. It was a testimony to the capability of the party-state, seemingly in a state of disarray, to muster the necessary resources for a highly complex and difficult coercive operation. Only then did the rapid deterioration of relations between Solidarity and the Polish state in the fall of 1981 emerge as an intrinsic part of the preparation for the internal military option.

On the eve of the imposition of martial law in Poland, the domestic and international situation was qualitatively different from the crisis situations in Hungary and Czechoslovakia. First of all, the open political crisis in Poland lasted eighteen months, including the summer of 1980. The protracted character of this crisis allowed both society to organize, and the party-state to regroup and adjust to a new political situation. As Staniszkis argues, by the fall of 1981,

all the elements that could lead to the emergence of a strong, authoritarian political system were present. In the first place a power deflation occurred, with the characteristic fragmentation of political forces, the polarized and factionalized PUWP facing Solidarity divided in terms of political versus strictly syndicalist practices. Another feature of power deflation was a visible loss of autonomy of the political system due to broadening of the political arena, politicization of the populace and in political mobilization of originally nonpolitical institutions such as the Catholic church and professional associations. . . . The gap between the formal organization of the political system and civil society was increasing; the 'social contract' rhetoric changed the style but not the structure of the Sejm and other elements of the political system. The PUWP functionaries seemed unable to find a new formula for their relations with society; they escaped into ritualized activity, trying in this way to erect a glass wall between themselves and the society.[105]

When Solidarity's National Committee met in Radom on December 3, the specter of the inevitable confrontation with the party-state was forcefully raised by all leaders, including the always moderate Walesa. It is clear, however, that Solidarity gravely underestimated the party-state's strength, capabilities, and determination. When the independent Congress of Polish Culture met in Warsaw on December 11, the chairman of the Polish Writers

Union, Jan Jozef Szczepanski, expressed concern: "I have heard an opinion that the Congress of Polish Culture will resemble the performance of ship's orchestra on the deck of Titanic." This very pessimistic comparison was not entirely off the mark. The last session of Congress of the Polish Culture, which planned to meet on December 13, was never held.

Poland under Martial Law and After

ON THE NIGHT of December 12–13, 1981, the most extensive internal military operation in Polish history began. Shortly after mid-night, thousands of Solidarity's leaders and advisers were arrested, the union's headquarters were seized, and the country's borders closed. All domestic and international communication networks were blocked, and the troops entered cities and took control of all important installations in the country. In retrospect, it is hard to resist a judgment that it was an almost perfectly executed repressive action. Large scale preparations lasting for months were kept secret successfully, and neither the Solidarity movement nor society at large was really prepared for what occurred. One of the most senior leaders of Solidarity, Zbigniew Bujak, later said: "That they could impose martial law never occurred to me, particularly as none of our advisers had been able to say firmly whether or not this was possible. The only person I know who foresaw a military dictatorship was Wiktor Kulerski. But he kept quiet about it because he didn't want—as he put it—to go around sowing defeatism."[1]

The repressive action launched by the Polish party-state has several distinctive features. First of all, in contrast to the other two cases, which involved a full-scale military invasion by the Soviet Union, this action was an internal military operation carried on exclusively by Polish military and police units and directed by Polish commanders. Although there is no doubt that the Soviets supported the operation and were involved in its preparation and had serious contingency plans for the military invasion,[2] it was the Polish party-state that delivered the blow that destroyed Solidarity. Moreover, following the Soviet military intervention in both Hungary and Czechoslovakia, there was an extended period of internal chaos that passed before the resistance was effectively eliminated and the party-state was able to fully recover its strength and control over its internal institutional structures and the political space. Yet no more than two weeks passed before the Polish state became the sole master of the country's political situation. Most of the strikes were crushed during the first four days of martial law, and on December 28 the last surviving strike, in the coal mine Piast, was declared over.

Despite its startling short-term success, the imposition of martial law did not break the political stalemate between the party-state elites and various forces within society that emerged during the Solidarity period. It also did not improve the state's capacity to deal with Poland's economic crisis. With the passage of time it became increasingly clear that the party-state's initial success in crushing the independent organizations was not followed by a consistent demobilization process through which the Polish party-state could again emerge as the unchallenged political force in the country and regain its capacity to resolve the country's crisis and reequilibrate the Soviet-type political regime. This faltered demobilization process, during which both sides of the conflict frequently changed their strategies and failed to achieve a convincing success, stretched over the entire decade, prolonging the political and economic difficulties that begun in the 1970s as well as political and institutional instability that reign during the 1980–81 crisis.

The first phase of the demobilization process that followed the military crackdown lasted almost three years. During this time, martial law was suspended on December 31, 1982, and finally repealed on July 22, 1983.[3] It was characterized by heightened political emotions, strong mobilization efforts, and determination on both sides. This was the heroic phase of the conflict marked by political repressions, outbursts of street demonstrations, and determined struggle of Solidarity's underground. After 1984, the demobilization process entered its second phase. During this time, organized political resistance and occasional street demonstrations had lost their momentum, and the strategy of building an "underground society" was exhausted. At the same time, however, the state elites were unable to achieve any major improvements in the economic situation, reform economic institutions, or successfully co-opt or neutralize the political opposition. This was a frustrating period for both sides of the conflict, as the majority of the population retreated from politics and alienated itself from both the state and the opposition. The post–martial-law regime firmly ruled the country but failed to solidify public support necessary for enhancing its ability to govern.

The last stage of the demobilization process, which led to the final collapse of state socialism in Poland, began in the spring of 1988, when after several years of relative social peace, strikes and protests again erupted in factories and universities across the country. During these strikes, the restoration of the Solidarity union became the major demand. The revived Solidarity movement became again present in the country's political life. Another wave of strikes hit the country during the summer of 1988, and by the end of August the Polish authorities finally agreed to meet with representatives of the opposition, despite resistance coming from important segments of the ruling elite. The famous roundtable negotiations, which gave the initial stimulus to historical changes in East Central Europe, began in Warsaw on February 6, 1989. An agreement was signed on April 5 that provided for re-legalization of Solidarity, Farmers Solidarity, and the Independent Student Union. The opposition also gained limited access to the official political process through semi-democratic elections that were scheduled for June 1989. The results of the roundtable negotiations set in motion a rapid process of liberalization and democratization, and the party-state elites very soon lost control over the events. The Solidarity-based political coalition had celebrated a political and moral triumph in the June elections, and by the fall of 1989, Poles established the first noncommunist government in the region since the Second World War. By January 1990, the Polish United

Workers' party ceased to exist. The roundtable negotiations were the final proof of the inability of the Polish party-state elites to reequilibrate the state-socialist regime and to restore domination of the Communist party. In short, the demobilization policies ended as a spectacular political failure. In this chapter, I analyze the conditions and causes that contributed to the breakdown of the demobilization process in Poland. I will argue that significant changes in the character and the role of the Polish state, as well as the survival and expansion of independent political society, made it impossible to rebuild institutions and restore the type of relationship between the state and society that typified state-socialist regimes. The failure to accomplish the regime's institutional restoration and reimpose such relations was, in my view, responsible for the ineffectiveness of the demobilization strategies and for ultimate collapse of the Polish party-state.

THE IMPOSITION OF MARTIAL LAW

Martial law was formally, although unconstitutionally, imposed by the Council of the State. In the middle of the night of December 12–13, its members were presented with a ready legal framework consisting of the martial law decree, decrees changing the constitution of the military tribunals and military prosecutor's office, and the decree on special procedures in cases of offenses and violations during martial law. These acts enhancing repressive capacity of the state were supplemented the next day by a series of more specific decrees issued by the Council of Ministers.[4] Yet it was not until January 25, 1982, that the imposition of martial law was retroactively approved by the Polish Parliament, together with decrees issued on December 13. At the same time, without any legal precedent, the existence of the Military Council of National Salvation (WRON) was announced. The council was headed by General Wojciech Jaruzelski, who at that time was also first secretary of the party, prime minister, and minister of national defense, and consisted of fifteen generals and five colonels. It declared itself to be the supreme authority in the country and very much resembled a classical military junta. This resemblance, however, was highly misleading. As Andrew Michta persuasively argued:

> despite outward appearances the change effected in 1981 within the structures of political power in Poland was not a military coup d'etat but a shift of key governmental posts from one functional group, the civilian apparat, to another, the top level military elite. The 1981 restructuring of Poland's ruling elite was the culmination of the long-term process of the gradual erosion of the party's power, paralleled by a steady . . . consolidation of the officer elite's role in Poland's domestic politics.[5]

In fact, in the recent testimony to the Committee of Constitutional Responsibility, General Jaruzelski admitted that the WRON was established on

December 12, 1981, one day before the imposition of martial law. Jaruzelski also revealed that it was a purely symbolic body and that during the first six months of the martial-law period, the real power was in hands of a directorate composed of the representatives of the government, military, Ministry of Internal Affairs, and the Communist party.[6]

The WRON announced that it would neither limit the scope of competency of the state administration or representative bodies of the state nor take over any of their legally defined duties. It was supposed to ensure the country's internal order and security until the "danger of an overthrow of the constitutional order" of the Polish state had passed and the proper functioning of the state administration and the economy was secured. But the WRON overstepped its self-imposed limitations almost immediately. Following an initial round of meetings, the WRON issued binding instructions to state authorities and military commissaries who represented the WRON at all levels of state administration and in all organizational units of the economy. It also instructed the parliament on specific aspects of its legislative work. In accordance with its promises, the council was dissolved when the country's political situation stabilized and martial law was officially lifted in July 1983.

The implementation of WRON's instructions was insured by the military commissars who were appointed to the ministries, central offices, provinces, towns and town districts, and enterprises as well as to party offices by the National Defense Committee (KOK). The military commissars were given extensive powers based on the martial law legal acts and instructed to "supervise the implementation of tasks aiming at the elimination of internal threat [and] normalization of public and economic life." Those military officers appointed as commissaries already had a knowledge of the administration and local problems, since they had also headed Field Operation Groups that were deployed across the country in the fall of 1981, weeks before martial law was declared. The commissaries provided an extralegal military supervising network extending throughout the whole country. According to George Malcher:

> In the first phase, before May 1982, commissaries headed operational groups in 1,059 enterprises and 1,064 localities. After May 1982, 528 commissaries and their teams covered 830 enterprises. In addition there were the commissaries in ministries and central offices and the separate supervision and inspection groups that worked for the commissaries in regions. It has been stated that the system of commissaries proved to be a most efficient instrument of supervision of the administration. With the lifting of martial law, nearly 8,000 commissaries ended their duties and were withdrawn.[7]

Moreover, for the duration of martial law, special inspection commissions were organized and sent to different regions and sectors of the economy to scrutinize the operation of the civilian sector. They had considerable powers and often were responsible for sacking incompetent, corrupt, or politically unreliable people in scrutinized institutions.

With the imposition of martial law, all the civil rights and freedoms defined in the constitution and international treaties were uniformly suspended as were all trade union activities and the activities of all the legally registered organizations and associations. The country's borders were sealed, all internal and external telecommunication networks were blocked, the most important factories, selected central institutions, and mass media were militarized, allowing the authorities to impose extraordinary duties and to arbitrarily regulate work conditions.[8] A nationwide curfew was declared and travel to places other than one's permanent residence was prohibited. Also, special rights were granted to state authorities, police, and military commanders; internment camps for Solidarity activists were established; and telecommunication and printing equipment and hunting arms were confiscated. Any violations of the martial-law regulations, especially attempts to organize protest actions or strikes, were threatened with severe legal penalties, including the death penalty. These regulations and their strict and open implementation were intended to intimidate the population and restrict its movement, to break all communication networks and seize any resources that collective actors within society may have had at their disposal, as well as to paralyze all organized resistance. This massive use of repressions and intimidation was the intended objective of martial law. Czeslaw Kiszczak, one of its main architects, characterized the nature of the military operation in the following way: "The general principle of martial law was to implement it with such a number of people and forces as to create a psychological pressure which would scare the other side, overwhelm it with its magnitude and impetus, and maximally discourage any effective resistance."[9] The imposition of martial law was also accompanied by an intensive propaganda campaign designed to discredit Solidarity, its leaders, and advisers and to establish some justification for the military operation and political repression.

The implementation of martial law regulations was swiftly executed. During the night of December 12–13, several thousand Solidarity activists, including most of the members of Solidarity's National Committee who participated in the session in Gdansk, were detained and sent to prisons and internment camps. Wales was detained and kept incommunicado in an unknown location. The communication networks were effectively broken, and all press and broadcasting facilities were taken over by the military. All programs went off the air except one radio program and informational TV broadcasting. Only two national and seventeen provincial party newspapers remained open, and these were taken over by the commissars appointed by the Military Council. Despite this massive military action, on December 14 strikes broke out in many enterprises, including almost all of the country's coal mines, steel mills, shipyards, and seaports. During the following nights, these strikes were broken by units of militarized riot police (ZOMO) and troops that stormed the factories using tanks, helicopters, and tear gas. The first deadly confrontation took place on December 16. During an attack on the Wujek coal mine, nine workers were killed and twenty-two were wounded. In a span of several days, the strikes were almost uniformly crushed and spontaneous street demonstrations that had erupted in several cities were brutally dispersed by the police. The sit-in strikes survived the longest in the Katowice steel mill, which was stormed by security forces on December 23, and in the Piast coal mine, where the miners surrendered on December 28.[10] The first group of strike organizers was tried and sentenced by the military courts just after Christmas. Thus, in a state of confusion following the military operation, open resistance of workers was swiftly broken, and the Polish military and police fully controlled the situation in the country. Jerzy Holzer and Krzysztof Leski write that "in December the extent of the resistance was significant, nevertheless, according to many, the imposition of martial law came easier than it could have been expected."[11]

Rumors set the number of people detained and arrested during martial law in the tens of thousands, but the actual number was much lower. On March 1, 1982, the minister of the interior, General Kiszczak, announced that between December 13 and February 26, 6,647 persons were interned, of whom 2,552 were released during this time. In addition to those interned, by January 5, 1,274 persons were arrested. However, thousands more people were detained for shorter periods ranging from a few hours to two days for curfew violations and for participating in demonstrations or strikes. In 1983 the government released more date concerning arrests. It was admitted that during 1982, 3,616 were arrested for political offenses and that by March 1983, 2,580 persons were sentenced to prison terms and fined for antistate activities. Moreover, 6,800 persons were fined for participation in unauthorized demonstrations and gatherings during which fifteen persons were killed and thirty-six wounded. In those enterprises, where police intervention was used to break up the strikes started on December 13, Solidarity activists and members were fired from their jobs. For example, two thousand employees were fired from the Lenin shipyard, fifteen hundred from Warski shipyard, and two thousand from Piast coal mine.[12]

The process of purging Solidarity activists in state institutions started with the WRON's instruction to the government, issued on December 16, that it conduct an extensive survey of all employees in state administration and dismiss all those found to be inefficient, corrupt, or politically unsuitable. This action gained momentum and was most widespread in the spring of 1982. As a result, more than 440 top administrators, including deputy premiers and provincial governors, were replaced. So were two hundred mayors and local village administrators and 650 top managers of industrial enterprises.[13]

The professionals most affected by the purge of politically unreliable elements were employees of the mass media. Most Solidarity members were barred from working in newspapers and broadcast stations. By spring, some periodicals and newspapers whose publications were suspended by the martial law decree, were gradually allowed to resume publication on the condition that verification of their personnel was concluded by special committees and declarations of loyalty were signed by those wanting to remain on the editorial boards. As a result of the verification and the boycott initiated by those who refused to go through the humiliating screening process, sixty editors-in-chief and twenty television directors were replaced. In addition, of the more than nine thousand members of the Polish Journalists Union, twelve hundred were dismissed and another thousand demoted.[14] Finally, the Polish Journalists Union, suspended on December 13, was dissolved by the authorities on March 20 for refusing to renounce its opposition to martial law. The mass media and the state administration were the only institutions that underwent the process of political verification. This method of removing politically unreliable employees was not extended to any other institutions, despite widespread expectations and fears. For example, schools, universities, and research institutes, although forced to subject their staffs to compulsory political instructions, were spared the verification procedure. The absence of purges within universities allowed them to remain centers of political opposition to the post-martial law regime. Although all organizations and associations were suspended following the imposition of martial law, some of them, especially those that promptly decided to cooperate with the regime, were soon allowed to resume their activities. But some professional associations were disbanded after the authorities failed to force them to change their leadership and pledge support for the imposition of martial law. The first organizations liquidated were the Independent Student Union, which was disbanded on January 5, and the Polish Journalists Union, which was disbanded in March 1982.

The most important issue both for the regime and the opposition, however, was the future of the trade unions. For the first several months, it was not clear what the intentions of the authorities were regarding the trade unions in general and Solidarity in particular.[15] It seems that if the regime had been able to induce a notable number of the Solidarity leaders into collaboration, the union would possibly have been restored, of course, in a different organizational form. But the authorities failed to get the union leadership to cooperate at all, and they were forced to opt for a decisive solution to the problem. In October 1982, the Polish Parliament passed a new law that effectively banned all trade-union organizations that existed before December 13, 1981. As a result, the core institutional foundation of the independent organization of Polish society was officially destroyed—an indication that any hopes for a compromise between the authorities and Solidarity were ill-founded. After outlawing Solidarity, all other remaining unrepentant professional organizations were banned as well. The Union of Polish Actors was outlawed in December 1982, and in 1983 the unions of Polish writers and painters were dissolved.

After the threat of large-scale protests was eliminated and after all organizations and associations that refused to endorse the state's policies were
dissolved, martial law was conditionally suspended by the Council of State
on December 31, 1982. The authorities believed that the country's political
situation was once again stable. As a result of the suspension of martial law,
almost all Solidarity activists detained in the internment camps were released, and most of the restrictions on movement and communication, such
as the censorship of mail and telephone conversations and special the per-
mits necessary for leaving the place of permanent residence, were revoked.
However, it was still not life as usual. In the words of Holzer and Leski:

> The legislation on special legal regulations during the suspension of martial law
> introduced emergency powers which gave the authorities significant room for ma-
> neuver. They could maintain the suspension of associations and organizations and
> had even the right to outlaw them. The prerogatives of self-management institu-
> tions in factories were restricted and authorities retained the right to dissolve
> them. Severe retributions in case of strikes were announced and the draconian
> penalties for illegal activities were maintained. Political prisoners could be re-
> leased but only through the act of individual clemency after a required petition.[16]

Martial law was finally lifted on July 22, 1983, but, as in the case of its
suspension, the Parliament enacted the special legislation to remain in force
for the time required to "overcome the socio-economic crisis." This new
legal act maintained, in a somehow relaxed form, repressive regulations that
were in force during martial law. Also, the granting of limited amnesty did
not significantly change the fate of most political prisoners and did not encourage those Solidarity activists who remained in hiding to stop their illegal
political activities. Thus, the regime's attempt to decree a return to the routine practices of the party-state was an obvious failure. Moreover, the very
notion of routine practices became problematic. There were major disagreements among the ruling elite concerning the regime's policies on different
issues, which led to the collapse of the original coalition whose decision it
had been to impose martial law. The post–martial-law regime was internally
divided along several political issues. These internal conflicts focused on
(1) the role of the communist party, (2) strategies of demobilization with
explicit references to the Hungarian and Czechoslovak models, (3) types of
economic policies, (4) the role of the trade union movement; and (5) the
strategies of dealing with the political opposition. In these political debates,
Jaruzelski's faction opted for more pragmatic policies, while the professional party apparatus and old party activists took a more ideologically orthodox stance. Given the cumulation of power in his hands, the reduced role
of the Communist party that had already taken effect in 1980–81, and the
support of the Soviet leaders, Jaruzelski controlled the political situation.
His policies based on the principle that "there is no return to the situation
either before December 1981 or before August 1980" were never seriously
challenged. Thus, the power of the pragmatic faction within the regime was
not seriously threatened during the entire post–martial-law period.

During the martial law period, the Polish party-state underwent a significant institutional and political evolution. The most striking features of this transition were the decline in power of the Communist party and the shift in the center of political gravity from party to state institutions, depoliticization of many important institutional spheres, and the change of the official legitimation claims. Abandoning Marxist-Leninist ideological claims as a foundation of its policies, the party-state elite had developed a new repressive legal framework by incorporating most of the legal restrictions and repressive regulations of the martial law decrees into a regular legal system, enhanced state's coercive capacity, and expanded its freedom to impose its political and economic decisions. These changes, however, did not solve the problems facing the post–martial-law regime. It confronted determined resistance of many strategic groups in society, lacked domestic support, and suffered international sanctions and isolation. Very soon, as Andrzej Walicki argues, "they realize[d] that reliance on naked force is not enough to secure a necessary minimum of voluntary cooperation—a minimum required for their own survival. As a consequence they [were] sincerely striving for a workable compromise with the principal forces of society, as well as for some limitation of their political responsibility."[17] Thus, the party-state remained increasingly weak behind the facade of repressive rules and coercive forces it had erected.

In the final analysis, martial law policies evidently failed to eradicate opposition movements, to fully recover the political space for the party-state and regenerate its institutions, and to generate popular support for the regime—in spite of its initial success in removing (at least momentarily) the direct challenge to the party-state's power. Most important, however, the post–martial-law state failed to deliver on its promise to stabilize the economic situation and to revert the progressing collapse of the Polish economy. It can be argued that the post–martial-law regime lacked the political will and ideological conviction to follow the path of either its Hungarian or Czechoslovak predecessors. In a certain sense, just as the Solidarity movement was characterized as a self-limiting revolution, the imposition of martial law could be characterized as a self-limiting counterrevolution. The overall leniency of the political repressions and the Polish ruling elite's hesitation to revert to neo-Stalinist political practices was, as I would suggest, the result of several factors. Among the most important were Western political pressures coupled with Poland's dependence on Western economic assistance and cooperation, the political succession crisis in the Soviet Union, and the exhaustion of Marxist-Leninist state idea, which was no longer able to supply the ruling elite with a credible political vision or believable self-justification for its rule.

The collapse of the Marxist-Leninist state-idea and the official political discourse, which can be traced back to the end of the 1960s, forced the Polish party-state to seek different foundations for its legitimation claims. The ruling elite could not plausibly justify its coercive action any longer by the general laws of history, objective interests of the working class, superiority of the socialist organization of society, unbreakable alliance with the Soviet Union, or indispensability and theoretical superiority of the Communist party. In a striking contrast to Hungary's and Czechoslovakia's post-crisis rulers, who claimed to lead the struggle in defense of socialism and of the achievements of the working class, the Polish regime explained the imposition of martial law as the choice of a "lesser evil." It was forced to revert to narrow geopolitical arguments: "We saved the country from an imminent national catastrophe" (meaning a Soviet military invasion) and from political and economic chaos. In this respect the Polish state experienced a fate similar to those of all military dictatorships. It defined itself as a classical "regime exceptional," and by doing this it abandoned communist regimes' 'historical mission' to offer a permanent alternative to political democracy and market economy. Its only justification was based on the claim to deliver efficiency, a better economic performance, and therefore better standards of living and economic security, as well as to put an end to injustice, corruption, and anarchy. When this claim failed, there was nothing left to justify the necessity and indispensability of the oppressive political rule.

The Emergence of the Underground Society

As I have argued before, the scope and strength of the resistance and opposition in Poland during martial law was a result not only of the self-limiting character of the Polish regime's demobilization policies but also of the characteristics of the 1980–81 political crisis. Poland experienced a prolonged period of political mobilization, which resulted in the emergence of a well-defined and symbolically validated rift between the state and society and the recovery of the public space controlled previously by the institutions of the party-state. This led to the independent self-organization of society based on firm institutional foundations and considerable resources. These factors helped to create an experienced army of grass-root organizers and leaders who established highly developed networks of communication and cooperation reaching all groups, institutions, and segments of society. The Solidarity movement crossed economic, ideological, and social barriers, secured significant material resources, and developed a powerful collective identity.[18] At no other point in the postwar history of the region had the party-state confronted such a powerful challenger. However, Polish society was unable to block the imposition of martial law or to defeat the state's demobilization policies. There were several reasons for this. First, Solidarity was taken by surprise and had to face a very well planned and executed coercive operation. Second, Polish society was exhausted after sixteen months of a deteriorating economic situation and constant political tensions and conflicts. Third, the Catholic church pleaded with the population to remain calm in order to avoid a bloody confrontation. Finally, there was the ethos of a nonviolent struggle, which was an integral part of Solidarity's identity.[19]

While Solidarity as the formal organization was under siege during the military action, with its leaders arrested, resources seized, organizational structures and communication networks destroyed, its members formed instantaneously the underground social and self-defensive organizations in reaction to the imposition of martial law. During this initial period, the Catholic church, as the only legally existing institution outside the direct control of the state,[20] spearheaded all efforts to effectively respond to the repressive military action. The church served as a focus and as an umbrella for independent activities. As early as December 14, Archbishop Jozef Glemp established the Primate's Committee for Assistance to the Prosecuted and Their Families after Franciszek Cardinal Macharski negotiated with General Kiszczak for permission to carry on these activities. The committee members included priests as well as lawyers, physicians, academics, writers, and artists affiliated with Solidarity. Within a few days, similar committees were formed in thirty-six other cities and dioceses across the country. These committees provided legal, medical, and material aid to persons who were detained and fired from jobs under martial law decree and their families. They also coordinated the distribution of aid sent to Poland by individuals and organizations from the West. The church's involvement in helping the victims of martial law was extensive. Archbishop Glemp made countless visits to the internment camps and hundreds of masses were celebrated in places of detention. Overall, during 1981–83 the Charity Committee of the Polish Episcopate received and distributed nearly 120,000 tons of food, medical supplies, and other goods coming from twenty-three countries. In 1984–86 the committee received 149,892 tons of food, 3,512 tons of medical supplies, 12,146 tons of clothing and shoes, and 594 tons and 159 train wagons of agricultural machines and equipment.[21]

The church unequivocally spoke out against violent resistance and encouraged moderation, reconciliation, and a new social accord between the state and society. In April 1982, Archbishop Glemp circulated a ten-point proposal prepared by the Primate's Social Council and designed as a platform for negotiations with the regime.[22] It also emphatically defended human rights and political freedoms as well as Solidarity's right to exist. Moreover, during the years following the imposition of martial law, church grounds became centers for a wide range of cultural, social, and political activities. The church opened its buildings to artists boycotting official institutions, who organized art exhibits and concerts and staged plays and shows. For example, in 1984 there were fifteen large art exhibits in which more than 580 artists showed their works and forty-five individual exhibits organized by churches in various cities.[23] The churches were also gathering points from which most manifestations and demonstrations were launched. Although neo-Stalinist radicals in the party contemplated a crackdown on church social activities and often openly attacked parish priests, especially those active in supporting the resistance, the powerful Polish Catholic church, with its Polish-born pope in Rome, was not a realistic target for repression by the isolated ruling elite. In fact, none of the concessions granted to the church during the Solidarity period were revoked, and its institutional and political gains as well as prestige were significantly expanded.[24]

While the Catholic church was able to openly establish a network of committees to provide aid to victims of repression, the Solidarity movement immediately begun the painstaking process of rebuilding its shattered structures and mobilizing its resources so as to continue its oppositional activities. The adjustment to a new repressive situation created by the imposition of martial law provided the dispersed organization committed to open activities and legality with daunting challenges. As David Ost notes, "Just as opposition leaders were not prepared for success in August 1980, they were not prepared for defeat sixteen months later."[25]

During the week following the imposition of martial law, underground oppositional networks were gradually and spontaneously formed on the basis of former Solidarity enterprise committees. At the same time, Solidarity leaders both in hiding and in prisons hotly debated the strategy and tactics for the union as a whole.[26] The consensus that emerged from these debates was aptly expressed by Adam Michnik in his letters from prison. First, while the general aim of the movement was to seek negotiations and a political agreement with the ruling elite, any cooperation with the state was rejected. Michnik wrote: "When a state's power has been confiscated by a band of gangsters who impose their ways on the people, then the attitude 'loyalty to the state' is simple complicity in crime. Resistance against such a 'state' is natural, and civil disobedience is the only attitude worthy of respect."[27] Second, the highly centralized and organized model of the underground movement was rejected. The opposition movement, according to Michnik, "should not be an underground state with a national government, a parliament, and armed forces. . . . Our country needs many things but it does not need self-appointed national rule."[28] Third, the vision of a broad, decentralized civic movement emerged as the only sensible alternative. Michnik argued:

> It is not terrorism that Poland needs today. It is widespread underground activity that will reconstruct society, spreading thorough towns and villages, factories and research institutions, universities and high schools. Underground Solidarity has to encompass all this. The institutional form of this movement should be left open. It must obviously include mechanisms for collecting money, help for those who are threatened by penal repression or by loss of their jobs. It must obviously include intellectual movement that will offer society a vision of a democratic Poland. It must include publishing enterprises, so . . . intellectual life in general, and social self-knowledge can flourish. Also needed is an umbrella institution—made up of Solidarity activists—which can deal with the fundamental question of national existence. . . . such a center is an indispensable condition for effective action.[29]

On April 22, 1982, after all hopes for the legal restoration of Solidarity were dashed, the union's leaders who had escaped arrest formed the Provisional Coordinating Commission of Solidarity (TKK). Provisional regional committees were also formed in most of the former Solidarity regions and the network of regional and local Solidarity structures was gradually expanded. In July, the TKK issued a program for the union entitled "Underground Society." The TKK outlined four objectives of the underground movement, namely: the boycott of official institutions and organizations; the defense of employees' economic interests; the struggle for independent educational, cultural, and intellectual life; and the preparation for a decisive general strike. The program sought to create a situation in which "the authorities were forced to seek a compromise with society." Thus, in 1982 underground Solidarity emerged as a loose network of groups organized on territorial, institutional, professional, and personal bases united around a set of common goals, values, and symbols. Various groups, however, pursued their own activities and devised their own programs and umbrella institutions; the TKK served as a moral authority and as a symbolic expression of unity among diverse, independent groups organized across the country. It is also worth noting that the underground Solidarity organization had a very limited capacity to launch and sustain a concerted nationwide protest action as was aptly proved by Solidarity's failure to effectively respond to its delegalization in October 1982.

It would be difficult to summarize the various activities, collective actions, and forms of organization that emerged in Polish society after the imposition of martial law. The most important initiatives during the most repressive period of martial law were the formation of mutual support networks that collected union dues and distributed financial, legal, and material aid to individuals prosecuted for their political activities and their families. For example, almost all fines (often very high) imposed by the courts as penalty for participation in demonstrations and other prohibited political activities were paid by the Catholic church or underground organizations collecting union dues. Another action organized during the initial period of martial law was a boycott of official institutions in order to discourage and isolate those who were collaborating with the regime and to put constant pressure on the authorities. To this purpose, professional organizations such as writers, journalists, and actors unions issued codes of moral conduct, outlining the norms of behavior and responsibilities of their members.[30]

The most visible of the oppositional activities were street demonstrations and protests organized on the thirteenth of every month and other noncommunist national holidays. Street protests were most frequent and dramatic in 1982, although they were usually confined to Solidarity strongholds and several big cities. The first significant nationwide protests took place on May 1 (Labor Day) and May 3 (the prewar national holiday banned by the Communist regime) followed by a successful protest action launched by the TKK on May 13. Other violent and widespread demonstrations during this year occurred on the anniversary of the Gdansk Agreements on August 31. According to official statistics, demonstrations were held in sixty-six cities and in thirty-four of the country's forty-nine provinces. In seven cities demonstrations were followed by violent clashes with the police in which four people were killed, hundreds wounded, and thousands arrested. These demonstrations not only showed the population's persistent support for Solidarity and their defiance of the authorities, but they also helped to built the distinctive collective identity of the resistance movement. Irena Grudzinska-Gross wrote that "the entire society lives by a calendar different from that of the government: the two sides have different sets of dates and saints to celebrate, different songs to sing and different dreams to dream."[31]

Street protests were most frequent in 1982 and 1983. In the years that followed, they exhausted their popular appeal and subsided. Celebrations of important national anniversaries became less confrontational. Nevertheless, street protests remained a potential threat and often forced the authorities to mobilize their coercive forces to prevent their occurrence and escalation. These demonstrations of police strength, however, served as a constant reminder of the repressive nature of the post–martial-law regime.

The most important components of underground Solidarity's activities were the formation of an independent education system and underground publishing and distribution networks. The discussion clubs, self-education groups, and underground universities flourished across the country. Networks of lecturers teaching history, literature, economics, and other social sciences were organized, and educational materials were prepared and distributed. Meetings of study groups were organized in churches, private apartments, and even in buildings of official organizations and institutions. Together with the underground educational activities, independent research on a wide range of subjects—for example, politics, economics, health, and environment—and independent polling of public opinion were organized and financed by various underground organizations. Also, archival centers for collection of documents and underground publications were formed. The most impressive dimensions of underground activities were the underground publishing and information and distribution networks.

In December 1982, General Boguslaw Stachura, deputy minister of internal affairs, announced that the security forces had liquidated 360 outlets producing illegal publications, confiscated 1,196 printing machines and 468 typewriters. They also seized 730 thousands leaflets, 340 editions of books and pamphlets, and 4,000 posters. Moreover, the security forces eliminated eleven clandestine Solidarity Radio stations. Despite these loses and the strict control of printing facilities and equipment and the rationing of paper, independent publishing flourished and expanded throughout the 1980s. During the first six months of martial law, 560 underground periodicals appeared, and in the next six months there were an additional 215 titles. In the first half of 1983, 169 new titles were published and in the second half, 83 titles. Among the eleven hundred to thirteen hundred periodicals that emerged after martial law, many survived until the end of the 1980s without interruption. At any given moment, there were approximately four hundred underground periodicals being published in Poland. The average circulation of small periodicals was between five hundred and two thousand copies, but *Tygodnik Mazowsze* printed on average fifty thousand copies of each weekly issue. It was estimated by both the opposition and the government that about three million people regularly read uncensored literature.[32] In addition to periodicals, independent publishing houses such as NOWa and Krag printed well over a thousand book titles by Polish and foreign authors with a run of between one thousand and ten thousand copies each. Books as well as periodicals were sold through distribution networks covering the entire country, and the proceeds together with the grants from Solidarity committees were used to maintain publishing houses and their publications, to finance new publications and to support other causes and independent activities. For example, a Solidarity campaign urging the boycott of elections in 1984 and 1985 were financed in part with profits from publishing. At the end of the decade, with declining political repression, the underground publishing comprised more and more profit-oriented entrepreneurial ventures with a prominent place not only in the underground culture but also in the underground economy.

Given that the opposition's activities were often fragmented, decentralized, and ephemeral, it would be very difficult to estimate their scope or the number of people involved. It would be, however, safe to assume that at least in major cities and major industrial complexes, there was hardly a person who did not encounter some type of underground activities or meet people involved in them. Moreover, public opinion surveys conducted in Poland indicate that by the end of the Solidarity period, one in five Poles had participated at least once in collective protest, and that the approval of different forms of protest, including strikes, demonstrations, and boycotts of state decisions, was growing.[33]

While the organized and vocal political opposition and independent culture became a permanent fixture in post–martial-law Poland, the forms, strategies, and magnitude of the opposition underwent significant changes during the several years following martial law. By 1983, underground-sponsored activities did not have the same pull they had in the two previous years. Even the pope's second visit to Poland, in June 1983, and Walesa's reception of the Nobel Prize did not have a strong mobilizing effect. By the middle of 1984, the strategy of building an "underground society" had slowly exhausted its momentum and capacity to mobilize broad popular support. Facing evident signs of contraction in the scope and intensity of their oppositional activities, Solidarity gradually attempted to move on toward more open forms of action, testing the limits of what was permissible. In this way, a certain period in the life of the underground movement came to an end. Although the ideals and values represented by Solidarity remained a symbol of popular opposition to the regime, Solidarity as an organization gradually lost its ability to mobilize active resistance. At the same time, the party-state wavered between granting political concessions to the opposition and continuing to repress independent activities. Following the amnesty granted in July 1984, 829 people were arrested for political reasons and 296 were sentenced. Thus, according to Holzer and Leski: "Four years after the imposition of martial law the authorities were still not able to destroy Solidarity and after a short pause, in the fall of 1984, again resorted to mass arrests. On the other hand, the attempts of Solidarity to extend the scope of activities and gradually come out 'above ground' were not successful either."[34]

One more attempt to break this political stalemate came in September 1986, when the government declared a general amnesty for political prisoners, launched a series of economic reforms, and moved toward the implicit recognition of the political opposition as an indispensable part of efforts to bring about the political stabilization.[35] The shift in the state's strategy during 1986 changed the rules of the political game and gave more breathing space to the Solidarity-based opposition. After receiving an unconditional release from prison in 1986, Solidarity's leaders were able to meet openly and arrive at an official union policy. As a result, the official Provisional Council of Solidarity (TRS) was formed. At the same time, however, there was a growing political diversity among various groups within the opposition still united under the banner of Solidarity. Many oppositional groups were gradually moving in different political directions and toward different strategies. In response to this situation, Solidarity's leaders decided to overhaul its organizational structures in October 1987. Both the underground TKK and the still unofficial but not clandestine TRS were dissolved, and a single National Executive Commission was formed, headed by Walesa and consisting of ten regional representatives. But this new situation was not perceived by everyone as the most desirable solution. Jacek Kuron registered the following complaint:

> We are failing to achieve any success, although after the release of political prisoners it is clear that the authorities regained their sensitivity to social pressure. . . . The most important force of Polish independent society, Solidarnosc, formed its present organizational structures during the first several months of so-called war. Today we are not able to adjust to a totally new situation. This maladjustment is the major cause of the present crisis of the movement. Organizational structures are right now a prime factor impeding the movement.[36]

Moreover, Kuron stressed that the various organizations the regime created to form an institutional buffer between the state and society had acquired a life of their own and pursued more independent policies. "When after December [the authorities] started to create various PRONs, neo-trade unions, councils, and committees it looked like a puppet-show. However, the experiences of Solidarity and the existence of independent competitors create the atmosphere of social pressure in which the proclaimed readiness to represent interests could not remain a sheer fiction. Official institutions became semi-authentic."[37] Thus, after 1986, demobilization policies of the Polish regime underwent a marked transformation. These policies became increasingly open and tolerant. One indication of this new attitude was relaxation of censorship and opening of official media. As a result, "politics and citizenship had become possible more than five years after martial law seemed to mark their doom."[38]

In early 1988, the political system created by the imposition of martial law began to unravel. Two waves of worker strikes rocked the country in the spring and summer, injected new political dynamism into the stalled system and raised hopes for a political change. In factories across the country, Solidarity's enterprise committees were revived and repeatedly attempted to apply for official recognition under the new law regulating the activities of trade unions. Solidarity again became present in the country's public life. The rising militancy of the workers reflected a changing political balance within the country and signified the final collapse of demobilization strategies pursued by the Polish regime for seven years. At the end of August, facing the spreading wave of strikes, the Polish regime publicly offered to begin negotiations with "representatives of various social and professional groups." On December 18, the Citizen's Committee was formed as an advisory body to Lech Walesa. Thus, a new political representation emerged that became a partner in the coming negotiations with the government. The failure of demobilization policies in Poland, however, cannot be attributed exclusively to the strength and determination of Poland's independent political society. In fact, the protest potential of society, its support for the political opposition, and the organizational effectiveness of the underground movement declined through the 1980s.[39] The failure of demobilization policies in Poland was more the reflection of the gradual disintegration of the party-state's institutional structures and the communist elite's political vision in which the imposition of martial law was a crucial component with far-reaching political consequences. As Casimir Garnysz observed in the middle of decade: "If Poland today resembles the state depicted in George Orwell's 1984, the resemblance is of a peculiar kind: a strong police state endowed with the most advanced means for suppressing civil unrest, yet a weak state, deeply afraid of its citizens; a state that can rule but cannot govern, and that has maneuvered itself into a spectacular civil-political stalemate."[40]

THE PARTY-STATE IN TRANSITION

In each of the two previously analyzed cases, the coercive military resolution of the political crisis succeeded in stopping the breakdown of the party-state's institutional structures, restored the balance of power between its core institutions, and launched the successful political demobilization process. The demobilization policies in Hungary and Czechoslovakia were based on and implemented through the institutions and organizations that formed a typical political structure of Soviet-type regimes. These institutions and organizations were rebuild, purged, and forced to resume their usual functions and activities. The central role of the Communist party in formulating and implementing state policies and in controlling all appointments in the administration, public institutions, and the economy through the nomenclatura system was reinforced. The state institutions, including coercive forces, judiciary, state administration, and representative bodies were not reformed and were fully subordinated to the party's hegemony. Mass and professional organizations, economic institutions, cultural institutions, and mass media were purged, politicized, and fully controlled. Moreover, in these two cases, the local power structures were the least affected by the political crisis and became institutional bases for the demobilization policies. Finally, because of weakness of the organized opposition, the party-state was never forced to make significant political concessions or to loosen its grip over society.

In Poland, however, the reverse seemed to be the case. The imposition of martial law furthered the decay of the orthodox model of the party-state and facilitated the shift toward statism. It also did not impede the decay tendencies and erosion of membership within the party-state's organizations, including the Communist party itself. First of all, the political role and position of the Communist party within the regime was seriously weakened. The state became the locus of power and authority as members of the military elite replaced many top party functionaries on the central and regional level. Moreover, the diminishing role of the party had drastic consequences on the local level. During the Solidarity period and after the introduction of martial law, the institutional foundations of party rule were destroyed by the limitation of the party's role and influence in enterprises, public institutions, and organizations. The anarchization of local structures of authority was further facilitated by the disintegration of traditional social networks. These social bases of power were split and fragmented as a result of political conflicts and polarization. Finally, the Polish regime was forced to suspend many traditional communist institutions and mass organizations that blocked the political space and extended the party-state control to all segments of society and significantly relaxed its control over others. The post–martial law regime only partially succeeded in building new surrogate institutional and legal buffers sheltering the core institutions of the state from a direct confrontation with various professional and social groups. And even in organizations they were able to restore—for example, trade unions—their control was significantly weakened.

There are three points that are crucial in understanding the evolution of the Polish party-state after martial law. First, the new regime had a distinct proreformist leaning and seriously intended to carry on significant changes in the organization and functioning of political institutions and the economy. Recently, General Jaruzelski, asked to justify the imposition of martial law, said: "I want to stress that martial law did not altogether halt the pace of gradual change, and—however paradoxically it may sound—without martial law there would have been no Round Table."[41] Similarly, General Kiszczak argued that "paradoxically there is general affinity of intentions and goals behind martial law and the 'round table' agreement. They constitute two opposite poles of the same policy—policy of fundamental and, at the same time, guarded reforms."[42] The ruling elite also remained sensitive to popular pressures and searched for a modus vivendi with society. Considerable freedom was allowed to the press and universities and inclusive policies were extended to anybody, irrespective of ideological position, who agreed to support the government. As Ost emphasizes: "Although many people expected that martial law would mean the death of all reform efforts, the government knew it could not return to the pre-August days. It thought it could do without Solidarity, but it knew it had to find some social support. The civil society that became conscious of itself after August 1980 could not just be bottled up to die. And so the period from 1982 to 1986 was marked by an effort to win some support from some sections of civil society."[43]

Second, the political evolution of the Polish regime during the 1980s and its demobilization policies were shaped by the persistence of the economic crisis in the 1980s. The demobilization policies in Poland unfolded against the background of a steadily deteriorating domestic economic situation and worsening external balances of payment. Neither the efforts of the Polish state nor its partners within the Council for Mutual Economic Assistance could stabilize the economic system and prevent the growing economic disaster with all its potentially explosive political consequences. Finally, in neither Hungary nor Czechoslovakia were demobilization policies carried out in such adverse international conditions. The post–martial-law regime, as Kaminski put it, "was isolated in the West and ignored by the East."[44]

I will analyze the economic and international dimensions of the Polish demobilization process in the next chapter. In the remainder of this chapter, I will look at the institutional transformations of the Polish party-state in the 1980s to document the shift of political authority from the party to the state and the departure of Jaruzelski's regime from the orthodox model of state-socialism. Furthermore, I will draw a clear distinction between the political evolution and policies of the Polish regime and political evolution of post-crisis regimes in Hungary and Czechoslovakia.

The formation of the WRON and the shift of power to the military Communist elite did not mean the demise of the PUWP. However, after the imposition of martial law, the Communist party was hidden behind the backs of the state and the military. According to Ost:

> There was never . . . any attempt to resurrect the idea of the infallibility of the Party. In fact, Party was hardly mentioned at all in the first days of 'the war.' . . . General Jaruzelski appeared and signed proclamations as Minister of defense, head of the new Military Council of National Salvation, and Premier, but his role as head of the Party was omitted. In this sense, martial law further weakened the already fragile theoretical underpinnings of the system. When the Party began to reappear publicly in 1982, there was never any question that it could run things by itself. That notion had been discredited forever.[45]

The Central Committee did not hold its first meeting until the end of February, at which time it publicly endorsed the imposition of martial law long after the Parliament gave its approval. The few other meetings it held during 1982 did not result in any major decisions or policy formulations. The political role of the Polish Communist party was waning in spite of all efforts to prevent this. Jaruzelski even contemplated the dissolution of the party. However, after discussions with Hungarians and Russians he decided that the cost and potential dangers outweighed the potential benefits.[46]

One of the causes of the party's declining political role was the massive membership losses it sustained. The party lost more than one-third of its members during the Solidarity period and after the imposition of martial law. Between the summer of 1980 and the Ninth Extraordinary Congress in July 1981, the party's membership decreased by 380,000, and during the period ending with the Tenth Congress in 1986, the party lost an additional 780,000 members. While the number of people who left the party is staggering by itself, the loses were disproportionally concentrated in crucial social categories—that is, among industrial workers, the youth, and the intelligentsia. Thereafter, party membership stabilized to around 2.1 million.[47] However, the majority of the party members remained passive and stayed in the party for opportunistic reasons. Moreover, as Kolankiewicz and Lewis emphasize, "it is clear than that the mere number of party members does not tell as very much about the stability of party's social bases or about its political strength within Polish society."[48]

The imposition of martial law brought the return of centralized decision making within the party. It also gave an occasion to undo the personnel changes that took place during the preparation for the Extraordinary Congress in 1981, when election procedures were significantly democratized. During the Solidarity period, criticism and pressure from below was directed against the professional party apparatus and as a result led to the replacement of 80 percent of the functionaries of the regional committees and 65 percent in the town, district, and factory committees. More than 50 percent of the secretaries of basic party organizations also went. The party, operating under martial law according to extraordinary rules that invalidated the existing statutes and accountability of its apparatus, moved quickly to remedy the democratic excesses of the previous period. Numerous basic party organizations in factories, institutions, and universities were dissolved, and in others the party's activities contrary to central directives were curtailed. The purge of lower-rank party functionaries followed. Within two months of the imposition of martial law, 349 secretaries of local and city organizations, 307 secretaries of factory committees, and 2,091 secretaries of the basic organizations were dismissed. In addition, eighteen hundred members of party committees on various levels were recalled and 53 percent (six thousand) of the professional party cadres were replaced. At the same time, almost one hundred thousand party members were expelled. Michta notes, "Jaruzelski's purge was directed against the apparatchiks from the

Gierek period who had survived the earlier purge by Kania, and against some of Kania's appointees, whom the general considered too weak or too prounion."[49]

In contrast to the purge on the local and regional levels, there were no significant changes in the national leadership of the party and only one member of the Politburo and three out of two hundred members of the Central Committee resigned or were removed. The stability of the top party leadership continued through the entire demobilization period. The Tenth Party Congress in 1986 did not bring any significant reshuffle of the highest party leadership. In a development similar to other two cases, the political leadership compiled by Jaruzelski in preparation for the imposition of martial law in 1981 showed considerable durability.

Despite stability in its top leadership, however, the power wielded by the Polish Communist party underwent a significant transformation in the 1980s. As Lewis convincingly argues in his well documented study, the party's authority in Soviet-type regimes was crucially dependent on the status and performance of the provincial party committees and their functionaries. However, in Poland starting in the mid 1970s, this level of party structure experienced a long period of gradual diminution of power and authority.[50] The challenges of the Solidarity period, as well as the imposition of martial law, were crucial watersheds in this process of political decline. Jacek Tarkowski writes:

> During the several months after August 1980, the entire system of local authority and administration of communities, which had been in existence for over thirty years, collapsed. Everywhere there were deep transformations in the structure of authority and influence and practically in all communities the mechanisms of horizontal integration disintegrated. The most conspicuous change was a shift in the structure of power and influence in which local chief executives [*naczelnicy*] and presidents, that is heads of the local state administration, moved to the top of this structure.[51]

Thus, already during the Solidarity period but even more so after the imposition of martial law, the state not only acquired relative autonomy from the Communist party, especially on the local level, but shifted the balance of power in its favor. In this way the most fundamental principle of institutional order of state socialist regimes was forsaken. In this respect, the period of demobilization policies in Poland and its institutional outcome remains in striking contrast to the other two cases of political demobilization. As Staniszkis emphasizes, the post–martial-law period was characterized by a fundamental conflict concerning the place of the Communist party in the political system.

> Jaruzelski's military group pursued the course of evolution toward a system in which the state remained as the decision-making center. The apparatus, on the other hand, especially on the provincial level, felt that its interests were in jeop-

ardy. Unintentionally, the introduction of a military regime contributed to the erosion of the 'leading role of the party' [and] the myth that there were no alternatives to the position of the party in the system collapsed.[52]

The state, however, faced an equally formidable challenge in attempting to regain its credibility, institutional strength, and authority, as well as to solve emerging political and economic problems.

The imposition of martial law placed formally all political power in hands of the WRON and military commanders. The work of the state administration, however, was not interrupted. In several weeks, all institutional components of the political system were revitalized and resumed their routine operations. This included the government and regional and local state organs, official political parties and groups represented in the Parliament and local councils, and the local representative bodies themselves.[53] However, the activities of many auxiliary state institutions (mass organizations and smaller professional associations) were entirely suspended, and this substantially inhibited the state's ability to penetrate society and control political space. Thus, while the core state institutions—including the coercive forces, the government, and the Parliament—remained fully operational and firmly behind martial law policies, the ruling elite was forced to rebuilt and consolidate its power within the political space and to establish institutional bridges between the state and society. Two strategies were employed in this process of institutional consolidation: first, was the effort to rebuild or reconquer existing but temporarily suspended auxiliary organizations such as trade unions, mass organizations, and professional associations; second, was an attempt to create new institutional bodies that would substitute for suspended organizations. They were allowed to acquire a semi-autonomous status to attract some support from the population, and bridge the gap between the state and society. These new institutions were designed to foster limited and controlled participation in the political process of all those who did not fundamentally oppose the imposition of martial law. It was hoped that such institutions would play the role of mediator during political conflicts and provide a modicum of social support for the regime.

Immediately after the imposition of martial law, the regime worked to build a new all-inclusive movement that would give the appearance of popular support for the regime's policies. By June 1982, the so-called Citizens Committees of National Salvation (OKON) were established in seven thousand localities. Initially, these committees were staffed by retired party apparatchiks and security police functionaries as well as hard-line party activists. The OKON groups transformed into a nationwide Patriotic Movement of National Revival (PRON), which was designed to replace the traditional national front organization that was moribund in Poland since 1980. The movement was organized according to the usual territorial pattern. In 1983, the PRON published its programmatic declaration, describing itself as a "platform for uniting all patriotic forces of the nation," and held its founding congress in May 1983. The movement, however, failed to attract mass membership, despite the fact that all state-controlled organizations were forced to sign the PRON declaration and join the movement. In 1986, the PRON had only 1.2 million individual members, and among those only 30 percent were not already members of official political parties.[54] In an effort to gain some public confidence, the PRON attempted to portray itself as an instrument of independent public opinion by appealing, for example, to the parliament and the Council of State for the lifting martial law and the granting of amnesties to political prisoners. But such political gestures and manipulations did nothing to improve the image of the organization, which was resolutely rejected by the majority of the population.

Other organizations created by the regime in order to replace suspended and dissolved professional organizations experienced a similar fate. The new Journalists Union of the Polish People's Republic, for example, was boycotted by the majority of journalists and failed to establish itself as something more than a thoroughly manipulated agent of the state. Also the constitutional changes, such as the creation of a Constitutional Tribunal, Tribunal of State, and Commission for Constitutional Responsibilities failed to give more credibility to the post—martial-law regime. Nor did the persistent efforts of the regime to set up semi-independent consultative bodies such as a Consultative Council to the chairman of the Council of State, and Consultative Conventions on the local level succeed. They failed to attract any significant interest or important personalities.

The most difficult problem in restoring the institutional structure of the party-state was rebuilding a state-controlled trade-union movement. The Polish Parliament had dissolved all trade-union organizations existing before the imposition of martial law, and the formation of new unions posed several crucial challenges for the regime. First, the union movement had to be different in structure and function from Solidarity as well as from the old, discredited trade-union organization with its highly centralized and bureaucratic structures. Second, there was a danger that the underground Solidarity activists might attempt a takeover of the new emerging unions and regain an institutional platform for their oppositional activities. And finally, new unions had to secure a significant level of autonomy if they wanted to attract any sizable membership and yet still be fully responsive to the state's influence and concerns. The drive for full independence of trade unions was at the center of Solidarity's self-limiting revolution, but the government realized that it was impossible to dispense with the unions in the longer run. To run the centralized economy more efficiently, it needed a reliable organization representing employees that could be integrated into the political system and ready to cooperate at least on economic issues. For these reasons the government made the restoration of the unions a slow and controlled process in which all possible risks were carefully considered.[55] The government chose a strategy of organizing highly fragmented and small unions based at first on individual enterprises but leaving open the possibility of developing the branch structure based on occupation and industrial sectors and the national level organization at the later day. The limit of one union per enterprise was an important element in this institutional design.

The new Trade Union Law enacted on October 8, 1982, provided that the unions were to be independent from the administrative and economic organs of the state but, at the same time, were to fully endorse the social ownership of the means of production and the leading role of the Communist party. Moreover, the rights, especially the right to strike, and other prerogatives of the unions were carefully restricted. The law specified a transitional period that would allow first for the formation of factory-level unions in 1983, then their sectoral national organizations in 1984, and finally union associations and confederations in 1985. Initially, factory-level founding committees attracted very little support. They were boycotted by employees and had a large number of retirees, who joined tempted by the benefits unions could offer. The new unions, however, experienced significant financial difficulties, given the fact that the assets of the former unions were concentrated on the national and regional levels not on the level of factories. They had, therefore, little incentives to attract or buy new members. This problem persisted. Even when national-level federations were formed, the distribution of assets belonging to former union organizations presented the government with serious problems. By the middle of 1983 approximately three million employees had joined the new unions, but membership rarely exceeded 20 percent of the workforce in any given enterprise.[56] Encouraged by the total boycott of the new unions by underground Solidarity, the Council of State in April 1983 gave permission for the formation of national trade-union organizations.[57] By the middle of 1984, more than one hundred national-level federations existed. By the end of 1984, the formal Council of All-Poland Alliance of Trade Unions (OPZZ) was established, which included representatives from each federation and delegates from some 400 enterprise-based unions. The chairman of the OPZZ, Alfred Miodowicz, was elected as a member of the party's Politburo in 1986.

After further relaxation of organizational restrictions, such as canceling the minimal requirement of fifty members in order to set up a union, the organization slowly grew and by the middle of 1984 claimed 4.5 million members and existed in 90 percent of the workplaces within the socialized sector of the economy. Under the October 1982 law, the new unions acquired all the assets of the former unions, including Solidarity. They were extensively endorsed and supported by the government and increasingly came to resemble the old Central Council of Trade Unions. In 1986, the trade union organization had 6.1 million members, including retirees, and was comprised of 133 federations. The level of unionization, however, was particularly weak in big cities, among skilled workers and in big enterprises, and the number of retirees and party members among the unions' membership was disproportionally high.[58] There was only a small increase in membership during the next two years before the re-legalization of Solidarity in 1989.

The emergence and consolidation of the new trade unions was only a partial success for the post–martial-law regime. There was a significant reluctance among important segments of the working class to joint the unions as well as a significant degree of distrust and passivity among those who joined or were forced to join them. The new unions never achieved the strength they had in the past and never played the role of an obedient "transmission belt" prescribed to them by the classical Leninist tradition. Moreover, deprived of any possibility to regain real political influence and eager to gain some credibility, the new unions lobbied for economic concessions, which additionally complicated the difficult economic pressures faced by the Polish party-state. The structure of the trade-union movement that evolved in Poland as a result of post–martial-law developments became perhaps the most important institutional legacy of state socialism. Poland is the only country in the former Soviet bloc that has a highly fragmented, competitive, and militant trade-union sector.

The situation in the trade-union movement reflected a broader phenomenon that was characterized by the inability of the existing mass organizations and state-sponsored associations to attract substantial membership and to exert enough pressure to force people to join the ranks of such organizations. On the other hand, even if conscious resistance subsided and people joined these organizations, there was the clear reluctance on the side of the members to become involved in any political activity. Besides, the state largely failed to provide enough resources and material incentives to make joining these organizations profitable. As a result, membership in the unions, mass and political organizations, youth organizations, and state-sponsored professional associations was notably lower in the 1980s than in the 1970s.[59] Thus, the post-martial law regime's efforts to revitalize the protective belt of auxiliary organizations and institutions failed; nor was the regime able to diminish society's alienation from the party-state sponsored organizations and rebuild the institutional bridges between the state and society. In this respect, the results of demobilization policies in Poland departed distinctively from political developments in Hungary and Czechoslovakia after the invasion.

The above analysis of the demobilization process clearly shows that, while the Polish party-state did not experience an institutional breakdown of its core institutions and did preserve its coercive and administrative capacity through the entire period of demobilization, it failed to reequilibrate a state-socialist regime in its traditional form. The Polish ruling elite faced widespread defiance and active resistance and opposition. It failed to restore and consolidate some important institutional elements of the regime, bridge the gap between the state and society, and secure public compliance with state policies. On the other hand, the regime did succeed in demobilizing the population to such a degree as to secure the uninterrupted functioning of the state administration's national and local structures. Moreover, after a two-year postponement, it finally organized local elections in 1984 and parliamentary elections the following year. However, while a new Parliament and local councils were elected, the electoral boycott organized by underground Solidarity was quite successful and indicated that the political domination of the post–martial-law regime was on shaky foundations. Based on the results of these elections, it became obvious that a return to routine political rituals was an unlikely possibility, and future electoral procedures and practices had to be significantly reformed. Moreover, despite the centralization and secure control of the national and local politics, the post–martial-law regime was not able to rebuild the effective auxiliary institutions, including trade unions and youth organizations; halt the defection of workers and intellectuals; break the considerable isolation of the ruling elites; and in this way to restore a specific type of relationship between the state and society characteristic of Soviet-type regimes. The 1988 worker strikes the and reorganization of Solidarity forces dramatically underscored the political stalemate that persisted in Poland during the entire demobilization process—a testimony to the failure of demobilization policies.

While I have argued that the failure of the demobilization policies in Poland should be seen above all as a domestic political failure, political choices and strategies of the post–martial-law ruling elites were shaped by other significant factors. The disastrous economic and social crisis that plagued Poland for the entire decade, which the post–martial-law regime was not able to reverse or even stop, was a equally powerful factor contributing to the unraveling of demobilization policies and disintegration of communist power in Poland. In the next chapter I will look more closely at the failure of the economic reform during the demobilization period and at the role of international factors in shaping demobilization policies employed by the Polish party-state elites.

The Political Crisis and the Failure
of Demobilization and Regime Reequilibration

AFTER THE SOLIDARITY movement was crushed through the imposition of martial law in December 1981, parallels were immediately drawn to the two previous cases of large-scale coercive demobilization in the region. A consensus among scholars seemed to emerge that the most likely scenario of the demobilization process in Poland would resemble the one in Hungary, with a highly repressive period of restoration and consolidation of institutional structures of the party-state followed by more pragmatic and reform-oriented policies within the economic and political sphere.[1] In fact, the Polish ruling elite openly expressed the desire to follow a "Kadarization" model, extensively consulted Hungarian experts, and encouraged publication of monographs and articles on post-1956 developments in Hungary. This was the most obvious example of the political learning process. The option to choose between strategies of demobilization, however, was unavailable to the Polish ruling elite. I have argued earlier in this work that the processes of demobilization in Hungary and Czechoslovakia were shaped by a unique combination of domestic and geopolitical conditions specific to each country and developed as a set of ruling elites' ad hoc responses to changing domestic and international constraints and developments. I have also argued that the nature and course of the political crises that preceded the demobilization process in both countries greatly affected the capacities of the resistance movements and institutional coherence of the party-states, as well as the range of political choices available to the individual regimes.

It should have been clear from the outset of the Polish demobilization process that, given the nature of the Polish political crisis, the type of coercive response, and the specific combination of domestic and international constraints, both the state's strategies and the possible outcomes of the demobilization process should vary significantly from those in Hungary and Czechoslovakia. The challenge to the state-socialist political order posed by the emergence of Solidarity was more fundamental and effective than the short-lived revolutionary challenge in Hungary and the self-limiting reform movement from above in Czechoslovakia. Furthermore, the demobilization policies of the Polish regimes unfolded in more complex and adverse international conditions both within the Soviet bloc and between the West and the East. Moreover, the imposition of martial law, which was designed to break the stalemate between the two sides of the political conflict and to give the ruling elite new means of action, failed to accomplish either.

Not surprisingly, therefore, during the successive stages of the demobilization process in Poland, it became increasingly clear that the defining characteristic of this process was the persistence of a political stalemate between the state elites and antiregime opposition. The post–martial-law regime experienced a gradual devaluation or exhaustion of its demobilization tactics, involving a combination of repressive measures, gestures of good will, nationalistic appeals, and limited concessions. It failed to reestablish full political control, secure a modicum of social support and legitimacy, and solve Poland's economic and political problems. Similarly, the underground opposition movement failed to mobilize enough resources and popular support to be able to seriously threaten the survival of the regime or to extract significant political concessions. At the same time, Polish society withdrew from politics, slipping into passive hostility and inaction. Thus, neither side of the conflict was able to impose its will on the other or to monopolize political resources and initiative. The party-state institutions failed to achieve exclusive domination of political space and to secure sufficient compliance and cooperation from the population, while the opposition movements and organizations failed to effectively challenge the state monopoly of power.

Until 1984, this persistent political stalemate was in its "hot" phase. This phase was characterized by a repeated escalation of the government's repressive measures, followed by acts of amnesty granted to political offenders. Neither successive waves of repression, however, nor four amnesties granted by the government between 1982 and 1986 succeeded in persuading the crushed Solidarity movement to accept defeat and withdraw from illegal political activities. Yet this period was also characterized by Solidarity's persistent efforts to rebuild its organizational structures, mobilize popular resistance, and sustain the boycott of official institutions and initiatives. Although initially successful, these efforts were equally disappointing in the long run. After 1984, the political stalemate in Poland shifted to its "cold" phase—characterized by gradual softening in the regime's repressive actions and policies, especially after the 1986 amnesty, and by a significant decline in the mobilizational capacity of the political opposition.

The local (1984) and general (1985) elections, which became a test of political capacity and strength for both sides, proved inconclusive. The high level of nonparticipation (25.1 percent in 1984 and 21.1 percent in 1985) underscored the Polish regime's persistent authority deficit. At the same time, the fact that so many people did vote showed that the boycott campaign organized by the underground opposition was not fully successful either. Inconclusive results of elections forced the ruling elite to rethink its demobilization strategies and compelled opposition leaders to revaluate their strategies of resistance. In 1986 and 1987, both sides began to search for some sort of accommodation that would not jeopardize their moral and political principles and simultaneously would allow room for compromise and negotiations. This effort amplified conflicts and divisions between soft-

and hard-liners within both the ruling elite and Solidarity underground movement. As a result the political opportunity structure was again re-opened after years of more repressive authoritarian policies.

The search for political accommodation was stepped up in 1988, when political and economic stability of the country was seriously threatened. Two waves of worker strikes and growing popular unrest fueled by the worsening economic situation shifted the balance of power in favor of the opposition, forcing the state to grant unprecedented political concessions to the opposition. The roundtable negotiations that took place in the spring of 1989 between the state (represented by those who introduced martial law) and the opposition movements (represented by former Solidarity leaders and advisers) were a symbolic end to the demobilization process and served as unmistakable proof of its ultimate failure.

In the last chapter, I traced the causes for the collapse of demobilization policies to three sets of conditions. The first was the capacity of resistance and opposition movements to survive in a highly repressive political environment after the imposition of martial law. The second was the failure of the Polish regime to rebuild the institutional structures of the party-state and to restore the peculiar type of relationship between the state and society that characterized Soviet-type regimes, as well as its inability to arrest the economic decline. Finally, there was a new and complex set of international pressures and constraints that decisively shaped the capacities of political actors on both sides of the domestic political conflict. The one-sided dependence on the Soviet Union, which had characterized the countries of the region in the 1950s and 1960s, gradually gave way in the 1970s and 1980s to an intricate net of global dependencies both in the political and economic dimensions. These dependencies resulted from the economic and political opening to the West and an unraveling of the Soviet economic and geopolitical domination of the region. This new international context imposed a much more constrained framework within which the post–martial-law regime was forced to operate. In the following section, I will look briefly at these three dimensions to see how the developments in each of them contributed to the ultimate failure of the demobilization process in Poland and in what respects political developments in Poland differed from those in Hungary and Czechoslovakia.

THE CAPACITY OF RESISTANCE AND OPPOSITION MOVEMENTS

In comparison to the Soviet military invasions of Hungary and Czechoslovakia, the coercive military resolution of the political crisis in Poland was not only executed by the domestic coercive forces but was also was much better prepared and, in the short run, more effective. The Military Council of National Salvation had from the very beginning full command of the Polish military and police and the full cooperation of central and local organs of the state administration. While repressive actions were certainly much more restrained in comparison to the bloody political terror that followed the Hungarian Revolution, they were also more severe than the immediate repressive measures following the Soviet invasion in Czechoslovakia. Solidarity had its offices and resources seized by the government, its leaders detained, and its communication networks destroyed. Nevertheless, the union was able to regroup and gradually rebuild its local and national structures into an underground movement. After a few confused weeks, underground presses and publications emerged across the country, clandestine factory and local committees were formed, union dues were collected and channeled to finance underground activities and to support the detainees and their families. Despite continual arrests, political trials, and other repressive measures, the activities of the underground movement gradually acquired an organized and professional character and the organized opposition became a permanent element in the political configuration of post–martial-law Poland. To explain this persistence and capacity of the political opposition to survive and to shape political developments in Poland, several important factors have to be taken into account. The first is connected with the internal characteristics of the opposition movement itself.

As I argued in the opening chapter, an oppositional movement's prospect for survival in the highly repressive environment following a military crackdown is directly linked to the nature of political mobilization before the coercive resolution of the crisis. In this respect the political crisis in Poland differed radically from those in Hungary or Czechoslovakia. The Solidarity movement was born as the result of a massive, country-wide popular mobilization with clearly articulated demands that led to the emergence of well-defined political cleavages and sides of the conflict. This was a movement coming from outside the party-state institutional structures; defying the existing mode of political domination; rejecting its ideological underpinnings, official political discourse, and legitimation claims; and seeking its own autonomous political and institutional expression. At the same time, it was a movement with a carefully limited and very effective political agenda—in the words of Andrew Arato, "a new type of movement that seeks to rebuild structures of social solidarity, bypassing state power altogether."[2]

Second, the Polish democratic opposition's strategy of political struggle, which evolved at the end of 1970s, envisioned the self-organization of society into a democratic movement, working to limit the state's influence and control over many areas of social life. The idea of the reconstitution of civil society on the basis of the rule of law and the guarantee of civil rights and expressed through a free public sphere and a plurality of independent movements and associations was present in all of the opposition documents. Although this political strategy was developed by the oppositional intellectuals, it found its successful realization in the trade union movement and became an effective political weapon in the hands of Solidarity's organizers and leaders. More importantly, the self-organization of Polish society after the 1980 August Agreements was based on the formation of new and the expansion of existing organic social networks found in localities and places of employment. These social bonds were additionally reinforced by the principle of decentralized and territorial organization adopted by Solidarity in 1980. The regional organization of Solidarity not only established powerful horizontal structures, countering the vertical organization of the party-state and its fundamental principle of societal fragmentation, but also allowed the movement to preserve and strengthen close relations with its social bases. Solidarity provided the vehicle to mobilize all segments of the Polish population and all professional groups and categories, but at the same time it preserved informal, localized networks of social relations as founding blocks of the formal organization of the movement. The movement was also successful in building the all-inclusive alliance between the workers, intelligentsia, students, peasants, private entrepreneurs, and the Catholic church, which produced a powerful and closely tied social and political force with well-defined constituencies, similar objectives, and overwhelming popular support. Public opinion polls conducted in Poland during the Solidarity period reveal the image of society broadly divided into two blocs reflecting the political cleavage between the state and society. Interestingly, standard socioeconomic variables do not play any important role in distinguishing these two blocs, which formed around organizational affiliations, symbols, and identities not around socioeconomic locations and interests. Thus, the Solidarity movement was successful in establishing all-inclusive, counterhegemonic political identity.[3]

Third, Solidarity gradually evolved from spontaneous political mobilization into well-established organizational structures that encompassed a growing number of people and expanded to all areas of social life and all parts of the country. As I mentioned before, the time span between the eruption of popular mobilization and a state's coercive counteraction is crucial in enhancing or diminishing the chances for the survival of the organized opposition. The political crisis in Poland, in contrast to Hungary and Czechoslovakia, lasted long enough (sixteen months) to transform mobilized masses into an integrated and well-organized movement able to monopolize considerable material and human resources and to develop a distinctive collective identity. While most of the movement's resources were dispersed and seized during martial law, a significant portion of printing equipment and paper was salvaged and immediately used in clandestine activities. The movement also was able to build a sizable cadre of experienced and committed grassroots leaders and activists who could carry on political activities, despite political repression and the arrest of most of the movement's elected leaders. Moreover, the adoption of a decentralized and segmented structure of the underground organization proved to be a great advantage. Disruption of the national or regional Solidarity's centers through arrests was less devastating in the situation where activities of the union were based on dispersed local initiatives.[4]

Fourth, students of social movements emphasize that the presence of powerful allies greatly enhances a movement's chances for survival or success, especially in nondemocratic regimes.[5] Largely because of the backing of the Catholic church, underground Solidarity was able to build effective self-defense networks and to provide wide-ranging support, aid, and protection to all of its members and sympathizers involved in underground activities and to those who suffered repressions. The church structure and institutions, unaffected by martial law regulations, formed an emergency safety net for the dispersed and prosecuted union organizations and often provided institutional outlets for various independent cultural and political activities. The political position and institutional autonomy of the church, as well as its traditional role as a defender and bearer of the national identity, combined with the religious homogeneity of the Polish population, were crucial factors strengthening the position of the resistance movement in Poland. Neither in Hungary nor in Czechoslovakia did the resistance movements have the support of such an organizationally, ideologically, and historically influential organization. Thus, after sixteen months of legal existence, the Solidarity movement developed strong popular roots, cross-class alliances, and informal social networks across the country, which were firmly grounded in organic social bases and relations. Moreover, after the crackdown, it had a powerful ally offering support, protection, and considerable resources. These characteristics allowed the movement to survive the destruction of its formal organizational structures and to endure under highly repressive policies of the post–martial-law regime.

Finally, the Solidarity movement was more than an organized social force. It also represented a distinct intellectual and symbolic formation that provided the movement with a collective identity and created an insurmountable division between the state and society. During the period of its legal existence, Solidarity was able to develop a distinctive alternative political discourse and to appropriate an important segment of national and patriotic values and traditions as well as their symbolic expressions into its own cultural idiom. The collective identity of the movement was built around those symbols, values, and traditions, which set the movement apart from the official political language, values, and ideology. Thus, the political crisis in Poland did more than destroy a significant part of the state's theoretical legacy and justifications, compromise its political declarations, and undermine the legitimation claims routinely employed by the party-state. More important, the crisis generated two well-defined political forces and created two separate cultural and political idioms appealing to different values and traditions and using different political calendars and symbols.[6] Solidarity emerged as a powerful defender of the Polish national tradition and values and as a representative of a powerful vision of reform and political change based on self-organization of democratic society against the totalitarian and alien state. It easily won the battle for national symbols and legitimation claims with the party-state elites, which in a short time was forced into a position of a guarantor of foreign political domination indispensable only as long as the geopolitical balance of power in Europe remained unaltered.

Solidarity's strong internal organization contributed to the relative ease with which it set up its underground activities, but there were several elements of the state' repressive strategies that directly or indirectly contributed to the movement's survival underground. I emphasized when analyzing the demobilization policies in Hungary and Czechoslovakia that the policy of open borders that followed the Soviet military intervention decimated the opposition and resistance movements by allowing thousands of determined opponents of the regime, as well as potential oppositional activists and leaders, to leave the country. The extent of this massive political emigration, which included the most dynamic, young, and educated segments of the population, made all efforts to organize and to sustain effective resistance and opposition much more difficult. In contrast with these two previous cases, the Polish regime sealed the country's borders and maintained very restrictive travel policies immediately after the imposition of martial law. As a result all those who would have emigrated for political reasons or for fear of political prosecution were trapped within the country and became a new elite of the resistance movement. When in the latter period of the demobilization process the regime realized dangerous consequences of its restrictive emigration policies and attempted to encourage or even to force opposition leaders to leave the country, Solidarity launched a counteraction urging all activists to endure the pressure and to stay in the country. It should be noted, however, that the significant relaxation of travel restrictions after the lifting of martial law caused a notable exodus from the country and can be seen as one of the important factors that contributed to the decline of capacity of the opposition after 1984.

Another element of the state's strategy that contributed to the survival of the organized opposition was the regime's self-limitation of repressive action. The legal framework of martial law allowed the repression to be carried to its ultimate limits, yet in reality, they were relatively mild and restricted. Poland was not subjected to organized political violence, and the regime's opponents were not systematically purged from the state's institutions and organizations. To be sure, there were cases of police killings and brutality that resulted in the death of those arrested, as well as mysterious "accidents" involving activists of the opposition; it should be stressed, however, that organized political repression was not carried to the full limits allowed by the law. Prison sentences rarely exceeded three years and substantial financial fines imposed on demonstrators and activists were paid by the Catholic church and underground organizations, making them less severe and quite ineffective as a deterrent. In addition, the safety net build by the church and underground organizations made largely ineffective a strategy of terminating employment as a punishment for the refusal to sign the declaration of loyalty and for the lack of political compliance that was so widely and effectively used in Czechoslovakia. In Poland, persons losing jobs for political reasons not only received material support but very often were employed by private enterprises or were able to set up private firms with the help of Solidarity funds and resources.

The Polish underground movement had one more important asset that was not feasible during the previous periods. No other movement in East Central Europe during the postwar period had so much international support from various political forces, governments, and international organizations on both sides of the political spectrum. Moreover, no other organization was allowed to maintain independent international contacts and relations. During the Solidarity period, Western trade unions became crucial political supporters of the Polish unions and provided massive material assistance to help establish Solidarity's organizational structures and to strengthen its resources.[7] This situation did not change after the imposition of martial law. Western union federations not only organized protest actions supporting the Solidarity movement on the international arena and issued repeated protests addressed to the Polish government but also provided assistance to Solidarity's organizations abroad and inside the country. Moreover, through the wide network of newly created Solidarity offices abroad and through a variety of organizations and institutions, both money and equipment were smuggled to Poland, greatly enhancing the capacity of the resistance movement. Thanks to high quality printing equipment, for example, the underground publishing houses could significantly expand their output and achieve an almost professional quality in their publications. As Zbigniew Brzezinski emphasizes: "There is no doubt that without this . . . support, it would have been very difficult to mount this kind of effort [i.e., underground oppositional activities] in Poland and to sustain it over five very difficult years."[8] Thus, the fact that after the imposition of martial law, Solidarity was morally, politically, and materially supported by Western trade unions, social movements, political parties, human rights organizations, governments, and international organizations had an important impact on both the oppositional capacity of the Solidarity movement and the effectiveness of repressive measures employed by the Polish party-state.

International political pressures and support provided the opposition movement in Poland with one more crucial asset. The eagerness of the Polish regime to improve its international reputation and persuade Western countries to lift their economic and political sanctions resulted in the regime's efforts to lift martial law regulations as quickly as possible and to limit the extent of repressive measures. The post–martial-law elites tried to convince the international community that they embraced the course of political moderation, despite facing determined domestic opposition and Soviet pressures. They also wanted to create at least the appearance of political stability and domestic legitimacy. Consider the regime's impatient and imprudent amnesties. Between 1982 and 1986, the Polish regime granted four successive amnesties to political prisoners, which had quite the opposite effect of Kadar's amnesties following the Hungarian Revolution. The Polish amnesties not only reduced the severity of penal repression but also meant that the granting of a state's pardon would no longer be effective as an element of the demobilization policy. Moreover, through its actions, the regime admitted that outside pressure was effective in shaping its policies. Thus, the repressive edge of the post–martial-law regime was significantly weakened by self-imposed limitations and the ruling elite's strategic errors in applying both coercive measures and political concessions. Any hope of repeating the Hungarian scenario of political demobilization, which concluded repressive policies with gestures of reconciliation willingly accepted by society, was quite naively entertained by the Polish ruling elite.

All factors listed above were responsible for the survival of comparatively strong, widespread, and organized resistance and opposition. In contrast to Hungary and Czechoslovakia, where all traces of independent social organizations and political activities were methodically erased by the regime in a very short time, in Poland the post–martial-law regime quickly exhausted the effectiveness of its demobilization strategies. It gradually relinquished its political control over many aspects of social and economic life, scaled down repression and its political ambitions, and accepted implicitly the existence of the political opposition. As the demobilization process progressed, it became clear that behind the tanks, riffles, tear-gas grenades, and repressive laws—as well as the rhetoric of saving Poland from the imminent Soviet military invasion and civil war—there was an empty shell of institutions and organizations whose political grounds and practical reasons for existence evaporated as soon as society took the political initiative into its own hands and challenged not only the unjust privileges and abuses of power but the very right of the party-state to rule.

THE CAPACITY AND STRATEGIES OF THE PARTY-STATE

The emergence of the Solidarity movement and the protracted political crisis in Poland created a situation in which self-organizing society's actors pushed back the power of the state and in the process limited its polymorphic character by liberating many spheres of social life from the state's direct control and command. The gradual retreat and displacement of the party-state control over many areas of political and social life endangered the very existence of many established institutions and organizations, including the Communist party itself. The Polish party-state, however, was able to insulate its core institutions and to preside over the countermobilization of the state's coercive forces and bureaucratic apparatus, which culminated in the imposition of martial law. The effort to halt the decay of the political structures of the state-socialist regime included the removal of Solidarity from the political scene, as well as the reform of the party-state institutions and practices. This task, according to Jan de Weydenthal,

> was tackled in three ways. First was the imposition of a basically provisional form of government that, while providing protective umbrella for the more protracted power-building operation, would also supply a model of correct work and organizational behavior; this was achieved by the militarization of the system. The second way involved a drastic change of personnel in directing positions in the party and the government to ensure that those positions would be filled by people free of external commitments and compliant to orders from above. Third was the creation of a new and legally binding framework for political operations that would give the refurbished institutions a basis for their future work.[9]

Still, while the Polish party-state implemented an amazingly complex and effective military crackdown operation and introduced a number of measures to prop up the capacity of party-state institutions, the reequilibration of the regime was not achieved. Following the imposition of martial law the ruling elites experimented with various institutional reforms and policy changes, but these efforts did not bring about political stability and administrative efficiency. I have already pointed to some causes behind this failure but in order to fully explain the collapse of demobilization policies in Poland it is necessary to look at the country's economic developments during the post—martial-law period. A disastrous economic crisis plagued Poland in the 1980s, undermining the efforts to reequilibrate the regime. It is possible that if the post–martial-law regime was able to arrest the economic decline, improve the economic performance, and raise living standards, demobilization policies may have succeeded, despite the existence of the organized political opposition.

In the previous chapter, I described the economic problems and difficulties that developed in the 1970s and eventually led to the economic crisis at the end of the decade. Without a doubt, the economic failure of the Gierek regime significantly contributed to the widespread popular unrest and the rise of Solidarity. The political crisis of 1980 and 1981, however, led to a further deterioration of the economic situation, causing a sharp decline in industrial production, pervasive shortages, and a subsequent destabilization of the consumer market. The beginning of the 1980s revealed the drastic decrease in industrial production in all sectors of the economy as well as a significant decline in levels of consumption, and in standards of living. Despite official statements that placed blame for the deterioration of the economic situation solely on Solidarity, only a part of these economic problems can be attributed to strikes and protest actions. The economic difficulties were largely the result of the regime's economic policies in the 1970s. In 1980 the Polish GNP dropped 6 percent, and in 1981, it further declined by 12 percent. Due to the crisis, about 40–50 percent of industrial capacity became idle, and exports declined by 19 percent.[10] At the same time, Polish foreign debt increased from $20.7 billion in 1979 to $25.5 billion in 1981 despite a sharp cut in Western imports. In the early 1980s, debt servicing substantially exceeded Polish foreign currency earnings, and the country was virtually bankrupt. As Kazimierz Poznanski argues, however, "although these indicators clearly showed that the economy had collapsed, the regime still had not developed either a solid program or the authority necessary to launch a package of anticrisis measures."[11]

Martial law was imposed, however, for political reasons, and during its duration politics took primacy over economics. Although party-state elites were concerned with the extent of the economic crisis and vigorously lobbied the Soviet Union for additional economic aid, martial law policies were not designed to stabilize a rapidly deteriorating economic situation in the country. Their goal was to terminate the agreement, which had been signed with striking committees in 1980, to halt the disintegration of the state and the Communist party and to destroy all independent organizations. Despite its rhetoric, the economic policies of the Jaruzelski regime fell far short of addressing the country's real economic ills. Andrew Michta writes:

> WRON's martial-law decrees demonstrate the military's "ideological" approach to the complexities of Poland's economic quagmire. They also bear witness to the new regime's lack of administrative experience and the often naive belief of the soldier that clearly formulated orders and discipline would always have the intended effect. The militarization of Poland's factories and the presence of army commissars at managerial posts were to reverse Poland's economic decline; systemic weaknesses were to be overcome by uncorrupted, principled individuals. Paradoxically, the underlying premise of this approach was that Poland needed not less but more centrally imposed economic decisionmaking.[12]

Difficult economic circumstances in which the post–martial-law regime was forced to operate closed one of the easiest alternatives for winning the population's support and compensating for political repression—significantly raising living standards and improving the consumer market situation. In contrast to the situations in Hungary and Czechoslovakia and other crises in the past, the Polish regime could not mobilize and use economic measures and resources to pacify political unrest and to buy political compliance. Quite the contrary, the rapidly deteriorating economic situation forced the regime to introduce highly unpopular measures in order to the prevent the imminent collapse of the consumer market, as well as austerity measures necessary to secure further foreign aid and relief from financial obligations. Thus, already in the spring of 1982, a massive increase in consumer prices was introduced, which depressed the real income of the population by approximately 20 percent. Price increases were introduced again in 1984 and 1985. Overall, during the first three years of the demobilization process, food prices increased 350 percent and prices of other consumer goods rose 250 percent.[13] Despite these drastic increases of prices, the inflationary pressures were not eliminated. Zbigniew Fallenbuchl argues that "faced with passive resistance of the population and 'a very limited trust in the authorities', the government had been trying to use 'money illusion' in order to reduce the full psychological impact of the economic crisis and its own policies."[14] Inflation on the order of 30–40 percent a year persisted during the 1980s and exploded in open hyperinflation in 1989.

Although the decline of the GNP was temporarily halted in 1983 and 1984, the national income in 1987 was still significantly lower than in 1978. So was the real income of the population and the level of investment in the economy, while the foreign debt soared to $37 billion. The only notable success of the Polish regime was the increase in coal output achieved through the massive concentration of resources in this hard-currency generating industry. Moreover, a classical method of stimulating growth by increasing investment was not available to the Polish regime, stripped of financial and other resources and facing not only a restive population but also very reluctant Western governments and financial institutions. Thus, in 1982, the government suspended sixteen hundred investment projects, among which only 444 were restarted later on.[15]

The gap left by Western economic sanctions was not compensated for by the Soviet Union and other partners within the Soviet bloc. At that time all state-socialist regimes in the region were already experiencing economic difficulties of their own and were unable to extend any significant economic aid to Poland. Also, Western financial institutions and governments were not willing to extend new credits or offer economic aid for political reasons.[16] Thus, the severe economic crisis persisted through the entire post–martial-law period and the numerous partial reform programs introduced by the regime failed not only to improve the overall economic situation of the country but also failed to arrest the process of economic decay and the anarchization of productive and distributive capacities of the economy. During this period, the country's financial crisis reached disastrous proportions and was reflected by a growing inflation and budget deficit, declining exports, and the collapse of domestic and international balances of payments. Although the need for economic reforms was one of the most fundamental justifications offered for the imposition of martial law, it is particularly striking that "a regime that had accorded so much priority to reform has yet achieved so little with that reform."[17] Poznanski concluded in his analysis of economic developments after the imposition of martial law with the following:

> In economic terms, military rule has not provided a framework for genuine recovery. Poland is enduring another period of immobilization and hence is unable to take advantage of many important policy alternatives. The austerity program is falling apart under continuous wage pressure from the workers. Intraparty traditionalists are sabotaging badly needed systemic reforms. No mechanism for promoting export to hard-currency markets has been developed so far, so that severe import restrictions serve as the major source of improvements in the balance of payments. The picture of the economy under Jaruzelski's rule is not altogether different from that which existed before the transfer of power to the military.[18]

This persistent economic stagnation had a severe impact not only on domestic consumption and the consumer market but led to a deterioration of the housing market and the welfare system and to a catastrophic environmental crisis. Housing shortages, the inadequacy of the child-care system, the decapitalization and the disastrous state of the educational system, and the near collapse of the health system were only the tip of the iceberg of the Polish social crisis. Moreover, the 1980s witnessed a rapid spread of poverty affecting some four million people, especially among the most vulnerable segments of the population, such as pensioners and multichild and single-parent families. While Poland was far from the poverty level of some Third World countries and there was no overt hunger or large-scale homelessness, nevertheless, as George Kolankiewicz and Paul Lewis emphasize: "In a situation where upwards of 54 percent of household expenditure goes towards the purchase of food, then any drop in real incomes must cause undernourishment in essentials such as protein and vitamins. The remainder of income goes towards shoes, clothing and housing. As a consequence, one in four workers are believed to be under-nourished."[19]

With the drastic decline of living standards, there was a significant expansion of social inequalities generated by the rampant development of the black market and the permissive attitude of the government toward the second economy. Inequalities increased within the state sector as well, generated by government's attempts to buy support of strategic groups of industrial workers, for, example miners, through expanding social and financial benefits and privileges. Due to its economic and political crisis, Poland presented probably the most visible example of the process, which Ivan Szelenyi and Robert Manchin identified in Hungary.[20] On the one hand, there was a rapid accumulation of privileges and resources by the new private entrepreneurs and a portion of the party and state elite who learned how to exploit market opportunities. On the other hand, the 1980s witnessed growing disadvantages among large segments of the population with no access either to the state's redistributive system or the market-generated income.

Therefore, in contrast to the post-crisis situation in Hungary and Czechoslovakia, the dramatic and multidimensional economic and social crisis that affected Poland in the 1980s presented a thorny background against which the ruling elites implemented their demobilization policies and attempted to reequilibrate the regime. Deprived of the easy redistributive measures successfully used by other regimes in previous political crises, such as immediate improvement of the market situation and increase in the population's real incomes, Poland's government was forced to impose drastic austerity measures to stabilize the economy. The inability to deal with the economic difficulties fueled the undercurrents of social unrest during the entire demobilization period and drastically diminished the effect of political measures and concessions offered by the regime in its effort to regain a modicum of credibility and acceptance. Both the Kadar regime in Hungary and the Husak regime in Czechoslovakia had significantly more room for maneuver and the capacity to quickly stabilize their economies. With the economic aid from the Soviet Union and other bloc countries, they could also offer notable economic concessions and improvements in living standards that had important demobilizing consequences.

Disastrous as the impact of Poland's failed economy was on the regime's efforts to recover after the crisis, I would argue that the failure of demobilization policies was first of all a political failure. The Polish state-socialist regime emerged from the political crisis of 1980–81 in a state of momentous institutional transformation. The Jaruzelski regime, as Kolankiewicz put it, "made its ideology an ideology of change [and] the dynamic of normalization was rooted in the regime's stated commitment to change rather than to defend [the] indefensible."[21] Accordingly, the country's legal framework, the relations among the regime's institutional orders, the locus of political authority and its theoretical and political underpinnings were fundamentally altered. These changes transgressed many of the institutional and ideological principles of state socialism. After martial law the Polish ruling elite decided to rebuild the institutional system in a notably different form and abandon the Marxist rhetoric altogether, accelerating the process of transition from totalitarian rule that began as far back as in 1956. Thus, the failure of demobilization policies in Poland was not so much a failure to restore the classical form of the Soviet-type regime but rather the failure to successfully manage the transition from an impaired totalitarian state to a new authoritarian bureaucratic system. This goal and failure of rebuilding the political institutions and practices of the Polish regime on different foundations made the demobilization process distinctly unique.

In his analysis of the demobilization process in Poland, Kolankiewicz argues that the political developments after martial law conform to the logic of inclusion identified by Ken Jowitt in his seminal analysis of the political developments in European state-socialist regimes.[22] I disagree with this assertion. The distinction between exclusionary and inclusionary strategies has a limited historical validity and can hardly be applied to political developments in Poland after 1981. This distinction may only be used as long as the fundamental principles of the sociopolitical order remain unchallenged by the elites and the ruled. Inclusionary strategies define to what extent participation in the political process is contingent upon the acceptance of other principles, such as those based on Marxist-Leninist ideology. In this sense, the notion of inclusionary and exclusionary strategies may be applied to the demobilization processes in Hungary and Czechoslovakia, where the principle of the Marxist-Leninist state-idea was fully endorsed and unequivocally accepted by the demobilizing regimes and was not effectively challenged by the opposition. On the one hand, the Hungarian demobilization process, described in Kadar's famous maxim "who is not against us is with us" may be seen as an example of the explicitly endorsed inclusionary strategy, especially in its late phase in the 1960s. On the other hand, the demobilization process in Czechoslovakia can be seen as an example of regressive political development in which the neo-Stalinist exclusionary strategy was revived and consistently used to limit political participation. In these two cases inclusionary and exclusionary strategies represented alternative types of political practices, which strived to establish a similar type of relationship between the ruling elite and the population and restore unchallenged domination of the Communist party. As I have argued, the choice between these two types of political practices was determined by the character of political crisis, patterns of political mobilization, and the strength and internal cohesion of the demobilizing regime.

The policies of the Polish regime in the 1980s, however, went beyond past strategies available to state-socialist regimes. As I have argued, in Poland the Marxist-Leninist state-idea disintegrated in the end of the 1970s, and the Marxist rhetoric was discarded by the ruling elites in favor of nationalistic and statist claims. After the imposition of martial law, the return to an orthodox model of state socialism was advocated only by small, highly conservative groups of party apparatchiks operating on the fringes of the power structure. The demobilization policies in Poland were not defined in terms of the class struggle against counterrevolution in order to protect the achievements of the working class but were presented as a struggle of forces representing order, stability, reforms, and the national interest against forces breeding institutional chaos and economic disaster and motivated by geopolitical irresponsibility. According to Kolankiewicz, the regime's political rhetoric was based on the following principles:

(a) continuity with the acceptable features of the 1980–81 workers' discontent and thus with the legitimate responses of the various political actors; (b) change and its associated rhetoric which served to distance the regime from those elements of the pre-1980 as well as the pre-1981 which it found unacceptable and encumbering; (c) diversity of opinions, views and interests which could not be denied but which requires reconciling in order to provide the necessary consensus; and (d) unity or 'national understanding' necessary for overcoming the crises.[23]

This transformation of the regime's political rhetoric did not produce intended results. The post–martial-law regime's appeal to national interest and traditions lacked any credibility and social resonance, given the appropriation of the national tradition and symbols into political discourse of Solidarity and the Catholic church. The language of class struggle and the principle of the Communist party's leading role disappeared from the official political discourse, undercutting the only exclusive political idiom of the party-state. Similarly, the legitimacy claims of the post–martial-law regime hardly referred to orthodox Marxist-Leninist principles and ideas. They were replaced by simple arguments appealing to the Polish "reason d'etat," national unity, and "realpolitik." And, as Michta argues, "if taken to its logical conclusion Jaruzelski's call for national unity as the unity of the 'entire Polish nation' meant repudiation of communism."[24]

This striking departure from Marxist-Leninist state-idea was reflected in the whole range of official pronouncements, specific policies, and actions undertaken by the Polish regime. First of all, as many commentators emphasized, the main focus of the restoration efforts was not the Communist party but the state, understood as a principal national institution. In Robin Remington's words, "The imposition of martial law effectively interrupted whatever remained of 'normal' functioning of the Polish Communist Party."[25] The notable transfer of power and decisions from the party organs to the state administration at all levels represented only one significant aspect of the political transformation. It could be argued that, if the Polish regime succeeded in building the intended array of fronts, citizen committees, councils and consultative bodies, the role of the Communist party in the political system would have definitively diminished even further. Another indication of the departure from an orthodox Marxist-Leninist state-idea was the fundamental change of the Polish legal system after martial law and the official emphasis on legality (*praworzadnosc*).

From the emergence of the Solidarity movement in 1980 until the delayed parliamentary election in 1985, the Polish Parliament enacted 203 bills, which covered all major areas of political, social, and economic life and introduced significant changes in the structure and prerogatives of the central state's institutions and organs. The scope of new legal regulations, often enacted in a way that violated the constitutional parliamentary procedures and in some cases contradicting the Polish constitution and international conventions signed by the Polish government, had no precedent in any other demobilization processes.[26] Following political crises, there were only minor changes introduced to the Stalinist legal framework in Hungary and Czechoslovakia which was put in place in the 1940s and 1950s. In Poland, however, the extent of changes introduced in the legal system can only be compared to the legislative upheaval brought about by the imposition of communist regimes in the late 1940s and early 1950s. Moreover, the transformation of the legal system in post–martial-law Poland took a very specific direction reflecting not only the regime's immediate political needs but also a fundamental change in its legal philosophy. Solidarity's report pointed out that the new legal framework was characterized by:

> 1. unparalleled admissibility of arbitrary action of the state organs in comparison to previous legal acts—that is, full discretion of state's organs in their relations with citizens, and, at the same time, the lack of protection against such actions on the side of citizens;
>
> 2. intensification of the repressive character of the law both through extension of the scope of behaviors and acts prohibited by the law and through increased severity of penalties but also through legalization as legitimate penal sanctions of such repressive measures as prohibition to practice a profession, dismissal from job, reduction of salaries etc.
>
> 3. prevention of functioning of independent civic associations and preclusion of collective action by the citizens.[27]

The Jaruzelski regime's obsession with legality underscores the shift toward an authoritarian system where the "lawlessness" and legal ambiguity that characterized state-socialist regimes[28] was replaced by a "legalization of illegality." The new laws provided a detailed specification of the rights and prerogatives of citizens and various organizations and institutions but, at the same time, they carefully specified and upheld the state's rights and dominant position in any situation threatening the state's interests. The power elite clearly followed a statist principle, attempting to build a "legal fortification" in order to secure its right to rule in the face of a society encroaching on the traditional prerogatives of the party-state's institutions and political elites.

I see this new legal philosophy as a reflection of a fundamental change in the relation between the state and society brought about by the political crisis in 1980–81. The Polish regime opted for depoliticization and only a partial recovery of control over the many aspects of social life that are traditionally tightly controlled by the state-socialist regimes. These included media and communication, education, and culture. The regime accepted the existence of a plurality of interests and values and the need for their independent organization and representation. It strove, however, to codify the boundaries between the state and society in order to protect the state from organized action from below and the emergence of any Solidarity-type movement in the future. Thus, the demobilization process in Poland reflected a fundamental change in the regime's political vision, ambitions, and goals. The often emphasized reformist rhetoric of the post–martial-law regime, and its obsession with legality indicates that the ruling elite painfully attempted to construct a new political order and a new justification for its right to rule. Under such an order, the regime's position would be guaranteed and legally protected in exchange for political concessions and a relaxation of its control over the political space. Accordingly, unlike Czechoslovak and Hungarian party-states, the Polish regime did not attempt to fully reconquer the political space by reimposing the subservient belt of auxiliary institutions and mass and professional organizations. It sought to establish only partial control over social organizations, which were allowed to function within the relatively open political space and to represent specific social interests as long as they did not challenge directly the state's right to rule. Therefore, David Ost is right arguing that the Polish political crisis that started in 1980 can be seen as an attempt to establish a form of neo-corporatist arrangement[29] in which the ruling elite seeks to preserve its absolute power over crucial areas of political and economic life and core institutions of the state. This attempt, as the events of 1989 aptly illustrate, proved to be a spectacular failure. As I argued elsewhere, a neo-corporatist solution in Poland was not, for a variety reasons, a viable political option.[30]

To reiterate, the collapse of the demobilization policies in Poland can only be partially attributed to the survival and pressure from the organized political opposition or the quagmire of failed economic policies. The overriding cause was the failure of the post–martial-law regime to accomplish a transition from the orthodox model of state socialism to a new authoritarian political arrangement based on the absolute domination of the national state over semi-autonomous political, economic, and social actors. As a result of this failure, further reinforced by the persistence of the economic crisis, a frustrated part of the ruling elite was prompted to seek accommodation with political opposition and divide responsibilities for governing the country. In this sense, the transition from state socialism in 1989 can justifiably be seen as initiated and organized from above.[31] Moreover, Poznanski is right when he emphasizes that "in 1989, the regime of Jaruzelski was not particularly weak, and there were no signs of rapid demoralization of army or police. There was also no evidence of unusual lack of order, with people feeling afraid for their lives or property. . . . power was taken over by the opposition thorough negotiations or rather handed over to them by the Communist party."[32]

The International Context of the Demobilization Period

The imposition of martial law and the destruction of the Solidarity movement was greeted with great relief by the Soviet Union and Poland's other neighbors. The Soviet bloc countries' propaganda switched from warnings, accusations, and attacks to uniform praise of the courage of the Polish party-state leadership in taking decisive action to stabilize the political situation, to revert the dangers of anarchy and counterrevolution, and to save the socialist system in Poland. All Soviet-bloc regimes rallied to throw their full political support behind the Polish regime and to shield it from international condemnations and pressures—just as they did after the military crackdowns in Hungary and Czechoslovakia. In March 1982, the Polish Communist party and state delegation headed by Jaruzelski received a hero's welcome in Moscow, and the communique issued by two sides after the meeting emphasized that "any attempts to resume actions aimed at causing economic disarray, at resumption of anarchy, disturbances, or at changing the social and political system will be cut short in the same resolute manner in the future as well."[33] The visit was followed by a flurry of consultations and meetings with the Soviets and other bloc leaders.[34] At the same time, however, the post–martial-law regime faced uniform condemnation from countries and international organizations outside the Soviet bloc.

From its outset, the Solidarity movement commanded unusual attention and sympathy from around the world. Timothy Garton Ash writes: "The range of support for Solidarity was unique. No other movement in the world was supported by President Reagan and Mr Carillo, Mr Berlinguer and the Pope, Mrs Thatcher and Tony Benn, peace campaigners and NATO spokesmen, Christians and communists, conservatives, liberals and socialists."[35] Mindful of past Soviet behavior, especially reinforced by the invasion of Afghanistan in 1979, NATO issued a warning to the Soviet Union in December 1980 that "any intervention [in Poland] would fundamentally alter the entire international situation. The Allies would be compelled to react in the manner which the gravity of this development would require."[36] Therefore, the imposition of martial law created a chorus of outrage and worldwide condemnation expressed by many governments, political parties, trade unions, and international organizations. West European governments condemned the Polish and Soviet regimes for violation of the Helsinki Accords, severed their political relations with Poland, and joined the international boycott of the new Polish regime. The United States called a special NATO session in January 1982 to condemn the imposition of martial law and to appeal for the restoration of civil liberties. Moreover, for the first time, economic sanctions were effectively used against a Warsaw Pact country. Poland was especially vulnerable to these sanctions because of her extensive economic relations with the West, enormous foreign debt, and desperate economic situation.

Although the NATO countries could never come to a full agreement on economic sanctions, the U.S. government promptly announced sanctions of its own against Poland and the Soviet Union. The members of the European Community only reluctantly followed the American move, imposing their own economic sanctions almost three months later. The importance of these economic sanctions can be illustrated by the fact that in 1981, Poland received from the United States alone $670 million in credits for food purchases, $70 million in surplus butter and dried milk, and a rescheduling of $80 million in debt payments due in 1981.[37] The imposition of martial law terminated entirely official U.S. economic aid. On December 23, 1981, President Reagan announced economic sanctions against Poland, which included the cancellation of the most-favored-nation status and the prohibition of Polish commercial aircraft from U.S. airspace. Moreover, Polish fishing rights in U.S. coastal waters were suspended, and so were the U.S. government-guaranteed credits. Humanitarian aid, however, to private organizations in Poland was exempted from the sanctions. Economic sanctions were also applied against the Soviet Union. This policy had two major objectives. In the words of Arthur Rachwald: "First, sanctions against Jaruzelski's Poland and against Moscow were intended to apply economic pressure to the entire Soviet bloc, which was already experiencing severe economic difficulties. . . . Continuing subsidies for Poland were unacceptable to the Western public, and because of martial law, the Soviet Union had to assume full economic responsibility for its satellite. The second U.S. policy objective was to use its economic leverage to press the military regime in Warsaw toward moderation and dialogue."[38] The U.S. government stopped short of declaring Poland insolvent, which would have been the ultimate economic sanction, for very calculated reasons. According to Rachwald: "Declaring the country bankrupt would exceed the policy objectives stated by the West, and would offer the martial law regime no incentives to alter its policies. The United States favored a flexible approach to Poland—a policy of carrots and sticks—even if that involved paying Jaruzelski's debts."[39] The

Reagan administration specified three conditions for lifting the sanctions: the repeal of martial law, the release of all political prisoners, and the resumption of a dialogue between the regime, Solidarity and the Catholic church.[40]

It is impossible to calculate Polish economic losses resulting from the sanctions. Their effect, however, is evident in economic statistics. Polish trade with the West declined from $7.5 billion in 1980 to only slightly more than $1 billion in 1983, the Polish debt to the Soviet bloc countries rose rapidly, and the amount Poland was able to borrow from the West declined from almost $5 billion in 1981 to $560 million in 1983 to $300 million in 1984–85.[41] The Polish government accused the West of causing the loss of $12.5 billion dollars in Polish earnings over the first three years of martial law and used this number as an excuse to explain the continuing economic crisis and its inability to stabilize the country's economic situation.

Given the extent the Polish economic crisis and the significant impact of the sanctions, Poland's ruling elites realized that all attempts to stabilize the economy were dependent on regaining Western credits and economic help. Thus, despite hostile propaganda toward the West, the Jaruzelski regime repeatedly attempted to negotiated the lifting of the sanctions. By doing this the regime showed its vulnerability and gave further proof of the sanctions' effectiveness. It could be argued that many domestic policies were designed to induce favorable reaction in the West, which could revoke economic sanctions. For example, after 1983 and 1984, the Polish government attempted to use amnesties to negotiate the lifting of the economic sanctions.[42] Thus, the Polish regime, in contrast to demobilizing regimes in Hungary and Czechoslovakia, faced not only embarrassing political isolation and international diplomatic pressures but also a real economic pressure, making its efforts to alleviate the economic crisis highly difficult if not impossible. Because of the Western economic sanctions, Poland tried to establish even more extensive economic relations within the Soviet bloc countries. Poland's dire needs provided new urgency for political and economic integration within the Warsaw Pact and the Council for Mutual Economic Assistance (CMEA). The council, however, was in a state of disarray, and was poorly equipped to substitute for Western economic aid and cooperation. In stark contrast to the past, when economic aid from other state-socialist regimes helped to stabilize the Hungarian economy after the revolution, the Soviet bloc countries were quite incapable of assisting Poland in solving her economic problems in the 1980s.

The Soviet bloc countries gave Poland firm political support—but what the country needed at that time was a massive infusion of credits, raw materials, and consumer goods into its economy to solve the acute economic shortages and to counterbalance the Western economic sanctions. The Soviet bloc countries, however, were experiencing growing economic stagnation and could not afford to offer any massive economic aid. And as de Weydenthal concludes:

Despite the Soviet media's frequent extravagant claims about the assistance the USSR was granting to Poland, many of the examples cited appeared to be merely recitals of standard Comecon trading arrangements that were already in place before martial law. [Thus] the overall Soviet contribution to Poland's economic recovery—if it can be so called—must be rated as marginal. Poland was in at least as desperate an economic condition after one year of martial law as it had been in 1981.[43]

Moreover, the Polish demobilization process coincided not only with economic difficulties in other East European countries but also with growing political turmoil and power struggles in the Soviet Union following the death of the long-reigning Soviet leader Leonid Brezhnev in November 1982.

Western economic sanctions were gradually lifted after 1984 in recognition of the Jaruzelski regime's relative political moderation and in order to encourage the Polish leadership to modify its internal policies. The United States withdrew its veto blocking Poland's membership in the World Bank and the International Monetary Fund in 1984, and in 1986 Poland was admitted to both organizations. In 1985 Jaruzelski was invited to France by President François Mitterrand. It was his first visit, although still unofficial, to a Western country, and France's invitation created considerable political controversy.[44] In 1986 the Polish government issued a general amnesty and tacitly recognized the existence of political opposition. In response, the Catholic church and Solidarity leaders, who earlier supported all measures against the Jaruzelski regime, appealed for the lifting of all economic sanctions. Gradually, political and economic relations with the West entered a phase of normalization. In 1987, after the visit to Poland by the U.S. deputy secretary of state, John C. Whitehead, the most-favored-nation status was restored and ambassadors were exchanged between the two countries. This progress, however, did not mean a return to the pre-December 1981 status quo ante. Rachwald points out:

> The breakthrough in U.S.-Polish relations had to wait until July 1989, when President Bush arrived in Poland to back up the new accord between Solidarity leader Lech Walesa and the minister of internal affairs, Czeslaw Kiszczak. The visit was intended to demonstrate U.S. support for the emerging pluralism in Poland and to achieve reconciliation between the two nations and their governments. In this respect, the visit marked a turning point in bilateral relations and created the foundations for future cooperation.[45]

The resumption of diplomatic contacts, however, added an important new element to Poland's domestic balance of power. During the entire demobilization process, the international community officially supported and recognized political opposition in Poland and sought simultaneous contacts with both the government and the opposition. Such a policy was intended not only to unsettle Poland's rulers but also to give a moral and political boost to the Solidarity movement. Following the precedent established by the pope during his 1983 visit to Poland, Whitehead met with Walesa and other opposition leaders, setting the pattern for all official visits by Western politicians and leaders to Poland. Their schedule included both the official meetings with government dignitaries and unofficial consultations with the church and Solidarity leaders.[46] From this brief overview of international reactions to the Polish crisis, it seem obvious that Western political and economic pressures and actions contributed to the collapse of the Polish demobilization policies. In contrast, the absence of credible Western economic and political leverage in Hungarian and Czechoslovak cases contributed to the success of their regimes' demobilization policies.

I mentioned in passing that the growing political turmoil in the Soviet Union had a crucial impact on the events in Poland. The political succession crisis in the Soviet Union provided a radically different set of geopolitical conditions for demobilization efforts of the Polish regime. The Soviet hard-line leader Leonid Brezhnev, who presided over the demobilization process in Czechoslovakia, died in November 1982. This event, which came in the most critical years of the demobilization process in Poland, left the Soviet Union immersed in a protracted struggle for succession and leadership. The succession crisis in the Soviet Union gave more freedom and flexibility to the internal policies of the Polish regime. The brief reigns of Yuri Andropov, who died in February 1984, and Konstantin Chernienko, who died in March 1985, preceded the rise of Michail Gorbachev, who set the Soviet Union on the course of internal reform and within five years dramatically changed the whole geopolitical situation on the European continent. The transition of power in the Soviet Union and its growing economic and political problems deflected Soviet attention from Poland's persistent problems. As a result, Jaruzelski's regime enjoyed much more room for domestic political maneuvers than did either Kadar or Husak. The Polish demobilization process was spared consistent Soviet political supervision and pressure to reimpose a more orthodox model of state socialism. The failure of the demobilization process in Poland is, therefore, a revealing testimony to the disintegration of the Soviet empire and to the profound change in geopolitical balance in Europe in the 1980s. However, without the collapse of the Jaruzelski regime's demobilization policies, one could wonder whether the "spring of nations" of 1989 would have been possible.

Conclusions: Patterns and Legacies of Political Crisis, Demobilization, and Regime Reequilibration in East Central Europe

CLASSICAL IMAGES of state socialism that have developed in contemporary social sciences were founded on a few simple presuppositions. These assumptions were thought to reflect fundamental qualities of all Soviet-type regimes and their common institutional and political identity that set them apart from industrial and democratic countries of the West. It was argued that despite their contrasting histories and traditions as well as their social, economic, and political differences in the interwar period, East European countries experienced forced imposition of identical political and economic institutions. Soviet-sponsored policies transformed their entire social and political order and created similar social structures and economic systems, and established repressive, ideology-driven political practices. As a result of these transformations, state-socialist regimes were considered to be, first, politically stable due to their repressive capacity and pervasive institutional and ideological control over everyday lives of their citizens. Second, they were seen as highly immobile, rigid, inert, and impervious to reform and change. Scholars argued that state-socialist regimes tended to pursue the same policies, despite repeated failures, and never succeeded in a major overhaul of their inefficient institutions. Third, they were considered to represent an extreme case of political and economic dependency. It was often argued that their domestic politics were merely a reflection of Soviet goals and policies. Thus, they were thought to be basically identical in their institutional design, social and economic structures, and policies. The analysis presented in this book challenges such a common political wisdom.

Hungary, Czechoslovakia, and Poland each experienced during its postwar history a major political crisis, which threatened its domestic political order and destabilized geopolitical relations in the region. The Hungarian Revolution of 1956, the Prague Spring of 1968, and Poland's "self-limiting" revolution of 1980 were critical turning points in these countries' political developments. They revealed profound internal political instability and the vulnerability of the Soviet-imposed regimes to the challenge from below. They left enduring legacies. Thus the impact of political crises on policies of these regimes was in many ways similar to the consequences of a major crisis in other political systems. Peter Gourevitch emphasizes that "Crises pry open the political scene, throwing traditional relationship into flux. Groups, institutions and individuals are torn loose from their moorings, their assumptions, their loyalties, 'cognitive road maps'. Circumstances become less certain, and solutions less obvious. Crises thus render politics more plastic." This was undoubtedly the case in East Central Europe.[1]

The crises I have analyzed in this book affected all levels of the party-states' political organization, destabilized their institutions and state-controlled organizations, weakened the states' coercive capacity, and divided ruling elites. Moreover, they opened the political opportunity structure, produced mass political mobilization, and posed a fundamental political challenge to the existence and policies of these regimes. In each of the three countries, the crisis provoked coercive responses from domestic and regional hard-line forces guarding the postwar political status quo in the region. In each case the political crisis was resolved by massive employment of coercive military means and involved a heightened level of political repression directed against reform movements and groups that rose to challenge these regimes. Hungary and Czechoslovakia suffered a massive military invasion of foreign troops sent by the Kremlin to reverse changes in domestic political institutions, terminate reform efforts, and preserve the politically dependent status of these countries. Poland experienced the imposition of martial law by the domestic military and police forces that decimated the Solidarity movement and delayed political and economic reforms for nearly a decade. In sum, these events exposed the inability of Soviet-dependent party-states to open their political system to genuine popular participation, reform their political institutions and their inefficient centrally planned economies, and modify their ideological principles and political practices. At the same time, however, these events generated policy changes and institutional adjustments that had decisive impact on the evolution of these regimes and demonstrated their considerable flexibility. In Hungary and Czechoslovakia, the process of reequilibration of the regime in the aftermath of the crisis was successfully accomplished. In Poland reequilibration efforts failed.

In the existing literature, these three crises have often been grouped together and described as similar examples of the political challenge to the Soviet-imposed communist rule. It has been argued that efforts to reform institutions and practices of state socialism provoked similar political responses of domestic and regional ruling elites and had similar consequences—the defeat of the reform movements, re-consolidation of the party-state, and return to orthodox political practices. As I have shown, however, the nature and political consequences of these crises varied significantly. The extent of the institutional breakdown of the party-state, the types of conflicts and cleavages and the patterns of popular mobilization were different. Similarly, coercive responses by regional or domestic forces, the nature and degree of political repressions, and the capacity of resistance and opposition movements were quite unique in each case. Moreover, the coercive resolution of each crisis produced varying short- and long-term political, economic, and social consequences. The purpose of this book, therefore, was to offer a comparative analysis of these events. I assumed that by comparing systematically their nature and consequences, we can better explain the differences among state-socialist regimes and the distinctive experiences of East Central European countries under communist rule.

The comparative approach I developed in this work was designed to avoid a persistent methodological problem common to many comparative analyses in the field of East European studies. While students of Eastern Europe have always strongly emphasized the crucial historical, cultural, and political differences between countries in the region, they too often employed simple macro-level models in their comparative research. This, unfortunately, led to simplistic and sometimes false analogies and hindered the analysis of important political differences between these countries, their particular political experiences, and sources of cross-regional diversity. Moreover, typical comparative approaches in the field of East European studies have been usually based on functional models, and their basic unit of analysis has been either a country or specific sets of institutions (parliaments, armies, trade unions, communist parties, etc.) or social groups (workers, peasants, party apparatchiks, intelligentsia, etc.) or selected socioeconomic processes (urbanization, collectivization, economic reforms, political opposition, etc.). The comparative strategy I have adopted here has shifted the focus away from abstract categories and formal institutions to real historical events. I have focused on analyzing specific historical trajectories of three countries of the region that experienced an open political crisis. My analysis shows the importance of political crisis situations in shaping political choices of the ruling elites and in generating institutional and policy adjustments. These crises revealed the changing nature of political conflicts and struggles as well as the different capacities of various collective actors and constraints they faced. This strategy allowed me to explore specific national patterns emerging within the seemingly uniform institutional structure of these countries. Despite their common geopolitical dependency on the Soviet Union, which characterized the entire post–World War II period, East Central European regimes that experienced political crises followed contrasting strategies of institutional survival and experimented with different types of policies and institutional adjustments. In short, I have argued that the development of state-socialist regimes was crisis-driven and the process of regime reequilibration in the aftermath of the institutional breakdown required considerable flexibility as well as institutional and policy changes and adjustments.

I have argued that major political crises and ways in which particular regimes responded to the crisis were more important in shaping political processes in these countries than the formal characteristics of their political and economic systems or their politically dependent status. Such events reshaped party-state institutions, produced institutional innovations, redefined relations between party-state's institutional orders, altered the relationship between the party-state and various groups and institutions within society, and modified the political practices of these regimes. Moreover, they transformed cultural categories, produced collective memories, and imposed constraints on people's behavior and actions for long periods following the crisis. In short, major political crises formed critical historical junctions setting in motion long-term, path-dependent developments that produced the most important cross-national differences among the state-socialist regimes. In addition, these three political crises and their aftermaths had long-lasting impact not only on Czechoslovakia, Hungary, and Poland but also on other Soviet bloc countries. They defined the political evolution of the entire region over the last four decades.

POLITICAL CRISES, DEMOBILIZATION, AND REGIME REEQUILIBRATION

At the beginning of this study, I noted that the comparison of the state-socialist regimes' responses to the major political crises raised a number of interesting puzzles. How and why was the Hungarian regime able to conclude the highly repressive period of demobilization with the establishment of a paternalistic regime characterized by the pragmatic approach to economic policies and relative flexibility in political and ideological matters? Why did the demobilization policies in Czechoslovakia remain highly repressive, produce political and economic stagnation, and freeze any attempts to introduce meaningful political and/or economic reforms for almost twenty years? And finally, why did the Polish regime fail to reequilibrate the state-socialist regime, restore the party-state's authority, demobilize political opposition, prevent large-scale collective protest, arrest the economic crisis, and introduce effective political and economic reforms? By employing a consistent analytical framework in all three cases, I believe the analysis presented here provides some illuminating answers.

When analyzing political developments in each country, I have focused on three sets of constraints that emerged as a result of the crisis and shaped demobilization and regime reequilibration processes that followed the crisis. These were (1) the capacity, institutional coherence, and strength of the party-state, (2) the capacity of resistance and opposition movements, and (3) the geopolitical constraints within which both state and opposition actors operated. I have argued that, in the most general sense, each demobilization and reequilibration process was shaped by conflicts among various collective actors and produced specific divisions within the party-state elites and within society at large. The contrasting capabilities, goals, strategies, and actions of these actors provided a crucial base for the variation, effectiveness, and outcomes among the demobilization processes. Moreover, these three sets of factors were analyzed against the background of long-term evolutionary processes of change, reflecting the fundamental contradictions and tensions of domestic and geopolitical relations in the region. Thus, a consistent and historically specific comparative framework was applied to all three cases under study.

I have argued that these cases, when examined in a comparative perspective, provided a unique opportunity to account for the broader, long-term processes of political change in state-socialist societies. The evolutionary change detectable in the postwar history of the region was punctuated by two periods of accelerated changes and institutional readjustments stimulated by the political crisis. The first followed the unraveling of Stalinist regimes in the 1950s and the second signaled the exhaustion of post-Stalinist inclusionary strategies and conditional accommodation between the party-state elites and various collective actors within society at the end of 1970s and in the 1980s. During these two periods, the political opportunity structure was significantly altered, opening access to participation for previously excluded groups, changing political alignments and dividing ruling elites. In both periods, however, the impetus for change came from different institutional locations, and different collective actors played the most crucial role in shaping the dynamic of the political crisis. The de-Stalinization crisis witnessed efforts to reform the institutions and practices of state socialism from above by the reformist factions within the ruling elites. Andrew Gyorgy emphasizes that in Hungary "the Nagy government was composed of lifelong, ardent communists, who believed in the cause of Marxism-Leninism while attempting to oppose the Soviet Union. Thus, the tragic events of October and November, 1956, can well be described as an internecine civil war among communists."[2] Similarly, Ivan Szelenyi describes the Prague Spring as a "struggle between reformed and unreformed Communists."[3] The "early risers" who challenged the Stalinist establishment were members of the elite—intellectuals, artists, and younger party activists. Using their resources and protected status they openly criticized abuses of power and demanded institutional and policy changes. They also opened access to political participation and created the opportunity for other groups to voice their grievances and press various demands. Sidney Tarrow argues: "One of the most remarkable characteristics of collective action is that it expands the opportunities of others. Protesting groups put issues on the agenda with which other people identify and demonstrate the utility of collective action that others can copy or innovate upon."[4] The leading role of intellectuals in the political crises of East Central Europe reflected specific institutional constraints, unequal distribution of political resources within society, exclusionary strategies employed by state-socialist regimes, and varied repressive capacity of the party-states.[5] In Hungary and Czechoslovakia, the opening of the political opportunity structure had different consequences. A protracted power struggle within the ruling elite facilitated rapid mass mobilization and a revolutionary uprising in Hungary, which soon led to the total institutional breakdown of the party-state. In Czechoslovakia, mass political mobilization remained highly constrained, leaving the institutional structures of the party-state intact. This contrasting nature of the political crisis shaped subsequent demobilization policies and resulted in the significantly different character of the reequilibrated postcrisis regimes. In both countries, however, party-state institutions and the dominant position of the Communist party were restored, opposition movements were destroyed, and the political initiative was securely monopolized by the ruling elites.

The post-Stalinist developments entailed a dual process that included, on the one hand, the institutional, political and economic decay of state-socialist regimes coupled with an identity crisis of the Communist party and, on the other hand, the reconstitution of an increasingly effective civil society able to organize, survive, and defend itself. In Poland, building on previous experiences of collective struggles, the challenge to party rule came from outside. Mass political mobilization based on a cross-class alliance culminated in the formation of a massive, independent trade-union movement and other organizations representing various social and professional groups. New organizations liberated political space previously controlled by the party-state organizations and established new boundaries and relations between the party-state and society. The crisis in Poland also signified a profound cultural revolution and the formation of an independent political discourse that undermined the ideological foundations of the Marxist-Leninist state-idea and eroded legitimacy claims of the ruling elites. The political initiative shifted from factions within the party-state to groups and organizations within society. Thus, the nature of the Polish crisis was different from other two cases. Its characteristics were responsible, above all, for the failure of the demobilization strategies employed by the Polish post–martial-law regime. Eight years after crushing Solidarity's self-limiting revolution, the Polish Communist party was forced to recognize the political opposition, to allow semi-free elections, and to permit the formation of a noncommunist government.

I have argued that the most important factors explaining these different political outcomes of the demobilization process can be found in the specific characteristics of the political crisis these countries experienced. In all three cases, the political crisis set in motion different patterns of relations among competing factions within the party-state and between the party-state and society. Following Andrew Arato, I have described these political crises as the popular revolution (Hungary), reform from above (Czechoslovakia), and reform from below (Poland).[6] In the two former cases the impetus for political change came from inside the regime—that is, from the liberal wings of the Communist party. In Poland the impetus for change came from outside the party-state institutional structures. The varied nature of political crisis and character of challengers produced different patterns of popular mobilization during the crisis. These patterns had different consequences for institutional orders of the party-state, and produced different levels of independent organization among collective actors within society. In turn, these characteristics of popular mobilization crucially shaped the capabilities of the resistance and opposition during the demobilization and regime reequilibration phase of the crisis. They also generated specific cleavages, conflicts, and divisions among the party-state elites, which significantly shaped the policy choices available to the demobilizing regimes.

The revolution in Hungary, crushed by Soviet intervention, set an unambiguous division between the Soviet-imposed party-state and society, which perceived Kadar's government as a tool of the antinational policy. Paradoxically, this highly polarized political situation and disintegration of the Communist party and other state institutions produced a strong party-state that was able to restore its institutional coherence, accommodate both reformist and conservative factions into the policymaking process, and give the regime more room for political maneuver and flexibility in shaping the demobilization process. The restored Hungarian party-state was able to preserve the political initiative and to choose and pursue more flexibly between both the Stalinist-type terrorist practices and more pragmatic policies of concessions, reforms, and humanization of the regime. Moreover, due to the rapidity of both the political mobilization during the revolution and the ensuing invasion, Hungarian society was deprived of the organizational resources and social networks needed to support prolonged political resistance and establish an effective opposition movement. Also, Western responses to the Hungarian crisis lacked of any credible political and economic leverage at that time and failed to have any significant impact on the policies of the Kadar regime and the Soviet leadership.

In Czechoslovakia and Poland the crises and their military terminations produced weak party-states, though for quite different reasons. In Czechoslovakia the level of popular mobilization was very low during the political crisis and society did not establish the organizational and social resources necessary to endure the state's demobilization policies. This was the result of the top-down nature of the reform process. Political initiative was monopolized by the Communist party factions and confined to the institutions and organizations of the party-state. Strategies of reformist groups within the Czechoslovak party-state involved a conscious effort to bloc popular mobilization. Moreover, it was the top party leadership that symbolized the political hopes and struggle for change. Thus, a well-pronounced cleavage between the state and society did not emerge and the political articulation of an anticommunist platform as well as the formation of independent organizations were hampered.

The party-state elites, however, were locked in paralyzing internal divisions and conflicts. Reformers were not able to eliminate hard-liners during the Spring of 1968, and the pro-Soviet faction failed to create "worker-peasant" government after the invasion. This prolonged period of political stalemate within the state was resolved by a shift toward highly repressive policies and neo-Stalinist practices that resulted in the eradication of all reformist groups and individuals within the party-state. The triumph of a conservative faction within the Czechoslovak ruling elite and the inability to accommodate more pragmatic groups within the post-invasion regime blocked any possibility of preserving the impetus for reforms or securing a shift toward more pragmatic policies. In addition, the Czechoslovak crisis unfolded in the most unfavorable international context possible. The Kremlin leadership was the most conservative since Stalin. This coincided with a high level of political insecurity in neighboring countries. The Soviet leadership and its East European allies feared and were poised to crush any reform efforts anywhere within the Soviet bloc in order to prevent the same from occurring in their own countries. Also, similar to the Hungarian case in the 1950s, the capacity of the West to influence Czech domestic developments was restricted and minimal. Such efforts were additionally impaired by American involvement in the Vietnam War and Western alliance attempts to induce the Soviets to sign arms control agreements.

In Poland the self-limiting revolution resulted in a sharp division between the state and society and a well-define political polarization. Almost from the beginning of the crisis the party-state elites confronted a mobilized society organized in complex territorial and professional networks. Facing such massive pressure, ruling elites were forced to surrender their control over vast areas of political and social life. This newly open political space was immediately taken over by independent organizations. Although these organizations were destroyed and de-legalized as a result of the imposition of martial law, social networks they created survived the military repression and provided the foundations for a strong opposition movement. During the years that followed martial law, neither the party-state elites nor the opposition movements were able to break the political stalemate and recover the political initiative. This situation produced a deepening decay of the regime and anarchization of its political and economic institutions. More important, however, was the fact that the Polish party-state elites, weakened by the prolonged political conflict and unable to reduce legitimacy deficit, began the serious process of institutional and political change designed to transform the nature of the country's political system and relations between the state and society. Post–martial-law rulers attempted to offer a modicum of political participation to semi-independent organizations in exchange for political support, reduce the role of the Communist party and mass organizations, and introduce elements of a market economy to boost the country's sagging economic performance. As I have argued, these attempts to move toward a more classical authoritarian system while at the same time pursuing a more market oriented economy failed. Poland's post–martial-law regime was caught in a contradictory effort to liberalize and reform the economy without the sufficient liberalization of the polity, while facing a restive population, organized opposition, and acute external pressures and constraints.

Another crucial element of the failure in Poland's demobilization and regime reequilibration process lies in the geopolitical dimension. The Polish post–martial-law regime had more autonomy in pursuing its domestic policies. The intra–Soviet bloc situation and the capacity of state-socialist regimes at that time were decisively shaped by the Soviet Union's prolonged political succession crisis during the 1980s and a sweeping regional economic crisis. Thus, the Polish ruling elites were less constrained politically but, at the same time, the economic aid offered to Poland by its partners was

TABLE 1. Major Factors Shaping Political Crises

	Hungary	Czechoslovakia	Poland
Nature of the crisis	popular revolution	reform from above	reform from below
Institutional capacity of core state institutions	collapse	high	high
Institutional capacity of the Communist party	collapse	high	moderate
Institutional capacity of auxiliary institutions	collapse	high	low
Viability of Marxist-Leninist state-idea	high	high	low
Intra-elite conflict	very high	very high	moderate
Main split	state/society	intrastate	state/society
Economic situation	serious	stable	severe
Economic and political concessions	high	low	high
Independent organization of society	fragmented	absent	highly effective
Political mobilization	rapid/high	slow/low	slow/high
Cross-class alliances	weak	weak	strong
Powerful ally	none	none	Catholic church
Dependence relations	semipermissive	rigid	permissive
Integration with the global economy	weak	weak	strong
Effectiveness of international pressures	low	low	high

highly insufficient. The differences in geopolitical situation applied also to the relationship with the West. Beginning in the mid-1970s, as a result of the Helsinki process, Western countries acquired a considerable political leverage vis-à-vis Poland and the other Soviet bloc countries. Similarly, opening of the East-bloc economies to Western trade, technologies, and credits for the first time in postwar history gave Western governments a credible economic leverage. Thus, political pressures and economic sanctions were effectively used to influence Poland's domestic policies as well as the Soviet behavior in the region.

In the preceding chapters I have specified a number of distinctive factors that account for the differences among analyzed cases. The first set of important conditions and constraints was generated by the nature and dynamic of the political crisis in each country. They are summarized in table 1, which provides only a simplified picture of my preceding analysis but emphasizes the major contrasts among the countries.

These differences applied to most of the crucial dimensions of social and political life and organization. They indicate that capacities of collective actors varied across the cases and that the constraints that shaped their actions during the crisis were different. The characteristics of each crisis formed the initial background for the coercive response to the crisis and formed the preconditions for the ensuing demobilization and regime reequilibration phase. In short, each crisis set the stage for the different coercive responses and strategies of the post-crisis regimes.

I have defined the process of political demobilization as the state's coercive reappropriation of political spaces opened during the crisis. The goal of demobilization efforts was reequilibration of the regime undermined by the crisis. In each case the ruling elites' strategies involved an attempt to restore the institutional structure of the party-state, reestablish hierarchical power distribution among institutional orders of the state, and reimpose the specific type of state/society relationship—based on pervasive political control and extreme monopolization of power and initiative by the Communist party—inherent in Soviet-type regimes. This emphasis of institutions, constraints, and capacities of collective actors sets this interpretation apart from the existing analyses of demobilization processes, which focus almost exclusively on the policy choices of top party and state leadership and constraints to such choices imposed by the Soviet Union. Thus, I have sought to expand explanatory categories traditionally employed in the field of East European studies. I have argued that political demobilization and regime reequilibration was a complex, highly disruptive, and costly social and political phenomenon that involved a wide variety of collective actors, political and social institutions, and resources. I have pointed out that the means and tactics employed by the political elites in power following the coercive response to the crisis differed from case to case. They were shaped most prominently by the degree of the state's institutional breakdown, the internal struggles and divisions among ruling elites, the capacity and strength of the party-state institutions, the capacity of the collective actors who were the subject of demobilization efforts, and by geopolitical constrains. The main factors and conditions that shaped the demobilization and regime reequilibration period in the three countries are summarized in table 2, which highlights the main differences. Each demobilization period is divided into two parts: the initial situation following the military action and a longer period of demobilization and reequilibration policies. Of course, they differ in length between cases.

In general, demobilization policies appeared to be shaped by highly contingent policy choices that, instead of being a simple implementation of the preconceived political scenario or the directives of the regional hegemon, were in fact ad hoc responses to the changing domestic and international situation and pressures. In all cases, demobilization policies were more or less innovative improvisations and led to a variety of unanticipated political and social consequences. While multiple political and economic factors contributed to the character and effectiveness of demobilization processes and successful reequilibration of the regime, I have focused more specifically on three dimensions crucial to our understanding of the demobilization phase of the crisis: (1) the patterns of cleavages and conflict among the party-state

TABLE 2. Major Factors Shaping Demobilization Processes

	Hungary	Czechoslovakia	Poland
Termination of the crisis	Soviet invasion	Warsaw Pact invasion	martial law
Effectiveness of demobilization policies	initial moderate	initial high	initial high
	next high	next high	next low
Level of repression	initial very high	initial low	initial high
	next moderate	next high	next low
Economic situation	improved	improved	aggravated
Institutional innovations	low	low	high
Economic concessions	initial moderate	initial moderate	initial moderate
	next high	next moderate	next low
Political concessions	initial moderate	initial low	initial low
	next low	next low	next high
Viability of Marxist-Leninist state idea	high	high	low
Recovery of the party-state	slow	fast	very slow
Exit emigration of opposition activists	initial high	initial high	initial low
	next low	next low	next moderate
Counterhegemonic discourse	absent	absent	present
Organized political opposition	destroyed	destroyed	present
Powerful ally	absent	absent	church
Collective protest	initial high	initial moderate	initial high
	next none	next none	next moderate
Soviet pressure	moderate	high	low
Effectiveness of Soviet economic assistance	high	moderate	low
Effectiveness of international pressures	low	low	high

elites and the capacity of the state that set the limits and constraints for state's demobilization strategies; (2) the patterns of popular mobilization that shaped the capacity of resistance movements against the party-state's demobilization efforts and strategies; and (3) the nature of geopolitical pressures and constraints that shaped both the policies of the regimes and the capacity of the opposition.

The Hungarian and Czechoslovak demobilization processes were successful and the state-socialist regime was reequilibrated on an equal or higher level of efficacy. The postcrisis ruling elites were able to rebuild the institutional structure of the party-states and restore all institutional means of political control. They reestablished hierarchical relations between institutional orders of the party-state, secured the monopolistic position of the Communist party, and restored party discipline. They reinstated full control of the media and other forms of information, reimposed strict supervision in education, and reduced the influence of nonparty groups and individuals in social and political life. In the process they effectively destroyed all independent forces and denied any means of organization and resistance to actors within society. There were, however, significant differences in the type of political practices that developed during the demobilization periods in both countries. In Hungary, the demobilization process that began with political terror resulted in the establishment of inclusionary political practices that transformed the Hungarian party-state into one of the most politically flexible and reform-oriented regimes in East Central Europe. In Czechoslovakia, the demobilization process produced a return to exclusionary neo-Stalinist practices that transformed the country from one of the most liberal into one of the most conservative regimes in the region and blocked all reform efforts for the next two decades. I have argued that these contrasting developments were the result of legacies produced by the crisis and configuration of power and influence among the factions of the postcrisis ruling elite.

In contrast, the demobilization process in Poland has to be evaluated as a striking political failure. The Polish party-state not only failed to reestablish its control over society, it also never fully recovered from the multi-dimensional political, social, and economic crisis that erupted in 1980. In short, a state-socialist regime was not reequilibrated. The failure of the Polish party-state elites was above all an institutional failure. As I have emphasized, the post–martial-law ruling elites did not restore the classical institutional architecture of the Soviet-type regime; instead, they transformed the relations and distribution of power among the party-state's core institutions. The state administration became a center of power at the expense of the Communist party. Moreover, they did not reimpose strict political control over all domains of social life. In fact, the Polish regime attempted to depoliticize many sectors of economic and social organization. It failed to reinstate full control over the media and other forms of communication, allowed the existence of semi-official political opposition, and abandoned Marxism-Leninism as its central legitimation claim. The post–martial-law regime weakened the boundaries between political insiders and outsiders and offered some access to the decision-making process to those who gave even minimal support for the regime, regardless of their ideological convictions. As a result, the Polish party-state evolved into a weak state with considerable despotic power and a severe lack of infrastructural power.[7] Bartlomiej Kaminski writes that in order "to assure a modicum of governability, the state had to rely on the institutions that were outside its political structure—mainly the Catholic Church."[8]

In turn, I have argued that the ability of the Hungarian and Czech regimes to restore all party-state institutions and organizations, secure the leading role for the Communist party, and establish the dominance of the Marxist-Leninist political discourse largely determined the course and the successful outcomes of their demobilization and regime reequilibration policies. It can be argued that in these two cases the success of demobilization policies was based on the strategy of "institutional incapacitation" through which political space was blocked by state-sponsored organizations and the resources and the capacity of groups that emerged during the crisis to challenge the party-state authority were destroyed.[9] The institutional restoration of the party-state, which extended state control to all domains of society, depressed the preconditions for collective action and blocked any effective pressure from below, which, according to Tarrow, "is a more effective strategy than its direct suppression."[10] Another important strategy successfully implemented in Hungary and Czechoslovakia that supplemented institutional incapacitation was the reestablishment of the official political discourse. It involved, in Jan Kubik's words, "the near-perfect saturation of the public domain with the official discourse (which thereby is posed to become the public hegemonic discourse), confining all independent thinking, visualizing, imagining, symbolizing, naming, classifying, and so on to the private domain and, therefore, preventing the public articulation of counterhegemonic discourse."[11] In Poland, the official political discourse disintegrated and national symbols and identities were reappropriated by nonstate political and social actors before and during the Solidarity period. Following the imposition of martial law, the Polish regime did not attempt to revive the Marxist-Leninist ideology and recover full control of the media and intellectual life. Instead, it constructed its official discourse on the pragmatic and nationalistic basis centered around the narrowly defined claim of preventing Soviet military invasion and saving the country from imminent civil war and economic disaster.

Demobilization efforts in Hungary and Czechoslovakia were centered on restoring the "leading role" of the Communist party, its central role among the party-state institutions, and party discipline. However, in Poland, the party's authority, capacity, and influence were remarkably curtailed. Post–martial-law elites abandoned the classical model of Soviet-type state organization and attempted to build "a new version of communist statism."[12] As a result, the Polish Communist party experienced a process of rapid decline after 1982. This affected its membership base, its power vis-à-vis other institutions and organizations, and its control of the nomenclatura system. The change in the party's membership during the postcrisis period, in comparison to Hungary and Czechoslovakia, presented in table 3, shows that the imposition of martial law did not reverse the membership decline. The Polish party was neither reconstructed (as in Hungary) nor purged (as in Czechoslovakia). Almost one-third of its members left on their own. Moreover, it lost its ideological teeth, a considerable part of its power, and persisted as a result of bureaucratic inertia.

A similar membership decline affected all state-sponsored mass organizations, especially new trade unions. By 1988 the official, monopolistic trade unions reactivated after suspension of martial law were able to claim only one-third of Poland's labor force as members.[13] Thus, the party-state's institutional capacity to penetrate all spheres of social life and enforce political

TABLE 3. Size of Communist Parties

		Party members	Percent of population
Hungary	September 1956	900,000	9.1
	December 1956	108,000	1.1
	June 1957	345,733	3.5
	December 1966	585,000	5.8
	1971	670,000	6.5
	1976	756,566	7.2
Czechoslovakia	1966	1,698,000	11.9
	January 1968	1,670,977	11.6
	July 1968	1,687,565	11.7
	April 1969	1,650,587	11.4
	1970	1,200,000	8.3
	1978	1,450,000	9.7
Poland	1978	2,929,000	8.4
	1980	3,092,000	8.7
	1981	2,691,000	7.5
	1984	2,117,000	5.7
	1987	2,149,000	5.7
	1988	2,132,000	5.5

Sources: Data for Hungary and Czechoslovakia come from Zvi Gitelman, "The Politics of Socialist Restoration in Hungary and Czechoslovakia," in *Revolutions: Theoretical and Comparative Studies*, ed. Jack A. Goldstone (San Diego: Harcourt Brace Jovanovich, 1986), 272. Data for Poland come from Antoni Sulek, "The Polish United Worker's Party: From Mobilization to Non-Representation," *Soviet Studies* 42, no. 3 (1990): 501. The percentage of population was calculated using population estimates from *The World Almanac and Book of Facts* (New York: Newspaper Enterprise Association 1980, 1981, 1982, 1986, 1988, 1989).

compliance was significantly reduced. Because the Polish party-state failed to recover its institutional strength and infrastructural power on the basis of a new authoritarian design of the state, the Poland's ruling elites were the first in the region to be forced to surrender their monopoly of power and to enter the process of controlled political transition from state socialism. I have argued that this breakdown of state socialism in Poland was not only the result of the failure of demobilization policies but also reflected the failed efforts of the Polish ruling elite to accomplish a transition from the classical state-socialist regimes to a new authoritarian political order.

In my case studies I have demonstrated that the capacity of oppositional political actors to survive demobilization efforts was directly linked to the character of the popular mobilization that preceded the demobilization phase of the crisis, and that a direct relationship existed between patterns of mobilization and demobilization. Empirical evidence distinctively demonstrated that the opposition movement's ability to survive in an extremely repressive environment, which characterized the political situation after the Soviet invasions or the imposition of martial law, depended on the speed and duration of mobilization, the adopted model of organization, the presence of independent allies, and the fate of opposition leaders. In the Polish case, political mobilization, following its initial peak in the summer of 1980, was gradual, long lasting and institutionalized. The Solidarity movement was more organized and centralized before coercive demobilization strategies were employed than were the opposition movements in Hungary and Czechoslovakia. Moreover, Solidarity developed a distinct movement identity, a collective-action frame, its own repertoire of collective protest, and alternative political discourse, which provided foundations for a broad cross-class movement of a truly national scope. Neither the Hungarian resistance nor Czech and Slovak opposition were able to develop a similarly powerful and distinct identity. After the military crackdown, the Solidarity movement was able to adopt a segmented and decentralized model of organization and could rely on some institutional bases independent of the state through its cooperation with the church. Finally, the "exit option" in the form of large-scale emigration of oppositional activists and leaders undercut the oppositional potential of Hungarian and Czechoslovak societies. In Poland, the imposition of martial law involved sealing the country's boarders and abolishing the freedom to travel. Paradoxically, these policies enhanced the Solidarity movement's ability to survive by preventing mass political exodus from the country. Thus, only in Poland did the pre– and post–martial-law conditions (i.e., a prolonged political conflict, the presence of the powerful and independent Catholic church, and autonomous self-organization of society) create the foundations for the survival of the political opposition and for effective resistance to the state's demobilization efforts. In the other two cases, the absence of those factors made oppositional groups and organizations highly vulnerable to the state's demobilization policies.

The historical events I have studied occurred in twelve-year intervals and distinctively reflected the gradual transformation of the relationship between the party-state and society that took place between the collapse of Stalinist policies and the unraveling of the inclusionary post-Stalinist project. I have argued that they had a consequential impact not only on the countries where the crises took place but also on other countries of the region, including the Soviet Union. These events showed not only the interactive nature of political crisis within a closely defined state system but also reflected a distinctive political learning process among ruling elites and opposition activists across the region. Similarly, they reflected the changing political and economic relations between East Central European countries and the Soviet Union, as well as the changing impact of the broader international context. The post-invasion regimes in Hungary and Czechoslovakia were effectively shielded from international pressures and sanctions by the Soviet Union and their East European allies. They provided not only political support but also significant economic aid, which assured a relatively fast

TABLE 4. Soviet Trade Surpluses with East
Central European Countries in Crisis
(millions of rubles)[1]

	Hungary	Czecho-slovakia	Poland
1956	5.5		
1957	128.6		
1958	34.8		
1967		−13.3	
1968		43.3	
1969		−4.5	
1970		−27.8	
1979			2.0
1980			809.7
1981			1,117.0
1982			651.0
1983			490.0

Source: Keith Crane, "Soviet Economic Policy Towards Eastern Europe," in *Continuity and Change in
Soviet-East European Relations*, ed. Marco Carnovale and William C. Potter (Boulder: Westview Press,
1989), 125.

economic recovery after the crisis and allowed the postcrisis regimes to improve standards of living and buy social peace. In the Polish case, the situation was much more difficult for the Jaruzelski regime. Following the
Helsinki agreements in 1975, Poland's regime was increasingly vulnerable
to Western political pressures, and its domestic policies were scrutinized by
human rights and other international organizations. Moreover, since the
beginning of the 1970s, Poland established links to the global economy and
became dependent on Western economic assistance and credits. Given the
extent of Poland's economic crisis, it was more affected by Western pressures and economic sanctions, which were not, and could not been compensated for by the Soviet bloc allies. The declining economic performance of
other state-socialist countries in the 1980s and the sheer size and needs of the
Polish economy made the amount of economic aid necessary to facilitate the
economic stabilization and recovery beyond the means of the Soviet bloc.
Thus, the lingering economic crisis contributed to the unraveling of the Polish regime's demobilization policies. In fact, the Soviet economic effort to
prop up the Polish regime was greater than in either Hungary or Czechoslovakia. Yet, it was not enough to sustain any lasting effect. The extent of the
Soviet economic aid in all three crises is illustrated by the Soviet trade surplus within a given country (table 4).

In conclusion, the political and economic failure of Poland's post–martial-law ruling elites to reequilibrate the state-socialist regime opened the

process of democratization, which swept all Eastern European regimes. This failure had complex sources. They included not only the political choices of ruling elites but also the nature and outcomes of political crises, the strategies of repressive action employed by the Polish regime, as well as broader domestic and international constraints. The extent of Poland's economic difficulties, its dependence on Western economic cooperation, and the economic decline of the Soviet bloc countries all played an important role. I have emphasized, however, the role of institutional factors and domestic policies. In a more general vain, the theoretical importance of the analysis I have presented lies primarily in the effort to explain why the party-states in similar countries—with seemingly uniform political systems and under seemingly stable geopolitical domination—employ such varied coercive and political strategies and produce such different outcomes while dealing with severe political crises. Moreover, this analysis suggests that the striking differences between patterns of disintegration of state-socialist regimes in 1989 in these three countries and the different trajectories of political and economic transformations emerging now in East Central Europe cannot be fully comprehended without understanding how these countries were stabilized and their populations demobilized after their respective crises. The negotiated transitions in Poland and Hungary and the popular upsurge in Czechoslovakia, which brought to an end communist rule in East Central Europe, may be directly linked to the past demobilization strategies employed in these countries and to their outcomes.

LEGACIES OF THE PAST AND DEMOCRATIC TRANSITIONS

The rapid, unexpected collapse of state-socialist regimes in East Central Europe in 1989 and the ensuing efforts at democratization and restructuring of the economy pose one of the most challenging set of puzzles for students of comparative politics today. The simultaneity of the breakdown, despite varied political and economic conditions in each country, reinforced a notion that these regimes were basically similar and kept in power by the Soviet military presence. Journalists and scholars alike sought to identify a single factor that could account for the simultaneous downfall of Hungarian reformists, Czechoslovakian hard-liners, and a Rumanian despot; and in fact they have singled out one element common to all countries in the region—"the Gorbachev factor." Gorbachev's policies undoubtedly contributed to the demise of these regimes. Internal crisis in the Soviet Union caused relaxation of geopolitical constraints and Soviet supervision over domestic policies of East European regimes. There were, however, crucial differences in responses of particular countries to this new situation and the way various state-socialist regimes were removed differed across the region. Moreover, their political experiences after 1989 have differed in many crucial respects. Despite such obvious differences, it seems that now, as in the past, scholars tend to treat these regimes as a single political type where general characteristics of the political system outweigh the possible contrasts between particular countries. In the past all East European regimes were considered as examples of basically identical state-socialist regimes, now they are considered to be democratizing regimes facing basically the same problems and challenges. I have argued in this book that East Central European regimes underwent complex processes of transformation and adjustment during the four decades of communist rule. Domestic political developments differed from country to country, producing varying consequences, institutional dissimilarities, and distinctive relations between the party-state elites and non-elite actors within society. These differences have created a variation of initial conditions in which the state-socialist regimes were removed and became significant factors shaping the progress of political and economic transitions in each country. As I have emphasized, each regime left its own imprint and distinct legacies, which should be carefully examined if we are to explain the present rapidly diverging trajectories of political, social, and economic changes taking place in the region.

I have argued in this book that the institutions and policies of state-socialist regimes have been shaped by domestic politics—specifically, by patterns of political conflict, mobilization and demobilization. The incidents of political crisis, institutional breakdown, and strategies of regime reequilibration left long-lasting political legacies and were the most important determinants of their recent history. As a result of these crises, fundamental changes and adjustments were introduced into the political and economic institutions and practices of these regimes, altering relations between institutional orders of the party-state and between the state and society. Following this argument, one should expect that the specific nature of their removal and the path of the democratization process in each country would depend on institutional and political legacies left by the old regime. And, in fact, despite the puzzling clustering of regime breakdowns, there are important differences in the way particular countries entered the transition process. Moreover, despite some political and economic similarities, growing differences have been emerging between countries of the region since 1989. Several years after the collapse of the communist rule, they are distinctive regions, or groups of countries, emerging within the former Soviet bloc. The new, postcommunist regimes have faced their own distinctive challenges and varied domestic conditions. They have pursued different strategies of political and economic reforms. Thus, David Stark is correct when he argues that we should "regard East Central Europe as undergoing a plurality of transitions in a dual sense: across the region, we are seeing a multiplicity of distinctive strategies; within any given country, we find not one transition but many occurring in different domains—political, economic, and social—and the temporality of these processes are often asynchronous and their articulation seldom harmonious."[14] These divergent paths of transition so easily detectable on the empirical level are often obscured by the scholars' attempts to construct a general model of regime change and transition.

In his paper on democratic transition, Giuseppe Di Palma argues that "the logic by which communist regimes may change does not differ as much as we think from that of other regimes."[15] Robert Bova echoes this assertion, claiming that, "however unique these developments have been . . . the transition from communism may, nevertheless, be usefully viewed as a subcategory of a more generic phenomenon of transition from authoritarian rule."[16] This new viewpoint that totalitarian regimes were not as unique as generations of scholars believed and that the individual peculiarities of particular countries can be disregarded for the sake of comparative generalizations has been shared by many politicians leading political and economic revolutions in the region. As Edmund Mokrzycki points out, "It was assumed, as a self evident fact, that East European societies, freed from communist control, reveal, at least in a preliminary form, characteristics common to West European societies."[17] Yet, the political experiences of the first years of transition indicate that the entrenched legacies of state socialism and historical trajectories of political developments in particular countries have shaped the transition process in a powerful way and have produced many unique features of the East Central European democratizations as well as growing differences among postcommunist regimes.

One of the most important elements in the whole body of scholarly literature on state-socialist regimes written during the last decade or so is the presentation of state socialism as a unique social, political, and economic system with its own specific dynamics and reproduction capabilities.[18] State-socialist regimes not only produced very distinct political and economic institutions but also formed a well-established pattern of attitudes, behavior, and habits corresponding to the constraints and requirements of the system.[19] Similarly, transitions from state socialism present a specific set of constraints and opportunities shaping the actions of collective actors and displaying many peculiarities absent in other types of transitions. Therefore, any effort to analyze the patterns of regime collapse and transition in East Central Europe requires a careful reexamination of the legacies left by decades of communist rule. Moreover, the case studies presented in this book showed how different institutional frameworks, intra-elite relations, and relations between the state and society were established as the result of past political crises and their resolution. Accordingly, to understand the emerging trajectories of political and economic transitions in the region, we have to include these political experiences in our analytical frameworks.

This leads me to another theoretical point. There is a marked theoretical shift reflected in the growing literature on democratization. From searching for social and economic preconditions for a stable democracy, scholars have switched "their attention to the strategic calculations, unfolding processes and sequential patterns that are involved in moving from one type of political regime to another."[20] This new approach—emphasizing political uncertainty, changing contingencies, structural indeterminacy, and significance of elite choices made during the founding moments of democracy—is a major advancement in our understanding of political transition processes. As Di Palma contends, political crafting is at the heart of transition to democracy, and successful democratizations are more a product of political will than structural conditions.[21] But this emphasis on historical contingency and elite choices carries a risk of excessive voluntarism. Ken Jowitt argues that this new approach assumes "near-absolute malleability of . . . political environments" and he charges the transition theory with "ignoring the Leninist legacy's impact on the range of viable political choices available to leaderships in the Soviet Union and Eastern Europe."[22] The emphasis on the sequential political process and political crafting, while rightly rejecting simplistic and mechanical interpretations of links between structural factors and political outcomes, puts too much weight on actions and strategies of political actors. They are accorded with power and capacity to negotiate and secure democratic outcomes of the transition and in turn may be portrayed as the main culprits of political failures due to their incompetence, ill will, or particularistic interests.

The path-dependency approach proposed recently by Terry L. Karl and Philippe Schmitter seeks to correct the voluntaristic bias of dominant theories in the field.[23] They argue that transitions should be placed within the framework of structural-historical constraints and include the impact of the "political institutional space inherited from the ancient regime." This approach was already applied in a very insightful way to understanding economic transformation in Eastern Europe. Stark argues that "the economic and political institutions that must be reconstructed on the ruins of state socialism cannot simply be chosen from among the economists' designs like selecting wares from the supermarket or choosing the winning blueprints in an architectural competition."[24] We have to acknowledge, however, not only the diversity of the initial conditions and the presence of inherited institutional constraints. We have to seriously examine specific historical experiences and their impact on the institutional structures of each country and probe their bearing on the transition process.

Looking at political experiences of postcommunist countries since 1989, it is clear that Eastern Europe represents distinctive sets of subregional developments. On the one hand, there are four (following the division of Czechoslovakia) Central European countries analyzed in this book where political and economic reforms are most advanced. They contrast with the Balkan countries and the former Soviet republics in a variety of ways. Poland and Hungary, through their negotiated political transitions, opened the democratization process in the region. In all three countries, the initial disintegration and political defeat of the communist parties and politicians was faster and more radical than elsewhere. Also, in contrast to other former Soviet-bloc countries, reorganized and renamed communist parties were not serious contenders in the first round of democratic elections, although reformed heirs of the communist parties were returned to power in Poland's 1993 and Hungary's 1994 elections. Finally, in all three countries, political and economic reforms were introduced more rapidly, and there was more of a consensus, both among the elites and the population, regarding the transition to a market economy and a liberal democracy. It would seem, therefore, that in these countries that experienced significant political crises and conflicts in the past, the legitimacy of communist rule was eroded to much higher degree. Moreover, they had alternative political elites who were able to capture political initiative and were more prone to experiment with more radical institutional alternatives. These countries also developed at least a rudimentary civil society composed of various political and social movements and groups as well as material and intellectual resources outside the party-state institutions. In addition, symbolic resources based on collective memories of struggles and defeats played an important role in the extrication of communists and in transitional politics in general. While the process of decay of the communist rule was more pronounced in the three countries analyzed in this book, there were, however, important differences among them as well. The analysis shows that such differences can be related to the nature of the specific political conflicts they experienced as well as to ways in which such conflicts were resolved and the party-state reequilibrated.

I have argued that one can identify several long-term processes that have led to the unraveling of East Central European state-socialist regimes. Following the turbulent period of de-Stalinization (in the 1950s and 1960s) and the exhaustion of the post-Stalinist project at the end of the 1970s, countries in the region entered a radically new stage of development, which can be characterized as a systemic crisis of state socialism. This new transitory phase was shaped by several distinct but, nevertheless, interconnected processes: (1) the failure of the centrally planned economies, (2) the profound identity crisis of the communist parties and the collapse of the Marxist-Leninist "state-idea," (3) the gradual disintegration of institutional structures of the party-state, and (4) the formation of independent political society.[25] These processes advanced with varying speed and intensity in different countries of the region, reflecting differences in their domestic political and economic developments. In this gradual, evolutionary process of state socialism's decline, the political crises analyzed in this book played a critical role. They produced a cumulation of changes, diffusion of ideas across the region, and institutional and policy adjustments in all countries. The decay of state socialism was the most advanced in Poland as a result of the 1980–81 political crisis and the failure of the demobilization strategies implemented after martial law. In Hungary, the successful reequilibration of the regime after the revolution of 1956 had specific long-term consequences. While the political structure of the party-state remained intact, the humanization of political practices, the process of economic reforms, and the opening of the second economy undermined the foundations of the communist rule. This situation can be traced back to the nature of demobilization policies following the crushed revolution of 1956. Ivan Szelenyi makes an interesting argument in this matter, comparing Polish and Hungarian roads to civil society. He argues that the self-organization of society in Hungary found its expression in the economy, while in Poland this self-organization by-passed the economy and was expressed within the polity.[26] In Czechoslovakia, the legacies of the demobilization policies had their most devastating effect. Both the Polish-style self-organization of civil society in the political arena and Hungary's pattern of "embourgeoisement" within the second economy were blocked, producing political and economic stagnation. According to Sharon Wolchik, while "Czech and Slovak leaders faced many of the same problems as leaders in other communist countries, their responses to these problems were influenced heavily by the end of the 1968 reform process and its economic and political repercussions."[27] The Czechoslovak party hard-liners who presided over the destruction of the Prague Spring desperately resisted any adjustment of their economic policies and political practices. In short, as a result of past crises, the three countries analyzed in this book differed in many crucial respects at the end of the 1980s. Therefore, when external guaranties of political order were effectively removed by the dominant regional power, the decomposition of traditional forms of communist power took place in markedly different ways.

Looking at the political events of 1989, one can distinguish three characteristic patterns by which communist parties surrendered their power and countries of the region entered the process of political transition. There were negotiated openings in Poland and Hungary where preliminary pacts between the party-state elites and the opposition forces were established. These pacts, outlining the stages and limits of political change and guarantees for all political actors, secured an orderly transfer of power and prevented mass political mobilization among the population. Timothy Garton Ash aptly described the transfer of power in these two countries as "refolutions," where revolutionary change was accomplished by reformist means.[28] Thus, Poland and Hungary initiated and led the process of democratization in the region. Their domestic transformation tested the limits of possible political change and provided a political impulse and a model for all other East European countries. In East Germany and Czechoslovakia, rapid, nonviolent political mobilization—or what Guillermo O'Donnell and Philippe Schmitter call "popular upsurge"[29]—forced in a short period of time significant political concessions and the total surrender of the communist elites. And, finally, in Romania a full-blown revolution laid open the path to political transition.[30] These differences in the political dynamic of the breakthroughs were only partially shaped by the geopolitical factors and the interactive nature of the 1989 revolutions. They were also a reflection of the different domestic situations and distinctive legacies of the communist rule in each country as well as the availability of symbolic and other resources collective actors had at their disposal.

One factor that facilitated these different patterns of transition and that can be traced back to the nature and outcomes of past political crises was the presence of well-developed cleavages and conflicts within the political leadership. At the beginning of 1989, political analysts explained the moves toward political and economic reforms in Poland and Hungary as well as their absence in Czechoslovakia by the existence of splits within the established leadership over the need to reform the economy and the desirability to retain the monopoly of power. They argued that the opening of the political opportunity structure, which allows society's activation to occur, happens only when the ruling elite are divided. The experiences of 1989 show, however, that the political change and society activation can occur even in absence of well-pronounced splits within the ruling elites (i.e., Czechoslovakia, East Germany, Bulgaria, Romania). Other factors, such as political diffusion or a demonstration effect combined with policy changes that affect the situation in other countries (for example, the decision of the Hungarian government to allow East Germans to emigrate to the West) may destabilize seemingly stable and united regimes. But these experiences also indicate that the existence of splits facilitates negotiated openings and a more orderly process of political transition. In Poland and Hungary, strong reformist factions within the regime were able to initiate the negotiation process with the opposition and thus prevent a large-scale collective protest and dangerous political confrontation. In Czechoslovakia, as a result of repressive and orthodox demobilization policies, the Communist party did not have a notable reformist faction, and links to existing opposition groups were not established. Therefore, the negotiated transition was not a viable political option. Despite the absence of open conflicts within the ruling elites, political events in other countries contributed to the popular perception that the political opportunity structure changed and imposed constraints on the use of repressive means by the ruling elites. This situation produced a rapid process of popular mobilization, a short period of nonviolent confrontation, and the swift capitulation of the Czechoslovak ruling elites. To explain this rapid political mobilization and the "velvet revolution," we must specify several additional factors that I believe have to do with legacies of the past political crisis and the strength and organization of independent political society.

In Poland, Czechoslovakia, and Hungary, there was at least rudimentary political opposition whose strength and capacity was shaped by the nature of demobilization policies following the past crises. Only in Poland has there been a mass movement with a fully developed organization, symbols, and collective identity. Political society in Poland has formed and maintained an alliance between intellectuals, workers, peasants and students. For years it had had extensive underground networks and some institutional basis through its cooperation with the Catholic church. In 1988, there were more than sixty independent groups, parties, and movements in addition to hundreds of smaller organizations. As I argued before, this situation can be explained by the nature of Poland's political crisis in 1980, the type of demobilization strategy employed by the Polish regime following the imposition of martial law, and its failure to reequilibrate the state-socialist regime.

In Czechoslovakia, due to the highly repressive nature of demobilization policies, groups organized around Charter 77 were not able to establish any significant links to important segments of the population and to form a mass opposition movement. In the second half of the 1980s, however, in response to growing political and economic stagnation and exhaustion of repressive strategies, there was growing political dissent and a multiplication of independent social and political groups. The survey of independent movements in Eastern Europe listed more than thirty such groups and organizations in Czechoslovakia.[31] Also, there was a significant revival of the Catholic church and religion. The petition demanding religious rights begun in 1987 (Thirty One Demands), was signed by more than six hundred thousand people. In 1988, there was the demonstration on the twentieth anniversary of the 1968 invasion, which drew an estimated one hundred thousand people, and in 1989 demonstrations on the anniversary of the Jan Palach's self-immolation protest were harshly broken up by the police. Thus the collective memory of the 1968 events had a visible impact of the mobilizational potential of Czechoslovak society.

In less repressive Hungary, there were hundreds of independent societies, circles, and clubs and more than twenty new and revived oppositional political movements and parties. Although Hungarian political society did not have the power and unity of the Polish opposition, nevertheless, it was much better developed than in Czechoslovakia. Moreover, the Hungarian opposition was reinforced by an accommodating posture of the reformist segments of the ruling elite. The Hungarian roundtable negotiations, initiated by the party-state's leadership shortly after the Polish elections in June, suggested that the ruling elite accepted the inevitability of a fundamental political change. The negotiations were designed to benefit and legitimize both the reformist faction within the ruling elite and the opposition movements that were invited to participate. But, as Andras Korosenyi notes, "There were no two strong, determined and self-confident characters in this political drama, as with Solidarity and the Communist party in Poland, but rather several hesitant second fiddlers. The Communists resigned under rather weak pressure . . . before the opposition could take power."[32]

Therefore, in these three countries, independent political society had preexisting organization, intrapersonal networks, and symbolic resources that constituted a springboard for political pressure and collective protest. When a multitude of domestic and external factors and pressures coincided in 1989, countries with a better-organized opposition and more divided party-state elites were more likely to negotiate the peaceful transfer of power than countries with weak and fragmented opposition, less disorganized state, and less divided elites. It is clear that the effective removal of external guarantees of political order by the Soviet Union in 1989 came at the moment when all

East Central European state-socialist regimes had exhausted or nearly exhausted the economic and political potentials of the socioeconomic order that was imposed on the region after the Second World War. I would suggest, however, that in spite of differences in the intensity of the economic crisis, the anarchization of state institutions, and the development of independent political society, countries with the recent history of struggles and defeats were in the forefront of political change in the region and became leaders of reform. In that sense the chain reaction of political breakthroughs, which started in Poland and ended in Romania, reflects not only the general internal fragility and economic crisis of all state-socialist regimes at the end of the 1980s and the weakness of the Soviet Union but also the impact and long term consequences of past political developments. Although the simultaneous collapse of all European state-socialist regimes obscured the different nature of political breakthroughs, the experiences of the first stages of political and economic transformations reveal striking differences among the countries of the region. Not only does the situation in Poland, Czechoslovakia, and Hungary differ from that in the Balkan countries and former Soviet republics, but these three countries display a notable variation in their domestic developments as well.

During first years following the collapse of communist rule, East Central European countries have defied many initial predictions and expectations. In Poland, the Solidarity movement broke into numerous, fiercely competing small political parties. Despite an orderly transition of power and a successful introduction of the ambitious economic recovery program, Poland has experienced political fragmentation and bitter political struggles, governmental instability, and a significant level of collective protest. The 1993 parliamentary elections returned to power ex-communist parties that paradoxically became responsible for consolidating Poland's new democracy and stabilizing the country's emerging market economy.[33] In Czechoslovakia, a joyful "velvet revolution" gave way to intense political divisions and struggles and the irreconcilable national conflict that split the country into two independent states in 1993. The collapse of the Czechoslovak federation happened in a surprisingly peaceful way. Since then, two new republics have pursued contrasting economic policies and have faced different challenges and problems. Different political forces have played a dominant role in each country's politics. In Hungary, the success of the initial political transition and the formation of a stable parliamentary system has given way to political and economic stagnation. New political parties have been loosing popular support and former communists were returned to power in the 1994 elections. Despite substantial foreign investment that the country have been able to attract, economic reforms have been stalled by governmental indecision and political divisions in the Parliament.

It is not possible to explain the turbulence of Polish politics, the fragmentation of the party system, the strength and militancy of the trade unions, or the role of the Catholic church, and the divisive impact of controversies about abortion, religion in public schools, and attempts to enshrine Christian values in the new Polish constitution without a careful examination of the strategies, policies, and outcomes of the demobilization process following the imposition of martial law. Similarly, the intensity of the ethnic conflict and differences of attitudes between Czechs and Slovaks on many issues that led to the collapse of the Czechoslovak federation, the orthodox nature and weakness of ex-communist parties and forces, and the initial eagerness of the new regime to impose restrictive decommunization policies are peculiar phenomenon of the Czechoslovak transformation. Understanding Czechoslovakia's predicament requires an analysis of the country's political experiences after the Soviet-led invasion of 1968. Finally, the political stability of Hungary's party-system and parliamentary politics, the apprehension of its citizenry over participation in its new democracy, a gradualist approach to economic transformations, and government's concerns about living standards cannot be explained without understanding the experiences and legacies of the crushed revolution of 1956. As George Schopflin emphasizes that sources of peculiarities of the Hungarian postcommunist politics "are partly to be found in the remote past, in the origins of the Kadar regime and in the ways in which that system was put together after the revolution of 1956."[34]

In this book I have intended to analyze historical experiences of three East Central European societies partially to show that the legacies of state socialism are quite different in each country and that their impact may become more evident with the progress of political and economic transformations. East Central Europe's "return to diversity" reflects these contrasting experiences of communist rule. From the vantage point of this research, I would argue that we need a more specific and historically grounded understanding of structural factors shaping processes of regime change and democratic transition. While historically evolving patterns of social structure, institutional resources, economic organization, and modes of relations between the state and society are powerful determinants of the political transition constraining the choices of collective actors, so are more illusive cultural constraints, such as collective memories, inherited political discourses, symbols, or forms of legitimization. These political and cultural factors play a major and autonomous role in shaping both the interest politics and institutional resources of postcommunist political actors. State-socialist societies were always quite diverse, and we have to take seriously their specific historical experiences if knowledge of the region and understanding of processes taking place there are to be expanded. I hope that this book contributes to such historically grounded understanding of East Central European politics.

NOTES

Preface and Acknowledgments

1. Albert Hirschman, "The Turn to Authoritarianism in Latin America and the Search for Its Economic Determinants," in *The New Authoritarianism in Latin America*, ed. David Collier (Princeton: Princeton University Press, 1979), 98.

2. See, for example, David Stark and Victor Nee, "Toward an Institutional Analysis of State Socialism," in *Remaking the Economic Institutions of Socialism*, ed. Victor Nee and David Stark (Stanford: Stanford University Press, 1989), 1–31; Ellen Comisso, "Where Have We Been and Where Are We Going? Analyzing Post-Socialist Politics in the 1990s," in *Political Science: Looking to the Future*, ed. William Crotty (Evanstone: Northwestern University Press, 1991), 77–122; Andrew C. Janos, "Social Science, Communism, and the Dynamics of Political Change," *World Politics* 44, no. 1 (1991): 81–112; Ken Jowitt, "Weber, Trotsky and Holmes on the Study of Leninist Regimes," *Journal of International Affairs* 45, no. 1 (1991): 31–49; Raymond C. Taras, ed., *Handbook of Political Science Research on the USSR and Eastern Europe* (Westport, Conn.: Greenwood Press, 1992).

3. Comisso, "Where Have We Been," 79.

4. Janos M. Rainer, "The Yeltsin Dossier: Soviet Documents on Hungary, 1956," *Cold War International History Project Bulletin*, no. 5 (Spring 1995), 22. See also Jiri Valenta and Jan Moravec, "Could the Prague Spring Have Been Saved?" *Orbis* 35, no. 4 (Fall 1991): 581–601; Mark Kramer, "New Sources on the 1968 Soviet Invasion of Czechoslovakia," *Cold War International History Project Bulletin* 2 (Fall 1992): 1, 4–13; Csaba Bekes, "New Findings on the 1956 Hungarian Revolution," *Cold War International History Project Bulletin* 2 (Fall 1992): 1–3; Janos M. Rainer, "The Other Side of the Story: Five Documents from the Yeltsin File," *New Hungarian Quarterly* 34, no. 129 (1993): 100–114.

5. See, for example, Wojciech Jaruzelski, *Stan Wojenny: Dlaczego . . .* (Warszawa: BGW, 1992); Witold Beres and Jerzy Skoczylas, *General Kiszczak mowi . . . Prawie wszystko* (Warszawa: BGW, 1991); Mieczyslaw F. Rakowski, *Jak to sie stalo* (Warszawa: BGW, 1991); *Pameti Vasila Bilaka: Unikatni svedectvi ze zakulisi KSC* (Prague: Agentury Cesty, 1991); Alexander Dubcek, *Hope Dies Last* (New York: Kodansha, 1993); Zbigniew Wlodek, ed., *Tajne Dokumenty Biura Politycznego: PZPR a Solidarnosc 1980–1981* (London: Aneks, 1992); Anna Karas, ed., *Sad nad autorami stanu wojennego* (Warszawa: BGW, 1993).

6. Andrew Janos, "Social Science, Communism, and the Dynamics," 82.

7. George Schopflin, *Politics in Eastern Europe, 1945–1992* (Oxford: Blackwell, 1993), 3.

8. Daniel N. Nelson, "Comparative Communism: A Postmortem," in Taras, *Handbook*, 303.

9. Adam Przeworski, for example, stated that "hundreds of macrohistorical comparative sociologists will write thousands of books and articles correlating background conditions with outcomes in each country, but I think they will be wasting their time." *Democracy and the Market* (Cambridge: Cambridge University Press, 1991), 3.

10. William H. Sewell Jr., "Three Temporalities: Toward a Sociology of the Event," CSST Working Papers, No. 58 (Ann Arbor: University of Michigan, October 1990), 17.

11. William H. Sewell Jr., *A Rhetoric of Bourgeois Revolution: The Abbe Sieyes and What Is the Third Estate?* (Durham: Duke University Press, 1994), 6.

12. William H. Sewell, "Three Temporalities," 23.

13. Kathleen Thelen and Sven Steinmo, "Historical Institutionalism in Comparative Politics," in *Structuring Politics: Historical Institutionalism in Comparative Perspective*, ed. Sven Steinmo, Kathleen Thelen, and Frank Longstreth (Cambridge: Cambridge University Press, 1992), 18.

14. See Peter Hall, *Governing the Economy: The Politics of State Intervention in Britain and France* (New York: Oxford University Press, 1986), 19.

15. Timothy Garton Ash, *The Magic Lantern: The Revolution of '89 Witnessed in Warsaw, Budapest, Berlin, and Prague* (New York: Random House, 1990).

16. See, for example, Laszlo Bruszt and David Stark, "Remaking the Political Field in Hungary: From the Politics of Confrontation to the Politics of Competition," *Journal of International Affairs* 45, no. 1 (1991): 201–45; Grzegorz Ekiert, "Transitions from State-Socialism in East Central Europe," *State and Social Structures Newsletters* 12 (1990): 1–6.

17. In this book I do not deal systematically with controlled transition from Stalinism in Poland in 1956. My selection included only cases in which there was a coercive, military response to the crisis either by the Soviet Union (Hungary, Czechoslovakia) or by domestic forces (Poland in 1981). I analyze the role of the 1956 transition in Poland's political developments in the paper "Rebellious Poles: Cycles of Protest and Popular Mobilization under State-Socialism, 1945–1989," Working Paper Series, no. 5, Advanced Study Center, International Institute, University of Michigan, 1995.

18. It should be stressed that single-country studies often used the event-centered strategy. The majority of books written on Hungary focused on the 1956 revolution or on its consequences, studies of Czechoslovakia were mostly concerned with the Prague Spring and its legacies, and most recent studies of Polish political and economic developments centered around the phenomenon of Solidarity.

CHAPTER 1

1. Helene Carrere d'Encausse, *Big Brother: The Soviet Union and Soviet Europe* (New York: Holmes and Meier, 1987), 296.

2. Poland represents here an extreme example of both the weakness of the party-state and the capacity of various social groups in society to challenge state authority and to launch a collective protest. Since 1956 mass protests have become a relatively routine way of exerting political pressure, transmitting collective grievances, and defending collective interests. Jadwiga Staniszkis, analyzing in detail Polish experiences during the last four decades, argues that the "regulation through crisis" was one of the most characteristic features of a political and economic system that lacks independent mechanisms of self-regulation. See *Poland's Self-limiting Revolution* (Princeton: Princeton University Press, 1984), 249–78; see also Wojtek Lamentowicz, "Adaptation through Political Crises in Post-War Poland," *Journal of Peace Research* 19, no. 2 (1982): 117–31. Polish exceptionalism, however, can be ex-

plained as the outcome of a specific political dynamics produced by consecutive political crises with the 1956 controlled transition from Stalinism as a crucial turning point setting in motion path-dependent developments. See Grzegorz Ekiert, "Rebellious Poles: Cycles of Protest and Popular Mobilization under State-Socialism, 1945–1989," Working Paper Series, no. 5, Advanced Study Center, International Institute, University of Michigan, 1995.

3. Manuel Antonio Garreton, "Popular Mobilization and the Military Regime in Chile: The Complexities of the Invisible Transition," in *Power and Popular Protest*, ed. Susan Eckstein (Berkeley: University of California Press, 1989), 261.

4. For the critique of one-actor models employed by scholars in analyses of state-socialist societies, see Elemer Hankiss, "Demobilization, Self-Mobilization, and Quasi-Mobilization in Hungary, 1948–1987," *East European Politics and Societies* 3, no. 1 (1989): 105–52.

5. Recently David Stark and Victor Nee criticized this limited focus of East European studies on party and state elites and advocated a new approach that "opens up society and economy and their relationship to the state as arenas of research." "Toward an Institutional Analysis of State Socialism," in *Remaking the Economic Institutions of Socialism*, ed. Victor Nee and David Stark (Stanford: Stanford University Press, 1989), 30. See also Ivan Szelenyi, *Socialist Entrepreneurs* (Madison: University of Wisconsin Press, 1988).

6. Dependent state-socialism combines, according to Valerie Bunce, "a Stalinist political economy—that is state ownership of means of production, central planning and a Leninist party—with external dependence on the Soviet Union for national security, political authority, markets and primary products." "Why Some Rebel and Others Comply: The Polish Crisis of 1980–81, Eastern Europe and Theories of Revolution," unpublished paper (1988), 10.

7. For the seminal work analyzing the role of the political opportunity structure in facilitating collective protest, see Charles Tilly, *From Mobilization to Revolution* (New York: Random House, 1978). See also Herbert Kitschelt, "Political Opportunity Structures and Political Protest: Antinuclear Movements in Four Democracies," *British Journal of Political Science* 16 (1986): 57–85, and Sidney Tarrow, *Power in Movement: Social Movements, Collective Action, and Politics* (Cambridge: Cambridge University Press, 1994). The cumulation of collective action and protests in specific historical periods is a general phenomenon observed in different societies and different political contexts. Scholars studying collective action concluded that such cycles of protest that produce wide variety of protest movements and collective actions alternate with periods of relative political quiescence. Albert Hirshman describes such times as periods of increased public involvement. See his *Shifting Involvements* (Princeton: Princeton University Press, 1982). Sidney Tarrow developed the most consistent analytical and empirical approach to cycles of protest in West European societies. See his *Democracy and Disorder* (Oxford: Clarendon Press, 1989), and *Power in Movement*. See also Mark Traugott, ed., *Repertoires and Cycles of Collective Action* (Durham: Duke University Press, 1995).

8. David Snyder and Charles Tilly, "Hardship and Collective Violence in France," *American Sociological Review* 37 (1972): 520–32.

9. Theda Skocpol, *States and Social Revolutions* (Cambridge: Cambridge University Press, 1979), 117.

10. Tarrow, *Power in Movement*, 99.

11. Sidney Tarrow, "National Politics and Collective Action: Recent Theory and Research in Western Europe and the United States," *Annual Review of Sociology* 14 (1988): 429–30.

12. Doug McAdam, "'Initiator' and 'Spin-off' Movements: Diffusion Processes in Protest Cycles," in *Repertoires and Cycles of Collective Action*, 224.

13. Sidney Tarrow, "Cycles of Collective Action: Between Movements of Madness and the Repertoire of Contention," in *Repertoires and Cycles of Collective Action*, 92–94.

14. The notion of state practices supplements Philip Abrams's distinction between the state idea and the state system, which I find very useful for understanding state-socialist regimes ("Notes on the Difficulties of Studying the State," *Journal of Historical Sociology* 1 [1988]: 58–90). While the notion of state system describes institutional structures and legal codes dominant in any given society, the category of state practices represents the set of a state's routine actions. They are induced and constrained by the institutional structures of the state as well as the underlying set of political preferences. This set of preferences can be described as a state idea. The state idea represents a principal cognitive framework for political actors. It not only gives directions to the state's actions and shapes its institutional design but also supplies the foundations of state's legitimacy and self-justification for power elites. Within a given state system, there is room for several quite independent and sometimes discrepant sets of practices. In Soviet-type regimes, the state system remained almost unchanged for more than four decades. It was designed to achieve a symbiotic relationship among the Communist party, the state apparatus, and economic institutions. It was characterized by considerable centralization and concentration of power, the penetration of party-state institutions into all realms of social life, and the elimination of self-regulators in the polity and economy. Party-state practices, however, both in the sphere of politics and economy in the post-Stalinist period, were significantly different from Stalinist practices, despite a relative stability of institutional and legal systems.

15. George Schopflin, *Politics in Eastern Europe, 1945–1992* (Oxford: Blackwell, 1993), 107.

16. In this context, one should question the suggestion, often formulated by scholars and recently, for example, by Staniszkis (*Poland's Self-limiting Revolution*, chap. 7), that most cases of collective protest were deliberately provoked by competing segments of power elites. Staniszkis argues that crises in Poland were intensified and used by various factions within the Communist party as a convenient tool of power politics. She describes this technique as an artificial process of a temporary reconstruction of public opinion from above in order to channel social tensions and to secure the transition of power within the ruling elite. Although Staniszkis's concept of artificial negativity is worthy of further exploration, her idea of crisis as a ritual drama remains entirely within a framework of "one-actor models."

17. The German uprising in 1953, however, may be seen more as a direct effect of a precarious geopolitical situation of East Germany than as a result of contradictory tensions produced by the state-socialist regime itself. In short, this crisis resulted from a combination of unresolved geopolitical status of the East German state with tensions generated by the formation of Stalinist regime on the domestic level. For the detailed analysis of these events, see Arnulf Baring, *Uprising in East Germany* (Ithaca: Cornell University Press, 1972).

18. For the account of the revolt, see Otto Ulc, "Pilsen: The Unknown Revolt," *Problems of Communism* 14, no. 3 (1965): 46–49.

19. For detailed analysis of the Polish events see, for example, Konrad Syrop, *Spring in October: The Polish Revolution of 1956* (London: Weidenfeld and Nicolson, 1957); Flora Lewis, *A Case History of Hope: The Story of Poland's Peaceful Revolution* (New York: Doubleday, 1958); Jakub Karpinski, *Count-Down* (New York: Karz-Cohl, 1982); Jaroslaw Maciejewski and Zofia Trojanowicz, *Poznanski Czerwiec 1956* (Poznan: Wydawnictwo Poznanskie, 1981); Zbyslaw Rykowski and Wieslaw Wladyka, *Polska proba Pazdziernik '56* (Krakow: Wydawnictwo Literackie, 1989).

20. For detailed analysis of the revolution, see, for example, Ferenc A. Vali, *Rift and Revolt in Hungary* (Cambridge: Harvard University Press, 1961); Paul Zinner, *Revolution in Hungary* (Freeport: Books for Libraries Press, 1962); Bill Lomax, *Hungary, 1956* (New York: St. Martin's Press, 1976).

21. For analyses of the March 1968 crisis, see, for example, Jerzy Eisler, *Marzec, 1968* (Warszawa: PWN, 1991); Bogdan Hillebrandt, *Marzec, 1968* (Warszawa: Wydawnictwo Spoldzielcze, 1986); Jakub Karpinski, *Count-Down*; Jack Bielasiak, "Social Confrontation to Contrived Crisis: March 1968 in Poland," *East European Quarterly* 22, no. 1 (1988): 81–105.

22. For accounts of the developments in Czechoslovakia, see, for example, Harold G. Skilling, *Czechoslovakia's Interrupted Revolution* (Princeton: Princeton University Press, 1976); Galia Golan, *The Czechoslovak Reform Movement* (Cambridge: Cambridge University Press, 1971), and Galia Golan, *Reform Rule in Czechoslovakia* (Cambridge: Cambridge University Press, 1973).

23. For analysis of the worker unrest in Poland, see, for example, Michael Bernhard, "The Strikes of June 1976 in Poland," *East European Politics and Societies* 1, no. 3 (1987): 363–92, Zygmunt Korybutowicz, *Grudzien, 1970* (Paris: Instytut Literacki, 1983); Jakub Karpinski, *Count-Down*; Roman Laba, *The Roots of Solidarity* (Princeton: Princeton University Press, 1991).

24. For analysis of mutual impact of political crises in Eastern Europe see, for example, Adam Bromke, "Poland," in *The Hungarian Revolution in Retrospect*, ed. Bela Kiraly and Paul Jonas (Boulder: East European Quarterly, 1978), 87–94; Otto Ulc, "How the Czechs Felt in 1956," *Central European Federalist* 14, no. 1 (July 1966): 23–28; Janos Tischler, ed., *Rewolucja wegierska 1956 w polskich dokumentach* (Warszawa: ISP PAN, 1995); Adam Bromke, "Czechoslovakia 1968—Poland 1978: a Dilemma for Moscow," *International Journal* 23, 4 (1978): 740–62. The theoretical challenge to account for the interactive nature of political crisis in Eastern Europe is addressed in a more systematic way by Laszlo Bruszt and David Stark, "Remaking the Political Field in Hungary," *Journal of International Affairs* 45, no. 1 (1991): 201–45.

25. See David Ost, "Towards a Corporatist Solution in Eastern Europe: The Case of Poland," *East European Politics and Societies* 3, no. 1 (1989): 152–74.

26. See Szelenyi, *Socialist Entrepreneurs*.

27. Walter W. Powell and Paul J. DiMaggio, "Introduction," in their *The New Institutionalism in Organizational Analysis* (Chicago: University of Chicago Press, 1991), 11.

28. Jadwiga Staniszkis, *Ontologia socializmu* (Warszawa: In Plus, 1989), 18. According to Staniszkis, revolts to defend material interests under state-socialism only

reproduce the state-socialist type of domination by invoking the redistributive role of the state.

29. See ibid., 18.

30. This fragmentation of society was reinforced by specific mechanisms of social stratification. According to Staniszkis, in the absence of a market that forms a unique constitutive mechanism of stratification, stratification is shaped by a multitude of overlapping principles producing segmented and discontinued social space (see ibid., 89–94).

31. For the distinction between parallel and auxiliary institutions that form characteristic elements of modern authoritarian systems, see Amos Perlmutter, *Modern Authoritarianism* (New Haven: Yale University Press, 1981), and for the analysis of the political importance of such institutions in totalitarian states, see Philip Selznick, *Organizational Weapon* (New York: McGraw-Hill, 1952).

32. See Jose Casanova, "Private and Public Religion," *Social Research* 59, no. 1 (1992): 17–57. It is important to emphasize that while human rights organizations and independent social movements were widely analyzed by the scholars, the role of religion and churches in the decay of state-socialism is often misunderstood and the least-explored aspect of East European political developments. For recent attempts to assess the role of religion see Jan Kubik, *The Power of Symbols against Symbols of Power: The Rise of Solidarity and the Fall of State Socialism* (University Park: Penn State University Press, 1994); Niels Nielsen, *Revolutions in Eastern Europe: The Religious Roots* (Maryknoll, N.Y.: Orbis Books, 1991); Maryjane Osa, "Resistance, Persistence and Change: The Transformation of the Catholic Church in Poland," *East European Politics and Societies* 3, no. 2 (1989): 268–99; and George Weigel, *The Final Revolution: The Resistance of Church and the Collapse of Communism* (New York: Oxford University Press, 1992).

33. For the discussion about peculiarities of legitimization in state-socialist regimes, see Thomas H. Rigby and Ferenc Feher, eds., *Political Legitimation in Communist States* (London: Macmillan 1982); Stephen White, "Economic Performance and Communist Legitimacy" *World Politics* 38, no. 3 (1986): 462–82; Paul Lewis, ed., *Eastern Europe: Political Crisis and Legitimation* (New York: St. Martin's Press, 1984); Jan Pakulski, "Legitimacy and Mass Compliance: Reflections on Max Weber and Soviet-Type Societies," *British Journal of Political Science* 16 (1986): 35–56; Grzegorz Ekiert, "Conditions of Political Obedience and Stability in State-Socialist Societies," CROPSO Working Paper Series, Harvard University (1989), no. 0005.

34. According to Ivan Szelenyi, the economic crisis that started in the 1970s had several unique features: (1) it was exceptionally long, (2) it caused a zero growth rate and a decline of living standards in several countries, and (3) it caused the slide of socialist countries from the semiperiphery to the periphery within the global economic system. "Eastern Europe in an Epoch of Transition: Toward a Socialist Mixed Economy," in *Remaking Economic Institutions*, ed. Nee and Stark, 210.

35. Among other things, the collapse of the ideological legitimation of party-states and their desperate attempts to find another source of social support recreated the important element of instability in the region. In the past, as Joseph Rothschild points out, "ethnonational tensions constituted interwar East Central Europe's most vivid and sensitive political problem and were, indeed, often exploited to obscure social and economic weaknesses" (*Return to Diversity* [New York: Oxford University Press, 1989], 12). The attempts of ruling elites in the region to restore legitimacy

on the basis of nationalistic claims revived these irredentist and revisionist debates, producing territorial claims and exploiting the issue of ethnic minorities.

36. According to Ferenc Feher and Agnes Heller, the events in Poland opened a new chapter in the history of state-socialist regimes and played a truly "world-historical role" in the region. Polish political experiences redefined the principles and practices of state-socialism and moved the state-society conflict beyond the intellectual and political limits of the post-Stalinist, revisionist project (*Hungary 1956 Revisited* [London: Allen and Unwin, 1983], viii).

37. In the middle of the 1980s, according to Timothy Garton Ash, in state-socialist societies the dominant Marxist-Leninist "ideology [was] not only dead but officially buried." See "Reform or Revolution," *New York Review of Books* 35, no. 15 (1988): 59. But the same applied to political discourses of the revisionist opposition. The language of Marxist reformation was equally dead. Miklos Molnar is right when he points out that "revisionism . . . fulfilled its historical role when it wrote the obituary of Stalinism." See "The Heritage of Imre Nagy," in *Ten Years After*, ed. Tamas Aczel (London: Macgibbon and Kee, 1966), 171.

38. Jerzy Urban, an official spokesman of the Polish regime, quite openly acknowledged this change in his confidential letter to the first secretary of the Polish United Workers party written in 1981. In this letter he contended, "We are facing disaster, since, in my opinion, the time has already passed when PZPR could affect a renewal, remodel the system of government, advance a program, and obtain the acceptance and support of society—in other words, stand at the head of a social movement and give it direction." "Letter to the First Secretary," *Uncaptive Minds* 1, no. 4 (1988): 3.

39. This new political discourse decoupled social analysis from the traditional Marxist language and was built around concepts of human and political rights, legalism, individual responsibility, personalism, and new-evolutionism. These ideas, according to Roger Scruton ("The New Right in Central Europe I: Czechoslovakia," *Political Studies* 36, no. 3 [1988]: 461), constituted "a decisive reaction against the previously accepted alternative of 'socialism with a human face,'" and, as Tony Judt ("The Dilemmas of Dissidence: The Politics of Opposition on East-Central Europe," *East European Politics and Societies* 2, no. 2 [1988]: 239) points out, reflected the "progressive abandonment of socialism." Such redefinition of political language facilitated an intellectual reconciliation between various opposition movements and the church as well as revindicated progressive national traditions. I would like to emphasize that contrary to Michael Shafir's assertion ("Political Stagnation and Marxist Critique: 1968 and Beyond in Comparative East European Perspective," *British Journal of Political Science* 14, no. 4 [1984]: 436) that "absence of a 're-formed Marxism' impetus is likely to result in political stagnation," it was precisely the collapse of revisionist ideas that created a new political dynamic and posed real threat to party-states.

40. For the penetrating discussion of the nature and dimensions of instability in state-socialist regimes, see Jan Kubik, "Social and Political Instability in Poland: A Theoretical Reconsideration," Program on Central and Eastern Europe Working Paper Series, Center for European Studies, Harvard University (1990), no. 1.

41. Doug McAdam points out that the political process model "stresses the confluence of three factors shaping the chances of movement emergence. The first is the level of organization within the aggravated population; the second the collective assessment of the prospects for successful insurgency within that same population;

and the third, an increase in the vulnerability or receptivity of the broader political system to challenge" ("'Initiator' and 'Spin-off' Movements," 221). See also his *Political Process and Development of Black Insurgency, 1930–1970* (Chicago: University of Chicago Press, 1982).

42. Karen L. Remmer, "Political Demobilization in Chile, 1973–1978," *Comparative Politics* 12, no. 3 (1980): 277.

43. Piotr Sztompka, "The Social Functions of Defeat," *Research in Social Movements, Conflicts and Change* 10 (1988): 183–84.

44. Mayer N. Zald, "Issues in the Theory of Social Movements," *Current Perspectives in Social Theory* 1 (1980): 64.

45. The cases of large-scale coercive demobilization stand apart from routine demobilization strategies and tactics used by party-states in the region as an instrument of political control. See Hankiss, "Demobilization, Self-Mobilization, and Quasi-Mobilization."

46. Juan Linz, who introduced this term, explored the issue of reequilibration of a political regime in the context of democracies that experienced the political crisis and institutional breakdown. See his *Crisis, Breakdown, and Reequlibration* (Baltimore: Johns Hopkins University Press, 1978).

47. George Urban, "Hungary: The Balance Sheet," in *Hungary Today*, ed. the editors of Survey (New York: Praeger, 1962), 8.

48. Rothschild, *Return to Diversity*, 208.

49. Vaclav Havel, "Letter to Dr. Gustav Husak," in *Vaclav Havel or Living in Truth*, ed. Jan Vladislav (London: Faber and Faber, 1986), 12.

50. See Zdenek Mlynar, "Normalization in Czechoslovakia after 1968," in Wlodzimierz Brus, Pierre Kende and Zdenek Mlynar, *Normalization Processes in Soviet Dominated Central Europe*, Research Project "Crisis in Soviet-Type Systems," (Koln: Index, 1982), no. 1, p. 32.

51. For example, a bibliography of the Hungarian revolution published in 1963 contained 2,136 entries and listed 428 books and 1,608 articles; see I. L. Halasz de Beky, *A Bibliography of the Hungarian Revolution, 1956* (Toronto: University of Toronto Press, 1963). For the period between 1958 and 1965, such a bibliography would contain, at most, a couple dozen entries. A similar situation exists in the case of the Prague Spring. In the Polish case, however, this disproportion is less striking due to the persistence of crisis and the continuous political instability of the country after the imposition of martial law.

52. Jiri Valenta, "Revolutionary Change, Soviet Intervention, and 'Normalization' in East-Central Europe," *Comparative Politics* 16, no. 2 (1984): 128.

53. Jan B. de Weydenthal, Bruce D. Porter, and Kevin Devlin, *The Polish Drama, 1980–1982* (Lexington, Mass.: Lexington Books, 1983), 296.

54. Wlodzimierz Brus, "The Prospect of Normalization in Poland," in Brus, Kende, and Mlynar, *Normalization Processes in Soviet-Dominated Central Europe*, 38.

55. As Laszlo Szemuely points out, "What happened in Hungary in 1957, was not the restoration of the political and economic regime which preceded October 1956; it was not 'normalization' but genuine consolidation." See "The First Wave of the Mechanism Debate in Hungary (1954–1957)," *Acta Oeconomica* 29, nos. 1–2 (1982): 16. Similarly, Zdenek Mlynar argues the "the term 'normalization of the situation' is in fact designed to obscure the reality of the forced restoration of a Soviet-type socio-political system" ("Normalization in Czechoslovakia," 3).

56. Linz (*Crisis, Breakdown and Reequilibration*, 87) applies the concept of reequilibration to the breakdown and reconstitution of democratic regimes and emphasizes the elite-level conditions and legitimacy requirements. The application of the concept to nondemocratic regimes implies a modification of reequilibration's conditions. First of all, it requires effective demobilization of challenging groups and forces, the restoration of institutional coherence of the party-state, and what is particularly important in dependent East European regimes, the acceptance and support of the Soviet leaders for a new leadership.

57. Pierre Kende, "The Post-1956 Hungarian Normalization," in Wlodzimierz Brus, Pierre Kende, and Zdenek Mlynar, *Normalization Processes in Soviet-Dominated Central Europe*, 11.

58. See Charles Bright and Susan Harding, "Processes of Statemaking and Popular Protest: An Introduction," in *Statemaking and Social Movements*, ed. Charles Bright and Susan Harding (Ann Arbor: University of Michigan Press, 1984), 5.

59. According to Jacques Rupnik, "the drastic changes in the role of the Communist Party and the State after the fall of A. Dubcek in April 1969 were proportional to those undertaken by the party during the Czechoslovak reform movement of 1968" ("The Restoration of the Party-State in Czechoslovakia since 1968," in *The Withering Away of the State*, ed. Leslie Holmes (London: Sage, 1981), 105). Similarly, in Poland the scope of institutional and political changes introduced after martial law significantly reshaped the institutional framework of the regime, the composition of political elites, the legal system, and the functioning of the economy. These innovations clearly surpassed the changes gained during the Solidarity period. In Hungary, Kadar's government reintroduced and even perfected certain elements of the Stalinist legacy by accomplishing, for example, the collectivization of agriculture. Yet, in the course of the demobilization process the Hungarian party-state also introduced some important innovations that clearly departed from the Stalinist scenario and laid foundations for the subsequent economic reforms and experimentation with the limited market economy. See Kende, "Post-1956 Hungarian Normalization"; Ferenc Feher, "Kadarism as the Model State of Khrushchevism," *Telos* 40, (1979): 19–31.

60. Anthony Oberschall, *Social Conflicts and Social Movements* (Englewood Cliffs: Prentice-Hall, 1973), 334.

61. The attempts to account for the similarities and differences between demobilization processes reflect these theoretical limitations of the field, as may be exemplified by Jiri Valenta's assertion that "the complex of factors that has conditioned the evolution toward domestic liberalization in Hungary and the retardation of the same process in Czechoslovakia include, in particular, the changing political climates in the USSR and Eastern Europe, Soviet perceptions of the overall domestic situations in the two countries, actual Soviet policies, Kadar's and Husak's personalities, and factional struggles within their leadership" ("Soviet Policy Toward Hungary and Czechoslovakia," in *Soviet Policy in Eastern Europe*, ed. Sarah M. Terry [New Haven: Yale University Press, 1984], 110–11). As this quotation illustrates, the main factors shaping demobilization policies lie within the geopolitical dimension and the intra-elite struggles at the pinnacle of political institutions, with a characteristic underestimation of other domestic factors and social realities underlying the processes of political demobilization. See also Zvi Gitelman, "The Politics of Socialist Restoration in Hungary and Czechoslovakia," in *Revolutions: Theoretical,*

Comparative, and Historical Studies, ed. Jack A. Goldstone (San Diego: Harcourt Brace Jovanovich, 1986), 268–80.

62. Most existing comparative works were written before 1980. As a result only the Hungarian and Czech crises are compared, sometimes with other, more limited crises. In one such work, Maria Hirszowicz (*Coercion and Control in Communist Societies* [Brighton: Wheatsheaf Books, 1986]) attempts to distinguish between "political normalization" (Poland 1956 and 1970) and "normalization based on military intervention" (Hungary 1956 and Czechoslovakia 1968). She argues that these two types of normalization are likely to produce contrasting regularities and consequences—liberalization and concessions in the later type and regressive tendencies and repressions in the former. This hypothesis, however, is questionable, given the case of Poland in 1980–81.

63. According to Zdenek Suda, the reason post-invasion Czechoslovakia "has not followed the example of Hungary or Poland after 1956 and indeed not even explored the room for independent policies . . . lies to a large extent in Gustav Husak's personality. Husak is not Janos Kadar, however similar certain aspects of the personal histories of the two men may be" ("Czechoslovakia: An Aborted Reform," in *East Central Europe* ed. Milorad M. Drachkovitch (Stanford: Hoover Institution Press, 1982), 258–59). Even such a knowledgeable scholar as Vladimir Kusin expresses regrets that Husak's "moderate intentions" were changed "beyond recognition." He blames Husak for the severity of Czechoslovak "normalization," claiming that "Husak has thus failed to make an imprint of his own on the decade of his rule. History books will remember him for unfulfilled promise. It is a pity; Czechoslovakia has been ripe for Kadarization since 1969–70, and Husak could have played the leading role" (*From Dubcek to Charter 77: A Study of "Normalization" in Czechoslovakia, 1968–1978* (Edinburgh: Q Press 1978), 667).

64. The theoretically compelling argument concerning the importance of leaders in monocentric polities was presented by Stanislaw Ossowski, "O osobliwosciach nauk spolecznych," in *Dziela* (Warszawa: PWN, 1967), 4:173–94.

65. Joel S. Migdal, *Strong Societies and Weak States* (Princeton: Princeton University Press, 1988), 263.

66. Jiri Valenta, "Soviet Policy," 108. See also Jiri Valenta, "Military Interventions: Doctrines, Motives, Goals, and Outcomes," in *Dominant Powers and Subordinate States: The United States in Latin America and the Soviet Union in Eastern Europe*, ed. Jan F. Triska (Durham: Duke University Press, 1986), 261–84.

67. Andrzej Korbonski, "Soviet–East European Relations in the 1980s: Continuity and Change," in *Continuity and Change in Soviet–East European Relations*, ed. Marco Carnovale and William C. Potter (Boulder: Westview Press 1989), 16. See also Terry, ed., *Soviet Policy in Eastern Europe*, and Karen Dawisha, *Eastern Europe, Gorbachev, and Reform* (Cambridge: Cambridge University Press, 1990).

68. See Feher, "Kadarism as the Model State"; and Ferenc Feher, "Kadarism as Applied Khrushchevism," in *Khrushchev and the Communist World*, ed. by Robert F. Miller and Ferenc Feher (London: Croom Helm, 1984), 210–279.

69. See Kende, "Post-1956 Hungarian Normalization."

70. See Jiri Valenta, "Soviet Policy" and "Revolutionary Change."

71. Kende, "Post-1956 Hungarian Normalization," 6.

72. Csaba Bekes, "New Findings on the 1956 Hungarian Revolution," *Cold War International History Project Bulletin* 2 (Fall 1992), 3; and Janos M. Rainer, "The Reprisals," *New Hungarian Quarterly* 33, no. 127 (1992): 118–27. For the former

estimates, see George Urban, "Hungary 1957–1961," Background and Current Situation, RFE Special Report (May 16, 1961), 19–20.

73. Mark Kramer, "The Prague Spring and the Soviet Invasion of Czechoslovakia: New Interpretations," *Cold War International History Project Bulletin* 3 (Fall 1993): 10.

74. See Kusin, *From Dubcek to Charter 77*, 11–13, and Vladimir Kusin, "Challenge to Normalcy: Political Opposition in Czechoslovakia, 1968–1977," in *Opposition in Eastern Europe*, ed. Rudolf L. Tokes (Baltimore: Johns Hopkins University Press, 1979), 42.

75. See Helsinki Watch Committee, *Violation of Human Rights in Poland, 1985* (London: Libra Books, 1985), 46, 74.

76. The concept of a new social contract was introduced by Antonin Liehm ("Intellectuals on the New Social Contract," *Telos* 23 [1975]: 156–64; *Nowa Umowa Spoleczna* [Warszawa: NOWA, 1978]; "The New Social Contract and the Parallel Polity," in *Dissent in Eastern Europe*, ed. Jane L. Curry [New York: Praeger, 1983]) during the debate concerning demobilization policies in Czechoslovakia and has become one of the most widely accepted explanatory concept in the field during the 1970s and 1980s. By virtue of its generality, the notion of a new social contract (the concept may be understood as a description of a general mechanism of maintaining stability in Soviet-type societies) is used to explain three quite different situations. First, it is employed to explain the effectiveness of demobilization policies in Czechoslovakia and to account for the relative passivity and compliance of the Czech population. Second, it is also used to explain the transition of Kadar's regime from a highly repressive period of demobilization policies to more "liberal" and softer strategies of demobilization. Finally, it is used to explain a specificity of the Polish case where the failure of the Polish regime to pursue effective demobilization policies is linked to the crisis in the Polish economy and the lack of capacity to provide the population with significant economic concessions.

77. Alain Touraine, "An Introduction to the Study of Social Movements," *Social Research* 52, no. 4 (1985): 753.

78. See Pierre Birnbaum, *States and Collective Action* (Cambridge: Cambridge University Press, 1988), 5.

79. Sidney Tarrow, "National States and Collective Action," *States and Social Structures Newsletter* 5 (1987): 2.

80. See, for example, Arend Lijphart, "Comparative Politics and the Comparative Method," *American Political Science Review* 65, no. 3 (1971): 682–93, and "The Comparable-Case Strategy in Comparative Research," *Comparative Political Studies* 8 (1975): 158–77.

81. See Charles C. Ragin, *The Comparative Method* (Berkeley: University of California Press, 1987), ix, 2–3.

82. David D. Laitin, "Hegemony and the State," *States and Social Structures Newsletter* 9 (Winter 1989): 3.

83. See Stefano Bartolini, "On Time and Comparative Research," *Journal of Theoretical Politics* 5, no. 2 (1993): 157–60.

84. Nancy Bermeo defines political learning as "the process through which people modify their political beliefs and tactics as a result of severe crises, frustrations, and dramatic changes in environment." She argues that "crises often force people to reevaluate the ideas that they have used as guides to action in the past. The changed ideas may relate to tactics, parties, allies, enemies, or institutions. The new ideas may

be true or false, justified or unjustified, polarizing or compromising. Their relevance . . . derives . . . from the fact that they are believed and used as guidelines for behavior" ("Democracy and the Lessons of Dictatorship," *Comparative Politics* 24, no. 3 (April 1992): 274.

85. For the purpose of my analysis I shall disregard the notion of demobilization that may be derived from natural history of social movements where demobilization is considered to be a typical phase in the life cycle of any social or political movement.

86. Tilly, *From Mobilization to Revolution*, 217.

87. Birnbaum, *States and Collective Action*, 35.

88. State capacity is defined here, following Karen Barkey and Sunita Parikh, "as the state's ability to implement strategies to achieve its economic, political, or social goals in society." They argue: "The state may acquire capacity through institutions such as the bureaucracy, or through resources such as external ties to entrepreneurs and finance capital [but it is also] determined by the state's relation to society. Resources, organization and state-society relations are constantly interacting with each other; these interactions in turn reshape the nature of state autonomy and capacity" ("Comparative Perspectives on the State," *Annual Review of Sociology* 17 [1991], 526). To apply this concept to state-socialist regimes, however, the notion of external ties has to include economic and political ties to the Soviet state. For dependent countries of Eastern Europe, resources provided by the Soviet Union often were more important than those offered by domestic actors.

89. The central political process under state-socialist regimes was often identified as all-pervasive political mobilization induced by the state and designed to enhance the political control, resources, and capacity of the state. The reason stated by many scholars for relying on political mobilization was directly linked to the revolutionary origin of these regimes. Robert Tucker, for example, emphasizing the mobilizational capacities and strategies of Soviet-type regimes, qualified them as "movement-regimes" ("Towards a Comparative Politics of Movement Regimes," *American Political Science Review* 55, no. 2 (1961): 281–89).

90. See Hankiss, "Demobilization, Self-Mobilization and Quasi-Mobilization."

91. See Jadwiga Staniszkis, *Ontologia socjalizmu*, 96. See also Jan Kubik, "Who Done It: Workers or Intellectuals? Controversy over Solidarity's Origins and Social Composition," *Theory and Society* 23 (1994): 441–66.

92. Tilly, *From Mobilization to Revolution*, 69.

93. Remmer, "Political Demobilization in Chile," 275.

94. Peter Hall, *Governing the Economy: The Politics of State Intervention in Britain and France* (New York: Oxford University Press, 1986), 17.

95. See, for example, Karl W. Deutsch, "Social Mobilization and Political Development," *American Political Science Review* 55, no. 3 (1961): 493–514.

96. See, for example, David Apter, *The Politics of Modernization* (Chicago: University of Chicago Press, 1965); Peter J. Nettl, *Political Mobilization: A Sociological Analysis of Methods and Concepts* (New York: Basic Books, 1967); Samuel P. Huntington, *Political Order in Changing Societies* (New Haven: Yale University Press, 1969).

97. See, for example, Obershall, *Social Conflict and Social Movements*; Tilly, *From Mobilization to Revolution*; Birnbaum, *States and Collective Action*; Scott G. McNall, *The Road to Rebellion: Class Formation and Kansas Populism, 1865–1900* (Chicago: University of Chicago Press, 1988); Craig J. Calhoun, *The Question of Class Struggle: Social Foundations of Popular Radicalism during the Industrial Rev-*

olution (Chicago: University of Chicago Press, 1982). Sidney Tarrow, "Struggle, Politics, and Reform—Collective Action, Social Movements and Cycles of Protest," Western Society Program, Paper No. 21, Ithaca: Cornell University (1989); Roger V. Gould, "Multiple Networks and Mobilization in the Paris Commune, 1871," *American Sociological Review* 56, no. 6 (1991): 716–30.

98. Tilly, *From Mobilization to Revolution*, 62–63.

99. Calhoun, *Question of Class Struggle*, 136.

100. John D. McCarthy and Mayer N. Zald, eds., *The Dynamics of Social Movements: Resource Mobilization, Social Control and Outcomes* (Cambridge: Winthrop, 1977), 1215.

101. This element of a movement's capacity to survive is a crucial one, and often underestimated by scholars. Pierre Birnbaum says that "even nowadays, the theoreticians of mobilization still tend too often to neglect this dimension, which is nevertheless inherent in social action, the ideologies developed by social groups being reducible neither to communal values alone nor to projects emanating from organizations of the associative type" (*States and Collective Action*, 36).

102. McNall, *Road the Rebellion*, 19.

103. Charles Tilly makes a similar observation, arguing that "lightning mobilization, if it occurs, does reduce the chances for the incremental challenging, testing, and coalition-formation which belong to the routine acquisition of power" (*From Mobilization to Revolution*, 201–2).

104. According to Claus Offe, social movements with a weak organization have inherent difficulty surviving even in a nonrepressive political environment. Such movements "have often tried to overcome this difficulty by defining certain days as occasions for collective action ... and certain locations are often charged with symbolic meaning and made the focuses of collective action." But, as Offe argues, "these are obviously weak and primitive methods for securing survival," especially in the situation in which there is a lack of "sufficiently abstract and inclusive definition of the collective identity of actors and their causes" ("Challenging the Boundaries of Institutional Politics," in *Changing Boundaries of the Political*, ed. by Charles S. Maier (Cambridge: Cambridge University Press, 1987), 91–92).

105. The importance of this defensive capability on social movements is suggested by Mayer N. Zald (see "Issues in the Theory of Social Movements," *Current Perspectives in Social Theory* 1 [1980], 68).

106. See Albert Hirschman, *Exit, Voice and Loyalty* (Princeton: Princeton University Press, 1970).

107. For the account of the Soviet involvement in the preparation of martial law, see Ryszard Kuklinski, "Wojna z narodem widziana od srodka," *Kultura* 4, no. 475 (1987): 3–57. See also Wojciech Jaruzelski, *Stan Wojenny* (Warszawa: BGW, 1992), 377–404; Witold Beres and Jerzy Skoczylas, *General Kiszczak mowi . . . Prawie wszystko* (Warszawa: BGW, 1991), 116–23; Jan Widacki, *Czego nie powiedzial General Kiszczak* (Warszawa: BGW, 1992), 135–46; Zbigniew Wlodek, ed., *Tajne dokumenty Biura Politycznego: PZPR a Solidarnosc, 1980–1981* (London: Aneks, 1992).

108. In general, the limits of tolerance applied by the Soviet Union to its client party-states was shaped by a variety of considerations. Most Western scholars have concluded that in a situation of domestic conflict the Soviet state resorted to military interventions only when certain ideological and military-strategic issues were at stake. Some scholars, for example, Christopher Jones ("Soviet Hegemony in Eastern

Europe: The Dynamics of Political Autonomy and Military Intervention," *World Politics* 29, no. 2 [1977]: 216–41), maintain that the only issue at stake was control over the local communist party. It seems, however, that these limits depend on a number of factors peculiar to the country and time and to the nature of the leadership in the Kremlin in a given moment (Charles Gati, *Hungary and the Soviet Bloc* [Durham: Duke University Press, 1986]; Jiri Valenta, *Soviet Intervention in Czechoslovakia, 1968* [Baltimore: Johns Hopkins University Press, 1979]; Terry ed., *Soviet Policy in Eastern Europe*).

109. The decision to use military force, as many scholars pointed out, was preceded by a prolonged and conflictual process of reaching a bureaucratic consensus within the power elites (see Jiri Valenta, *Soviet Intervention*; Michael G. Fry and Condolenzza Rice, "The Hungarian Crisis of 1956: The Soviet Decision," *Studies in Comparative Communism* 16, nos. 1–2 (1983): 85–98; Janos M. Rainer, "The Yeltsin Dossier: Soviet Documents on Hungary, 1956," *Cold War International History Project Bulletin*, no. 5 (Spring 1995): 22, 27–27..

110. Ken Jowitt, "Moscow 'Centre,'" *East European Politics and Societies* 1, no. 3 (1987): 296–352.

111. According to James F. Brown: "Cohesion in this context means a situation where—allowing for some degree of diversity caused by differing local conditions—there is a general conformity of both domestic and foreign policies as well as an identification of the institutions implementing these policies in both the Soviet Union and its East European dependencies. Viability can be defined as a degree of confidence, credibility, and efficiency in the East European states that would increasingly legitimize Communist rule there and consequently reduce the Soviet need for a preemptive preoccupation with the region" (*Eastern Europe and Communist Rule* (Durham: Duke University Press, 1988), 42).

112. Eric P. Hoffmann, "Soviet Foreign Policy Aims and Accomplishments from Lenin to Brezhnev," in *Soviet Foreign Policy: Classic and Contemporary Issues*, ed. Frederic J. Fleron Jr., Eric P. Hoffmann, and Robbin F. Laird (Hawthorne: Aldine de Gruyter, 1991), 50.

113. See James F. Brown, "The East European Setting," in *Eroding Empire*, ed. Lincoln Gordon (Washington, D.C.: Brookings Institution, 1987), 19.

114. William Zimmerman, "Soviet Foreign Policy and World Politics," in *Soviet Foreign Policy*, ed. Fleron, Hoffmann, and Laird, 124.

115. Jan F. Triska, "Introduction," in *Dominant Powers and Subordinate States*, ed. Triska, 9–10.

116. Cal Clark and Donna Bahry, "Dependent Development: A Socialist Variant," *International Studies Quarterly* 27, no. 3 (1983): 271–93.

117. See Valerie Bunce, "The Empire Strikes Back: The Evolution of the Eastern Bloc from a Soviet Asset to a Soviet Liability," *International Organization* 39, no. 1 (1985): 1–46; Paul Marer and Kazimierz Poznanski, "Costs of Domination, Benefits of Subordination," in *Dominant Powers and Subordinate States*, ed. Triska, 371–99; Keith Crane, "Soviet Economic Policy towards Eastern Europe," in *Continuity and Change in Soviet–East European Relations*, ed. Carnovale and Potter, 75–111.

118. See William Pfaff, "Reflections: Where the Wars Come From," *New Yorker*, Dec. 26, 1988, pp. 83–91.

119. See Paul M. Kennedy, *The Rise and Fall of Great Powers* (New York: Random House, 1987).

PART I

1. Charles Gati, *Hungary and the Soviet Bloc* (Durham: Duke University Press, 1986), 158.

2. Sandor Balogh and Sandor Jakab, *The History of Hungary after the Second World War, 1944–1980* (Budapest: Corvina, 1986), 171.

3. *Hungary Today* (New York: Praeger, 1962), 3.

4. In spite of the myth of Kadar as enlightened reformer, it should be stressed that he never went beyond the reform program drafted by the Hungarian Stalinist leadership in 1953 (see Jerzy R. Nowak, *Wegry: Burzliwe lata, 1953–1956* [Warszawa: Almapress, 1988], 83; William Robinson, *The Pattern of Reform in Hungary* [New York: Praeger, 1973], 7–12). In some respects he did not go as far as his Stalinist predecessors. During the decades of Kadar's reign, his regime introduced few political reforms. Also the 1968 economic reforms did not initiate any significant structural changes that could set Hungary apart from other East European state-socialist regimes. What really changed in Hungary was a shift in political and economic practices that did not produce and depend on any significant structural changes of the polity and economy and any real extension of liberties. These more liberal practices and relative tolerance were, however, always overshadowed by the threat of return to direct political repression. This potential or latent repressiveness was in the view of many scholars the main condition of political stability in Hungary for the decades that followed the revolution. See Bill Lomax, "Hungary—The Quest for Legitimacy," in *Eastern Europe: Political Crisis and Legitimation*, ed. Paul G. Lewis (New York: St. Martin's Press, 1984), 68–109, and Istvan Lovas and Ken Anderson, "State Terrorism in Hungary: The Case of Friendly Repression," *Telos* 54 (1982–83): 77–87.

5. See Andrzej Korbonski, "The Revolution and East Central Europe," in *The First War between Socialist States: The Hungarian Revolution of 1956 and Its Impact*, ed. by Bela K. Kiraly, Barbara Lotze, and Nanador F. Dreisziger (New York: Brooklyn College Press, 1984), 355–69.

6. Gati, *Hungary and the Soviet Bloc*, 159.

7. I shall use selectively the following sources in order to present the background and illustrate the analytical points and arguments. The first are official Marxist interpretations of the events advanced in Hungary and other East European societies. See, for example, Janos Berecz, *1956, Counter-Revolution in Hungary* (Budapest: Akademiai Kiado, 1986); Janos Molnar, *A Nagybudapesti Kozponti Munkastanacs* (Budapest: Akademiai Kiado, 1969); Ivan Szenes, *A kommunista part ujjaszervezese Magyarorszagon, 1956–1957* (Budapest: Kossuth Konyvkiado, 1976); Janos Molnar, *Ellenforradalom Magyarorszagon, 1956-ban* (Budapest: Akademiai Kiado, 1967); Arpad Szabo, *A Magyar Forradalmi Honved Karhatalom* (Budapest: Zrinyi Katonai Kiado, 1976); and Nowak, *Wegry*. Although these are expedient and ideologically and politically tainted, they can nevertheless provide some useful details and facts. The second group of works lists Western scholarship on the revolution. See, for example, Ferenc A. Vali, *Rift and Revolt in Hungary* (Cambridge: Harvard University Press, 1961); Paul E. Zinner, *Revolution in Hungary* (Freeport: Books for Libraries Press, 1962); Bill Lomax, *Hungary, 1956* (New York: St. Martin's Press, 1976). On the Hungarian economic reforms introduced in 1968, see Robinson, *Pattern*. The third source list consists of papers written for collections prepared for the

tenth and twentieth anniversaries of the revolution. See, for example, Tamas Aczel, ed., *Ten Years After* (London: Macgibbon & Kee, 1966); Francis Wagner, ed., *The Hungarian Revolution in Perspective* (Washington, D.C.: F. F. Memorial Foundation, 1967); Bela K. Kiraly and Paul Jonas, eds., *The Hungarian Revolution of 1956 in Retrospect* (Boulder: East European Quarterly, 1978), and occasional articles in journals. While the literature on the revolution is immense, only a few more systematic accounts of the demobilization period can be found. See George R. Urban, "Hungary, 1957–1961: Background and Current Situation" (Radio Free Europe, Special Report, May 16, 1961); Janos Kis, "The Restoration of 1956–1957 in a Thirty Year Perspective," in his *Politics in Hungary: For a Democratic Alternative* (New York: Columbia University Press, 1989), 31–84; Andrew Felkay, *Hungary and USSR, 1956–1988* (New York: Greenwood Press, 1989); and Gati, *Hungary and the Soviet Bloc.* Finally, I shall include post-1989 analyses based on newly discovered information. See, for example, Bill Lomax, ed., *Hungarian Workers' Councils in 1956* (New York: Columbia University Press, 1990); Csaba Bekes, "New Findings on the 1956 Hungarian Revolution," *Cold War International History Project Bulletin* 2 (1992); Janos M. Rainer, "The Yeltsin Dossier: Soviet Documents on Hungary, 1956," *Cold War International History Project Bulletin* 5 (Spring 1995): 22, 24–27; Daniel F. Calhoun, *Hungary and Suez, 1956: An Exploration of Who Makes History* (Lanham: University Press of America, 1991); Johanna Granville, "Imre Nagy, Hesitant Revolutionary," *Cold War International History Project Bulletin* 5 (Spring 1995): 23, 27–37.

8. Janos Kis, "The End and the Beginning," in his *Politics in Hungary: For a Democratic Alternative* (New York: Columbia University Press, 1989), 9.

CHAPTER 2

1. See, Joseph Rothschild, *Return to Diversity* (New York: Oxford University Press, 1989), 76–125. For a more detailed analyses of the immediate postwar period in Hungary, see Charles Gati, "The Democratic Interlude in Post-War Hungary," *Survey* 28, no. 2 (1984): 99–134), which provides a well-documented overview of the political dimension of Hungarian developments during the first three years, and Part One of his book *Hungary and the Soviet Bloc,* 13–123. Similarly, Andrew B. Gollner, "Foundations of Soviet Domination and Communist Political Power in Hungary, 1945–1950," *Canadian-American Review of Hungarian Studies* 3, no. 2 (1976): 73–105, offers an interesting analysis that emphasizes the economic dimension the Soviet and the HWP policies during the same period. For more general accounts see Hugh Seton-Watson, *The East-European Revolution* (New York: Praeger, 1956); Peter A. Toma and Ivan Volgyes, *Politics in Hungary* (San Francisco: Freeman, 1977); Bennett Kovrig, *Communism in Hungary: From Kun to Kadar* (Stanford: Hoover Institution Press, 1979); Miklos Molnar, *From Bela Kun to Janos Kadar* (New York: Berg 1990).

2. Rothschild, *Return to Diversity*, 98.

3. In the 1945 parliamentary election, six participating political parties acquired the following share of popular vote: Smallholders 57 percent, Social Democrats 17.4 percent, Communists 17 percent, National Peasants 6.9 percent, Citizen Democrats 1.6 percent, and Radicals 0.9 percent. In spite of these results, on the basis of the agreement with the Soviets, the Smallholders party was not allowed to form the government and the Communists remained in control of the crucial ministries. In

the 1947 parliamentary elections, four new parties entered the contest, pulling away the popular vote from the Smallholders. This time the votes were divided in the following way: Communists 22.3 percent, Democratic Populist (Catholic) 16.4 percent, Smallholders 15.4 percent, Social Democrats 14.9 percent, Independence party 13.4 percent, National Peasants 8.3 percent, list headed by priest Istvan Balogh 5.2 percent, Radicals 1.7 percent, Christian Women's League 1.4 percent, and Citizen Democrats 1.0 percent. In spite of these results, however, the Hungarian Workers party, backed by the Soviet Military Command, controlled key elements of state machinery from the very beginning: the Ministry of Interior and the Supreme Economic Council—a supra-ministerial committee established in 1945 with formidable powers over the economy.

4. For the compelling presentation of this argument see Gati, "Democratic Interlude." See also Gollner, "Foundations of Soviet Domination"; and Rothschild, *Return to Diversity*, 97–104.

5. According to Peter Toma and Ivan Volgyes (*Politics in Hungary*, 5), in 1945 and 1946 approximately twenty-five thousand Hungarians were tried as war criminals by the people's courts and about 2 percent of those were executed. Between January 1945 and March 1948, a total of 39,514 Hungarians were brought to trial for political offenses and 19,273 were convicted.

6. Gollner, "Foundations of Soviet Domination," 85. After the Communists consolidated their power in 1948, the outstanding war reparations to the Soviet Union were reduced by half.

7. In 1946 gross industrial production was below 60 percent of its value in 1938, and the average wages of urban workers were about 50 percent of the 1938 level. See Ferenc Erdei ed., *Information Hungary* (Budapest: Akademiai Kiado, 1968), 297.

8. For a detailed analysis of Communist policies against the churches during this period, see Robert Tobias, *Communist-Christian Encounter in East Europe* (Indianapolis: School of Religion Press, 1956); Steven Polgar, "A Summary of the Situation of the Hungarian Catholic Church," *Religion in Communist Lands* 12, no. 1 (1984): 11–41; Miklos Tomka, "Church and Religion in a Communist State, 1945–1990," *New Hungarian Quarterly* 32, no. 121 (1991): 59–69; Tamas Majsai, "Protestants under Communism," *New Hungarian Quarterly* 32, no. 123 (1991): 58–67.

9. In 1948, all primary and secondary schools administered by churches, communities, or private owners were nationalized, and the nationwide centralized system of eight-year general schools was established. The importance of this action can be illustrated by the fact that before the secularization of schools, the Catholic church alone controlled more than half of all schools in Hungary.

10. Nationalization of the economy was a gradual and carefully designed process. In 1945, land reform was carried through and some important agricultural assets and forests were nationalized. In 1946 coal and bauxite mines were nationalized, and in 1947 so were the banks. Factories and enterprises employing more than one hundred employees were grabbed by the state in 1948. In 1949 firms employing more than ten people were expropriated by the state. In the process, the handicraft industry and private retail trade were destroyed. According to Ferenc Erdei (*Information Hungary*, 301), the number of those engaged in handicraft, which at the end of 1948 had been 339,000, dropped to 53,000 by February 1953.

11. Paul E. Zinner, *Revolution in Hungary* (Freeport: Books for Libraries Press, 1962), 127.

12. By 1953 production fell below the 1949 level (see Erdei, *Information*, 356) and more than 10 percent of tillable land was left uncultivated (see Janos Berecz, *1956, Counter-Revolution in Hungary* [Budapest: Akademiai Kiado, 1986], 37).

13. The development of a country of steel was the professed goal of the plan, and as Janos Berecz (*1956, Counter-Revolution*, 36) admits, at the beginning of the first five-year plan, expenditures for military and civilian purposes were almost identical. Moreover, the mechanism of central planning brought havoc to industrial production. In 1953 alone the yearly plan was corrected 225 times. In the letter to the head of Planning Office written in 1956, the Statistical Office head confessed that because of several thousand changes introduced to the plan, the office no longer knew the objectives of the plan. See Jerzy R. Nowak, *Wegry: Wychodzenie z kryzysu, 1956* (Warszawa: Ksiazka i Wiedza, 1984), 13.

14. The extent of the political terror during the Stalinist period is astonishing for a country with a population of around ten million. The number of political prisoners reached 150,000 at the beginning of the 1950s, and at least two thousand people were executed. Between 1952 and 1955, more than 10 percent of the Hungarian population was in one way or another the subject of police action (see Ferenc A. Vali, *Rift and Revolt in Hungary* [Cambridge: Harvard University Press, 1961], 64; Berecz, *1956, Counter-Revolution*, 35). In political purges during the Stalinist period, more than 350,000 members of the Communist party were expelled, and more Communists were executed between 1949 and 1953 than under the Horthy regime (see Gollner, "Foundations of Soviet Domination," 97; Zinner, *Revolution in Hungary*, 131–38). Even the membership of the party's Central Committee did not give any guarantees. Of ninety-two men elected to it at the party congresses in 1948 and 1951, forty-six had been removed by 1954. See David Pryce-Jones, *The Hungarian Revolution* (London: Ernest Benn, 1969), 36.

15. For example, until the purges of state bureaucracies that started in 1947, 80 percent of all officeholders were old Horthyite bureaucrats (see Rothschild, *Return to Diversity*, 98).

16. Rothschild, *Return to Diversity*, 153.

17. With 1949 as 100, per capita real income of worker and employee populations was 102.8 in 1950, 97.8 in 1951, 87.5 in 1952, 91.0 in 1953, 115.0 in 1954, 121.8 in 1955, and 129.3 in 1956. See Nigel Swain, *Hungary: The Rise and Fall of Feasible Socialism* (London: Verso, 1992), 83. For data on trade and investment distribution, see Swain, *Hungary*, 76–79.

18. In 1954 a number of people employed in the state administration was three times higher than at the end of 1930s, reaching 280,000. A similar situation affected the economy. In machine-making industry alone, the number of administration employees rose by 357 percent over 1938, reaching 243,000, while at the same time the number of workers rose only by 212 percent (Nowak, *Wegry: Burzliwe lata, 1953–1956* [Warszawa: Almapress, 1988], 57).

19. See Lomax, "Hungary—The Quest for Legitimacy," in *Eastern Europe: Political Crisis and Legitimation*, ed. Paul G. Lewis (New York: St. Martin's Press, 1984), 72.

20. Quoted in Bill Lomax, "The Hungarian Revolution of 1956 and the Origin of the Kadar Regime," *Studies in Comparative Communism* 18, nos. 2–3 (1985): 89.

21. George Schopflin, *Politics in Eastern Europe, 1945–1992* (Oxford: Blackwell, 1993), 105.

22. In his speech Nagy promised to curtail irresponsible industrialization, forced

collectivization and police terror. He promised to increase of the production of consumer goods and agricultural investments, improve living standards, and a return to collective leadership and socialist legality. Peasants were permitted to leave collective farms, and small businessmen and artisans to reopen their shops. He assured that police terror would be relaxed, deportation stopped, concentration camps liquidated, and political prisoners granted amnesty. He also promised better treatment of the middle class and intelligentsia. See William Juhasz, ed., *Hungarian Social Science Reader, 1945–63* (New York: Aurora Editions, 1965), 156–63.

23. Lomax, "Hungarian Revolution," 90. See also Bill Lomax, "25 Years Later—New Light on 1956," *Labour Focus on Eastern Europe 5*, nos. 3–4 (1982): 14–16. This issue includes also Nagy's famous secret speech delivered during the June 27 Central Committee meeting (8–10).

24. Bill Lomax, "Hungarian Revolution," 91.

25. Initially new measures brought some improvements in agriculture and light industry. The production of consumer goods rose 12.4 percent. Also by cutting investments, lowering prices of many goods, and raising wages, living standards of the population were boosted. In 1954 the real wages of workers and state employees increased by 15 percent (see Nowak, *Wegry: Burzliwe lata*, 50).

26. Nagy's fall is commonly associated with the ouster in the Soviet Union in March 1955 of Malenkov, who was considered to be a main proponent of more consumption-oriented economic policies. However, as one of the Hungarian leaders during that time argues, most of authors link the struggle between Rakosi and Nagy "to personal conflicts within the Moscow leadership, while neglecting its deeper roots which existed in Hungary." See Andras Hegedus, "Additional Remarks by a Major Participant in the Hungarian Revolution of 1956," *Studies in Comparative Communism* 18, nos. 2–3 (1985): 118.

27. According to Lomax (*Hungary, 1956* [New York: St. Martin's Press, 1976], 51): "The majority of the opposition members . . . were drawn from those younger intellectuals who had enthusiastically joined the Communist Party . . . soon to become the most loyal and uncritical disciples of Stalinism. Once disillusioned by the revelations of the early fifties, it was these former militants who were destined to become the most passionate and determined opponents of the regime and the pacesetter of the opposition."

28. Paul Jonas, "Economic Aspect," in *The Hungarian Revolution of 1956 in Retrospect*, ed. Bela K. Kiraly and Paul Jonas (Boulder: East European Quarterly, 1978), 36.

29. Paul Kecskemeti, *The Unexpected Revolution* (Stanford: Stanford University Press, 1961), 1.

30. Tamas Aczel, "Intellectual Aspect," in *The Hungarian Revolution of 1956 in Retrospect*, ed. Kiraly and Jones, 32.

31. For the analysis of the Soviet involvement, see Andrew Felkay, *Hungary and USSR, 1956–1988* (New York: Greenwood Press, 1989), 54–55.

32. Lomax, "Hungarian Revolution," 94.

33. Vali, *Rift and Revolt*, 209.

34. Schopflin, *Politics in Eastern Europe*, 125–26.

35. Zinner, *Revolution in Hungary*, 106. Miklos Molnar makes a similar point when he argues that "the cause of the HCP's impotence was not of a material nature. Nor was it a political error or a poor analysis of the situation. It was of moral impotence. If the situation had been misjudged, the total demoralization of the party was

at the root of the misjudgment." *A Short History of the Hungarian Communist Party* (Boulder: Westview Press, 1978), 120–21.

36. Miklos Molnar, "The Heritage of Imre Nagy," in *Ten Years After*, ed. Tamas Aczel (London: Macgibbon and Kee, 1966), 162.

37. Miklos Molnar, *Budapest, 1956* (London: Allen and Unwin, 1971), 266.

38. The top party-state leadership clearly did not anticipate such a development. According to Janos Berecz, "In Budapest, for example, there were practically no combat-ready garrison troops, nor was there any defense plan for the special armed forces to counter an armed attack launched by the domestic enemy" (*1956, Counter-Revolution*, 114).

39. Lomax, *Hungary, 1956*, 115.

40. See Csaba Bekes, "New Findings on the 1956 Hungarian Revolution," *Cold War International History Project Bulletin* 2 (1992).

41. The only major case of a direct armed assault on the party institutions was an obscure siege of the party's Budapest city headquarters launched by the marginal insurgent groups on October 30. The siege ended up in the brutal shooting of many defenders of the building (mostly AVH functionaries), including the secretary of the party in Budapest Imre Mezo (see Lomax, *Hungary, 1956*, 124–28).

42. Molnar, *Short History*, 121. The paralysis of the Central Committee of the party during the first four days of the revolution is illustrated by the failure to implement plans for the joint Hungarian and Soviet military action against the insurgent centers that were prepared by the special military committee appointed by the Central Committee. Only on October 28 were the hard-liners within the Central Committee effectively defeated, and Nagy was finally able to establish his authority over the leading bodies of the party. The various plans for an internal military solution, however, were draw up by the military committee and finally abandoned only after the Soviet leaders decided to invade Hungary (see Lomax, "Hungarian Revolution," 96–98).

43. See Molnar, *Short History*, 59.

44. Quoted in Nowak, *Wegry: Burzliwe*, 164. The vivid illustration of this collapse is the fact that on December 1, 1956, the new Hungarian Socialist Workers Party established shortly after the Soviet intervention listed only 37,818 members (see Molnar, *Short History*, 48). Moreover, when the provisional Central Committee of the HSWP met for the first time on November 11, it had only twenty-three members, who represented wide spectrum of views ranging from those favouring an accommodation with Imre Nagy and reformers to those seeking a Stalinist restoration. In February 1957, the party's Central Committee still had a mere thirty-seven members, down from seventy-one before the revolution (see Thomas Schreiber, "Changes in the Leadership," in *Hungary Today* [Durham: Duke University Press, 1986], 45, and Lomax, "Hungarian Revolution," 107).

45. Lomax, *Hungary, 1956*, 96–98.

46. Lomax, *Hungary, 1956*, 128.

47. The formations of the Frontier Guards were established after 1948 and placed under the control of the Ministry of Interior and the security police. The Guards were organized in eleven area commands, each of which comprised three to four mobile battalions (see Bela K. Kiraly, "The Hungarian Revolution and Soviet Readiness to Wage War against Socialist States," in *The First War between Socialist States*, ed. Kiraly, Lotze, and Dreisziger, 13). See also Vali, *Rift and Revolt*, 72, and

Laszlo Nagy, "Military Aspects of the Hungarian Revolution," *Saturn* 3, no. 5 (1957): 15.

48. Published in Paul E. Zinner, ed., *National Communism and Popular Revolt in Eastern Europe* (New York: Columbia University Press 1956), 408.

49. See Berecz, *1956, Counter-Revolution*, 120, and Tibor Meray, *That Day in Budapest* (New York: Funk and Wagnalls, 1969), 274.

50. Meray, *That Day*, 265.

51. For his personal account of the revolution, see Sandor Kopacsi, *In the Name of Working Class* (New York: Grove Press, 1987).

52. Kiraly ("Hungarian Revolution," 12) points out that "in September 1948, the Hungarian *honvedseg* had consisted of two undermanned, under equipped rifle divisions and one engineering division. No armored forces or air forces had existed to speak of. The honvedseg had been purposefully left to disintegrate and amounted to nothing that would warrant being called an army." For a brief overview of the situation of the Hungarian army in the years before the revolution, see Ivan Volgyes, "Hungary," in *Soviet Allies: The Warsaw Pact and the Issue of Reliability*, ed. Daniel N. Nelson (Boulder: Westview Press, 1984), 184–92, and Bela K. Kiraly, "Hungary's Army under the Soviets," *East Europe* 7 (1958): 3–14.

53. See, for example, Jonathan R. Adelman, *Revolutions, Armies and War: A Political History* (Boulder: Lynne Rienner, 1985), and Theda Skocpol, "Social Revolutions and Mass Military Mobilizations," chap. 12 in her *Social Revolutions in the Modern World* (Cambridge: Cambridge University Press, 1994).

54. Berecz, *1956, Counter-Revolution*, 119.

55. Ibid., 114.

56. Meray, *That Day*, 262.

57. Kiraly, "Hungarian Revolution," 22.

58. See Philip Selznick, *The Organizational Weapon* (New York: McGraw-Hill, 1952). For the discussion of the nature and role of auxiliary institutions in fascist and communist regimes, see Amos Perlmutter, *Modern Authoritarianism* (New Haven: Yale University Press, 1981), 12–16.

59. See Leszek Nowak, *Property and Power: Toward Non-Marxist Historical Materialism* (Dordrecht: Reidel, 1983).

60. See Elemer Hankiss, "Demobilization, Self-Mobilization, and Quasi-Mobilization, 1948–1987," *East European Politics and Societies* 3, no. 1 (1989): 106–8.

61. For the insightful discussion of the stabilizing role of social organizations under Chinese communist regime, see Andrew Walder, *Communist Neo-Traditionalism: Work and Authority in Chinese Industry* (Berkeley: California University Press, 1986).

62. *Szabad Nep*, Aug. 28, 1956.

63. Among these new youth organizations some were influenced by the religious considerations such as the KISZ (Christian Youth Association) and others by the revolutionary ideals, such as the Hungarian Revolutionary Youth Party, the Revolutionary Young Workers' Association, and the Hungarian Unified Youth Association.

64. Radio Free Europe, Background Reports, Jan. 17, 1957, p. 3.

65. Lomax, *Hungary, 1956*, 71.

66. For the government and party statements on Oct. 28, 1956, see Zinner ed., *National Communism and Popular Revolt in Eastern Europe*, 428–32.

67. *Szabad Nep*, Oct. 29, 1956.

68. General Bela Kiraly, the leader of the council, described the organizational difficulties faced by the military leaders: "The existing Armed Forces had to be turned into organizations loyal to the revolutionary government; the unreliable organizations had to be dissolved; spontaneously created freedom-fighter groups, which had already proven themselves in battle, had to be organized into one single new force." As a result the National Guard was formed, which unified and integrated freedom-fighter groups and those army and police units that had joined the revolution during the first several days. On Oct. 31, the consolidation of the major freedom-fighter groups into the National Guard and establishment of its central headquarters were successfully concluded. On Nov. 3, the Frontier Guard units were integrated into the Army ("The Organization of National Defense during the Hungarian Revolution," *Central European Federalist* 14, no. 1 [1966]: 14, 19).

69. Wiktor Woroszylski, *Dziennik Wegierski, 1956* (Warszawa: Biblioteka Wiezi, 1990), 33.

70. Hungarian Peoples Republic, *The Counter-Revolutionary Conspiracy of Imre Nagy and His Accomplices* (Budapest: Information Bureau of the Council of Ministers, 1958), 101.

71. Several parties, such as the Democratic People's party, the Hungarian Radical party, and the Hungarian Independence party, represented a conservative political current. Others, like the Catholic People's party, the Christian People's party, the Christian Democratic party, the Hungarian Christian party, and the Catholic Alliance, were based on religious inspiration. There were also some far-right parties, such as the Party of Hungarian Revolutionaries (see Lomax, *Hungary, 1956*, 132–36).

72. Bela K. Kiraly, "The Armed Forces and the Working Class in the Hungarian Revolution, 1956," *New Politics* 1, no. 1 (1986): 194.

73. Lomax, *Hungary, 1956*, 140.

74. See Bekes, "New Findings," 2. See also Lomax, ed., *Hungarian Workers' Councils in 1956* (New York: Columbia University Press, 1990).

75. Edmund O. Stillman, *The Ideology of Revolution* (New York: Free Europe Press, 1957), 13.

76. See Bekes, "New Findings," 2.

77. Bill Lomax, *Hungary, 1956*, 74.

78. Woroszylski, *Dziennik*, 20.

79. Quoted in Lomax, *Hungarian Workers' Councils*, xix.

80. Aczel, "Intellectual Aspect," 31.

81. Zinner, *Revolution in Hungary*, 190.

82. Quoted in Lomax, *Hungary, 1956*, 55.

83. Zinner, *Revolution in Hungary*, 191.

84. See *Revolt in Hungary* (New York: Free Europe Press, 1956), 4.

85. Stillman, *Ideology*, 16.

86. Ibid., 25.

87. For the analysis of peculiarities of the communist political discourse, see Jan Kubik, "John Paul II's First Visit to Poland and the Collapse of the Official Marxist-Leninist Discourse," CROPSO Working Paper Series, Harvard University, no. 0025 (1989).

88. For the analysis of relations between Hungarian and Soviet leaders before the revolution see Lomax, "Hungarian Revolution," and Charles Gati, "Imre Nagy and Moscow, 1953–1956," *Problems of Communism* 35, no. 3 (1986): 32–49.

89. Quoted in Janos M. Rainer, "The Yeltsin Dossier: Soviet Documents on Hungary, 1956," *Cold War International History Project Bulletin* 5 (Spring 1995): 25.

90. Ibid.

91. Nagy, "Military Aspects," 13–14.

92. According to Laszlo Nagy, thirty-five tanks and about two thousand men deserted their units during this phase of the revolution ("Military Aspects," 19).

93. On Nov. 1, Khrushchev, Malenkow, and Molotow met with Polish leaders. The next day they met party leaders from Czechoslovakia, Romania, and Bulgaria. Finally Khrushchev met with Tito on the night of Nov. 2–3 to inform him about the planned invasion. For accounts of Soviet actions, see Jiri Valenta, "Soviet Decision Making and the Hungarian Revolution," in *The First War between Socialist States*, ed. Kiraly, Lotze, and Dreisziger, 265–78; Charles Gati, *Hungary and the Soviet Bloc* (Durham: Duke University Press, 1986), 148–55; Lomax, "Hungarian Revolution," 99; and Strobe Talbott, ed., *Khrushchev Remembers* (Boston: Little Brown, 1970), 461–64.

94. Vali, *Rift and Revolt*, 362.

95. Gati (*Hungary and the Soviet Bloc*, 154) quotes Khrushchev, who during the meeting with Yugoslav leaders in Brioni said: "If we let things take their course the West would say we are either stupid or weak, and that's one and the same thing. We cannot possibly permit it, either as Communists and internationalists or as the Soviet state."

96. Vali, *Rift and Revolt*, 366.

CHAPTER 3

1. Pierre Kende, "The Post-1956 Hungarian Normalization," in *Normalization Processes in Soviet-Dominated Central Europe*, Wlodzimierz Brus, Pierre Kende, and Zdenek Mlynar, Research Project, Crisis in Soviet-Type Systems, no. 1 (Koln: Index, 1982), 6.

2. As Ferenc Vali emphasizes, "all fighting took place exclusively between Hungarians and Soviet armed forces; a limited number of Hungarian Security police personnel had placed themselves at the disposal of the Soviet Command, but these rendered only noncombatant services" (*Rift and Revolt in Hungary* [Cambridge: Harvard University Press, 1961], 384).

3. See Bela Kiraly, "The Hungarian Revolution and Soviet Readiness to Wage War against Socialist States," in *The First War between Socialist States: The Hungarian Revolution of 1956 and Its Impact*, ed. Bela K. Kiraly, Barbara Lotze, and Nandor F. Dreisziger (New York: Brooklyn College Press, 1984), 28–30. Kiraly also points to the role of Soviet officials in obstructing any military response from the Hungarian government. He recalls that "when the defense perimeter of Budapest was penetrated by the Soviet troops, I insisted that either the Prime Minister or I as Supreme Commander should announce by radio (the only way we could reach all the fighting forces) that we were in a state of war with the USSR. Andropov [Soviet ambassador to Hungary] still claimed that no such Soviet policy existed [and] used his diplomatic immunity to remain in the nerve center of the revolution and to disinform the government, so the Hungarians would be confused about Soviet intentions up the very last minute" ("The Armed Forces and the Working Class in the Hungarian Revolution of 1956 and Its Impact," *New Politics* 1, no. 1 [1986]: 197).

4. See Vali, *Rift and Revolt*, 384–86. According to recently discovered evidence, by mid-November the Soviet security forces arrested and handed over to the Hungarian authorities 1,326 people (see Csaba Bekes, "New Findings on the 1956 Hungarian Revolution," *Cold War International History Project Bulletin* 2 [1992]: 3).

5. Paul Zinner, *Revolution in Hungary* (Freeport: Books for Libraries Press, 1962), 339. Also Bill Lomax reports that "Soviet command dealt directly with the Central Workers' Council, completely over the heads of the Kadar government, and in so doing effectively recognized the Central Council as the representative organ of the Hungarian workers. Indeed, each member of the Central Council was even issued with a special Soviet pass authorising the bearer to travel freely after curfew, as well as a permit to carry arms" (*Hungary, 1956* [New York: St. Martin's Press, 1956], 158).

6. Janos Berecz, *1956, Counter-Revolution in Hungary* (Budapest: Akademiai Kiado, 1986), 213.

7. See ibid., 214.

8. See Arpad Szabo, *A Magyar Forradalmi Honved Karhatalom* Budapest: Zrinya Katonai Kiado, 1976), 144.

9. Janos Kadar, *Socialism and Democracy in Hungary* (Budapest: Corvina Kiado, 1984), 81–82.

10. Vali, *Rift and Revolt*, 436.

11. Ibid., 437.

12. Kiraly, "Hungarian Revolution," 28.

13. See Vali, *Rift and Revolt*, 439, and Ivan Volgyes, "Hungary," in *Soviet Allies: The Warsaw Pact and the Issue of Reliability*, ed. Daniel L. Nelson (Boulder: Westview Press, 1984), 201.

14. Berecz, *1956, Counter-Revolution*, 184.

15. *Az MSzMP honvedelmi politikajarol* (Budapest: Zrinyi, 1974), 26.

16. Volgyes, "Hungary," 191.

17. See Jerzy R. Nowak, *Wegry: Wychodzenie* (Warszawa: Ksiazka i Wiedza, 1984), 108. According to the party document quoted above, altogether 20 percent of the former officer corps refused to sign up the declaration (p. 27). For more information about the Hungarian army during this period, see Peter Gosztony, "Zur Geschichte des ungarischen nationalen Wiederstandes in der Anfangsperiods des Kadar-Regimes," *Osteuropa* 18, nos. 10–11 (1968): 805–24; Michael Csizmas, "Die ungarische Volksarmee nach der Revolution," *Osterreichische Militarische Zeitschrift* 2 (1967): 134–45.

18. Jorg Konrad Hoensch, *A History of Modern Hungary, 1867–1986* (London: Longman, 1988), 224.

19. Volgyes, "Hungary," 192.

20. See Nowak, *Wegry: Wychodzenie*, 136.

21. Volgyes, "Hungary," 202.

22. Bill Lomax, *Hungary, 1956*, 148–49.

23. As Francois Bondy sarcastically stated, "The Kadar regime presented the ultimate paradox of contemporary Communism: a 'People's Government' resolutely opposed to the people, a 'Worker's State' in bitter class conflict with the workers" ("Epilogue: Winter 1956–7," in *The Hungarian Revolution*, ed. Melvin J. Lasky [New York: Praeger, 1957], 291).

24. Janos Kis, "The Restoration of 1956–1957," in his *Politics in Hungary: For a Democratic Alternative* (New York: Columbia University Press, 1989), 36.

25. As Bela Kiraly points out: "The general strike for political purposes was used differently before and after November 4. Before the second Soviet aggression, strikes were called to help Imre Nagy consolidate his government power vis-à-vis Stalinist counterrevolution. After November 4 the strikes were aimed at the consolidation of the power of the Workers' Councils and to prevent the consolidation of Kadar's counterrevolutionary regime" ("The Armed Forces and the Working Class in the Hungarian Revolution, 1956," *New Politics* 1, no. 1 (1986), 208).

26. Lomax, *Hungary, 1956*, 147.

27. It was led by two economists, G. Adam and G. Markos, and forty-four institutions were listed among its members, including the Writers Association, the Journalists Association, the University Revolutionary Council, the Hungarian Academy of Sciences, research institutions, artists and youth associations (see Kis, "Restoration of 1956–1957," 37).

28. Vali, *Rift and Revolt*, 394.

29. Zinner, *Revolution in Hungary*, 343.

30. The CWC presented the following major demands to the government on Nov. 14: (1) Re-appointment of Imre Nagy as premier; (2) barring of former AVH men from new police force and guarantee that new police would not be used for party purposes; (3) release of all freedom fighters including Pal Malater; (4) withdrawal of Soviet troops from Hungary; (5) guarantee that radio and press will tell the truth; (6) end of one-party system and guarantee of free elections as soon as possible; (7) trade agreements to be published and disadvantageous agreements cancelled; (8) deportations to be stopped (Radio Free Europe, Background Information, Nov. 18, 1957, p. 2). But the CWC, faced with a clever strategy of the government to keep the meetings going on and fearing that the continuation of the strike might provoke the Soviet repressive action, also made some concessions. After the heated debate, which divided the delegates, the CWC decided to call off the strike from 19 November but warned that if the main demands were not met, the CWC would call for a new strike (see Lomax, *Hungary, 1956*, 155–58; Kis, "Restoration of 1956–1957," 46–48).

31. Kis, "Restoration of 1956–1957," 44.

32. The parliament of the worker councils was designed to have 156 members elected by district in Budapest and county worker councils in the countryside. Moreover, the biggest factories were to have their own delegates. The parliament would elect a thirty member presidium that than would co-opt twenty representatives of universities, the army, the police, the organizations of intellectuals and political parties (see Janos Molnar, *A Nagybudapesti Kozponti Munkastanacs* [Budapest: Akademiai Kiado, 1969], 63–64).

33. See Lomax, *Hungary, 1956*, 59–60.

34. On Nov. 22, Imre Nagy and other members of his government were arrested by the Soviet police after they left the Yugoslav Embassy with Kadar's written guarantee of safe conduct. The whole episode is often quoted as an example of Kadar's total impotence during the first months of his rule, during which the Soviet police de facto ruled the country.

35. See Molnar, *A Nagybudapesti*, 67–68.

36. Kis, "Restoration of 1956–1957," 45.

37. "It would be an inaccuracy," Kis points out "to describe the meetings between Nov. 14 and 16 as negotiations. Kadar kept the CWC delegates for five to six hours, while his associates took them aside one by one, interrogated them and lectured them" ("Restoration of 1956–1957," 46).

38. One of the most contentious issues was the council's right to appoint and remove managers of enterprises and the right to strike. Another was government's attempt to reestablish party cells in factories, which was opposed by the councils. As Sandor Racz, the president of CWC put it: "We are and will be the leaders of Hungary. There is no need for the [Communist party] organization[;] it must be removed from factories" (quoted in Kiraly, "Armed Forces," 204). Both issues constituted necessary prerogatives of and foundations for the restoration of the party-state.

39. Zinner, *Revolution in Hungary*, 343.

40. In its appeal to workers on Nov. 27, 1956, the CWC emphasized that "we have never, in course of our negotiations, deviated from aims and basic demands of the glorious national revolution of October 23rd" ("Appeal of the Central Workers' Council of Greater Budapest to All Factories, District and County Councils," *The Review* 4 [April 1960]: 108). However, after the suspension of the strike on Nov. 19, as Kis points out: "A nation-wide strike for the immediate departure of the Soviet troops, for the return of the Imre Nagy government to office or for the restoration of the multi-party system was never again launched. The CWC maintained its basic demands, but they slipped down the list of priorities and, during the weeks that followed, it made efforts only where it could hope to achieve something" ("Restoration of 1956–1957," 47).

41. According to Lomax: "At the beginning of December Malenkov was dispatched to Hungary by the Soviet leadership to urge tougher measures, and after a three day meeting of the Central Committee a governmental decree banned the revolutionary committees, while organisers of the underground press like Miklos Gimes and Gyula Obersovszky were taken into custody, and several hundred workers' council activists . . . arrested" ("Hungarian Revolution," 104). At the same time the Soviet commander in Hungary, General Grebennik, was replaced by the secret police general, Ivan Serov, who took charge of the operations aimed at the speedy suppression of all resistance. But as Janos Kis argues, it is difficult to find out "what role was played in bringing about the changes in the leadership's standpoint by shifts in the internal balance of forces and of how extensive direct Soviet intervention might have been" (" Restoration of 1956–1957," 54).

42. In the provinces the situation remained particularly tense. "Away from the capital," as Janos Kis argues "the local organs of state power and the new local government organs paid less heed to the nascent, though uncertain, ground-rules emerging between the government and the CWC. In many places, there was open fighting between the territorial workers' councils and the old local authority over positions of power" (" Restoration of 1956–1957," 52).

43. Radio Free Europe, Background Information, Nov. 18, 1957, 4.

44. Kis, "Restoration," 56.

45. See ibid., 57, and Lomax, *Hungary, 1956*, 169.

46. By that time the majority of councils cease to exist. As Antal Apro stated in his speech on Sept. 19 in Kecskemet: "The overwhelming majority of the workers' councils was dissolved because in many places their activities were both economically and politically harmful and their composition was wholly unsuitable. But the govern-

ment and the party are of the opinion that we must create factory committees to take place of the workers' councils, factory committees led by the trade unions"(quoted in Thomas Schreiber, "Changes in the Leadership," *in Hungary Today*, ed. editors of *Survey* (New York: Praeger, 1962), 50).

47. *Nepakarat*, Nov. 17, quoted in Schreiber, "Changes," 51.

48. Factory councils were to be formed in all state's productive enterprises and other institutions under the leadership of the chairman of the factory trade-union committee. Two-thirds of its members were to be trade-union officials elected by the trade-union committee. The remaining one-third could be elected by the workers. The factory chief managers, the secretary of the party organization, and the secretary of Communist Youth Union were automatically members of the council (see Radio Free Europe, Background Report, Nov. 19, 1957, p. 2).

49. George Urban, "Hungary, 1957–1961: Background and Current Situation," *Radio Free Europe Special Report*, May 16, 1961, p. 4.

50. For a detailed analysis of the use of law in Hungary after the Soviet invasion, see Urban, "Hungary, 1957–1961," 38–79; the reports of the International Commission of Jurists (*The Hungarian Situation and the Rule of Law* [Hague: Tri Press, 1957]; and Laszlo Varga, *Human Rights in Hungary* (Gainesville, Fla.: Dunabian Research and Information Center, 1967).

51. According to the ordinance of Mar. 19, 1957, for example, any persons "who could not, for lack of existing evidence, be criminally prosecuted, could be expelled from their permanent or ordinary place of residence or from a fixed part of the country and/or subjected to police supervision" (quoted in Urban, "Hungary, 1957–1961," 6).

52. Quoted in Vali, *Rift and Revolt*, 398.

53. See Bekes, "New Findings," 3, and Janos M. Rainer, "The Reprisals," *New Hungarian Quarterly* 33, no. 127 (1992): 118–27.

54. Quoted in American Friends of Captive Nations, *Hungary under Soviet Rule* (New York: American Friends of Captive Nations, 1958), 22.

55. Urban, "Hungary, 1957–1961," 52–54.

56. Tibor A. Marczali, "Criminal Law in Communist Hungary," *Slavic Review* 23, no. 1 (1964): 99.

57. Quoted in ibid., 99.

58. Urban, "Hungary, 1957–1961," 60.

59. See Bekes, "New Findings on the 1956," 3.

60. The decree law no. 9/1957 extended the rights of the Public Prosecutor Office to include the right to supervise societies, clubs, and social organizations and to participate in all meetings of such organizations.

61. For more detailed accounts of the relationship between the state and the church in postwar Hungary, see Steven Polgar, "A Summary of the Situation of the Hungarian Catholic Church," *Religion in Communist Lands* 12, no. 1 (1984): 11–41; Charles E. Kovats, "The Path of Church-State Reconciliation in Hungary," in *Eastern Europe's Uncertain Future* ed. Robert R. King and James F. Brown (New York: Praeger, 1978), 301–11; Miklos Veto, "The Catholic Church," in *Hungary Today*, ed. the editors of *Survey* (New York: Praeger, 1962), 58–64; Robert Tobias, *Communist-Christian Encounterin East Europe* (Indianapolis: School of Religion Press, 1956); Andrzej Kaminski, "Anachronizm czy meczenstwo," *Krytyka* 16 (1983): 218–28; Pedro Ramet, *Cross and Comissars: The Politics of Religion in Eastern Europe and the USSR* (Bloomington: Indiana University Press, 1987); and

Pedro Ramet, *Catholicism and Politics in Communist Societies* (Durham: Duke University Press, 1990).

62. Kadar's government did not uphold the rehabilitation of Mindszenty enacted by Nagy's government during the revolution, and the cardinal remained in the American Embassy until November 1971, rejecting the proposition of amnesty in exchange for the resignation as the head of Hungarian Catholic church and emigration. He left Hungary as "the prisoner which escaped from the place of detention" and was relieved of his position after the agreement between the Kadar government and Vatican in 1974. He died in Vienna in 1975.

63. See Urban, "Hungary, 1957–1961," 137. This decree, which contained detailed instructions regarding the church appointments, was retroactive to Oct. 1, 1956, thus allowing the Office of Church Affairs to remove all church officials elected or appointed during the revolution.

64. To avoid the repetition of the prerevolutionary situation with the state sponsored and controlled movement of priests operating within the church, the Bench of Catholic Bishops in cooperation with the National Peace Council established an independent peace organization under the name of Opus Pacis, which represented those bishops and priests who were inclined to collaborate with the state. This preemptive move did not result, however, in regaining control over the state agents within the church.

65. See Urban, "Hungary, 1957–1961," 152.

66. See Bill Lomax, "The Hungarian Revolution of 1956 and the Origin of the Kadar Regime," *Studies in Comparative Communism* 18, nos. 2–3 (1985): 98–99.

67. Quoted in Berecz, *1956, Counter-Revolution*, 209.

68. Gyorgy Marosan, minister in Kadar's government, outlined on Feb. 2, 1957, the stages of reconstitution of the party-state: "The reconstitution of the Party constitutes the fourth phase of the return to normalcy." The first three phases were (1) armed repression of the revolt, (2) the renewal of contacts with other communist nations, and (3) the reorganization of the police (quoted in Francois Bondy, "Epilogue," 306).

69. Lomax, "Hungarian Revolution," 101–102.

70. As Bill Lomax points out "in his first pronouncements as head of the new government Kadar did not perform any drastic about-turn, but continued to speak very much in the spirit of his statements during the revolution . . . when he described the revolution as a 'glorious uprising' that had 'achieved freedom for the people and independence for the country.' In his first appeal on 4 November, he continued to speak of the events of 23 October as a 'mass movement' of 'honest patriots' with 'noble aims' and 'genuine and legitimate demands'" ("Hungarian Revolution," 101).

71. Berecz, *1956, Counter-Revolution*, 176.

72. Vali, *Rift and Revolt*, 391.

73. Ibid., 386.

74. For example, Bill Lomax argues that "in the early years of his regime [Kadar] was rather weak, inexperienced, and at times [a] naive politician whose main failing often lay in underestimating the cynicism and Machiavellianism of others. It is also my belief that in the first months after the crushing of the revolution, Kadar was head of the government in name only and far from being master of the situation. The real power in Hungary at that time lay with the Soviet army and the KGB, and while Soviets had chosen Kadar to be the figurehead of the new regime, their main confi-

dant remained Ferenc Munnich who, as minister in charge of the armed forces and state security, held the reins of power in the first months of the new regime" ("Hungarian Revolution," 102).

75. Janos Kadar, *Selected Speeches and Interviews* (Budapest: Akademiai Kiado, 1985), 183.

76. See Vali, *Rift and Revolt*, 390.

77. Lomax, "Hungarian Revolution," 106.

78. Kadar frankly admitted the government concerns about displaced functionaries. He said that "while we were working here in Budapest on the strengthening of the central authority, around us the storm waves of the counter-revolution were still sweeping. For weeks we were in charge of the center, but the Workers' Councils ruled in the plants. . . . They chased away hundreds and hundreds of worker-directors, and hundreds upon hundreds were displaced from the ministries and trusts. Since then, we have reinstated these people, with a few exception" (quoted in Andrew Felkay, *Hungary and the USSR, 1956–1988* [New York: Greenwood Press], 108).

79. Berecz, *1956, Counter-Revolution*, 210.

80. For the overviews of the party reconstruction and data on membership, see Miklos Molnar, *A Short History of the Hungarian Communist Party* (Boulder: Westview Press, 1978), 59; Ivan Szenes, *A kommunista part ujjaszervezese Magyarorszagon, 1956–1957* (Budapest: Kossuth Konyvkiado, 1976), 144; Berecz, *1956, Counter-Revolution*, 211.

81. According to George Urban ("Hungary, 1957–1961," 80), for example, at the end of December 1956, there were only 340 party members in the Csepel Iron Works, which employed thirty-eight thousand workers, and the situation was similar in all factories in the country. Moreover, workers in general were opposed to reintroducing of party organizations in places of work. Workers formed 24.2 percent of party's membership in April 1957, compared to 30.3 percent in January 1956, with one-quarter the total number of members at the beginning of 1956 (see Nowak, *Wegry: Wychodzenie*, 163).

82. According to Ferenc Vali , during April 1957, 118,000 people joined the party, which may be explained by the fact that "at that time the cadre system had been re-established making Party affiliation the prerequisite of the a great number of jobs." Thus by 1958 among 400,000 party members, "approximately 50,000 [were] functionaries of the Party, 130,000 [were] members of the new security agencies regrouping former members of the AVH, frontier guards, and militia men; and another 50,000 [were] government and municipal employees. Thus . . . less than half of the members [were] persons not directly and exclusively dependent on the Party or on the state for their material existence" (*Rift and Revolt*, 402, 403).

83. Molnar, *Short History*, 61.

84. There were scarcely any new faces in the new government and the Politburo build by Kadar after the invasion. As George Urban ("Hungary, 1957–1961," 80) points out: "Of the 41 government appointments made at the end of January [1957], the holders of 13 were the same as before the Revolution. A further 19 had been in prominent positions under either Rakosi or Gero or both. Among those holding important posts were five members (or alternate members) of Gero's Politburo [and] nine out of 10 members of the new Politburo had held Party office under Rakosi or Gero and the same was true of the large majority of the new Central Committee." See also Nowak, *Wegry: Wychodzenie*, 164.

85. Vali, *Rift and Revolt*, 402.

86. Molnar, *Short History*, 49.

87. Kende, "Post-1956 Hungarian Normalization," 7.

88. Lomax, "Hungarian Revolution," 106. Similarly Janos Kis argues that there were three currents within the emerging Communist party with quite pronounced tactical differences. These included Kadar's centrist group, the old communists group representing the pure proletarian policy of the Hungarian Soviet Republic of 1919 and the Stalinist group. As Kis points out: "In the eyes of the supporters of the ancient regime, Kadar himself was the principal traitor"; therefore, "the Kadar group had the greatest personal interest in eliminating the pro-Rakosi forces that were gathering strength within the party" ("Restoration," 14). It can be argued, therefore, that the anti-Stalinist position of Kadar's regime had less to do with ideological differences but rather with the practical struggle for political survival.

89. In this spirit the guidelines on recruitment to the party adopted by the Provisional Central Committee on Nov. 22, 1956, and published in *Nepszabadsag* excluded applicants from three categories: those whom "the leadership does not regard as worthy of membership by reason of the serious political errors they committed during the rule of the Rakosi-clique," those who "committed crimes against the people and the party under Rakosi leadership," and finally those who "murdered communists or other progressive people as participants in the uprising or incited others to this end, by plundering, engaging in financial speculation or generally taking part in arbitrary acts of terror" (quoted in Kis, "Restoration," 42).

90. Quoted in Berecz, *1956, Counter-Revolution*, 216.

91. Quoted in ibid., 205.

92. *Revolt in Hungary* (New York: Free Europe Press, 1956), 102.

93. See Sandor Balogh and Sandor Jakab, *The History of Hungary after the Second World War, 1944–1980* (Budapest: Corvina, 1986), 155.

94. Urban, "Hungary, 1957–1961," 45.

95. Kis, "Restoration," 65.

96. Quoted in Balogh and Jakab, *History of Hungary*, 165.

97. Vali, *Rift and Revolt*, 418.

98. Ibid., 419–20.

99. Ibid., 397.

100. Quoted in Urban, "Hungary, 1957–1961," 16.

101. Quoted in ibid., 39.

102. See ibid., 38–39.

103. Ibid., 39. To this end the Budapest Chamber of Lawyers enacted a confidential ruling stating that "Socialist lawyers are debarred, on pain of incurring disciplinary action, from giving legal aid to class enemies."

104. This intention of the government was openly endorsed at the meeting of the Provisional Central Committee at the beginning of December. The committee decided that "the Communists must mobilize all the honest working people to defend the trade unions, the traditional organs safeguarding the interests of the working class against the attacks of the class enemy" (quoted in Berecz, *1956, Counter-Revolution*, 223).

105. Quoted in *Revolt in Hungary*, 97.

106. See Kis, "Restoration," 50–51.

107. As Kis argues "at the outset, the relations between the CWC and the Trade Union Council was decidedly hostile. The workers leaders had not the least intention

of having anything to do with the Gaspar group. Early in December, however, relations between the two bodies improved somewhat. The CWC was having problems with finding a headquarters and preferred to accept the offer of the trade Union Council to that of the government" ("Restoration," 51ff).

108. See Radio Free Europe, Background Report, May 9, 1959.

109. *Hungary under the Communists* (New York: Praeger, 1957), 374.

110. Urban, "Hungary, 1957–1961," 183.

111. Balogh and Jakab, *History of Hungary*, 163.

112. Radio Free Europe, Background Report, Nov. 29, 1960, 2.

113. Radio Free Europe, Background Report, Aug. 28, 1957, 6.

114. Quoted in Urban, "Hungary, 1957–1961," 185.

115. Ibid., 186.

116. See *Hungary under Soviet Rule*, 34.

117. Quoted in Urban, "Hungary, 1957–1961," 114.

118. Quoted in ibid., 116.

119. To put this number into a perspective, the "socialist sector" in the agriculture in 1960 comprised 333 state farms, 4,507 farmer cooperatives, and 217 specialist cooperatives. See Marida Hollos and Bela C. Maday, eds., *New Hungarian Peasants: An East Central European Experience with Collectivization* (New York: Columbia University Press, 1983), 12.

120. Balogh and Jakab, *History of Hungary*, 172–73.

121. William Robinson, *The Pattern of Reform in Hungary* (New York: Praeger, 1973), 38.

122. According to George Urban, the reason for stopping the collectivization was that "Kadar's intention was not to go beyond a gradual and non-violent extension of kolkhozes and that, in the heat of battle, the operation assumed a momentum and speed of its own which the central authorities, seeing the drive succeed beyond their wildest expectations, were unwilling or possibly powerless to control. The activists specially trained for collectivization were selected Party toughs [who] gained their wings under Rakosi. It was only in March 1959 that the Political Committee realized the extent of the upheaval and ordered a halt. By this time irreparable damage had been done both to the Government's reputation as a representative of more human methods, and to the economy" ("Hungary, 1957–1961," 236).

123. Quoted in Bologh and Jakab, *History of Hungary*, 186.

124. Urban, "Hungary, 1957–1961," 237–38.

125. There were also more pragmatic considerations. Urban points out: "A fully socialized agriculture must have been considered an easier factor to fit into the second Five-Year Plan than one which consisted of a socialist and private sector. For export purposes, too, official purchases were more likely to reach the expected quotas if the Government had the whip-hand over the whole production process. The same goes for home consumption" ("Hungary, 1957–1961," 241).

126. Ibid., 246.

CHAPTER 4

1. Leszek Kolakowski, "Swiadomosc narodowa i rozklad komunizmu," in *1956 w dwadziescia lat pozniej z mysla o przyszlosci* (London: Aneks, 1978), 29.

2. For years, for example, it has been argued that the trial and execution of Imre Nagy and other leaders of the revolution was directed by the Kremlin. Ferenc A. Vali

argued that "Kadar had no important part to play in Nagy's fate. His role was restricted to that of Cat's paw of the Soviets" (*Rift and Revolt in Hungary* [Cambridge: Harvard University Press, 1961], 443). Recently uncovered evidence, however, shows that the decision was made by the Central Committee and the Hungarian party during sessions on Dec. 21, 1957, and Feb. 14, 1958. When it was noted that the date set for Nagy's trial coincided with a scheduled East-West summit meeting, Kadar "offered two alternatives: either to have the trial take place as scheduled and pass a light sentence, or to postpone the trial and pass sever sentences as originally planned. The Committee eventually voted, at Kadar's suggestion, for the latter option" (see Csaba Bekes, "New Findings on the 1956 Hungarian Revolution," *Cold War International History Project Bulletin* 2 [1992]: 3).

3. For a detailed elaboration of this argument, see Ferenc Feher and Agnes Heller, *Hungary 1956 Revisited* (London: Allen and Unwin, 1983).

4. Istvan Lovas and Ken Anderson, "State Terrorism in Hungary: The Case of Friendly Repression," *Telos* 54 (1982–83), 79.

5. Elemer Hankiss, "Demobilization, Self-Mobilization and Quasi-Mobilization, 1948–1987," *East European Politics and Societies* 3, no. 1 (1989): 122.

6. See, for example, William Gamson, *The Strategy of Collective Protest*, 2d ed. (Belmont, Calif.: Wadsworth, 1990); Craig J. Jenkins and Charles Perrow, "Insurgency of the Powerless: Farm Worker Movements (1946–1972)," *American Sociological Review* 42 (1977): 249–68.

7. Sidney Tarrow, "Struggle, Politics, and Reform—Collective Action, Social Movements and Cycles of Protest," Western Societies Program, Paper no. 21 (Ithaca: Cornell University, 1989), 35.

8. Miklos Molnar, *A Short History of the Hungarian Communist Party* (Boulder: Westview Press, 1978), 101.

9. The notion of collective action frame was developed by David Snow and Robert Benford in order to account for the critical role of ideological and symbolic factors in collective action. They argue that each historical period produces a small number of "master frames" that stimulate and guide collective action. See their "Ideology, Frame Resonance, and Participant Mobilization," in *From Structure to Action: Comparing Social Movements across Cultures*, ed. Bert Klandermans, Hanspeter Kriesi, and Sidney Tarrow (Greenwich: JAI, 1988): 197–218. See also Sidney Tarrow, *Power in Movement: Social Movements, Collective Actions, and Politics* (Cambridge: Cambridge University Press, 1994), 118–34.

10. For the insightful analysis of the dominant political discourse under state-socialism see Jan Kubik, "John Paul II's First Visit to Poland and the Collapse of the Official Marxist-Leninist Discourse," CROPSO Working Paper Series, no. 0025 (Cambridge: Harvard University, 1989.)

11. Mihaly Vajda, *The State and Socialism* (London: Allison and Busby, 1981), 126.

12. Hankiss, "Demobilization, Self-Mobilization and Quasi-Mobilization," 123–31.

13. See Ivan Szelenyi, *Socialist Entrepreneurs: Embourgeoisement in Rural Hungary* (Madison: University of Wisconsin Press, 1988), 5.

14. See Istvan Rev, "The Advantage of Being Atomized: How Hungarian Peasants Cope with Collectivization," *Dissent*, Summer 1988, 335–49.

15. Feher and Heller, *Hungary 1956 Revisited*, 157.

16. Janos Kis, "The Restoration of 1956–1957," in his *Politics in Hungary: For a Democratic Alternative* (New York: Columbia University Press, 1989), 75.

17. Paul Zinner, *Revolution in Hungary* (Freeport: Books for Libraries Press, 1962), 338.

18. Janos Kadar, "The Basis of Consensus," *New Hungarian Quarterly* 23, no. 86 (1982): 18.

19. Janos Kadar, *Selected Speeches and Interviews* (Budapest: Akademiai Kiado, 1985), 63–64 (emphases mine).

20. The average number of days per year when Parliament was in session was 8.5 between 1961 and 1970 and 7.5 between 1971 and 1980. Laws passed by Parliament were often replaced by mandatory Law Decrees issued by the Presidential Council of the Republic. Between 1957 and 1986 there were only thirteen interpellations. See Hankiss, "Demobilization, Self-Mobilization and Quasi-Mobilization," 109.

21. This struggle for the recovery of exclusive control of political space was the specific element of demobilization strategies, and Kadar many times stressed party-state's intentions on this issue. In his radio speech on Dec. 31 he said, for example, "We accept the institution of these Workers Councils in principle, but they must be directed by Communists." In a similar fashion he justified his opposition to the CWC at the beginning of December. He complained that the Central Council "had engaged in politics" and "had raised questions concerning the political order and had thus, in the natural course of events, effectively come into conflict with the power of the State. That is why we are now opposed to regional Workers Councils" (quoted in Francois Bondy, "Epilogue: Winter 1956–7," in *The Hungarian Revolution*, ed. Melvin Lasky [New York: Praeger, 1957], 298, 301). Such statements clearly indicate that any attempt to break into the political sphere and "engage in politics" was the most serious violation of state's rights and prerogatives.

22. See George Urban, "Hungary, 1957–1961: Background and Current Situation," *Radio Free Europe Special Report*, May 16, 1961, pp. 14–22.

23. The notion of "humanization" as distinct from liberalization was introduced by Wojtek Lamentowicz ("Eastern Europe and the Emergence of Civil Society: Starting Point of the Long Process," paper presented at the 83d Annual Meeting of the American Sociological Association in Atlanta, Aug. 28, 1988). It describes the phenomenon of softening repressive policies without granting any political rights to the population, which was common to post-Stalinist regimes in East Central Europe.

24. Quoted in Andrew Felkay, *Hungary and the USSR, 1956–1988* (New York: Greenwood Press), 158.

25. According to William Robinson: "The introduction of a new and more tolerant policy toward the intellectuals was perhaps most noticeable in the case of the technical intelligentsia and the economists. The increased attention and more favorable treatment accorded these people were reflected not only in the press but also in the requirements that the basic Party organizations invite non-Party specialists to their discussions of the new political guidelines issued prior the 1959 and 1962 Party Congresses. Moreover, it was expected that the opinions of such people on the matters contained in these documents would be solicited, and that their advice would be given sober consideration" (*The Pattern of Reform in Hungary* [New York: Praeger, 1973], 41).

26. Janos Kis, "Can 1956 Be Forgotten?" in *Politics in Hungary: For a Democratic Alternative* (New York: Columbia University Press, 1989), 28.

27. Feher and Heller, *Hungary 1956 Revisited*, 151–53, ix.

28. Kis, "Restoration," 34.

29. Bela Kiraly, "The Armed Forces and the Working Class in the Hungarian Revolution," *New Politics* 1, no. 1 (1986): 209.

30. Kis, "Restoration," 70–71.

31. For example, William Robinson (*Pattern of Reform*, 46–48) lists six factors that account for the repressive character of demobilization policies pointing to internal struggle and difficulties as well as to Soviet involvement and pressures.

32. Kadar, *Selected Speeches and Interviews*, 60.

33. Kadar repeated this sincere justification for the use of political terror many times. He clearly viewed repression as legitimate and necessary means of political struggle. In his speech on Nov. 26, 1956, he expressed this idea in a graphic way: "It would be extremely unwise to pursue the path of concessions made to the will of the counter-revolutionary forces. Our opinion is that one cannot placate a tiger, and that one can tame it and make it peaceful only if one beats it to death" (quoted in Bondy, "Epilogue," 295).

34. According to George Urban, "while one cannot speak of dogmatic and revisionist factions in the Hungarian Party, public criticism of both extremes has been so frequent and sometimes so acrimonious that the existence and attraction of these rival tendencies (if not actual groups) cannot be doubted. It is clear where the Party divides into those who stand to the left and those (if any) who stand to the right of Kadar" ("Hungary, 1957–1961," 12).

35. Feher and Heller, *Hungary 1956 Revisited*, 147.

36. Minutes of the Nation Conference of the HSWP in 1957. Quoted in Kis, "Restoration," 69–70.

37. See, Nigel Swain, *Hungary: The Rise and Fall of Feasible Socialism* (London: Verso, 1992), 88–94.

38. See Jerzy R. Nowak, *Wegry: Wychodzenie* (Warszawa: Almapress, 1988), 135.

39. Urban, "Hungary, 1957–1961," 210.

40. See ibid., 234.

41. Ivan T. Berend, "Continuity and Change of Industrialization in Hungary after the Turn of 1956/57," *Acta Oeconomica* 27, no. 3–4 (1981): 227.

42. See Andrzej Korbonski, "CMEA, Economic Integration, and Perestroika, 1948–1989," *Studies in Comparative Communism* 23, no. 1 (1990): 47–72.

43. This recurrence of earlier characteristics of the economic development resulted from the restoration of structural and institutional frameworks of the party-state after the revolution. As Laszlo Antal emphasized: "Practical experiences unambiguously show that within the framework of a given mechanism the possibilities of economic policy to influence relevant characteristics of development are strongly limited. Namely, the power positions, the resulting primary interests and relations, thus possibilities for enforcing interests . . . do not change considerably" without the fundamental change of economic and political structures ("Historical Development of the Hungarian System of Economic Control and Management," *Acta Oeconomica* 27, nos. 3–4 (1981): 252).

44. Berend, "Continuity and Change," 244–45.

45. For the analysis of the committee recommendations, see Robinson, *Pattern of Reform*, 19–21.

46. In the official evaluation of the proposal, Ivan Szurdi emphasized: "The principle of economic efficiency could not be recognized as the 'sole and unlimited principle of action.' State directives were also necessary in order to 'strengthen the socialist elements' of society, to 'limit the prevailing capitalist sector' (i.e., agriculture), and to 'group the small-scale farms into cooperatives.' Without such directives, he concluded, the policy of the Communist Party would be unable to prevail with sufficient force in the state direction of the economy" (quoted in Robinson, *Pattern of Reform*, 23).

47. Antal, "Historical Development," 259.

48. Robinson, *Pattern of Reform*, 52.

49. Antal, "Historical Development," 259.

50. It is important to note that the reform proposal implemented in 1968 was not, as Laszlo Szamuely emphasizes, "the posterior implementation of the 1957 plans taken out of the archives and dusted. It offered more in every respect, went further, stood on a much firmer theoretical foundations, not to speak of political soil" ("The First Wave of the Mechanism Debate in Hungary [1954–1957]," *Acta Oeconomica* 29, nos. 1–2 [1982]: 18). For the analysis of the introduction, main features and consequences of the NEM, see Robinson, *The Pattern of Reform*; Swain, *Hungary*, 85–115; Janos Kornai, "The Hungarian Reform Process: Visions, Hopes and Reality," in *Remaking the Economic Institutions of Socialism*, ed. Victor Nee and David Stark (Stanford: Stanford University Press, 1989), 32–94.

51. See Robert T. Jerome, Jr., "Sources of Economic Growth in Hungary," *East European Quarterly* 22, no. 1 (1988): 112–13.

52. See Bill Lomax, "The Hungarian Revolution of 1956 and the Origin of the Kadar Regime," *Studies in Comparative Communism* 18, nos. 2–3 (1985): 87–113.

53. Charles Gati, *Hungary and the Soviet Bloc* (Durham: Duke University Press, 1986), 187.

54. See Jiri Valenta, "Soviet Decisionmaking and the Hungarian Revolution," in *The First War between Socialist States: The Hungarian Revolution of 1956 and Its Impact*, ed. Bela Kiraly, Barbara Lotze, and Nandor F. Dreisziger (New York: Brooklyn College Press, 1984), 270, and Janos M. Rainer, "The Yeltsin Dossier: Soviet Documents on Hungary, 1956" *Cold War International History Project Bulletin* 5 (Spring 1995): 22, 24–27."

55. Hans J. Morgenthau, "The Revolution in U.S. Foreign Policy," *Commentary* 23, no. 2 (1957): 102–3. See also Bennett Kovrig, "Rolling Back Liberation: The United States and the Hungarian Revolution, in *The First War between Socialist States*, 279–90; Janos M. Rainer, "Their Men in Budapest," *New Hungarian Quarterly* 32, no. 122 (1991): 131–35, and for declassified U.S. government documents on the 1956 crisis, see U.S. Department of State, *Eastern Europe*, vol. 25 of *Foreign Relations of the United States, 1955–1957* (Washington, D.C.: Government Printing Office, 1990).

56. Kovrig, "Rolling Back Liberation," 287. See also Brian McCauley, "Hungary and Suez, 1956: The Limits of Soviet and American Power," in *The First War between Socialist States*, 291–316; Csaba Bekes, "New Findings," 3; Daniel F. Calhoun, *Hungary and Suez, 1956: An Exploration of Who Makes History* (Lanham: University Press of America, 1991).

57. Kovrig notes, "By the time that the Hungarian crisis received full play at the United Nations, the speeches, observed [U.S. ambassador to the UN] Lodge at that time, 'had some of the quality of funeral orations.' The funeral was for two victims: The Hungarian Revolution and the American policy of liberation" ("Rolling Back Liberation," 284).

58. Charles Gati, *Hungary and the Soviet Bloc*, 218. While this is a commonly accepted view, some commentators argued that a more active American response could have helped to consolidate Nagy's government and possibly delay or forestall the Soviet intervention (see Kovrig, "Rolling Back Liberation," 286–87).

59. For the detailed account of intrabloc meetings after the revolution, see Andrew Felkay, *Hungary and the USSR*, 103–50.

60. See ibid., 165–66.

61. See ibid., 111.

62. Vali, *Rift and Revolt*, 401.

63. Andrew Felkay, *Hungary and the USSR*, 113. The final acknowledgement for Kadar's role in saving socialism in Hungary and successfully accomplishing the restoration of the party-state came on April 4, 1964, when Khrushchev handed him the title Hero of the Soviet Union accompanied by the Lenin Prize with Gold Cluster, which the Supreme Soviet of the Soviet Union awarded him for his "outstanding role in the fight against the common enemies of the Soviet and Hungarian people."

64. Felkay, *Hungary and the USSR*, 150. Also Gati emphasizes that "to gain sufficient room for 'Kadarization' at home, Kadar had regarded it essential not to take foreign policy positions different from those of the Kremlin. To the extent differences had existed at all, they had to do with issues related to economics" (*Hungary and the Soviet Bloc*, 173).

65. See Gati, *Hungary and the Soviet Bloc*, 174.

66. Feher and Heller, *Hungary 1956 Revisited*, x.

67. See Tamas Hofer, "The Demonstration of March 15, 1989 in Budapest: A Struggle for Public Memory," Program on Central and Eastern Europe Working Paper Series, Center for European Studies, Harvard University, no. 15 (1991).

68. Rainer, "Their Men in Budapest," 131.

69. George Schopflin, "From Communism to Democracy in Hungary," in *Post-Communist Transition: Emerging Pluralism in Hungary*, ed. Andras Bozoki, Andras Korosenyi, and George Schopflin (London: Pinter, 1992), 96.

Part II

1. Harold G. Skilling, *Czechoslovakia's Interrupted Revolution* (Princeton: Princeton University Press, 1976), 824.

2. Antonin J. Liehm, "It Was You Who Did It!" in *The Prague Spring: A Mixed Legacy*, ed. Jiri Pehe (New York: Freedom House, 1988), 172.

3. Already in March 1946, President Gottwald's Communist party had more than a million members, twice as many as the second strongest party—the National Socialists. In the May 1946 elections, the Communists pulled 38 percent of the votes (the National Socialist won 18.29 percent), emerging as the dominant party in the country. In November 1948, there were more than 2.5 million party members—no less than 21 percent of the entire population. This number dropped in the 1950s as the result of purges and stabilized around 1.7 million in the 1960s. See Sharon L. Wolchik, *Czechoslovakia in Transition* (New York: Pinter 1991), 88–91; Zdenek

Suda, *Zealots and Rebels: A History of the Ruling Communist Party of Czechoslovakia* (Stanford: Hoover Institution Press 1980). A high level of membership in other party-state organizations is emphasized by Vladimir Kusin, *Political Grouping in the Czechoslovak Reform Movement* (London: Q Press, 1972), 5.

4. Zdenek Suda, "Czechoslovakia: An Aborted Reform," in *East Central Europe: Yesterday, Today, Tomorrow*, ed. Milorad M. Drachkovitch (Stanford: Hoover Institution Press, 1982), 255.

5. Galia Golan, "Comment: Reform Movements and the Problem of Prediction," *Studies in Comparative Communism* 8, no. 4 (1975): 432.

6. For the elaboration of this argument see, Agnes Heller and Ferenc Feher, *From Yalta to Glasnost* (Oxford: Basil Blackwell, 1990), chap. 5.

7. Otto Ulc, *Politics in Czechoslovakia* (San Francisco: Freeman, 1974), 22. The results of public opinion polls conducted during this period strongly support this conclusion. See Jaroslaw Piekalkiewicz, *Public Opinion Polling in Czechoslovakia, 1968–1969: Results and Analysis of Surveys Conducted during the Dubcek Era* (New York: Praeger, 1972), and Zvi Y. Gitelman, "Public Opinion in Czechoslovakia," in *Public Opinion in European Socialist Systems*, ed. Walter D. Connor and Zvi Y. Gitelman (New York: Praeger, 1977), 83–103.

8. The reform movement in Czechoslovakia did not attempt to redesign the existing political system or introduce changes that were incompatible with socialist organization of the economy. As Suda argues "the whole reform movement of 1968 could be defined simply as the application of rules and laws that long had been dead letters, but nevertheless existed" ("Czechoslovakia: An Aborted Reform," 256).

9. Ivan Svitak, *The Czechoslovak Experiment, 1968–1969* (New York: Columbia University Press, 1971), 4.

10. See, for example, Harold G. Skilling, *Czechoslovakia's Interrupted Revolution*; Vladimir Kusin, *Political Grouping in the Czechoslovak Reform Movement* (London: Q Press, 1972); Vladimir Kusin, *The Intellectual Origins of the Prague Spring: The Development of Reformist Ideas in Czechoslovakia, 1956–1967* (Cambridge: Cambridge University Press, 1971); Galia Golan, *The Czechoslovak Reform Movement* (Cambridge: Cambridge University Press, 1971); Galia Golan, *Reform Rule in Czechoslovakia* (Cambridge: Cambridge University Press, 1973); Alex Pravda, *Reform and Change in the Czechoslovak System: January–August 1968* (Beverly Hills: Sage, 1975). The bibliography, compiled in 1974, lists some six hundred books on the Prague Spring published in the West; see Vladimir Kusin and Zdenek Hejzlar, *Czechoslovakia 1968–1969: Annotation, Bibliography, Chronology* (New York: Garland, 1974).

CHAPTER 5

1. Only after the Munich crisis was the Communist party banned from all political activity, and the majority of its leadership fled the country before Germany completed the occupation of Czechoslovakia in March 1939. See Zdenek Suda, *Zealots and Rebels: A History of the Ruling Communist Party of Czechoslovakia* (Stanford: Hoover Institution Press 1980); and Jacques Rupnik, *Histoire du parti communiste tchecoslovaque* (Paris: Presses de la fondation nationale des sciences politiques, 1981).

2. Joseph Rothschild, *Return to Diversity* (New York: Oxford University Press, 1989), 91.

3. Karel Kaplan argues that already by 1945 "the economic reforms put an end to private finance capital and to the power of industrialists and landlords. The bourgeoisie was so weakened that it could no longer determine the direction of economic change, a responsibility that now fell on the public sector. The various reforms went a long way toward leveling out society. The two social extremes had been removed, namely finance capital and the poorest classes, the latter having considerably improved their position through the distribution of property confiscated from the Germans and from wartime collaborators" (Karel Kaplan, "Czechoslovakia's February 1948," in *Czechoslovakia: Crossroads and Crises, 1918–88,* ed. Norman Stone and Eduard Strouhal (New York: St. Martin's Press, 1989), 149. See also Hans Renner, *A History of Czechoslovakia since 1945* (London: Routledge, 1989), 5.

4. On the Czech lands the Communists gained 40 percent of votes, the Socialists 24 percent, the Populists 20 percent, and the Social Democrats 16 percent. In Slovakia the Democratic party won 62 percent of votes, the Communists 30 percent, the new Party of Freedom and the Labor party 4 and 3 percent, respectively. As a result of the elections, in the National Assembly the Communist party had 114 seats, Social Democrats 37, National Socialists 55, Populists 46, and Democrats 43. Thus, the political forces of the left had a majority of seats in the country, while the center-right Democratic party won in Slovakia. See *Dejiny Ceskoslovenska v datech* (Praha: Svoboda, 1968), 468.

5. Renner, *History of Czechoslovakia,* 12.

6. See Otto Ulc, "Czechoslovakia," in *Communism in Eastern Europe,* ed. Teresa Rakowska-Harmstone and Andrew Gyorgy (Bloomington: Indiana University Press, 1984), 101, and Suda, *Zealots and Rebels,* 197. These assets controlled by the communists allowed from the very beginning the establishment of clientelistic networks where political support was traded for immediate material gratification. According to Renner: "Klement Gottwald and his party managed to turn the expulsion of the Germans in the Czech border region into considerable political gains. First, the CPCz succeeded (like its Polish counterpart) in getting control over the evacuated areas. . . . In a true 'gold rush' manner numerous applicants were helped to new property by means of political corruption. This reprehensible practice meant that to the new occupants were handed over, along with a house and piece of land, their membership card of the communist party" (*History of Czechoslovakia,* 7). See also Alfred M. de Zayas, *Nemesis at Potsdam: The Expulsion of the Germans from the East* (Lincoln: University of Nebraska Press, 1988), and Radomir Luza, *The Transfer of Sudeten Germans: A Study of Czecho-German Relations, 1933–1962* (New York: New York University Press, 1964).

7. Renner, *History of Czechoslovakia,* 6.

8. See Pavel Tigrid, "The Prague Coup of 1948: The Elegant Takeover," in *The Anatomy of Communist Takeovers,* ed. Thomas T. Hammond (New Haven: Yale University Press, 1975), 399–432. See also Karel Kaplan, "Czechoslovakia's February 1948"; and Francois Fejto, *Le Coup de Prague, 1948* (Paris: Editions du Seuil, 1976).

9. The Democratic party, which opposed the Communists from the very beginning, was disbanded; the Czechoslovak National Socialist party was reorganized and renamed the Czechoslovak Socialist party; the Czechoslovak Popular party was penetrated by Communist agents and set at odds with the Catholic church hierarchy; the Social Democrats were forced to merge with the Communists. Leaders of remaining non-Communist parties (People's party in the Czech lands and Freedom and the

Slovak Revival parties) were replaced by expedient third-rate politicians, and at the same time thousands of members of these parties were arrested and detained. Also, the Communist party of Slovakia was fully incorporated into the CPCz, becoming its regional organization. See Paul Zinner, *Communist Strategy and Tactics in Czechoslovakia, 1918–1948* (Princeton: Princeton University Press, 1963).

10. Already in the spring of 1947, a communist minister of agriculture introduced a draft of the bill designed to nationalize all private farms owning more than fifty hectares of land. In the next step, in January 1948, the Communists demanded nationalization of all enterprises employing more than fifty workers. One month after the coup, the Communist government enacted both the nationalization of enterprises employing more than fifty workers and nationalization of farms larger than fifty hectares. In February 1949, in order to speed up collectivization of agriculture, the new law on agricultural cooperatives was enacted. Overall, by the end of 1955, 43 percent of land was controlled by state farms and cooperatives. Collectivization was concluded in 1960, when 88 percent of land was controlled by the state. The small businesses were also systematically destroyed. By 1956, only forty-seven thousand private enterprises remained in retail and services, which was a little over 10 percent of businesses in operation in 1948. For more detailed analysis, see Martin Myant, *The Czechoslovak Economy, 1948–1988* (Cambridge: Cambridge University Press, 1989), 42–55.

11. See Renner, *History of Czechoslovakia*, 23; Pedro Ramet, "Christianity and National Heritage among the Czechs and Slovaks," in *Religion and Nationalism in Soviet and East European Politics*, ed. Pedro Ramet (Durham: Duke University Press, 1989), 277–78; Karel Kaplan, "Church and State in Czechoslovakia from 1948–1956," in *Religion in Communist Lands* 14, nos. 1–3 (1986): 59–72, 180–93, 273–82. Sabrina P. Ramet, "The Catholic Church in Czechoslovakia, 1948–1991," *Studies in Comparative Communism* 24, no. 4 (1991): 377–93.

12. According to official data, the party had 2,674,838 members and candidates in 1948, while in 1956 the membership of the party was reduced to 1,417,989. See Gordon Wightman and Archie H. Brown, "Changes in the Levels of Membership and Social Composition of the Communist Party of Czechoslovakia," *Soviet Studies* 27, no. 3 (1975): 396–417.

13. Rothschild, *Return to Diversity*, 134–35. For detailed analysis of political repression during the Stalinist period, see Karel Kaplan, *Report on the Murder of the General Secretary* (Columbus: Ohio University Press, 1990), and for the official report on political trials, which was prepared by a special committee during the Prague Spring, see Jiri Pelikan, ed., *The Czechoslovak Political Trials, 1950–54: The Suppressed Report of the Dubcek's Commission of Inquiry* (Stanford: Stanford University Press, 1971); and for personal accounts, see Artur London, *The Confession* (New York: Ballantine Books, 1970); Eugen Loebl, *Sentenced and Tried: The Stalinist Purges in Czechoslovakia* (London: Elek Books, 1969); Josefa Slanska, *Report on My Husband* (London: Hutchinson, 1969); Heda Margolius Kovaly, *Under a Cruel Star: A Life in Prague, 1941–1968* (Cambridge: Plunkett Lake Press, 1986).

14. Rothschild, *Return to Diversity*, 97.

15. See Jerzy Tomaszewski, "Czechoslowacka Republika Socialistyczna," in *Dzieje Panstw Socjalistycznych*, ed. Jerzy Ciepielewski (Warszawa: PWN, 1986), 73.

16. Myant, *Czechoslovak Economy*, 1.

17. As a result of a currency reform designed to establish a market equilibrium with stable prices implemented on 1 June 1953, most of the savings of the population

were wiped out. In response 129 factories went on strike involving 32,359 workers. The major demonstrations took place in Pilzen where the army was employed to restore the order and hundreds of workers were arrested. See Myant, *Czechoslovak Economy*, 63–64; Otto Ulc, "Pilsen: The Unknown Revolt," *Problems in Communism* 14, no. 3 (1965): 46–49.

18. Otto Ulc, *Politics in Czechoslovakia* (San Francisco: Freeman, 1974), 3.

19. Renner, *History of Czechoslovakia*, 26.

20. In contrast to the first five-year plan, the targets of the second five-year plan (1956–60) were overfulfilled, and as Martin Myant suggests, "the dominant feeling towards the end of the Second Five Year Plan was one of success" (*Czechoslovak Economy*, 90).

21. Renner, *History of Czechoslovakia*, 29.

22. According to Myant, the fact that in the 1950s Czechoslovakia had "the misfortune to avoid a major political crisis or economic failure," resulted in the absence of important policy adjustments, and "the country stuck to the same concept of growth based on heavy industry. That left it especially susceptible to both chance and predictable external changes: over-confidence led to an underestimation of the dangers" (*Czechoslovak Economy*, 92). He argues that "the only alternatives—given the structural weaknesses of the Czechoslovak economy after the growth strategy of the 1950s—were to cut living standards or to run into debt" (ibid., 100).

23. See Myant, *Czechoslovak Economy*, 97–106.

24. Ibid., 111.

25. Renner, *History of Czechoslovakia*, 38.

26. Ibid., 40.

27. Myant, *Czechoslovak Economy*, 118.

28. Vladimir Kusin, *Political Grouping in the Czechoslovak Reform Movement* (London: Q Press, 1972), 69. See also Dusan Humsik, *Writers against the Rulers* (New York: Random House, 1971). Alexander Dubcek acknowledged that the writers revolt "was truly significant because some three quarters of the Writers' Union members—novelists, poets, playwrights, and editors—were Communists who had constituted a prestigious force solidly supportive of the Party since before the war" (*Hope Dies Last* [New York: Kodansha, 1993], 113).

29. Renner, *History of Czechoslovakia*, 42.

30. Jiri Valenta, *Soviet Intervention in Czechoslovakia, 1968* (Baltimore: Johns Hopkins University Press, 1979), 29.

31. Kusin, *Political Grouping*, 2.

32. One could only speculate whether the Czechoslovak party-state and the Communist party leaders would ultimately control and survive the political process that they set in motion in the long run. It seems that political liberalization would lead to calls for a genuine democratic system. See Pavel Tigrid, "And What If the Russians Did Not Come," in *Prague Spring*, ed. Pehe, 77–87.

33. See, Vladimir Kusin, *The Intellectual Origins of the Prague Spring: The Development of Reformist Ideas in Czechoslovakia, 1956–1967* (Cambridge: Cambridge University Press, 1971), and Galia Golan, *The Czechoslovak Reform Movement* (Cambridge: Cambridge University Press, 1971).

34. Renner, *History of Czechoslovakia*, 50. See also William Shawcross, *Dubcek* (New York: Simon and Schuster, 1990), 85–103.

35. This was because of the years he had spent in the Soviet Union, living there as a child and later on as a student at the Higher Party School in Moscow. See Dubcek, *Hope Dies Last*, 24–30, 66–73.

36. During the first few weeks after the replacement of Novotny, there were no important personnel changes in top party posts. The only exception was the replacement of the conservative head of the Eight Department of the Central Committee, Miroslav Mamula, by general Vaclav Prchlik, a radical supporter of reforms. Moreover, new members of the Presidium included two reformers, Josef Boruvka and Josef Spacek; two dogmatists, Emil Rigo and Vasil Bilak; and one uncommitted conservative, Jan Piller. These changes certainly reflected a desire to keep balance between political factions within the party's leadership.

37. See Giuseppe Di Palma, *To Craft Democracies* (Berkeley: University of California Press, 1990).

38. Kusin reports a characteristic episode from this period, when Ludvik Vaculik, one of the most outspoken supporters of the reform met with the workers at Skoda Works in Pilsen in March 1968. He found the workers divided into two groups: "The one said nothing, the other was again divided into those who were suspicious of the new developments and those who were willing to go ahead if only instructions from above . . . were forthcoming. In characteristic reflection of workers attitude one of discussants declared: 'We need not have our own programme; the Party's programme will tell us what the trade unions should do' " (*Political Grouping*, 13).

39. Ivan Svitak, *The Czechoslovak Experiment, 1968–1969* (New York: Columbia University Press, 1971), 352.

40. Renner, *History of Czechoslovakia*, 52.

41. Ibid., 61. See also Frank L. Kaplan, *Winter into Spring: The Czechoslovak Press and the Reform Movement, 1963–68* (Boulder: Westview Press, 1977).

42. Renner, *History of Czechoslovakia*, 55. It is clear that the divisions within the Czechoslovak leadership were never clear cut and constant. As Valenta points out, they "exhibited a wide range of views from antireformist to radical, which were based not only on different perceptions of reform but also on different evaluations of the forthcoming Party congress . . . and the extent of Soviet pressure, and on differing bureaucratic and personal interests (such as a simple opportunism and fear about loss of privileges). Thus, the views of some leaders differed from issue to issue, and the various coalition affiliations altered during the crisis" (*Soviet Intervention in Czechoslovakia*, 37). See also Harold G. Skilling, *Czechoslovakia's Interrupted Revolution* (Princeton: Princeton University Press, 1976), 493–525, and Zdenek Mlynar, *Nightfrost in Prague* (New York: Karz, 1980), 146–246.

43. For the full text of the Action Program, see Robin A. Remington, ed., *Winter in Prague* (Cambridge: MIT Press, 1969), 88–137.

44. Milan Hauner, "The Prague Spring—Twenty Years After," in *Czechoslovakia: Crossroads and Crises*, ed. Norman Stone and Eduard Strouhal, 217.

45. See, for example, Pehe, ed., *Prague Spring*; and Norman Stone and Eduard Strouhal, eds., *Czechoslovakia: Crossroads and Crisis*, chaps. 12–16.

46. Kusin, *Political Grouping*, 6.

47. See Renner, *History of Czechoslovakia*, 59. For a detailed analysis of public opinion surveys conducted during the Prague Spring, see, for example, Jaroslaw A. Piekalkiewicz, *Public Opinion Polling in Czechoslovakia, 1968–69: Results and Analysis of Surveys Conducted during the Dubcek Era* (New York: Praeger, 1972), and Zdenek Strmiska, "The Prague Spring as a Social Movement," in *Czechoslovakia: Crossroads and Crises*, ed. Stone and Strouhal, 253–267.

48. Ulc, *Politics in Czechoslovakia*, 101.

49. For the text of the Manifesto see Remington, ed., *Winter in Prague*, 196–203.

50. Valenta, *Soviet Intervention*, 41.

51. For a detailed analysis of the geopolitical context of the Prague Spring, see Skilling, *Czechoslovakia's Interrupted Revolution*; Valenta, *Soviet Intervention*; and Karen Dawisha, *The Kremlin and the Prague Spring* (Berkeley: University of California Press, 1985). For new archival findings on the Prague Spring, see Mark Kramer, "New Sources on the 1968 Soviet Invasion of Czechoslovakia," *Cold War International History Project Bulletin* 2 (Fall 1992): 1, 4–13, and Kramer "The Prague Spring and the Soviet Invasion of Czechoslovakia: New Interpretations," *Cold War International History Project Bulletin* 3 (Fall 1993): 2–13, 54–55.

52. Valenta, *Soviet Intervention*, 65.

53. For a detailed account of negotiations, see ibid., 71–85, and Mlynar, *Nightfrost in Prague*.

54. Valenta, *Soviet Intervention*, 88.

55. Ibid., 91.

56. In the new party statutes prepared for the Extraordinary Congress, the only proposed structural change, as Golan points out, "was federation of the party, i.e. replacement of the regional organs by 'national' bodies. Organizational measures to eliminate the system of parallel party organizations for every area or organization of society were rejected at the time. Presumably it was felt that such a move was premature, particularly given Soviet concern, as it was, that the party was losing its leading role" (*Czechoslovak Reform Movement*, 302).

57. Most of these changes, however, were the result of the generation change. As Barbara Wolfe Jancar argues in her detailed analysis of changes within Czechoslovak party elites, the exchange of personnel taking place in 1968 was to a significant degree a result of the normal transition of power from the party veterans to younger leaders. See *Czechoslovakia and the Absolute Monopoly of Power* (New York: Praeger 1971), 132–82.

58. According to Ulc, "Dubcek's credo was that Party's ethics demanded that people be dealt with in a human, dignified, humanistic way. Anxious to avoid the semblance of a purge, the emphasis was on persuasion, appeal to good will, and the prospect of a comfortable retirement. As we know, there was few takers, the majority biding its time and thirsting for revenge" (*Politics in Czechoslovakia*, 101–2).

59. Jancar, *Czechoslovakia and the Absolute Monopoly*, 232.

60. According to Ulc, at the end of 1968, the Socialist Party had some fifty thousand members and the People's Party had sixty thousand members (*Politics in Czechoslovakia*, 35). See also Kusin, *Political Grouping*, 162–93.

61. Golan, *Czechoslovak Reform Movement*, 307.

62. See Condoleezza Rice, "Czechoslovakian Secret Police," in *Terror and Communist Politics: The Role of the Secret Police in Communist States*, ed. Jonathan R. Adelman (Boulder: Westview Press, 1984), 165.

63. Ulc, *Politics in Czechoslovakia*, 68.

64. Rice, "Czechoslovakian Secret Police," 169.

65. See Condoleezza Rice, *The Soviet Union and the Czechoslovak Army, 1948–1983* (Princeton: Princeton University Press, 1984), 73.

66. See Jiri Valenta and Condoleezza Rice, "The Czechoslovak Army," in *Communist Armies in Politics*, ed. Jonathan R. Adelman (Boulder: Westview Press, 1982), 138, and Condoleezza Rice, *Soviet Union and Czechoslovak Army*, 79.

67. Rice, *Soviet Union and Czechoslovak Army*, 111. For the detailed discussion of the reform proposal advanced during the Prague Spring within the army, see ibid., 122–37.

68. Quoted in ibid., 148.

69. According to Kusin, the membership of the unions in 1968 was as follows: architects, 1,920; theatrical artists, 1,734; film and television artists, 554; journalists, 4,000; composers, 860; writers, 610, and fine artists, 3,380 (*Political Grouping*, 83).

70. For a more detailed analysis of the trade-union structure, see Kusin, *Political Grouping*, 17–25.

71. Ibid., 13.

72. According to Kusin, the reported number of preparatory committees and established councils that came to existence during the Prague Spring vary depending on the source. Prime Minister Cernik stated that as of Oct. 1, 1968, 131 councils had been registered and some 140 preparatory committees established out of seven hundred enterprises in Czechoslovakia (*Political Grouping*, 33). For a more detailed analysis of the worker-council movement in Czechoslovakia during 1968–69, see Vladimir C. Fisera, ed., *Workers' Councils in Czechoslovakia* (London: Allison and Busby, 1978); and Karel Kovanda, "Czechoslovak Workers' Councils, 1968–69," *Telos* 28 (1976): 36–54.

73. Kusin, *Political Grouping*, 36.

74. Jancar, *Czechoslovakia and the Absolute Monopoly*, 190–91.

75. The CSM comprised the Pioneer organization for children between age eight and fifteen and the youth organization for people between age fifteen and twenty-five. Its organizational structure was identical to the structure of the Communist party, including district, regional, and central committees. The central committee had its presidium and secretariat, and the congress was the highest authority of the organization. According to its statute, the CSM was "the reserve force of the communist Party" and its activities were based on Party's policy. The statute emphasized that the union "guides young people toward mastering Marxism-Leninism" and "the greatest honor for a member of CSM is to be admitted to the Communist Party."

76. See Ulc, *Politics in Czechoslovakia*, 115.

77. Kusin, *Political Grouping*, 126.

78. Ulc, *Politics in Czechoslovakia*, 115.

79. As Kusin emphasizes: "The odds in the Party leadership of the day, even with its reformist majority, were against the endorsement of new parties. This seemed to be the result of foreign disapproval as much as of a built-in ideological barrier and a genuine fear of a return to 'capitalist' parliamentarism" (*Political Grouping*, 168). See also ibid., 170–76.

80. See Kusin, *Political Grouping*, 176–81, and Arnulf I. Simon, "Czechoslovakia's KAN: A Brief Venture in Democracy," *East Europe* 18, no. 6 (1969): 20–22.

81. See Kusin, *Political Grouping*, 181–91, and Jaroslav Brodsky, "Czechoslovakia's 231 Club," *East Europe* 18, no. 6 (1969): 23–25.

82. Ulc, *Politics in Czechoslovakia*, 37.

83. See Kusin, *Political Grouping*, 205–10.

84. Ibid., 209.

85. See, Kramer, "Prague Spring and the Soviet Invasion," 4–6.

86. Valenta, *Soviet Intervention*, 15.

87. Zdenek Suda, "Czechoslovakia: An Aborted Reform," in *East Central Europe: Yesterday, Today, Tomorrow*, ed. Milorad M. Drachkovitch (Stanford: Hoover Institution Press, 1982), 258.

88. On May 14, despite reluctance of Czechoslovak leaders, the joint "general staff exercises" of the Warsaw Treaty Organization took place in northern Czecho-

slovakia, which included large armored and infantry detachments. Although maneuvers were due to end on June 30, by the second week of July, 16,000 Soviet troops were reported to be still in Czechoslovakia.

89. See, for example, Golan, *Czechoslovak Reform Movement*, 316–29; Valenta, *Soviet Intervention*; Skilling, *Czechoslovakia's Interrupted Revolution*, 261–333; Karen Dawisha, The *Kremlin and the Prague Spring* (Berkeley: University of California Press, 1985); Michel Tatu, "Intervention in Eastern Europe," in *Diplomacy of Power*, ed. Stephen S. Kaplan (Washington, D.C.: Brookings Institution, 1981), 205–64.

90. Valenta, *Soviet Intervention*, 155.

91. Ken Jowitt, "Moscow 'Centre,'" *East European Politics and Societies* 1, no. 3 (1987), 321.

92. See George Schopflin, "The Political Structure of Eastern Europe as a Factor in Intra-Bloc Relations," in *Soviet–East European Dilemmas*, ed. Karen Dawisha and Philip Hanson (London: Heinemann 1981), 61–83.

93. For example, while the feelings among Slovaks that they were exploited and offended by the Czechs were widespread and the national question was one of the issues that decisively contributed to the crisis of Czechoslovak Stalinism, "no specifically Slovak political party or organization," as Kusin points out "devoted to gaining a greater share of political power for its members came into being or was even contemplated" (*Political Grouping*, 143).

94. Ibid., 195.

95. Ibid., 118–19.

96. Galia Golan, *Reform Rule in Czechoslovakia* (Cambridge: Cambridge University Press, 1973), 239.

97. Golan, *Czechoslovak Reform Movement*, 275.

98. Rice, "Czechoslovakian Secret Police," 165.

99. Ulc, *Politics in Czechoslovakia*, 67.

100. Kusin, *Political Grouping*, 38.

101. Golan argues: "Conservatives continued their efforts to separate the workers from the reformers, specifically by pointing to the loss in benefits or job security the former would suffer from the reform. Regime promises of increased welfare benefits, greater job mobility, and the actual reduction of the work week to forty hours were in part designed to counter these efforts" (*Czechoslovak Reform Movement*, 283).

102. Svitak, *Czechoslovak Experiment*, 78.

103. For the summary of all visits and meetings between the Warsaw Pact members that dealt with the internal situation in Czechoslovakia, see Jancar, *Czechoslovakia and the Absolute Monopoly*, 264–65.

CHAPTER 6

1. For the text of the TASS statement, see Philip Windsor and Adam Roberts, *Czechoslovakia, 1968: Reform, Repression and Resistance* (New York: Columbia University Press, 1969), 176–77. The "invitation letter" send by the small group of hard-line senior officials led by the Slovak Communist party leader Vasil Bilak was turn over to the Czechoslovak government by Boris Yeltsin only in 1992. See Mark Kramer, "The Prague Spring and the Soviet Invasion of Czechoslovakia," *Cold War International History Project Bulletin* 2 (Fall 1992): 2–4.

Blazyca, George. "The Polish Economy under Martial Law: A Dissenting View." *Soviet Studies* 37, no. 3 (1985): 428–36.

Bondy, Francois. "Epilogue: Winter 1956–7." In *The Hungarian Revolution*, edited by Melvin Lasky, 289–318. New York: Praeger, 1957.

Bova, Russell. "Political Dynamics of the Post-Communist Transition: A Comparative Perspective." *World Politics* 44, no. 1 (1991): 113–38.

Bozoki, Andras, Andras Korosenyi, and George Schopflin, eds. *Post-Communist Transition: Emerging Pluralism in Hungary*. London: Pinter, 1992.

Bright, Charles, and Susan Harding, eds. *Statemaking and Social Movements*. Ann Arbor: University of Michigan Press, 1984.

Brodsky, Jaroslav. "Czechoslovakia's 231 Club." *East Europe* 18, no. 6 (1969): 23–25.

Bromke, Adam. "Czechoslovakia 1968—Poland 1978: A Dilemma for Moscow." *International Journal* 23, no. 4 (1978): 740–62.

———. "The Opposition in Poland." *Problems of Communism* 27, no. 5 (1978): 37–51.

———. "Poland." In *The Hungarian Revolution in Retrospect*, edited by Bela Kiraly and Paul Jonas, 87–94. Boulder: East European Quarterly, 1978.

———. "Poland under Gierek: A New Political Style." *Problems of Communism* 21, no. 5 (September–October 1972): 1–19.

Broue, Pierre. *Ecrits a Prague sous la censure, aout 1968–juin 1969*. Paris: EDI, 1973.

Brown, James F. "The East European Setting." In *Eroding Empire: Western Relations with Eastern Europe*, edited by Lincoln Gordon, 8–38. Washington, D.C.: Brookings Institution, 1987.

———. *Eastern Europe and Communist Rule*. Durham: Duke University Press, 1988.

Brumberg, Abraham, ed. *Poland: Genesis of a Revolution*. New York: Random House, 1983.

Brus, Wlodzimierz. "Economics and Politics: The Fatal Link." In *Poland: Genesis of a Revolution*, edited by Abraham Brumberg, 26–41. New York: Random House, 1983.

Brus, Wlodzimierz, Pierre Kende, and Zdenek Mlynar. *Normalization Processes in Soviet-dominated Central Europe*. Research Project "Crisis in Soviet-type Systems" no. 1. Koln: Index, 1982.

Bruszt, Laszlo. "The Negotiated Revolution in Hungary." *Social Research* 57, no. 2 (1991): 365–87.

Bruszt, Laszlo, and David Stark. "Remaking the Political Field in Hungary: From the Politics of Confrontation to the Politics of Competition." *Journal of International Affairs* 45, no. 1 (1991): 201–45.

Brzezinski, Zbigniew. "East-West Relations after Czechoslovakia." *East Europe* 18, nos. 11–12 (1969): 2–10.

———. "Solidarity and US Foreign Policy." In *Solidarity and Poland: Impacts East and West*, edited by Steve W. Reiquam, 28–35. Washington, D.C.: Wilson Center Press, 1988.

———. "US Policy toward Poland." In *Creditworthiness and Reform in Poland*, edited by Paul Marer and Wlodzimierz Sliwinski, 315–21. Bloomington: Indiana University Press, 1988.

Bugajski, Janusz. *Czechoslovakia: Charter 77's Decade of Dissent*. The Washington Papers, no. 125. New York: Praeger, 1987.

Bunce, Valerie. "The Empire Strikes Back: The Evolution of the Eastern Bloc from a Soviet Asset to a Soviet Liability." *International Organization* 39, no. 1 (1985): 1–46.

———. "Why Some Rebel and Others Comply: The Polish Crisis of 1980–81, Eastern Europe and Theories of Revolution." Unpublished paper, 1988.

Calhoun, Craig J. *The Question of Class Struggle: Social Foundations of Popular Radicalism during the Industrial Revolution.* Chicago: University of Chicago Press, 1982.

Calhoun, Daniel F. *Hungary and Suez, 1956: An Exploration of Who Makes History.* Lanham: University Press of America, 1991.

Carnovale, Marco, and William C. Potter, eds. *Continuity and Change in Soviet–East European Relations.* Boulder: Westview Press, 1989.

Casanova, Jose. "Private and Public Religion." *Social Research* 59, no. 1 (1992): 17–57.

Cave, Jane. "Worker Response to Martial Law: The December Strikes." *Poland Watch* 1 (1982): 8–18.

Checinski, Michael. "Polish Secret Police." In *Terror and Communist Politics: The Role of the Secret Police in Communist States*, edited by Jonathan Adelman, 17–78. Boulder: Westview Press, 1984.

———. *The Postwar Development of the Polish Armed Forces.* Santa Monica, Calif.: Rand Corporation, 1979.

Chirot, Daniel. "The Corporatist Model of Socialism." *Theory and Society* 2, no. 9 (1980): 363–81.

Chrypinski, Vincent. "The Catholic Church in Poland, 1944–1989." In *Catholicism and Politics in Communist Societies*, edited by Pedro Ramet, 117–41. Durham: Duke University Press, 1990.

———. "Church and State in Poland after Solidarity." In *Sisyphus and Poland: Reflections on Martial Law*, edited by Joseph Black and John Strong, 145–57. Winnipeg: R. P. Frye, 1986.

Ciepielewski, Jerzy, ed. *Dzieje Panstw Socialistycznych.* Warszawa: PWN, 1986.

Ciolkosz, Lidia. "The Uncensored Press." *Survey* 24, no. 4 (1979): 56–67.

Clark, Cal, and Donna Bahry. "Dependent Development: A Socialist Variant." *International Studies Quarterly* 27, no. 3 (1983): 271–93.

Collier, David, ed. *The New Authoritarianism in Latin America.* Princeton: Princeton University Press, 1979.

Comisso, Ellen. "Where Have We Been and Where Are We Going? Analyzing Post-Socialist Politics in the 1990s." In *Political Science: Looking to the Futured*, ed. William J. Crotty, 77–122. Evanston: Northwestern University Press, 1991.

Connor, Walter D., and Zvi Y. Gitelman, eds. *Public Opinion in European Socialist Systems.* New York: Praeger, 1977.

Crane, Keith. "Soviet Economic Policy towards Eastern Europe." In *Continuity and Change in Soviet–East European Relations*, edited by Marco Carnovale and William C. Potter, 75–133. Boulder: Westview Press, 1989.

Crotty, William J. *Political Science: Looking to the Future: Comparative Politics, Policy, and International Relations.* Evanston: Northwestern University Press, 1991.

Csepeli, Gyorgy, and Antal Orkeny. *Ideology and Political Beliefs in Hungary: The Twilight of State-Socialism.* New York: Columbia University Press, 1992.

Csizmas, Michael. "Die ungarische Volksarmee nach der Revolution." *Osterreichische Militarische Zeitschrift* 2 (1967): 134–45.

Curry, Jane L. ed. *Dissent in Eastern Europe*. New York: Praeger, 1983.

Cviic, Christopher. "The Church." In *Poland: Genesis of a Revolution*, edited by Abraham Brumberg, 92–108. New York: Random House, 1983.

Czerwinski, Edward J., and Jaroslaw Piekalkiewicz, eds. *The Soviet Invasion of Czechoslovakia: Its Effects on Eastern Europe*. New York: Praeger, 1972.

Davies, James C. "Toward a Theory of Revolution." *American Sociological Review* 27 (1962): 5–19.

Dawisha, Karen. *Eastern Europe, Gorbachev, and Reform*. Cambridge: Cambridge University Press, 1990.

————. *The Kremlin and the Prague Spring*. Berkeley: University of California Press, 1985.

————. "The 1968 Invasion of Czechoslovakia: Causes, Consequences, and Lessons for the Future." In *Soviet–East European Dilemmas*, edited by Karen Dawisha and Philip Hanson, 9–25. London: Heinemann, 1981.

Dawisha, Karen, and Philip Hanson, eds. *Soviet–East European Dilemmas*. London: Heinemann, 1981.

Dejiny Ceskoslovenska v datech. Praha: Svoboda, 1968.

d'Encausse, Helene Carrere. *Big Brother: The Soviet Union and Soviet Europe*. New York: Holmes and Meier, 1987.

Deutsch, Karl W. "Social Mobilization and Political Development." *American Political Science Review* 55, no. 3 (1961): 493–514.

de Weydenthal, Jan B. "Martial Law and the Reliability of the Polish Military." In *Soviet Allies: The Warsaw Pact and the Issue of Reliability*, edited by Daniel N. Nelson, 225–49. Boulder: Westview Press, 1984.

————. "Poland." In *Yearbook of International Communist Affairs*, edited by Richard F. Staar, 425–49. Stanford: Hoover Institution Press, 1983.

de Weydenthal, Jan B., Bruce D. Porter, and Kevin Devlin. *The Polish Drama, 1980–1982*. Lexington, Mass.: Lexington Books, 1989.

de Zayas, Alfred M. *Nemesis at Potsdam: The Expulsion of the Germans from the East*. Lincoln: University of Nebraska Press, 1988.

Di Palma, Giuseppe. "Democratic Transitions: Puzzles and Surprises from West and East." Program on Central and Eastern Europe Working Paper Series, no. 4. Cambridge: Center for European Studies, Harvard University, 1990.

————. *To Craft Democracies*. Berkeley: University of California Press, 1990.

Donosy (Electronic News Bulletin, available from listproc@fuw.edu.pl or http://info.fuw.edu.pl/donosy) Apr. 1, 1993.

Drachkovitch, Milorad M., ed. *East Central Europe: Yesterday, Today, Tomorrow*. Stanford: Hoover Institution Press, 1982.

Drewnowski, Jan, ed. *Crisis in East European Economy: The Spread of the Polish Disease*. New York: St. Martin's Press, 1982.

Dubcek, Alexander. *Hope Dies Last*. New York: Kodansha, 1993.

Eckstein, Susan, ed. *Power and Popular Protest*. Berkeley: University of California Press, 1989.

Eidlin, Fred H. *The Logic of "Normalization": The Soviet Intervention in Czechoslovakia of 21 August 1968 and the Czechoslovak Responses*. New York: Columbia University Press, 1980.

Eisler, Jerzy. *Marzec 1968*. Warszawa: PWN, 1991.

Ekiert, Grzegorz. "Conditions of Political Obedience and Stability in State-Socialist Societies." CROPSO Working Paper Series, no. 0005. Cambridge: Department of Sociology, Harvard University, 1989.

———. "Democratization Processes in East Central Europe: A Theoretical Reconsideration." *British Journal of Political Science* 21, no. 3 (1991): 285–313.

———. "Peculiarities of Post-Communist Politics: The Case of Poland." *Studies in Comparative Communism* 25, no. 4 (1992): 341–61.

———. "Public Participation and Politics of Discontent in Post-Communist Poland." Program on Eastern and Central Europe Working Paper Series, no. 30. Cambridge: Center for European Studies, Harvard University, 1994.

———. "Rebellious Poles: Cycle of Protest and Popular Mobilization under State-Socialism, 1945–1989." Working Paper Series, no. 5. Advanced Study Center International Institute, University of Michigan, 1995.

———. "Recent Elections in Poland and Hungary: The Coming Crisis of Ritualized Politics." CROPSO Working Paper Series, no. 0014. Cambridge: Department of Sociology, Harvard University, 1989.

———. "Transitions from State-Socialism in East Central Europe." *State and Social Structures Newsletters* 12 (1990): 1–6.

Erdei, Ferenc, ed. *Information Hungary*. Budapest: Akademiai Kiado, 1968.

Fallenbuch, Zbigniew. "Anatomy of Stagnation." In *Pressures for Reform in the East European Economies*, edited by the U.S. Congress, Joint Economic Committee, 2:102–36. Washington, D.C.: Government Printing Office, 1989.

———. "The Polish Economy under Martial Law." *Soviet Studies* 36, no. 4 (1984): 513–27.

———. *Polityka gospodarcza PRL*. London: Odnowa, 1980.

Farrell, R. Barry, ed. *Political Leadership in Eastern Europe and the Soviet Union*. Chicago: Aldine, 1970.

Feher, Ferenc. "Kadarism as Applied Khrushchevism." In *Khrushchev and the Communist World*, edited by Robert Miller and Ferenc Feher, 210–29. London: Croom Helm, 1984.

———. "Kadarism as the Model State of Khrushchevism." *Telos* 40 (1979): 19–31.

Feher, Ferenc, and Andrew Arato, eds. *Crisis and Reform in Eastern Europe*. New Brunswick, N.J.: Transaction, 1991.

Feher, Ferenc, and Agnes Heller. *Hungary 1956 Revisited*. London: Allen and Unwin, 1983.

Feher, Ferenc, Agnes Heller, and Gyorgy Markus. *Dictatorship over Needs*. New York: Basil Blackwell, 1983.

Fejto, Francois. *Le Coup de Prague, 1948*. Paris: Editions du Seuil, 1976.

Felkay, Andrew. *Hungary and the USSR, 1956–1988*. New York: Greenwood Press, 1989.

Fisera, Vladimir C., ed. *Workers' Councils in Czechoslovakia*. London: Allison and Busby, 1978.

Fleron, Frederic, Jr., Eric P. Hoffmann, and Robbin F. Laird, eds. *Soviet Foreign Policy: Classic and Contemporary Issues*. Hawthorne, N.Y.: Aldine de Gruyter, 1991.

Frentzel-Zagorska, Janina, and Krzysztof Zagorski. "East European Intellectuals on the Road of Dissent: The Old Prophecy of a New Class Re-examined." *Politics and Society* 17, no. 1 (1989): 89–113.

Fry, Michael, and Condoleezza Rice. "The Hungarian Crisis of 1956: The Soviet Decision." *Studies in Comparative Communism* 16, nos. 1–2 (1983): 85–90.

Gamson, William A. *The Strategy of Social Protest.* 2d. ed. Belmont, Calif.: Wadsworth, 1990.

Garnysz, Casimir. "Polish Stalemate." *Problems of Communism* 33, no. 3 (1984): 51–59.

Garreton, Manuel Antonio. "Popular Mobilization and the Military Regime in Chile: The Complexities of the Invisible Transition." In *Power and Popular Protest*, edited by Susan Eckstein, 259–77. Berkeley: University of California Press, 1989.

Gati, Charles. "The Democratic Interlude in Post-War Hungary." *Survey* 28, no. 2 (1984): 99–134.

———. *Hungary and the Soviet Bloc.* Durham: Duke University Press, 1986.

———. "Imre Nagy and Moscow, 1953–1956." *Problems of Communism* 35, no. 3 (1986): 32–49.

Gebert, Konstanty. *Magia slow: Polityka francuska wobec Polski po 13 grudnia 1981 roku.* London: Aneks, 1991.

Gerlach, Luther P., and Victoria H. Hine. *People, Power, and Change: Movements of Social Transformation.* Indianapolis: Bobbs-Merrill, 1970.

Gitelman, Zvi Y. "The Politics of Socialist Restoration in Hungary and Czechoslovakia." *Comparative Politics* 13 (1981): 187–210. Reprinted in *Revolutions: Theoretical, Comparative, and Historical Studies*, edited by Jack Goldstone, 268–80. San Diego: Harcourt Brace Jovanovich, 1986.

———. "Public Opinion in Communist Political Systems." In *Public Opinion in European Socialist Systems*, edited by Walter D. Connor and Zvi Y. Gitelman, 1–40. New York: Praeger, 1977.

Glowny Urzad Statystyczny. *Maly Rocznik Statystyczny 1990.* Warszawa: GUS, 1990.

———. *Rocznik Statystyczny 1991.* Warszawa: GUS, 1991.

Golan, Galia. "Comment: Reform Movements and the Problem of Prediction." *Studies in Comparative Communism* 8, no. 4 (1975): 430–35.

———. *The Czechoslovak Reform Movement.* Cambridge: Cambridge University Press, 1971.

———. *Reform Rule in Czechoslovakia.* Cambridge: Cambridge University Press, 1973.

Goldfarb, Jeffrey C. *Beyond Glasnost: The Post-Totalitarian Mind.* Chicago: University of Chicago Press, 1989.

Goldstone, Jack A., ed. *Revolutions: Theoretical, Comparative, and Historical Studies.* San Diego: Harcourt Brace Jovanovich, 1986.

Gollner, Andrew B. "Foundations of Soviet Domination and Communist Political Power in Hungary: 1945–1950." *Canadian-American Review of Hungarian Studies* 3, no. 2 (1976): 73–105.

Gomulka, Stanislaw. *Growth, Innovation and Reform in Eastern Europe.* Madison: University of Wisconsin Press, 1986.

Gomulka, Stanislaw, and Jacek Rostowski. "The Reformed Polish Economic System, 1982–1983." *Soviet Studies* 36, no. 3 (1984): 386–405.

Goodwyn, Lawrence. *Breaking the Barriers: The Rise of Solidarity in Poland*. New York: Oxford University Press, 1991.

Gordon, Lincoln, ed. *Eroding Empire: Western Relations with Eastern Europe*. Washington, D.C.: Brookings Institution, 1987.

Gosztony, Peter. "Zur Geschichte des ungarischen nationalen Wiederstandes in der Anfangsperiods des Kadar-Regimes." *Osteuropa* 18, nos. 10–11 (1968): 805–24.

Gould, Roger V. "Multiple Networks and Mobilization in the Paris Commune, 1871." *American Sociological Review* 56, no. 6 (1991): 716–30.

Gourevitch, Peter A. "Breaking with Orthodoxy: The Politics of Economic Policy Responses to the Depression of the 1930s." *International Organization* 38, no. 1 (Winter 1984): 95–129.

Granville, Johanna. "Imre Nagy, Hesitant Revolutionary." *Cold War International History Project Bulletin* 5 (Spring 1995): 23, 27–37.

Gross, Jan T. "Social Consequences of War: Preliminaries to the Study of Imposition of Communist Regimes in East Central Europe." *East European Politics and Societies* 3, no. 2 (1989): 198–214.

Grudzinska-Gross, Irena. "Culture as Opposition in Today's Poland." *Journal of International Affairs* 40, no. 2 (1987): 387–90.

Gueyt, Remi. *La mutation tchecoslovaque: analysee par un temoin, 1969–1969*. Paris: Editions ouvrieres, 1969.

Gyorgy, Andrew. "The Hungarian Revolution of 1956." In *The Anatomy of Communist Takeovers*, edited by Thomas Hammond, 596–603. New Haven: Yale University Press, 1975.

Hahn, Werner G. *Democracy in the Communist Party: Poland's Experience Since 1980*. New York: Columbia University Press, 1987.

Halamska, Maria. "Peasant Movement in Poland." *Research in Social Movements, Conflicts, and Change* 10 (1988): 147–60.

Halasz de Beky, I. L. *A Bibliography of the Hungarian Revolution, 1956*. Toronto: University of Toronto Press, 1963.

Hall, Peter. *Governing the Economy: The Politics of State Intervention in Britain and France*. New York: Oxford University Press, 1986.

Hammond, Thomas T., ed. *The Anatomy of Communist Takeovers*. New Haven: Yale University Press, 1975.

Hankiss, Elemer. "Demobilization, Self-Mobilization, and Quasi-Mobilization in Hungary, 1948–1987." *East European Politics and Societies* 3, no. 1 (1989): 105–52.

Hauner, Milan. "The Prague Spring—Twenty Years After." In *Czechoslovakia: Crossroads and Crises, 1919–1988*, edited by Norman Stone and Eduard Strouhal, 207–30. New York: St. Martin's Press, 1989.

Havel, Vaclav. "Letter to Dr. Gustav Husak." In *Vaclav Havel or Living in Truth*, edited by Jan Vladislav, 3–35. London: Faber and Faber, 1986.

Hegedus, Andras. "Additional Remarks by a Major Participant in the Hungarian Revolution of 1956." *Studies in Comparative Communism* 18, nos. 2–3 (1985): 118.

Heller, Agnes, and Ferenc Feher. *From Yalta to Glasnost*. Oxford: Basil Blackwell, 1990.

Helsinki Watch Committee. *Poland under Martial Law*. New York: U.S. Helsinki Watch Committee, 1983.

————. *Violation of Human Rights in Poland.* London: Libra Books, 1985.

Hillebrandt, Bogdan. *Marzec 1968.* Warszawa: Wydawnictwo Spoldzielcze, 1986.

Hirschman, Albert. *Exit, Voice and Loyalty.* Princeton: Princeton University Press, 1970.

————. *Shifting Involvements.* Princeton: Princeton University Press, 1982.

Hirszowicz, Maria. *Coercion and Control in Communist Societies.* Brighton: Wheatsheaf Books, 1986.

Hochman, Jiri. "Words and Tanks." In *The Prague Spring: A Mixed Legacy,* edited by Jiri Pehe, 27–40. New York: Freedom House, 1988.

Hoensch, Jorg Konrad. *A History of Modern Hungary, 1867–1986.* London: Longman, 1988.

Hofer, Tamas, "Demonstration of March 15, 1989 in Budapest: A Struggle for Public Memory." Program on Central and Eastern Europe Working Paper Series, Center for European Studies, Harvard University, no. 15 (1991).

Hoffmann, Eric P. "Soviet Foreign Policy: Aims and Accomplishments from Lenin to Brezhnev." In *Soviet Foreign Policy: Classic and Contemporary Issues,* edited by Frederic Fleron Jr., Eric P. Hoffmann, and Robbin F. Laird, 49–71. Hawthorne, N.Y.: Aldine de Gruyter, 1991.

Hollos, Marida, and Bela C. Maday, eds. *New Hungarian Peasants: An East Central European Experience with Collectivization.* New York: Columbia University Press, 1983.

Holmes, Leslie, ed. *The Withering Away of the State.* London: Sage, 1981.

Holzer, Jerzy. *Solidarnosc, 1980–1981.* Paris: Instytut Literacki, 1984.

————. "Stan wojenny: Dla Polski czy dla socjalizmu?" *Gazeta Wyborcza* 130, June 7, 1994, pp. 19–21.

Holzer, Jerzy, and Krzysztof Leski. *Solidarnosc w podziemiu.* Lodz: Wydawnictwo Lodzkie, 1990.

Humsik, Dusan. *Writers against the Rulers.* New York: Random House, 1971.

Hungarian Peoples Republic. *The Counter-Revolutionary Conspiracy of Imre Nagy and His Accomplices.* Budapest: Information Bureau of the Council of Ministers, 1958.

Hungary Today. New York: Praeger, 1962.

Hungary under the Communists. New York: Praeger, 1957.

Huntington, Samuel P. *Political Order in Changing Societies.* New Haven: Yale University Press, 1969.

International Commission of Jurists. *The Hungarian Situation and the Rule of Law.* Hague: Tri Press, 1957.

Jancar, Barbara Wolfe. *Czechoslovakia and the Absolute Monopoly of Power.* New York: Praeger, 1971.

Janos, Andrew. "Social Science, Communism, and the Dynamics of Political Change." *World Politics* 44, no. 1 (1991): 81–112.

Jaruzelski, Wojciech. *Stan Wojenny: Dlaczego . . .* Warszawa: BGW, 1992.

Jenkins, J. Craig, and Charles Perrow. "Insurgency of the Powerless: Farm Worker Movement (1946–1972)." *American Sociological Review* 42 (1977): 249–68.

Jerome, Robert T., Jr. "Sources of Economic Growth in Hungary." *East European Quarterly* 22, no. 1 (1988): 107–18.

Jonas, Paul. "Economic Aspect." In *The Hungarian Revolution of 1956 in Retrospect,* edited by Bela Kiraly and Paul Jonas, 33–38. Boulder: East European Quarterly, 1978.

Jones, Christopher D. "Soviet Hegemony in Eastern Europe: The Dynamics of Political Autonomy and Military Intervention." *World Politics* 29, no. 2 (1977): 216–41.

Jowitt, Ken. "Inclusion and Mobilization in European Leninist Regimes." *World Politics* 28, no. 1 (1975): 69–97.

———. "Moscow 'Centre.'" *East European Politics and Societies* 1, no. 3 (1987): 296–352.

———. "Weber, Trotsky and Holmes on the Study of Leninist Regimes." *Journal of International Affairs* 45, no. 1 (1991): 31–49.

Judt, Tony. "The Dilemmas of Dissidence: The Politics of Opposition in East Central Europe." *East European Politics and Societies* 2, no. 2 (1988): 185–241.

Juhasz, William, ed. *Hungarian Social Science Reader, 1945–63*. New York: Aurora Editions, 1965.

Kadar, Janos. "The Basis of Consensus." *New Hungarian Quarterly* 23, no. 86 (1982): 7–22.

———. *Selected Speeches and Interviews*. Budapest: Akademiai Kiado, 1985.

———. *Socialism and Democracy in Hungary*. Budapest: Corvina Kiado, 1984.

Kalinovska, Milena. "Czechoslovakia Ten Years After." *Religion in Communist Lands* 6, no. 3 (1978): 100–110.

Kaminski, Andrzej. "Anachronizm czy meczenstwo." *Krytyka* 16 (1983): 218–28.

Kaminski, Bartlomiej. *The Collapse of State Socialism*. Princeton: Princeton University Press, 1991.

———. "Systemic Underpinnings of the Transition in Poland: The Shadow of the Roundtable Agreement." *Studies in Comparative Communism* 24, no. 2 (1991): 173–90.

Kaminski, Ted. "Underground Publishing in Poland." *Orbis* 31, no. 3 (1987): 313–29.

Kaplan, Frank L. *Winter into Spring: The Czechoslovak Press and the Reform Movement 1963–68*. Boulder: Westview Press, 1977.

Kaplan, Karel. "Church and State in Czechoslovakia from 1948–1956." *Religion in Communist Lands* 14, nos. 1–3 (1986): 59–72, 180–193, 273–282.

———. "Czechoslovakia's February 1948." In *Czechoslovakia: Crossroads and Crises, 1918–1988*, edited by Norman Stone and Eduard Strouhal, 147–68. New York: St. Martin's Press, 1989.

———. *Political Persecution in Czechoslovakia, 1948–1972*. Research Project "Crises in Soviet-Type Systems" no. 3. Koln: Index, 1983.

———. *Report on the Murder of the General Secretary*. Columbus: Ohio University Press, 1990.

Kaplan, Stephen S., ed. *Diplomacy of Power*. Washington, D.C.: Brookings Institution, 1981.

Karas, Anna, ed. *Sad nad autorami stanu wojennego*. Warszawa: BGW, 1993.

Karl, Terry. "Dilemmas of Democratization in Latin America." *Comparative Politics* 23, no. 1 (1990): 1–21.

Karl, Terry, and Philippe C. Schmitter. "Modes of Transition in Latin America, Southern and Eastern Europe." *International Social Science Journal* 128 (1991): 269–84.

Karpinski, Jakub. *Count-Down*. New York: Karz-Cohl, 1982.

———. *Dziwna wojna*. Paris: Instytut Literacki, 1990.

———. "Polish Intellectuals in Opposition." *Problems of Communism* 36, no. 4 (1987): 44–57.

Kavan, Jan. "From the Prague Spring to a Long Winter." In *The Prague Spring: A Mixed Legacy,* edited by Jiri Pehe, 103–29. New York: Freedom House, 1988.

Kawalec, Stefan. *Demokratyczna Opozycja w Polsce.* Warszawa: Glos, 1979.

Keane, John, ed. *Civil Society and the State.* London: Verso, 1988.

Kecskemeti, Paul. *The Unexpected Revolution.* Stanford: Stanford University Press, 1961.

Kemme, David M., ed. *Economic Reform in Poland: The Aftermath of Martial Law, 1981–1988.* Greenwich, Conn.: JAI Press, 1991.

Kemme, David, and Keith Crane. "The Polish Economic Collapse: Contributing Factors and Economic Costs." *Journal of Comparative Economics* 8 (1984): 25–40.

Kende, Pierre, and Krzysztof Pomian, eds. *1956, Varsovie—Budapest: La deuxieme revolution d'Octobre.* Paris: Seuil, 1978.

Kennedy, Michael. *Professionals, Power and Solidarity in Poland.* Cambridge: Cambridge University Press, 1991.

Kennedy, Paul. *The Rise and Fall of Great Powers.* New York: Random House, 1987.

King, Robert R., and James F. Brown, eds. *Eastern Europe's Uncertain Future.* New York: Praeger, 1978.

Kiraly, Bela K. "The Armed Forces and the Working Class in the Hungarian Revolution, 1956." *New Politics* 1, no. 1 (1986): 193–212.

———. "The Hungarian Revolution and Soviet Readiness to Wage War against Socialist States." In *The First War between Socialist States: The Hungarian Revolution of 1956 and Its Impact,* edited by Bela K. Kiraly, Barbara Lotze, and Nandor F. Dreisziger, 3–31. New York: Brooklyn College Press 1984.

———. "Hungary's Army under the Soviets." *East Europe* 7 (1958): 3–14.

———. "The Organization of National Defense during the Hungarian Revolution." *Central European Federalist* 14, no. 1 (1966): 12–22.

Kiraly, Bela K., and Paul Jonas, eds. *The Hungarian Revolution of 1956 in Retrospect.* Boulder: East European Quarterly, 1978.

Kiraly, Bela K., Barbara Lotze, and Nandor F. Dreisziger, eds. *The First War between Socialist States: The Hungarian Revolution of 1956 and Its Impact.* New York: Brooklyn College Press, 1984.

Kis, Janos. *Politics in Hungary: For a Democratic Alternative.* New York: Columbia University Press, 1989.

Kitschelt, Herbert. "Political Opportunity Structures and Political Protest: Antinuclear Movements in Four Democracies." *British Journal of Political Science* 16, no. 1 (1986): 57–85.

Kittrie, Nicholas N., and Ivan Volgyes, eds. *The Uncertain Future: Gorbachev's Eastern Bloc.* New York: Paragon House, 1988.

Klandermans, Bert, Hanspeter Kriesi, and Sidney Tarrow, eds. *From Structure to Action: Comparing Social Movements across Cultures.* Greenwich, Conn.: JAI Press, 1988.

Klein, George. "The Role of Ethnic Politics in the Czechoslovak Crisis of 1968 and the Yugoslav Crisis of 1971." *Studies in Comparative Communism* 8, no. 4 (1975): 339–69.

Kolakowski, Leszek. "The Intelligentsia." In *Poland: Genesis of a Revolution,* edited by Abraham Brumberg, 54–67. New York: Random House, 1983.

Kolakowski, Leszak. "Swiadomosc narodowa i rozklad komunizmu." In *1956 w dwadziescia lat pozniej z mysla o przyszlosci*, 24–29. London: Aneks, 1979.

Kolankiewicz, George. "Poland and the Politics of Permissible Pluralism." *East European Politics and Societies* 2, no. 1 (1988): 152–82.

———. "Polish Trade Unions 'Normalized.'" *Problems of Communism* 36, no. 6 (1987): 57–69.

———. "The Regime Responses to Solidarity." In *Solidarity and Poland: Impacts East and West*, edited by Steve Reiquam, 5–13. Washington, D.C.: Wilson Center Press, 1988.

Kolankiewicz, George, and Paul G. Lewis. *Poland: Politics, Economics and Society*. London: Pinter, 1988.

Kolarska, Lena, and Andrzej Rychard. "Lad Polityczny i Lad Ekonomiczny." In *Polacy '81*, edited by Wladyslaw Adamski et al., 197–267. Warszawa: IFiS PAN, 1982.

Kolarska-Bobinska, Lena. "Civil Society and Social Anomy in Poland." *Acta Sociologica* 33, no. 4 (1990): 277–88.

Kopacsi, Sandor. *In the Name of Working Class*. New York: Grove Press, 1987.

Korbonski, Andrzej. "CMEA, Economic Interpretation, and Perestroika, 1948–1989." *Studies in Comparative Communism* 23, no. 1 (1990): 47–72.

———. "Ideology Disabused: Communism without a Face in Eastern Europe." In *The Uncertain Future: Gorbachev's Eastern Bloc*, edited by Nicholas Kittrie and Ivan Volgyes, 39–56. New York: Paragon House, 1988.

———. "The Polish Army." In *Communist Armies in Politics*, edited by Jonathan Adelman, 103–28. Boulder: Westview Press, 1982.

———. "The Revolution and East Central Europe." In *The First War between Socialist States: The Hungarian Revolution of 1956 and Its Impact*, edited by Bela Kiraly, Barbara Lotze, and Nandor Dreisziger, 355–70. New York: Brooklyn College Press, 1984.

———. "Soviet-East European Relations in the 1980s: Continuity and Change." *Continuity and Change in Soviet–East European Relations*, edited by Marco Carnovale and William Potter, 5–26. Boulder: Westview Press, 1989.

———. "Soviet Policy toward Poland." In *Soviet Policy in Eastern Europe*, edited by Sarah Terry, 61–92. New Haven: Yale University Press, 1984.

———. "Victim or Villain: Polish Agriculture since 1970." In *Background to Crisis: Policy and Politics in Gierek's Poland*, edited by Maurice Simon and Roger Kanet, 271–98. Boulder: Westview Press, 1981.

Korda, B. "A Decade of Economic Growth in Czechoslovakia (1962–73)." *Communist Studies* 28, no. 4 (1976): 499–523.

Kornai, Janos. "The Hungarian Reform Process: Visions, Hopes and Reality." In *Remaking the Economic Institutions of Socialism*, edited by Victor Nee and David Stark, 32–94. Stanford: Stanford University Press, 1989.

Korybutowicz, Zygmunt. *Grudzien 1970*. Paris: Instytut Literacki, 1983.

Kovalev, S. "Sovereignty and the Internal Obligations of Socialist Countries." *Pravda* (Sept. 26, 1968). Translated in *Current Digest of the Soviet Press* 20, no. 39 (Oct. 16, 1968): 10–12.

Kovaly, Heda Margolius. *Under a Cruel Star: A Life in Prague, 1941–1968*. Cambridge: Plunkett Lake Press, 1986.

Kovanda, Karel. "Czechoslovak Workers' Councils, 1968–69." *Telos* 28 (1976): 36–54.

————. "Czechoslovakia in Transition." *Telos* 31 (1977): 143–47.

Kovats, Charles. "The Path of Church-State Reconciliation in Hungary." In *Eastern Europe's Uncertain Future*, edited by Robert King and James F. Brown, 301–11. New York: Praeger, 1978.

Kovrig, Bennett. *Communism in Hungary: From Kun to Kadar.* Stanford: Hoover Institution Press, 1979.

————. "Rolling Back Liberation: The United States and the Hungarian Revolution." In *The First War between Socialist States*, edited by Bela K. Kiraly, Barbara Lotze, and Nandor F. Dreisziger, 279–90. New York: Brooklyn College Press, 1984.

Kramer, Mark. "New Sources on the 1968 Soviet Invasion of Czechoslovakia," *Cold War International History Project Bulletin* 2 (Fall 1992): 1, 4–13.

————. "Poland, 1980–1: Soviet Policy during the Polish Crisis." *Cold War International History Project Bulletin* 5 (Spring 1995): 1, 116–39.

————. "The Prague Spring and the Soviet Invasion of Czechoslovakia: New Interpretations." *Cold War International History Project Bulletin* 3 (Fall 1993): 2–13, 54–55.

Krzeminski, Ireneusz. *Czego chcieli, o czym mysleli? Analiza postulatow robotnikow Wybrzeza z 1970 i 1980.* Warszawa: IS UW, 1987.

Kubik, Jan. "John Paul II's First Visit to Poland and the Collapse of the Official Marxist-Leninist Discourse." CROPSO Working Paper Series, no. 0025. Cambridge: Harvard University, 1989.

————. *The Power of Symbols against the Symbols of Power: The Rise of Solidarity and the Fall of State Socialism in Poland.* University Park: Penn State University Press, 1994.

————. "Social and Political Instability in Poland: A Theoretical Reconsideration." Program on Central and Eastern Europe Working Paper Series, no. 1. Cambridge: Center for European Studies, Harvard University, 1990.

————. "Who Done It: Workers or Intellectuals? Controversy over Solidarity's Origins and Social Composition." *Theory and Society* 23 (1994): 441–66.

Kuczynski, Pawel. "Dwa modele swiadomosci politycznej: Analiza ruchu spolecznego, 1980–81." In *Demokracja i Gospodarka*, edited by Witold Morawski, 461–90. Warszawa: Instytut Socjologii UW, 1983.

Kuczynski, Waldemar. *Po wielkim skoku.* Warszawa: NOWA, 1979.

Kuklinski, Ryszard. "The Crushing of Solidarity." *Orbis* 32, no. 1 (1988): 7–32.

————. "Wojna z narodem widziana od srodka." *Kultura* 4, no. 475 (1987): 3–57.

Kurczewski, Jacek. "The Old System and the Revolution." *Sisyphus* 3 (1982): 21–32.

Kuron, Jacek. "Krajobraz po bitwie." *Aneks* 48 (1987): 3–13.

Kusin, Vladimir V. "Challenge to Normalcy: Political Opposition in Czechoslovakia." In *Opposition in Eastern Europe*, edited by Rudolf Tokes, 26–59. Baltimore: Johns Hopkins University Press, 1979.

————. *From Dubcek to Charter 77: A Study of "Normalization" in Czechoslovakia, 1968–1978.* Edinburgh: Q Press, 1978.

————. *The Intellectual Origins of the Prague Spring: The Development of Reformist Ideas in Czechoslovakia, 1956–1967.* Cambridge: Cambridge University Press, 1971.

————. *Political Grouping in the Czechoslovak Reform Movement.* London: Q Press, 1972.

Kusin, Vladimir V., and Zdenek Hejzlar. *Czechoslovakia, 1968–1969: Annotation, Bibliography, Chronology.* New York: Garland, 1974.

Laba, Roman. *The Roots of Solidarity.* Princeton: Princeton University Press, 1991.

Laitin, David. "Hegemony and the State." *States and Social Structures Newsletter* 9 (Winter 1989): 1–4.

Lamentowicz, Wojciech. "Adaptation through Political Crises in Post-War Poland." *Journal of Peace Research* 19, no. 2 (1982): 117–31.

―――. "Eastern Europe and the Emergence of Civil Society: Starting Point of the Long Process." Paper presented at the 83d Annual Meeting of the American Sociological Association in Atlanta, Aug. 28, 1988.

Lasky, Melvin J., ed. *The Hungarian Revolution.* New York: Praeger, 1957.

Lechowicz, Leszek. "The Mass Media under Martial Law." *Poland Watch* 1 (1982): 41–50.

Lepak, Keith John. *Prelude to Solidarity: Poland and the Politics and the Gierek Regime.* New York: Columbia University Press, 1988.

Lewis, Flora. *A Case History of Hope: The Story of Poland's Peaceful Revolution.* New York: Doubleday, 1958.

Lewis, Paul G. *Political Authority and Party Secretaries in Poland, 1975–1986.* Cambridge: Cambridge University Press, 1988.

―――. "Political Institutionalisation and Party Development in Post-Communist Poland." *Europe-Asia Studies* 46, no. 5 (1994): 779–99.

Lewis, Paul G., ed. *Eastern Europe: Political Crisis and Legitimation.* New York: St. Martin's Press, 1984.

Liehm, Antonin J. "Intellectuals on the New Social Contract." *Telos* 23 (1975): 156–64.

―――. "It Was You Who Did It!" In *The Prague Spring: A Mixed Legacy*, edited by Jiri Pehe, 171–75. New York: Freedom House, 1988.

―――. "The New Social Contract and Parallel Polity." In *Dissent in Eastern Europe*, edited by Jane Curry, 173–81. New York: Praeger, 1983.

―――. *Nowa Umowa Spoleczna.* Warszawa: NOWA, 1978.

Lijphart, Arend. "The Comparable-Case Strategy in Comparative Research." *Comparative Political Studies* 8 (1975): 158–77.

―――. "Comparative Politics and the Comparative Method." *American Political Science Review* 65, no. 3 (1971): 682–98.

Linz, Juan. *Crisis, Breakdown, and Reequilibration.* Baltimore: Johns Hopkins University Press, 1978.

Lipski, Jan Jozef. *KOR.* London: Aneks, 1983.

―――. *KOR: A History of the Workers' Defense Committee in Poland, 1976–1981.* Berkeley: University of California Press, 1985.

Littell, Robert, ed. *The Czech Black Book.* New York: Praeger, 1969.

Loebl, Eugen. *Sentenced and Tried: The Stalinist Purges in Czechoslovakia.* London: Elek Books, 1969.

Lomax, Bill. "The Hungarian Revolution of 1956 and the Origin of the Kadar Regime." *Studies in Comparative Communism* 18, nos. 2–3 (1985): 87–113.

―――. *Hungary, 1956.* New York: St. Martin's Press, 1976.

―――. "Hungary—The Quest for Legitimacy." In *Eastern Europe: Political Crisis and Legitimation*, edited by Paul G. Lewis, 68–110. New York: St. Martin's Press, 1984.

―――. "25 Years Later—New Light on 1956." *Labour Focus on Eastern Europe* 5, no. 3–4 (1982): 14–16.

Lomax, Bill, ed. *Hungarian Workers' Councils in 1956.* New York: Columbia University Press, 1990.

London, Artur. *The Confession.* New York: Ballantine Books, 1970.

Lopinski, Maciej, Marcin Moskit, and Mariusz Wilk. *Konspira: Solidarity Underground.* Berkley: California University Press, 1990.

Lovas, Istvan, and Ken Anderson. "State Terrorism in Hungary: The Case of Friendly Repression." *Telos* 54 (1982–83): 77–86.

Luza, Radomir. *The Transfer of the Sudeten Germans: A Study of Czecho-German Relations, 1933–1962.* New York: New York University Press, 1964.

Maciejewski, Jaroslaw, and Zofia Trojanowicz. *Poznanski Czerwiec, 1956.* Poznan: Wydawnictwo Poznanskie, 1981.

Maier, Charles S., "Why Did Communism Collapse in 1989." Program on Eastern and Central Europe Working Papers Series, no. 7. Cambridge: Center for European Studies, Harvard University, 1991.

Maier, Charles S., ed. *Changing Boundaries of the Political.* Cambridge: Cambridge University Press, 1987.

Majsai, Tamas. "Protestants under Communism." *New Hungarian Quarterly* 32, no. 123 (1991): 58–67.

Malcher, George C. *Poland's Politicized Army: Communists in Uniform.* New York: Praeger, 1984.

Mann, Michael. "The Autonomous Power of the State: Its Origin, Mechanisms and Results." *Archives Europeennes de Sociologie* 25, no. 2 (1984): 185–213.

Manticone, Ronald C. *The Catholic Church in Communist Poland, 1945–1985.* New York: Columbia University Press, 1986.

Marciniak, Piotr. "Horyzont programowy strajkow 1980 r." *Studia nad Ruchami Spolecznymi* 2 (1989): 131–200.

Marczali, Tibor Arthur. "Criminal Law in Communist Hungary." *Slavic Review* 23, no. 1 (1964): 92–102.

Marentz, Paul. "Economic Sanctions in the Polish Crisis." In *Sisyphus and Poland: Reflections on Martial Law,* edited by Joseph Black and John Strong, 109–24. Winnipeg: R. P. Frye, 1986

Marer, Paul, and Kazimierz Poznanski. "Costs of Domination, Benefits of Subordination."In *Dominant Powers and Subordinate States,* edited by Jan Triska, 371–99. Durham: Duke University Press, 1986.

Marer, Paul, and Wlodzimierz Sliwinski, eds. *Creditworthiness and Reform in Poland.* Bloomington: Indiana University Press, 1988.

Marody, Miroslawa, and Antoni Sulek, eds. *Rzeczywistosc polska i sposoby radzenia sobie z nia.* Warszawa: Universytet Warszawski, Instytut Socjologii 1987.

Mason, David S. "Poland's New Trade Unions." *Soviet Studies* 39, no. 3 (1987): 489–508.

―――. *Public Opinion and Political Change in Poland, 1980–1981.* Cambridge: Cambridge University Press, 1985.

McAdam, Doug. " 'Initiator' and 'Spin-Off' Movements: Diffusion Processes in Protest Cycles." In *Repertoires and Cycles of Collective Action,* edited by Mark Traugott, 217–39. Durham: Duke University Press, 1995.

―――. *Political Process and the Development of Black Insurgency, 1930–1970.* Chicago: University of Chicago Press, 1982.

McAdams, A. James. "Crisis in the Soviet Empire: Three Ambiguities in Search of a Prediction." *Comparative Politics* 20, no. 1 (1987): 107–18.

McCarthy, John D., and Mayer N. Zald, eds. *The Dynamics of Social Movements: Resource Mobilization, Social Control, and Outcomes.* Cambridge: Winthrop, 1977.

McCauley, Brian. "Hungary and Suez, 1956: The Limits of Soviet and American Power." In *The First War between Socialist States*, edited by Bela Kiraly, Barbara Lotze, and Nandor Dreisziger, 291–316. New York: Brooklyn College Press, 1984.

McNall, Scott G. *The Road to Rebellion: Class Formation and Kansas Populism, 1865–1900.* Chicago: University of Chicago Press, 1988.

Meray, Tibor. *That Day in Budapest.* New York: Funk and Wagnalls, 1969.

Micewski, Andrzej. *Kosciol—Panstwo, 1945–1989.* Warszawa: Wydawnictwa Szkolne i Pedagogiczne, 1994.

Michnik, Adam. *The Church and the Left.* 1977. Chicago: University of Chicago Press, 1993.

———. *Letters from Prison and Other Essays.* Berkeley: University of California Press, 1985.

Michta, Andrew A. *Red Eagle: The Army in Polish Politics, 1944–1988.* Stanford: Hoover Institution Press, 1990.

Migdal, Joel S. *Strong Societies and Weak States.* Princeton: Princeton University Press, 1988.

Miller, Robert F., and Ferenc Feher, eds. *Khrushchev and the Communist World.* London: Croom Helm, 1984.

Mlynar, Zdenek. *Nightfrost in Prague.* New York: Karz, 1980.

Mlynar, Zdenek, and Aleksander Muller, eds. *Ceskoslovensko 1968—Polsko 1981: A krize Sovetskych systemu.* Koln: Index, 1983.

Mokrzycki, Edmund. "Dziedzictwo realnego socjalizmu, interesy grupowe i poszukiwanie nowej utopii." *Kultura i Spoleczenstwo* 35, no. 1 (1991): 7–16.

Molnar, Janos. *A Nagybudapesti Kozponti Munkastanacs.* Budapest: Akademiai Kiado, 1969.

———. *Ellenforradalom Magyarorszagon, 1956-ban.* Budapest: Akademiai Kiado, 1967.

Molnar, Miklos. *Budapest, 1956.* London: Allen and Unwin, 1971.

———. *From Bela Kun to Janos Kadar.* New York: Berg, 1990.

———. "The Heritage of Imre Nagy." In *Ten Years After*, edited by Tamas Aczel, 153–74. London: Macgibbon and Kee, 1966.

———. *A Short History of the Hungarian Communist Party.* Boulder: Westview Press, 1978.

Morawski, Witold, ed. *Demokracja i gospodarka.* Warszawa: Instytut Sociologii UW, 1983.

Morgenthau, Hans J. "The Revolution in U.S. Foreign Policy." *Commentary* 23, no. 2 (1957): 101–5.

Mrela, Krzysztof. "System's Identity Crisis: Revolt and Normalization in Poland." In *The Crisis—Problems in Poland*, Research Project "Crises in Soviet-Type Systems," Study 12a, 3–57. Koln: Index, 1987.

Myant, Martin. *The Czechoslovak Economy, 1948–1988.* Cambridge: Cambridge University Press, 1989.

Nagy, Laszlo. "Military Aspects of the Hungarian Revolution." *Saturn* 3, no. 5 (1957): 11–26.

Nee, Victor, and David Stark, eds. *Remaking the Economic Institutions of Socialism.* Stanford: Stanford University Press, 1989.

Nelson, Daniel N. "Comparative Communism: A Postmortem." In *Handbook of Political Science Research on the USSR and Eastern Europe*, edited by Raymond C. Taras, 302–15. London: Greenwood Press, 1992.

Nelson, Daniel N., ed. *Soviet Allies: The Warsaw Pact and the Issue of Reliability.* Boulder: Westview Press, 1984.

Nettl, J. Peter. *Political Mobilization: A Sociological Analysis of Methods and Concepts.* New York: Basic Books, 1967.

Nielsen, Niels C. *Revolutions in Eastern Europe: The Religious Roots.* Maryknoll, N.Y.: Orbis Books, 1991.

Nixon, Richard. "U.S. Foreign Policy for the 1970s: A New Strategy for Peace." A Report to the Congress by R. Nixon, President of the United States, Washington, D.C.: Feb. 18, 1970, pp. 138–39.

Nowak, Jerzy R. *Wegry: Burzliwe lata, 1953–1956.* Warszawa: Almapress, 1988.

———. *Wegry: Wychodzenie z kryzysu, 1956.* Warszawa: Ksiazka i Wiedza, 1984.

Nowak, Leszek. *Property and Power: Toward Non-Marxist Historical Materialism.* Dordrecht: Reidel, 1983.

NSZZ Solidarnosc. *Polska 5 lat po sierpniu.* London: Aneks, 1986.

Oberschall, Anthony. *Social Conflicts and Social Movements.* Englewood Cliffs: Prentice-Hall, 1973.

O'Donnell, Guillermo, and Phillippe Schmitter. *Transitions from Authoritarian Rule: Tentative Conclusions about Uncertain Democracies.* Baltimore: Johns Hopkins University Press, 1989.

Osa, Maryjane. "Resistance, Persistence, and Change: The Transformation of the Catholic Church in Poland." *East European Politics and Societies* 3, no. 2 (1989): 268–99.

Ossowski, Stanislaw. "O osobliwosciach nauk spolecznych." In *Dziela*, by Stanislaw Ossowski, 4:173–94. Warszawa: PWN, 1967.

Ost, David. "November 1982: Opposition at a Turning Point." *Poland Watch* 2 (1983): 70–84.

———. *Solidarity and the Politics and Anti-Politics.* Philadelphia: Temple University Press, 1990.

———. "Towards a Corporatist Solution in Eastern Europe: The Case of Poland." *East European Politics and Societies* 3, no. 1 (1989): 152–74.

Pakulski, Jan. "Legitimacy and Mass Compliance: Reflections on Max Weber and Soviet-Type Societies." *British Journal of Political Science* 16 (1986): 35–56.

Pankow, Wlodzimierz. "The Roots of the Polish Summer: A Crisis of the System of Power." *Sisyphus* 3 (1982): 33–47.

Paul, David W. *Czechoslovakia: Profile of a Socialist Republic at the Crossroads of Europe.* Boulder: Westview Press, 1981.

Pehe, Jiri. "An Annotated Survey of Independent Movements in Eastern Europe." Radio Free Europe Background Report 100, June 13, 1989.

Pehe, Jiri, ed. *The Prague Spring: A Mixed Legacy.* New York: Freedom House, 1988.

Pelczynski, Zbigniew. "Solidarity and the Rebirth of Civil Society." In *Civil Society and the State*, edited by John Keane, 361–80. London: Verso, 1988.

Pelikan, Jiri. *Socialist Opposition in Eastern Europe.* New York: St. Martin's Press, 1973.

Pelikan, Jiri, ed. *The Czechoslovak Political Trials, 1950–54: The Supressed Report of the Dubcek Government's Commission of Inquiry.* Stanford: Stanford University Press, 1971.

———. *The Secret Vysocany Congress: Proceedings and Documents of the Extraordinary Fourteenth Congress of the Communist Party of Czechoslovakia.* London: Allen Lane, 1971.

Perez-Diaz, Victor M. *The Return of Civil Society.* Cambridge: Harvard University Press, 1993.

Perlmutter, Amos. *Modern Authoritarianism.* New Haven: Yale University Press, 1981.

Pfaff, William. "Reflections: Where the Wars Come From." *New Yorker,* Dec. 26, 1988, pp. 83–90.

Piekalkiewicz, Jaroslaw. *Public Opinion Polling in Czechoslovakia, 1968–1969: Results and Analysis of Surveys Conducted during the Dubcek Era.* New York: Praeger, 1972.

Polgar, Steven. "A Summary of the Situation of the Hungarian Catholic Church." *Religion in Communist Lands* 12, no. 1 (1984): 11–41.

Pomian, Krzysztof. "Religione e politica in Polonia." In *Una nuova pace constantiniana,* edited by Giuseppe Ruggieri, 114–58. Casale Monferrato: Marietti, 1985.

———. *Wymiary polskiego konfliktu.* London: Aneks, 1985.

Powell, Walter W., and Paul J. DiMaggio, ed. *The New Institutionalism in Organizational Analysis.* Chicago: University of Chicago Press, 1991.

Poznanski, Kazimierz. "Economic Adjustment and Political Forces: Poland since 1970." *International Organization* 40, no. 2 (1986): 455–88.

Poznanski, Kazimierz, ed. *Constructing Capitalism: The Reemergence of Civil Society and Liberal Economy in the Post-Communist World.* Boulder: Westview Press, 1992.

Pravda, Alex. "Poland 1980: From 'Premature Consumerism' to Labour Solidarity." *Soviet Studies* 34, no. 2 (1982): 167–99.

———. *Reform and Change in the Czechoslovak Political System: January-August 1968.* Beverly Hills: Sage, 1975.

———. "The Workers." In *Poland: Genesis of a Revolution,* edited by Abraham Brumberg, 68–92. New York: Random House, 1983.

Preibisz, Joanna M. *Polish Dissident Publications: An Annotated Bibliography.* New York: Praeger, 1982.

Pryce-Jones, David. *The Hungarian Revolution.* London: Ernest Benn, 1969.

Przeworski, Adam. *Democracy and the Market.* Cambridge University Press, 1991.

Rachwald, Arthur. *In Search of Poland: The Superpowers' Responses to Solidarity, 1980–1989.* Stanford: Hoover Institution Press, 1990.

Ragin, Charles C. *The Comparative Method.* Berkeley: University of California Press, 1987.

Raina, Peter. *Independent Social Movements in Poland.* London: London School of Economics, 1981.

———. *Ks. Jerzy Popieluszko: Meczennik za wiare i ojczyzne.* Olsztyn: Warminskie Wydawnictwo Diecezjalne, 1990.

———. *Political Opposition in Poland, 1954–1977.* London: Poets and Painters Press, 1978.

Raina, Peter, ed. *Kosciol w Polsce, 1981–1984.* London: Veritas, 1985.

Rainer, Janos M. "The Other Side of the Story: Five Documents from the Yeltsin File." *New Hungarian Quarterly* 34, no. 129 (1993): 100–114.

———. "The Reprisals." *New Hungarian Quarterly* 33, no. 127 (1992): 118–27.

———. "Their Man in Budapest." *New Hungarian Quarterly* 32, no. 122 (1991): 131–35.

———. "The Yeltsin Dossier: Soviet Documents on Hungary, 1956." *Cold War International History Project Bulletin* 5 (Spring 1995): 22, 24–27.

Rakowska-Harmstone, Teresa, and Andrew Gyorgy, eds. *Communism in Eastern Europe*. Bloomington: Indiana University Press, 1984.

Rakowski, Mieczyslaw F. *Jak to sie stalo*. Warszawa: BGW, 1991.

Ramet, Pedro. *Catholicism and Politics in Communist Societies*. Durham: Duke University Press, 1990.

———. "Christianity and National Heritage among the Czechs and Slovakis." In *Religion and Nationalism in Soviet and East European Politics*, edited by Pedro Ramet, 264–85. Durham: Duke University Press, 1989.

Ramet, Sabrina. "The Catholic Church in Czechoslovakia, 1948–1991." *Studies in Comparative Communism* 24, no. 4 (1991): 377–93.

———. *Cross and Comissars: The Politics of Religion in Eastern Europe and the USSR*. Bloomington: Indiana University Press, 1987.

Rein, Martin, Gosta Esping-Andersen, and Lee Rainwater, eds. *Stagnation and Renewal in Social Policy*. Armonk: Sharpe, 1987.

Reiquam, Steve W., ed. *Solidarity and Poland: Impacts East and West*. Washington, D.C.: Wilson Center Press, 1988.

Remington, Robin A. "The Leading Role of the Polish Military: Implications." In *Sisyphus and Poland: Reflections on Martial Law*, edited by Joseph Black and John Strong, 43–64. Winnipeg: R. P. Frye, 1986.

Remington, Robin A., ed. *Winter in Prague*. Cambridge: MIT Press, 1969.

Remmer, Karen L. "Political Demobilization in Chile, 1973–1978." *Comparative Politics* 12, no. 3 (1980): 275–301.

Renner, Hans. *A History of Czechoslovakia since 1945*. London: Routledge, 1989.

Rev, Istvan. "The Adventures of Being Atomised: How Hungarian Peasants Cope with Collectivization." *Dissent*, Summer 1988, 335–49.

Revolt in Hungary. New York: Free Europe Press, 1956.

Rice, Condoleezza. "Czechoslovakian Secret Police." In *Terror and Communist Politics: The Role of the Secret Police in Communist States*, edited by Jonathan Adelman, 155–74. Boulder: Westview Press, 1984.

———. *The Soviet Union and the Czechoslovak Army, 1948–1983*. Princeton: Princeton University Press, 1984.

Rigby, Thomas H., and Ferenc Feher, eds. *Political Legitimation in Communist States*. London: Macmillan, 1982.

Robinson, William. *The Pattern of Reform in Hungary*. New York: Praeger, 1973.

Robinson, William, ed. *August 1980: The Strikes in Poland*. Munich: Radio Free Europe Research, 1980.

Rothschild, Joseph. *Return to Diversity*. New York: Oxford University Press, 1989.

Ruggieri, Giuseppe, ed. *Una nuova pace constantiniana*. Casale Monferrato: Marietti, 1985.

Rupnik, Jacques. *Histoire du parti communiste tchecoslovaque*. Paris: Presses de la fondation nationale des sciences politiques, 1981.

Rupnik, Jacques. "The Restoration of the Party-State." In *The Withering Away of the State*, edited by Leslie Holmes, 105–24. London: Sage, 1981.

Rykowski, Zbyslaw, and Wieslaw Wladyka. *Polska proba Pazdziernik '56*. Krakow: Wydawnictwo Literackie, 1989.

Sanford, George. "The Polish Communist Leadership and the Onset of the State of War." *Soviet Studies* 36, no. 4 (1984): 494–512.

———. "Polish People's Republic." In *Marxist Governments: A World Survey*, edited by Bogdan Szajkowski. London: Macmillan, 1981.

Schmid, Alex P. *Soviet Military Interventions since 1945*. New Brunswick: Transaction Books, 1985.

Schopflin, George. "From Communism to Democracy in Hungary." In *Post-Communist Transition: Emerging Pluralism in Hungary*, edited by Andras Bozoki, Andras Korosenyi, and George Schopflin, 96–110. London: Pinter, 1992.

———. "The Political Structure of Eastern Europe as a Factor in Intra-Bloc Relations." In *Soviet–East European Dilemmas*, edited by Karen Dawisha and Philip Hanson, 61–83. London: Heinemann, 1981.

———. *Politics in Eastern Europe, 1945–1992*. Oxford: Blackwell, 1993.

Schreiber, Thomas. "Changes in the Leadership." In *Hungary Today*, edited by the editors of *Survey*, 39–48. New York: Praeger, 1962.

Scott, James C. *Domination and the Arts of Resistance*. New Haven: Yale University Press, 1990.

Scruton, Roger. "The New Right in Central Europe I: Czechoslovakia." *Political Studies* 36, no. 3 (1988): 449–63.

———. "The New Right in Eastern Europe II: Poland and Hungary." *Political Studies* 36, no. 4 (1988): 562–85.

Selznick, Philip. *The Organizational Weapon*. New York: McGraw-Hill, 1952.

Seton-Watson, Hugh. *The East European Revolution*. New York: Praeger, 1956.

Sewell, William H., Jr. *A Rhetoric of Bourgeois Revolution: The Abbe Sieyes and What Is the Third Estate?* Durham: Duke University Press, 1994.

———. "Three Temporalities: Toward a Sociology of the Event." CSST Working Papers, no. 58. Ann Arbor: University of Michigan, October 1990.

Shafir, Michael. "Political Stagnation and Marxist Critique: 1968 and Beyond in Comparative East European Perspective." *British Journal of Political Science* 14, no. 4 (1984): 435–459.

Shawcross, William. *Dubcek*. New York: Simon and Schuster, 1990.

Simecka, Milan. *The Restoration of Order: The Normalization of Czechoslovakia, 1969–1976*. London: Verso, 1984.

Simon, Arnulf I. "Czechoslovakia's KAN: A Brief Venture in Democracy." *East Europe* 18, no. 6 (1969): 20–22.

Simon, Maurice D., and Roger E. Kanet, eds. *Background to Crisis: Policy and Politics in Gierek's Poland*. Boulder: Westview Press, 1981.

Skalnik Leff, Carol. *National Conflict in Czechoslovakia*. Princeton University Press, 1988.

Skilling, Harold G. *Charter 77 and Human Rights in Czechoslovakia*. London: Allen & Unwin, 1981.

———. *Czechoslovakia's Interrupted Revolution*. Princeton: Princeton University Press, 1976.

———. "The Interrupted Revolutions." In *Sisyphus and Poland: Reflections on*

Martial Law, edited by Joseph Black and John Strong, 65–82. Winnipeg: R. P. Frye, 1986.

———. "Leadership and Group Conflict in Czechoslovakia." In *Political Leadership in Eastern Europe and the Soviet Union*, edited by R. Barry Farrell, 276–93. Chicago: Aldine, 1970.

Skocpol, Theda. *Social Revolutions in the Modern World*. Cambridge: Cambridge University Press, 1994.

———. *States and Social Revolutions*. Cambridge: Cambridge University Press, 1979.

Slanska, Josefa. *Report on My Husband*. London: Hutchinson, 1969.

Smolar, Aleksander. "The Polish Opposition." In *Crisis and Reform in Eastern Europe*, edited by Ferenc Feher and Andrew Arato, 175–252. New Brunswick: Transaction, 1991.

———. "The Rich and the Powerful." In *Poland: Genesis of a Revolution*, edited by Abraham Brumberg, 42–53. New York: Random House 1983.

Smrkovsky, Josef. "Nedokonceny rozhovor: Mluvi Josef Smrkovsky." *Listy* 4, no. 2 (1975): 3–25.

Snow, David, and Robert Benford. "Ideology, Frame Resonance, and Participant Mobilization." In *From Structure to Action: Comparing Social Movements across Cultures*, edited by Bert Klandermans, Hanspeter Kriesi, and Sidney Tarrow, 197–217. Greenwich: JAI, 1988.

Snyder, David, and Charles Tilly. "Hardship and Collective Violence in France." *American Sociological Review* 37 (1972): 520–32.

Spielman, Richard. "The Eighteenth Brumaire of General Wojciech Jaruzelski." *World Politics* 37, no. 4 (1985): 562–85.

Staar, Richard F. "The Opposition Movement in Poland." *Current History* 80 (April 1981): 149–53.

Staar, Richard F., ed. *Transition to Democracy in Poland*. New York: St. Martin's Press, 1993.

———. *Yearbook of International Communist Affairs 1982*. Stanford: Hoover Institution Press, 1983.

Staniszkis, Jadwiga. *The Dynamics of Breakthrough in Eastern Europe*. Berkeley: University of California Press, 1991.

———. "Martial Law in Poland." *Telos* 54 (1982–83): 87–100.

———. *Ontologia socializmu*. Warszawa: In Plus, 1989.

———. *Poland's Self-limiting Revolution*. Princeton: Princeton University Press, 1984.

Stark, David. "Introduction." *East European Politics and Societies* 6, no. 1 (1992): 1–2.

———. "Path Dependence and Privatization Strategies in East Central Europe." *East European Politics and Societies* 6, no. 1 (1992): 17–54.

Stark, David, and Victor Nee. "Toward an Institutional Analysis of State Socialism." In *Remaking the Economic Institutions of Socialism*, edited by David Stark and Victor Nees, 1–31. Stanford: Stanford University Press, 1989.

Steinmo, Sven, Kathleen Thelen, and Frank Longstreth, eds. *Structuring Politics: Historical Institutionalism in Comparative Perspective*. Cambridge: Cambridge University Press, 1992.

Stillman, Edmund O. *The Ideology of Revolution*. New York: Free Europe Press, 1957.

Stone, Norman, and Eduard Strouhal, eds. *Czechoslovakia: Crossroads and Crises, 1918–88.* New York: St. Martin's Press, 1989.

Strmiska, Zdenek. "The Prague Spring as a Social Movement." In *Czechoslovakia: Crossroads and Crises, 1918–88,* edited by Norman Stone and Eduard Strouhal, 253–67. New York: St. Martin's Press, 1989.

Strzelecka, Jolanta. "The Functioning of the Sejmu since December 13, 1981." *Poland Watch* 7 (1984): 55–74.

Suda, Zdenek. "Czechoslovakia: An Aborted Reform." In *East Central Europe: Yesterday, Today, Tomorrow,* edited by Milorad Drachkovitch, 243–65. Stanford: Hoover Institution Press, 1982.

———. *Zealots and Rebels: A History of the Ruling Communist Party of Czechoslovakia.* Stanford: Hoover Institution Press, 1980.

Sulek, Antoni. "The Polish United Workers' Party: From Mobilization to Non-Representation." *Soviet Studies* 42, no. 3 (1990): 499–511.

Sulik, Boleslaw. "March of a Pole: Interview with Jaruzelski" *East European Reporter* 4, no. 4 (1991): 100–102.

Summerscale, Peter. "The Continuing Validity of the Brezhnev Doctrine." In *Soviet–East European Dilemmas,* edited by Karen Dawisha and Philip Hanson, 26–40. London: Heinemann, 1981.

Svitak, Ivan. *The Czechoslovak Experiment, 1968–1969.* New York: Columbia University Press, 1971.

———. "The Premature Perestroika." In *The Prague Spring: A Mixed Legacy,* edited by Jiri Pehe, 177–86. New York: Freedom House, 1988.

Swain, Nigel. *Hungary: The Rise and Fall of Feasible Socialism.* London: Verso, 1992.

Swidlicki, Andrzej. *Political Trials in Poland, 1981–1986.* London: Croom Helm, 1987.

Syrop, Konrad. *Spring in October: The Polish Revolution of 1956.* London: Weidenfeld and Nicolson, 1957.

Szabo, Arpad. *A Magyar Forradalmi Honved Karhatalom.* Budapest: Zrinyi Katonai Kiado, 1976.

Szajkowski, Bogdan. *Next to God . . . Poland: Politics and Religion in Contemporary Poland.* London: Pinter, 1983.

Szajkowski, Bogdan, ed. *Marxist Governments: A World Survey.* London: Macmillan, 1981.

Szamuely, Laszlo. "The First Wave of the Mechanism Debate in Hungary (1954–1957)." *Acta Oeconomica* 29, nos. 1–2 (1982): 1–24.

Szczypiorski, Andrzej. *The Polish Ordeal.* London: Croom Helm, 1982.

Szelenyi, Ivan. "Eastern Europe in an Epoch of Transition: Towards a Socialist Mixed Economy." In *Remaking the Economic Institutions of Socialism,* edited by Victor Nee and David Stark, 208–32. Stanford: Stanford University Press, 1989.

———. "The Prospects and Limits of the East European New Class Project: An Auto-critical Reflection on the Intellectuals on the Road to Class Power." *Politics and Society* 15, no. 2 (1986–87): 103–44.

———. *Socialist Entrepreneurs: Embourgeoisement in Rural Hungary.* Madison: University of Wisconsin Press, 1988.

Szelenyi, Ivan, and Robert Manchin. "Social Policy under State-Socialism." In *Stag-*

nation and Renewal in Social Policy, edited by Martin Rein, Gosta Esping-Andersen, and Lee Rainwater, 102–39. Armonk: Sharpe, 1987.

Szenes, Ivan. *A kommunista part ujjaszervezese Magyarorszagon, 1956–1957*. Budapest: Kossuth Konyvkiado, 1976.

Sztompka, Piotr. "The Intangibles and Imponderables of the Transition to Democracy." *Studies in Comparative Communism* 24, no. 3 (1991): 295–311.

———. "The Social Functions of Defeat." *Research in Social Movements, Conflicts and Change* 10 (1988): 183–92.

Talbott, Strobe, ed. *Khrushchev Remembers*. Boston: Little Brown, 1970.

Taras, Raymond C. *Ideology in a Socialist State: Poland, 1956–1983*. Cambridge: Cambridge University Press, 1984.

Taras, Raymond C., ed. *Handbook of Political Science Research on the USSR and Eastern Europe*. Westport, Conn.: Greenwood Press, 1992.

Tarkowski, Jacek. "Wladze lokalne wobec kryzysu i kryzys wladzy lokalnej." In *Rzeczywistosc polska i sposoby radzenia sobie z nia*, edited by Miroslawa Marody and Antoni Sulek, 179–203. Warszawa: Uniwersytet Warszawski, Instytut Socjologii, 1987.

Tarrow, Sidney. "Cycles of Collective Action: Between Moments of Madness and the Repertoire of Contention." In *Repertoires and Cycles of Collective Action*, edited by Mark Traugott, 89–115. Durham: Duke University Press, 1995.

———. *Democracy and Disorder*. Oxford: Clarendon Press, 1989.

———. "National Politics and Collective Action: Recent Theory and Research in Western Europe and the United States." *Annual Review of Sociology* 14 (1988): 421–40.

———. "National States and Collective Action." *States and Social Structures Newsletter*, no. 5 (1987): 1–4.

———. *Power in Movement: Social Movements, Collective Action, and Politics*. Cambridge: Cambridge University Press, 1994.

———. "Struggle, Politics and Reform—Collective Action, Social Movements and Cycles of Protest." Western Societies Program, Paper no. 21. Ithaca: Cornell University, 1989.

Tatu, Michel. "Intervention in Eastern Europe." In *Diplomacy of Power*, edited by Stephen Kaplan, 205–64. Washington, D.C.: Brookings Institution Press, 1981.

Terry, Sarah M. "External Influences on Political Change in Eastern Europe: A Framework for Analysis." In *Political Development in Eastern Europe*, edited by Jan Triska and Paul M. Cocks, 277–314. New York: Praeger, 1977.

Terry, Sarah M., ed. *Soviet Policy in Eastern Europe*. New Haven: Yale University Press, 1984.

Tesar, Jan. "Opozycja w Czechoslowacji." *Kontakt* 1–2 (1989): 121–33.

Tigrid, Pavel. "And What if the Russians Did Not Come." In *Prague Spring: A Mixed Legacy*, edited by Jiri Pehe, 77–87. New York: Freedom House, 1988.

———. "The Prague Coup of 1948: The Elegant Takeover." In *The Anatomy of Communist Takeovers*, edited by Thomas Hammond, 399–432. New Haven: Yale University Press, 1975.

———. *Why Dubcek Fell*. London: Macdonald, 1971.

Tilly, Charles. *From Mobilization to Revolution*. New York: Random House, 1978.

Tilly, Charles, Louise Tilly, and Richard Tilly. *The Rebellious Century, 1830–1930*. Cambridge: Harvard University Press, 1975.

Tischler, Janos, ed. *Rewolucja wegierska 1956 w polskich dokumentach*. Warszawa: ISP PAN, 1995.

Tobias, Robert. *Communist-Christian Encounter in East Europe*. Indianapolis: School of Religion Press, 1956.

Toch, Marta. *Reinventing Civil Society: Poland's Quiet Revolution, 1981–1986*. New York: U.S. Helsinki Watch Committee, 1986.

Tokes, Rudolf L., ed. *Eurocommunism and Detente*. New York: New York University Press, 1978.

———. *Opposition in Eastern Europe*. Baltimore: Johns Hopkins University Press, 1979.

Toma, Peter A., and Ivan Volgyes. *Politics in Hungary*. San Francisco: Freeman, 1977.

Tomaszewski, Jerzy. "Czechoslowacka Republika Socjalistyczna." In *Dzieje Panstw Socjalistycznych*, edited by Jerzy Ciepielewski, 60–89. Warszawa: PWN, 1986.

Tomka, Miklos. "Church and Religion in a Communist State, 1945–1990." *New Hungarian Quarterly* 32, no. 121 (1991): 59–69.

Traugott, Mark, ed. *Repertoires and Cycles of Collective Action*. Durham: Duke University Press, 1995.

Touraine, Alain. "An Introduction to the Study of Social Movements." *Social Research* 52, no. 4 (1985): 749–87.

Touraine, Alain, et al. *Solidarity: Poland 1980–1981*. Cambridge: Cambridge University Press, 1983.

Triska, Jan, ed. *Dominant Powers and Subordinate States: The United States in Latin America and the Soviet Union in Eastern Europe*. Durham: Duke University Press, 1986.

Triska, Jan, and Paul M. Cocks, eds. *Political Development in Eastern Europe*. New York: Praeger, 1977.

Tucker, Robert C. "Towards a Comparative Politics of Movement Regimes." *American Political Science Review* 55, no. 2 (1961): 281–89.

Tymowski, Andrzej. "The Underground Debate on Strategy and Tactics." *Poland Watch* 1 (1982): 75–88.

Ulc, Otto. "Czechoslovakia." In *Communism in Eastern Europe*, edited by Teresa Rakowska-Harmstone and Andrew Gyorgy, 100–120. Bloomington: Indiana University Press, 1984.

———. "How the Czechs Felt in 1956." *Central European Federalist* 14, no. 1 (July 1966): 23–28.

———. "The 'Normalisation' of Post-Invasion Czechoslovakia." *Survey* 24, no. 3 (1979): 201–13.

———. "Pilsen: The Unknown Revolt." *Problems of Communism* 14, no. 3 (1965): 46–49.

———. *Politics in Czechoslovakia*. San Francisco: Freeman, 1974.

———. "Those Who Left: A Current Profile." In *The Prague Spring: A Mixed Legacy*, edited by Jiri Pehe, 143–55. New York: Freedom House, 1988.

U.S. Department of State. *Foreign Relations of the United States, 1955–1957: Eastern Europe*. Vol. 25. Washington, D.C.: Government Printing Office, 1990.

Urban, George R. "Hungary: The Balance Sheet." In *Hungary Today*, edited by the editors of Survey, 7–18. New York: Praeger, 1962.

———. "Hungary, 1957–1961: Background and Current Situation." *Radio Free Europe Special Report*, May 16, 1961.

Urban, Jerzy. "Letter to the First Secretary." *Uncaptive Minds* 1, no. 4 (1988): 2–7.

Vajda, Mihaly. *The State and Socialism.* London: Allison and Busby, 1981.

Valenta, Jiri. "Military Interventions: Doctrines, Motives, Goals, and Outcomes." In *Dominant Powers and Subordinate States,* edited by Jan Triska, 261–84. Durham: Duke University Press, 1986.

———. "Revolutionary Change, Soviet Intervention, and 'Normalization' in East-Central Europe." *Comparative Politics* 16, no. 2 (1984): 127–51.

———. "Soviet Decisionmaking and the Hungarian Revolution." In *The First War between Socialist States: The Hungarian Revolution of 1956 and Its Impact,* edited by Bela Kiraly, Barbara Lotze, and Nandor F. Dreisziger, 265–78. New York: Brooklyn College Press, 1984.

———. *Soviet Intervention in Czechoslovakia, 1968.* Baltimore: Johns Hopkins University Press, 1979.

———. "Soviet Policy Toward Hungary and Czechoslovakia." In *Soviet Policy in Eastern Europe,* edited by Sarah M. Terry, 93–124. New Haven: Yale University Press, 1984.

Valenta, Jiri, and Jan Moravec. "Could the Prague Spring Have Been Saved?" *Orbis* 35, no. 4 (Fall 1991): 581–601.

Valenta, Jiri, and Condoleezza Rice. "The Czechoslovak Army." In *Communist Armies in Politics,* edited by Jonathan Adelman, 129–48. Boulder: Westview Press, 1982.

Vali, Ferenc A. *Rift and Revolt in Hungary.* Cambridge: Harvard University Press, 1961.

Varga, Laszlo. *Human Rights in Hungary.* Gainesville, Fla.: Dunabian Research and Information Center, 1967.

Veto, Miklos. "The Catholic Church." In *Hungary Today,* edited by the editors of *Survey,* 58–64. New York: Praeger, 1962.

Vladislav, Jan, ed. *Vaclav Havel or Living in Truth.* London: Faber and Faber, 1986.

Volgyes, Ivan. "The Hungarian and Czechoslovak Revolutions." In *The Soviet Invasion of Czechoslovakia: Its Effects on Eastern Europe,* edited by Edward J. Czerwinski and Jaroslaw Piekalkiewicz. New York: Praeger, 1972.

———. "Hungary." In *Soviet Allies: The Warsaw Pact and the Issue of Reliability,* edited by Daniel N. Nelson, 184–224. Boulder: Westview Press, 1984.

Wagner, Francis, ed. *The Hungarian Revolution in Perspective.* Washington, D.C.: F. F. Memorial Foundation, 1967.

Walder, Andrew G. *Communist Neo-Traditionalism: Work and Authority in Chinese Industry.* Berkeley: California University Press, 1986.

Walicki, Andrzej. "The Main Components of the Situation in Poland." *Politics* 19, no. 1 (1984): 4–17.

———. "Notes on Jaruzelski's Poland." In *Crisis and Reform in Eastern Europe,* edited by Ferenc Feher and Andrew Arato, 335–91. New Brunswick, N.J.: Transaction, 1991.

Watts, Larry. "Civil-Military Relations in Eastern Europe: Some Reflections on the Polish Case." *Nordic Journal of Soviet and East European Studies* 2, no. 4 (1985): 1–93.

Weigel, George. *The Final Revolution: The Resistance of Church and the Collapse of Communism.* New York: Oxford University Press, 1992.

Weschler, Lawrence. *The Passion of Poland.* New York: Pantheon Books, 1984.

White, Stephen. "Economic Performance and Communist Legitimacy," *World Politics* 38, no. 3 (1986): 462–82.

Wiatr, Jerzy J. *The Soldier and the Nation: The Role of the Military in Polish Politics, 1918–1985*. Boulder: Westview Press, 1988.

Widacki, Jan. *Czego nie powiedzial General Kiszczak*. Warszawa: BGW, 1991.

Wightman, Gordon, and Archie Brown. "Changes in the Levels of Membership and Social Composition of the Communist Party of Czechoslovakia." *Soviet Studies* 27, no. 3 (1975): 396–417.

Windsor, Philip, and Adam Roberts. *Czechoslovakia, 1968: Reform, Repression and Resistance*. New York: Columbia University Press, 1969.

Wlodek, Zbigniew, ed. *Tajne Documenty Biura Politycznego: PZPR a Solidarnosc, 1980–1981*. London: Aneks, 1992.

Wolchik, Sharon L. *Czechoslovakia in Transition*. New York: Pinter, 1991.

Woodall, Jean. "New Social Factors in the Unrest in Poland." *Government and Opposition* 16, no. 1 (1981): 37–57.

The World Almanac and Book of Facts. New York: Newspaper Enterprise Association, 1980, 1981, 1982, 1986, 1988, 1989.

Woroszylski, Wiktor. *Dziennik Wegierski, 1956*. Warszawa: Biblioteka Wiezi, 1990.

Wright, Mark. "Ideology and Power in the Czechoslovak Political System." In *Eastern Europe: Political Crisis and Legitimation*, edited by Paul Lewis, 110–53. New York: St. Martin's Press, 1984.

Zald, Mayer N. "Issues in the Theory of Social Movements." *Current Perspectives in Social Theory* 1 (1980): 61–72.

Zaleski, Eugene. *Kryzys gospodarki polskiej: Przyczyny i srodki zaradcze*. London: Instytut Romana Dmowskiego, 1983.

Zielonka, Jan. "Poland: The Experiment with Communist Statism." In *The Crisis— Problems in Poland*, Research Project "Crises in Soviet-Type Systems," Study 12a, 59–82. Koln: Index, 1987.

———. *Political Ideas in Contemporary Poland*. Aldershot: Avebury, 1989.

Zimmerman, William. "Soviet Foreign Policy and World Politics."In *Soviet Foreign Policy: Classic and Contemporary Issues*, edited by Frederic Fleron, Jr., Eric P. Hoffmann, and Robbin F. Laird, 119–31. Hawthorne, N.Y.: Aldine de Gruyter, 1991.

Zinner, Paul E. *Communist Strategy and Tactics in Czechoslovakia, 1918–1948*. Princeton: Princeton University Press, 1963.

———. *Revolution in Hungary*. Freeport: Books for Libraries Press, 1962.

Zinner, Paul E., ed. *National Communism and Popular Revolt in Eastern Europe*. New York: Columbia University Press, 1956.

About the Author

GRZEGORZ EKIERT is Associate Professor of Government at Harvard University.

INDEX

Action Program (Czechoslovakia, 1968), 122–23, 139–43, 145, 147, 164, 170
Afghanistan, 254, 300
Albania, 22
Andropov, Yuri, 63, 304
Apro, Antal, 84, 356n.46
Austria, 69, 79
auxiliary organizations of party-state, 11, 336n.31
 in Czechoslovakia, 122, 147, 151, 153–54, 180–81, 188–93, 206, 373n.68
 in Hungary, 38, 47, 54, 91–94, 106
 in Poland, 225, 240–42, 250–51, 274, 278, 281, 317, 397n.59
AVH Security Police. *See* coercive forces in Hungary

Babiuch, Edward, 248
Benes, Edvard, 126
Bilak, Vasil, 174, 180, 371n.36, 374n.1
Brezhnev, Leonid, 22, 136, 157, 198, 304
Brezhnev Doctrine, 116, 158, 210–11, 378n.43
Bruzek, Miloslav, 191, 193
Bujak, Zbigniew, 257, 395n.26
Bulgaria, 7, 142, 327

Cernik, Oldrich, 139, 163, 176, 180, 377n.25
Charter '77, 195, 328
China, 32, 64, 111
churches
 in Czechoslovakia, 129, 156, 193, 328
 in Hungary, 15, 43, 80–81, 357n.61
 in Poland, 17, 102, 216–17, 225–26, 231, 234–36, 241, 266–68, 287–88
Cisar, Cestmir, 165, 180
civil society, 286, 390n.71
coercive forces
 in Czechoslovakia, 147–48, 163, 185–86, 205–06
 in Hungary, 51–54, 67–69, 71, 350n.47
 in Poland, 248–50, 278
Cold War, 32, 34, 102
communist parties, 317–18
 in Czechoslovakia, 121, 127–88, 145, 160, 166–67, 179–83, 184, 204–07, 208, 329, 366n.3, 369n.12, 381n.19
 in Hungary, 37, 43–44, 49–51, 83–87,

106, 109, 350nn.42 and 44, 359nn.81, 82, and 84
 in Poland, 218–19, 227–28, 243–47, 265, 274–78, 317
comparative communism, x
corporatism, 228–29, 299
CMEA (Council for Mutual Economic Assistance), 22, 113, 141, 143, 254, 275, 302
CSM (Czechoslovak Youth Union). *See* auxiliary organizations of party-state in Czechoslovakia
cycles of protest, 5, 13
Czechoslovakia
 churches, 129, 156, 193, 328
 communist coup (1948) 128, 155
 communist party, 121, 127–28, 145, 160, 166–67, 179–83, 184, 204–08, 329, 366n.3, 369n.12, 381n.19
 Czech-Slovak relations, 130, 134, 171, 183–85, 196–97, 203, 209–10, 329, 378n.62
 economy, 126–27, 129–30, 132–33, 208–09, 212, 368n.3, 369n.10
 independent organizations, 126, 152–56, 158–59, 175–76, 193–98, 368n.9
 international context, 156–58, 210–14, 319
 intra-elite divisions, 123, 134–35, 141, 145, 177, 185, 199, 208
 party-state institutions, 35, 122, 128, 144–47, 153–54, 172–73, 183–93, 205–06
 political demobilization, 124, 129, 173, 169–70, 174, 180–97, 200–08, 328
 political discourses, 140–01, 203
 political mobilization, 122–23, 139, 144, 158–60, 170–72, 200–04
 political repression, 23, 124, 129, 165, 177, 178–81, 194
 protest and resistance, 154, 168–70, 173, 200
 reform movement, 122–23, 139–42, 146–47, 159–60, 172, 200
 Soviet policy toward, 127, 136, 142–44, 156–58, 161–64, 174–75, 198–200, 205–06, 210–11, 306

dependency theory, 33
Dery, Tibor, 107

About the Author

GRZEGORZ EKIERT is Associate Professor of Government
at Harvard University.